TOWARD
EVIDENCE-BASED
PRACTICE

Also Available from Lyceum Books, Inc.

Advisory Editors: Thomas M. Meenaghan, *New York University*
Ira Colby, *University of Houston*

ESSENTIAL SKILLS OF SOCIAL WORK PRACTICE: ASSESSMENT,
INTERVENTION, AND EVALUATION
by Thomas O'Hare

A PRACTICAL GUIDE TO SOCIAL SERVICE EVALUATION,
by Carl F. Brun

SOCIAL WORK EVALUATION: ENHANCING WHAT WE DO
by James R. Dudley

WHAT IS PROFESSIONAL SOCIAL WORK?,
by Malcolm Payne

USING STATISTICAL METHODS IN SOCIAL WORK PRACTICE WITH SPSS,
by Soleman H. Abu-Bader

EVIDENCE-BASED PRACTICES FOR SOCIAL WORKERS,
by Thomas O'Hare

USING EVIDENCE IN SOCIAL WORK PRACTICE: BEHAVIORAL PERSPECTIVES,
by Harold E. Briggs and Tina L. Rzepnicki

CLINICAL ASSESSMENT FOR SOCIAL WORKERS: QUALITATIVE AND
QUANTITATIVE METHODS, 2E,
edited by Catheleen Jordan and Cynthia Franklin

JOEL FISCHER
University of Hawai'i

TOWARD EVIDENCE-BASED PRACTICE

VARIATIONS ON A THEME

LYCEUM
BOOKS, INC.

Chicago, Illinois

© Lyceum Books, Inc., 2009

Published by
LYCEUM BOOKS, INC.
5758 S. Blackstone Ave.
Chicago, Illinois 60637
773+643-1903 (Fax)
773+643-1902 (Phone)
lyceum@lyceumbooks.com
http://www.lyceumbooks.com

6 5 4 3 2 1   09 10 11 12

ISBN 978-1-933478-55-5

Library of Congress Cataloging-in-Publication Data
Fischer, Joel.
Toward evidence-based practice : variations on a theme / Joel Fischer.
    p. cm.
 Includes bibliographical references.
 ISBN 978-1-933478-55-5
 1. Social service—Evaluation. 2. Social case work. 3. Evaluation research (Social action programs)
I. Title.
 HV41.F473 2008
 361.3'2—dc22

                                                                2008063054

It is unwise to be too sure of one's own wisdom. It is healthy to be reminded that the strongest may weaken and the wisest might fall.
—Mahatma Gandhi

If you would be a real seeker after truth, it is necessary that at least once in your life, you doubt, as far as possible, everything.
—René Descartes

The only true wisdom is knowing you know nothing.
—Socrates

Renee, without you, I am nothing. Thank you . . . for everything.
—Joel Fischer

Contents

Foreword

Toward Evidence-Based Practice: Variations on a Theme is chock-full of understanding, insight, and reflection on the field of social work and its struggle toward evidence-based practice. It is an essential and concise summary of where we came from and how we got to the point of empirically supported interventions—all illustrated by one of social work's most controversial, if not downright provocative, scholars, Joel Fischer. Much of this reputation is due to how Fischer has advocated so strongly for research and research-based practices in social work. As his dear friend, Harvey Gochros (1978), once observed in the foreword to another Fischer book, kings in Greek city-states would kill the messenger who brought them news they did not like. It was simply too easy, then, to also want to "kill" Fischer because he howled about how the field was not meeting its goals of helping people with effective interventions. It is no wonder he provoked anger in social work academics and practitioners alike. After all, who wanted to hear that? Moreover, new and innovative ideas are typically seen as controversial and provocative.

And yet, the messenger could not be killed, the hollering continued, and Fischer fought his righteous fight. My, how times have changed! Eventually the perspective of effective social work practice prevailed in many forms, especially in clinical practice. Empirical-clinical practice, and, now, evidence-based practice were once controversial approaches, but today are considered almost commonplace.

Provoking change must be satisfying, and Fischer's nifty volume shows just how much change actually has occurred, with twenty-three readings covering the past forty years of social work research and practice. As Stuart Kirk (2005, personal communication) once commented, "How does he [Fischer] keep up the enthusiasm decade after decade after decade?"

These readings are accompanied by introductory comments that tie the original issues at the time to issues of today. Not surprisingly, the readings begin with Fischer's early, controversial publication, "Is Casework Effective?," published in 1973. And this is only the prologue. The book follows with other significant, often groundbreaking, works of Fischer, up to his most recent publication in *Reflections*, which atones for his "sin" of "destroying social work." Well, perhaps he did do a little destroying. But if so, the field of social work is far better for it. Attempting to produce evidence of change was introduced into evidence-based practice in no small degree because of Joel Fischer, and this book illustrates how and why.

The book also shows, however, that Fischer is not beyond error. Fischer even admits, in the introduction to Part II, that he probably was wrong in thinking that changes occurring at the time were revolutionary rather than evolutionary. Other errors are just errors. Most noticeable is in the epilogue, where he misspelled the word "irresistible" and instead wrote "irrepressible" in reference to a kind, supportive, and caring colleague, a spell-check error, I would assume. Additionally, the title is altogether too modest; I believe this book would be more appropriately subtitled, *The Joel Fischer Reader*. Small errors, all things considered.

In summary, there is more wisdom in this book than in a forest full of owls. Yes, provoking change must be satisfying after all these decades.

Kevin Corcoran, PhD, JD
Vancor Point of View
Yachats, Oregon

Reference

Gochros, H. L. (1978). Foreword. In Fischer J., *Effective casework practice: An eclectic approach*. New York: McGraw-Hill.

Preface

Outside of a dog, a book is man's best friend. Inside of a dog, it's too dark to read.
    —Groucho Marx

I was watching TV one night with my wife, Renee, when she turned to me, and without any warning, said, "Why don't you put together a collection of your own work into a book of readings?"

I am not making this up.

I thought for a second, and replied, "Hmm; lemme think about that."

I can't say that I thought at the time that it was a great idea. But it certainly was different from the suggestions my wife usually has for me while sitting around, such as: "Honey would you take out the garbage?" or "I think you better take Schmoopie out for her walk."

This new suggestion promised to be more work, but, after all, as a professor for almost forty years, that IS the kind of work they pay me for.

So, with only a little more pestering from Renee, and with Groucho's encouragement, I decided to go for it. This book is the result.

Renee, this book is for you.

It's also, I hope, for students, faculty, and practitioners in social work; for beginners; and for those with experience, who may recognize in these pages some of their own struggles in coming to grips with the bombardment of new knowledge that has taken place over the past forty years.

What I am trying to do here is trace the path of a forty-year journey—my journey, of course, but also the social work profession's—as we, collectively, moved through different eras of knowledge development for practice. These eras have been enormously fruitful in changing the face of our profession as we advance, baby steps at a time, toward more effective ways of helping our clients.

I am using my own work as an exemplar, one might say, for the changes in social work over the past years. I must acknowledge at the outset: Since this journey is comprised of my own work and my reflections on it from the point of view of today's world, the journey, obviously, will be from *my* perspective. I do not mean in any way that other perspectives on the changes in the field over the past several decades are wrong, less deserving, or in any way less fruitful. After all, when a profession or its knowledge changes, the changes are a result of multiple factors, including political, empirical, social, and so forth. If we know anything at all as social workers, we know that there are multiple influences on virtually all changes.

On the other hand, precisely *because* of those multiple influences, practitioners, professors, researchers, and theorists can easily flounder. One of the most serious questions that any profession faces is how do we control all those factors in order to best understand our clients and provide the best, most effective, services to them? Ultimately, because social work cares most about finding ways to help our clients in a demonstrable way, what all of us really want to find are the methods and means of helping that, in some way, are most powerful in demonstrably helping.

That search—*our* search—is *exactly* the focus of this book.

I want to acknowledge, and I realize that this makes for a lot of up-front acknowledging, that this book is not about *all* the faces of social work, nor is it intended to deal with all the methods of practice, and not even all the changes. The focus of *Toward Evidence-Based Practice* is, well, just that. My career is focused on examining the literature for the best ways of helping our clients in direct practice, and, mainly, what we might call *clinical practice* at that. And you can tell from the title that I am assuming that the past 40 years has been a march, uneven as the steps may have been, toward evidence-based practice as the latest attempt by our field to try to define the best ways of finding and developing knowledge for effective practice.

You will find later on, especially in some of my own commentary later in the book, that I am not completely convinced that evidence-based practice is the *ultimate* or *perfect* or even the *last* step in this journey, certainly for me, but perhaps also for our profession. But as we try to perfect—that's too "high falutin"—maybe I should say as we *develop* our knowledge base, evidence-based practice seems like a pretty important step ahead.

As part of my, uh, "acknowledgments" about the focus of this book being largely on clinical practice, I want you to know something about me. And that is that I do not even think that clinical practice is the most *important* part of what we do as social workers. Although I have not written much about it, I believe our collective and individual advocacy and organizing activities, where we do our best to fight for the rights of oppressed and underserved populations, are really where it's at. Much of my time in Hawai'i is spent in social justice activities including legislative lobbying with NASW for welfare rights; demonstrating against the war in Iraq and against the militarization of my university; supporting the indigenous people of Hawai'i, the Native Hawaiians, in their struggle for self-determination; working in favor of environmental and animal protections . . . the broad range of social justice activities that are at the heart of what I believe is the *main mission* of social work. I do not experience my scholarly work on clinical practice and my social justice activities as a discrepancy. They are just complementary parts of the ways I am trying to be a complete social worker.

However, I apologize in advance to those readers who may find that these omissions are an important gap in the book. I agree.

Let me explain, then, what this book *does* contain and how it is organized.

Purpose

It seems to me that there often may be a major disconnect between what social work students are learning today and how that knowledge has evolved over the years. A concrete example of that disconnect is that many students of today are not even familiar with the term "casework," perhaps thinking that whatever descriptor of direct practice that they learn must be the only one or the correct one. Yet, the term "casework" was the predominant one used to discuss direct practice in social work for many decades—and you will find it in many of the chapters in this book, especially the earlier ones—before it essentially was abandoned in most schools of social work around the country in favor of such terms as "direct practice," "clinical practice," "practice with individuals and groups," "micro practice," and so on.

Linking students and even faculty and practitioners to some of the history of their own practice can provide an understanding of the substantive nature of the changes in the field over the years. This will, I hope, lead to a greater capacity for analytic scrutiny of what appears to be true for them today.

The major purpose of this book, then, is to examine the past forty years of changes in social work research and practice as a basis for not only understanding the practice of today, but for realizing how today's practice actually is very much linked to the practice of the past. I propose to do that by providing a selection of twenty-three readings from my own work. The readings cover four decades of the development of research and practice in social work, four decades that I characterized earlier as explosive because, viewed through the lens of time, they really seemed to lead to major changes in how we conceptualize and practice social work. These readings were especially selected to reflect and help analyze those changes.

Now, I have to say that *I* was one of the social workers who was advocating for the changes at many of these points in time. This is not to say that topics I advocated for did not change over time because, as you will see, they certainly did. At least one cannot say that I'm not flexible. But there also was, I believe, a certain consistency in my work around some core beliefs about practice and research, in particular, the quest for increasingly more effective practice; hence, the subtitle of this book, *Variations on a Theme*. Looking back, as I have, through the mechanism of these chapters, I believe I was able to capture in these works some of what seemed to be the most significant of the changes over those four decades. This also is a way of saying that I was a *part* of the movement to change social work. Because all the chapters in this book are written by me, I hope it does not appear that I am saying I *was* the movement.

Very briefly, I want to explain *why* I think it is important for social work practitioners to be on a permanent journey in the search for more effective means of helping their clients. I am going to do that by telling you a story. This is a *true* story, one that I have been telling at the start of every class since the 1970s. Some of my repeat students can even shout out the punch line if they really wanted to do so, but mercifully no one ever has. I tell this story in my classes using the actual name, and with the permission, of the person to whom this story actually happened. Here, just in case, I'll call her "Barbara."

Barbara is a former colleague of mine at the University of Hawai'i, School of Social Work. Barbara was having trouble with her vision, so she went to an ophthalmologist. The doctor examined her and said, "Well, Barbara, I have bad news. You have glaucoma. And the glaucoma is so advanced, that we cannot use the first line of treatment, eye drops, to treat it. We're going to have to do surgery." "Omigod," Barbara said. "What kind of surgery?"

"Well," said the doctor, "there basically are two types. The first is what I call 'conventional surgery.'" In conventional surgery, I use a scalpel to make tiny incisions in your eyeball to relieve the pressure that is building up and is the primary cause of glaucoma. This surgery is very successful, though it has serious side effects. You will be hospitalized for the surgery and after the operation for two to three days, depending on how things go. Then, your eye will be bandaged for at least two weeks. During those weeks, you will be pretty much confined to bed. You cannot do any lifting for a period of months, and you will have double vision for approximately one month, maybe longer. Some patients even are confined to their homes far longer than two weeks. It just depends on each case. Once your first eye gets better, we do the whole thing again on the other eye."

"That sounds awful!" Barbara exclaimed. "But you mentioned there were two types of surgery. What's the other one?"

"The other surgery is much newer," said the doctor. "It's called laser surgery. Here, the incisions are made by pulsating beams of light that do an almost perfect job of making those incisions. With laser surgery, the effectiveness is even better than with conventional surgery and there are almost no side effects. Laser surgery is outpatient surgery. You can go home after a few hours, you wear a bandage for just one day, but two weeks at night while you are sleeping. You can even go back to work the next day if you want, though I usually recommend staying at home another day. You may have double vision for a couple of days, I recommend no heavy lifting for awhile, and except for follow-up care, that's it."

"Huh?" was all Barbara managed to say at first. When she recovered from the shock at the seriousness of conventional surgery and the comparative ease of laser surgery, she finally said, "Well, obviously I want the laser surgery."

"Of course. That's what I would have recommended anyway," the doctor said.

"But if laser surgery is so superior," Barbara asked, "why would you even bother telling me about the old surgery?"

"You know how it is," the doctor replied. "When you or someone in your family has a new disease, you end up hearing from everyone else who also had it. They're going to tell you how they were treated. I can tell you right now that most opthalmologists are still using the conventional surgery despite its far inferior outcomes. I didn't want you to think that, with so many others getting the conventional surgery, you had done the wrong thing by getting the newer treatment."

"But why," Barbara asked, "would all those opthalmologists be doing the conventional treatment when a far better treatment is available?"

"Because," the doctor replied, *"that's all they know!"*

Once again, I swear I am not making this story up. That is exactly how "Barbara" told it to me!

It seems to me that all of us as professionals have to maintain a continuous vigil so that we do not become the type of practitioners who do what they do only because *"that's all they know."* What we know at any given point may indeed be worth knowing. It may be the best we have to offer at that time. But continuing to practice with only that knowledge, and ignoring new and better knowledge as it appears, is the certain path to professional obsolescence. This book is my attempt to illustrate my forty-year struggle to avoid my own professional obsolescence, and to try to communicate to others what I was finding in the literature and in practice so that they too would have a fighting chance to make headway in their own professional struggles.

This book is not, however, a history text. It is a book about what seemed to be cutting-edge changes at a given point in time throughout the past forty years that appear to me to be relevant to *today's* practice and evaluation approaches. For example, one of the focal points of these readings is the efforts in social work for many, many years to attempt to integrate research/evaluation and practice. Several of the chapters address this issue, an issue that is considered by many in our field as virtually resolved today.

Each reading is accompanied by introductory comments that place the reading not only in historical context but attempt to relate the reading to the social work of the twenty-first century. I also try to add personal comments and insights regarding my impressions of the state of research and practice at the time each chapter originally appeared.

Organization

In order to accomplish what I said I would be trying to accomplish, I have organized the book, largely on the basis of chronology, into four main parts, plus a prologue and an epilogue. Each of the parts represents a specific decade.

Obviously, dividing historical events into nice, neat ten-year categories does not necessarily correspond to real life. Things happen without regard to concern about what decade a change might fit into; changes also appear as trends over time, again without concern about whether the changes occur over years that remain within decades or overlap across decades.

And so it is in social work. Organizing this book into decades implies far more order than there actually is in the processes of change, let alone the changes themselves. Thus, the organization of this book into decades is largely an artificial device for clarity. Oh, the decades actually existed all right! They were great decades. But whether a brief history of forty years of social work is best organized by decades is another matter. That question is open for debate.

The first publication is the prologue, which is the reprint of one article, "Is Casework Effective?" I'll have a little more to say about it in the introduction to the prologue. (I realize prologues usually don't have introductions, but this prologue, as you will see from the epilogue, is kinda dear to my heart.)

Part one consists of several chapters that were originally written in the 1970s. I view that period of time as a major part of the foundation of the move toward evidence-based practice and away from some of our older conceptions of practice, so I thought it might be a clever idea to call part one "Foundations."

Part two is comprised of chapters from the 1980s. I view this time period as a kind of reexamination of issues from the 1970s as well as a consolidation of some of what we learned from the work in the previous decade. So, part two is called "Building on Foundations."

Part three contains chapters from the 1990s. I see social work in that decade as continuing the changes from the previous decade, but taking more advantage of newer ideas and methodologies as well. So, I call part three "Connecting the Past with the Future."

Part four encompasses work from the twenty-first century. (It seems much loftier, doesn't it, to say "twenty-first century" than to say "the decade from 2000 to 2010?") There is almost a culmination here of many of the variations on the themes from the earlier years. So part four is called "Toward Evidence-Based Practice." This is the shortest of the four parts since there are several more years left in this century at the time of writing this preface. I complete this part with many hopes and dreams for the movement of social work practice into both more scientific and even more humane endeavors.

The epilogue is a publication that essentially explains, I hope, what I said earlier in this preface about the prologue being "dear to my heart." I hope you will understand why I have bracketed all the chapters in this book with the articles I have chosen for the prologue and epilogue.

Finally, I have included some material in the appendix that I hope will help faculty and students with enhanced development of their interviewing and technical skills.

Acknowledgments

My wife, Renee, is the heart and soul of this book. I'm not going to say, "Without her, I wouldn't be here." That is much too much of a cliché. It's much too corny. Aw, heck: It's the absolute truth.

I want to thank Schmoopie Fischer for her support and patience. She is just as sweet as ever (although after I spend roughly two hours on the computer, without fail, she does come to the door and whine, "Enough already, daddy. Let's go for a walk.").

I very much appreciate the contributions to this book by my friend Kevin Corcoran. He not only wrote the foreword, but he also was instrumental in helping this book see the light of day.

Finally, I want to thank publisher David Follmer for believing in both me and this project.

To all of you: Me Ke Aloha Pumehana.

Joel

Prologue

It doesn't matter how beautiful your theory is, it doesn't matter how smart you are. If it doesn't agree with experiment, it's wrong.
—Richard Feynman, Nobel Laureate

In all affairs, it's a healthy thing now and then to hang a question mark on the things you have long taken for granted.
—Bertrand Russell

I may be wrong, but I doubt it.
—Charles Barkley, former NBA star, and many, many others

I realize that it defies publishing convention a little by actually introducing a prologue, but because this article was so central to everything else in this book, I thought I'd give it a shot.

"Is Casework Effective?", published in 1973, sets the more or less empirical tone for this book by presenting a review of the early outcome research in social work. This review has two dire conclusions. The first is that there appeared to be no studies with adequate methodology that could lead to a conclusion that anything social workers did led to demonstrably positive changes in clients.

The second conclusion was that many of the clients of professional social workers actually did worse than similar clients in control groups or in groups treated by nonprofessionals. I called that phenomenon "the deterioration effect," in line with what some researchers had found in the outcome studies of psychotherapy by non-social work professional personnel (Bergin, 1971).

This review of research was very stimulating to me, and to others in the field. I am using the term "stimulating" in all its possible meanings. I won't discuss that result any more here, since that impact is the entire topic of the epilogue. Suffice it to say that that article got that part of my professional career off to a bang.

Reference

Bergin, A. E. (1971). The evaluation of therapeutic outcomes. In Bergin, A. E., & Garfield, S. L. (Eds.), *Handbook of psychotherapy and behavior change: An empirical analysis*. New York: John Wiley and Sons.

Is Casework Effective?
A Review

The core of professional practice is a commitment to competence—a commitment that most directly refers to a concern with the effective carrying out of professional services. Unfortunately, social casework, the largest segment of the social work profession, has been criticized consistently and most dramatically for its failure to demonstrate clearly effectiveness in helping clients.[1] Much of the criticism leveled at casework, however, has been based either on ideological grounds, with little apparent concern for research data to support such criticism, or on an inadequate review of research, for example, using only one study, from which the critic attempts to draw conclusions for the entire profession. One can hardly be confident in conclusions derived from such methods of evaluation.

Although there was a flurry of interest in the question of casework effectiveness raised by the publication of *Girls at Vocational High,* the issues raised at that time are far from settled.[2] In fact, they never have been thoroughly discussed. It seems as if, by some tacit arrangement, major contenders in the issue of effectiveness had agreed to let the matter drop.

The thesis of this paper is that the issue of effectiveness of practice always must be of paramount concern to the profession and cannot be brushed aside. A convergence between the professional values of commitment to the scientific method and the desire to promote capably the well-being of our clients demands such a stance.[3] It is surprising then that although the issue of effectiveness frequently is a topic of discussion, and there have been some attempts to examine aspects of the research on this subject, no comprehensive review of all the available

Fischer, J. (1973). *Social Work, 18,* 5–20. Reprinted with permission of National Association of Social Workers.

[1] *See,* for example, Scott Briar, "The Current Crisis in Social Casework," *Social Work Practice, 1967* (New York: Columbia University Press, 1967), pp. 19–33.

[2] Henry J. Meyer, Edgar Borgatta, and Wyatt Jones, *Girls at Vocational High: An Experiment in Social Work Intervention* (New York: Russell Sage Foundation, 1965). For examples of the issues raised at that time, *see* Earl Ubell, "Social Casework Fails the Test," *New York Herald Tribune* (October 4, 1964); and Briar, op. cit.

[3] Scott Briar and Henry Miller, *Problems and Issues in Social Casework* (New York: Columbia University Press, 1971).

major evaluative research on casework effectiveness is available in the social work literature.[4]

This article is an attempt to provide such a review. Its aim is to examine casework effectiveness in such a way as to generate reliable conclusions that can be scrutinized and tested through independent investigation. Utilizing analytic criteria of demonstrated validity, this review will present the findings of major extant evaluative research and will extrapolate from these studies conclusions as to whether professional casework practice has indeed been found to be effective.

What Is Social Casework?

To draw conclusions about how effective casework is, it is first necessary to consider just *what* casework is, that is, what is to be examined. Hartman poses this well:

> Because people who define themselves as caseworkers define the practice so differently, and because no one has been elected to determine the definition, I assume that we can all carve out our area, practice it, teach it and write articles about it as long as the community, clients, universities and editors will support us.[5]

She also reviews a number of definitions of social casework that reflect the major streams of casework since its earliest days.

However, for research purposes, the definitions reviewed by Hartman neglect a most crucial variable—exactly what it is that caseworkers do. Complicating this problem is the increasing recognition that caseworkers do many things in many ways, all of which legitimately can be called casework.[6] This confusion in specification of casework methodology, to paraphrase Raimy's definition of psychotherapy, points to a view of casework as a set of undefined techniques, applied to unspecified problems, with unpredictable outcome. For this approach, rigorous training is recommended.[7]

In a most general sense, then, casework could be defined—at least for the purpose of reviewing studies that evaluate casework—as the services of professional caseworkers. Specification of the details of these services generally has been held to be less important than agreement that the services should be provided by persons whose educational qualifications have met the standards of the profession.

---

[4] Attempts to examine aspects of this research have been made by Scott Briar, "Family Services," in Henry S. Maas, ed., *Five Fields of Social Service: Reviews of Research* (New York: National Association of Social Workers, 1966): Briar, "Family Services and Casework," in Maas, ed., *Research in the Social Services: A Five-Year Review* (New York: National Association of Social Workers, 1970); and Ludwig L. Geismar, "Implications of a Family Life Improvement Project," *Social Casework*, 52 (July 1971), pp. 455–465.

[5] Ann Hartman, "But What Is Social Casework?" *Social Casework*, 52 (July 1971), p. 419.

[6] Robert W. Roberts and Robert H. Nee, eds., *Theories of Social Casework* (Chicago: University of Chicago Press, 1970).

[7] Victor Raimy, ed., *Training in Clinical Psychology* (Englewood Cliffs, N.J.: Prentice-Hall, 1950), p. 93.

And these qualifications traditionally have consisted of a master's degree from an accredited graduate school of social work (MSW).

The implication is that educational criteria relate to a presumed basic minimum competence in the practice of casework for all those who have been educated as caseworkers, but that it is not necessary to specify the exact nature or kind of casework. Thus any conclusion about the general success or failure of casework reached from reviewing the research can be made only if two conditions are met: (1) the services evaluated are performed by professional caseworkers and can be shown to have some central core of relevance to casework practice and (2) success or failure is the *rule* in the studies evaluated, cutting across a variety of clients, approaches, and situations. Although the issue of specification of practice methodology is important, lack of specification does not preclude drawing conclusions on a broader level—the level that examines the effectiveness of services offered by professional caseworkers, no matter which techniques and methods have been used in these services.

Almost as difficult as defining casework, however, is the problem of specifying just what is meant by "effectiveness" (or "success" or "improvement"). Obviously, the effects of intervention can show up in a number of ways, from subtle psychological changes to objective, observable changes in school grades, delinquency rates, and other performance dimensions. There might be some validity in drawing general conclusions about the effectiveness of casework from changes in only a few measures of outcome, since those few measures might really be the only appropriate indicators of the kinds of changes casework services are capable of producing. However, the scope of potential changes resulting from casework intervention would suggest that one would have more confidence about conclusions when positive changes can be demonstrated using varying types of criterion measures in one study and across several studies.

Actually, the selection of outcome indicators is a task that must be determined in advance in each study.[8] Effectiveness would then mean that differences in scores significantly favor one group over another in achieving a goal specified in advance by the researcher. Thus this review is constrained by the fact that results can only be reported in relation to the measures included in the primary investigations, even though there may have been other unknown, potentially important effects of the services.

Selection of Studies

The purpose of a study of casework effectiveness is to examine whether the services were successful in helping clients.[9] A minimum requirement for establishing that whatever changes in clients could be found were actually a result of the

---

[8] Elizabeth Herzog, *Some Guide Lines for Evaluative Research* (Washington, D.C.: U.S. Department of Health, Education & Welfare, 1959).

[9] This type of study should be distinguished from other types of outcome research that might examine the *effects* of services (e.g., along such dimensions as continuance-discontinuance) which may be unrelated to the question of whether the services were *effective*.

specific services provided is the use of a control procedure. So evidence of change in clients is not necessarily evidence that the changes came about because of the casework services, and evidence of no change cannot be taken as a demonstration that the services had no effect (e.g., that intervention might have prevented deterioration). In either situation the researcher cannot draw definite conclusions unless some form of control has been introduced to minimize alternative explanations. As Nagel points out succinctly:

> . . . data must be analyzed so as to make possible comparisons on the basis of some *control* group, if they are to constitute cogent evidence for a causal inference. The introduction of such controls is the minimum requirement for the reliable interpretation and use of empirical data.[10]

Therefore, a minimum requirement for selection of studies for this review was that some form of control group of clients was utilized in the study.

Beginning with recent reviews, major social work journals, dissertation abstracts, and unpublished agency reports were surveyed from the 1930s to the present. Over seventy studies were located that purported to examine the effectiveness of casework services. However, although these studies contained much valuable information, most neglected to include a control group in their design. Because of the difficulty in drawing a valid conclusion regarding cause and effect without a control group for comparison, the bulk of these studies had to be excluded from this review.

Two major types of control were utilized in the studies eventually selected: (1) untreated control—a group that purportedly received no treatment at all and (2) a specific form of "other-treated control." In the second type of study the experimental group received the services of professional MSW caseworkers and the control group received services from nonprofessionals (e.g., non-MSW public assistance or probation workers). Despite obvious differences in the two categories of studies, certain assumptions basic to professional education and practice are utilized in this review.

Essentially, these assumptions are as follows: given client groups with similar problems appropriate for social work intervention (1) caseworkers with professional degrees should achieve more successful results than nonprofessional workers and (2) a program of professional intervention should achieve more successful outcome with clients than either no treatment at all or nonspecific or haphazardly selected treatment. Considerable research points to the fact that there are few pure control groups. Even when nominally in a control group, people often seek help from a variety of sources, such as family, friends, the clergy, and so forth. In such cases it is assumed that a program of professional intervention should, on the whole, achieve more efficacious results.[11]

---

[10] Ernest Nagel, "Methodological Issues in Psychoanalytic Theory," in Sidney Hook, ed., *Psychoanalysis, Scientific Method and Philosophy* (New York: New York University Press, 1959), p. 53.

[11] *See* Allen E. Bergin, "The Evaluation of Therapeutic Outcomes," in Bergin and Sol L. Garfield, eds., *Handbook of Psychotherapy and Behavior Change: An Empirical Analysis* (New York: John Wiley & Sons, 1971).

Thus in line with the definition of casework as the services offered by professional caseworkers, this review will attempt to ascertain whether such services have been found to be more effective than no treatment or other nonspecific or nonprofessional services with which they have been compared.

Several other types of studies were excluded from this review in the hope that their omission would permit greater precision in drawing conclusions by minimizing potential biasing and the confounding effects which could have occurred if they had been included. Studies examining casework services outside the United States proper were not included.[12] Since the effectiveness of MSW caseworkers was the object of attention, several well-known studies examining only the services of nonprofessionals also were not reviewed.[13] Those studies that examined variations in types of professional casework without utilizing an untreated or nonprofessionally treated control group were excluded as well.[14] Further, those studies in which it appeared that caseworkers were only a small minority of the treatment team providing services to clients in the experimental group were omitted.[15] However, when there was lack of clarity in the text of the report as to certain characteristics of the study (e.g., number or proportion of caseworkers involved or the exact nature of their training), such studies were included. This was done because it was thought that the chance rejection of an appropriate study could detract more from the generality of conclusions than the chance inclusion of an inappropriate study.

Eleven studies were located that met the minimum criteria for inclusion in this review: (1) services were provided by professional caseworkers for the experimental group and (2) an "untreated" or nonprofessionally treated control group was used. The criteria used to analyze these studies were derived from available texts on the evaluation of research.[16] In general, the studies were analyzed along

[12] *See,* for example, E. Matilda Goldberg, *Helping the Aged* (London, England: Allen & Unwin, 1970): Rosa A. Marin, *A Comprehensive Program for Multi-Problem Families: Report on a Four-Year Controlled Experiment* (Rio Piedras: Institute of Caribbean Studies, University of Puerto Rico, 1969); and P. M. Kuhl, *The Family Center Project and Action Research on Socially Deprived Families* (Copenhagen: Danish National Institute of Social Research, 1969).

[13] *See,* for example, John H. Behling, "An Experimental Study to Measure the Effectiveness of Casework Service" (Columbus, Ohio: Franklin County Welfare Department, 1961) (mimeographed); Geismar, op. cit.; Alvin Rudoff and Irving Piliavin, "An Aid to Needy Children Program: A Study of Types and Responses to Casework Services," *Community Mental Health Journal,* 5 (January 1969), pp. 20–28; and Edward E. Schwartz and William C. Sample, "First Findings from Midway," *Social Service Review,* 41 (June 1967), pp. 113–151.

[14] *See,* for example, Margaret Blenkner, Julius Jahn, and Edna Wasser, *Serving the Aging: An Experiment in Social Work and Public Health Nursing* (New York: Community Service Society, 1964); and William J. Reid and Ann W. Shyne, *Brief and Extended Casework* (New York: Columbia University Press, 1969).

[15] *See,* for example, Donald G. Langsley, Frank S. Pittman III, and Kalman Flomenhaft, "Family Crisis Therapy—Results and Implications," *Family Process,* 7 (September 1968), pp. 145–158.

[16] *See* Donald T. Campbell and Julian C. Stanley, *Experimental and Quasi-Experimental Designs for Research* (Chicago: Rand McNally Co., 1963); Herzog, op. cit.; Julian Meltzoff and Melvin Kornreich, *Research in Psychotherapy* (New York: Atherton Press, 1970); and Tony Tripodi, Philip Fellin, and Henry S. Meyer, *Assessment of Social Research* (Itasca, Ill.: F. E. Peacock Publishers, 1969). For a summary of the criteria used in these texts *see* Joel Fischer, "Framework for the Analysis of Outcome Research" (Honolulu: School of Social Work, University of Hawaii, 1971), (Mimeographed.)

the following dimensions: (1) formulation of the problem, (2) research design and method of data collection, (3) methods of data analysis, and (4) the authors' conclusions. Because of space limitations, detailed analysis of each study is not included here, except when problems in design either obscured potential findings or produced incomplete conclusions.

Except for a few situations in which methods traditionally defined as group work or community organization were used, the studies reviewed here " . . . addressed the practice of social casework . . . for the most part practiced 'classically.'"[17] Thus it could be assumed, and the studies themselves demonstrate, that each examines the practice of professional caseworkers, that there is indeed in all of the studies a central core of relevance to casework practice.

Since many readers may be unfamiliar with the results of these studies, the following sections present brief summaries, detailing the types of clients included, the nature and length of service, crucial aspects of the research method, and, of course, the findings. These summaries are so presented because such a review of the content of the studies is a necessary substantive basis for forming conclusions regarding the state of casework practice. For clarity of exposition, the studies are grouped into two categories according to whether they used one or the other of the two types of control groups already described.

Untreated Controls

Berleman and Steiner   This study attempted to measure the impact of a service program on the prevention of juvenile delinquency.[18] The researchers studied 167 black seventh-grade boys to determine past evidence of acting out and to predict future acting-out behavior. Four "high-risk" categories were formed from this group, and the boys were randomly assigned from these categories to experimental and control groups. Owing to attrition and other factors, the experimental group eventually consisted of twenty-one boys and the control group of twenty-six. Three trained social workers provided intensive individual and group services to the experimental group for five months. The dependent variable of juvenile delinquency was operationally defined as acting-out behavior and measured by school and police disciplinary records. Outcome was assessed between the preservice and service periods and at two postservice periods. No significant differences were found between the groups on the criterion measures of acting-out behavior at any of the service or postservice periods.

Craig and Furst   This study was also designed to influence delinquency rates.[19]

---

[17] Carol Meyer, "Implications of Evaluative Research Findings for Curriculum Concerned with Intervention on the Micro-System Level." Paper prepared for the Symposium on the Effectiveness of Social Work Intervention, Fordham University, New York, New York, January 14–15, 1971.

[18] William C. Berleman and Thomas W. Steiner, "The Execution and Evaluation of a Delinquency Prevention Program," *Social Problems,* 14 (Spring 1967), pp. 413–423.

[19] Maude M. Craig and Philip W. Furst, "What Happens After Treatment? A Study of Potentially Delinquent Boys," *Social Service Review,* 39 (June 1965), pp. 165–171.

It included boys who rated high in predictions of probable delinquency (according to the Glueck Social Prediction Table, designed to predict future delinquency) as well as a small group of referrals from teachers. On the basis of matching, twenty-nine first-grade boys were assigned to an experimental group and twenty-nine to a control group. The boys in the treatment group were given intensive child guidance therapy by psychiatric social workers and other clinic professionals. The median length of clinic contact was fifty months. Delinquency records (presumably police and court records) were inspected over a ten-year interval and revealed the same number of delinquents in the experimental and control groups. In addition, school behavior reports, based on teacher evaluations, for nondelinquent boys were compared. These reports also revealed that the groups were not significantly different.[20]

McCabe This study attempted to use social work intervention to diminish the deleterious effects of a "pathological environment" on intellectually superior children.[21] From a larger group of predominantly black and Puerto Rican children in the second to fourth grades, who had demonstrated superior ability on IQ tests, sixty-seven children were matched and randomly assigned to treatment and control groups. Forty-two children were placed in treatment groups and twenty-five in control groups. Social workers conducted a program of intervention grounded in principles of ego psychology. They concentrated most of their efforts on small-group services to both the children and their parents.

Outcome was operationalized in terms of the children's intellectual functioning, the parents' functioning, and the family's overall functioning and measured fifty-eight indicators of change. These measures included items from intelligence and school achievement tests, behavior rating scales, and scales of parental and family functioning. The researchers compiled an overall index of outcome that showed no significant differences between the experimental and control groups. In addition, of fifty-eight measures, only one statistically significant difference— reading achievement—favored the experimental group. The overall impact of this intensive service program, even if the one significant difference was not just a statistical artifact, was negligible.

Meyer, Borgatta, and Jones The purpose of this large-scale study was to examine "the extent to which social casework is effective in prevention" with potentially problematic subjects.[22] The study subjects were four cohorts of high school girls, selected from the entire population of one school and identified on the basis of school records as "potential problem cases." Eventually, by random assignment, 189 were referred to the experimental group and 192 to the untreated control group.

Services were provided by trained social workers from an agency specializing in the problems of adolescent girls. Both individual and group services were provided, although after the first year of the three-year program, group treatment was

---

[20] The statistics used were not specified in the report.

[21] Alice McCabe, *The Pursuit of Promise* (New York: Community Service Society, 1967).

[22] Meyer, Borgatta, and Jones, op. cit., p. 3.

the primary mode of service. Three of the cohorts were included in analyses of all the data, while the last cohort, which had been exposed to treatment for two instead of the normal three years, was included only on selected measures.

Measures of outcome included a variety of subjective and objective criteria: school achievement and behavior ratings, personality and sociometric data, and client and worker ratings. Of the dozens of criteria by which experimental and control groups were compared, there were significant differences between the groups on only one of twelve factors of the Junior Personality Quiz. Although several other criteria tended to favor the experimental groups, no other between-group differences were statistically significant. To quote the authors: " . . . the conclusion must be stated in the negative when it is asked whether social work intervention with potential problem high school girls was . . . effective."[23]

Miller   The goal of this study was to prevent adolescent delinquency—operationally defined as the amount of law-violating behavior—in a lower-class urban district.[24] As part of a large-scale "total community delinquency control project," an experimental group of 205 gang members was matched with a control group of 172 gang members. Over a period of three years, the experimental group received both individualized and group services, with emphasis on group services. Although data on several outcome indicators were reported, the only clear comparison between experimental and control groups was on the number of court appearances. On this measure, there was no discernible difference between the groups. Reviewing the overall impact of the project, the author asked rhetorically: "Was there a significant measurable inhibition of law violating . . . behavior? The answer . . . is 'No.'"[25]

Powers and Witmer   This was the first controlled study to examine the effects of casework intervention.[26] A well-designed delinquency prevention project, it matched and then randomly assigned 325 "predelinquent" boys to an experimental group and 325 to a control group. Direct individualized services were provided predominantly by caseworker-counselors. The mean length of contact per boy was four years and ten months.

Outcome was measured by court and police records, ratings of social adjustment, and psychological inventories. No significant difference was found between experimental and control groups on all major methods of evaluation. As frequently happens in the evaluation of services, the workers involved believed they had substantially helped a greater proportion of their clients than the more objective outcome measures revealed. This is an important indicator of the need for control groups and objective criterion measures.[27]

---

[23] Ibid., p. 180.

[24] Walter B. Miller, "The Impact of a Total Community Delinquency Control Project," *Social Problems,* 9 (Fall 1962), pp. 168–191.

[25] Ibid., p. 187.

[26] Edwin Powers and Helen Witmer, *An Experiment in the Prevention of Delinquency—The Cambridge–Somerville Youth Study* (New York: Columbia University Press, 1951).

[27] *See,* for example, Harvey Gochros, "The Caseworker–Adoptive Parent Relationship in Post-Placement Services," *Child Welfare,* 46 (June 1967), pp. 317–326.

Of the six studies utilizing untreated control groups reviewed so far, all dealt primarily with children and adolescents, most in preventive rather than remedial terms. However, although most of the studies were conceptualized as prevention efforts, outcome indicators (e.g., personality measures, school achievement) are mainly the same as would be used in evaluating the effectiveness of remedial efforts. The overall outcome was clear: none of the studies revealed that their program had any significant effect on the clients when outcome measures for experimental and control groups were compared.

Other-treated Controls

Blenkner, Bloom, and Nielsen This study evaluated the effects of a program of services for the aged. A group of 164 aged persons were referred to community agencies for protective services because they had difficulty in caring for themselves. From this group 76 were randomly assigned to an experimental group and 88 to a control group. For one year the experimental group received intensive individualized services from experienced caseworkers; the goal was to do "whatever is necessary to meet the needs of the situation."[28] The control group received ordinary community services from a variety of agencies. Outcome was operationalized in terms of four major aspects of the clients' lives and situations: competence, environmental protection, affect, and effect on others.

Data were collected through structured interviews and ratings by observers. There were no significant differences between the experimental and control groups on most measures. Measures of "physical environment" and "concrete assistance" (both in the area of protection and not further delineated) and relief of stress on collaterals significantly favored the experimental group. However, most of the apparent gains in relation to these variables were explainable by a higher rate of institutionalization for experimental group subjects. In fact, overall findings from the initial part of the study led the project staff to consider the hypothesis that intensive service actually accelerates decline and to further examine follow-up data.

When data were examined at a five-year follow-up, there were significant differences between the experimental and control groups. That is, the experimental group members were found to have significantly higher rates of institutionalization and death than the control group members. Thus with survival being the ultimate outcome criterion, the effects of this intervention program favored the control, rather than the experimental group.

Brown Brown reported the findings of a program intended to evaluate the effectiveness of intervention with low-income multiproblem families.[29] Fifty multiproblem families receiving Aid to Families with Dependent Children (AFDC) were randomly assigned to an experimental group and fifty to a control group. The

---

[28] Margaret Blenkner, Martin Bloom, and Margaret Nielsen, "A Research and Demonstration Project of Protective Services," *Social Casework,* 52 (October 1971), p. 489.

[29] Gordon E. Brown, ed., *The Multi-Problem Dilemma* (Metuchen, N.J.: Scarecrow Press, 1968).

experimental group received intensive family-centered services from professional caseworkers with reduced caseloads, while the control group received the usual services of the public assistance agency. The program lasted thirty-one months, and the dependent variable of family functioning was operationalized as movement on the Geismar Scale of Family Functioning and the Hunt-Kogan Movement Scale. There were no significant differences between the groups, which led the researchers to conclude as follows: "Whatever was done by these workers for these clients cannot be demonstrated to have had a beneficial effect. . . ."[30]

Geismar and Krisberg   This was another study dealing with the effect of reaching-out family-centered casework on low-income multiproblem families.[31] The treatment group consisted of thirty of the most "seriously disorganized" families in one housing project. The control group was composed of fifty-one families from another housing project, all of whom were receiving AFDC and associated services. The control group differed from the treatment group on several variables. That is, it contained a far higher percentage of black families and families with absent fathers and demonstrated higher levels of family functioning at the pretest on the main criterion measure, the Geismar Scale of Family Functioning. In addition, the control and experimental groups lived in different geographic areas.

Services to the treatment group utilized various methods, primarily intensive direct services and use of environmental resources. Outcome was assessed on the Geismar scale twice for the control group and three times for the experimental group over the eighteen-month experimental period. At the conclusion of the project, the experimental group showed a gain of just under seven steps in mean "total family functioning," while the control group gained less than one scale step. The authors concluded that this demonstrated a significant effect of treatment.

Unfortunately, the data do not support this conclusion. The initial differences previously noted between the experimental and control groups—several possibly crucial variables for which the two groups were not comparable—makes any conclusion of effectiveness or noneffectiveness potentially misleading. With neither matching nor the more preferable randomization of assignments to the experimental and treatment groups, and such obvious noncomparability, any gain for the experimental group can be explained as a "selection-maturation" artifact.[32]

The treatment workers supplied information on the families' social functioning for the experimental cases, and a different group of trained researchers supplied this information for the control group, which introduced an obvious and critical source of bias. And since the scores at pretest were more extreme in a negative direction for the experimental than for the control group, any positive change from pre- to post-test may be a product of statistical regression, independent of

---

[30] Ibid., p. 127.

[31] Ludwig Geismar and Jane Krisberg, *The Forgotten Neighborhood* (Metuchen, N.J.: Scarecrow Press, 1967).

[32] Campbell and Stanley, op. cit. A selection-maturation artifact refers to an interaction that occurs when the selection of subjects for experimental and control groups results in groups with different potentials for rates of change.

the effects of the experimental variable.[33] In fact, the mean total family functioning score for the experimental families at the conclusion of treatment was still more than three steps below the pretest scores of the control group.[34] Thus the only conclusion that can be drawn from this study is that no definite conclusion about the effectiveness of the intervention program is possible.

Mullen, Chazin, and Feldstein This study utilized more satisfactory design procedures.[35] Eighty-eight new public assistance families were randomly assigned to an experimental group and sixty-eight to a control group. The experimental families received intensive professional casework services aimed at decreasing rates of family disorganization and enhancing family functioning. Control families received standard public assistance services. Eleven areas of family functioning, based on ratings of structured interviews, were used as criterion measures. At the conclusion of up to two years of service, no significant differences in family functioning were found between the experimental and control groups.

Webb and Riley The last study to be reviewed here was an attempt to affect the "life adjustment" of female probationers, aged 18 to 25.[36] Using random assignment, twenty-six recent probationers were assigned to an experimental group and thirty-two to a control group. The experimental group received intensive individualized services from family agency caseworkers for one year, and the control group received the usual probation services.

The dependent variable of life adjustment was operationalized as several dimensions of the Minnesota Multiphasic Inventory and a form of semantic differential. Subjects were also rated on sixteen "behavior correlates" by probation officers. The authors reported that the project was successful because six of twelve psychological measures showed significant improvement in the experimental group and only one of twelve showed significant improvement in the control group. In addition, five of sixteen behavior correlates "reflected markedly improved ratings of the experimental group as compared to the control group."[37]

These conclusions cannot be sustained, however, because Webb and Riley, at least on the psychological dimensions, did not include between-group statistical measures. They only reported that the experimental group improved significantly on selected measures and that the control group did not. However, if the authors

[33] Statistical regression refers to a general tendency for those groups selected for treatment because of extremely negative scores to show evidence of improvement at a later point in time, irrespective of the treatment.

[34] Although a design using analysis of covariance techniques for equating experimental and control groups on pretest measures might have reduced uncertainty, such a design is hampered when the covariate is not perfectly reliable and when the samples are drawn from such obviously disparate populations. *See* F. M. Lord, "Large-Sample Covariance Analysis when the Control Variable is Fallible," *Journal of the American Statistical Association,* 55 (1960), pp. 437–451.

[35] Edward Mullen, Robert Chazin, and David Feldstein, *Preventing Chronic Dependency* (New York: Community Service Society, 1970).

[36] Allen P. Webb and Patrick Riley, "Effectiveness of Casework with Young Female Probationers," *Social Casework,* 51 (November 1970), pp. 113–115.

[37] Ibid., p. 569.

had utilized a more appropriate statistical test—an analysis of covariance with pretest scores as the covariate (or even a t-test between the experimental and control group means if the pretest scores were equivalent)—the difference *between* groups, which is the crucial measure in evaluating overall impact of an experimental variable, may not have been significant. This is especially true in the several instances in which the differences between the groups were so slight. Again, the only conclusion that can be reached in this study is that the data were not presented in such a way as to justify a conclusion either of no effect or of significant effect.

The studies reviewed in this section contained a wider variety of clients and programs than those studies reviewed in the previous section. However, of the five studies, three clearly revealed little or no significant differences between the experimental and control groups and two provided inconclusive results.

Summary Analysis of Studies

Tables I.1 and I.2 provide a summary of all the studies reviewed. Six of the eleven studies dealt primarily with children as clients, three with low-income multiproblem families, one with the aging, and one with female probationers, aged 18–25. Most studies dealt with predominantly low-income subjects, although this was not uniformly the case. Both sexes and several ethnic groups were represented. Over two thousand separate cases, including a high percentage of families with multiple members, were involved. The group of studies reviewed here demonstrated a great diversity in criterion measures, ranging from subjective to objective measures that deal with several aspects of both personal and social functioning. Judgment, descriptive, and performance data were utilized and collected in a variety of ways, from psychological inventories and questionnaires, to worker and client ratings, to observed behaviors. While these measures individually could be faulty as indicators of change resulting from casework services, together they provide a wealth of information about the effects of casework services. More than one source of data was used to draw conclusions in almost all the studies. A wide variety of services was offered, although perhaps because many of the studies were conducted in the same time period, they reflect some uniformity in caseworker orientation, which is related to psychodynamic theoretical perspectives and/or "family-centered reaching-out" approaches.

Most of the studies provided at least minimally acceptable designs wherein experimental and control groups were assigned either through matching, randomization, or a combination of the two.[38] Frequently, however, the independent variable

---

[38] Randomization is an attempt to ensure that every potential subject has an equal chance of being assigned to an experimental or control group and is the preferable approach in attempting to avoid bias. Matching of subjects is often used when randomization is not possible. Since it would be desirable to have experimental and control groups demonstrate pretest equivalence on outcome measures (and perhaps other relevant life measures such as age) and also have an equal chance of being assigned to treatment or control groups, the optimum design would include both matching and randomization procedures. Randomization alone often produces equivalence, but this still must be examined separately by the researcher to determine whether equivalence between groups has in fact been attained.

was inadequately defined, so that the precise nature of the casework techniques used was unknown. This, however, may be less a fault of the research than, as noted earlier in this paper, of the theory and field that spawned it. There were no attempts to control for various traits and characteristics of the caseworkers (e.g., style, personality, techniques) and few attempts to examine differential characteristics of clients, especially in relation to differential responses to treatment.

Although these last flaws detract somewhat from the ability to analyze comprehensively all aspects of the results of these studies, they do not detract from the more general conclusions that can be drawn from this review. Of all the controlled studies of the effectiveness of casework that could be located, nine of eleven clearly showed that professional caseworkers were unable to bring about any positive, significant, measurable changes in their clients beyond those that would have occurred without the specific intervention program or that could have been induced by nonprofessionals dealing with similar clients, often in less-intensive service programs. In the two additional studies, the results were obfuscated by deficiencies in the design or the statistical analysis. Thus not only has professional casework failed to demonstrate that it is effective, but lack of effectiveness appears to be the rule rather than the exception across several categories of clients, problems, situations, and types of casework.

Deterioration of Clients

One of the most disturbing conclusions from the field of psychotherapy research is the finding that in a high proportion of psychotherapy studies, as many clients receiving professional services deteriorate as improve.[39] Averaged together and compared with a control group, the experimental group would therefore show no differences; thus the true effects of the experimental variable would be concealed. A reanalysis of the studies in this review shows a parallel phenomenon. In slightly under 50 percent of the studies, clients receiving services in the experimental group were shown either to deteriorate to a greater degree than clients in the control group or to demonstrate improved functioning at a lesser rate than control subjects.

For example, Berleman and Steiner, in examining the percentage of boys with school disciplinary records, concluded that there was no overall difference between the groups.[40] However, further analysis reveals that the percentage of boys in the experimental group with school disciplinary records was far higher (X^2 was significant beyond .01) than the percentage of boys in the control group. The study of Blenkner, Bloom, and Nielsen was already reviewed with regard to the deterioration of clients in the experimental group. That is, the experimental group subjects had a significantly higher death rate than those in the control group.[41]

The study by McCabe of educationally superior children revealed several areas

[39] Bergin, op. cit.
[40] Berleman and Steiner, op. cit., p. 421.
[41] Op. cit.

Table I.1 Summary of Studies Reviewed: Untreated Control Groups[a]

Author and Year	Clients			Caseworkers		
	Number	Characteristics	Method of Selection	Orientation	Major Approach	Setting for Services
Berleman and Steiner (1967)	E = 21 C = 26	Black seventh-grade boys with school disciplinary problems and police records	Matching, random	Undetermined	Intensive, direct individualized, and group services	Settlement house, home, and school
Craig and Furst (1965)	E = 29 C = 29	First-grade boys rated as "probable delinquents" on Glueck Social Prediction Scale	Matching	Undetermined, possibly psychodynamic	Intensive child guidance therapy	Child guidance clinic
McCabe (1967)	E = 42 C = 23	Mainly "intellectually superior, socially disadvantaged" black and Puerto Rican children	Matching, random	Ego psychology	Groups, some individual services	Office
Meyer, Borgatta, and Jones (1965)	E = 189 C = 192	High school girls, varied races and socioeconomic statuses, identified as "potential problems"	Random	Ego psychology, diagnostic casework	Group services, individualized services	Office
Miller (1962)	E = 205 C = 172	Lower-class gang members, varied ethnic backgrounds, both sexes	Matching	Psychodynamic, group dynamics	Group and individualized services	Streets, homes, schools
Powers and Witmer (1951)	E = 325 C = 325	Predelinquent boys aged 10–17, screened through teacher reports and test data. A variety of socio-economic classes and ethnic groups	Matching, random	Dynamic psychology	Direct individualized services	Homes, school, office

in which experimental group members declined at a higher rate than control group members or in which control group members improved at a higher rate than experimental group members.[42] On the overall index of functioning, 50 percent of the experimental group members declined, compared to only 38 percent of the control group members. The greatest decline was found in the black clients: eight out of fourteen in the experimental group deteriorated—presumably as a result of

[42] Op. cit.

Table I.1   Summary of Studies Reviewed: Untreated Control Groups[a] (*continued*)

Length and Amount of Contact	Assessment Procedure		Outcome
	Dependent Variable	Criterion Measures	
L = 5 months A = median—75 hours per client	Acting-out behavior	School disciplinary records, police records	No significant difference between E and C groups
L = 5 years (median 50 months) A = Unknown	Delinquency rates	Teacher's behavior reports, delinquency records	No significant difference between E and C groups
L = 3 years overall A = 90.5 meetings	Intellectual functioning of children, parental functioning, family functioning	Intelligence tests, school achievement, behavior rating scales, ego functioning scales, ratings of parental and family functioning	No significant difference between E and C groups
L = 1 contact to 3 years A = median— 17 contacts	School behavior, social functioning	Client and worker ratings, school grades, school-related behaviors, teacher ratings, personality and attitude inventories	No significant difference between E and C groups
L = 3 years A = 3.5 contacts per week	Law-violating behavior (delinquency)	Number of court appearances	No significant difference between E and C groups
L = 8 years (mean of 4 years, 10 months per boy) A = 27.3 contacts per year	Frequency and seriousness of delinquency, social adjustment	Court records, police statistics, ratings of seriousness of offenses, ratings of social adjustment, psychological inventories	No significant difference between E and C groups

[a]In this table "L" stands for length, "A" stands for amount of contact, "E" stands for experimental group, and "C" stands for control group.

treatment—whereas only one black control group member did so. The outcome pattern was reversed for Puerto Rican clients. Thus the overall effect was that the black and Puerto Rican clients canceled each other out so that no significant differences could be observed. McCabe further reported that means on both ego and family functioning indicators for black subjects tended to increase (indicating more positive outcome) to a greater extent for control group members than for experimental group members. This suggests treatment may have retarded normal improvement.

The delinquency control project by Miller also showed evidence of this phenomenon. In several areas related to trends in disapproved behavior and in illegal acts, the experimental group showed statistically significant increases rather than the hypothesized desired decreases.[43] However, since no figures were reported for

---

[43] Op. cit., pp. 180–183.

Table I.2 Summary of Studies Reviewed: Other-Treated Control Groups[a]

Author and Year	Clients			Caseworkers		
	Number	Characteristics	Method of Selection	Orientation	Major Approach	Setting for Services
Blenkner, Bloom, and Nielsen (1971)	E = 76 C = 88	Mentally impaired aged in need of protective services; noninstitutionalized	Random	Undetermined, probably psycho-dynamic, "social therapy"	Intensive direct services, use of environmental resources	Office and home
Brown (1968)	E = 50 C = 50	Multiproblem families receiving AFDC	Random	Multiproblem, family centered	Intensive direct services, use of environmental resources	Office and home
Geismar and Krisberg (1967)	E = 30 C = 51	Low-income multiproblem families, pre-dominantly white	Unclear, mainly post-hoc matching	Reaching-out, family centered	Intensive direct services, use of environmental resources, multimethod	Office, home, neighborhood
Mullen, Chazin, and Feldstein (1970)	E = 88 C = 68	Newly dependent public assistance recipients, mixed ethnic group, families with at least 2 members	Random	Psychodynamic	Direct individ-ualized services	Undetermined, probably office, home
Webb and Riley (1970)	E = 26 C = 32	Female probationers aged 18–25; variety of ethnic groups	Random	Psychodynamic	Direct individ-ualized services	Office

the control group, there is no way of knowing whether such deterioration was an effect of treatment or of other circumstances.

The Powers and Witmer study showed that although some of the clients in the delinquency program seemed to benefit from treatment, a substantial proportion actually were handicapped by it. The authors concluded that "the apparent chance distribution of terminal adjustment ratings . . . was due to the fact that the good effects of the study were counterbalanced by the poor."[44]

Geismar and Krisberg revealed that 10 percent of the experimental group members in their study deteriorated in social functioning over the course of the project. A comparable breakdown was not available to examine such possible decline in the control group.[45]

In three of the five studies (Berleman and Steiner, McCabe, and Powers and Witmer) control procedures made it appear likely that decline in the experimental

[44] Op. cit., p. 455.
[45] Op. cit.

Table I.2 Summary of Studies Reviewed: Other-Treated Control Groups[a] (*continued*)

Caseworkers / Control Group Workers	Length and Amount of Contact	Assessment Procedure — Dependent Variable	Assessment Procedure — Criterion Measures	Outcome
Variety of community workers, generally not social workers or not MSWs	L = 1 year A = mean of 31.8 per case	Competence, environmental protection, affect, effect on others	Ratings from structured interviews, observer ratings, clinical ratings, death and institutionalization rates	Experimental group had higher death and institutionalization rates. Also higher on "physical environment," "concrete assistance," and relief of collateral stress
Public assistance workers—BAs	L = 31 months A = median of 2+ per month	Family functioning	Geismar Scale of Family Functioning, Hunt-Kogan Movement Scale	No significant difference between E and C groups
Public assistance workers—BAs	L = 18 months A = mean of 4.4 direct contacts per month	Family functioning	Geismar Scale of Family Functioning	Major movement within E group. Major differences between E and C groups at pretest not handled statistically
Public assistance workers—BAs	L = up to 2 years A = median of 15 direct interviews	Individual and family disorganization, family functioning	Ratings of structured interviews with clients in 11 areas of family functioning	No significant differences in family functioning between E and C groups
Non-MSW probation workers	L = 1 year A = median of 6 to 9 interviews	Life adjustment	MMPI, Semantic Differential, behavior ratings	No between-group measures reported. Reported "improved" scores on 5 of 16 behavior ratings favoring E group and on 5 of 12 psychological measures favoring E group

[a]In this table "L" stands for length, "A" stands for amount of contact, "E" stands for experimental group, and "C" stands for control group.

group was actually a result of the treatment, while in two studies (Miller and Geismar and Krisberg) there is evidence to suggest that such deterioration took place. It was not always clear that the deteriorated group was sufficient in number to offset statistically the number of clients who may have improved and thereby produce a finding of no significant difference between experimental and control groups. However, even the evidence presented here is strong enough to suggest that, as with psychotherapy, the results of casework may be for better or for worse![46] At the least, future research should attempt to specify the influence, whether personal

[46] Charles Truax and Robert Carkhuff, *Toward Effective Counseling and Psychotherapy* (Chicago: Aldine Publishing Co., 1967).

(e.g., personality characteristics of caseworkers) or situational, that might account for this variation in effects.

Conclusion

This article has been concerned primarily with a presentation of research findings related to practice, rather than with an analysis of practice per se. But the disturbing nature of the results of these studies does suggest some areas for further questioning.

It is possible that the type of casework used in these studies really was not representative of the mainstream of casework practice. There appeared to be, for example, a disproportionate number of studies concentrating on work with children, especially with juvenile delinquents. Also since most of the studies dealt with low-income clients and few with middle-class clients, it might be argued that the high rate of failure was merely an artifact of the general inability of caseworkers to help clients when other more powerful environmental forces hold sway. And, although the nature of the problem is important, the methods used may reflect outdated forms of casework.

Most of the studies were conducted in the 1950s and 1960s and reflect the dominant modes of practice in those decades. Compared at least to the services offered in the earlier studies, the nature of casework practice has undergone many alterations, although there is as yet no controlled evidence that newer schools of casework have been able to demonstrate success in helping clients.[47]

But caseworkers do have to act, even in the face of such discouraging evidence, since practice can never be painted in terms of absolute success or failure. Making judgments in the face of uncertainty of knowledge has long been a characteristic of most of the helping professions. A variety of emerging approaches to practice are available as the search for more effective methods of intervention continues.[48] Perhaps future research will be able not only to validate new methodologies, but, as in the studies in which client deterioration was evident, more clearly define the elements of the old forms that enhance effectiveness.

Nevertheless, this review of the available controlled research strongly suggests that at present lack of evidence of the effectiveness of professional casework is the rule rather than the exception. A technical research corollary to this conclusion, and a comment frequently appearing in the social work literature, is that "we also lack good scientific proof of ineffectiveness."[49] This assertion, however, taken alone, would appear to be rather insubstantial grounds on which to support a profession.

[47] Roberts and Nee, op. cit.

[48] *See* Joel Fischer, *Interpersonal Helping: Emerging Approaches to Social Work Practice* (Springfield, Ill.: Charles C Thomas, 1972).

[49] Mary E. MacDonald, "Reunion at Vocational High: An Analysis of 'Girl's at Vocational High'" *Social Service Review,* 40 (June 1966), p. 188. *See also* Cooper and Krantzler, op. cit.

Part 1
The 1970s: Foundations

Whatever people in general do not understand, they are always prepared to dislike; the incomprehensible is always the obnoxious.
—Letitia E. Landon

A question that sometimes drives me hazy;
Am I or the others crazy?
—Albert Einstein

There is wisdom in turning as often as possible from the familiar to the unfamiliar: It keeps the mind nimble, it kills prejudice and it fosters humor.
—George Santayana

There seems to be considerable opinion, represented in the quotations above, that change may be difficult, but is often necessary. We sometimes seem so rooted in old ideas that, as Nobel laureate Max Planck said, the only way for change to occur in a field like a profession is for the old generation to die out, and the younger generation taught the new ideas from the beginning.

So, do these ideas apply to social work? What exactly are some of the "old" ideas, or, even more precisely, what are some of the *problems* with some of our old ideas in the years leading up to, say, the 1970s, where the materials in this book begin?

The field of direct practice in social work had a distinctly different look and feel in those days compared to our field in the first part of the twenty-first century. My impressions and observations then, in the broadest sense, were that: the effectiveness of practice was more or less assumed, mainly taken for granted; the warmth and empathy of practitioners, likewise, were taken as givens; there was a rather monolithic perspective in our theoretical orientation(s), as seen in the rather limited choice of textbooks for practice used in schools of social work; there simply was a far more limited range of approaches to practice available to social workers, as could be seen in the literature of the time. Finally, data about our many practices were missing from social work, in that most of our teaching and practice was conducted in the absence of empirical data—research evidence—supporting whatever methods we were using.

So, even as I was starting out in social work, in the mid-1960s, some distinct impressions were forming. Of course, I was looking at the field through the lenses of my own experiences in practice and through what was available in the literature. Such observations obviously are fallible. But the impressions were strong enough to me that they informed my whole academic and practice career in trying to find answers to some of the problems I perceived in our field. I hope the chapters of this book will illustrate that search.

Interestingly, the article republished in the prologue, "Is Casework Effective?" actually helped crystallize for me with empirical data some of the perceptions that I had about the social work practice enterprise. In a publication in 1978 (Fischer, 1978), I described a number of problems with our direct social work practice enterprise that I will, mercifully, only summarize here. These were problems and criticisms of the field that a small number of social work authors and researchers were beginning to identify. Many of these observations actually were supported by research evidence, as in the article in the prologue. These problems, then, are summarized as follows:

1. Social work interventions tended to be inefficient.
2. There was a lack of specific knowledge regarding interventions for changing the client's proximate environment and relevant others.
3. Our approaches to practice did not make adequate use of change agents in the client's natural environment.
4. Traditional approaches paid disproportionate attention to diagnosis and assessment and insufficient attention to *intervention* (this would become an important theme for me, as will be seen in some of the chapters in this book).
5. Most traditional approaches relied mainly on "talking therapy," with clients treated the same way no matter what the problem.
6. Many of our approaches focused more on client self-understanding (insight) than on changes in actual functioning.
7. Clients frequently were not involved with their own treatment.
8. A high percentage of clients dropped out of treatment before treatment could "work."
9. Practitioners and clients often did not agree on goals for treatment, let alone have a mutual understanding of what the intervention process is all about.
10. Social workers often were more bureaucratically-oriented rather than client-oriented.
11. There was little or no evidence that what social work educators taught was successfully learned, let alone translated into benefits for the client.
12. Social work had yet to develop effective ways of engaging and helping low-income and culturally different clients.
13. There was little or no evidence that any approaches in social work were

effective, with several studies even showing that clients of professional social workers actually *deteriorated* compared to clients in no treatment control groups.

That was quite a list—intimidating, in fact. Nevertheless, we in the field had the opportunity to take observations such as these, which really varied from the predominating beliefs at the time, in two broad ways: to paraphrase Brown's (1968) comments, as a challenge to be disputed phrase by phrase or as a challenge to reexamine assumptions on which the beliefs rest.

I took the leap at the time to hypothesize *why* these problems may have come about (Fischer, 1976, 1978). My first hypothesis was that our prevailing theoretical orientations for practice, almost exclusively derivatives of one form or another of psychoanalytic theory, had led to the inability to find positive results in research. It was the basic impotency of our practice approaches that seemed to me to be at the heart of the effectiveness issues. Moreover, I thought that many of the ways we *approached our clients* had the imprint of psychoanalytic thinking and that those forms of thinking were not inherently useful for social work clients.

Second, I hypothesized that social work had paid far more attention in our knowledge base to knowledge about *understanding* our clients and far too little attention to knowledge geared toward *helping* our clients. In other words, social work was seriously lacking in *intervention* technology, specific techniques designed to bring about planned change in clients and/or clients' situations. Most of what we engaged in was "the talking cure," another result, I'm sure, of overreliance on psychoanalytic theories. In other words, once we *understood* a situation, we did not have the commensurate capacity to *change* it.

Now, of course, there were, and still are, differing opinions about these observations, my hypotheses about them, and certainly about the accuracy of any of these ideas individually or as a whole. And our field may not have been quite as monolithic or as limited as I may have portrayed it.

Nevertheless, these observations formed the basis for virtually all of the articles to follow as I searched for answers to these most worrisome issues.

Chapters in Part 1

Chapter one actually was titled "Introduction" in the original publication, so it seems like the perfect place to start. Although this chapter originally was the introduction to another book, it serves here as an introduction to the frame of reference and some of the themes that carried over for many years in other works. Surprisingly, this introduction, with only a little editing, still seems to work for this completely different book, published well over thirty years after the original book.

Chapter two, "A Framework for the Analysis and Comparison of Clinical Theories of Induced Change" was my attempt to contribute to the literature of critical analysis in our field. It defines the focus of the analysis (clinical theories of *change*, not solely of understanding), and then provides and defines the criteria one might use to analyze clinical theories. My attempted statement here was simply that our practitioners cannot be expected to make intelligent and rational choices about their interventions without having the skills and tools to critically analyze available intervention approaches. I still believe that as firmly today as I did thirty-five years ago.

Chapter three is "Introducing New Technology Into Social Agencies: The Case of Behavior Modification." Written with Harvey Gochros, this chapter addresses one of the core issues for evidence-based practice and for every new technology (technology is defined simply as *applied knowledge*) that social workers might be considering adopting. Will it be *used?* It (almost) goes without saying that technology, such as intervention techniques and programs, that is not used is worthless to social workers and to their clients. (There is an assumption here that the technology is *worth* using, but that is a different issue, one that is addressed in the next chapter.) In this chapter, the argument is that intervention technologies must make their way into, and be adopted in, social agencies since that is where the overwhelming number of social workers doing direct practice are employed. Therefore, with most people suspicious of new technologies at first, there needs to be some strategic thought put into *how* a new technology can be successfully introduced in agencies. This chapter presents strategies for doing just that, including discussion of barriers to new information and changing negative attitudes toward that information.

Chapter four, "Do Social Workers Understand Research?" written with Stuart Kirk, is one of my favorite studies. I guess I shouldn't make fun, but Stuart and I enjoyed this entire process. We surveyed a national sample of National Association of Social Workers (NASW) members, and using a survey experimental design, determined that social workers' judgments about the quality of research and its implications for practice were significantly affected by whether the findings of a study were positive or negative. Thus, as one example, respondents believed that the study made an important contribution to the field if the results were positive while disbelieving the study was important if the results were negative. The critical message here, I believe, is that social workers must be more able to evaluate empirical work freed from certain biases that affect how they view the results of research. These results also shed some light on possible reactions of social workers to negative results of actual research when those results are counter to many professionals' beliefs, such as the article reprinted in the prologue (see the epilogue for the aftereffects, or should I say, "aftershocks," of that article). Devaluing what one does not want to believe ultimately can contribute to the decay in a profession's body of knowledge and the practices of its practitioners.

Chapter five is titled "An Eclectic Base for Practice." In this chapter, I discuss the basic principles that would inform my practice for the rest of my career through today: *eclectic practice.* I believed then and I believe now that it is impossible to be an effective practitioner by ignoring any parts of the literature that describe interventions that demonstrably can improve the lives of our clients. Thus, remaining stuck in the mire of a single perspective or theory means practitioners will approach all new knowledge with blinders on, seduced as they may be by the tenets of the approach to which they adhere. My solution: develop principles and criteria for helping practitioners make reasoned and intelligent selection from the literature of what works. My thesis: As long as an approach deals with the problems and issues that we deal with in social work, and as long as that approach is consistent with social work values, then that approach is a candidate for serious consideration by social workers. Few social workers today adhere to a solitary theoretical orientation, but the central concern of eclecticism then and now is that what one selects to use to help clients should be selected using clear and systematic criteria. This chapter presents a way of conceptualizing and using that knowledge-selection process. The chapter also fleshes out some of the ideas touched on in chapter one; in particular, ideas about the most important areas of knowledge for practice and the criteria we can—and perhaps, should—use to *select* that knowledge.

Chapter six is titled, "Building Research into Practice." The purpose of this chapter is to provide an overview of what I believe is one of the most important components of effective practice, practitioner-oriented evaluation designs. We now call these designs single-system designs because they can be used to evaluate all cases, from individuals to families to groups to larger collectivities, but as you will see from this chapter, they have a long history of other terms by which they were designated. These designs help us provide answers that all professions need in order to establish a shared body of knowledge and to be compelling in their professionalism. Those answers have to do with establishing the effectiveness of our interventions. It is my belief that every case should be evaluated as rigorously as the case and situation allows (see chapter 12 for measurement tools that can be used with these designs). Without more or less objective evaluation, we may not be able to clearly understand where we as individual practitioners and as a field are going, both with individual cases and in general. As Lewis Carroll wrote in *Alice in Wonderland:*

Alice: Would you tell me, please, which way I ought to go from here?
Cat: That depends a good deal on where you want to get to.
Alice: I don't much care where—
Cat: Then it doesn't matter which way you go.
Alice: —so long as I get somewhere.
Cat: Oh, you're sure to do that if you only walk long enough.

Maybe single-system designs and the measurement procedures described in chapter 12 can help provide a short-cut on the road to effective practice.

Chapter seven is the last chapter in part one. It is titled, "Does Anything Work?" In this chapter, I review the results of outcome research in several fields, social work, of course, but also psychotherapy and counseling, criminal justice, psychiatric hospitalization, and education. This work was stimulated by "Is Casework Effective?" and by wondering what the status of the outcome research was in other fields. Well, I found out. In all those fields, the research appeared to indicate that, at best, professionals were operating with little or no empirical evidence validating their effectiveness since lack of evidence of effectiveness seemed to be the rule rather than the exception. In addition, there seemed to be a pattern of deterioration that was eerily similar to the one I found in the social work studies.

I hope that some of the hypotheses I used in this chapter to try to explain this trying set of results have relevance even to the practice of today.

References

Brown, G. E. (1968). *The multi-problem dilemma*. Metuchen, N.J.: Scarecrow Press.

Carroll, Lewis. (1865). *Alice's adventures in wonderland*. London: Macmillan.

Fischer, J. (1976). *The effectiveness of social casework*. Springfield, IL: Charles C. Thomas.

Fischer, J. (1978). *Effective casework practice: An eclectic approach*. New York: McGraw Hill.

Chapter 1
Introduction

"Interpersonal helping"—the topic of this book—encompasses a wide variety of interventive practices, methods and techniques. In the broadest sense, interpersonal helping can be described as informed, purposeful intervention either directly with, or on behalf of, a given person or persons (client). The goal of such intervention is to bring about positive changes either directly in the client's functioning, or in environmental factors immediately impinging on the client's functioning. These interventions are intended to enhance aspects of the client's feelings, attitudes and/or behaviors in such a way that his personal and social functioning will be more satisfying and beneficial to him.

Although broad in scope, this definition nevertheless excludes from the rubric "interpersonal helping" a variety of potential interventions. Use of the term "purposeful" excludes any chance or unplanned change such as might occur through accidental encounters between, say, professional helpers and clients. Unintended by-products of other endeavors—e.g. the "warm" teacher who coincidentally to her teaching modifies pupil feelings and attitudes—would also be excluded. Similarly, use of the term "informed" suggests the importance of utilizing principles and procedures derived systematically from an identifiable body of knowledge, as opposed to reliance on luck, faith or intuition (although such characteristics may be powerful change factors in their own right as noted by Frank, 1961).

This implies that the intervener—or helper—is qualified to do his job, mainly on the basis of his familiarity with, and competence in, the utilization of intervention knowledge on behalf of his clients. Again, this rules out "naturally helpful" individuals, such as the kind and understanding neighbor, teacher or physician, who unwittingly apply successful interventive tactics. Obviously, these individuals can have most beneficial effects on people, but they are not a primary object of concern in this book.

In selecting the term "client," there is an attempt to convey the idea that a more or less formal process of identification—by the client, helper and/or society—has

Fischer, J. (1973). *Interpersonal Helping*. Springfield, IL: Charles C. Thomas. Reprinted with permission of Charles C. Thomas.

led to the determination that some aspect of dysfunctionality (Fischer, 1969) exists in the life of a given person (the client). The client himself may be voluntary or involuntary,[1] aware of his problem(s) or not, an apt participant in the helping process or not. But there should be a clear designation by the helper of whom he is to help. This implies that the client, himself, may not be the actual target for action, although he is to be the beneficiary of that action (Pincus and Minahan, 1970). Intervention may proceed in his environment—home or school, for example—but the helper will have identified the ways in which such intervention will affect the person(s) on whose behalf he is intervening. The term client also connotes a customer or consumer of services. Such a designation almost inherently contains a greater degree of dignity and worth than an appellation such as "patient," which suggests elements of sickness and of disease. Further, the term "patient" also implies an intervention strategy so circumscribed as to deal with individuals solely on a direct basis in a quasimedical way, while the notion of "client" implies a broader purview for intervention, encompassing social and environmental factors.

This definition of interpersonal helping also calls for an emphasis on the *functioning* of the client. This is not to disparage the value of independent changes in attitudes, feelings and so on. In fact, changes in these dimensions are hard enough to come by as the research on outcome shows. Nevertheless, the point of view expressed here is that such changes as can be attributed to the helper's intervention should have results demonstrable in improved personal and social functioning in the variety of roles which constitute daily living.[2]

Clearly, such a sweeping definition of interpersonal helping does not set explicit limits on the kinds of knowledge which a practitioner might utilize. Except for the suggestion here that this knowledge must deal with interventive principles and procedures, the criteria for knowledge selection will be discussed in the following section. However, there does remain the matter of discussing the helper's group affiliation—profession and discipline.

Interpersonal helping provides a broad umbrella encompassing a number of the activities which traditionally have been included under such designations as psychotherapy, casework, and counseling and guidance, performed by social workers, psychologists, counselors and psychiatrists. In fact, in areas where research has been conducted, primarily views and attitudes toward clients and preferences for therapeutic techniques, little or no differences arising from professional affiliation can be detected (Strupp, 1955, 1958, 1960; McNair and Lorr, 1964; McNair, Lorr and Callahan, 1963; Eels, 1964; Henry et al., 1970). Far more importantly, there is no evidence that the profession of the helper leads to any difference in his *success* with clients (Poser, 1966; Meltzoff and Kornreich, 1970). There may be

---

[1] There are few truly "voluntary" clients, despite such an assumption in most of the literature on interpersonal helping. Aside from the obvious institutionalized and legally coerced client, most clients come to "treatment" under pressure from family, peers, employers, etc. or the unwanted pressure of their own problems. (See Miller, 1968, for a discussion of the value dilemmas involving nonvoluntary clients.)

[2] This emphasis on functioning is also congruent with social work's long-standing focus on problems of social functioning.

professional differences in status and prestige, and ability to influence *colleagues,* but no differences that can be attributed to profession in the ability of helpers to help their clients.

This suggests that whatever the official designation of the process—whether, for example, it be called psychotherapy or casework—within the limits of an inter-personal influence process where the helper attempts to intervene in the psycho-social problems of clients, the various professions may be engaged in a uniform enterprise (Henry et al., 1970). This has been demonstrated empirically, and can be demonstrated conceptually to the extent that the approaches to intervention used by members of different professions draw systematically upon a common core of knowledge (e.g. "psychodynamic theory"). As a corollary to that notion, it might be suggested that when professionals are in fact engaged in similar activities, it would behoove them to be utilizing the best knowledge available, whether or not that knowledge has been developed by members of one's own profession.

This, of course, does not mean that differences between the various profes-sions are lacking. Clearly, a variety of professional differences do exist, in matters of training, interests, spheres of functioning, societal mandates, areas of special-ization, and so on. Overlap exists most obviously, though, in the area of clinical or therapeutic endeavors. And this suggests that when such overlap does occur, knowledge that has common relevance must be made available to all practitioners who might be able to put it to use. While social workers—to whom this book is largely directed—obviously derive a considerable portion of their knowledge from fields other than social work, the perspectives, opinions and new developments external to social work often suffer either in translation to social work terms, or through pure neglect.

Although a substantial part of the profession does engage in clinical activities, social workers are not only clinicians or therapists. As one of its unique features, social work traditionally has featured a broadly-based practice which, even in the direct service component, deals with such dimensions of practice as restoration, provision and prevention (Boehm, 1959). Thus, it would seem to be setting up a straw man to argue, for example, that casework and psychotherapy are one and the same. The caseworker, generally operating from a far broader base than the field of psychotherapy alone can provide, traditionally has supplied a wide range of services to clients. What can be argued, though, is first, the literature has not accurately reflected this broadly-based practice; second, much of the direct service literature until only recently has been preoccupied with development of rather narrow models for practice (see Fischer, 1971 re: Roberts and Nee, 1970); and third, there is a considerable amount of well-defined knowledge available that is appropriate for social work, and that could be integrated into a more flexible and comprehensive practice approach.

In essence, this orientation contains within it an appeal that social workers (and other professionals) remain open to new ideas and emerging developments in practice, and that carefully thought-out criteria be utilized to distinguish between fads, and the selection of knowledge that can be translated into constructive gains for clients. In short, the professional cannot afford premature closure around one approach, expecting to use that approach indefinitely without either awareness of new developments, or willingness to examine and utilize new developments when they are available. This book is an attempt to provide not only the tools for analysis, but a selection of knowledge from multidisciplinary sources that hopefully will update professional practice in these areas, and stimulate a broadly conceived practice resting on a careful, informed scrutiny of a number of alternatives.

A Frame of Reference

The question obviously arises as to how knowledge selected from presumably divergent perspectives can be meaningfully integrated in a volume such as this, let alone in actual practice. In the past, many social workers have opted for a form of theoretical integration. Freudian-based ego psychology was used to "understand people," and to pull together a variety of perspectives ranging from role theory to personality development to casework practice principles. But, despite noble efforts to the contrary, this resulted in a rather unidimensional picture of man, and a clearly circumscribed practice theory. Change principles were derived from a narrow base composed of part-Freud (and his theoretical descendants) and part "practice wisdom." But since the practice wisdom itself was largely a reflection of Freudian and neo-Freudian thinking, the end-product of this ingrown and circular process was clearly lacking in the breadth necessary for a comprehensive base for practice. More importantly, use of a single "theoretical orientation," whatever its nature, as an integrating base for practice generally precludes the consideration of clearly divergent new developments in intervention technology as viable alternatives for practice.

The frame of reference utilized here is atheoretical, but grounded in certain values and principles which cut across various theoretical (and professional) domains. This section of the book contains an explication of those principles.

Since social work is ultimately a profession deeply rooted in, and committed to, a number of value positions, the most appropriate way to introduce an approach to practice for social work is through a recapitulation of what might be considered the principal value premises underlying the approach. Two value propositions could be identified as furnishing direction for the contents of this book, and perhaps the social work enterprise as a whole. They can be viewed as the primary values in a hierarchy of several values.[3] They are: (a) respect for the dignity and worth—or more appropriately, the humanity—of every individual; and (b) a commitment endorsing man's responsibility to his fellow man. These values almost automatically render irrelevant the argument that individualized helping is a waste of time or energy with little or no palpable return. For while it is not necessary to engage all people in an individualized helping process, and it may not always be effec-

---

[3] See *Values in Social Work: A Re-Examination,* NASW (1967), for a comprehensive discussion of major values underlying the practice of social work.

tive when we do, the primacy of these values indicates it would be even more disastrous if, when appropriate, we were not to *try*. Taken together, these two premises point toward an unabashed recognition of the inherent meaningfulness of the person-to-person approach, and the desirability of countering what might be contended are the increasing processes of dehumanization and impersonalization of modern society.

Thus, two levels of principles for examining a variety of alternatives for practice can be derived from these preeminent ethical considerations. At the broadest level, in making selections from among alternatives for practice and in integrating those selections into a practice framework, the first principle involves the extent to which utilization of an approach would be congruent with the primary values of the profession. Secondly, in actual application, a specific procedure can be evaluated as ethically suitable if its utilization does not demean—more, enhances or maintains—the dignity and individuality of the persons involved, and can be implemented in a way consonant with the values of both client(s) and helper(s).

As another dimension, the area of knowledge to be examined, per se, has characteristics which can be utilized both as criteria for evaluation and as principles of integration. Obviously, given the explosion of knowledge in the social and behavioral sciences in recent decades, the educator and theorist, not to mention the practitioner, needs guidelines to aid in wending his way through the constantly expanding maze of ideas. It would probably be gratuitous to note that social work has long avowed the importance of knowledge for practice which deals with both social *and* psychological characteristics of human beings, particularly as related to the practice goal of enhancing client social functioning.[4] What may be less obvious, though, is that a substantial proportion of this knowledge is only minimally related to the explicit process of intervention into dysfunctional spheres of human existence. In large part, available knowledge has served mainly to bolster professional *understanding* of human behavior (no mean accomplishment in itself), with very little to say about how maladaptive aspects of that behavior might be *changed*.

A graphic presentation might suffice at this point for facilitative purposes. Figure 1 is a representation of the two major areas of knowledge from the social and behavioral sciences which, in a gross sense, are potentially available to practitioners in the area of interpersonal helping.

Causal knowledge, by far the bulk of the knowledge developed in the behavioral sciences, essentially serves as an aid in understanding the development of both adaptive and maladaptive behavior, and is devoted to answering the question: why did this state of affairs come about? This is, of course, valuable information for the practitioner, and crucial in assessing cases and situations. Intervention knowledge, on the other hand, prescribes principles and procedures for inducing change in (by and large) problematic situations, and seeks to answer the question: what

---

[4] That such avowals have not always kept pace with realities of practice seems clear from the earlier example of overdependence on ego psychology as a theoretical orientation, and examples to be discussed in the following section.

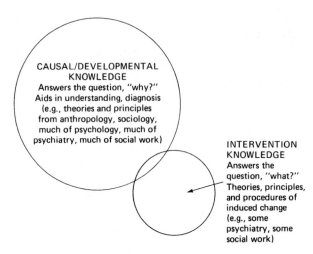

Fig. 1   Areas of knowledge potentially available to practitioners.

can be done in this situation and will it be effective? Clearly, there is some overlap between these two areas of knowledge. Perhaps equally as clear is the necessity for establishing some priorities for knowledge development and selection. The position taken throughout this book is that the priority for professional practice is in the area of knowledge dealing specifically with interventive methodology.

Statements such as the above may appear to be mere truisms. By definition, a professional practice rests on a body of knowledge the purpose of which is to supply the practitioner with the capacity to influence (or control or change) "natural" events. In fact, practice theory, per se, can be described as being composed of two major elements. The first involves a systematic explication of diagnostic principles (with the goal of understanding the phenomena of concern). The second part involves a systematic explication of principles of change, and procedures for implementing those principles. Hypothetically, the diagnostic and treatment principles are to be utilized together. Unfortunately, what can be demonstrated is, first, there appears to be little or no relationship between diagnosis and treatment in major areas of traditional practice (Fischer, 1971), and second, the bulk of our current professional knowledge lies in the causal-diagnostic realm, at the expense of intervention methodology, and to the extent that some approaches even fail to prescribe any procedures for influencing client-change (see, e.g. Fischer, 1972; Roberts and Nee, 1970; Ford and Urban, 1963). This contributes to what might be termed the "etiological pitfall" (Bennis et al., 1961), wherein practitioners are caught up in a process of trying to understand how the client came to be the way he is, without a concomitant ability to influence changes in those dimensions even were they to be successfully understood. Diagnostic knowledge, in and of itself, while important, is an insufficient basis for effective intervention, and is of real consequence only to the extent that it complements knowledge dealing with intervention.

Thus, an important principle both for selection of the contents of this book, and for integrating diverse approaches in practice, lies in the extent to which an approach deals with interventive practices, whether of an individual-psychological or social-environmental nature. This includes a systematic explanation of how induced change comes about, and prescription of procedures so that the change principles might be implemented by the practitioner.

The latter part of this criterion bears particularly careful scrutiny. A number of approaches ostensibly dealing with interventive practices nevertheless equivocate on the matter of delineating techniques. Since theories, or principles of theories, cannot themselves be applied with people, an absence of specific techniques which detail how to carry out change efforts means that a helping person would not actually be able to implement the approach (see e.g. Perlman, 1970; Smalley, 1970).

Specification of interventive procedures alone, while serving to narrow the field considerably, is still insufficient as a sole criterion for adequate selection from among the dozens of available approaches to intervention (see, e.g. Ford and Urban, 1963; Patterson, 1966). Thus, a crucial additional criterion for establishing the value of an approach, and applied whenever possible in the selection of articles for this book, is the extent to which there is empirical validation of successful intervention with clients when change procedures are implemented. In other words, when research establishes the efficacy of an approach, it must be considered a prime candidate for adoption for practice.

At least three implications stem from major reliance on research. In the first place, use of research findings provides clear guidelines for use in evaluation. This would tend to diminish a helter-skelter approach to knowledge selection wherein a practitioner adopts an approach because a theorist uses flowery phrases, seems impressive in his erudition, or the approach somehow "sounds good."

Second, the complexity of most theories precludes total theoretical validation. Hence, it would appear to be a near-impossibility to bring together entire theories, or comprehensive systems of change, especially on the basis of research evidence of effectiveness. Actually, research tends to be carried out on selected portions of theory, in this case, on specific change principles and procedures. So, instead of attempting to integrate several complete theories, a number of different principles and procedures, perhaps selected from different theories and used in a complementary fashion, might form the basis for practice. Thus, their utilization can be decided upon given the particular nature of the client, problem or situation. This can be accomplished on the basis of an appropriate assessment, and evidence that implementation will be efficacious.

The preceding relates to the third implication of using research as an important aid in integrating diverse approaches to practice. Presumably, the studies upon which a judgment is based illustrate the conditions under which an approach is successfully utilized. This, in turn, suggests an implicit, or even explicit, client/diagnostic typology which demonstrates the types of problems and clients where a given approach can be effectively applied. Combination of effective approaches, then, can supply not only a complementary range of interventive procedures, but a range of problem-situation configurations where the procedures can be applied. The goal, of course, is the maximum in technical flexibility for the practitioner in response to the large variety of potential client problems.

In essence, what is proposed here is that the greater the degree of scientifically validated input in practice, the greater the degree of competence can be exercised by the practitioner on behalf of his clients. This does not exclude the use of intuition or "horse sense"—the art of practice. The point is not that professionals should be automatons unfeelingly implementing an intervention technology. The point *is* that a rigorous foundation for practice, involving the testing and evaluation of concepts and propositions, will provide a more successful base for the use of less clearly defined dimensions.

Unless posed as an alternative to the approach which has clear and considerable empirical validation, lack of research on effectiveness does not automatically render an approach without merit. In fact, a wide range of criteria exist for evaluation of such approaches on structural, substantive and ethical grounds. In some situations, and in the absence of research evidence to the contrary, such approaches may be the intervention of choice. What is looked for ultimately is some Gestalt, some careful piecing together of a complex of analytic factors. When a number of approaches can be evaluated as satisfactory on the variety of criteria suggested here, and can be seen to complement each other based on clearly defined prescriptive statements for their utilization, some degree of integration for practice can be demonstrated to have occurred.

Such integration may be facilitated through use of a framework for assessment such as the one developed by Atherton, Mitchell and Schein (1971 a and b). These authors have devised a classification scheme of client problems as related to personal roles and the structure of social systems. The problem typology is divided into three major categories: (a) Problems related to performance of legitimate and acceptable roles (e.g. impairment of role performance because of illness; or problems in role transition); (b) Problematical roles (e.g. outsider role; or stigmatized role); and (c) Problems in the structure of social systems (e.g. nonavailable roles; or excessive role expectations). Within each category, a variety of "points for intervention" are identified. Based upon these points for intervention, Atherton et al. have identified eleven roles—several of which are discussed in this book—for the change agent: broker, interpreter, psychosocial and sociobehavioral counselor, educator, mediator, advocate, crisis intervener, role model, catalyst, and agent of social change.

Through their attempt to systematize the assessment-intervention process, Atherton et al. offer an advantageous method of looking at the multiplicity of practice functions dealt with in this book. Implicit in their work, also, is the necessity for the professional helper to be equipped with an eclectic knowledge base to be able to flexibly meet the demands of the great number and variety of problems encountered in practice.

Social Work Tradition and an Example from Practice

There are clear potential problems of confusion and uncertainty involved both in utilizing knowledge derived from a variety of sources, and in functioning in a variety of roles. Why, therefore, should the practitioner, especially the social work practitioner, have to contend with such difficulties? Obviously, in the first place, experience points to the fact that the diversity of problems and situations encountered in practice dictates the necessity for a response in kind: diversity of knowledge and roles to more adequately deal with such situations as they arise. But beyond this is an element partly composed of professional mandate, of societal sanction, of practice experience, and of agency or institutional concerns, which, cumulatively, serves to interrelate and enhance values and knowledge and the realities of day to day practice. For want of a better term, this element might be called "tradition."

In social work, particularly, tradition operates powerfully to shape aspects of our practice. For example, one of the points of view expressed in this book is that it is a responsibility of the direct service practitioner to take on a mediating function, working to coordinate individuals with institutions. This could be seen partly as an expression of awareness and concern about the importance of interactional factors—psychological and social—influencing human behavior. But more than that, this point of view has been expressed, often implicitly, from social work's earliest days, from Richmond[5] to Hamilton (1952) to Reynolds (1963); identified by Wilensky and Lebeaux (1958) as social work's liasion function, and described in this book as a "broker" function.

Actually, like Topsy, traditional practices have a habit of "just growing up." There is, perhaps, at some point in time an "unmet need," and individual practitioners, agencies or institutions take action to attempt to fill the gap. So, as Tevya notes in "Fiddler on the Roof": "You may ask, 'How did this tradition get started?' I'll tell you. I don't know. But it's a tradition." And the traditions become developed (and even "conceptualized") and incorporated into practice. Thus, social workers have come to perform a mediating function, ranging in activity from helping a bedridden client deal with a hospital staff, to aiding a client in wending his way through a bureaucratic maze to secure a basic right, to the application of pressure to influence institutions to respond to the needs of individuals. And these functions are performed for an important reason: they are necessary, and very few other people are doing them in an organized or systematic way.

The interrelation of values, knowledge and tradition can be clarified by examining a prototypical form of social work, practice in a school setting. The practitioner in a school participates in a variety of activities (Vinter and Sarri, 1965): direct services aimed at remediation of individual pupils' problems and facilitation of growth

---

[5] Mary Richmond stated: "I have spent twenty-five years of my life in an attempt to get social casework accepted as a valid process in social work. Now I shall spend the rest of my life in trying to demonstrate to social caseworkers that there is more to social work than social casework." Quoted in Bruno (1948), pp. 186, 187.

and development; mediation between pupil and school personnel; consultation to teaching personnel; and a bargaining or lobbying function—advocacy on behalf of students whom the social worker has identified as clients.

A number of points can be illustrated by these activities. Whatever the form of intervention, the social worker's efforts are on behalf of the student as identified client (but not necessarily with the student as target). In fact, an important corollary to the value positions identified in the preceding section, and aptly stated in the Code of Ethics of the National Association of Social Workers, demands such a stance: "I regard as my primary obligation the welfare of the individual or group served, which includes action for improving social conditions." Another point which can be illustrated is the necessity for the practitioner to possess a wide repertoire of interventive measures—some with few obvious similarities—to adequately conduct his job. Additionally, all of the interventions in the school can be seen not only in terms of remediation or treatment, but within the context of prevention: direct intervention with the child to forestall further disruption, and consultation if not advocacy to alter the system to provide a more beneficial effect on the functioning of its constituents. And finally, it can be seen that a process of assessment is necessary as a basis for making decisions as to what form of intervention is appropriate at what point.

Again using the school system as an example, the practitioner's job at point of contact, say, with a student newly referred by a teacher, would be to begin an assessment process incorporating the following dimensions: (a) identifying (for himself) the child as his client, but not immediately accepting the child as the target for intervention; (b) assessing both personal and interpersonal circumstances based on the principle that a broad range of psychosocial variables are pertinent;[6] (c) making the judgment as to where intervention would be most efficacious; (d) implementing the intervention (which could involve a combination of approaches); and (e) evaluating the results of intervention. In sum, this process involves a continuous interaction between the practitioner's values, knowledge and a tradition of services. Together, these dimensions provide a system for decision-making which could lead to intervention at any level—in this example, from the individual child, to the family, teacher or broader school system.

It is the thesis of this book that it is dysfunctional for a profession involved in interpersonal helping to become overly dependent on one theoretical perspective. It is dysfunctional for two primary reasons: (a) exclusive reliance on one orientation frequently precludes systematic, objective examination of other orientations; and (b) no single theoretical perspective—at least to this date—has been able to successfully address the wide range of problems that practitioners encounter.

---

[6] As contrasted, say, to only psychological. This precludes immediate assignment to psychotherapeutic treatment since a form of intervention into the impinging social system might be more relevant. Immediate acceptance of the child into treatment implies that the problem rests mainly with the child as deviant, thereby hastening a labelling process (see Siporin, 1965). Despite social work's avowal of the importance of social phenomena, practitioners often still attend more readily to psychological variables (Fischer, 1970).

And, as the above example illustrates, use of a number of discrete approaches in practice does not preclude employment of an overall perspective or orientation that serves to aid the practitioner in comprehending the array of forces which he confronts. As suggested in this book, that orientation might be integrated less at a theoretical level than at a level at which values, knowledge and tradition interrelate to provide a broad framework for professional practice. The framework utilized in this book also assumes the appropriateness of an interactional model of human behavior in which individual and social phenomena interact in definable ways to produce numerous forms of dysfunctionality (see Vinter, 1967). This in turn leads to the necessity for the practitioner to be equipped with a variety of approaches to both individual and social intervention.

References

Atherton, C., Mitchell, S., and Schein, E. (1971A). Locating points for intervention. *Social Casework, 52(3),* 131–142.

Atherton, C., Mitchell, S., and Schein, E. (1971B). Using points for intervention. *Social Casework, 52(4),* 223–233.

Bennis, W., Benne, K. and Chin, R. (Eds.). *The Planning of Change.* New York, Holt, Rinehart & Winston, 1961.

Bergin, A. and Garfield, S. (Eds.). *Handbook of Psychotherapy and Behavior Change.* New York, Wiley & Sons, 1971.

Boehm, W. *Objectives of the Social Work Curriculum of the Future.* New York, Council on Social Work Education, 1959.

Bruno, F. *Trends in Social Work.* New York, Columbia University Press, 1948.

Eells, J. Therapists' views and preferences concerning intake cases. *J Consult Psychol, 28:*382, 1964.

Fischer, J. Theories of social casework: A review. *Social Work, 17(1):* 1972.

Fischer, J. Portents from the past: What ever happened to social diagnosis? *International Social Work, 13(2):*18–29, 1970.

Fischer, J. Negroes and whites and rates of mental illness: Reconsideration of a myth. *Psychiatry, 32(4):*428–446, 1969.

Ford, D. and Urban, H. *Systems of Psychotherapy.* New York, Wiley & Sons, 1963.

Frank, J. *Persuasion and Healing.* Baltimore, John Hopkins Press, 1961.

Goldstein, A., Heller, K. and Sechrest, L. *Psychotherapy and the Psychology of Behavior Change.* New York, Wiley & Sons, 1966.

Goldstein, A. and Simonson, N. Social psychological approaches to psychotherapy research. In Bergin, A. and Garfield, S. (Eds.). *Handbook of Psychotherapy and Behavior Change.* New York, Wiley & Sons, 1971, pp. 154–196.

Hamilton, G. *Theory and Practice of Social Casework.* New York, Columbia University Press, 1951.

Henry, W., Sims, J. and Spray, S. L. *The Fifth Profession.* San Francisco, Jossey-Bass, 1971.

McNair, D. and Lorr, M. An analysis of professed psychotherapeutic techniques. *J Consult Psychol, 28*:265–271, 1964.

McNair, D., Callahan, D., and Lorr, M. Therapist 'type' and patient response to psychotherapy. *J Consult Psychol, 26*:425–429, 1962.

Meltzoff, J. and Kornreich, M.: *Research in Psychotherapy*. New York, Atherton, 1970.

Miller, H. Values dilemmas in social casework. *Social Work, 13 (1)*:27–34, 1968.

Patterson, C. *Theories of Counseling and Psychotherapy*. New York, Harper & Row, 1966.

Perlman, H. H. The problem-solving model in social casework. In Roberts, R. and Nee, R. (Eds.). *Theories of Social Casework*. Chicago, University of Chicago Press, 1970, pp. 129–181.

Pincus, A. and Minahan, A. Toward a model for teaching a basic first-year course in methods of social work practice. In Ripple, L. (Ed.): *Innovations in Teaching Social Work Practice*. New York, C.S.W.E., 1970, pp. 34–57.

Poser, E. The effect of therapists' training on group therapeutic outcome. *J Consult Psychol, 30*:283–289, 1966.

Reynolds, B. *An Uncharted Journey*. New York, Citadel Press, 1963.

Roberts, R. and Nee, R. (Eds.). *Theories of Social Casework*. Chicago, University of Chicago Press, 1970.

Simon, B. Social casework theory: An overview. In Roberts, R. and Nee, R. (Eds.). *Theories of Social Casework*. Chicago, University of Chicago Press, 1970, pp. 353–397.

Siporin, M. Deviant behavior theory in social work. *Social Work, 10*:59–67, 1965.

Smalley, R. The functional approach to casework practice. In Roberts, R. and Nee, R. (Eds.). *Theories of Social Casework*. Chicago, University of Chicago Press, 1970, pp. 77–129.

Strupp, H. *Psychotherapists in Action*. New York, Grune & Stratton, 1960.

Strupp, H. The performance of psychiatrists and psychologists in a therapeutic interview. *J Clin Psychol, 22*:219–226, 1958.

Strupp, H. Psychotherapeutic technique, professional affiliation and experience level. *J Consult Psychol, 19*:97–102, 1955.

Values in Social Work: A Re-Examination. New York, National Association of Social Workers, 1967.

Vinter, R. (Ed.) *Readings in Group Work Practice*. Ann Arbor, University of Michigan Press, 1967.

Vinter, R. and Sarri, R. Malperformance in the public school: A group work approach. *Social Work, 10 (1)*:3–14, 1965.

Wilensky, H. and Lebeaux, C. *Industrial Society and Social Welfare*. New York, Russell Sage Foundation, 1958.

Chapter 2
A Framework for the Analysis and Comparison of Clinical Theories of Induced Change

In the process of knowledge-building for social work, one of the profession's great strengths and one of its most serious weaknesses lies in its "integrative" nature: the tendency to select from other areas knowledge appropriate for the practice of social work. The strength of this orientation is the potential flexibility such selection allows our profession; unattached as we hypothetically are to a specific professional theory, we are free to seek out and utilize from other disciplines whatever may be efficacious in work with our clients. The flaw in the process, though, lies in the paucity of available material that can serve as a reasoned guide for the study and selection of material from sources external to the profession. We therefore tend to be rather haphazard in our choices, and, as the periodic upheavals in the state of both our knowledge and our practice might well testify, frequently fail to evaluate critically what we do select, often to the detriment of our client populations.

The purpose of this paper is to propose a framework for the analysis of clinical theories of induced change—that is, theories of therapy[1]—in an effort to help correct what has been essentially a dysfunctional position for the profession. The framework is focused on clinical change theories for three reasons. First, a considerable portion of the curriculum in most schools of social work is structured around education in the theories and practice of intervention with individuals, families, and small groups (for example, the "methods" as opposed to the human-behavior courses), and a substantial part of our knowledge base is similarly concerned. Second, most social work practitioners are employed in agencies whose primary function is the provision of such direct services. Third, there is a dearth of readily accessible analytic material, particularly with a social work emphasis, dealing directly with clinical theories of induced change. This is not to say that several writers have not suggested criteria that are appropriate to the purposes intended here (see, for example, Hall and Lindzey [5], Ford and Urban [3], Thomas [13], Briar [1]); in fact, some of the applicable material, particularly from the prototypic work of Ford

Fischer, J. (1971). *Social Service Review*, 45, 446–454. Reprinted from *The Social Service Review* Vol. 45, No. 4, December 1971.

[1] For definitions and a discussion of the distinction between theories of induced change and other related theories (for example, personality theories) see Fischer (2).

and Urban (3), has been modified for inclusion in this framework. Rather, the point is that much of this work has utilized assessment criteria that are either too gross to provide guidelines for detailed, intensive analysis of theoretical material, or that basically tend to be focused on areas of knowledge other than clinical theories.

The goals of development of this framework are twofold:

1. It can serve as a guide in the study of clinical theories by pointing out some of the significant questions that a clinical theory might address. Thus, some of the uncertainty and confusion that might confront a reader of many of the complex theories of therapy can be minimized, and some of the superfluous theoretical material bypassed.

2. Based on the way in which a theory is constructed around these dimensions, and the way it does or does not address the criteria—which is the substance of the analysis—an evaluation of the theory can take place: a judgment about the value of a given theory (or aspects of a theory) for the practice of social work.

There are two basic approaches to studying theory. The first is to step within the boundaries of the theory itself, learn what the theorist has to say, and then accept or reject it on the basis of ambiguous, poorly defined, or (as often happens) no criteria. This might be called the descriptive method since the reader, after considerable study, is generally prepared only to describe what the theory states. The second approach involves the development of a number of criteria—external to any specific theory—which a theory should or could address or around which it is constructed, and then stepping outside the boundaries of the theory to this external frame of reference and assessing the theory against those criteria. This is the analytic orientation, the frame of reference utilized here. The most important advantages this orientation offers lie in its utilization of standardized guidelines for studying diverse theories, and, although some bias is inevitably present, in its objectivity. That is, every theory is evaluated against the same criteria.

There are five basic areas in which clinical theories can be analyzed: (*a*) structural characteristics; (*b*) characteristics as a theory of therapy; (*c*) empirical status; (*d*) assumptions about the nature of man and moral implications; and, as a summary device, (*e*) applicability for social work.[2] Each of these five categories has numerous subclassifications. The extent to which the various theories address each of these criteria varies considerably. But, in this, of course, lies the analysis.

Structural Characteristics

In the most general sense, a theory is any more or less formalized explanatory conceptualization of the relationship of variables. The "basic building blocks" of theory construction are the concepts, generalized class names representing certain abstracted properties of the class (7). Propositions are statements about relationships between concepts (formal) and/or observable events (empirical). All theories

---

[2] With minor modifications, this framework is also applicable to the evaluation of selected social work approaches, such as contained in Roberts and Nee (8).

can be analyzed along several dimensions of their logical structure (that is, in addition to the actual content of the theory).[3] Of major significance for the nature of the construction of a theory is the extent to which it varies along the dimension of formality-informality. Formal theories are tightly organized, deductive systems arranged in a consistent, interdependent whole. Informal theories, on the other hand, tend to be inductive, loosely organized collections of empirical propositions. The formality or informality of a theory is generally related to the theorist's preference for nomothetic or idiographic study. The nomothetic focus of a theory refers to a concern with general statements applicable to several members of a given class, while an idiographic focus refers to the intensive study of an individual subject (see, for example, Skinner [12]), with all the potential concomitant law-making limitations this entails.

Since a major goal of theory development is the explanation of selected phenomena—in this case, the principles and procedures of therapeutic behavior change—an important analytic criterion is explanatory ability. The theory must facilitate understanding of the dimensions it seeks to explain, based on a clear and logical ordering of pertinent knowledge and clarification of the relationships between relevant variables. The theory, in other words, should prevent "the observer from being dazzled by the full-blown complexity of natural or complex events" (5:14). Many theories, though, tend to reductionistic explanations, wherein higher-level phenomena are explained at lower, more basic levels of analysis, which lead in the extreme to oversimplification. All theories are also to some extent deterministic; that is, they seek to establish causal relationships. But in the extreme—for example, Freud's psychic determinism—meaning is attributed to all behavior. That is, every form of behavior is assumed to have an antecedent condition which, somehow, can be ascertained. Finally, theories can also be more or less comprehensive, dependent upon the range of phenomena which they purport to explain. For example, Freud's theory of personality attends to a wide range of developmental phenomena, but his theory of therapy is far more circumscribed, as it deals with only limited client groups, diagnostic categories, and technical interventions.[4]

Theories, and particularly the concepts of which they are constructed, can be analyzed as to their level of abstraction, from concrete (molecular) to molar. The kinds, variety, and amounts of events to which they refer are functions of their complexity. While the more abstract theory, of course, can be more inclusive, it can also fall prey to a lack of clarity and explicitness, and thus produce confusion and conceptual muddiness. The concepts and propositions should be logically related and also clearly formulated in relation to the areas of central concern to the theory. The assumptions should be clear and germane to the context of the theory. In essence, theories must be internally consistent. A related hazard is the possibility of

---

[3] For more extensive discussions of the structural dimensions of theories, see Hall and Lindzey (5), chapter 1; Marx (7); Ford and Urban (3), section 1; and Rychlak (11).

[4] Throughout this paper, the work of Freud, Rogers, and Wolpe is used for illustrative purposes. These three approaches were selected because each represents a major and distinct thrust in the clinical field.

reification of concepts, wherein concepts are treated less as abstractions and more as actual entities in themselves (for example, "her ego is weak").

A most critical function of theory lies in its potential for generating predictions, for establishing knowledge about the nature of B, given the characteristics of A. This directly utilitarian aspect of theory is a function not only of the construction of its propositions as testable hypotheses, but of the operationalization of its concepts. The concepts used in a theory must be tied to empirical referents so that major elements of the theory are measurable and confirmable or disconfirmable. If its major concepts are not accessible to operationalization, not only is the theory untestable, and hence minimally useful in facilitating empirical investigation, but lack of identifiable referents will lead different observers to make different interpretations and observations based on the theory. Thus, the explanatory and clarifying ability of the theory will also be greatly diminished. Measurement problems, of course, are minimized if the emphasis in the theory is on utilization of concepts that are focused on observable phenomena, rather than on the use of inferential constructs, which are unobservable and difficult to operationalize.

A major function of a theory lies in its ability to stimulate related study, generate empirical research, and add to the development of a body of knowledge which, both quantitatively and qualitatively, produces a range of scholarly endeavors. Similarly, a theory must be flexible, able to stand the test of a range of empirical findings and incorporate them within its domain. This does not mean that a theory must explain everything, but an adequate theory should be adaptable to the results of empirical research focused on the area of concern to the theory. Moreover, a theory has more utilitarian value if it is somewhat congruent with other theories in the same area. Finally, a traditional principle of science has dealt with theoretical parsimony—the notion that, when two theories arrive at similar explanations, it is wiser to accept the simpler of the alternative explanations.

Characteristics as a Theory of Therapy

The heart of the assessment of a clinical theory—and the aspect of the analysis differentiating it from other types of theories—lies in careful examination of its specific characteristics as a theory of therapy, that is, what the position of the theory is along several content dimensions. A theory of therapy, as an interrelated system intended to explain diverse phenomena of the therapeutic endeavor, can in fact be identified by an enumeration of those dimensions. Its utilitarian value can best be assessed by the manner in which it addresses those criteria. This assessment, however, consists of more than a mere description of what a theorist might say; it calls in addition for a careful, critical examination of both explicit and implicit characteristics of the theory, watching for the possibility of propositional contradictions embedded in the theory. For example, a theorist may state that, in his system, the client determines the goals, but careful reading of the theory may reveal that the theorist has already made a priori determinations of the nature of most or all psychosocial disorders and the necessary forms of treatment for those disorders. In other words, the major decisions may have been made even before meeting a given client, thus eliminating any realistic potential for setting of goals by the client.[5]

Given the focus on theories of therapeutic change, it is nevertheless helpful, but not always necessary, if a theory articulates with both a theory of normal development and a theory of behavior disorder. The degree of necessity for this articulation is decreased when the theorist suggests that behavior change can be carried out without knowledge of antecedent conditions, that is, when the method of changing behavior is independent of the acquisition of that behavior.[6] Freud's theory of therapy, for example, is deeply rooted in his theories of normal and abnormal development; it is practically impossible to proceed in Freudian psychoanalysis without careful examination of developmental features. On the other hand, the behavior therapy of Joseph Wolpe (16) is only tenuously connected to developmental theory, and, in fact, the therapist may implement change procedures without knowledge of the developmental history of an individual.

A theory of induced change should identify the client unit of concern, that is, whether, based on the theory, a therapist is equipped to deal with an individual client, a family, a group, or a combination of the three units. A critical function of a theory of therapy is a careful detailing of the behavior (broadly defined; see [3]) to which a therapist should attend. This means that the theory should specify not only the kinds of problems that should be included as objects of therapeutic attention, but also those that should be excluded. For example, a "symptom" might be seen only as a derivative phenomenon (Freud) or as an important focus of therapeutic effort (Wolpe). Further, a theory of therapy should define the superordinate goals of the system, so that the reader will be clear, not only about the behavior to be focused upon, but to what the behavior will be changed. Therapeutic systems also vary in their emphasis on specification of objectives. Not only is there probably an inverse relationship between the generality of such statements and their utility, but the greater the degree of specification of outcome statements, the more likely it is that specific and precise therapeutic operations will arise (3).

Related, of course, to statements about the goals of the system are questions about who should select the goals. A theory might state that the client sets the goals, that the therapist (by way of his theory) sets the goals, or some combination of the two. Whichever way the theorist presents his case, it should be clear and congruent with both the assumptions and the remainder of the content of the theory. Some systems also place heavy emphasis on careful assessment of the client's problems and situation, and hence result in a "differential diagnosis." This process is important, not only as an individualizing procedure, but as a way of organizing the pertinent facts. However, unless there is a direct relationship between assessment and treatment, the value of any diagnostic procedure is minimal. For a system such

[5] The distinction, perhaps, is between paying lip service to what might be a particular value (the client determines his own goals), and the assumptions and actual content of the theory.

[6] For a discussion of the potential independence of theories of change, see Fischer (2). The opposing point of view is presented in Ford and Urban (3).

as Wolpe's, careful assessment is particularly important since it suggests which one of several available intervention procedures should be implemented. On the other hand, Rogers (9) dispenses with diagnosis altogether, since it is philosophically and ethically objectionable to Rogers, who views objective diagnosis by an outside observer (the therapist) as practically impossible, and who espouses essentially one form of treatment for all problems anyway.

There are multiple focal points for intervention which could be emphasized by a theory of therapy. A theory might focus its treatment on phenomena occurring in the present or those occurring in the past. Similarly, a theory might place emphasis on interpersonal or intrapsychic behavior. Closely related to the above, a theory might emphasize change of observable behavior as a primary therapeutic objective, or be more concerned with the client's achieving some form of self-understanding or insight. Actually, many of these dimensions might be combined in a given system, and there is considerable blurring of the fine lines between the two extremes of each bipolar dimension. Nevertheless, for purposes of discussion, it might be assumed that such "ideal types" as a "present-interpersonal-observable behavior" constellation or a "past-intrapsychic-insight" emphasis could exist. Clearly, then, each feature or set of features would require a different perspective from client and therapist, since each set involves important implications regarding the assumptions of the theory, as well as the process of intervention itself. Summarily, the former constellation (or elements of it) not only could lead to more tangible and accessible intervention procedures (for example, focus on communication or on altering environmental contingencies), but would allow more direct measurement of outcome. The latter constellation, on the other hand, would require a process of intervention designed to tap phenomena which appear to be less accessible for manipulation (for example, emphasis on history-taking and on reordering and re-thinking past experiences), and the measurement of therapeutic success or failure would be more difficult.

The heart of a theory of therapy lies in four types of statements: (*a*) principles regarding extinguishing unwanted (or dysfunctional) behavior; (*b*) specification of procedures and techniques for extinguishing unwanted behavior; (*c*) principles regarding the development of new behavior; and (*d*) specification of procedures and techniques dealing with the production of new behavior. Two basic distinctions are involved: the first between "principles" and "procedures," the second between eliminating unwanted behavior and developing new behavior.

Principles of behavior change are propositions stating how and why problematic behavior may be altered. Statement of these principles generally is a precondition for a discussion of therapeutic techniques utilized to implement the change principles. The techniques consist of a set of conditions that can be varied by the therapist (3); a clear statement of therapeutic procedures is the crux of the therapeutic system, as it details what it is that the therapist has to do in order to produce changes in the client's behavior. As an example of the preceding material, Wolpe's principle of reciprocal inhibition is a principle by which behavior change occurs;

Wolpe's procedure of systematic desensitization is a technique for implementing the principle.

Wolpe's technique of systematic desensitization might also serve to illustrate the distinction between extinguishing unwanted behavior and developing new behavior. Systematic desensitization is a procedure primarily concerned with eliminating maladaptive behavior. To induce development of new behavior, Wolpe might call on other procedures, such as behavior rehearsal (16). This distinction is crucial; too often, theorists develop material dealing only with principles and procedures for eliminating behavior; for the adherent to such a theory who is faced with a client in need of new forms of functional behavior, only one-half of the job of therapy would be possible within the confines of such a theory. A related concern is the necessity for development of principles and procedures for transfer of change from the therapy situation to the extratherapy milieu. The ultimate goal of all theories of therapy is to produce lasting changes in the client's real-life situation. The therapist cannot always rely on automatic carry-over of in-therapy changes to the client's external situation; a whole new set of procedures may be called for. At the least, the theorist should attend to this issue and offer a discussion of how his therapy proposes to handle it.

Some theories of therapy are limited in their development of a range of procedures for changing behavior. For example, Rogers utilizes, in large part, only one type of interview procedure, of a reflective mode (9). Other systems, for example Wolpe's (16), have, in addition to verbal interventions, considerable technical diversity, differentially applied on the basis of assessment of the client's problems. Some systems emphasize a systematic approach by the therapist, wherein each stage of therapy is carefully planned, objectives are determined, and specific programs are implemented and evaluated. A critical analytic criterion for social work is whether or not the theory makes provision for an environmental approach to behavior change. If, for example, the theory assumes that the source of the problem is internal and that treatment must of necessity deal with the client's reworking of his own experience, provision for "environmental manipulation," or some form of rearranging of environmental elicitors or maintainers of dysfunctional behavior, is less likely to occur. Finally, given the emphasis on delineating the functions of the therapist, a theory should also address the question of specification of in-treatment client behaviors, of what a client should do and/or talk about in therapy. Some theories also allow the therapist to explain his principles and procedures to the client, thus facilitating client understanding of the program and, presumably, facilitating client cooperation as well.

Theories of therapy vary considerably in the emphasis placed on the planned use of relationship, that is, in statements detailing how the therapist is to utilize the constellation of factors generally thought of as composing "the relationship" (for example, warmth, acceptance, genuineness, etc.). Similarly, there can be considerable variation in theorists' views of the degree of structure recommended for the relationship. This may involve such dimensions as strictness-permissiveness, directiveness-nondirectiveness, and emphasis on a planned versus an unplanned approach. Furthermore, some theorists, as does Rogers, see the major source of therapeutic change in the therapist's personality (the relationship, in itself, is viewed as "curative"), whereas others, for example, most behavior therapists, emphasize technical procedures as the basic change element in therapy. Each perspective, of course, leads to a distinctly different approach to the development of therapeutic principles and procedures.

Some theories of therapy are intended to deal only with selected client groups or diagnostic categories. Hence, their applicability to a range of both clients and problems is an important analytic criterion. Thus, if the theory placed great value on the client's psychological sophistication, verbalness, and intellectual capacity or educational attainment, large categories of clients would be viewed as inaccessible to, or unsuited for, treatment. Both Freud and Wolpe, for example, also state that their systems are intended primarily for neurotic (or non-psychotic) clients. Related to these criteria is the degree to which the theory is culturally specific. Many theorists, based on their own life experiences, intentionally or unintentionally develop approaches so that there are particular cultural groups for whom their system is most applicable. The efficiency of the treatment process—or the length of time required for successful treatment to take place—must also be considered. It appears that, if all other things, including effectiveness, are equal, "that form of treatment is best that does it least and does it fastest" (2:20). Finally, an area that most clinical theories tend to neglect is the establishment of clear criteria for termination of treatment, including statements about when the process ends, who decides, and what the basis for the decision is.

Empirical Status

A most important ingredient in assessing the ultimate value of a theory of therapy lies in the degree of successful empirical verification of (*a*) its content and (*b*) its effectiveness in successfully changing clients' behavior. Success is a function not only of the degree to which the concepts and propositions are constructed so as to be testable (as discussed in the section dealing with structural characteristics of theory), but of the extent to which the theorist emphasizes the necessity for empirical testing. For many years, for example, Rogers stood by the necessity for the scientific investigation of the propositions contained in his theory. But beyond this orientation (or attitude) toward the use of scientific procedures, there should be actual attempts at conducting research, and a demonstration of success in measuring aspects of the theory. In fact, each of the content criteria specified above can be examined to assess its empirical status: the degree to which research has validated the position of a particular theorist regarding each dimension. For example, Rogers and his colleagues have been able to operationalize and reliably measure the basic ingredients of Rogers's theory—the therapist's attitudinal orientation or therapeutic conditions (10, 14). Not only is such successful measurement crucial for the transmission (or teaching) of a theory; it is even more critical in the actual implementation of the theory in practice—the model is there to be followed. Of course, successful measurement of concepts and propositions then allows the examination of the relationship to outcome of the important elements of the theory, of the idea that the theorist's procedures are in fact producing the changes intended (3).[7]

The issue of outcome—or success in validating effectiveness with clients—is second to none in the evaluation of a clinical theory of induced change. Presumably, a search for the most effective means of providing help to clients is the *raison d'être* for the development of a theory of therapy, and is also an important reason for undertaking an intensive review of it. Once the theorist has made clear how outcome should be determined (that is, answered the questions—what is success and how can it be assessed? [1]), and some measurable goals have been developed, the critical job of actually validating the results of therapy remains. For the student of a theory of therapy, the task is twofold: first, to become aware of the research that examines the effectiveness with clients of a particular approach; second, to be able to evaluate the quality of the research as well, so as not to be confused by inadequate research methodologies or incorrect interpretations of data.[8]

Assumptions About the Nature of Man and Moral Implications

All theories of therapy have embedded in them a view about the nature of man, ranging from an image of man as essentially "ugly," a seething cauldron of primordial drives, to a view of man as a creative, self-actualizing being. Related to this view is the degree to which the theorist is optimistic about the therapy process itself. For example, Freud thought personality very difficult to modify, and the analytic process, he suggested, was an interminable one (4). On the other hand, on the basis of the view that all behavior is learned and therefore adaptable, behavior therapists tend to view the therapy process with optimism and consider most forms of behavior modifiable. Furthermore, theorists differ with regard to their view of man as responsible. As Ford and Urban (3) note, some theorists see "man as a pilot," able to exercise control over his own behavior. Others view "man as a robot," at the mercy of the environment and not responsible for the direction of his behavior.

Some theorists fail to attend to the value issues which are so critical in both the theory and the practice of methods of induced change. This neglect may be due to

---

[7] Note the work of Rogers (10), and Truax and Carkhuff (14), studying the relationship of the therapeutic conditions to successful outcome, and Lang's review of studies of the procedure of systematic desensitization (6).

[8] Actually, the most useful question to ask may not always be "does a given theory 'work'?" since there are so many potential intervening and confounding variables; in fact, even the demonstrated treatment success of adherents to a particular theory does not necessarily prove the efficacy of the theory. Rather, a more valuable and certainly more precise question might be: what methods, based on what theory (the relationship to outcome must be demonstrated), with what therapists, working with what clients, with what kinds of problems, in what situations, are most successful?

an oversight or a judgment that values are not appropriate areas for discussion in theories of therapy. Other theorists devote considerable attention to such issues. Either way, a careful reading of the theory should reveal whether or not a theorist places a primary value on man's dignity and individuality, or whether such concerns are secondary to other issues. Further, analysis should reveal whether the theorist considers it important for the therapist to attempt to avoid imposing his own values on the client and, if so, how he proposes that this can be accomplished. It is clear, at any rate, that throughout the process of theorizing about and practicing therapy—from decisions about goals to implementation of procedures—value questions do exist.

Two other important assumptions of theories of therapy deal with use of the disease model and use of the medical model, two characteristics which are generally lumped together. However, there seems to be some heuristic value in separating them in the analysis of a theory. The disease model, in the first place, refers to a set of assumptions about the nature of the problem (or pathology or maladaptive behavior). Behavior would be considered disturbed (or "diseased") because of some underlying cause ("the patient is sick"); symptoms are viewed as symbolic and less worthy of attention than "the basic cause," the ferreting out of which should be the "proper" focus of the therapist's efforts. The major alternative to the disease model is the "psychological" (or behavioral) model (15), in which both adaptive and maladaptive behaviors are seen as learned through similar processes, no underlying causes (diseases) are presumed, and the focus is on overt, objectively identifiable behaviors (the "symptoms" are the problem).

The medical model, on the other hand, deals with assumptions about the nature of treatment; like the disease model, in which dysfunctional behavior is considered as analogous to a physical illness, an adherent to the medical model might proceed in treatment as would a physician treating a physical illness. The therapist-doctor is considered the expert, who has the knowledge to "cure" the patient through the therapist's prescriptions for behavior change. Quasi-medical terminology is utilized ("patient," "cure," "treatment"). Practice is conducted in the privacy of an office, within the context of the therapist-patient relationship, or in "consultation" with a small group, with the therapist in full control of treatment. Such an approach prevents the therapist from dealing with the social situation and working in the environment (that is, away from the client), since the theory is circumscribed to include only statements regarding behavior change accomplished through the application of techniques directly to the client (that is, in therapy); it is, in essence, the clinical approach.[9]

Theories of therapy can also be assessed by the degree to which an attempt is made to minimize client dependency. Is a by-product of the process of therapy a decrease in the competence and decision-making ability of the client, based on

---

[9] It is possible for a theory to be heavily weighted toward the medical model but not the disease model. Wolpe, for example, while decrying the disease model of psychopathology, quite consistently adheres to the medical model of treatment (16).

enforced dependency on the therapist? Or are the conditions so arranged that the client will be able to maintain some degree of independence, some sense of integrity, during the process of therapy? Related to this criterion is the importance that a theorist attributes to the client's perspective. This ranges from the client's opportunity to share in the process of goal determination to an attempt actually to "begin where the client is." Similarly, theories vary in the extent to which they maintain the client's reality orientation, ranging from an unconscious-historical-pathology focus, to a present-problem-oriented interactional focus.

Finally, theories of therapy may be examined by considering the extent to which they permit therapist involvement. Must the therapist stay removed from the situation in a passive, neutral, "objective" posture, or does the theory make provision for an open encounter in which the therapist takes active interest in the well-being of the client? While not as clearly an ethical dimension, each theory might also be assessed by viewing its position on technical flexibility, on whether or not it emphasizes "what works." In such an approach, the therapist actively searches for procedures that will benefit the client, as opposed to placing all of his technical eggs in one basket by utilizing only one basic procedure, regardless of the problem. Theories should also make some provision for controlling for incompetent practitioners, whether it be through training, examination, quality of past experience, or some other form of evaluative process.

Applicability for Social Work

The last section of this framework deals with criteria for selecting aspects of a theory for social work. Utilization of these criteria is based on the assumption that all of the above criteria have been analyzed, that is, the selector is thoroughly knowledgeable about the theory. The first criterion has to do with whether or not the theory has relevance to the phenomena with which social work is concerned. Clearly, the profession is not interested in the adaptation of theories of physics, but is concerned with induced behavior change. If this criterion has been met, the second deals with the issue of value convergence between the theory in question and the social work profession. The profession has developed its own ethical and philosophical position, rooted in the worth and dignity of its clients; a theory of therapy whose assumptions or content contradict this position is, at best, questionable for adaptation for social work practice.

The next criterion deals with the degree of empirical validation of aspects of the theory. Of course, because of their complexity, such theories can rarely if ever be validated *in toto.* Most important, though, for a theory of therapy, is substantial empirical evidence of success in work with clients. Selection of aspects of theory must also take into account its heuristic value: the theory should serve as a tool for guiding empirical investigation, for ordering relevant knowledge, and for facilitating understanding of complex phenomena.

Adoption or use of a particular theory must mean that its principles and procedures are teachable within the social work curriculum. If, to learn a theory, the student must spend many years of preparation, or the cost of implementing training in or practice of the theory would be excessive, the theory would simply be impracticable for social work. A final dimension for assessment involves the utility of a theory, including the degree to which the crucial elements of the theory are identifiable and accessible for manipulation (13) and, of major consequence for a clinical theory, the extent to which the theory provides specific prescriptions for action. There would be little advantage in adopting a theory the major provisions of which are not available for direct action by the practitioner.

Framework for Analysis

As a summary device, and to aid in the utilization of this framework in the analysis of theories, all the criteria have been abstracted and included in the Appendix.

A theory—or several theories in comparison—can be rated on each criterion on a four-point scale:

1 = clear discussion of criterion; strong emphasis or high value placed by theory on criterion in question
2 = addresses criterion, but incomplete
3 = inadequately addresses criterion and/or position is highly dubious
4 = does not deal with criterion; little emphasis or value placed on criterion by theory

Thus, rating a theory "1" on any given criterion would indicate that either the theorist or the reader of the theory considers the theory to be heavily weighted on that dimension—for example, highly reductionistic (No. 5); clear specification of principles regarding extinguishing unwanted behavior (No. 34); strong emphasis on empirical testing (No. 54); or highly positive view of the nature of man (No. 59). A higher rating does not necessarily indicate that a given theory is "better" on a specific dimension than a lower rating, but differential ratings should supply information about where a particular theory stands on each dimension.

This table is not offered as a finely honed, precise scientific instrument, but as a heuristic guide to aid in the process of theory analysis. In actuality, most of the categories are not independent, and there is a clear question about the relative weighting of dimensions; some items obviously are more important than others. Nevertheless, the framework, as summarized in the table, is offered in the spirit that the use of criteria such as those proposed here will result in a more scholarly, yet, at the same time, more pragmatic approach to the assessment of relevant theories. Implicit in this view is the notion that such analysis is not a simple task, nor is it one that should be considered lightly, for the careful evaluation of available knowledge from the social and behavioral sciences has direct implications for the success or failure of work with clients.

Appendix

Framework for Analysis of Theories

Item	Theory			
A. Structural Characteristics	A	B	C	D
1. Formality	–	–	–	–
2. Informality	–	–	–	–
3. Explanatory ability	–	–	–	–
4. Internal consistency	–	–	–	–
5. Reductionism	–	–	–	–
6. Determinism	–	–	–	–
7. Comprehensiveness	–	–	–	–
8. Level of abstraction	–	–	–	–
9. Clarity	–	–	–	–
10. Explicitness	–	–	–	–
11. Reification of concepts	–	–	–	–
12. Capacity to generate predictions	–	–	–	–
13. Construction of propositions as testable hypotheses	–	–	–	–
14. Operationalization of concepts	–	–	–	–
15. Focus on observables	–	–	–	–
16. Stimulation of related study	–	–	–	–
17. Flexibility	–	–	–	–
18. Congruence with other theories	–	–	–	–
B. Characteristics as a Theory of Therapy	A	B	C	D
19. Articulation with theory of normal development	–	–	–	–
20. Articulation with theory of behavior disorder	–	–	–	–
21. Dependence on knowledge of antecedent conditions	–	–	–	–
22. Identification of client-unit	–	–	–	–
23. Detailing of behaviors to which therapist should attend	–	–	–	–
24. Delineation of goals of the theory	–	–	–	–
25. Emphasis on specification of objectives	–	–	–	–
26. Description of who should set goals	–	–	–	–
27. Use of differential assessment	–	–	–	–
28. Relationship between assessment and treatment	–	–	–	–
29. Focus on the present	–	–	–	–
30. Emphasis on interpersonal behavior	–	–	–	–
31. Emphasis on intrapsychic behavior	–	–	–	–
32. Emphasis on change of observable behavior	–	–	–	–
33. Emphasis on self-understanding	–	–	–	–

34. Specification of principles regarding extinguishing
    unwanted behavior   _ _ _ _
35. Specification of techniques (re: 34)   _ _ _ _
36. Specification of principles regarding development of
    new behavior   _ _ _ _
37. Specification of techniques (re: 36)   _ _ _ _
38. Specification of principles for transfer of change   _ _ _ _
39. Specification of techniques (re: 38)   _ _ _ _
40. Range of procedures for changing behavior   _ _ _ _
41. Emphasis on systematic approach by therapist   _ _ _ _
42. Provision for environmental approach   _ _ _ _
43. Specification of in-treatment client behaviors   _ _ _ _
44. Facilitation of client understanding of program   _ _ _ _
45. Planned use of relationship   _ _ _ _
46. Degree of structure in relationship   _ _ _ _
47. Source of change in therapist's personality   _ _ _ _
48. Source of change in technical procedures   _ _ _ _
49. Applicability to range of clients   _ _ _ _
50. Applicability to range of problems   _ _ _ _
51. Degree of cultural specificity   _ _ _ _
52. Efficiency   _ _ _ _
53. Specification of criteria for termination   _ _ _ _

C. Empirical Status	A	B	C	D
54. Emphasis on empirical testing	_	_	_	_
55. Success in measuring aspects of theory	_	_	_	_
56. Clarity about how outcome should be determined	_	_	_	_
57. Relationship to outcome of elements of theory	_	_	_	_
58. Success in validating effectiveness	_	_	_	_

D. Assumptions and Moral Implications	A	B	C	D
59. Positive view of nature of man	_	_	_	_
60. Optimism about therapy process	_	_	_	_
61. View of man as responsible	_	_	_	_
62. Attention to value issues	_	_	_	_
63. Primary value on man's dignity and individuality	_	_	_	_
64. Attempt to avoid imposition of therapist's values on client	_	_	_	_
65. Use of disease model	_	_	_	_
66. Use of psychological model	_	_	_	_
67. Use of medical model	_	_	_	_
68. Attempt to minimize client dependency	_	_	_	_
69. Importance of client's perspective	_	_	_	_

	A	B	C	D
70. Maintenance of reality orientation	–	–	–	–
71. Therapist involvement	–	–	–	–
72. Emphasis on what works	–	–	–	–
73. Controls for incompetent practitioners	–	–	–	–

E. Applicability for Social Work	A	B	C	D
74. Relevance to phenomena of concern	–	–	–	–
75. Value convergence	–	–	–	–
76. Degree of empirical validation	–	–	–	–
77. Heuristic value	–	–	–	–
78. Teachability	–	–	–	–
79. Utility	–	–	–	–

References

1. Briar, Scott. "Analysis of Intervention Theories." Mimeographed. Berkeley: University of California, 1967.
2. Fischer, Joel. *An Eclectic Approach to Therapeutic Casework.* In press.
3. Ford, Donald, and Urban, Hugh. *Systems of Psychotherapy.* New York: John Wiley & Sons, 1963.
4. Freud, Sigmund. "Analysis Terminable and Interminable." In *Collected Papers,* Vol. V. Translated by Joan Rivière. London: Hogarth Press, 1950.
5. Hall, Calvin, and Lindzey, Gardner. *Theories of Personality.* New York: John Wiley & Sons, 1957.
6. Lang, Peter. "The Mechanisms of Desensitization and the Laboratory Study of Human Fear." In *Behavior Therapy: Appraisal and Status,* edited by Cyril Franks, pp. 160–91. New York: McGraw-Hill Book Co., 1969.
7. Marx, Melvin. "The General Nature of Theory Construction." *In Theories in Contemporary Psychology,* edited by Melvin Marx, pp. 4–46. New York: Macmillan Co., 1963.
8. Roberts, Robert W., and Nee, Robert, eds. *Theories of Social Casework.* Chicago: University of Chicago Press, 1970.
9. Rogers, Carl. "A Theory of Therapy, Personality, and Interpersonal Relationships as Developed in the Client-centered Framework." In *Psychology: A Study of a Science,* Vol. II, edited by S. Koch. New York: McGraw-Hill Book Co., 1959.
10. Rogers, Carl, et al. *The Therapeutic Relationship and Its Impact: A Study of Psychotherapy with Schizophrenics.* Madison: University of Wisconsin Press, 1967.
11. Rychlak, Joseph. *A Philosophy of Science for Personality Theory.* New York: Houghton Mifflin Co., 1968.
12. Skinner, B. F. "A Case History in Scientific Method." *American Psychologist* 11 (1956): 221–33.

13. Thomas, Edwin. "Selecting Knowledge from Behavioral Science." In *Building Social Work Knowledge,* pp. 38–48. New York: National Association of Social Workers, 1964.
14. Truax, Charles, and Carkhuff, Robert. *Toward Effective Counseling and Psychotherapy.* Chicago: Aldine Publishing Co., 1967.
15. Ullman, Leonard, and Krasner, Leonard. *A Psychological Approach to Abnormal Behavior.* Englewood Cliffs, N.J.: Prentice-Hall, 1969.
16. Wolpe, Joseph. *The Practice of Behavior Therapy.* New York: Pergamon Press, 1969.

Chapter 3

Introducing New Technology into Social Agencies: The Case of Behavior Modification

There seems to be a pattern in the introduction of new practice concepts into social work practice (Carter and Stuart, 1970). First, a few social workers introduce the ideas into practice and the social work literature. As the ideas spread, others in the field may inspect the ideas, often with a negative bias, and achieve consensus in rejecting the new and restating their allegiance to the established. As the number of people who experiment with the approach increase, some in the field begin to rephrase their evaluation in terms of the ideas having some, but limited, applications (Bruck, 1968). Or sometimes, the ideas may be viewed as all right, but nothing really new. Subsequently, the field may bifurcate (as it did in the functional-diagnostic schism) or—as seems to be happening in the case of the introduction of behavior modification—the concepts slowly begin to be infused into the mainstream of social work practice.

The introduction of behavior modification approaches into agencies is not a simple matter, but is often accompanied by a diversity of problems. Such problems can contribute to the failures of attempts to help clients through the use of behavior modification.

It is a paradox that the more effective and widely applicable behavior modification appears to be, even with client groups often considered untreatable (Atthowe and Krasner, 1968; Franks, 1969; Ayllon and Azrin, 1968; Bandura, 1969; Schafer and Martin, 1969; Rimm and Masters, 1974; O'Leary and Wilson, 1975), the more hesitant practitioners are to use it. Such resistance can be understood, in part at least, as a reaction from those who balk at any new approaches. But understanding of the problem by itself may be insufficient to produce change. The practitioner who believes that the use of behavior modification can make a substantial contribution to effective practice must go beyond mere understanding of this possibility to assessing what behavior modification might have to offer for the problems he or she deals with, what specific aspects of behavior modification might be applied,

Gochros, H. L. and Fischer, J. (1975). Paper presented at the 20th Anniversary N.A.S.W. Symposium, Hollywood by the Sea, Florida.

and what strategies can be used to shape the acceptance of these approaches into a social work organization.

The introduction into agency practice of behavior modification procedures by the social worker should be compatible with and support the objectives of his organization—as long as these objectives are professionally defensible. Such objectives may include not only the immediate goals of improved services to the client, but such long-range goals as maintaining community support and improving staff morale. The effective social worker studies his organization as he would any other target system, to understand the goals, response patterns, and reinforcements that affect those who are significant to his organization's functioning. The assessment of the variables that might influence the way behavior modification approaches are introduced—or whether they should be introduced at all—includes a review of the resources and the priorities of the organization and the probabilities that behavior modification will be effective in view of such variables as the manpower, physical resources, and sources of agency power; the problems to which the organization gives priority; and to the social worker's own skills, and those of his colleagues.

This chapter will survey the issues involved in introducing behavioral modification in social work settings, some of the common problems encountered in using this approach, and suggestions for overcoming such problems.

Demands on the Delivery System

The use of behavior modification, like any other method of practice, makes certain demands on the service delivery system that utilizes it. At the same time, social workers are well aware of the influence the delivery system has in controlling the professional decisions and choices made within the system. Behavioral approaches shape and are shaped by the organizations in which they are used. Their departure from some traditional approaches often exaggerates these problems. The effectiveness of behavior modification is therefore dependent to a large extent on how well the social worker resolves the various potential conflicts between the demands of the behavioral procedures and the demands of the delivery system.

The potential conflicts in the reciprocal relationship of delivery system demands and a system of practice concepts are varied and appear in many forms (Tharp and Wetzel, 1968; Sarri and Vinter, 1967). Many failures of behavior modification can be traced to such conflicts. Some of the more common problems will be discussed here along with some possible ways of overcoming them.

Informal Agency Obstacles

Social work agencies must be viewed as social systems as well as bureaucracies (Sarri and Vinter, 1967, p. 88). They are bureaucracies in the sense that they are established and maintained to accomplish specified goals, and are organized and structured in such a way as to ensure that these goals are attained at a high level of productivity with the most efficient means available. If clear and rational presentations of the effectiveness of behavior modification are made, there can be little rational resistance by the agency bureaucracy.

But the agency is also a group of professionals in a social system that often reacts in subtle, unwritten, and informal ways to pressures both from within and outside of the agency, which often conflict with the goals established by the bureaucratic aspects of the organization (Sarri and Vinter, 1967). The patterns by which the social system operates change over time as outside events influence the agency, and as there is personnel turnover within the agency or as staff members modify their perceptions. It is the informal, sometimes irrational factors within the social system of the agency that may have the most profound effects on the introduction of new approaches into the agency's program.

Often, organizations tend to resist change. There is comfort and safety in established procedures and policies. Inertia in organizational change is often the product of the distribution of power within the organization itself. The administrator and senior supervisors may represent a gerontocracy, having considerable power over the introduction of new policies and procedures in their agency. They may also be the individuals in the agency who are furthest away from practice as well as from their formal social work education. As a result, if they were educated as caseworkers, they were reinforced for learning and accepting a psychodynamic approach to human behavior and case management. In fact, if their graduate education followed the common pattern of much of the first half of this century, their challenges to this conceptualization may have been met with accusations of resistance and implicit psychological deficits.

Commitment to the psychodynamic model has traditionally received considerable reinforcement. It was almost universally accepted by peers and provided a fairly reinforcing technology for the practitioner—reinforcement by clients who stated that they were benefitted by the social worker's help, and protection from the aversive consequences of those clients who withdrew or refused to improve with the rationalization that they were probably untreatable in the first place. Furthermore, talk therapies based on the psychodynamic model provided fairly easy (you do not have to leave your office), enjoyable (long talks with many clients are very reinforcing) experiences for the worker. It also provided social workers with an opportunity to model their behavior after that of the much admired psychiatric treatment of the day. Indeed, the high priority placed on insight therapy as the apex of a large proportion of social work intervention typologies clearly emulated the psychiatric model.

Executives and supervisors who have been reinforced for many years for such an orientation may resist giving up this approach, except through token acceptance of some procedures in some situations. It is painful to question the patterns of a professional lifetime. While practitioners' questions and arguments may have considerable thought behind them, it is important for them—in trying to convince administrators and supervisors of the desirability of change—to be aware of the potential threat that a new approach may engender.

Administrators, supervisors, and line workers all operate according to the same laws of learning that influence our clients', and our own, behavior. They will tend to engage in behaviors which are reinforced and avoid those which are aversive. In this light, it may be useful to consider some of the potentially reinforcing and aversive properties of psychodynamic and behavior modification models for the practitioner, supervisor, and administrator, a delineation described in table 1.

Influencing Staff Attitudes

Hopefully, behavior modification will be considered by staff through an open evaluation of its merits. Acceptance of demonstrations of behavior modification can be facilitated by finding means of showing what the introduction of this technology (i.e., applied body of knowledge) into the agency can do not only for the clients but for the staff and agency as well. This requires the staff person advocating these procedures to understand what is reinforcing to staff and what aspects of the approach are aversive. All too often, the mistake is made of using logical debate as the only means of influencing staff attitudes. As noted earlier, the agency—when seen as a social system—is often controlled by nonrational factors.

It is necessary, then, for the social worker to assess the agency's attitudes, conceptions, and experiences with the practice of behavior modification, as well as to honestly explore his own attitudes about the agency. What do the various staff members anticipate to be the consequences of the use of behavior modification? What dangers or negative consequences do they expect? There often may be realistic bases for staff concern. Descriptions of professionals using behavior modification strategies as "arrogant, patronizing, and brusque" are frequent enough to raise questions as to their validity (Guyett, 1972). The development of civility and friendliness on the part of those introducing new approaches into a social agency is not just a nicety, but a necessity for making new ideas more acceptable and less threatening and creating an atmosphere in which there is willingness for *all* staff to share each other's experiences.

There are many procedures that can facilitate the use of behavior modification procedures in an agency that is mildly to strongly opposed to their use. Many approaches other than open and logical discussion of the issue may seem devious and in conflict with the openness ideally characteristic of the use of behavior modification. Some of the ways in which practitioners have been able to create more responsive attitudes toward behavior modification among fellow staff members, supervisors, and administrators are:

1. The practitioner first using this approach tries it out in a limited scope, such as with a particular set of problems in an agency special project, on one ward, in one cottage, and so forth. Objective records are kept and shared with those who have been involved with the project.
2. Suggestions can be made by the social worker to model after other local

Table 1   Qualities of Traditional Approaches and Behavior Modification That May Be Reinforcing and Aversive for Administrators, Supervisors, and Practitioners

	Reinforcing	Aversive
Traditional Approaches	Extended relationships with respecting and admiring people	Time-consuming
	Frequent reports (from those who continue) of being helped in general terms	Research indicates often unsuccessful and frequently leads to deterioration for clients
	Fascinating and intricate diagnostic procedures	Tends to treat clients as "sick"
	Doesn't require leaving own convenient and comfortable office	Verbalized changes in office may not affect behavior in outside world
	Is generally expected by large percentage of clients and colleagues	In consultation, approach is largely limited to understanding psychodynamics with unclear implications for interventions
	Similar to what other prestigious professions do	
Behavior Modification	Data seem to support effectiveness in a wide range of settings	New, requires changes
	Provides clear evidence of success when there is success	There may be little direct contact with the target
	Provides clear guidelines for practice (e.g., specific techniques)	Weekly reinforcement, through clients' gratitude, may not be forthcoming
	Facilitates egalitatian relationships with clients and mediators	Technology may be considered strange by clients; concerns over "bribery," etc.
	For consultation, provides a clear, easily transmissable, action-oriented approach	Often requires working effectively and closely with mediators (e.g., houseparents, teachers, etc.)
	Client improvement, which clearly relates to the intervention	Does not build on common knowledge base
	Greater range of tools for range of problems	Takes more precise, clear cut planning rather than depending on more global definitions of core of problem (e.g., "unresolved goal")
	Learning something new and revitalizing, being in on "ground floor" of new developments	Seems to be what "psychologists do"
	Efficient—generally demanding less time expended by social worker per case, more rapid turnover of cases	Is talked against by many social work educators and leaders
	Makes effective use of paraprofessionals, geometrially increasing potential for reaching people in need	Not enough experts to provide the consultation needed to practitioners as they first learn to use it
	Makes direct link between assessment and intervention	May be challenged, carefully scrutinized, and depreciated by colleagues

agencies, or similar agencies in other communities, which face the same problems and have successfully used behavior modification.

3. Through informal relations with a select group of paraprofessionals affiliated with the agency (e.g., foster parents, cottage personnel, outreach workers), the social worker can discuss the approach and explore ways in which they and the social worker might attempt to apply the technology with a particularly difficult situation. The procedures are explained in simple language and progress shared with the participants.

4. The social worker volunteers to work collaboratively on a case with one of the more skeptical but concerned members of the staff. If allowed to do so, he should then be open with the coworker and offer him appropriate reinforcement for joint participation.

5. The social worker should analyze his own behavior from a behavioral point of view to maximize his use of positive reinforcement and minimize his use of punishment or aversive behavior. For instance, any implications that the technologies used by colleagues are bad or unethical should be avoided. A low-key approach is likely to create less resistance. Share ideas with colleagues, avoiding lectures. Again, the principles of reinforcement apply to the worker's own behavior and that of his colleagues. It is not effective to attempt to influence people by making them feel stupid. Praise, positive criticism, and the pleasure of successful problem-solving can much more effectively change behavior. Rather than saying, "Your approaches clearly don't work, are outmoded, and behavior modification is the only intelligent approach," it may be more effective and honest to say, "There are many ways of approaching this kind of case. I (or others) have found it useful to use this approach."

6. The social worker should avoid jargon. While it may be conceptually useful to name approaches, it may be more acceptable to colleagues, supervisors, and mediators to functionally describe an approach than to label it. For instance, saying that, "I want to teach Tom how to be more comfortable with the things that make him uptight," may find a more responsive reception than saying, "I am going to apply systematic desensitization to Tom." Indeed, the term behavior modification itself has generated a constellation of myths in the field (Morrow and Gochros, 1970) and to some, it has become associated with a cold, computer-like, laboratory-oriented image. These images are understandably aversive to people in the helping professions. They can be avoided by offering functional descriptions of recommended procedures rather than abstract labels.

7. Before offering consultation or recommendations for procedures, the social worker should establish his credibility for being successful in these approaches. For example, a school social worker offered to help a teacher work with some of the particularly difficult behaviors of one of her students. After some progress was made, the teacher mentioned her project to other teachers who began to approach the social worker for help with some of their

problems. Later, some of the teachers suggested the worker offer a seminar on strategies of classroom management.

8. The social worker can offer praise and encouragement for those who begin to apply behavior modification in their own practice, but should not oversell. There are many factors which may lead to failures in the approach. These can be anticipated. It is also facilitating to take the tactic of, "Let's try this and see if it works a little bit better."

9. The social worker should start introducing concepts of behavior modification with those who have the most immediate contact with clients rather than trying to influence those who are further removed. For example, a rural child welfare worker sent letters home with all the children identified as "retarded" in the county inviting parents to an evening session on "child management." In the sessions, she offered "some things that seem to work with common problems experienced by parents of 'retarded' children." The parents asked for additional sessions and ultimately organized a countywide association of parents of retarded children that focused on helping parents teach their children necessary skills and deal with common behavioral problems.

Bureaucratic Obstacles

The social system aspects of the agency are not the only source of problems in developing behavior modification programs. The bureaucratic demands of organizations may create obstacles for the social worker (Tharp and Wetzel, 1969, p. 141). Some agencies cannot—or will not—provide the flexibility for allowing individualized plans for individual cases. Some agencies (particularly schools and institutions) are oriented to the convenience of staff through their policies and schedules, and offer little tolerance for individualized programs for particular clients. There is also pressure in bureaucracies to treat all consumers alike. Nondiscrimination is a basic social work value, but its inappropriate, inflexible application can impede individualized intervention programs.

An example of the complex problems introduced by such bureaucratic rigidity is provided by Tharp and Wetzel (1969, p. 141). A plan was developed in which a child was allowed to play in after-school football games as a reinforcement for good behavior at school in the morning. The school principal objected to the plan for two reasons: (1) he did not believe the school could restrict this child from the after-school football program when it was the right of all other children (bureaucracies are oriented to treating all individuals alike); and, more important, (2) there was no communication channel in the school for sending information from the student's morning teacher to the afternoon football coach. Both the teacher and the coach felt it would be inappropriate for their respective roles to have them report to each other.

Since most social work practice is carried out in bureaucratic settings, the friction between bureaucratic demands and the delivery of individualized services remains a major concern. Certainly this friction can create a major problem in the utilization of behavior modification. In describing problems in casework practice, Briar (1973, p. 24–25) suggests:

> Every attempt by the agency to routinize some condition or aspect of professional practice amounts to a restriction of professional discretion, and for that reason probably should be resisted, in most instances, by practitioners. But it will not be enough to resist bureaucratic restriction. We will need to roll back the restrictions that already constrain practice in order to gain the freedom essential to experiment, to discover new and better ways of helping the clients to whom we are primarily responsible.

Agency practice, and along with it basic administrative demands, are probably essential to the equitable and widespread distribution of social services. But the agency should remain the servant of these services, not their master. The extent to which administrative procedures can be stretched or relaxed to meet individual case needs requires constant exploration and reevaluation.

In cases such as the previously mentioned, for example, if an adequate plan cannot be devised within the existing bureaucratic arrangements, the social worker may have to assume the role of advocate or broker for his client for getting the various individuals in the clients' natural environment to bend their bureaucratic roles to meet the demands of the intervention plan. This may require finding ways of obtaining and developing extrinsic reinforcement systems that do not frighten those who are concerned with limited agency budgets. This problem is, of course, compounded when the worker operates in a separate bureaucracy from the one influencing the client, and thus has less access to the individuals involved (for example, a family agency worker dealing with a child in an institution). But even in such situations the basic formula remains: removing aversive consequences and finding reinforcement for those in the client's environment for participating in change efforts. At any rate, a variety of strategies may be necessary for removing bureaucratic obstacles to efficient and effective services. Such strategies are part of the broad spectrum of social work practice skills essential for competent practice in bureaucracies. Many of these strategies are articulated in the social work literature (e.g., Patti and Resnick, 1972; Pruger, 1973).

Case Consultation

Although the first sections of this chapter discussed problems in implementing behavior modification into agencies in general, and focused largely on the clinical values of behavior modification, there is another aspect of its use that can be of particular benefit to agencies. Because behavior modification provides a body of knowledge that is easily understood and readily translated into intervention, it is well suited to consultation, an increasingly important function of a wide range of social work agencies. Further, the principles of behavior modification provide direction for, and understanding of, the consultation process itself.

Depending on the needs and requests presented by the consultee, the social worker familiar with behavior modification can be helpful in four ways: 1) by providing basic information about how behavior is learned, and how it can be changed, in direction, frequency, duration, or intensity; 2) by helping the consultee consider how these basic concepts can be applied to understanding common learning experiences that tend to affect the behavior of those client groups with which the consultee works, such as particular age and cultural groups, subcultures, and institutional populations (e.g., oppressed minorities, adoptive parents, the aged, institutional offenders, etc.); 3) by considering how this knowledge can be related to developing assessment procedures and options for interventive strategies and programs in a particular setting (e.g., prison, home for the aged, school for the retarded, etc.) in which the consultee is working; and 4) by applying behavior modification assessment and interventive strategies and techniques to specific problems or cases that consultees are confronting in their practice.

A growing body of knowledge on the consultation process is being developed and is available for use by social workers (e.g., Caplan, 1970). Obviously, prior to the beginning of consultation, the consultant should thoroughly familiarize himself with the specific agency's organization, formal and informal structure, and problems. In terms of the specific use of behavior modification, the consultant should try to create a relationship with the consultee(s) that will positively reinforce the consultee's efforts to learn, evaluate, and subsequently utilize the ideas emanating from the consultations. Such a relationship will enable the consultee to objectively evaluate the extent to which the practices and/or personnel in his organization, and perhaps the consultee himself, may in some measure be sustaining—or even reinforcing—the very behaviors the consultee wishes to alter. The social worker may facilitate such explorations by helping the consultee develop objective observation and reporting procedures that will systematically record not only the pinpointed target behaviors, but antecedent and consequent events as well. Using such objective procedures introduced by the consultee reduces the aura of subjective blame or guilt associated with the problems.

Based on these assessment procedures, the social worker can explore with the consultee alternative interventive strategies that might be applicable given the nature of the problem, the setting in which the problems occur, the capacities of those available to plan and mediate interventions and the presence of other resources that may be required for various interventive strategies. The social worker may then inform the consultee of procedures used successfully in situations similar to that encountered by the consultee, or may help the consultee think through innovative uses of the available resources for particular interventions where there is no known precedent. If called for, the social worker may help the consultee evaluate whether referral is preferable, and if so, explore the options available for referral.

If the consultee is to proceed with intervention, the social work consultant may offer assistance with—and offer to role play or model—some of the suggested interventive procedures, and, perhaps, do some of the direct mediation under the observation of the consultee or other potential mediators. The consultant then follows through if possible as any subsequent problems emerge during intervention.

Throughout the process of consultation, the social worker must evaluate the effect of the consultation process on the behavior of the consultee. Certainly the consultations themselves should not be allowed to become aversive to consultees by overwhelming them, or by making them feel incompetent. The consultee should be helped to approach the consultation with neither unrealistic expectations nor fear of embarrassment.

Going along with consultees or agencies step by step without expecting them to take on more than they can handle at any point can avoid failure and consequent discouragement (along with a wholesale rejection of the behavior modification approach), and increases the chances of success and the positive reinforcement of change efforts.

The consultee's attempts to carry out plans derived from consultation are further reinforced by the awareness that the social worker understands and appreciates the consultee's goals, problems, and limitations, and offers help in overcoming realistic obstacles that may impede an interventive plan. Another source of reinforcement is the social worker's enthusiasm and praise as positive results of intervention begin to appear. On the other hand, the social worker can help consultees anticipate and respond constructively to failures, recognizing the resulting frustrations, anger, and, occasionally, the guilt, evaluating as well as possible the sources of failure and planning a revised approach. And, of course, the consultant should always be available for follow-up, to provide additional consultation, or simply positive reinforcement for obtained results.

Behavior modification, in essence, offers a variety of important factors that can be helpful in consultation by: 1) facilitating functioning in the role of the consultant, 2) providing a specific body of knowledge as the topic of consultation, and 3) enhancing the consultation process, per se. Thus, professional social workers may find not only that they, as consultees, may benefit from such consultation, but that, functioning as consultants, they can greatly increase their own efficiency in providing services to others by consulting both with other social workers and with a wide range of nonprofessionals and people in the natural environment.

Summary

This chapter considered some of the impediments to the acceptance of behavior modification programs in social work organizations. Sources of resistance to accepting these approaches can be lodged in both the formal bureaucratic structures and the informal, sometimes nonrational reactions of staff. Another source of resistance can be related to the approach used by the social worker in introducing behavior modification, if he fails to apply an understanding of the factors influencing the attitudes and behaviors of staff and administration in their reactions to the approach. Some procedures for understanding and overcoming inappropriate resistances are suggested. Finally, the use of behavior modification in consultation was discussed as a way of facilitating both the efficiency and effectiveness of agency services.

References

Atthowe, J. M., Jr. & Krasner, L. (1968). Preliminary report on the application of contingent reinforcement procedures (token economy) on a "chronic" psychiatric ward. *Journal of Abnormal Psychology, 73,* 37–43.

Ayllon, T., & Azrin, N. H. (1968). *The token economy.* New York: Appleton-Century-Crofts.

Bandura, A. (1969). *Principles of behavior modification.* New York: Holt, Rinehart, and Winston.

Briar, S. (1973). Effective social work intervention in direct practice: Implications for education. In S. Briar (Ed.), *Facing the challenge.* New York: CSWE.

Bruck, M. (1968). Behavior modification theory and practice: A critical review. *Social Work, 13,* 43–55.

Caplan, G. (1970). *The theory and practice of mental health consultation.* New York: Basic Books.

Carter, R. C., & Stuart, R. B. (1970). Behavior modification theory and practice: A reply. *Social Work, 15,* 37–50.

Franks, C. M. (Ed.) (1969). *Behavior Therapy: Appraisal and Status.* New York: McGraw-Hill.

Morrow, W. R., & Gochros, H. L. (1970). Misconceptions regarding behavior modification. *Social Service Review, 44,* 293–307.

O'Leary, K. D., & Wilson, G. T. (1975). *Behavior therapy: Application and outcome.* Englewood Cliffs, NJ: Prentice-Hall.

Patti, R. J., & Resnick, H. (1972). Changing the agency from within. *Social Work, 17*(4), 48–57.

Pruger, R. (1973). The good bureaucrat. *Social Work, 18*(4), 26–32.

Rimm, D. C., & Masters, J. C. (1974). *Behavior therapy: Techniques and empirical findings.* New York: Academic Press.

Sarri, R. C., & Vinter, R. D. (1967). Organizational requisites for a socio-behavioral technology. In E. J. Thomas (Ed.), *The socio-behavioral approach and applications to social work.* New York: Council on Social Work Education.

Schaefer, H. H., & Martin, P. L. (1969). *Behavioral therapy.* New York: McGraw-Hill.

Tharp, R. C., & Wetzel, R. J. (1969). *Behavioral modification in the natural environment.* New York: Academic Press.

Chapter 4

Do Social Workers Understand Research?

It is widely accepted among social work educators that the profession should be scientifically based and grounded in empirical research. This is reflected in both the Council on Social Work Education's official MSW curriculum policy statement[1] and the CSWE Task Force Report on Research in the MSW Curriculum.[2] This latter report states that the MSW curriculum should prepare students for intelligent consumption of, and participation in research. And at the 1973 Annual Program Meeting of CSWE, a keynote speaker proposed that the curriculum be restructured in a way that would make evaluative research a core component of training for effective practice.[3] In short, there can be no doubt that the interface of research and practice is crucial to the profession.

The role of research in social work and social work education has recently taken on added significance, as research studies have increasingly shown that some conventional practice methods are not demonstrably effective.[4] This has provoked a wide range of opinion, ranging from calls to make radical changes in practice, to denunciations of the research as poorly designed, methodologically weak, or

Kirk, S. A. & Fischer, J. (1976). *Journal of Education for Social Work, 12,* 63–70. Reprinted with permission of the Council of Social Work Education.

The authors want to thank Sondra Dockham, Lee Hajas, Morris Masuda, and Iris Nitta for their assistance with this study.

[1] Council on Social Work Education. "Curriculum Policy for the Master's Degree Program in Graduate Schools of Social Work." *Social Work Education Reporter,* Vol. 17, No. 4 (December 1969), pp. 25R–27R.

[2] Edward W. Francel et al., "Task Force Report on Research in MSW Curriculum," *Social Work Education Reporter,* Vol. 16, No. 1 (March 1968), pp. 13, 20–21.

[3] Scott Briar, "Effective Social Work Intervention in Direct Practice: Implications for Education," in *Facing the Challenge: Plenary Session Papers from the 19th Annual Program Meeting* (New York: Council on Social Work Education, 1973).

[4] See Joel Fischer, "Is Casework Effective? A Review," *Social Work,* Vol. 18, No. 1 (January 1973), pp. 5–20; Steven P. Segal, "Research on the Outcome of Social Work Therapeutic Interventions: A Review of the Literature," *Journal of Health and Social Behavior,* Vol. 13, No. 1 (March 1972), pp. 3–17; Scott Briar, "The Current Crisis in Social Casework," *Social Work Practice, 1967* (New York: Columbia University Press, 1967), pp. 19–33; and Edward J. Mullen and James R. Dumpson, *Evaluation of Social Intervention* (San Francisco: Jossey-Bass, 1972).

using unrepresentative samples of workers and clients. But it has also evoked numerous calls for more and better research, particularly outcome research, in the hopes that effective social work intervention can be documented, developed, and disseminated.

The assumption has been that the production of research studies concerning practice will have an impact on what practitioners do. It is not known, however, to what extent the research that is reported to practitioners actually influences their professional behavior, or perhaps even more basically, whether they are able to understand, critically assess, and consume such research. Previous research on this topic is not very encouraging. It tends to show that social workers seem to value the idea of research,[5] but find their research courses unhelpful,[6] seldom use research studies in their professional lives or to improve their skills,[7] may actually be resistant to research on their professional activities,[8] and may not be very knowledgeable about common statistical symbols.[9]

Building a scientifically based social work, therefore, involves both producing quality research of relevance to practice and having that research critically consumed and utilized by social workers in their daily practice. Most of the research mentioned above dealt with the attitudes of social workers toward research or the extent to which they drew on research studies in their practice. These studies tended to assume that social workers were able to critically assess research and make intelligent use of it. But is this the case? Can social workers recognize good research from inadequately designed studies? And are their decisions concerning the use of research governed by its quality or by their biases concerning its findings? These are the questions addressed in this study.

Method

Survey Experiment

In order to study these major questions, a survey experiment was selected as the best method for data collection. A survey experiment involves presenting respondents with systematically varied experimental stimuli—in this case, in written form. Such a design has several advantages: it allows the researcher to survey

---

[5] Joseph W. Eaton, "Symbolic and Substantive Evaluative Research." *Administrative Science Quarterly,* Vol. 6, No. 4 (March 1962), pp. 421–42.

[6] Aaron Rosenblatt, "The Practitioner's Use and Evaluation of Research," *Social Work,* Vol. 13, No. 1 (January 1968), pp. 53–59.

[7] *Ibid.;* and Betsy-Lea Casselman, "On the Practitioner's Orientation Toward Research," *Smith College Studies in Social Work,* Vol. 42, No. 3 (June 1972), pp. 211–33.

[8] S. Aronson and C. Sherwood, "Research Versus Practitioner: Problems in Social Action Research," *Social Work,* Vol. 12, No. 4 (October 1967), pp. 89–96; and Michael A. LaSorte, "The Caseworker as Research Interviewer," *American Sociologist,* Vol. 3, No. 3 (August 1968), pp. 222–25.

[9] Patricia Weed and Shayna R. Greenwald, "The Mystics of Statistics," *Social Work,* Vol. 18, No. 2 (March 1973), pp. 113–15.

a sufficiently large sample to enhance the generalizability of the findings, and at the same time it allows for the experimental manipulation of the key independent variables in the study. In this study these variables were the effect of good and bad research design and positive and negative findings on respondents' perceptions, judgments, and evaluation of social work research.

A 2 by 2 factorial design was developed using a summary of a hypothetical study of planned, short-term casework treatment. This summary was presented to respondents with the two major independent variables being systematically varied. There were four versions of the summary: good design with positive findings, good design with negative findings, bad design with positive findings, and bad design with negative findings. Each study summary was composed of six parts:

1. A brief introduction (the same in all four versions).
2. A statement of the purpose of the study—to measure the effectiveness of planned, short-term casework for young adults (the same in all versions).
3. A statement of the study sample: 100 unmarried men and women, ages 21–35, experiencing a variety of interpersonal problems (the same in all versions).
4. A statement of the treatment procedure and method of the study (the same in all versions). The study design, however, was varied. Half the summaries described the use of a control group with clients being randomly assigned to a treatment or control group, while the other half made no mention of a control group.
5. A statement of measurement procedures including a variety of instruments specifically designed to measure the effects of casework, applied both before and after treatment (same in all versions).
6. A statement of results, varied by positive or negative findings. In the control group versions, comparisons were made between the control and experimental groups, with half the summaries showing a significant positive difference favoring the experimental group, and half showing no difference. In the no-control group versions, comparisons were made only between pre- and post-test results, with half the summaries showing a significant positive change over the course of treatment, and the other half showing no change.

Design Variations

As mentioned above, 50 percent of the study summaries were described as using good designs, that is, using control groups, while the remaining 50 percent were described as using inadequate designs, that is, no control group. These distinctions were based on the authoritative work on experimental designs by Campbell and Stanley. In their book they distinguish between a variety of designs based, in major part, on their ability to control for major threats to internal validity. One of the weakest, but most commonly used designs, is the "one-group pretest-postest design" in which an entire sample receives some treatment and is measured before and after treatment; this design will be referred to as the "bad" design. Such a design controls for only two of eight possible sources of internal invalidity, and fails to control for such factors as history, maturation, testing, instrumentation, regression, and the interaction of selection with these.[10]

A stronger design described by Campbell and Stanley is the experimental "pretest-postest control group design" which controls for all eight sources of internal invalidity by randomly assigning subjects to a treatment and control group and testing them before and after treatment. This procedure was described in the other half of the study summaries and is referred to here as the "good" design.

In addition to the research summaries, the mailed survey contained three parts: (1) a section on personal and professional information, (2) a section on the respondents' attitudes toward research and its role in social work, and (3) the dependent variables, a section which dealt specifically with the respondents' assessment of the study summary. This paper will deal mainly with the responses to the latter section. There were 14 items in this section dealing with the respondents' judgements about the methodological soundness of the study, its general importance, and its impact on the respondents' professional practice. All items were in the form of statements that required a response on a 6-point Likert-type scale ranging from Strongly Agree to Strongly Disagree.

Sample

A 2 percent random sample of NASW members was drawn from the 1972 NASW Directory of Professional Social Workers, which resulted in an initial mailing of 1,102 letters stating that a research questionnaire would be mailed in several weeks, discussing the purpose of the research, and asking cooperation. Of these, 159 were returned by the post office for a variety of reasons, most commonly because the person had changed address. The remaining 943 were mailed questionnaires. Of these, which presumably reached the intended respondent (questionnaires were returned anonymously in self-addressed stamped envelopes), 470 (50 percent) were returned, a generally high return rate for a survey of NASW members.

The 470 were compared with the latest figures on NASW membership as a whole. The sample was 57 percent female, 68.5 percent married, and 88.3 percent Caucasian, almost identical with the NASW figures of 60 percent female, 65 percent

---

[10] D. T. Campbell and J. C. Stanley, *Experimental and Quasi-Experimental Designs for Research* (Chicago: Rand McNally, 1963). The important qualitative distinctions between the control group and the no-control group designs are recognized by almost all standard research texts. For example see E. Herzog, *Some Guidelines for Evaluative Research* (Washington, D.C.: Government Printing Office, 1959); C. Selltiz, M. Jahoda, M. Deutsch, and S. Cook, *Research Methods in Social Relations* (New York: Holt, Rinehart, and Winston, 1959); and T. Tripodi, P. Fellin, and H. Meyer, *The Assessment of Social Research* (Itasca, Ill.: Peacock, 1969).

married, and 90.1 percent Caucasian.[11] In addition, respondents were nearly identical to the membership of NASW as a whole on a range of professional variables, including master's degree specialty, major method of practice, practice settings, and current employment status. This suggests that the sample for this study was representative of NASW as a whole, and that the results were therefore probably applicable to the entire professional membership.

Results

The data reported here were analyzed by a series of two-way analyses of variance, which require equal N's per cell. To achieve this equality, questionnaires were randomly selected from each of three conditions until their N's were the same as the N of the cell with the lowest rate of entirely completed questionnaires. This procedure left a total of 316 questionnaires with 79 respondents in each cell. Comparisons among respondents in each of the four cells on the basis of demographic and professional background variables revealed no significant differences among any of the groups. This suggests that randomization procedures had produced four groups that were equivalent in terms of major background characteristics.

The findings are grouped into three types of dependent variables: (1) items pertaining to respondents' evaluation of the methodological soundness of the study, (2) items pertaining to respondents' perceptions of the importance of the study, and (3) items concerning the implications and use of the findings in the respondents' own practice. (There were no statistically significant interaction effects—design by findings—on any of the 14 items.)

Evaluation of Methodological Soundness

Table 4.1 presents a summary of the results of the two-way analysis of variance for all six items asking respondents to evaluate the methodological soundness of the study summary. The main effects of the two independent variables were remarkably consistent. On four out of six items, respondents with good designs rated the study summary as significantly more methodologically sound than respondents with bad designs. Respondents with good designs differed to a statistically significant degree from respondents with bad designs in concluding that the study they read had an excellent design (item 3), adequately controlled for alternative explanations (item 4), would be used again if examining similar issues (item 5), and was equally as good as an optimal casework research design (item 6).

The effects of the findings contained in the case summary were even more consistent than the effects of design. Although respondents tended to recognize the differences between good and bad designs, they were strongly influenced by the findings of the study, with the design variable held constant. On all items, the

[11] Grant Loavenbruck, "NASW Manpower Survey Finds Increase in Pay for Most Members," *NASW News,* Vol. 18, No. 3 (March 1973), pp. 10–11.

Table 4.1 Effects of Design and Findings on Judgments about Methodological Soundness

Item	Variables	Marginal Means[a]	F-ratio	Level of Significance
1. The way this study was designed allows one to conclude that this treatment experience was effective or not effective	Good Design	3.43	1.72	n.s.
	Bad Design	3.65		
	Positive Findings	3.22	15.51	.01
	Negative Findings	3.87		
2. The data presented in this study are inadequate for drawing any major conclusions	Good Design	2.40	.82	n.s.
	Bad Design	2.27		
	Positive Findings	2.49	4.45	.05
	Negative Findings	2.18		
3. Overall, the research design of this study is excellent	Good Design	3.51	17.52	.01
	Bad Design	4.13		
	Positive Findings	3.58	10.45	.01
	Negative Findings	4.06		
4. This study adequately controls for alternative explanations of the findings	Good Design	4.22	12.29	.01
	Bad Design	4.69		
	Positive Findings	4.23	11.00	.01
	Negative Findings	4.68		
5. If I were interested in studying similar issues, I would not conduct a study in the same manner	Good Design	3.45	9.06	.01
	Bad Design	3.00		
	Positive Findings	3.50	13.61	.01
	Negative Findings	2.95		
6. In comparing this study to an optimal casework research design, with the clients randomly assigned to treatment and control groups, I would rate this study as equally good	Good Design	3.12	53.50	.01
	Bad Design	4.17		
	Positive Findings	3.46	6.99	.01
	Negative Findings	3.84		

[a]Responses were to a 6-point Likert-type scale with 1 = strongly agree and 6 = strongly disagree.

group of respondents whose summaries showed no positive effect of casework treatment evaluated the design of the study as being significantly less methodologically sound than did the respondents with summaries showing positive findings. Respondents with negative findings differed to a statistically significant degree from those with positive findings in concluding that the study they read did not allow for conclusions regarding the effectiveness of treatment (item 1), that the data presented did not allow for the drawing of major conclusions (item 2), did not have an excellent design (item 3), did not adequately control for alternative explanations (item 4), would not be used again to examine similar issues (item 5), and was not as good as an optimal research design (item 6). It must be remembered that ideally the findings should not have had any influence on respondents' judgements about the methodological soundness of the study; the methodological adequacy of a study is in no way dependent on or related to the findings that the study produces.

Perceived Importance of Study

Table 4.2 presents a summary of the results of the analyses for the four items calling for the respondents to make judgements about the importance of the study and the knowledge it produced. A slightly different pattern from that found with the items evaluating the methodological soundness of the study was found here. In no instance did the findings produce a significant difference between the groups. On the other hand, on three out of four of the items, respondents with good designs judged the study they read as significantly more important than respondents with bad designs. Thus respondents with good designs differed to a statistically significant degree from respondents with bad designs in judging the study in regard to its general importance to social work; better designed studies were viewed as more important than poorly designed ones.

Perceived Implications for Personal Practice

The third category of items on the questionnaire called for the respondents to make judgements about the implications of the study they read for their personal

Table 4.2   Effects of Design and Findings on Judgments of the Importance of Study

Item	Variables	Marginal Means[a]	F-ratio	Level of Significance
7. I believe that this study makes an important contribution to social work's body of knowledge	Good Design	3.84	1.70	n.s.
	Bad Design	4.03		
	Positive Findings	3.82	2.17	n.s.
	Negative Findings	4.04		
8. I would bring this study to the attention of my colleagues	Good Design	3.49	7.46	.01
	Bad Design	3.93		
	Positive Findings	3.74	.12	n.s.
	Negative Findings	3.68		
9. The findings in the study are relevant to the practice of social work in general	Good Design	3.09	5.87	.05
	Bad Design	3.45		
	Positive Findings	3.16	2.22	n.s.
	Negative Findings	3.38		
10. If the full report were readily available to me, I would read the full report	Good Design	2.06	13.85	.01
	Bad Design	2.54		
	Positive Findings	2.28	.08	n.s.
	Negative Findings	2.32		

[a]Responses were to a 6-point Likert-type scale with 1 = strongly agree and 6 = strongly disagree.

Table 4.3 Effects of Design and Findings on Judgments of Implications for Personal Practice

Item	Variables	Marginal Means[a]	F-ratio	Level of Significance
11. I consider the findings of this study to be very helpful for my own practice	Good Design	3.99	1.80	n.s.
	Bad Design	4.20		
	Positive Findings	3.95	3.34	n.s.
	Negative Findings	4.23		
12. To use the findings of this study, I would have to make specific changes in my own practice	Good Design	4.01	.20	n.s.
	Bad Design	4.08		
	Positive Findings	4.30	9.06	.01
	Negative Findings	3.78		
13. The treatment procedures used in this study are similar to those I use in my own practice	Good Design	3.58	.02	n.s.
	Bad Design	3.60		
	Positive Findings	3.35	9.19	.01
	Negative Findings	3.83		
14. I would not be inclined to use the knowledge gained from this study in my professional practice	Good Design	3.61	2.45	n.s.
	Bad Design	3.36		
	Positive Findings	3.80	16.47	.01
	Negative Findings	3.16		

[a]Responses were to a 6-point Likert-type scale with 1 = strongly agree and 6 = strongly disagree.

practice. Table 4.3 summarizes these results. There were no significant effects of the study design on any of the four items pertaining to impact on personal practice.

On three out of four items (plus a strong tendency in the same direction on the fourth item), the findings of the study summary produced a statistically significant difference between groups. The results were consistent with those in the previous categories. Respondents with negative findings were significantly less inclined to use the knowledge gained from this study in their own practice (item 14). Respondents with negative findings also differed significantly from respondents with positive findings in believing that to use such knowledge they would have to make specific changes in their own practice (item 12), and that the treatment procedures described in the study were not similar to those used in their own practice (item 13). In other words, when reading a study showing that casework is effective, regardless of the quality of the research methodology, social workers tended to believe that the treatment procedures used were similar to their own and that they would not have to make changes in their own practice. But when confronted with the same study with negative findings, they believed their own treatment procedures were different from those described in the study and that they would have to make specific changes in their practice in order to use the findings. Finally, respondents with negative findings in comparison with those with positive findings, tended to believe that the findings were not very helpful for their own practice, an effect just short of significance at the .05 level.

Conclusion

There can be little doubt that for social work to be a vibrant and effective profession it must ensure that its practice is grounded as much as possible in empirical research. Research, as recognized by most social work educators, must be an integral part not only of training, but also of practice. It is discouraging to find, as past surveys have, that social workers do not view research courses as helpful in graduate school, do not read much research after graduation, and rarely find research studies helpful in their practice.

The study reported here has suggested that social workers, even when they are presented with potentially useful research information, often fail to assess and utilize it in a completely objective fashion. Social workers can and did distinguish between studies with good and bad designs. When reading studies with control groups, they evaluated them as methodologically more sound and more important to the profession than uncontrolled studies. But even more consistent, and undoubtedly more disturbing, was the revelation that the findings of the study exerted a strong biasing effect on social workers' judgements of the research. When reading a study with positive findings of the effectiveness of casework treatment, respondents evaluated the study as methodologically superior, and generally as having greater implications for practice than the same study reporting negative results. This biasing effect was so great that social workers reading the study with positive results tended to believe that the treatment procedures described were similar to their own, while those confronted with negative findings tended to deny that this was so!

Although this resistance to negative findings may not be unique to social work, and indeed may be common in the physical sciences[12] as well as in other professions, it can impede the development of a scientifically based social work practice. It is true that some social work research is not very relevant to practice problems, either because it is poorly conducted or addressed to insignificant practice issues, and practitioners' resistance to research reports may at times be well-founded. But it is equally likely that their professional biases and their inability to accurately assess research reports inhibits the development of effective practice.

[12] Reginald K. Carter, "Clients' Resistance to Negative Findings and the Latent Conservative Function of Evaluation," *American Sociologist,* Vol. 6, No. 2 (May 1971), pp. 118–24; and Thomas S. Kuhn, *The Structure of Scientific Revolutions* (Chicago: University of Chicago Press, 1962).

Chapter 5
An Eclectic Base for Practice

Chapter One called for caseworkers to be aware of and use, when appropriate, knowledge from diverse sources, regardless of whether that knowledge is derived from within or outside the profession. Such a stance, though, does suggest some questions regarding the knowledge base for the practice of social casework: (1) Are there any limitations to the types of knowledge caseworkers should use; (2) how should caseworkers select that knowledge; and (3) how can caseworkers organize such knowledge into an integrated, effective approach?

This chapter will pursue these questions and attempt to deal with them through the explication of a model for the development of an eclectic approach to the practice of casework. As noted previously, casework is not a unitary phenomenon—in terms of methods, approach, or even roles. Thus, although the major focus of this and subsequent chapters is on the clinical/behavior change role, the basic principles discussed here are applicable to knowledge selection and utilization in the several roles of social casework.

Knowledge for Casework

Two broad classes of knowledge are potentially available for casework practice. Figure 5.1 is a graphic representation of these areas of knowledge, which could include formulations from any of or all the social and behavioral sciences.

The first class, causal/developmental knowledge, contains by far the bulk of the knowledge developed in the social and behavioral sciences. This knowledge essentially serves as an aid in understanding the *development* of behavior (both adaptive and maladaptive). Use of causal/developmental knowledge focuses on answering the question, "Why did a given state of affairs come about?" Thus, a caseworker might use such knowledge to understand how and why a particular individual developed as he or she did. Classical examples of causal/developmental knowledge might be the bulk of Freudian theory, e.g., dealing with psychosexual development,

Fischer, J. (1978). *Effective Casework Practice: An Eclectic Approach.* New York: McGraw-Hill. Reprinted with permission of McGraw-Hill.

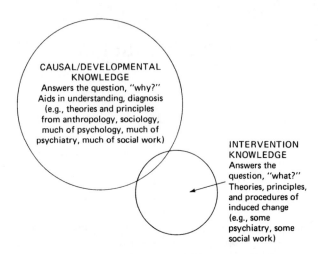

Fig. 5.1   Areas of knowledge potentially available to caseworkers.

Erikson's stages of life (Erikson, 1950), or any body of knowledge that focuses on *understanding* human behavior (whether in terms of personality, organizations, or society). In schools of social work, formal recognition of the presumed importance of this knowledge has been institutionalized in course sequences such as "Human Behavior and the Social Environment" and "Human Development." This knowledge traditionally has been assumed to be of value to the caseworker in the assessment of individuals, cases, and situations, in that understanding why an individual developed as he or she did was a major part of the diagnostic formulation.

Intervention knowledge, on the other hand, is intended to be used to prescribe principles and procedures for inducing change in behaviors and/or situations. Intervention knowledge focuses on the questions, "What can be done to modify this situation, and will it be effective?" A far smaller proportion of the social and behavioral sciences is devoted to producing such knowledge. Even a field such as psychiatry, a profession ostensibly devoted to intervention, has produced a far larger proportion of research and theory to help practitioners *understand* problematic conditions than to actually specifically *change* those conditions.

Obviously, as figure 5.1 illustrates, there is some overlap between these two areas. This could be seen, for example, in the production of knowledge where understanding specific developmental aspects is a precondition (or provides specific guidelines) for intervention, or in an approach that might incorporate both causal/developmental material *and* interventive procedures, thereby specifically relating diagnosis to treatment. But, as suggested in the Introduction, the latter, particularly, has not been the case in the vast majority of traditional approaches to casework practice (Simon, 1970; Turner, 1974). Even more importantly, there often is a lack of recognition of the real and significant differences in terms of substance and implications between these two broad classes of knowledge.

Caseworkers for years have attempted to use causal/developmental knowledge—the sum total or end product of which is the "diagnostic formulation"—as a substitute for intervention knowledge, on the assumption that understanding how a problem came about also provides information about how to change that problem. Thus, a body of knowledge such as Freudian or psychodynamic theory, which is largely causal/developmental, came to be viewed as a sufficient basis for casework intervention in several casework approaches (Roberts & Nee, 1970; Turner, 1974). In other words, it was assumed that understanding an individual's developmental history was sufficient for carrying out treatment, that *understanding* somehow was the key ingredient, or could be equated with *intervention*. Such a conception could be portrayed by redrawing figure 5.1 as two virtually overlapping concentric circles.

But by its very nature, causal/developmental knowledge describes and explains only problem *development*. An entirely different set of principles and procedures is necessary to provide guidelines for *changing* the problem. This is so even if understanding the cause and development of a problem is, within the context of a given theory, a necessary precondition for intervention. For example, in orthodox Freudian psychoanalysis, it is crucial for the analyst to understand the early life history and psychodynamics of each client. But the tools for intervention, say, the therapist's interpretations which lead to client insight, are a separate or additional body of knowledge with which the analyst must be equipped. Again, as particularly evident in the traditional approaches to social casework, causal/developmental knowledge is often tentatively, if at all, related to intervention knowledge and does not provide the tools necessary for actually carrying out intervention, or even, as with the bulk of traditional casework approaches, for *selecting* intervention plans. Thus, the predominant view of the base of casework practice as residing in "knowledge about human behavior," rather than knowledge specifically about *changing* human behavior, may account for at least part of the current confusion and upheaval in social casework regarding therapeutic efficacy.

Another major implication of heavy reliance on causal/developmental knowledge in casework has been a preoccupation with searching for and working with causes in most problem situations, as represented, e.g., in the taking of extensive and detailed social histories of clients. This generally assumes that there *are* specifiable causes for each problem. However, the notion of specific causality is part and parcel of the disease model of psychopathology, in which social and psychological problems tend to be thought of basically as analogous to physical health and illness. Such a model logically leads to the necessity for discovering the etiology of each "illness," as though it were some internal infection. Then, "treatment" is focused on ferreting out and dealing with this underlying cause, as a physician might use medicine to destroy some internal bacterium that was causing symptoms of fever and aches and pains.

However, all the work of the social and behavioral sciences has produced very little *validated* data as to just what *are* the specific "causes" of most of the problems with which caseworkers deal. Few variables have been identified that, given their presence, say, in the early history of an individual, uniformly lead to accurate predictions of the occurrence of maladaptive social functioning at a later point. In fact, there seem to be numerous salient factors (multicausality) in people's lives which, in often idiosyncratic ways, in particular patterns of interaction between people and their environments, may in some cases lead to future difficulties, but in others not produce discernible effects.

The focus on causality, which has led to heavy reliance in the practice of casework on the collection of extensive life histories of our clients, the better to see the "causes" of their problems, appears on the surface to have the ring of logic to it. It is, no doubt, reasonable to assume that every person is a product of his or her past experiences. But, in actual practice, an orientation to "etiology" may not be particularly helpful. In the first place, such retrospective data often simply are inaccurate, because of either the unintended distortions of memory or the desire of some clients to tell caseworkers what they think they "should" say, rather than what actually happened. Further, research comparing the histories of people identified (through a variety of means) as disturbed or "abnormal" with histories of those people not so identified ("normals") has not been able to distinguish between the histories of the two groups (e.g., Renaud & Estess, 1961; Schofield & Ballan, 1959). In other words, when facts about adult functioning, i.e., whether it has been generally adaptive or generally maladaptive, are unknown, experts cannot distinguish between groups of adequately functioning or poorly functioning people on the basis of their life histories.

In fact, considerable research refutes the common assumption in social casework that there is a linear relationship between specific disruption in early life (say, toilet training, feeding practices, separation) and later problems in social functioning (Orlansky, 1948; Caldwell, 1964). Indeed, one comprehensive review of research concluded that no factors of parent-child interaction could be found to be unique in any diagnostic groups, nor to distinguish these groups from controls (Frank, 1965), a view seconded in a recent review in the social work literature (Whittaker, 1976). Thus, it would appear as though something could be found in everybody's life history which, interpreted in light of later events, seems to be "pathogenic." Particularly for the clients of caseworkers, then, who already have been identified (or identified themselves) as having problems in social functioning, such retrospective analysis almost always results in the discovery of something that is considered an etiological or pathogenic factor in the client's life histories—a divorce in this family, an alcoholic mother in that—whether these incidents actually were specifically related to current problems or not.

Even if caseworkers *were* able to make such etiological or historical diagnoses, however, and to correctly identify factors in a client's early life history that actually led to later problems in social functioning, there is no evidence that such accuracy has (and little reason to believe it *would* have) a positive effect on the outcome of casework intervention. This is because, in the first place, to the extent that a problem is an enduring one, it has probably become functionally autonomous from its early life history "cause" (i.e., its existence has become independent of the cause).

Thus, even knowing the actual causal events would be of little help in current modification efforts. But even more importantly, the current level of knowledge in the social and behavioral sciences simply precludes us from taking direct interventive action on such "causal" variables even if we could accurately identify them. In other words, knowing that an individual was a subject of punitive toilet training, or is "fixated at the oral stage," is one thing; being able to do something about it may be something else altogether. Another, parallel, example of this would be the tendency of some scholars to attribute many of today's social problems to changes that occurred in our society during the 1800s. Of course, knowing that this is the case provides little help in trying to resolve those problems.

The point is not to deny the importance of any individual's life experiences. Every theoretical approach to human behavior recognizes the significance of past events in shaping present behavior. On the other hand, many approaches, particularly those derived from psychodynamic sources, hypothesize that specific events in an individual's early life history are predictive of later life "personality" or even ability to function adequately. But the evidence for such assumptions is, at best, equivocal (Mischel, 1968). In fact, research on human development is clear in showing that even apparently severely disruptive early life experiences (ranging from punitive toilet training to maternal deprivation) may be counterbalanced by any one or more of a number of subsequent facilitative experiences. Approaches that assume the importance, or immutability, of specific early life experiences may be basing their assumptions on irrelevant factors. Research, to date, has been unable to identify specific early life events that uniformly lead to disruptive behavior in later life. Thus, the caseworker who assumes their importance and searches for such events to attempt to give meaning or understanding to a client's current behavior is likely simply to be barking up the wrong tree.

The fact that a large proportion of caseworkers hold to such assumptions about human behavior presents serious problems for the field, particularly in terms of misdirecting practice. For example, adherence to such notions may lead some caseworkers to spend a considerable part of their practice time with clients searching for and analyzing such historical factors, a practice which, in realistic terms, is largely futile. Adhering to the assumptions about the central importance of early life history may lead caseworkers to believe that the "best" approach is one that somehow attempts to deal with such factors, and to regard any approach to casework intervention that does not as being superficial, as being capable of providing "only symptomatic relief." And finally, continuing adherence both to these assumptions and to the theories that spawned them, in the face of research that they are not tenable, points to a serious question regarding caseworkers' lack, or nonuse, of rigorous criteria for assessing and selecting the knowledge they utilize. While it may not be possible to find and select underpinnings for practice that are completely validated in research, continuing use of principles and assumptions that are, at best, unvalidated and, at worse, invalidated, points to the need for a systematic evaluation of whatever approaches happen to be in vogue to assess their actual, rather than desired, value for practice.

Another major implication of caseworkers' preoccupation with causal/developmental knowledge is that it has led to a situation in which we are far more sophisticated in our diagnostic than our intervention knowledge. This is a condition which seems to be an anomaly in a profession whose prior commitment, whose raison d'être in fact, is the development of effective methods of *intervention*. This is not to say that understanding our clients through a process of sensitive assessment is not important. *But understanding is not helping*. Causal/developmental knowledge is important mainly to the extent that the understanding of persons-in-situations which it provides articulates with specific notions about how to bring about change, i.e., when the assessment is stated in terms which are amenable directly to interventive measures. (The fact that it is known, or assumed, that an individual is suffering from, say, an "unresolved Oedipal complex" is not the same as stating in terms amenable to intervention what to do about such a situation. The diagnosis in such a case clearly does not lead to selection of specific procedures for inducing change.)

A recent study of caseworkers in a children's agency, reported by Middleman and Goldberg (1974), lends empirical support to the notion that caseworkers often spend undue amounts of time with diagnostic concerns. In that study, diagnostic evaluations consumed a minimum of 11½ to 13 hours per child and sometimes took up to 21½ hours. As Briar and Miller (1971, pp. 144–145) succinctly state:

> Clients generally do not come to caseworkers simply to be diagnosed—they want and legitimately expect to be helped. . . . In many social agencies, it is not uncommon for staff conferences convened to discuss cases to devote fifty-eight minutes to "diagnosis" and two minutes to intervention planning, with little apparent connection between the two.

Again, the point is not that, in and of themselves, understanding and assessment of clients are not key social work tasks. Rather, it is that the kind of understanding and assessment that caseworkers traditionally have utilized—focused on historical factors or those in the remote past which appear to have "caused" the present problems—seem unnecessary. Among the other reasons discussed here, factors related to the origins of a problem often disappear and simply do not explain the continued existence of the problem.

Thus, the type of "causal analysis" that a caseworker *would* undertake would involve a search for those factors that appear to be maintaining or affecting the problem *currently*. Perhaps this is more clearly illustrated by distinguishing between the traditional "causal (historical) analysis" and what might be termed "analysis of *controlling* conditions," or those that might be currently "causally connected" with the problem. Hence, the worker would locate the variables that seem to be sustaining the current problem. Then, he or she would attempt to determine those factors that seem most significant in affecting the current problem, particularly in the context of selecting as a focus for intervention from among several that may be operating and that would be most susceptible to the worker's change efforts. In other words, there would be an interaction between the significance or relevance of the factors and the worker's ability to affect them. There would be little value in selecting factors that have scanty relevance in maintaining the problem, or that are indeed important but cannot be translated directly into interventive efforts.

The statements above, calling for a direct relationship between assessment and intervention, may appear mere truisms. By definition, a professional practice rests on a body of knowledge the purpose of which is to supply the practitioner with the capacity to influence (or control or change) events. In fact, practice theory, per se, can be described as being composed of two major elements. The first involves a systematic explication of diagnostic principles with the goal of understanding the phenomena of concern and as a guide to selection of methods of intervention. The second part, then, involves a systematic explication of principles of induced change and procedures for implementing those principles, with the goal of intervening (or inducing change) in the phenomena of concern. Hypothetically, the assessment and intervention principles are utilized together, with one leading to the other. Unfortunately, in many traditional approaches to casework practice there appears to be little or no relationship between "diagnosis" and "treatment"; i.e., the in-depth assessment does not lead to or enhance the selection of intervention procedures (Fischer, 1975a). The second fact is that the bulk of the current knowledge used by professional caseworkers lies in the causal/developmental realm, at the expense of interventive methodology, and to the extent that most casework approaches even fail to prescribe any procedures for influencing client change (i.e., that would tell the caseworker what to do).

This focus contributes to what might be termed "the etiological pitfall" (Bennis et al., 1961), wherein caseworkers are caught up in a process of trying to understand how and why clients came to be the way they are, without a concomitant ability to influence changes in those dimensions even were they to be successfully understood. Causal/developmental knowledge, in and of itself, while important, is an insufficient basis for effective intervention and is of real consequence only to the extent that it complements knowledge dealing with intervention.

All this, however, is not intended as an argument for the removal of courses presenting causal/developmental knowledge from schools of social work, or for considering this knowledge irrelevant to the practitioner. And it is certainly not an argument for the abandonment of a careful assessment process in social casework. Indeed, a great deal of information derived largely from causal/developmental knowledge areas would appear to offer important aids to caseworkers in understanding and assessing their clients and the clients' situations. For example, role theory (Strean, 1974) provides an important perspective for the caseworker in examining the many ways people interact with each other in different contexts, including the worker-client relationship. Systems theory (Hearn, 1974) is particularly important as a framework for viewing and understanding the complex interactions between client and environment and the ways in which different milieus impinge on each other. Similarly, it would appear to be very difficult for the caseworker to practice effectively, especially with clients from different ethnic, class, or cultural groups, without an adequate understanding of the influence of culture in general on behavior, as well as understanding the possibilities of specific group effects on individual behavior, whether these be racial factors in the interview (Kadushin, 1972), or specific cultural effects on behavior (e.g., Lewis and Ho's 1975 report on work with Native Americans). Of course, it should be clear that while, in all these instances, the knowledge can add substantially to caseworkers' abilities to assess and understand situations, such knowledge does not necessarily or automatically prescribe what to do in those situations. Thus, the extent to which utilization of such knowledge actually benefits caseworkers' interventive practices is unclear.

Thus, while knowledge for assessment is important, the inexorable need to seek out the *causes* of every problem, particularly through anamnestic or historical analysis, should not be so inexorable. In fact, for much of social casework, it may not be necessary to be concerned with causal/developmental knowledge at all. The grounds for this conclusion, which were explored here, in sum, are: (1) such analysis is generally inaccurate; (2) enduring problems tend to be functionally autonomous from early causation; (3) such an emphasis misdirects practice efforts, not only in work with specific clients, but in overemphasizing causal/developmental knowledge at the expense of intervention knowledge; (4) there is no evidence that understanding historical causality is related to successful interventive efforts; and (5) even were we to be successful in understanding historical causality, we do not possess the kind of interventive repertoire that allows us to take direct action on this understanding. A sixth, and perhaps the most important, reason for downgrading the search for "causality" as part of casework practice is that there are numerous examples in the literature, many of which will be discussed in subsequent chapters, that testify to our ability to effectively help a wide variety of people suffering from a broad range of problems without knowing the causes of those problems. Factors influencing the genesis of problems simply may not have to be involved at all in efforts to successfully intervene into those problems. (For an interesting discussion of the paradox of predicting changes without understanding how the problem came about or even without understanding completely why a specific technique, when implemented, brought about a particular effect, see Dubin, 1969, chapter 1. In the same chapter, Dubin also describes several reasons why *understanding* a given system does not necessarily provide the basis for changing or making predictions about that system.)

The key point here is that the priorities in social casework education and practice must be shifted from an emphasis on the use of systems that are mainly concerned with developing an elaborate diagnostic methodology to more appropriate utilization and development of interventive knowledge as the primary foundation for practice.

Intervention Knowledge

The preceding section, for the variety of reasons summarized at the end of the section, provided a basis for a major change in emphasis and priorities—both in schools of social work and in practice—from prevailing allegiance to and utilization of causal/developmental knowledge to a continuing focus on the development and use of intervention knowledge. Again, although this may seem to be an obvious priority for social casework, the facts are that intervention knowledge has been consistently downgraded and/or underutilized in the profession.

The preceding section also elaborated the basis for considering the development of approaches to intervention in ways that may be independent of causal/developmental knowledge. Among the primary reasons for doing so is the fact that principles and procedures of intervention, of induced change, empirically have been demonstrated to be effective in helping people, independent of knowledge about the cause of their problems. This is still a minority position in both casework and related fields (e.g., Ford & Urban, 1963, in the field of psychotherapy), where traditional mythology still seems to prevail, arguing, in essence, that intervention knowledge must be firmly rooted in causal/developmental knowledge (e.g., theories of therapy must be grounded in theories of personality). This position is adhered to even in the face of research evidence that it need not be the case and that intervention principles and procedures can be applied effectively without recourse to an elaborate causal/developmental undergirding.

Technical definitions of "intervene" include, "to come in or between by way of . . . modification" *(Webster's Seventh New Collegiate Dictionary)* and "to come between in action" *(The American College Dictionary)*. The fact that caseworkers (and other helping professionals) increasingly are adopting the use of the term "intervention," then, suggests increasing acceptance of the notion that caseworkers do in fact take an active role in planning and carrying out action to influence the behavior, activities, and/or situations of others. Intervention knowledge, generically speaking, would include that knowledge which helps caseworkers *induce change* in those phenomena with which they are concerned. Intervention knowledge is not concerned simply with change alone (since such change may be accidental or largely developmental). To be useful for professional practice, the change must be guided and predictable (Ford & Urban, 1963) and, as suggested in the definition of casework services as interpersonal helping, informed and purposeful, utilizing principles and procedures derived systematically from an identified body of knowledge.

The main purpose of intervention knowledge is to provide guidelines for practice, for actually inducing change in the life situations of others. This change may be brought about in two general ways: (1) By altering directly the client's behavior or manners of responding, feelings, cognitions, or all these; and (2) by altering any of the social systems in which the client functions. Any given body of intervention knowledge, e.g., a single theory of psychotherapy or behavior change, or a theory of casework, might be comprehensive enough to encompass both kinds of change within its framework. But it is far more typical that intervention knowledge derived from a single source is either so circumscribed as to deal only with a single type of induced change, or pays lip service to both types of change while only actually dealing with one type (as witness the claims of many traditional casework approaches that they are both clinically and socially oriented while almost completely omitting detailed attention to the latter).

Intervention knowledge can range from comprehensive theories of change, to principles and procedures derived from such theories but utilized independently of the constraints of practice within the context of any theory, to principles and procedures developed inductively from clinical observations and empirical research. In other words, intervention knowledge (and this is also true of causal/developmental knowledge) runs the gamut from theory to research and includes a broad range of middle level propositions derived from either or both.

Hypothetically, intervention knowledge can go into great detail describing numerous dimensions, such as the items presented in chapter two, the framework for analysis of theories for casework. Thus, a given specific body of intervention knowledge might: contain principles with excellent predictive validity; be clear about the behaviors toward which the worker should attend and about what is expected of the client; clearly describe who should set the goals in the intervention process; be clear about the relationship between assessment and intervention; be clear about how the "therapeutic relationship" should be utilized by the worker; clearly present principles explaining the way unwanted behavior might be extinguished and desired behavior developed, and prescribe specific techniques or procedures for implementing those principles; describe principles and procedures for transfer of change from the locus of intervention to the natural environment; prescribe specific criteria for termination; and specify the specific clients and/or problems for which the approach is intended. The approach might even identify exactly how success can be measured and even present research evidence validating its utilization. In fact, any given approach hypothetically might address all the criteria described in chapter two.

On the other hand, an intervention approach might consist of only one procedure, inductively derived from clinical observation and research, which might be applicable in only specific and highly circumscribed situations.

Again, the above discussion is mainly intended to describe the wide range of alternatives which the rubric "intervention knowledge" is meant to convey. But there does appear to be a certain minimal level or floor beyond which intervention knowledge cannot go without losing its identification as intervention knowledge. This minimal level is the fact that intervention knowledge, to be suitable for application in practice, must contain *techniques*—procedures for *implementation,* for inducing or guiding change with clients. Without this, intervention knowledge merges into that fuzzy never-never land where philosophy, values, and causal/developmental knowledge become almost indistinguishable. This is not to say that any of these is irrelevant; only that without techniques, intervention knowledge is of limited worth to practitioners.

Unfortunately, many caseworkers seem to have developed an aversion to techniques, or perhaps more accurately, to the word "techniques." This word seems to connote a mechanistic, dehumanized, or oversimplified approach to complex human problems. Possibly this aversion stems from confusion over the nature of techniques. In the context of the worker's relationship with the client, however, "something" has to be done by the worker, or else he or she would be sitting passively, unengaged in therapeutic intervention. So the question is, what does the worker actually *do?*

The worker obviously does not "do" theory. A theory, a complex set of ideas, observations, facts, etc., in itself cannot be applied to a person. There must be some way of translating the theory, or a principle of the theory, into action. The technique is that translation, that application in action. The technique or procedure of helping is merely the way the worker attempts to use some principles, or use the theory, to make it "come alive" in application with clients. Without techniques, caseworkers could never accomplish their goals or even offer any services. Techniques are the expression in action and in a precise form of what the caseworker should actually *do* in a given situation and with a given client or problem. Techniques, in other words, form the core of the technology of social casework—the applied or practical methods of achieving practice objectives.

Caseworkers seem generally always to have known this. Most of the traditional casework approaches recognize the necessity for the use of techniques as a way of implementing each approach (e.g., Perlman, 1970, p. 161; Hollis, 1973; Reid & Epstein, 1972). However, while the *recognition* of the necessity for techniques has been present, the *development* of such techniques, as pointed out previously, has lagged considerably, to the point where there are few if any definitive guidelines available in traditional approaches as to what techniques to apply, to what kinds of problems, with what kinds of clients, in what kinds of situations. While some efforts have been made in this direction (e.g., Hollis, 1968, 1973), these techniques are poorly developed and vague. To date, they have remained merely catalogs or descriptions of what social workers do, not prescriptive statements as to what they should do and when and why they should do it.

Further, the notions of "relationship" and "techniques" are in no way antithetical. Even such complex interactions as the relationship between worker and client are expressed through techniques, through what the worker does. In fact, systems for specifically training these presumably complex and subtle skills of relationship have been developed (see the appendix of this book).

Now, obviously (or, it is hoped) the techniques should not be the master of the worker. Rather, the worker must be able to select techniques in a flexible, open manner, appropriate to the specific situation, and not be confined, say, to the use of only one technique with all problems because that is the only technique known. The development of an expanded repertoire of interventive procedures is the essence of professional skill and preparation for practice.

Toward Eclectic Casework Practice

The emphasis in this chapter has been on the diverse sources from which intervention knowledge can be derived. There has been little focus on intervention *theories* per se. An intervention theory is an interrelated system of more or less general propositions used as principles of explanation of some specified interventive (or therapeutic or clinical) process. Such theories, of course, can range from comprehensive and expansive general systems to mid- and lower-range theories concerned with a more constricted variety of phenomena.[1] The potential content of such theory is summarized in the framework in chapter two with regard to clinical (or casework or therapy) theories and includes any number of different dimensions, such as specifying which problems are the focus of intervention, how and why intervention should proceed, when intervention can be considered successful (or not successful), and what procedures should be used.

Frequently, however, the call for intervention knowledge to be rooted in "theory" is a function of confusion between *personality* theory (causal/developmental knowledge) and *intervention* theory (intervention knowledge). Intervention systems can be, and often are, theories (as formally defined) unto themselves, whether or not they are articulated with causal/developmental theories (say, a theory of personality development). But it should be clear that intervention theories need *not* be derived from theories of personality, although sound theoretical principles regarding structure, content, and so on need not be abrogated only because the intervention approach is not derived from personality theory. Further, the distinction between causal/developmental theory and intervention theory should not obscure the fact that certain theoretical *principles* may underlie certain aspects of both types of theory (as, for example, the learning principle of counter-conditioning is presumed to underlie the behavior therapy technique of systematic desensitization; Wolpe, 1973). Such principles may also be relevant to causal/developmental theory, but their key significance in the context of this discussion is that they also explain aspects of the intervention theory and hence are more germane as casework knowledge. The term "theory," then, is not synonymous with personality theory, or causal/developmental theory, or psychological (or social) theory, or even intervention theory, but can be differentially applied to any of these.

There are numerous potential advantages to the use of a theory of intervention (Turner, 1974, pp. 12–14; Ford & Urban, 1963). Use of such a theory can:

1. Allow classification of the phenomena of concern, and hence, imposes order on heterogeneous events.
2. Facilitate generalization from one situation to another.
3. Facilitate prediction of outcomes.
4. Allow the development of orderly, consistent procedures for observing the relationships between events.
5. Help us explain our orientation and activities to others.
6. Allow the development of means for modifying behaviors.
7. Provide assurance for the worker.

---

[1] Turner (1974, pp. 8–11) has described ten different approaches to theory and theory-building in social work that he has identified after a comprehensive search through the clinical social work literature.

In other words, a theory of intervention can be *useful,* a way of observing, understanding, planning, predicting results, and implementing intervention. As Kurt Lewin once pointed out, there is nothing as practical as a good theory.

On the other hand, there are several problems in the use of theories per se. Indeed, because of their more or less comprehensive nature, it is difficult to "adhere" to more than one, or at best two theories. Hence, these problems are made most obvious when, as is the case with many professionals, the *practitioner,* as opposed to the individual who is guided by a theory in the *development* of techniques, uses only one or two theories as a base for practice:

1. While there may be nothing as practical as a good theory, there is nothing as unfortunate as a *bad* theory. A theory may lead to inaccurate or incorrect predictions, weak or ineffective interventions, and guide practice in the wrong (unhelpful) directions.

2. Theories tend to channel both knowledge and perceptions of their users into unitary molds and narrow perspectives, thereby leading practitioners to attempt to force a number of significantly different people (clients) and problems into an incompatible jell, with disastrous results. For example, the increasing use of family therapy has seemed on the surface to be a major increment to caseworkers' knowledge, given the long-term concern of caseworkers with helping families. (Actually, family therapy is not a unitary phenomenon since there are several different approaches to it; see Erickson and Hogan, 1972.) However, as perceived by casework theorists (Scherz, 1970; Sherman, 1974), family therapy appears as a fairly loose conglomeration of principles derived from a psychodynamic base on one hand and communication theory on the other. Hence, the main focus of the interview, in addition to and often in contradistinction with conventional casework practices, is on family communication patterns, often to the exclusion of other salient topics (Fischer, 1974b). Indeed, a nationwide study of a cross section of professionals who utilized family therapy showed that 85 percent take as a primary goal for *all* families, irrespective of background or problem, improved communication, while such dimensions as improved individual behavior ("symptom") and improved task performance were seen as primary goals by only 23 and 12 percent, respectively (Group for the Advancement of Psychiatry, 1970). While this almost exclusive focus on communication may be salutary in some instances, family therapy emphasizing communication, particularly open and direct communication, often is applied in practice without differential assessment of its applicability, in other words, in most cases where family problems appear to predominate. This more or less universal application ignores the fact that a large percentage of our clients—particularly those from lower income groups—not only may not benefit from careful examination of and attempts to change their communication patterns along the lines of more "open" and direct communication, but may even be harmed by such a focus. This is because emphasis on such communication is largely a middle- and upper-class phenomenon—in essence, a middle-class value—but tends to be incongruent with and, in some cases, perhaps dysfunctional for the life-style of many lower-income or culturally divergent groups in our society.

3. When efforts at change are guided more or less by a single theory, the results are nonsensical. Not only are people and their problems too complicated for the use of only one approach to resolve all problems, but, on the face of it, clearly the numerous different roles and activities of caseworkers are unlikely to be adequately subsumed under a single theory.

4. No single theoretical perspective has successfully addressed the wide range of problems that practitioners encounter. There is no empirical evidence that one theory of intervention produces consistently superior results across the *total* range of people or problems.

5. One of the major bases for selecting a theory of intervention is empirical validation in research that its application results in effectiveness. However, the complexity of most theories precludes their total validation. Actually, research generally tends to be carried out on selected portions of theory, in this case, on specific principles and procedures of induced change. So criteria for selection on the basis of empirical evidence should be limited to the principles and procedures that have been validated in research, thereby avoiding the common mistake of assuming that because one aspect of a theory has been more or less validated, the entire theory is adoptable (e.g., if only one procedure of behavior modification had been validated in research, it would not mean that the whole approach—all the procedures—should be adopted).

6. The largest part of the content of many intervention theories is "excess baggage," basically irrelevant to the core tasks of intervention. For example, Rogers (1959) has developed a very complex, in-depth theory of therapy (in association with his theory of personality; see Ford & Urban, 1963). This aspect of his work, indeed, that which forms the bulk of it, is generally less well-known than Rogers' advocacy of "the necessary and sufficient conditions of psychotherapy" (Rogers, 1957, 1962) which revolve around such conditions as empathy, warmth, and genuineness. The reasons for this paradox are simple: when it comes to practicality, whatever the complexities of Roger's theory, the main therapeutic task of the therapist is to provide those conditions to the client, an occurrence that can take place independent of even knowing Roger's theory. A similar condition exists with many other approaches, as for example, with regard to the possibilities of the clinician implementing Wolpe's technique of systematic desensitization (Wolpe, 1969b) without knowing much at all about Wolpe's very complex neurological theorizing which underlies it (see Ford & Urban, 1963).

7. The fact that so many competing theories of intervention even exist—well over fifty in the clinical field alone!—suggests that they all cannot be equally valid, or perhaps even more obviously, that none has achieved either sufficiently widespread acceptance or sufficiently broad empirical validation to stand alone as the "optimum" approach. Indeed, the burden of proof regarding the development of evidence on the validity of an approach must rest with its adherents. It is neither justified nor appropriate for adherents of one or another "school" to insist that their approach is "best" because *others* have not disproved or invalidated it.

8. So many principles and procedures may influence the modification of behav-

ior—e.g., positive reinforcement, insight, extinction, "faith," reciprocal inhibition, social modeling, counter-conditioning, cognitive dissonance, situational manipulation—that it seems "the best strategy at this point would be to consider the hypothesis that different kinds of responses may be governed by different principles and may require different procedures for their modification" (Ford & Urban, 1967, p. 345). Indeed, this is bolstered by the finding in extensive research (Bergin, 1971; Meltzoff & Kornreich, 1970) showing very low intercorrelations between different measures of change (outcome measures). This suggests that behavior change, when it exists, may be multifactorial, and that divergent processes of change can be affected by divergent processes of intervention.

9. Finally, exclusive reliance on selected theories as integrating bases for practice frequently precludes the objective, systematic examination of other orientations. Theories frequently become the master of the practitioner rather than the guide to practice, and adherence to the approach becomes a matter of faith rather than rational decision making. In this way, questions or criticisms about the approach become dismissed out of hand, and cannot be subjected to examination in empirical research. This "faith" can reach the point where results of research, even when available, are ignored unless positive to one's own approach.

That this concern about the constricting influence of, or overdependence on, one theoretical perspective is not far-fetched can be seen in the history and current situation of much of social casework. Caseworkers traditionally have used psychodynamic theory, particularly Freudian-based ego psychology, to "understand people" and as the core theoretical framework to "pull together" a variety of other perspectives which ranged from role theory to theories of personality development to casework practice principles. Unfortunately, reliance on this theoretical orientation typifies the inappropriate use for interventive purposes of a perspective largely concerned with causal/developmental dimensions. Further, use of this heavily intrapsychically oriented framework focuses social casework away from its primary concern with psycho-*social* knowledge and social functioning. In addition, use of this theoretical orientation resulted in a rather unidimensional picture of human beings and a clearly circumscribed practice theory. Whatever principles of change were used were derived from a narrow base composed of part Freud (and his theoretical descendants) and part "practice wisdom." But since the practice wisdom itself was largely a reflection of Freudian and neo-Freudian thinking, the end product of this ingrown and circular process was clearly lacking in the breadth necessary for a comprehensive base for practice. Even more importantly, use of this theoretical orientation as an integrating base shut out the consideration of clearly divergent new developments in intervention technology as viable alternatives for practice.

Now, it would be simplistic to conclude that the psychodynamic approaches themselves are responsible for all the current problems in casework, or even that all casework is psychodynamically based. While most of the major casework approaches do owe considerable allegiance to the psychodynamic model, casework has made tremendous strides in broadening its knowledge base in the 1960s and

1970s. This can be seen in increasing attempts to utilize a variety of nonpsycho-analytic perspectives ranging from role and system theory to family therapy and communication theory (Turner, 1974). However, as mentioned before, the extent to which such approaches have actually enhanced the effectiveness of practice is open to serious question since most are either not primarily concerned with in-terventive practices but more with assessment and diagnostic concerns (e.g., role and systems theory) or have not produced clear research evidence of effectiveness even when they are focused on intervention (e.g., communication-based family therapy; Wells et al., 1972; Sigal et al., 1976).

Actually, many professionals are not even *aware* that they adhere to one or another theory or "school." An obvious example of this lies in the fact that some teachers of casework, when presenting one or another of the traditional casework approaches, avoid or do not clarify the fact that the approach is based on psy-choanalytic (or ego psychological) theory, that it is basically a psychodynamically oriented approach. Hence, students who embrace that approach as their major one would be adhering to an ego psychological, or psychoanalytic, theoretical orientation. Instead, the casework approach usually is presented simply as just "casework," or, at best, psychosocial, functional, or problem-solving casework. (The implication also is that there is only one approach to casework.)

An even more subtle, and far more pervasive, illustration of the lack of aware-ness of adherence to one theory or school lies in unwitting use of a theory to guide practice and as a basis for a particular world view. One social work educator re-cently asked a class of twenty-five students to identify from a long list of theories the one they considered both most useful and closest to their own orientation. None of the students selected any of the psychoanalytic theories. However, when following up this anonymous survey, the educator found that the bulk of, if not all, the students accepted, almost in toto, some of the key assumptions, percep-tions, and conceptualizations of psychoanalytic ego psychology (including such phenomena as the existence of intrapsychic structures, among them the superego and the unconscious, the importance of internal conflict and repression, defense mechanisms, and the importance of the transference)—to the point where they clearly were the students' predominant approaches to understanding both the development and the modification of human behavior.

The point is not that use of such concepts is right or wrong, good or bad. Rather, the point is that such use often tends to be totally divorced from critical thinking about what approach is being utilized, and, especially, about why. Untested pos-tulates, assumptions, and pure speculation are utilized as though they are proved facts. Indeed, not only might a theory, at least in the broadest sense, completely guide a professional's practice without the professional being aware that this was the case, but the idea that one must question critically the use of such concepts, or even that there is a major and crucial distinction between a hypothesis (a proposi-tion or prediction for testing) and established fact (or, at least, concepts with some degree of empirical validation) might not even have entered that professional's frame of reference.

Obviously, such an uncritical perspective, whether one is aware of it or not, could characterize anyone's thinking, whether an adherent of one theory or of many. But it is particularly dangerous, and probably more extensive, among practitioners who do adhere to only one orientation. This is for several reasons.

As mentioned previously, adherence to only one theory often tends to prevent practitioners from adopting, or even objectively considering, others. A false sense of confidence develops, based on presumed security and comfort from "mastering" a specific body of knowledge. Proponents of only one school—whether it be psychoanalysis or behavior modification—tend to form "cults" for the defense and advancement of their approach ("Society for the Advancement of . . . "). One is able to claim special knowledge and expertise, rather strong enticements to professionals. Indeed, a sense of group solidarity against "outsiders" (adherents of competing approaches) can increase the cohesiveness of members of the school. Further, many adherents to single schools become adherents as students, before they have had either the experience or the training to overcome such premature identifications through knowledge about and/or objective evaluations of available approaches (Thorne, 1973). In short, adherence to a special school becomes mainly a matter of faith, unassailable by appeals to reason or challenging evidence.

It appears, then, in sum, to be unnecessary to think in terms of a unitary theoretical perspective. It also appears to be highly undesirable as well because the current state of our knowledge strongly suggests the possibility that more than one approach to intervention may be necessary. In fact, all the above evidence points to the necessity to begin development of a framework for practice that can make use of the best knowledge available from a number of diverse orientations, or, specifically, the development of an *eclectic* approach to casework practice.

An Overview of Eclecticism

Eclecticism formally is defined as " . . . not following any one system as of philosophy, medicine, etc., but selecting and using whatever is considered best in all systems" (*The American College Dictionary,* 1957, p. 381). An eclectic approach to casework practice, then, would consist of a variety of interventive principles and procedures, derived from different systems of induced change, including even those that may appear to be incompatible on the surface, in large part on the basis of their demonstrated effectiveness, and applied with people and problems where the evidence indicates that such application has a substantial chance to produce successful outcome. Such an outcome-oriented approach would be empirically based, grounded in the development and use of interventive techniques that are developed and/or adapted through a process of rigorous and systematic testing, implementation, and retesting.

An eclectic approach would be atheoretical in that its focus would be on integrating principles and procedures, whether derived deductively or inductively, rather than attempting to integrate complex theories of intervention. This is because of the variety of reasons presented above, including: the problems of the practitioner becoming overidentified with one theory and therefore excluding others, even those with evidence of success; the fact that a variety of principles, perhaps *derived* from different theories, very likely are needed to explain and alter different behaviors; the fact that specific procedures may be validated in research but theories rarely are; and the sheer unworkability of trying to integrate completely divergent, comprehensive theories.

Unfortunately, however, the notion of eclecticism seems objectionable to many caseworkers. This is a rather strange phenomenon since one of the major hallmarks of social work is presumably its integrative nature—willingness to utilize a diverse knowledge base and to avoid dependence on only one theoretical perspective. Of course, the problem of an aversive reaction to eclecticism is not limited to social caseworkers, but also can be found in members of related disciplines. As an example of the distaste aroused by the concept of eclecticism, Joseph Wolpe, one of the major developers of modern behavior therapy, has disdainfully accused the intellectual position of eclecticism as being "inevitably barren" because the eclectic " . . . has no consistent rules to guide either his thoughts or his actions" (Wolpe, 1969a, p. xii). That mere mention of the term "eclectic" might almost automatically elicit such reactions in a very paradoxical way, independent of what eclecticism actually means, might be seen in the completely antithetical statement by Wolpe that, unequivocally, he (and behavior therapists in general) " . . . will always do *what the evidence* indicates . . . [we] will in appropriate circumstance willingly employ other methods that have empirically been shown to be effective" (Wolpe, 1969a, p. ix). The concept of eclecticism, in short, not only appears to arouse negative emotional reactions and resistance among professionals even when they do, or aver they will do, in practice just what eclecticism suggests, but also appears to have an aura of the unscientific, of having no systematic basis to guide its implementation.

But such ideas seem rooted in a basic misconception about the nature and potentialities of a *systematic* approach to eclecticism. Eclecticism is not a disordered conglomeration of disparate methods thrown together into an expedient potpourri (Wolberg, 1966). Rather, eclecticism involves the selection and studied amalgamation of intervention procedures of demonstrated effectiveness from varied sources that can be used compatibly and in ways that reinforce each other. These different procedures in implementation complement each other and serve to buttress weaknesses that occur in the individual systems from which they were derived. Further, even though the synthesis seems harmonious at any given moment, it is subject to constant study and reorganization as new or different procedures with evidence of effectiveness become available (Wolberg, 1966).

The mere fact of the existence of literally dozens of different interventive approaches dealing with areas of potential concern to social casework might suggest that none has unequivocal evidence of superiority to all the others. And obviously not all these systems have something to offer in terms of demonstrated success with particular problems. Eclecticism is not a camouflage for some mushy supertheory that attempts to integrate every approach under the sun only because the approach exists. But a variety of approaches do have to be studied through systematic analysis on preselected criteria (such as those presented in the next section) in the event that they do in fact offer the promise of adding effective procedures to the interventive repertoire of caseworkers.

Essentially, eclecticism refers to a commitment to being guided in practice by what is most effective for our clients. This commitment takes precedence over devotion to any theory or theoretical orientation. If our primary allegiance becomes attached to a particular theoretical orientation, rather than to the basic value of our responsibility to effectively help the people we serve, the entire casework enterprise would be in danger of drowning in a sea of misguided irrelevance. Casework can be casework independent of the theories or procedures used by caseworkers. Adherence to one theory or approach is neither a necessary nor sufficient condition for the existence of casework. It is hoped that this notion will be a liberating one for caseworkers, since it divorces casework from the unnecessary constraints of any theoretical orientations currently in vogue. Casework is not ego psychology nor behavior modification nor "a problem-solving process," although caseworkers might use one or more of these. Indeed, to some extent, it appears as though the long-lasting overdependence on narrow and unitary conceptions of casework not only led some caseworkers into the blind alley of ineffective practice, but also hindered examination of new and potentially more effective approaches as they appear.

Practicing from an eclectic base requires the ultimate in flexibility and open-mindedness on the part of practitioners. The knowledge used at any given point in time will almost inevitably change. This requires a critical evaluative stance by caseworkers and actually calls for far more work and a higher degree of competence than did our previous largely unitheoretical stance since caseworkers must be able to study and analyze a variety of diverse approaches.

Further, caseworkers cannot become complacent and satisfied with any one approach, no matter how efficient or effective it appears at any single point in time. Caseworkers must continuously guard against the disastrous conformity of paying total allegiance to only one approach. Thus, as professionals who claim to be capable of helping our clients, we must take the responsibility of ensuring that we are, in fact, capable of helping and of competently utilizing the vast amount of knowledge generated by our own profession and professions engaged in endeavors related to ours. This means, in short, that we look wherever we can for methods that "work." If anything, this is a distinguishing characteristic of *professional* practice.

It would be easy for caseworkers to adopt systematic eclecticism as a slogan and to pay lip service to this rigorous form of practice, while at the same time continuing traditional practices. This, in fact, appears to be happening in a large proportion of situations where caseworkers claim that they are indeed eclectic and utilizing a variety of procedures based on whatever will help the client. But the extensive research on both the process and the outcome of casework (see Fischer, 1975a) tends to refute this notion. In fact, in most situations, particularly in clinical practice, no matter what the nature of the client's problems, caseworkers tend to rely mainly on their old standbys—the interview and the use of only one or two verbal procedures. This may be comfortable for the worker but is hardly helpful for the client.

Eclectic caseworkers maximize their own potential for becoming *effective* caseworkers. Eclectic caseworkers owe no allegiance to any theory or dogma. They can not and will not exclude techniques of demonstrated efficacy from their practice merely on grounds of newness or because they are "uncomfortable with them." In short, eclectic caseworkers can be as effective as they are open to new ideas, " . . . the contributions of any and all systems as they become, at a given point in time, necessary to effect translations to human benefits" (Carkhuff, 1971, p. 130).

Selecting and Integrating an Eclectic Approach

The key questions that obviously arise in considering the utilization of principles and procedures derived from a number of presumably diverse sources are first, what guidelines are there for selection of such principles and procedures and, second, how can this material be meaningfully integrated in actual practice?

Traditionally, a variety of means for selection of practice material have been used. Many caseworkers selected their practice approach on the basis of what they learned or what they were exposed to in school, i.e., what they already *knew*. This has the ring of logic to it, of course; one should use what one learns and what one knows. But, in the first place, the approaches presumably taught in most schools of social work were extremely narrow and constraining of a broadly defined practice; in fact, most of these approaches never even provided information as to exactly what caseworkers were to *do* in practice. Second, if an individual uses *only* or mainly what he or she has been exposed to in school, as many caseworkers have tended to do, new or different approaches, perhaps more effective approaches, will not be considered. Third, this custom assumes that what a worker learns in school is (a) "right," (b) effective, and (c) the last word. But the two years that most caseworkers spend in M.S.W. programs are hardly enough time to learn and develop competence in using the variety of approaches that are available for effective practice. It would seem that, in addition to the teaching of certain practice skills in the social work program, a more desirable objective, already present in some schools, would be to teach students how to *analyze* and *select* approaches as they become available, thereby providing both the base and the framework for continuing professional development. If anything, professional education should be only the first step in a long professional career of educational pursuits. As Dubos (1967, p. 425) has noted in relation to the use of knowledge in practice by professionals: "The intellectual equipment most needed is that which makes it possible to adapt rapidly to new situations, as they constantly arise in the ever-changing world."

A second typical selection criterion, highly related to, and in a sense derived from, the first criterion, could be termed *worker comfort*. ("I don't use that approach; I'm not very comfortable with it.") But since "comfort" is largely a function of exposure and experience (who could be comfortable with a new approach the first time they use it?), this provides a perfect rationale for not using a new approach. It also leads to institutionalization of the myth that the only approaches which work are the ones a worker is comfortable with, again, a rationale preventing the use of new approaches since the worker cannot be "comfortable" with them. No caseworker who adheres to this "comfort myth" would ever select *another* professional on that basis. (How many caseworkers would choose a dentist who is "uncomfortable" with, and therefore does not use, high-speed drills or pain killers, or a physician who is "uncomfortable" with, and therefore does not use, antibiotics in the treatment of bacterial infections?)

Another common selection criterion is the prestige of the theorist or experienced practitioner who espouses a particular approach (Ford & Urban, 1963). Thus, younger practitioners would defer to the judgment of professionals whom they respect and admire, particularly if these "elder statesmen" are articulate or entertaining in the way they present their ideas. But prestige "tends to operate as a pressure toward conformity and as a brake on innovation" (Ford & Urban, 1963, p. 18). And obviously, the prestige of the theorist may be totally unrelated to the effectiveness of his or her approach.

A final common dimension for selecting an approach has to do with consensus among experts and peers (Ford & Urban, 1963). Since "everybody is doing it," a single practitioner, or even a group of practitioners, finds it difficult to deviate from the norm. Not only are the pressures for conformity great, but actual employment success may depend on acceptance of the approach promulgated by the director and workers in an agency.

All these selection criteria have one common underlying dimension: they have little or nothing to do with whether an approach, or a procedure derived from an approach, actually works, i.e., leads to effective results. They avoid systematic analysis of competing alternatives, and they ignore the use of rigorous criteria for evaluating different approaches.

An example of several of these selection criterion problems lies in the widespread use of communication-oriented family therapy, which, as noted previously, has become one of the bulwarks of casework practice (Scherz, 1970, Sherman, 1974). Few schools of social work do not either offer courses in family therapy or integrate this material into their core practice courses. Most family service agencies consider family therapy to be one of their key service components. And nationwide research (Group for the Advancement of Psychiatry, 1970) has revealed a great deal of commonality in opinions of who the most influential family theorists are, with the most influential theorists being those who hold changing communication patterns central to their approach (e.g., in order of influence in the survey, the top four were Satir, 1964, Ackerman, 1966, Jackson, 1968, Haley, 1963). However, despite this tremendous impact and powerful influence on casework education and practice, the research evidence on the effectiveness of the communication-based approaches to family therapy is best described as "equivocal" (e.g., Wells et al., 1972; Sigal et al., 1976). At the same time, as will be described in detail in Part Two, several approaches with evidence of effectiveness amounting in the aggregate to several hundred studies virtually have been ignored in the social work literature, in social work education, and in practice.

The development of an eclectic approach, contrary to widely accepted myths about eclecticism, is an attempt to bring order and systematization to the selection of approaches for practice. Clear, specific criteria for selection are delineated against which each approach is evaluated. New approaches are carefully elaborated, assessed, and validated in relation to each other and to their potential use with clients. The criterion of effectiveness—does this procedure with this client with this problem *work,* i.e., produce predictable, positive results?—is given top priority. The special order and efficiency that are best produced by being systematic, and which are at a premium for the busy practitioner, are maintained and enhanced.

An important issue related to the selection of divergent approaches has to do with the apparently confusing nature of such selection. It could seem as though caseworkers would have at their beck and call only a jumble or helter-skelter of techniques and no real way of "putting them all together."

Part of this issue derives from the traditional means of alleged integration of practice through the use of a common base in ego psychology and/or in "casework method." The historical high point of this "integration" was probably in the 1940s and 1950s when, except for the heretical Rankians, almost all caseworkers followed the party line (Freudian). That era may have been the high point of integration, but it may also have been the low point for effectiveness, and certainly for relevance and innovation. Not only did this presumed integration lead most caseworkers to practice with less than optimal effectiveness, but because any deviation from the norm was seen as radical heresy, it precluded the search for different and more effective means of intervention and placed the highest professional premium on conformity.

The kind of eclecticism advocated here eschews any form of *theoretical* integration (i.e., integrating divergent perspectives in the base of a particular theory), but develops an atheoretical integration grounded in certain values and propositions which cut across theoretical domains and are integrated at the level of *professional* (rather than theoretical) practice. Each dimension provides an aspect of philosophical, conceptual, and/or empirical evidence for use or nonuse of a given procedure by caseworkers. Significantly, the dimensions to be explicated here contain characteristics which can be utilized both as criteria for *evaluation* and *selection* of different approaches and as principles of *integration*. These dimensions are considered the key selection and integration criteria of the criteria presented in chapter two.

Casework is deeply committed to a number of value positions. These values could be thought of as the first major dimension to consider in selection of components for that approach (see *Values in Social Work: A Re-Examination,* NASW, 1967, and Bartlett, 1970, for comprehensive discussions of major values underlying the practice of social work). These values are discussed in chapter one.

A second major dimension for utilization in both selection and integration involves the area of knowledge to be examined. With the explosion of knowledge in the social and behavioral sciences in recent decades, the educator and theorist, not to mention the practitioner, needs guidelines for wending through the constantly expanding maze of ideas. As Bartlett (1970) has noted, the profession must identify an area of central concern that is (1) common to the profession as a whole; (2) meaningful in relation to the profession's values and goals; (3) practical in terms of available and attainable knowledge and techniques; and (4) sufficiently distinctive so that it does not duplicate what other professions are doing. For casework and social work as a whole, this area is "social functioning"—not only the behavior of individuals as they attempt to cope with life tasks and environmental demands, but the active and exchanging relationships with their environment along with the feedback and consequences to both flowing from that relationship (Bartlett, 1970, Chapter 6; see also Butler, 1970). Given the profession's avowal of the importance of knowledge for practice that will lead to the enhancement of client social functioning, a key dimension for evaluation of knowledge is that the knowledge to be examined would be pertinent to both social and psychological characteristics of human beings, i.e., to their social functioning, rather than exclusively concerned with internal or intrapsychic functioning on one hand or strictly social or sociological on the other.

A related criterion for knowledge selection and integration for practice lies in the extent to which an approach deals with *interventive practice* (rather than largely causal/developmental understanding). This includes a systematic explanation of how induced change comes about (the principles) plus prescription of procedures or techniques so the change principles can be implemented by the practitioner.

The latter part of the above criterion—the need for techniques—has been given particularly careful scrutiny in this book. As has been pointed out, most traditional approaches to casework equivocate on the matter of delineating techniques, to the point where most fail to prescribe any. Since theories, or principles of theories, cannot themselves be applied, an absence of specific techniques which detail ways to carry out change efforts means that the caseworker would not know how to actually implement the approach. Application of specific techniques provides the built-in advantage, in fact, necessity, of identifying and making accessible to manipulation by the worker specific interventive activities. In other words, the extent to which an approach includes specific techniques is the extent to which an approach meets the criterion of *utility* (see chapter two).

These points might be elaborated as follows. The heart of knowledge for practice lies in four types of statements: (1) Principles regarding extinguishing unwanted (or dysfunctional) behavior; (2) specification of procedures and techniques for extinguishing unwanted behavior; (3) principles regarding the development of new, desired (functional) behavior; and (4) specification of procedures and techniques dealing with the production of new behavior. Two basic distinctions are involved, the first between "principles" and "procedures," the second between eliminating unwanted behavior and developing new behavior.

Principles of behavior change are propositions stating how and why problematic behavior may be altered. Statement of these principles generally is a precondition for a discussion of therapeutic techniques utilized to implement the change principles. The techniques consist of a set of conditions that can be varied by the worker (Ford & Urban, 1963); a clear statement of therapeutic procedures is the crux of the therapeutic system, as it details what the worker must do in order to produce changes in the client's behavior. As an example of the preceding material, Wolpe's (1969; 1973) principle of reciprocal inhibition is a principle by which behavior change occurs; Wolpe's procedure of systematic desensitization is a technique for implementing the principle.

Wolpe's technique of systematic desensitization might also serve to illustrate the distinction between extinguishing unwanted behavior and developing new behavior. Systematic desensitization is a procedure primarily concerned with eliminating maladaptive behavior. To induce development of new behavior, Wolpe might call on other procedures, such as behavior rehearsal. This distinction is crucial. Too often, theorists develop material dealing only with principles and procedures for eliminating behavior. For the adherent to such an approach who is faced with a client in need of new forms of functional behavior, only one-half of the job would be possible within the confines of such an approach.

The next, particularly important, criterion for evaluating, selecting, and integrating the variety of principles and procedures necessary in the development of an eclectic approach to practice is the extent to which there is empirical validation of successful intervention with clients when change procedures are implemented. In other words, when research establishes the efficacy of an approach, it must be considered a prime candidate for adoption for practice. In order to properly assess what works and with whom, the necessity for empirically grounding practice becomes readily apparent. This requires extensive use of what has been called the "scientific method" of rational and orderly procedures of observation and testing as the most productive avenue of inquiry, as a governing principle both in evaluating and selecting knowledge and in integrating that knowledge in practice. This is simply to say that in a profession committed to bringing about positive change in the life situations of its clients, the most desirable knowledge is that knowledge which will tell us what is effective in accomplishing our aims.

A number of implications stem from major reliance on research. In the first place, research findings provide the clearest possible guidelines for evaluation. Obviously, however, there are numerous levels of research ranging from intensive case studies with various forms of measurement to elaborate complex factorial designs utilizing random assignment and control groups. Thus, it behooves caseworkers to be able to evaluate the rigor and adequacy of research and the extent to which generalizations can be made (to other workers, clients, problems).

Now, because of the nature of research, it is very difficult if not impossible to unequivocally *prove* anything. It is only possible to increase the confidence with which one draws conclusions about specified phenomena. Use of research findings as a guide to practice is not infallible. Individual studies must be put into the perspective of both the theory or approach which generated them and other studies which support or contradict them. Generally speaking, the greater the degree of replication of findings (assuming adequacy of research methodology), the greater the degree of confidence one can place in conclusions. But decision making for an eclectic approach is a never-ending process since, at any time, new findings might invalidate old. However, practitioners must make judgments because they are continuously rendering services, and so those judgments should be tempered by the best that research can offer at any given point in time.

This may be so at almost any level of research. For example, a technique such as systematic desensitization (which, in a variety of controlled studies, has been found superior to an absence of treatment and to other methods in reducing maladaptive anxiety and, as a total package, superior to selected aspects of the desensitization technique itself) obviously meets the criterion of selection by reason of demonstrated effectiveness in research. But, assuming for the moment all other things to be equal, even less-rigorous research can provide guidelines. Say, technique X in several studies with problem A has produced roughly a 78 percent "improved" rate, while technique Y, in several studies using clients with the same problem, consistently achieved roughly a 55 percent "improved" rate. On the basis of these figures, pending more rigorous evaluation, and assuming everything else to be equal, technique X likely would be the technique of choice.

Even assuming that two techniques have been demonstrated in research to have exactly the same rates of effectiveness, there are a variety of other criteria, summarized in chapter two, on which to assess those techniques. For example, these questions would be relevant: which is most efficient; is one less aversive to the client (or worker) than the other; is the worker more competent in using one than the other; does one have clearer guidelines for implementation than the other; and is one more appropriate to this particular type of problem?

In fact, even given similar rates of improvement for clients with two different techniques, further or more intensive research might reveal that, while the overall rates were the same, these rates might have served to conceal other factors (e.g., demographic variables, anxiety level) that might account for variations *within* the rates of success for each of the methods. Thus, unmarried men with high anxiety levels might respond better to technique X while married women with low anxiety levels might respond better to technique Y. Knowing these variables and using this knowledge to aid in technique selection could help in the more discriminating use of each technique and actually increase the overall success rates of *both* techniques since their use could then be focused on the clients most able to benefit from them.

Another major implication of relying on research relates to the fact that, as mentioned previously, research dealing with interventive practices generally is carried out on selected portions of the approach, rather than on complex and comprehensive theories themselves. These components tend to be the principles, and more frequently, the procedures derived from the approach. Hence, to the extent that research does validate anything about an interventive approach, it would be a specific procedure, which, in combination with other similarly validated procedures, would form the working foundation for an eclectic approach to effective practice.

The preceding discussion relates to the third major implication of using research as a primary aid in selecting and integrating diverse approaches to practice. Presumably, the studies upon which a judgment is made to select a procedure illustrate the conditions under which the procedure is successfully utilized. This in turn has the makings of a very explicit client/problem typology which would demonstrate the kinds of problems and clients where a given procedure has been and could be applied effectively. This approach is in contrast to the traditional one which starts with a diagnostic category based on psychodynamics and tries to develop an intervention approach on the basis of those dynamics. Instead, the reverse is suggested here—starting with the techniques themselves and client responses to those techniques and developing a typology of techniques to be used according to the nature of client responses. Combination of several effective techniques, then, can supply not only a complementary range of interventive procedures, but a range of problem/situation configurations where the procedures can be most successfully applied. The goal, of course, is the maximum in technical flexibility for the worker in response to the large variety of potential client problems.

In essence, this proposal holds that the greater the degree of scientifically validated input in practice, the greater the degree of competence that can be exercised by caseworkers on behalf of their clients. This is not intended to exclude the use of intuition or "horse sense"—the "art" of practice. The point is not that professionals should be automatons, unfeelingly implementing an intervention technology. But the point *is* that a rigorous foundation for practice, involving the careful and systematic testing and evaluation of its component parts, will provide a firmer and more successful base for the use of less clearly defined dimensions.

This focus on research and specification of techniques—in addition to being indicated as a major source of increased effectiveness for practice—is also intended to help the social work student, and some practicing professionals, avoid what Laing (1970) call the "knot," where the notion is advanced that effective practice involves intuitive knowledge not amenable to explicit formulation, even in principle (Argyris & Schön, 1974):

There is something I don't know
    that I am supposed to know.

I don't know *what* it is I don't know,
    and yet am supposed to know.

And I feel I look stupid
    if I seem both not to know it
    and not know *what* it is I don't know.

Therefore, I pretend I know it.
    This is nerve-wracking
    since I don't know what I must pretend to know.

Therefore I pretend to know everything.
    (Laing, 1970, p. 56)

Unless posed as an alternative to the approach or procedure that has clear and considerable empirical validation, lack of research on effectiveness does not automatically render an approach without merit. As noted above the criteria presented here by and large consist of a summary of the key criteria from the framework in chapter two that presents a description of numerous criteria for evaluating interventive approaches. A wide range of criteria is available for evaluating each approach on structural, substantive, empirical, and ethical grounds. Thus, every approach should be assessed as to its internal consistency, the clients and problems for which it is intended, the goals of the approach, the extent to which client and worker behaviors in treatment are specified, the range of procedures available in the approach, and so on. In some situations, and in the absence of research evidence to the contrary, one of these approaches may be the intervention of choice. For example, a new procedure may be developed and designed specifically for use with a particular type of problem. In the absence of research showing other procedures to be effective with the problem, and assuming an appropriate overall evaluation of the procedure on the dimensions presented here and in chapter two, the procedure may very well be the best for that problem at that point in time in the development of practice theory and research.

What ultimately is sought is a careful piecing together of a complex of specific analytic factors. When a number of procedures can be evaluated as satisfactory on the variety of criteria suggested here, and can be seen to complement each other on the basis of clearly defined prescriptive statements for utilization with a range of clients and problems, some degree of integration for practice can, in fact, be demonstrated to have occurred.

This discussion is intended to illustrate that the use of a number of presumably discrete approaches does not preclude employment of an overall perspective or orientation to aid caseworkers in comprehending the vast array of forces they confront. As suggested in this and the preceding chapter, that orientation is integrated less at a "theoretical" level than at a level where values, knowledge, and tradition interrelate to provide a broad and comprehensive framework for professional practice. That framework is diagrammed in figure 5.2. As should be obvious, the framework is intended to represent the derivation only of *casework* activities. Thus, the entire range of *social work* roles and activities in which caseworkers, as social workers, engage, involving social action, institutional and organizational change, reform, and so on, are not depicted. But their basis in values, knowledge, and tradition and differential application through a process of assessment is part of the total range of services which provide key and distinctive features to the profession of social work.

Objectives and Goals

The major goals for eclectic casework are consistent with those of social work as a whole—prevention of problems in social functioning; remediation of problems in social functioning that have already occurred or facilitation of adaptive

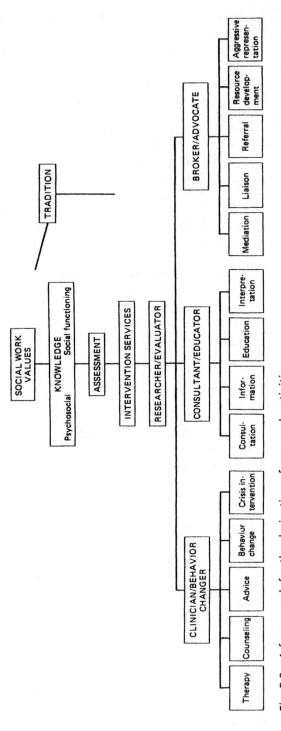

Fig. 5.2 A framework for the derivation of casework activities.

functioning; and the development of resources to enhance social functioning. These goals can be worked toward in a variety of ways in any number of different programs, and in a variety of different settings such as medical, educational, psychiatric, and vocational. However, in order to achieve some sense of direction for the enterprise and to point out what appears to be an underlying conception cutting across all these major goals, it seems appropriate to establish a superordinate criterion as a guideline for the derivation of individualized goals for each client. Taking into account the traditional and worthwhile focus of the profession on client social functioning, it appears as though an emphasis on the goal of *social adjustment* would best reflect that concern, and would be both realistic and attainable in casework intervention.

The concept of "social adjustment" is one that generally is repugnant to many caseworkers, conjuring up, as it does, images of turning our clients into a group of conforming robots, or of a profession devoted only to maintaining the status quo. But, it is hoped, this would not be the case. Social adjustment, a term with many popular variants such as "adaptation" and "coping," refers merely to the ability of a person to deal with the serious conflicts and problems of life, the situations that may be conceived as social tasks, life situations, or problems of living. These are experienced primarily as pressures from their social environment (Bartlett, 1970).

This conception is recognition of the fact that people do not exist in vacuo, but live in a complex series of relationships with other people and their environment. Employment of a social adjustment criterion can lead to realistic, objective planning of intervention for clients and the use of *attainable* goals, and is based on the fact that vague goals such as "enhancement of creativity," "enhancement of maturity" or "enhancement of ego functioning" not only do not lead to any specifiable intervention procedures, but may not be accomplishable no matter what techniques are used. Utilization of such elaborate, nebulous, and somewhat mystical goals may be asking too much of the available knowledge in casework.

The reluctance to acknowledge use or acceptance of a social adjustment criterion by many caseworkers is difficult to explain in relation to research on this topic. One nationwide study, utilizing a sample of caseworkers and psychotherapists, found that implicitly or explicitly, when it comes to actual practices, practitioners do indeed use a social adjustment criterion anyhow (Goldman & Mendelsohn, 1969). But the most important reason for use of social adjustment as a guideline in establishing objectives in practice is that extensive research with a variety of samples indicates that a substantial portion of our *clients* define their problems in terms of social adjustment (Gurin et. al., 1960; Mayer & Timms, 1969b; Bergin, 1971; Beck & Jones, 1973).

The behavioral manifestation of social adjustment is social functioning. The term "social functioning" essentially refers to the sum of an individual's activities in interaction with other individuals and/or situations in the environment as delineated through the enactment of roles. And role performance basically is made up of a series of behaviors an individual is expected to perform by virtue of membership in particular social groups (Boehm, 1959). If problems in social adjustment—or social functioning—arise, they are most likely to be problems in the performance of certain behaviors. Actually, most problems are not problems until they are observable, or, more accurately, are not *labeled* as problems until they involve an observable failure to adequately handle social responsibilities. Thus, if our practice is to be oriented by the goals which most directly affect the real-life experiences of our clients, the most reasonable arena for casework activity would seem to involve behavioral objectives, or objectives whose achievement can be ascertained in the actual *functioning* of the client. Such general and vague goals as "enhance self-esteem" or "increase ego strength" can be replaced by delineating which specific behaviors will accomplish the desired ends, how the client will be behaving (i.e., what he or she will actually be *doing*) when the aims are achieved, and the conditions under which the behavior can be expected to occur (Bandura, 1969).

This fact itself has several important implications for casework intervention. It allows the goals of casework to be stated in highly individualized forms for each client, detailing the particular behaviors of concern. It allows the development of very specific objectives for each individual. This helps the client and caseworker know whether that objective has been achieved. Specific objectives allow more exact specification of the interventive procedures necessary to accomplish the individualized objectives. The definition of the ends, therefore, helps define the means whereby they can become implemented, pointing to the procedures that may be relevant to accomplish these objectives (Ford & Urban, 1964). Use of specific, behavioral objectives also permits the development of clear, distinct outcome measures for the purposes of assessment and evaluative research. Finally, the use of specific objectives (which should not be confused with *inconsequential* objectives), relevant to client social functioning, also appears to lead to more effective intervention. Those approaches with evidence of greatest success, to be reviewed in subsequent chapters, are, in large part, those that rely most heavily on specific behavioral objectives.

Actually, and perhaps somewhat surprisingly, use of the social adjustment criterion and specific objectives is not necessarily antithetical to the increasingly popular goal of "enhancing self-actualization" for our clients. A self-actualized person would be someone who lives an enriching life, who develops and utilizes his or her unique capabilities or potentialities free of the emotional turmoil and inhibitions of the less actualized (Shostrom, 1966). Thus, the goals of eclectic casework, stated in terms of self-actualization, might be to (1) maximize the control one has over oneself and the environment, and (2) maximize the development and use of one's own abilities as well as environmental opportunities.

On the other hand, where social adjustment and specific behavioral objectives play a part is in the definition for each individual client of what self-actualization actually is. This means specifying, when a client is or becomes "self-actualized," what behaviors he or she will be performing and under what conditions those behaviors can be expected to occur. Without such specific definition, "self-actualization" may be a worthless concept. What self-actualization turns out to be varies with every individual and must begin with what each client wants or needs to be. "Self-actualization" can no more be applied as an indiscriminate and global goal for every client than can "social adjustment."

Behavioral objectives for each client are developed through skilled assessment of the client's problems and strengths. This includes a shift from the traditional *why* questions to the use of *what* questions (Ullmann & Krasner, 1969). Thus, the caseworker might ask, What is the client doing? Under what conditions are particular behaviors being performed? What are the effects of those behaviors, i.e., what changes occur after they are performed? What situations are being avoided? What environmental circumstances seem to be related to or maintaining the behavior? What environmental circumstances can be altered to diminish maladaptive behavior and increase or strengthen adaptive behavior? Most important the caseworker asks, what does the client want and what are the most efficient and effective means at my disposal for getting there? And a whole variety of assessment tools, instruments, and procedures are available to help the worker in making such assessments (Bergin, 1971; Bergin & Strupp, 1972; Waskow & Parloff, 1975).

All these questions must be phrased in terminology directly related to interventive possibilities. An assessment process such as this would be ridiculous if it did not result in the differential use of intervention procedures, i.e., if all problems were treated in, by and large, the same way. An interventive repertoire must be developed that allows taking overt action on the understanding of the problem developed in the assessment. As discussed earlier in this chapter, much of the traditional focus on historical causality basically can be dispensed with. In fact, to the extent that any form of causality is relevant to casework practice, it should be *functional causality*. Thus, in pursuing a functionally related cause, the caseworker would assess those factors within the current life situation of the client that are *actively* or *currently* related to or maintaining the problem and that *feasibly* can be affected by the worker's intervention procedures.

Eclecticism: Criticisms, Issues, and a Point of View

Eclecticism, in contrast to conventional orientations, because of its very nature—non adherence to unitary "schools," lack of "cultism," insistence on objective and rational evaluation, and the need for systematic, careful (and rather difficult) work in studying available approaches—is unlikely to attract a vocal or enthusiastic group of supporters. As Thorne (1973, p. 448) points out: "Eclecticism is simply one scientific mode for handling . . . data objectively but uncommitted to prior ideological positions." But, as noted in this chapter, the idea of eclecticism as a base for practice does tend to elicit from professionals a number of objections, frequently based on misconceptions; on the other hand, the use of eclecticism also raises several legitimate issues. The purpose of this section is to summarize and review these criticisms and issues (see also Thorne, 1973), not only to highlight them but in an attempt to correct possible misunderstandings.

Perhaps the most common criticism of eclecticism is that it consists of a grab bag of procedures, selected without a consistent, underlying rationale. As Wolpe

(1971, p. 404) comments, " . . . it is the nature of eclecticism that these ingredients [the components of practice] are on the whole determined by idiosyncrasy and not by principle." Of course, a main purpose of this chapter has been to puncture this myth, to present the specific principles that *are* used to guide the selection of methods for practice. Indeed, this systematic use of selection criteria far exceeds the rigor that could be expected from adherents to any unitary theoretical orientation, who, because they are limited by the nature of their theory, often have no more than one (if that many) procedure to "select," or who select methods only on the basis of what their theory has to offer, independent of empirical validation. The selection of methods for practice by the eclectic, on the other hand, above all else is grounded in the search for evidence of effectiveness.

A related criticism is that in actual practice (no matter how the methods are selected in principle) the eclectic utilizes a "shotgun approach," blindly trying one procedure, then another, until, finally, one "works." Again, the guidelines presented in this chapter dealing with technique selection in actual practice are intended to dispel this notion. In addition, the heart of eclectic practice is in sensitive and accurate assessment of the individual case/situation with the goal of selecting the correct procedures to apply in intervention. And those procedures are selected on the basis of familiarity with the practice and research literature with an eye primarily to answering the following question: What procedure is effective with what kind of problem with what client in what circumstances?

A common objection is that the eclectic tends to be a "jack of all trades, master of none," knowing a little about a good deal but a great deal about very little. This criticism might be seen in Gurin's (1973) comment that " . . . in becoming more eclectic they may lose the competence to do anything well." Of course, an eclectic approach is not (necessarily) a generalist or generic approach (although there may be a good many advantages in the generalist perspective). The eclectic does not attempt to learn a little bit about this, a little bit about that, then mix all this knowledge up to achieve, as this criticism implies, a little bit of knowledge about everything. The eclectic would indeed attempt to be comprehensive in *study* of what is available. But in selection and implementation for practice—and this is the crucial aspect of eclecticism—the eclectic is highly specific, with special in-depth competence in the methods of practice used. The very essence of eclecticism is just the opposite of selecting a little bit of something from everything.

A series of criticisms related to the above point revolves around the assumption that what is "best" for the practitioner is to have in-depth knowledge in one school or theory, presumably because this is the only way to become highly skilled and hence produce the most positive effects. Otherwise, the argument runs, the practitioner operating from an eclectic base will be only a technician, mechanically applying methods with neither in-depth knowledge nor individualized guidelines.

Of course, these, and all the other criticisms, may be more or less true, if the stereotyped perceptions of eclectism, and, correspondingly, its actual practice, also are true. But eclecticism that is implemented according to the framework proposed here can avoid those pitfalls. The eclectic practitioner conducts a careful individualized assessment of the client/problem/situation configuration which leads to careful individualized selection and implementation of procedures. This is based on knowledge of the research and practice literature and use of the framework for technique-selection presented earlier in this chapter. The eclectic practitioner can and should be as highly skilled in the use of single methods or techniques as are practitioners whose training is *only* in that school, *if* skill in those single methods or techniques is warranted by evidence of effectiveness. And that is just the point of eclecticism. The eclectic must have optimal levels of competence in the use of those procedures whose merit has been determined by a base other than blind faith or the fact that they are part of one's "own" theory. There is little advantage in possessing in-depth knowledge of one school or theory—knowing all its methods and procedures—when there is no evidence that such knowledge is related to successful outcome with clients. Eclectic practitioners can be judged not on how much they know of one approach but on the superordinate criterion—how effective they are.

Since this is an approach that, at least in part, proceeds from what is already known about interventive practices, it might appear as though eclecticism could be a rather stagnant orientation. There may appear to be an implication that caseworkers should wait for others to develop validated procedures while we remain content with only what is already known. But the various components brought together into an eclectic approach to casework practice, at any given time, would likely be far from exhaustive or the "final word." Caseworkers must live with the awareness that as new research is generated, some currently acceptable conclusions may be negated. Thus, basic to appropriate utilization of an eclectic approach are certain principles: (1) What works is what is important; it is, after all, the client who is our primary concern; (2) research interest must be built in from the outset. This means awareness of what others are finding in their research, plus the ability to conduct our own research, both with individual cases and for the field, ultimately, of an experimental-evaluative nature. This attitude, one hopes, can be engendered by awareness that the components of an eclectic approach are indeed not the last word on effective procedures, and that it is the caseworker's responsibility to search continually for new and better ways to help his or her clients. Thus, each segment of an eclectic approach is, and should be, chosen, in part, because of its emphasis on or susceptibility to evaluation in research.

An eclectic approach to the practice of casework cannot be developed or taught in a vacuum. In a complete casework program, it could be taught in accord with both empirically derived and theoretical material of diverse backgrounds in order to produce a practitioner knowledgeable in several areas relating to assessment of, and provision of services to, clients. Consequently, an intrinsic and essential characteristic of this approach is the assessment of every client with great skill and sensitivity in order to employ those procedures which, based on empirical evidence, seem most likely to be effective in modifying his or her problems.

Utilization of this perspective requires the development of a set of specific techniques that can be differentially applied under specifiable conditions to particular problem behaviors or cases (Strupp & Bergin, 1969). As emphasized earlier, specific objectives and plans must be made for each client, so there will be indications early in the process whether a particular plan is succeeding. If one plan is not successful, another can be substituted, since, of utmost importance, the caseworker is not hampered by practicing within the limits of a single theory. Several alternatives—depending on the knowledge, skill, and imagination of the caseworker—may be available.

Now it may seem as though this approach is a retreat to an overly technical, method-centered approach, recently under fire from so many of the critics of social casework. But if the techniques work, if our clients are helped, that is an *advance,* not a retreat. Further, the major intent of an eclectic approach is to find the procedures that fit the client, rather than forcing the client to fit the procedure, i.e., using only one technique, no matter what the nature of the client or the problem, as traditionally often was the case.

Nor should it be assumed that this is a plea for casework to operate independently of, or in opposition to, environmentally oriented programs of social change. Casework is only one arm of social work intervention, in which that intervention is applied selectively at a particular problem level. And it is not necessary to believe that, with a program of individualized services, all problems are the result of personality inadequacies or character deficits. Rather, a simple, more fundamental assertion is made: regardless of causality, a number of problems can be *resolved* through individualized services.

Problems may arise, however, in attempting to fit together within a single framework a number of apparently divergent procedures. But the evaluation of compatibility, as well as the testing of differential applicability, is a problem for future research. At this time, there seem to be no *inherent* reasons why any number of elements cannot be combined into a productive, uniform whole, integrated and organized on the basis of the principles suggested in this chapter.

Some caseworkers might argue that using such a variety of techniques will cause a great deal of confusion due to the absence of a single comprehensive theory, or at least a single method of casework, for integrative purposes. But, as this book has attempted to illustrate, not only has there never *been* a single theory or method of casework, but also, caseworkers, in practice, appear often to have developed purely idiosyncratic ways of dealing with clients and in many instances to respond with whatever seems to be a good idea at the time. Further, when only one theory is used, clients are perceived in a highly constricting way and forced into unitary molds. In addition, alternative approaches to practice tend to be avoided, and conformity rather than innovation becomes the norm. And, of course, an eclectic approach is indeed systematic and integrated, but in terms of atheoretical, professional, ethical, and empirical principles, rather than in terms of "theory." Thus, caseworkers utilizing a systematic eclectic approach will be provided with the consistency and structure that is typically attributed to the use of a single theory, without many of the liabilities of such a confining orientation.

A common argument among caseworkers is that we need "our own" theory in order to be clearly defined and recognized as a profession. But this seems both un-necessary and undesirable in view of the fact that there are just too many principles explaining the changing of behavior, and too many disparate methods involving differing goals and techniques, to assume that in the near future they could all be encompassed in a unifying, comprehensive theory of induced change.

At best, in addition to the unifying principles described in this chapter, the field may develop somewhat unifying procedural guidelines that cut across different procedures (e.g., assessment, intervention, evaluation). So, to the question of how we can be defined as a profession without a specific theory or body of knowledge uniquely our own, the answer might be, "How can we, *as a profession,* afford to ignore *any* knowledge, whatever the source, that will help us in effectively carrying out our job?" Use of such knowledge is central in distinguishing the professional from the lay person.

The approach advocated here also is intended to avoid problems associated with other attempts to develop eclectic approaches to practice (e.g., Carkhuff & Berenson, 1977; Thorne, 1973; Martin, 1971, 1972). Carkhuff and Berenson (1977), for example, suggest an adaptation of an eclectic approach which is centered around what they call the "primary factors" of empathy, warmth, and genuineness, and includes as "secondary dimensions" a variety of currently popular orientations such as "psychodynamic approaches," "behavioristic conditioning procedures," the "nondirective approach," and "educational and vocational counseling." Although much of their proposal is sound empirically, their assumption regarding eclecticism appears to be that every approach, just because it is there, must have *some* success, so all approaches should be used differentially. Carkhuff and Berenson (1977) hy-pothesize that the *appropriate* application of one of these secondary dimensions, in addition to the primary factors, will increase effectiveness about 10 percent or more, while the *inappropriate* application of such approaches will add nothing or even detract, possibly contributing to deterioration of the client.

Several problems are presented by such a conception of eclecticism. In the first place, a number of different procedures, not to mention theories, are grouped un-der most of the Carkhuff and Berenson "secondary dimensions." For example, the dimension "psychodynamic approaches" actually consists of a variety of undiffer-entiated approaches to practice. Second, the assumption that because an approach exists it must have *something* to offer is an untenable one. The key question is, Are there any procedures derived from any given approach which, with specified clients or problems, produce a higher success rate than any other procedures? Third, "appropriate" and "inappropriate" applications are undefined, left up to the imagination of the practitioner; there are no clear guidelines for implementation of this "eclectic" approach.

Finally, Carkhuff and Berenson (1977) make the mistake of not only ignoring what works and starting with effective techniques rather than approaches that already exist, but appear to suggest that the novice practitioner must learn *all* ap-proaches on the grounds that they *may* have occasion to use them. Indeed, that this is not an isolated occurrence of what might be termed "the omniscient-eclectic syndrome" can be seen also in Thorne's (1973) fervent advocacy of an eclectic approach wherein he states: "The best trained eclectic *knows all there is to be known about everything* . . . " (Thorne, 1973, p. 450; emphasis added). Such a condition—i.e., learn everything that is available—presents a patently impossible and insurmountable task for the learner. The fact that it is actually advocated by some eclectics may account for the reluctance of some practitioners to more thoroughly explore the eclectic position—few want to attempt the impossible. At any rate, because most approaches do not meet the criteria for selection presented in this chapter, "knowing everything" is clearly unnecessary.

The eclectic approach developed by Martin (1971, 1972), while not suggesting that practitioners learn everything there is to know about everything, attempts to integrate at least two perspectives—the therapeutic conditions of empathy, warmth, and genuineness and some behavioral techniques. While appropriately based on research evidence that such perspectives can be effective, Martin (1971, 1972) then makes the error of trying to integrate these two major thrusts in clinical practice on the basis of theory regarding the *development* of maladaptive behavior, rather than on the *evidence of effectiveness* generated by research. Thus, he concludes that neurotic problems involving internalized conflicts in which the individual's impulses become fear cues are most effectively treated in empathy-oriented psychotherapy, whereas externalized conflict, in which the individual has both approach and avoidance tendencies for some object outside himself or herself, is best treated by behavioral (or "direct reconditioning") procedures (Martin, 1971, pp. 155–158).

This perspective presents several problems also. Martin (1971, p. 157) himself acknowledges that the distinctions between internalized and externalized conflicts are "somewhat arbitrary." Using such a framework requires that the practitioner have "a clear understanding of the etiology of each client's unique problems" (Martin, 1971, p. 159). As pointed out previously in this book, that is a difficult task at best, an impossible task at worst. Thus, guidelines for using such an approach, to say the least, hardly are clear. Also, Martin (1971) ignores the research showing that making this etiological distinction is unnecessary because practitioners using each of the suggested approaches (empathy-oriented therapy and behavioral procedures) have reported success with a far wider range of problems than Martin gives them credit for. In fact, problems that would fall under the rubrics of "internalized and externalized conflicts" have been successfully treated with both approaches, thereby negating the importance of this distinction for interventive purposes. Placing such heavy emphasis on causal/developmental/etiological diagnosis, as is generally the case with most traditional approaches, can preclude the possibility that, with any given pattern of behavior, regardless of its developmental characteristics, if a given technique can be demonstrated to be effective, it is the technique of choice. Further, Martin's approach also tends to exclude the possibility, except for vaguely defined conditions in his framework, of *combining* both empathy-oriented and behavioral procedures to work on aspects of the same problem. Such a perspective has distinct therapeutic advantages, does not require making judgments on the basis of vague etiological diagnoses, and, most importantly, has empirical support in the research literature.

At this point, suffice it to say that the eclectic approach presented in this book is intended to be above all else an *empirical approach*. The vagaries of in-depth causal/developmental analysis are eschewed in favor of a perspective that argues: what can be empirically determined to be effective is what should be used.

Thus, an eclectic approach requires making explicit and rational the criteria that are used to select procedures for practice. It demands of the practitioner a constellation of knowledge, skills, and attitudes that require the utmost in flexibility, and demands, in education, *training for the future*. This involves the ability to continuously analyze and evaluate new approaches as they appear.

It is perhaps obviously important for agencies and individual practitioners to be regularly engaged in such analytic efforts. But it is equally obvious that the time and energy required to be so engaged are in rather short shrift in practice because of all the pressures of caseload, meetings, etc. On the other hand, in order to ensure such on-going evaluation, regular seminars could be built in to the schedule of every agency, at which new approaches and research could be analyzed, using criteria such as those suggested in this chapter and in chapters two and eleven. In addition, regular workshops could be scheduled to develop competence in using new approaches. These could be coordinated with educational institutions in the area, schools of social work, departments of psychology, and so on, to ensure fresh input. Similarly, instead of the traditional consultation practices where psychiatrists or other professionals are hired merely to reinforce an already entrenched, shared system of beliefs, consultation could serve to implement, continue, refresh, update, and help evaluate the new knowledge developed at such seminars and workshops. But the key issue in such programs, or in any adaptation of an eclectic perspective, is not merely *newness* of an approach. It is all too easy to become intrigued with a new approach merely *because* it is new. The key ingredients involve those dimensions discussed in this and other chapters—most significantly, not newness but *effectiveness:* Will this procedure be the very best one available for helping this client with this problem at this time? The criteria presented in this book are intended to help caseworkers make the crucial distinction between fads and legitimate, *helpful* therapeutic procedures. And above all else, these criteria are presented here with the intention and hope of helping caseworkers become more *effective*.

References

Ackerman, N. W. (1966). *Treating the Troubled Family*. New York: Basic Books.

American College Dictionary. (1957). New York: Random House.

Argyris, C., & Schon, D. A. (1974). *Theory in Practice: Increasing Professional Effectiveness*. San Francisco: Jossey-Bass.

Bandura, A. (1969). *Principles of Behavior Modification*. New York: Holt.

Bartlett, H. (1970). *The Common Base of Social Work Practice*. New York: National Association of Social Workers.

Beck, D. F., & Jones, M. A. (1973). *Progress on Family Problems.* New York: Family Service Association of America.

Bennis, W., Benne, K., & Chin, R. (Eds.). (1961). *The Planning of Change.* New York: Holt.

Bergin, A. E. (1971). The evaluation of therapeutic outcomes. In A. E. Bergin & S. L. Garfield (Eds.), *Handbook of Psychotherapy and Behavior Change: An Empirical Analysis.* New York: Wiley, pp. 217–270.

Bergin, A. E., & Strupp, H. H. (1972). *Changing Frontiers in the Science of Psychotherapy.* Chicago: Aldine-Atherton.

Boehm, W. (1959). *The Social Casework Method in Social Work Education.* New York: Council on Social Work Education.

Briar, S., & Miller, H. (1971). *Problems and Issues in Social Casework.* New York: Columbia.

Butler, R. M. (1970). *Social Functioning Framework.* New York: Council on Social Work Education.

Carkhuff, R. R. (1971). *The Development of Human Resources.* New York: Holt.

Carkhuff, R. R., & Berenson, R. (1977). *Beyond Counseling and Therapy* (2nd Ed.). New York: Holt.

Caldwell, B. (1964). The effects of infant care. In M. Hoffman & L. Hoffman (Eds.), *Review of Child Development Research,* (Vol. 1). New York: Russell Sage Foundation, pp. 9–87.

Dubin, R. (1969). *Theory Building.* New York: Free Press.

Dubos, R. (1967). *Man Adapting.* New Haven: Yale.

Erickson, G. D., & Hogan, T. P. (Eds.). (1972). *Family Therapy: An Introduction to Theory and Technique.* Monterey, Calif.: Brooks/Cole.

Erickson, E. (1950). *Childhood and Society.* New York: Norton.

Fischer, J. (1974). The Mental Research Institute on Family Therapy: Review and Assessment. *Family Therapy, 1,* 105–140.

Fischer, J. (1975). *Casework Theory, Research, and Practice: The Current State of the Art.* Unpublished paper. Honolulu: University of Hawaii, School of Social Work.

Ford, D., & Urban, H. (1963). *Systems of Psychotherapy.* New York: Wiley.

Frank, G. H. (1965). The role of the family in the development of psychopathology. *Psychological Bulletin, 64,* 191–205.

Goldman, R., & Mendelsohn, G. (1969). Psychotherapeutic change and social adjustment. *Journal of Abnormal Psychology, 74,* 164–172.

Group for the Advancement of Psychiatry. (1970). *Treatment of Families in Conflict.* New York: Science House.

Gurin, A. (1973). Report on selected efforts to develop a new curriculum for the social professions. In H. M. Barlon (Ed.), *Higher Education and the Social Professions.* Lexington: University of Kentucky, College of Social Professions, pp. 29–51.

Gurin, G., et al. (1960). *Americans View Their Mental Health.* New York: Basic Books.

Haley, J. (1963). *Strategies of Psychotherapy.* New York: Grune & Stratton.

Hearn, A. (1974). General systems theory and social work. In F. J. Turner (Ed.), *Social Work Treatment.* New York: Free Press, pp. 343–371.

Hollis, F. (1968). *A Typology of Casework Treatment.* New York: Family Service Association.

Hollis, F. (1973). *Casework: A Psycho-Social Therapy,* (2nd Ed.). New York: Random House.

Jackson, D. (Ed.). (1968). *Communication, Family and Marriage.* Palo Alto, Calif.: Science and Behavior Books.

Kadushin, A. (1972). The racial factor in the interview. *Social Work, 17,* 88–99.

Laing, R. D. (1970). *Knots.* New York: Pantheon.

Lewis, R. G., & Ho, M. K. (1975). Social work with Native Americans. *Social Work, 20,* 379–382.

Martin, D. G. (1971). *Introduction to Psychotherapy.* Belmont, Calif.: Brooks/Cole.

Martin, D. G. (1972). *Learning-Based Client-Centered Therapy.* Belmont, Calif.: Brooks/Cole.

Mayer, J. E., & Timms, N. (1969). Clash in perspective between worker and client. *Social Casework, 50,* 32–40(a).

Meltzoff, J., & Kornreich, M. (1970). *Research in Psychotherapy.* New York: Atherton.

Middleman, R. R., & Goldberg, G. (1974). *Social Service Delivery: A Structural Approach to Social Work Practice.* New York: Columbia University Press.

Mischel, W. (1968). *Personality and Assessment.* New York: Wiley.

NASW (1967). *Values in Social Work: A Re-Examination.* New York.

Orlansky, H. (1948). Infant care and personality. *Psychological Bulletin, 49,* 1–48.

Perlman, H. H. (1970). The problem-solving model in social casework. In R. Roberts & R. Nee (Eds.), *Theories of Social Casework.* University of Chicago Press, pp. 129–180.

Reid, W., & Epstein, L. (1972). *Task-Centered Casework.* New York: Columbia.

Renaud, H., & Estess, F. (1961). Life history interviews with 100 normal American males: "pathogenicity" of childhood. *American Journal of Orthopsychiatry, 31,* 786–802.

Roberts, R., & Nee, R. (Eds.) (1970). *Theories of Social Casework.* University of Chicago Press.

Rogers, C. R. (1957). The necessary and sufficient conditions of therapeutic personality change. *Journal of Consulting Psychology, 21,* 95–103.

Rogers, C. R. (1959). A theory of therapy, personality and interpersonal relationships as developed in the client centered framework. In S. Koch (Ed.), *Psychology: A Study of a Science* (Vol. II). New York: McGraw-Hill.

Rogers, C. R. (1962). The interpersonal relationship: The core of guidance. *Harvard Educational Review, 32,* 416–429.

Satir, V. (1964). *Conjoint Family Therapy.* Palo Alto, Calif.: Science and Behavior Books.

Scherz, F. H. (1970). Theory and practice of family therapy. In R. Roberts & R. Nee (Eds.), *Theories of Social Casework*. University of Chicago Press, pp. 219–264.

Schofield, W., & Ballan, L. (1959). A comparative study of the personal histories of schizophrenic and nonpsychiatric patients. *Journal of Abnormal and Social Psychology, 59,* 216–225.

Sherman, S. N. (1974). Family Therapy. In F. J. Turner (Ed.), *Social Work Treatment*. New York: Free Press, pp. 457–494.

Shostrom, E. L. (1966). *Manual for the Personal Orientation Inventory*. San Diego, Calif.: Educational and Industrial Testing Service.

Sigal, J. J., et al. (1976). The problems in measuring the success of family therapy in common clinical settings. *Family Process, 15,* 225–233.

Simon, B. K. (1970). Social casework theory: an overview. In R. Roberts & R. Nee (Eds.), *Theories of Social Casework*. University of Chicago Press, 353–396.

Strean, H. S. (1974). Role theory. In F. J. Turner (Ed.), *Social Work Treatment*. New York: Free Press, pp. 314–342.

Strupp, H., & Bergin, A. E. (1969). Some empirical and conceptual bases for coordinated research in psychotherapy. *International Journal of Psychiatry, 7* (whole no. 37).

Thorne, F. C. (1973). Eclectic Psychotherapy. In R. Corsini (Ed.), *Current Psychotherapies*. Itasca, Ill.: Peacock, pp. 445–486.

Turner, F. J. (Ed.). (1974). *Social Work Treatment*. New York: Free Press.

Ullman, L. P., & Krasner, L. A. (1969). *A Psychological Approach to Abnormal Behavior*. Englewood Cliffs, N.J.: Prentice-Hall.

Urban, H. B., & Ford, D. H. (1971). *Some Historical and Conceptual Perspectives on Psychotherapy and Behavior Change*. New York: Wiley, pp. 3–35.

Waskow, I. E., & Parloff, M. B. (1975). *Psychotherapy Change Measures*. Washington: National Institute of Mental Health.

Wells, R. A., Dilkes, T. C., & Trivelli, N. (1972). The results of family therapy: A critical review of the literature. *Family Process, 11,* 189–207.

Whittaker, J. K. (1976). Causes of childhood disorders: new findings. *Social Work, 21,* 91–96.

Wolberg, L. (1966). *Psychotherapy and the Behavioral Sciences*. New York: Grune & Stratton.

Wolpe, J. (1969a). Presidential address, Second Annual Meeting of the Association for the Advancement of Behavior of Therapy. In R. Rubin & C. Franks (Eds.), *Advances in Behavior Therapy*. New York: Academic Press.

Wolpe, J. (1969b). *The Practice of Behavior Therapy*. New York: Pergamon.

Wolpe, J. (1971). The compass of behavior therapy. *Behavior Therapy, 2,* 403–405.

Wolpe, J. (1973). *The Practice of Behavior Therapy* (2nd Ed.). New York: Pergamon.

Chapter 6
Building Research into Practice

The purpose of this chapter is to focus on the process of *technique building and validation* in practice with individuals. It is hoped that this will encourage explicitness in the kind of outcome-oriented approach that can serve as the foundation for clinical experimentation and innovation.

A general term for such practice-oriented research has been proposed by Chassan (1967) who distinguishes between the "extensive" and "intensive" models of research. The extensive design refers primarily to the testing of hypotheses with respect to groups of subjects, e.g., controlled group experimental designs (it also has been called "nomothetic research," i.e., research concerned with statements regarding general classes of events; Marx, 1963). Such a design might profitably, in fact, should, be used when there is substantial evidence from practice that its hypotheses can be validated. This is not to negate the importance of hypothesis-testing with the potential for discarding untenable positions such as already has occurred in the field of casework. Rather, the point is that *at the current stage of knowledge development in social casework, research modeled on the extensive design would likely be most successful if informed in advance by the replicated results of numerous studies based on the intensive model.*

The intensive or practice-oriented design (also called $N = 1$ or single-organism design) is used for research that pertains to single-case studies, more or less formalized to the extent that conclusions about effectiveness in individual cases can be established by varying certain conditions over a period of time (it also is called "idiographic research," referring to the intensive study of a single subject; Marx, 1963). This differs significantly from the extensive model where conclusions can be generated only about group effects and where, as a result, the possible variations in effects between individuals, except in the grossest sense, may be lost.

The prototypic intensive design is the time-series design, the characteristics, method, analysis, elaborations and variations, and problems of which have been spelled out in several recent publications (Hersen & Barlow, 1976; Campbell &

Fischer, J. (1978). *Effective Casework Practice: An Eclectic Approach.* New York: McGraw-Hill, 88–102. Reprinted with permission of McGraw-Hill.

Stanley, 1963; Gottman et al., 1969; Gottman, 1973; Glass et al., 1973; Hudson, 1975). Basically, the time-series design consists simply of measuring the extent of a given problem on a repeated basis over a period of time. Thus, successive observations are conducted throughout a programmed intervention to assess the characteristics of, and fluctuations in, the change process (Gottman et al., 1969). The observations may consist of an actual counting of problematic behaviors, repeated administration of a questionnaire, use of data recorded for other purposes (e.g., attendance records), or even repeated recordings of subjective reports of distress.

Of course, simple recording of repeated measures does not provide a basis for normal comparisons between non-intervention periods and intervention periods (Hudson, 1975). Hence, an important variation of the simple time-series design is available, called the "interrupted time-series design." In this design, a repeated series of observations are again taken over a period of time. However, they are begun before any formal intervention process has begun (the baseline); these observations continue during and after the intervention process. Then, the worker can compare any differences in client performance between the baseline and intervention periods. This process, with 0 being the observation, testing, or assessment and X being the intervention, could be diagrammed as follows (Campbell & Stanley, 1963):

$$X \rightarrow$$
$$0_1 \ 0_2 \ 0_3 \ 0_4 \ 0_5 \ 0_6 \ 0_7 \ 0_8$$

Because time-series data are collected on only one person over time, they tend to be serially correlated (the terms serial correlation, autocorrelation, and serial dependency can be used interchangeably); that is, there is a danger that they are sequentially dependent and that any changes which can be detected are due not to the intervention but to chance variations in, and the repeated observation of, the individual (technically, that it is possible to predict changes in the behavior of the individual in the future simply by knowing his or her behavior in the past, say, during baseline). There are two basic ways this can be examined. One is through the use of statistical procedures to examine the significance of the serial correlations and the statistical significance of any observed changes. For example, serial correlation may be determined by simply pairing successive observations and computing a correlation coefficient (called autocorrelation of lag 1), with statistical significance indicating the presence of serial correlation. (See Gottman et al., 1969; Gottman, 1973; Glass et al., 1973; Hersen & Barlow, 1976; and Gottman and Leiblum, 1974, for these and other procedures for statistically testing time-series designs and for procedures to follow when the data are serially correlated, and Hudson, 1975, for somewhat more elementary and accessible tools for analysis.)

Another way, certainly more feasible for most line workers who have minimal experience with, interest in, or time for, conducting complicated statistical procedures with all their clients, is to place the recordings on a simple chart, and then to look for discontinuities in the data. The key word is *discontinuities,* i.e., major changes in the level of behavior observed, particularly as related to the onset of intervention. The basic purpose of these observations is to attempt to rule out competing hypotheses that offer likely alternative explanations of the shift or change in the time series other than the effect of the intervention (Campbell & Stanley, 1963). In other words, the goal is to determine whether the intervention, or some other factor, had any effect on the observed changes.

There are three key dimensions to examine in looking at changes across phases of a time-series design (Hersen & Barlow, 1976). The first is change in *level,* i.e., changes in the amount, frequency, intensity, or duration of the behavior, particularly at the point where intervention is introduced. The second is change in *slope,* a change in the trend of the data between phases. The third is whether or not there is *drift* in the data across phases. Several patterns involving these three dimensions are possible, then, and some of these are illustrated in Figure 6.1 redrawn from Hersen and Barlow (1976, pp. 280, 281) and Gottman and Leiblum (1974, p. 159). On all these charts, the horizontal axis consists of observations or measurements over time, the vertical axis consists of some hypothetical behavior, and the broken vertical line indicates the dividing point between the preintervention and intervention phases.

As can be seen from Figure 6.1, there are several possibilities for combining patterns and changes in level, slope, and drift, including some that are not illustrated but simply are combinations of these five patterns. With regard to discontinuities in

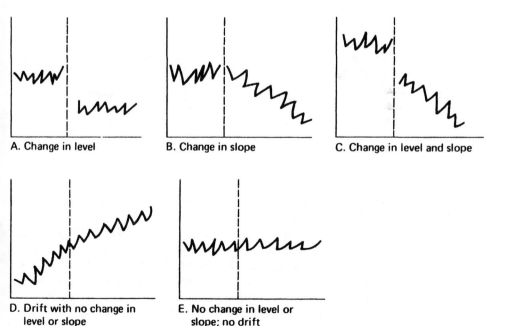

A. Change in level   B. Change in slope   C. Change in level and slope

D. Drift with no change in   E. No change in level or
   level or slope   slope; no drift

Fig. 6.1   Varying patterns of data for time-series designs: level, slope, and drift.

the data, which refer mainly to clear breaks in level between preintervention and intervention phases, the two series of measures with the clearest discontinuities are series A and series C. Series B, with no immediate change in level but a change in slope, would be next easiest to interpret visually regarding changes in behavior. Finally, series D, illustrating a continuous trend of drift over time with no change in level or slope, can best be interpreted as changes that likely would have occurred independent of intervention. This is because the drift (or trend) was present prior to intervention and simply carried over into the intervention phase. (Statistics are available in the references cited above to avoid interpreting changes as significant when drift, and hence, serial correlation, is present in the data.)

Now, it is important to note that, in actual practice, perfect patterns are unlikely, and the worker may have to make a judgment on a far less certain basis than appears in series A or C. Second, a major purpose of such evaluation is to examine changes in behavior. Hence, a change in a desired direction, objectively measured, *is* a change and can be used as an important source of feedback to worker and client. The judgment becomes more complicated when the worker attempts to make a clear determination as to whether his or her techniques brought about the change. Hence, fluctuations in the baseline period present more of a problem for that kind of determination, to the extent that it literally may be impossible to make an unequivocal judgment on the basis of such observations as to the relationship between the worker's use of a specific technique and changes in client behavior.

The purpose of this introduction was to present a brief overview of the basic characteristics of time-series designs as a prototypical model of intensive designs. Actually, the rigor of different intensive designs varies tremendously. For example, the first illustration of one model of intensive design to be discussed in the next section—the experimental investigation of single cases, developed and extended largely by behaviorists—is most directly related to the time-series design and also probably includes some of its most rigorous and ingenious applications. Other models, to be discussed in later sections, though less rigorous, offer different methods for assessment and evaluation that may be selected depending on the nature of the case, problem, and skills of the worker.

In essence, intensive designs offer numerous advantages for implementation in casework practice. First, they focus on individual clients; variations in effect from one client to another can be assessed. Second, they are the only designs that provide a continuous record of changes in the target problem over the entire course of the intervention. Third, they are practice-based and practitioner-oriented; they provide continuous assessment and outcome data to the worker who can then monitor progress and, because of the inherent flexibility of such designs, make changes in the nature of the intervention if so indicated. Fourth, at least in their more rigorous forms, they can function as quasi-experimental designs, testing for the relationship between interventive procedures and client change, and ruling out at least some alternative hypotheses as explanations of the changes. Fifth, such designs function as heuristic tools, especially when coupled with carefully kept logs of potentially relevant nonexperimental events. Thus, they can serve as a source of post hoc hypotheses regarding observed but unplanned changes in program variables (Gottman et al., 1969). Sixth, intensive designs avoid the problem of outside researchers coming in and imposing a research regime; they are organized and run by and for the practitioner, for his or her and the client's benefit. Finally, several replications of intensive, individualized case studies can form the basis for an informed, properly conceived study based on the extensive model. Thus, the two models of research can work hand in hand. The intensive case study, which tends to be limited in generalization potentials beyond a specific client and a specific worker, can provide the basic data for generating hypotheses for more elaborate group experimental designs following the extensive model. And conclusions from research using such extensive designs can, in turn, form the empirically validated basis for effective practice.

This point of generalization (i.e., to what extent are findings from intensive designs applicable to other clients, problems, workers, situations) bears some brief mention. Thomas (1975) suggests there are some possibilities when results from single-case research may be generalized:

1. When variability between subjects is known to be negligible so that replication would be redundant
2. When one case in depth clearly exemplifies many
3. When negative results from one case are sufficient to suggest the need for at least revision, and possibly even rejection, of the principles which generated that intervention
4. When the behavior studied is very unusual, and there is limited opportunity to study it
5. When the practitioner wants to focus on a problem by defining questions and variables that may lead to more refined approaches

Indeed, Hersen and Barlow (1976) argue that replications of single case experiments may provide sufficient evidence for generalization. That is, they suggest that a series of single-case experimental designs *with similar clients* in which the original experiment is *directly replicated* several times provides generalizable conclusions. Among other reasons, this is because treatment proceeds with individual clients whose characteristics presumably are clearly defined, and the positive results, if replicated with several clients, can readily be translated by the practitioner into applications in his or her own work with similar clients. Further, because each client serves as his or her own control, and the effects of variations in the environment or in the individual client can be observed when treatment is withdrawn (perhaps to be reapplied in a succeeding phase), these nontreatment influences can be estimated. Of course, such replications do not ensure generalization across workers and settings. For these, Hersen and Barlow (1976) suggest the use of *systematic replications,* that is, varying settings, workers, or even clients on a procedure previously demonstrated as successful with homogeneous clients.

On the other hand, it should be pointed out that the rules or laws of evidence regarding generalizations from single cases are rudimentary, if they exist at all. It is not at all clear how many successful replications are necessary before one may conclude that results are generalizable, or whether 100 percent of the replications must be successful or 90 percent or 80 percent, and so on. Much of the generalization process from single-case studies consists of practitioners or researchers picking up on clues from the literature, and examining the results of previous case studies in application with their own clients. Hence, the recommendation above—that the replicated results of single-case studies can be used as a basis for conducting more broadly based group experimental designs, where the rules of evidence for generalization are more clear-cut and established—seems to be the optimum process for utilizing research data to inform practice.

Again, the object of this chapter is to present models for studying the intervention process in terms of the application of specific techniques with individual clients and problems. These approaches vary in both rigor and methodology, but all have at least a modicum of potential in accomplishing the crucial tasks of, first, providing a degree of systematization and objectification to practice; second, developing techniques; and, third, presenting different methods for observing, collecting data about, and evaluating the effectiveness of practice with each and every client. It is hoped that use of such procedures will encourage making explicit the kind of outcome-oriented approach that can serve as the foundation for continuing experimentation and innovation in practice.

Experimental Investigations of Single Cases

Intensive study of single cases is actually one of the foundations of research in a number of social and behavioral sciences, spanning the disciplines of sociology, psychiatry, psychology, anthropology, and social work. While the strategies or methods may vary, both within and among these disciplines, the concern with understanding *individuals* and their relationships with any number of pertinent variables through intensive case studies transcends all the disciplines. Although, as indicated above, there are numerous models of intensive case study designs, one that appears to be of particular relevance to casework practice is the experimental investigation of single cases. This design has been developed to its highest degree of rigor by researchers with a behavioral orientation (Baer et al., 1968; Bushell & Burgess, 1969; Skinner, 1966; Yates, 1970; Howe, 1974; Hudson, 1975; Browning & Stover, 1971; Leitenberg, 1973; Thomas, 1975; McNamara & MacDonough, 1972; Jones, 1974; Kazdin, 1975; Honig, 1966; for the most recent and comprehensive work, see Hersen & Barlow, 1976). But because the use of this design requires a number of the features considered to be desirable for a broader orientation to practice, it would be unfortunate if its origins in behavior modification research prevented caseworkers with a broader, more eclectic orientation from adapting this design for general casework practice. (For an example of the use of one version of this design to evaluate "psychosocial casework," see Haynes, 1976.)

The use of this design requires the following: (1) Objective identification of techniques; presumably, any technique that can be clearly designated as to when it is being applied and when it is not can be used; (2) objective identification of the behavior(s) which it is desirable to change; (3) a method of observing, preferably in the natural environment, the occurrence or nonoccurrence of those behaviors (the target behaviors). (It would seem that regardless of whether the caseworker is using such a design, all three of these dimensions should be incorporated into practice as routinely as possible.) Given the above, the experimental investigation of single cases, in its more rigorous forms, can be used to demonstrate, first, that the techniques used are (or are not) actually affecting the target behaviors, and, second, that the target behaviors are (or are not) changing. Thus, use of this design can provide the worker with an ongoing evaluation of the effectiveness of the intervention program, can provide the necessary feedback to form the bases for deciding whether to reevaluate a given program and perhaps try a different interventive strategy, and can also provide clients with important feedback as to the success of the program with which they are involved (and possibly maintain their motivation to continue on the basis of objective knowledge of positive results).

The features of this design have been spelled out in considerable detail in the references cited above, and so only the key dimensions need be presented here. Further, only the most basic of several variations of this design will be presented (e.g., Thomas, 1975, and Hersen & Barlow, 1976, have identified and described some twenty variations of single-case experimental designs).

The first and perhaps most important variation of this design is called the A-B-A-B (or reversal) design. In essence, this design attempts to determine whether the changes in a target behavior are lawfully related to the experimental operations, or techniques, that were intended to produce them (Yates, 1970, p. 381). The basic procedures involve, first, identifying a target behavior which one desires to change and counting how many times it occurs (frequency), the length of time it occurs (duration), the number of intervals of time during which at least one instance of behavior occurs, the intensity of its occurrence, or all these, over a period of time long enough to provide base-rate information.

There are numerous methods for selecting and recording this information, a process that usually is negotiated between the client and the worker. For example, Howe (1976) has discussed and provided guidelines for using client's observations in research. Hiebert (1974) has discussed outcome criterion selection and then recording methods from the viewpoint of the client (e.g., self-observations, keeping records), from the viewpoint of significant others (e.g., parents' observations of a child's behavior), from the viewpoint of society (e.g., school grades, incarcerations), and from the viewpoint of the worker (structured questionnaires, qualitative and quantitative assessments of change).

Finally, Fischer and Gochros (1975, Chapter 10) have described a variety of methods for recording information. For example, a simple checklist can be used on which one jots down either a note or just a check mark each time a desired or undesired behavior occurs. Such simple procedures as moving coins or card chips from one pocket to another when a target behavior occurs, or even wearing a golf-score counter on the wrist to click off behaviors as they occur, can be used. Of course, with all recording procedures, it is important to ensure reliability, agreement among individuals observing the behavior as to just what the behavior is, independent of the assessment strategy used, and clarity and accuracy of observation, even if the observer is the client himself or herself. (Strategies for assessing and ensuring reliability are presented in Kazdin, 1975, Chapter 4, and Hersen & Barlow, 1976, Chapter 4.)

The base-rate information is called the baseline and is collected in a systematic, planned way, before any intervention begins. This baseline information is then charted, with the frequency or the duration put on the vertical axis, and the period of time over which it was recorded put on the horizontal axis. Say, a woman seeks help from a caseworker, complaining about her husband's "lack of communication." During the assessment process, the worker and client decide that one part of the problem is that the husband rarely initiates conversations. The worker suggests that the client select one hour per day, say, at mealtime, to record the number of times her husband initiates a conversation. This would be done simply by jotting down on a piece of paper each time he initiated a conversation (guidelines for the determination of indicators that a conversation had been initiated would also be discussed). This record could then be translated onto the chart as illustrated in Figure 6.2.

This is the first step in the evaluation process, the baseline or A phase, and actually forms the foundation for succeeding phases. The next step, resting on the baseline, is to identify the techniques necessary to change the behavior and to implement these techniques. This is the first intervention period, phase B, and data continue to be recorded in the same manner as previously. In the case described

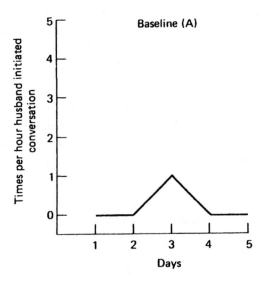

Fig. 6.2   Number of times husband initiated conversation during baseline period (A).

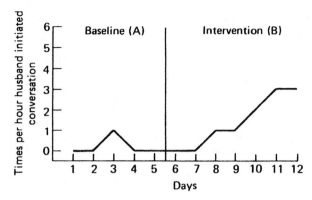

Fig. 6.3 Number of times husband initiated conversation during baseline (A) and first intervention (B) periods.

above, assume that the worker and client decide on the use of positive reinforcement every time the husband does speak, in an effort to both increase his overall frequency of speaking and his initiation of conversations (and, of course, to change the wife's pattern of responses to her husband's communication). The chart would then be presented as in Figure 6.3. This design is the foundation and most basic of these designs. It is called, simply, the A-B design.

During the baseline period, the husband initiated a conversation only once. But by the end of the first intervention period, he was initiating comments with his wife at the spectacular (for him) rate of four times per hour. At this point, it is safe to conclude that the target behavior has definitely increased since the start of intervention. The next step can be to find out whether this increase was related to the techniques suggested by the worker. This calls for reversing or, perhaps more accurately, withdrawing the procedure, returning to baseline conditions and removing the technique. This condition is called reversal, or once again, baseline or A, since the conditions are intended to approximate the original preintervention period. The reversal is particularly helpful when, as suggested in the introduction to this chapter, there is considerable fluctuation in the baseline data, and the discontinuity between baseline and intervention is not crystal clear. In this case, the wife was asked to stop providing positive reinforcement for her husband's conversation. The results are shown in Figure 6.4.

Figure 6.4 demonstrates that the behavior had decreased (although not to its original level) and also strongly suggests that the decrease was related to the removal of the technique. To draw a definitive conclusion regarding the rate of behavior and its relation to the specific technique, the worker then had the client reinstitute her provision of positive reinforcement. This is the second intervention period (B), and the results are illustrated in Figure 6.5.

Once again, the husband and wife are "communicating." And, as Figure 6.5 shows, the frequency with which the husband initiated a discussion with his wife

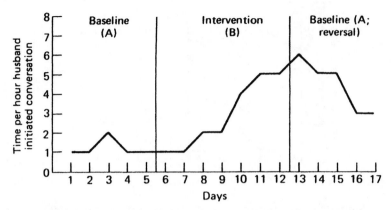

Fig. 6.4   Number of times husband initiated conversation during baseline (A), first intervention (B), and second baseline (A, reversal) periods.

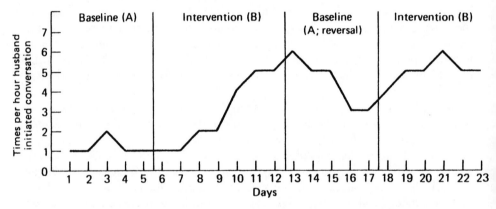

Fig. 6.5   Number of times husband initiated conversation during baseline (A), first intervention (B), second baseline (A), and second intervention (B) periods.

was clearly related all along the line to the technique that was used and whether it was being applied or withdrawn.

While the case illustration used here was both hypothetical and oversimplified, it did serve to exemplify how such a design, called the A-B-A-B design, could be incorporated into casework practice. The basic features, in review, include clearly identifying a target behavior and finding a way to measure it, then selecting a technique that is also clearly defined so that its use and nonuse can be objectively related to the observed changes in the target behavior. This design has numerous advantages for casework practice. The criterion for success—the change in behavior—is clearly identified for both worker and client and is built right into the research design. The client serves as his or her own control, and it is possible to tell with each case whether a technique works. It is not necessary for the practitioner to learn sophisticated statistical procedures. Further, the time involved for each study is based solely on changes in the target behavior itself. The data collected give ongoing evaluative feedback to the worker as to the effect of what he or she is doing, and provide the basis for making changes in the intervention program if such changes are necessary. The A-B-A-B design, in sum, is an excellent way of bridging the gap between research and practice.

But such a design cannot be the end product of research into practice effects. In the first place, a technique generally cannot be validated in toto using this design. At best, the A-B-A-B design shows that a given technique was clearly related to behavior change for this worker with this client with this problem. In other words, even after several successful replications, group experimental research ordinarily would be necessary to establish the effectiveness of a given technique across the range of workers and clients. Further, the recording process might seem particularly time-consuming, and it may prove difficult to find someone willing to actually engage in such recording (although these problems are present in any study where data collection is involved). And some workers may object to the reversal stages on ethical grounds and particularly when the first intervention period seems to have produced successful results in changing the target behavior. Few caseworkers would want to reestablish undesirable behaviors in actual practice just to prove a point. And rightly so!

Actually, though, research has established that behavior in the reversal period often does not return completely to the baseline or preintervention level. Further, demonstrating to clients and significant others involved in the program by use of reversal that their efforts are indeed producing changes can stimulate an increased desire to participate in the program. Finally, variations of the A-B-A-B design, where that design is not possible, might be utilized.

The first alternative to the reversal or A-B-A-B design is called the "multiple baseline" design (Baer et al., 1968). The multiple baseline design also is used to minimize the possibility that behavior changes are due to chance, but does so by either (1) collecting baseline data on more than one target behavior, (2) collecting baseline data on the same target behavior but in more than one setting, or (3) collecting baseline data on more than one but similar clients. Then, intervention techniques are applied and focused either on one of the behaviors or the behavior in one of the settings, or on one of the clients, while continuing to record data on all the behaviors or from all the settings, and/or on all the clients. Once the initial target behavior is seen to change, intervention is systematically introduced with the next target behavior or in the next setting. A multiple baseline design using four different behaviors is illustrated in Figure 6.6.

Since multiple baseline designs do not require the reversal condition, they seem a feasible alternative to the A-B-A-B design as a way of establishing basic data about the effects of the variety of techniques that would compose the eclectic caseworker's interventive repertoire. Further, when used across settings (i.e., recording the same

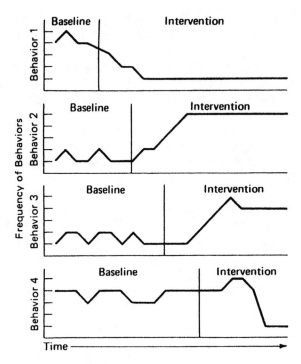

Fig. 6.6   Multiple baseline design using four different behaviors.

behaviors but in different locations), the multiple baseline design can support (or refute) conclusions about the generalization of the changes to more than one place.

Of course, the multiple baseline design does contain some disadvantages. At least two behaviors (or settings or clients) are needed. Further, there is difficulty in assessing effects when the behaviors vary a great deal in type or occurrence. Finally, and perhaps most importantly, if two or more behaviors of one client are used and the behaviors are not independent (that is, changes in one affect the other), the multiple baseline design cannot be used. Unfortunately, it is generally difficult, if not impossible, to tell in advance which behaviors will be independent, and which will not, so that the appropriateness of using the multiple baseline design may have to be determined on a post hoc basis. But despite these problems and because of its other advantages under conditions when such problems as these do not exist, the multiple baseline design appears to be a feasible and useful method of evaluation of technique effectiveness.

The second alternative to use of the reversal design is called the A-B design; it consists of the first two parts of the reversal design, the baseline and the first intervention periods. This design is illustrated in Figure 6.7 and can easily be built into everyday practice as a continuing method of evaluation. The A-B design admittedly cannot provide conclusive evidence as to the relationship between the application of a technique and a change in behavior, since no reversal period is used. On the

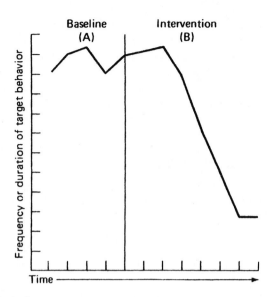

Fig. 6.7 The A-B design.

other hand, the A-B design does provide evidence as to whether there is a change in target behavior and thus is an excellent way of building outcome-oriented feedback into practice.[1]

As mentioned above, there often is no need for use of statistical procedures to assess the significance of changes in such cases. This primarily is because the criterion for success in practice is social or practical significance rather than statistical significance. Thus, whether or not an outcome is statistically significant is largely irrelevant if the intervention is socially and practically without meaning. Further, if these designs become too complicated and weighted down by the necessity for use of statistics, their basic value of simplicity and feasibility for use by practitioners becomes diluted.

On the other hand, there are times when the use of statistics can greatly aid in the interpretation of data (a review of these procedures is available in Hersen & Barlow, 1976, Chapter 8):

1. When baseline data are not stable, to rule out the effects of a trend (drift) and to establish and remove the effects of serial dependency
2. When exploring new variables with unestablished effects or when results appear ambiguous
3. To separate chance fluctuations from intervention effects
4. To find nondramatic but reliable effects that may lead to further experimentation and important theoretical or clinical developments

---

[1] For variations and extensions of these designs, see Hersen and Barlow, 1976; see Glass et al., 1973, for several additional variations of time-series designs.

In addition to the use of statistics for the assessment of significance, and visually examining the data for discontinuities, for the worker interested in generating slightly more rigorous data, three rather simple methods are available. One method (Gottman & Leiblum, 1974) is simply to create a boundary around the observations in the baseline and then to assume that changes beyond those boundaries in the desired direction are, indeed, reliable indicators of change. This procedure is illustrated in Figure 6.8 where the horizontal axis represents the period of time of the program and the vertical axis represents the target behavior, say, number of minutes of studying per day. Changes in number of minutes of studying per day beyond the boundary and in the desired direction would then be taken as evidence that the changes indicate a clear discontinuity from the baseline.

Unfortunately, there are limitations in use of these boundaries as well as issues about their use. First, for example, they are most effective when the baseline is fairly stable and when serial correlation (or autocorrelation) is not a problem. These problems may be overcome by use of simple statistical procedures (see Gottman & Leiblum, 1974, pp. 142–151), but once again, this limits their usefulness in everyday practice. Second, it is not always clear where to draw the boundaries, i.e., how far away from the baseline is sufficient to indicate a desired change. This can be overcome statistically by simply calculating a standard deviation for the baseline data and plotting the boundary two standard deviations above and below the mean as shown in Figure 6.8. If two successive observations drift outside the boundary either in a positive or negative direction, the changes are statistically significant (Gottman

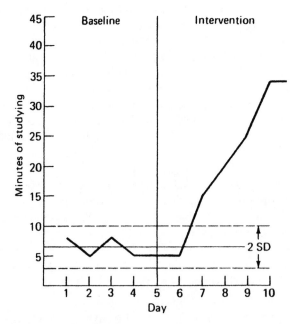

Fig. 6.8   Changes in target behavior of studying as indicated by boundaries placed two standard deviations around baseline observations.

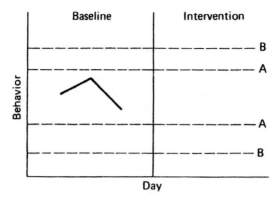

Fig. 6.9 Two methods of plotting boundaries, with method B being more likely to ensure a conclusion of important effect if drift exceeds boundary.

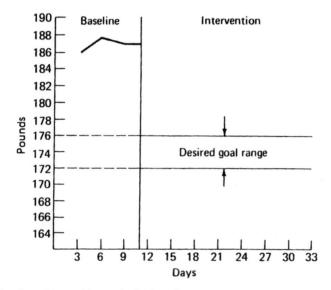

Fig. 6.10 Setting the goal boundaries in advance.

& Leiblum, 1974, p. 143). Failing this, a good rule of thumb is that the further away from the baseline the boundaries are plotted and the further the drift out of the band, the more likely it is that one can assume an important effect (see Figure 6.9).

A second method for examining the meaningfulness of effects is simply to set a goal (short- or long-term), plot it on a chart, and conclude that if the target behavior reaches the boundaries of the desired goal, the program has been successful (i.e., the goal achieved). For example, Figure 6.10 illustrates the setting of a goal for weight loss, wherein the desired target range is between 172 and 176 pounds.

A third method for examining the significance of effects has been described by Bloom (1975; Bloom & Block, 1977). He presents a simple probability table to determine whether (again in cases where there is an absence of serial correlation) it is likely that the number of desired events occurring in the intervention period could have occurred by chance alone as compared with the given proportion of events from the baseline period. As with reading any probability table, the practitioner simply compares the proportions of these two categories of events (from pre- and post-intervention periods) in Bloom's table to determine whether or not changes (both positive and negative) were statistically significant.

Again, for all these methods it is important to distinguish between two endeavors. The first is attempting to isolate the effects of a given technique, i.e., the relationship between application of a technique and a specific outcome. For this, a high degree of rigor is necessary, e.g., as is present in the A-B-A-B design. The second endeavor is simply collecting data to determine whether or not a behavior changes as feedback to worker and client. This requires less rigor and hence is more feasible (e.g., the A-B design), but also makes it difficult to conclude that it was the worker's intervention per se that produced the observed changes. Of course, in either situation, the careful monitoring of client progress is bound to add major increments in both objectification and systematization to practice.

The research methods described in this section can prove of particularly high value in the process of knowledge building for casework practice. With clearer specification of techniques and objectives basic to their utilization, a complementary process relating research to practice can occur. Caseworkers can test their techniques with every client and *be clear* as to the effects they are producing. Then, with numerous successful replications varying clients, behaviors, settings, and workers, hypotheses can be developed for testing in extensive, group experimental designs to provide a firm and expanding basis for effective practice.

References

Baer, D. M., et al. (1968). Some current dimensions of applied behavior analysis. *Journal of Applied Behavior Analysis, 1,* 91–97.

Bloom, M. (1975). *The Paradox of Helping: Introduction to the Philosophy of Scientific Practice.* New York: Wiley.

Bloom, M., & Block, S. (1977). Evaluating effectiveness and efficiency in one's own practice. *Social Work, 13,* 130–136.

Browning, R. M., & Stover, D. O. (1971). *Behavior Modification in Child Treatment.* Chicago: Aldine.

Bushell, D., & Burgess, R. L. (1969). Characteristics of the experimental analysis. In R. L. Burgess & D. Bushell (Eds.), *Behavioral Sociology.* New York: Columbia, 145–174.

Campbell, D. T., & Stanley, J. C. (1963). *Experimental and Quasi-Experimental Designs for Research.* Chicago: Rand McNally and Co.

Chassan, J. B. (1967). *Research Design in Clinical Psychology and Psychiatry.* New York: Appleton-Century-Crofts.

Fischer, J., & Gochros, H. L. (1975). *Planned Behavior Change: Behavior Modification in Social Work*. New York: Free Press.

Glass, G. V., Willson, V. K., & Gottman, J. M. (1973). *The Design and Analysis of Time-Series Experiements*. Boulder, Colo.: Laboratory of Educational Research Press.

Gottman, J. M. (1973). N-of-one and N-of-two research in psychotherapy. *Psychological Bulletin, 80,* 93–105.

Gottman, J. M., & Leiblum, S. R. (1974). *How to Do Psychotherapy and How to Evaluate It*. New York: Holt.

Gottman, J. M., McFall, R. M., & Barnett, J. T. (1969). Design and analysis of research using time series. *Psychological Bulletin, 72,* 299–306.

Haynes, J. (1977). *An Evaluation of Psychosocial Casework Using the Single-Subject Design: First Findings*. March 1. Paper presented at Council on Social Work Education, 23rd Annual Program Meeting. Phoenix, Arizona.

Hersen, M., & Barlow, D. H. (1976). *Single Case Experimental Designs*. New York: Pergamon.

Hiebert, S. (1974). Who benefits from the program? Criteria selection. In P. O. Davidson, F. Clark, & C. A. Hamerlynck (Eds.), *Evaluation of Behavioral Programs*. Champaign, Ill: Research Press, 33–54.

Honig, W. (Ed.). (1966). *Operant Behavior: Areas of Research and Application*. New York: Appleton-Century-Crofts.

Howe, M. W. (1974). Casework self evaluation: a single-subject approach. *Social Service Review, 48,* 1–23.

Howe, M. W. (1976). Using clients' observations in research. *Social Work, 21,* 28–33.

Hudson, W. W. (1975). Elementary techniques for assessing single-client/single-worker interventions. *Social Service Review, 51,* 311–326.

Jones, R. R. (1974). Design and analysis problems in program evaluation. In P. O. Davidson, F. W. Clark, & L. A. Hamerlynck (Eds.), *Evaluation of Behavioral Programs*. Champaign, Ill: Research Press, 1–31.

Kazdin, A. E. (1975). *Behavior Modification in Applied Settings*. Homewood, Ill.: Dorsey.

Leitenberg, H. (1973). The use of single-case methodology in psychotherapy research. *Journal of Abnormal Psychology, 82,* 87–101.

McNamara, J. R., & MacDonough, T. S. (1972). Some methodological considerations in the design and implementation of behavior therapy research. *Behavior Therapy, 3,* 361–378.

Marx, M. H. (1963). The general nature of theory construction. In M. H. Marx (Ed.), *Theories in Contemporary Psychology*. New York: Macmillan, 4–46.

Skinner, B. F. (1966). What is the experimental analysis of behavior? *Journal of Experimental Analysis of Behavior, 9,* 213–218.

Thomas, E. J. (1975). Uses of research methods in interpersonal practice. In N. A. Polansky (Ed.), *Social Work Research* (Rev. Ed.). University of Chicago Press, 254–283.

Yates, A. (1970). *Behavior Therapy*. New York: Wiley.

Chapter 7
Does Anything Work?

The years of the 1970s have been dubbed "the age of accountability" (Briar, 1973), and one of the direct implications of focusing on accountability is to examine whether any of the helping professions can actually demonstrate that what they are doing is effective.

This is not a frivolous question. The helping professions, depending on which ones are included in the definition, consume billions of dollars of our nation's resources, and consist of hundreds of thousands of professionals in thousands of settings providing countless hours of services to a vast number of clients and consumers. And the most basic assumption underlying these services is that they are effective. In accountability terms, this means that clients and consumers, and the communities that support those services, have the right to expect that the services will be effective.

This is not to say that guaranteed performance—total effectiveness irrespective of the situation—can be expected. None of the human services professions can promise that. But it *is* to say that once a field has defined a claim and shown it to be within acceptable bounds of realization, that field has created an expectation that it must fulfill by performance (Tropp, 1974). In other words, the burden of proof must be on the professionals in that field to demonstrate the effectiveness of the services they offer.

The purpose of this paper is to review the results of effectiveness research in several of the helping or human services professions in an effort to examine whether or not the bulk of that research supports the claims of efficacy of the professionals within each of the fields. The fields that will be reviewed are: social work practice, psychotherapy and counseling, corrections, psychiatric hospitalization, and elementary and secondary education. The professionals that do the bulk of the work in those fields include social workers, psychiatrists, clinical psychologists, counselors, and teachers.

Fischer, J. (1978). *Social Service Research, 1,* 215–243. Reprinted with permission of The Haworth Press.

There are, of course, several other professions and fields that could have been included in this review, but, apart from considerations of space, the following criteria for making these selections were used:

1. Availability of research. Some professions (e.g., lawyers) do not have an abundance of, and cannot even agree upon, criteria for conducting research on effectiveness. To that extent, it is to the credit of the professions involved in this discussion that such research is available.
2. There are certain similarities in the practice of the professions that were included. These will be discussed in a later section of this paper and essentially consist of the declared importance within each of the professions of "the professional use of self." That is, with some variation across the different fields, it is generally the functioning of the professional as a person (whether this be in direct therapeutic contacts with the client or through integration and selective use of technology) that is presumed to be the most crucial factor in obtaining effects, and the use of any technology is generally considered to be of secondary importance.
3. The final criterion is one resembling "face validity" in that all the professions included here generally strive to achieve changes in social and personal functioning for their clientele, whether these changes are behavioral, cognitive, affective, or some combination of these.

The research that will be reviewed consists of the following: (a) controlled studies examining the effectiveness of professionals versus either no intervention whatsoever or nonprofessionals working with similar problems;[1] and (b) where the above type of research is unavailable (e.g., in certain types of educational research where it is impossible to develop a "no treatment" control group consisting of children with no schooling), controlled studies examining the differential effects of two or more types of programs operated by professionals, or studies without formal control groups, but utilizing sophisticated "causal" statistical models such as multiple regression analyses to analyze the effects of professional intervention.

The main question this review is examining is: Can professional intervention in the areas delineated above be shown to be effective, that is, to have a positive effect compared to no intervention or nonprofessional intervention, or even to make a significant difference in outcome when various types of professional programs are compared with each other? Now, the main purpose of this review is to determine whether any general conclusions or rules—major directions indicated by the bulk of the evidence—can be derived regarding the research on effectiveness, within and/or across these several fields. Thus, any possible exceptions to these rules—and generally there are bound to be exceptions in the form

---

[1] For a discussion of the similarities and differences between no-treatment controls and other-treated or nonprofessionally treated controls, see Fischer (1976).

of individual studies contradicting general trends—although of potential importance, will not be a central focus here. Of course, by necessity, the criteria used to assess outcome will be those developed within each profession and within each study. Thus, no single superordinate criterion of effectiveness—cutting across all the professions—is available.[2] Thus, the search in this review is for *anything* that "works."

Reviews of Research

In this section, overviews of the findings of the outcome research in the five fields will be presented. Studies were located by beginning with recent reviews of research within each field, utilizing computerized search systems such as MEDLINE and ORBIT, and through the use of abstracting services including *Social Work Abstracts, Psychological Abstracts,* and *Sociological Abstracts.* This review includes research conducted through 1975. Of necessity, individual studies—amounting in the aggregate to several hundred—cannot be presented. Instead, the results of effectiveness research within each area will be summarized with an eye toward developing some general statements regarding outcome research in these fields in the conclusion of this paper. Wherever possible, for the convenience of the reader, since hundreds of studies are involved, reference will be made to sources that contain in-depth reviews and analyses of the individual studies within each of the five areas. Each of these sources can then be perused to obtain the original references and analyses of the individual studies.

Social Work

Social workers operate in perhaps the widest variety of settings with the broadest range of clientele of any of the professional groups reviewed here. The settings include in- and outpatient clinics, hospitals, child and family service agencies, community centers, and schools. The clientele range from low-income minority groups with whom social workers act as facilitators in community organization and advocates to obtain services, to upper middle-class clientele with emotional problems with whom social workers perform the social work variation of psychotherapy—social casework. Social workers work with individuals, families, groups, and communities in an effort to enhance the social functioning of their clientele, using a variety of methods of practice ranging from direct intensive individualized contact to social advocacy. The beginning professional degree in social work is the master of social work (MSW), although, recently, this has been modified to include individuals with BSW degrees and social work experience.

---

[2] For detailed discussion of the issue involved in comparing studies using a variety of definitions of effectiveness, different outcome criteria, and varying samples of professionals and clients, see Fischer (1975a, 1976).

Unfortunately, the results of effectiveness research in social work practice are among the grimmest of all the areas reviewed here.

Seventeen controlled studies of the effectiveness of social work practice in the United States were located, all of which used professional MSW social workers providing services to the experimental group. (Several studies that purport to examine the effectiveness of social work practice—e.g., many of those reviewed in Mullen & Dumpson, 1972—were omitted from this review because services to an experimental group were not provided by practitioners with the professional social work degree or the studies did not have a no-treatment or nonprofessionally treated control.) Each of these studies recently has been described and analyzed in detail by Fischer (1976). The results of those studies are consistent across all types of service programs, all types of clients and problem categories, no matter what the outcome indicator or criterion measure. In none of the studies was there clear evidence that professional social work services produced results superior to no treatment at all, or in any way better than the minimal services provided by nonprofessional workers to a contrast group of clients. Thirteen of the studies clearly showed no differences between the groups. In the additional four studies, definitive conclusions could not be drawn because of major deficiencies in research methodology and design. (For elaboration of these points and related issues, e.g., differences in levels of evidence necessary to draw conclusions with positive versus negative findings, see Fischer, 1976.) In essence, not a single controlled study could be located providing clear evidence that any form of social work is effective.

In analyzing the general effects of any form of intervention, it is possible to overlook other trends in the data. For example, it might be shown that certain clients seen by certain professionals using certain methods may have improved, whereas other combinations of clients by professionals by methods may have been unsuccessful. Reanalysis of the data in these 17 studies does show such a secondary trend, but it is, to say the least, not an encouraging one (see Fischer, 1976, chap. 4, for details of this reanalysis). In 12 of the studies, almost three-quarters of them, clients receiving services from professional social workers were shown to deteriorate.

The deterioration found in these studies involved at least one of three types of phenomena, occurring on one or more of the outcome indicators used in the study: (a) clients in the experimental group fared more poorly than subjects in the control group, even though both groups were comparable at the beginning of treatment; (b) clients in the experimental group demonstrated improved functioning at a lower rate than control subjects, again, with both groups equivalent at pretest; and/or (c) clients in the experimental group scored more negatively at posttest than they had at pretest. These were not readily observable findings, since these data often were buried in the comparisons of general effects between groups. Similarly, the strength of the findings varied between studies; frequently, the differences reached statistical significance, whereas at other times, the deterioration became obvious only when analyzing trends in the data. Nevertheless, the evidence on the presence of deterioration among clients of professional social workers appears sufficiently strong to warrant special attention in future research in an attempt to ferret out the causes of this phenomenon.

Psychotherapy and Counseling

The endeavor of psychotherapy is difficult to define because many of the professionals in the fields reviewed here believe they do "it," but call it by different names. Despite long-standing interprofessional squabbles, there is increasing acceptance of the notion that a broad range of helping professionals engage in psychotherapy, including psychiatrists, social workers, psychologists, counselors, occupational therapists, nurses, and the clergy. However, the bulk of the research that has been identified as "psychotherapy and counseling research" has been conducted with psychiatrists and clinical psychologists, and to a lesser extent, counselors, most of whom have doctorates (MD, PhD, or EdD). The defining characteristic of psychotherapy (this review does not include behavior modification research) seems to be the presence of an intense person-to-person relationship (usually one therapist and one client, although, at times, the therapist works with small groups of clients) in which the therapist attempts, through a combination of the power of his relationship with the client and the application of techniques derived from psychological principles, to help the client modify problematic personal characteristics involving feelings, values, attitudes, and behaviors (Meltzoff & Kornreich, 1970).

Although the research in this area has been extensive—involving well over 100 controlled studies, plus hundreds of less reliably controlled reports—results are frequently ambiguous so that an unequivocal overall conclusion on effectiveness is difficult (see Bergin, 1971, pp. 217–270; Bergin & Suinn, 1975, pp. 509–556; Luborsky, Singer, & Luborsky, 1975; Meltzoff & Kornreich, 1970; Truax & Carkhuff, 1967).

Early reviews of psychotherapy outcome concluded that conventional psychotherapy had not demonstrated its effectiveness (Eysenck, 1952, 1966). These conclusions have been updated and seconded, particularly with regard to traditional, psychodynamically oriented therapies, by more recent reviews (Rachman, 1971).

On the other hand, a review by Meltzoff and Kornreich (1970) of 101 controlled studies concluded that 80% of the studies yielded positive results, with 20% yielding null or negative results. However, those conclusions have been questioned in subsequent publications. Another, apparently pro–behavior therapy (or anti–traditional therapy) reviewer, using most of the same criteria as Meltzoff and Kornreich, reanalyzed the 101 studies and found that only 2 of the 101 studies provided clearcut support for the effectiveness of psychotherapy (Brody, 1972). Another report by a researcher who admits his bias toward viewing results as favorable toward psychotherapy (Luborsky, 1972) concluded that many of the studies reviewed by Meltzoff and Kornreich could not be used to develop reliable conclusions mainly because of design inadequacies (Luborsky et al., 1975). He and his colleagues reviewed 33 controlled studies and concluded that only 20 of these, out of more than 100 controlled studies as reported by Meltzoff and Kornreich and others, show an effect favoring psychotherapy.

Another review of 166 (mainly uncontrolled) outcome studies concluded that client variables seem to be the ones most highly correlated with positive outcome, whereas type of therapy itself was not (Luborsky, Chandler, Auerbach, Cohen, & Bachrach, 1971). Similarly, in reviewing all controlled studies in which any form of psychotherapy was compared with the use of psychopharmacotherapy, the results showed that the psychopharmacological agent alone was superior to psychotherapy alone in 7 studies, there was no difference in 1, and in no studies was psychotherapy found to be superior (Luborsky et al., 1975).

In all, then, it seems as though an unequivocal conclusion about effectiveness cannot be reached; psychotherapy has neither proven its case for effectiveness nor has it been completely refuted. However, it does appear as though the bulk of the research in this area either cannot be used to reach a conclusion, because of design deficiencies, or shows null or negative results. Furthermore, while a tentative conclusion might be that psychotherapy *can* work, because some controlled studies are available with positive results, it is not at all clear that it is psychotherapy—particularly the methods and skills of the therapist—that is the effective ingredient. That is because, as with any study in which an experimental group is contrasted with a control group, it is usually not clear as to what part of the experimental interventions—if it *was* the experimental intervention—led to the successful outcome. It could be the psychotherapy per se, that is, that which psychotherapists presumably have been trained to do, or it could be the therapist's "personality," the attention given to the client, or any combination of these in interaction with client problem and personality. This is further complicated by the fact that while there are some studies showing positive effects for "psychotherapy," the type of therapy usually is undifferentiated. That is, the studies with positive results include such a hodgepodge of methods and approaches, including some that simply are undefined, that no consistent pattern relating any clear type of conventional psychotherapy to positive outcome can be identified. This further bolsters the contention that the positive results may be due more to undefined or nonspecific factors operating in psychotherapy than to the therapy itself.

In addition to the large number of studies showing simply that psychotherapy was not more effective than no treatment, there are other reasons to question the general social value of psychotherapy. In the first place, a considerable body of research has shown that up to 50% of clients drop out of treatment on an unplanned basis after the first interview, and that up to 80% drop out before six interviews (Baekeland & Lundwall, 1975; Briar, 1966, pp. 9–50; Eiduson, 1968; Garfield, 1971, pp. 271–298). Indeed, some studies have reported that only 9 out of every 100 clients assigned to therapy receive the "optimum discharge" evaluation of "maximum benefit: improved" (Graziano & Fink, 1973). Thus, psychotherapy appears to reach—and hold—only a very small percentage of those people who may need it.

A second reason for questioning in general the value of psychotherapy lies in what Bergin (1971, pp. 217–270) calls "the deterioration effect" and Graziano and Fink (1973) call "second-order effects." In the first case, Bergin has reported some 48 studies (some of which showed greater variability, both positive and negative, for the experimental than the control group at posttest) in which some form of deterioration of psychotherapy clients has occurred (Lambert, Bergin, & Collins, 1977). In the second case, the argument is that a variety of negative second-order effects may overweigh in importance even the potential good that psychotherapy may accomplish. These second-order effects include the high dropout rate, labels and sick roles assigned the clients, and the demands imposed by the professional system such as fees and schedules.

It may just be that the clearest conclusion that can be drawn at this stage is that psychotherapy and counseling may be for better or for worse, that is, under some conditions (which, again, future research must attempt to specify) may either help or harm clients (Truax & Carkhuff, 1967). The evidence is clear that psychotherapy is not uniformly effective. Although the research does suggest that psychotherapy or some aspect thereof can be effective, the current state of the literature does not provide a clear answer as to whether or not the potential positive benefits are sufficient to offset the negative side effects and investment of time, energy, and financial resources that also ensue.

Corrections

The correctional (or criminal justice) establishment has long been torn between the opposing camps of rehabilitation and punishment. On one hand, the rehabilitationists argue that only through helping and changing the individual (who has committed or is likely to commit a crime) can any dent be made in the amount of crime in our society. The advocates of punishment argue that it is only through the threat of a long and difficult incarceration (if not capital punishment) that the number of criminal offenses can be decreased. But both groups agree on one central idea: The main purpose of the correctional establishment is to prevent crime, that is, keep new crimes from being committed.

There are a number of ways the correctional establishment seeks to accomplish this with individuals who have already committed crimes. (The putative effects of correctional programs in preventing individuals who have never been apprehended from committing crimes, i.e., deterrence, a phenomenon that has rarely if ever been systematically studied, will not be discussed here; see, e.g., Glaser, 1974; Jeffrey, 1971.) Offenders can be incarcerated rather than placed on probation. They can be incarcerated for longer rather than shorter periods. They can be educated and/or treated in the institution. They can be supervised closely in smaller than normal case loads. And they can be discharged from institutions outright versus supervised on parole (Robison & Smith, 1971). With all these programs, the major indicator of success is recidivism—do individuals recommit crimes and/or are they resentenced to institutions? Although even this presumably simple measure brings with it a variety of methodological and philosophical problems, properly applied, recidivism rates would seem to be the most important single measure of how well correctional programs perform.

The correctional workers who implement these programs include psychiatrists and other physicians, psychologists, social workers, teachers, and a range of "non-professional" personnel including guards, cottage parents, probation and parole officers with varying qualifications, and so on.

Despite the variety of programs available and the disparity in the personnel administering them, the results of controlled research examining the effectiveness of correctional programs have been rather consistent. To date there is no evidence supporting any program's claim of superior rehabilitative efficacy (Robison & Smith, 1971). In examining over 200 studies involving hundreds of thousands of individuals, the correctional programs that have been reported to date appear to have had no appreciable effect on recidivism (Carney, 1977; Martinson, 1974; Shireman, Mann, Larsen, & Young, 1972; Upton, Martinson, & Wilks, 1975; Waldo & Chiricos, 1977).

These programs include educational and vocational training, providing individual counseling and therapy, group counseling, transforming the institutional environment, providing medical treatment, work release, varying the sentence, and decarcerating the convict (providing a variety of forms of treatment and/or intensive supervision in the community). This is not to say that there have been no instances of success in terms of single studies reporting positive results. Rather, these successes have been very few and far between, with little identifiable pattern regarding forms of correctional intervention that are effective upon replication.

The costs of the correctional system, to society and to the inmates it presumably treats, are immense. In fiscal terms alone, support of the criminal justice system amounts to several billion dollars per year with very little return in terms of crime reduction, rehabilitation, or public safety (Raspberry, 1976). In fact, the criminal justice system has its own form of deterioration in that recidivism rates generally tend to be higher the more extensively an individual becomes involved with the system. Although this is almost certainly a result of the interaction between the characteristics of the individuals coming into the system and the programs themselves, such results at best fall short of any deterrent, rehabilitative, or even pragmatic goal for the correctional system, and, at worst, make a mockery of the system.

Psychiatric Hospitalization

In the mid-1960s there was a general belief that the new community mental health center movement would soon make the notion of the psychiatric hospital obsolete. This has not been the case. Although in some areas psychiatric hospitalizations—certainly in the large, stereotypical, custodially oriented state hospitals—have decreased, in others these effects have not uniformly appeared (Chu & Trotter, 1974; Kirk & Therrien, 1975; Wilder, Karasu, & Kligler, 1972). At any rate, one or another form of psychiatric hospitalization is still generally considered to be one of the (if not *the*) key means for dealing with a variety of psychiatric (emotional, behavioral, social) problems.

The experience with psychiatric hospitalization varies widely from geographic area to area. In some locales, hospitalization is limited to 30 days of intensive inpatient care in psychiatric wings of medical hospitals, whereas in others, especially for the poor, large state hospitals with minimal facilities, resources, and staff are the norm. Generally, the staff includes psychiatrists, psychologists, social workers, nurses, specialized therapists (art, dancing, vocational, etc.), and a variety of other nonprofessional staff (who often have the most regular contact with the inmates). In assessing the effectiveness of psychiatric hospitalization, it is usually difficult to separate the interactive effects of staff, program, medications, and hospitalization per se.

Surprisingly, despite the importance of psychiatric hospitalization as a major ingredient in most current conceptions of the resources necessary for the treatment of mental and emotional problems, there has been a rather small amount of research, particularly experimental research, evaluating the efficacy of hospitalization per se. (This is due to the obvious problem in developing a comparable control group of untreated subjects. Most outcome studies in this area tend to be either uncontrolled—e.g., percentages of recidivism—or program comparisons—e.g., hospitalization versus community-based programs.) There are slightly more studies evaluating different types of psychiatric hospitalization (e.g., different therapeutic programs), and a few studies evaluating differences between long-term and short-term hospitalization. (Reviews of studies on psychiatric hospitalization are available in Anthony et al., 1972; Ericson, 1975; Paul, 1969; Stuart, 1970. Additional recent studies include Bockoven & Solomon, 1975; Davis, Dinitz, & Pasamanick, 1974; Dyck, 1974; Glick, Hargreaves, & Goldfield, 1974; Glick, Hargreaves, Raskin, & Kutner, 1975; Herz, Endicott, & Spitzer, 1975; Hogarty, Goldberg, & the Collaborative Study Group, 1973; Hogarty, Goldberg, Schooler, Ulrich, & the Collaborative Study Group, 1974; Lipsius, 1973; Mosher, Menn, & Matthews, 1975; Scheer & Gail, 1974; Smith, Kaplan, & Siker, 1974; Stein, Newton, & Bowman, 1975; Stein, Test, & Marx, 1975.) Most studies use similar outcome criteria: in-hospital changes, recidivism (does the discharged patient return?), and the success of posthospital community adjustment.

The first and most important conclusion that can be formulated from the research is that there is as yet no clear evidence that psychiatric hospitalization is actually necessary. In most instances, when psychiatric hospitalization is contrasted with programs designed to keep people in the community, the community programs prove equal or superior to hospitalization in preventing or reducing future problems. In fact, much of the research suggests that once hospitalized, a high percentage of patients remain hospitalized for several years, if not the rest of their lives. For those who eventually are discharged, up to 50% and more eventually are readmitted. In addition, several studies show that people either do not change when in psychiatric hospitals or, more importantly, that any changes that do come about when in the hospital are not maintained after discharge.

A second finding from research on psychiatric hospitalization is that, with few exceptions, short-term hospitalization is as effective or more effective than long-term hospitalization in reducing or preventing future problems (e.g., recidivism, adjustment problems).

And finally, again with some few exceptions, traditional methods of treating hospitalized patients, including individual therapy, group therapy, work therapy, and drug therapy, do not affect differentially discharged patients' community functioning including recidivism rates (Anthony, 1972).

The rather surprising results on psychiatric hospitalization must be viewed in light of serious potential deterioration effects occurring for those individuals who are eventually hospitalized. These effects include: increased rather than decreased behavioral problems with increasing length of hospitalization; community and self-labeling effects; development of a pattern of chronicity and becoming established in the "patient role," even after eventual discharge; and finally, a possible increase in morbidity rates for hospitalized individuals (Chu & Trotter, 1974; Goffman, 1961, 1963; Spitzer & Denzin, 1968; Stuart, 1970). In view of the fact that many cases of psychiatric hospitalization bear no relation to the extent of the individual's psychiatric problems but to social and cultural variables affecting significant others' willingness to care for them, it appears that demonstrated alternatives to psychiatric hospitalization are available involving a range of community-based programs. Thus, it is not at all clear, and certainly remains unproved, that psychiatric hospitalization—certainly in the form of long-term care, but possibly even in relation to short-term treatment—provides a viable means for dealing with the social and psychological disorders that traditionally were assumed to come under their purview.

Education

Of all the areas of research reviewed here, research on education seems to produce the most interesting reactions in both professionals and the lay public. Perhaps this is due to the fact that virtually every adult in the United States has had some experience with the elementary and secondary educational system, producing a corps of some 150 million "experts" on what is "right" and what is "wrong" in this field.

Indeed, educational research totals thousands of studies each year, including many of the most sophisticated methodologies utilized in the helping professions (for recent reviews, see Shulman, 1976; Travers, 1974). Of those, only a small percentage can be considered studies of effectiveness, yet even this small percentage adds up to a total of several hundred studies.

Fortunately, a number of excellent reviews are available that analyze this research (Averch et al., 1972; Coleman, 1975; Dunkin & Biddle, 1974; Gage, 1972;

Jamison, Suppes, & Wells, 1974; Jencks et al., 1971; Rosenshine & Furst, 1971; Stephens, 1967; Walker & Schaffarzick, 1974). These reviews examine any number of variables potentially affecting educational outcome, including school resources (e.g., teacher characteristics, attributes of the school), background characteristics of students, the effects of differences in curricula, peer influences, and so on. Student outcomes generally involve cognitive achievement measured by scores on standardized tests, although at times noncognitive variables are also examined (e.g., attitudes, motivation).

In no other area reviewed does the expression seem more appropriate that "the effects often are more apparent than real." The facts are that research has not identified a variant of the existing system, including school resources, processes, organization, and aggregate levels of funding, that is consistently related to students' educational outcome (Averch et al., 1972). For example, one review examined research investigating school attendance, instructional television, educational independent study and correspondence courses, size of classes, individual consulting and tutoring, concentrating counseling on selected students, students' involvement, amount of time spent in study, distraction by jobs and extracurricular activities, size of school, qualities of teachers as rated by principals and supervisors, nongraded schools, team teaching, ability grouping, progressivism versus traditionalism, discussion versus lecture, group-centered versus teacher-centered approaches, the use of frequent quizzes, and programmed instruction (Stephens, 1967). None of these variables were found to produce consistent and significant differences in student achievement.

Similarly, two more recent reviews of scores of controlled studies investigating the effectiveness of alternative instructional media and traditional versus innovative curriculum units reached similar conclusions: Each of the programs does equally well, or, none does any better than any other (Jamison et al., 1974; Walker & Schaffarzick, 1974). (The general finding that there appears to be no consistent differences between various methods of instruction as evaluated on the basis of student performance on exams has been replicated with college students as well—Milton, 1972.) In fact, no matter what the type of investigation, the results appear to be the same—no consistent effects of any educational variables on educational outcome. It is results such as these that have led Jencks et al. (1971) in their influential volume, *Inequality*, to conclude that differences between schools and differences between educational programs in schools (e.g., curricula) have rather trivial, if any, long-term effects.

There appears to be one exception to this rule. In study after study, a student's background—socioeconomic status of his family—is shown to have a strong influence on his educational outcome (Averch et al., 1972).

Now, again, as pointed out by several researchers in this field, this is not to say that none of the studies show positive effects of one or another type of educational variable. Rather, it is that there is a general lack of any consistent patterns indicating that varying the nature of the educational inputs of the school would influence student learning to an important degree (Averch et al., 1972; Jamison et al., 1974). However, as Averch et al. put it, these results do not mean that school resources fail to affect student outcomes. It just means that research so far has failed to show that school resources *do* affect student outcomes.

When considered simply in terms of the billions of dollars in educational expenditures alone, these results are at best disquieting. Further, these findings have to be viewed in light of other disturbing occurrences involving the educational system, such as high school dropout rates that range up to 40% to 60% in some schools; the increasing number of lawsuits around the country with regard to parents of high school graduates suing their departments of education because their graduated children cannot read adequately; a significant decline in many students' IQ scores the longer they attend schools ("These Schools Lower I.Q.," 1977); and a recent report by the United States Office of Education which concluded that over 23 million adult Americans, 1 in every 5, lack the basic know-how to function effectively in modern society while another 43 million adults (1 in 3) have just the minimum competence required to be effective citizens, consumers, wage earners, or family members (Wentworth, 1975). This latter study was said to mark a trend among educators to look beyond classroom skills and judge education's effectiveness on the basis of whether Americans are learning to cope with the "real world." The apparent answer: To date, they are not.

Implications

In reviewing the research from these several areas of professional endeavor, the conclusion seems unavoidable that very little if anything has been shown to "work," or, that at best, professionals have had difficulty in demonstrating what works. On criteria selected by the professionals and researchers within each field, the bulk of the research in all the fields shows no apparent overall, significant, positive effect of professional intervention. It is, of course, an unrealistic expectation that *everything* should work, or that *every* study should show positive results of professional services. On the other hand, it appears reasonable to expect that at least a *majority* of the studies in any given field should show positive results before professionals in that area can even begin to believe that, on the whole, they are providing effective services.

On the contrary, however, quite an opposite picture has emerged. In none of the areas of professional endeavor reviewed here—social work practice, psychotherapy and counseling, corrections, psychiatric hospitalization, and elementary and secondary education—do the majority of studies show positive or discriminable effects of professional intervention, or effects supporting the key assumptions regarding professional competence within each field. Studies showing negative or null effects clearly are the rule rather than the exception. In addition, in several of the areas reviewed here, a pattern of deterioration also appears to exist, in which clients of professionals actually do *less* well after receiving services or in comparison with people with similar problems who receive no professional services whatsoever. In essence, to paraphrase Friedson (1970), the claims of "expertise" by many professionals in these fields seem based on *imputed* knowledge and *assumed* effectiveness rather than factual evidence.

The Professional Reaction

As Brown (1968) has noted: "The central finding of a social research study has a disturbing effect when at variance with commonly accepted values. For some, the finding then becomes a challenge to be disputed phrase for phrase; for others, a challenge to reexamine assumptions on which the values rest" (p. 7).

Unfortunately, within each field, as negative findings are reported, the latter type of reaction—in which professionals work to improve services on the basis of research showing the need for improvement—has been a far less common reaction among human services professionals than the former—outrage, derision, emotionality, defensiveness. In fact, since Eysenck (1952) published his first review of the effects of psychotherapy to the present day, the pages of the professional literature have been filled with a litany of common reactions as each profession, in turn, is confronted with the facts of negative findings regarding its practice. (For example, in the field of psychotherapy and counseling, see Astin, 1961; for the field of education, see Moynihan, 1968; for the field of social work, see "Letters to the Editor" and "Points and Viewpoints," 1973.) The negative findings generally are disregarded or ignored; they are discounted or explained away; the research and the researchers are attacked as unprofessional and unscholarly; and, by and large, the professionals in each area continue to practice as they had in the past, unaffected by the findings and, quite possibly, ineffectively.

The problem seems to be that many professionals fail to recognize the difference between *assertions* of effectiveness and *evidence* of effectiveness. What is needed is not declarations by professionals that they are effective, but the production of scientifically acceptable evidence—research showing positive effects of professional intervention—*demonstrating* that they are effective. This is, by and large, what is missing in all of the areas reviewed here. And, as noted in the introduction of this paper, the burden of proof for establishing the efficacy of the services in any field must be on the professionals in those fields.

Some Hypotheses

To say the least, this is a serious situation. But reviewing the research and recognizing that such a situation actually exists does little to explain it, and certainly nothing to remedy it. The first task, then, is attempting to understand just how such a situation could possibly have come about.

It is, of course, difficult, if not impossible, to explain unequivocally all the reasons for the preponderance of null and negative findings in the research on the effectiveness of the helping professions. But a series of explanations, offered here as tentative hypotheses, may provide some basis for more adequately understanding the present state of affairs.

First, and perhaps most obviously, it simply is extremely difficult to overcome the pervasive effects of the natural environment, and a generally oppressive environment at that. This may be the most basic reason of all for the consistent lack of effectiveness of professional intervention. Boiled down to its most essential terms, few if any professionals have contact with their clients or consumers in a way intensive or extensive enough to make changes substantial enough to overcome environmental factors. These factors, though often nonspecific, presumably include family, peer group, and cultural influences, the overall societal system with its attendant social and economic discrimination and deprivations, as well as nonenvironmental but potentially crucial effects of heritability, biochemical or physiological characteristics, and so on.

A second reason—potentially more amenable to control by professionals—lies in the nature of professional education in the United States. In addition to the consistency of the null and negative findings on practice, there are few if any programs of *professional education* in any of the helping professions that have demonstrated in controlled research their success in graduating effective professional practitioners. It often is not clear that the students in graduate programs even learn what they are taught. It rarely if ever has been demonstrated that what they are taught is translatable into effective practice. Thus, a demonstrated empirical basis for professional education in the United States—both in terms of the educational inputs, what is taught, and the outputs or products, presumably competent practitioners—is almost totally absent. Even when innovations (or presumed innovations) are introduced, they often are justified with unsubstantiated "logic" or "theory," and the innovations are disseminated in programs of professional education before they are validated in research (Rosenshine & Furst, 1971).

Thus, not only are the claims of effectiveness by practitioners apparently based largely on myths and wishful thinking, but the claims to competence in *educating* effective practitioners by those who educate professionals appear also to be, if not mythical, largely unsubstantiated.

A third possible explanation that may be related at least in part to the lack of success in demonstrating effective practice—and one obviously closely related to the preceding—involves the hypothesis that the theories and methods used by most professionals in practice are deficient in so many critical areas that the outcome in research and practice could hardly be expected to be any different. As indicated in the introduction to this paper, most of the helping professions covered in this review—in their educational and practice processes—pay more attention to the person of the professional than to what the person actually does. This may be for theoretical, philosophical, and/or practical reasons. But, be these as they may, over the years most of these helping professions have failed to develop a structured technology—techniques and procedures—that can be differentially applied with their clients, consumers, or students, depending on the nature of the client and the problem. Again, this varies somewhat across the professions, from the structure offered by the teacher's curriculum and teaching aids[3] to the almost complete lack of structure for the traditional psychotherapist. But to the extent that this absence of a specific technology does pertain, it would appear to be difficult, if not impossible, for the practitioner to guide and predict change. When approaches to or theories of practice are selected, by individual professionals or entire segments of a profession, they often are selected without the use of any rational or logical criteria whatsoever. Thus, "faith" in the theory, emotional appeal, or the prestige of the theorist may be extremely influential in having new approaches adopted, but rarely are new approaches selected on the basis of research evidence that implementing them will lead to effective practice. The theoretical and practical approaches used by most practitioners apparently receive so much reinforcement from teachers, peers, agencies, consultants, and, intrinsically, from the feeling that one is competent in what he is doing and has made the correct choice, that the potential reinforcement that could come from practice effectiveness—actually making a positive, discernible impact on the problems of the client—is overshadowed. Most of the helping professions have concentrated on theories—from Freud to Piaget to Erikson—that help practitioners understand their clients but not change them, emphasizing diagnosis at the expense of intervention. Thus, systematic ways for professionals to implement their theories—the techniques or procedures, what the practitioner is actually supposed to do—either have been given scant attention or ignored altogether.

This problem in the helping professions might be highlighted in terms suggested by Stone (1975) with regard to the field of mental health. The facts seem to point to a necessary and important distinction between technical services on one hand and personal human care on the other, in that for many of the client problems with which professionals currently deal, it may be that enlightened, humane care is the most effective or only treatment. In fact, as described above, only modest amounts of effective technical expertise exist, and that which does has been exaggerated and greatly oversold in the United States. This has led to the development of a huge array of human services professionals, as reviewed in this paper, few of whom have significant technical skills. Instead, a good deal of what they do is to provide personal care while attempting to attach a meaningful human relationship on what poses as a technical service. And the results of this appear in the literature as a major tendency toward the absence of effective results across all the helping professions.

Finally, one of the possible reasons for the consistent pattern of negative and null results has been, as suggested in the previous section, a general unwillingness of most professionals to be guided in their practice by the results of empirical research. This is especially so in the clinging to old methods of practice largely on the basis of faith and commitment in the face of evidence that the old methods may not be effective. But it also appears to be true, as the following section will

---

[3] Even this has been questioned as not constituting a clear and systematic body of substantive or technical knowledge (see Lortie, 1969).

illustrate, in view of a common unwillingness to examine the potential utility of new methods, even when they are accompanied by evidence of success.

The introduction of this paper presented several criteria for selecting the fields that were included for this review. As this section also has argued, there may be considerable justification for viewing—certainly in their most important respects— these fields and the professionals practicing in them as more similar than dissimilar. All the fields seem to have developed rather weak technological bases for conducting their interventive practices. None of the fields have clear evidence attesting to the effectiveness of their educational processes. And none of the fields—nor the professions involved—have demonstrated clearly through research showing evidence of their effectiveness in providing professional services, the justification for their existence as they are presently constituted.

Does Nothing Work?

The facts are that it does appear that very little "works," that is, that very little of what professionals control—their input—seems to have much of a positive effect on outcome. But that is not to say that absolutely nothing works. In fact, throughout the research across most of the fields, there are some positive exceptions. These exceptions might be categorized into two classes. The first category, as noted in the earlier reviews of research for each field, is the series of inconsistent, but clearly present, positive findings that show up here and there throughout the research. The second category involves those approaches to practice that have produced consistent positive results, whether within one or more of the fields.

The first class of events, the inconsistent positive findings, occurred in almost all of the five fields reviewed. That is to say, with the possible exception of social work practice, each of the fields did produce some studies showing positive results. Of course, their very inconsistency presents serious problems in attempting to determine the meaning of the results and just how important they are. Many of the positive findings were never replicated; either further studies were not conducted on these variables or the studies that were conducted did not reproduce the positive findings. Second, as discussed previously with regard to the field of psychotherapy, often the independent variables were not clearly specified (other than, e.g., just "psychotherapy") so that it is impossible to know just what aspect of the input had the effect. Further, this was complicated by the fact that even when the independent variable was specified, it is not always clear that this was responsible for the positive effects. Other variables (e.g., attention, enthusiasm, the "experimenter effect") may very well have accounted for the results.

Thus, while there is some reason to be encouraged that positive results are possible, there is little reason to be overly optimistic that any substantial, immediate results that could change the overall picture presented here will occur in the near future based solely on the selective use of these inconsistent positive findings.

The second category of positive findings involves those that show up with some consistency, either within one field or across more than one. These too are few and far between, but there are some. Perhaps the most striking of these is the research on behavior modification. Four out of five of the areas reviewed here (with the exception of social work practice which, despite some interest in this area, has yet to produce controlled research documenting positive results for professional social work practitioners using behavior modification) contain a number of studies showing the positive, significant effects of the application of behavior modification procedures. In fact, in the aggregate, there are over 200 controlled studies showing effective results using behavior modification, studies spanning the areas of psychotherapy and counseling, corrections, psychiatric hospitalization, and education (Bergin & Suinn, 1975, pp. 509–556; Craighead et al., 1976; Gambrill, 1977; Kazdin, 1975, 1977; Morrow, 1971; O'Leary & Wilson, 1975; Rimm & Masters, 1974; Robin, 1976). Importantly, a number of these studies utilize factorial designs wherein behavior modification was contrasted with other forms of intervention or where one aspect of a behavioral program (or even of a single technique) was contrasted with another (or with the entire technique). Thus, when positive results are obtained, it often is clear that the technique or program per se is responsible for the change. This conclusion is bolstered by the results of over 150 published, rigorous single case studies using the A-B-A-B reversal design (in which a baseline of occurrence of the target behavior is obtained, the program implemented, then withdrawn, then reimplemented), demonstrating the relationship between the specific techniques or program used and the resulting outcome.

Now there are several other reasons—in addition to effectiveness—as to why behavior modification appears to be a crucial addition to the armamentarium of the practitioners in the fields under review here. There is generally a clear connection between assessment and intervention using behavior modification. Once the problem is analyzed, there are relatively clear guidelines as to what the practitioner should do. More particularly, the field of behavior modification offers specific, structured techniques to implement in practice, a clear technology that goes beyond (but does not ignore) the "professional use of self." The principles and procedures of behavior modification are clear and easily communicated; they can be taught readily to professionals and lay people alike. In fact, this latter point, permitting, even necessitating, the use of mediators in the natural environment (e.g., parents, teachers), geometrically increases professionals' potential for helping their clients by the fact that they do not have to deal with each one themselves. Behavior modification allows, and frequently consists of, environmental intervention, working in the situations where the problems actually occur, and systematically applying empirically demonstrated laws of behavior to the altering of human problems. Behavior modification also tends to be more efficient than traditional approaches. And, finally, behavior modification is applicable to a wide range of clients and problems, cutting across the concerns of all the helping professions in all five of the areas reviewed here. So it seems as though behavior modification may be able to fill a number of the technological and empirical gaps in the approaches that currently are being used by many practitioners in these five fields.

However, there are several factors—both of a philosophical and empirical nature—mitigating against the helping professions becoming unduly enamored with the field of behavior modification. The first, simply stated, is that overallegiance to one approach often precludes examining new approaches as they become available, even new approaches with evidence of effectiveness. The history of the helping professions clearly demonstrates the problems professionals have had in giving up cherished old ideas when new and better ideas become available. Some 15 years ago, behavior modification was in its infancy—virtually unknown. Fifteen years from now it is difficult to predict what new technologies will become available. But whatever does appear must be evaluated as objectively as possible, free from the shackles of clinging to one and only one approach, whether it be behavior modification or any other orientation.

A second reason for not adopting behavior modification, at least as a sole approach, lies in the findings of research on behavior modification. Frequently, the effectiveness research on behavior modification falls short of really demonstrating effectiveness—at least on the target variables of most concern. In many studies, there is clear evidence that behavior modification can change behavior, but the behavior may not be the most socially significant outcome behavior, or the positive results do not generalize to the natural environment. This is most apparent in the corrections and psychiatric hospitalization areas but, to lesser degrees, has occurred at times in other areas as well (see, e.g., O'Donnell, 1977; Kazdin, 1977; Forehand & Atkeson, 1977). Thus, as an example, in corrections, the key question is: Will recidivism be reduced? Behaviorists have conducted a score of controlled studies showing effective use of behavior modification to change selected behaviors in the field of corrections; but, of these, only a handful actually address recidivism. (For reviews of this research, see Braukman & Fixsen, 1975, pp. 191–231; Davidson & Seidman, 1974; Milan & McKee, 1974, pp. 745–776.) Similarly, in the psychiatric hospitalization literature, it is clear that behavioral procedures implemented in hospitals have a significant effect on changing patient behavior, but rare indeed are the studies that show the use of behavior modification leading to substantially increased discharge rates and substantially better community adjustment or recidivism rates (Kazdin, 1977).

These problems often are not the case in the other fields. Often the positive effects of working with specific behaviors generalize to more global areas or to the natural environment, and even more often, the specific behaviors *are* the problem. However, it is still essential for behaviorists to demonstrate clearly and convincingly that changing a series of specific behaviors, as they are able to do, is going to have a substantial effect on more serious and more important dimensions (such as recidivism in hospitals and correctional institutions). Thus, behaviorists must demonstrate in all these areas the rigor and the relevance that they demand of researchers and practitioners from other approaches.

A third and final reason for not being tied to only one approach such as behavior modification, despite its impressive record of achievements, is that there *are* other approaches with evidence of success. As one example (see Fischer, 1978, for other examples of approaches to therapeutic practice with evidence of effectiveness), there is a substantial body of research, including studies in four of the five areas of professional endeavor described here (again, with social work practice as the exception), illustrating the significant and positive effects of the communication of the interpersonal skills of empathy, warmth, and genuineness on a range of client and student behaviors (Aspy & Roebuck, 1974a, 1974b; Carkhuff, 1969, 1971; Carkhuff & Berenson, 1976; Truax & Carkhuff, 1967; Truax & Mitchell, 1971, pp. 299–344). Further, these interpersonal skills demonstrably can be learned in special training courses and workshops (Fischer, 1975b). Now the research on these communication skills is neither as extensive nor as elegant as much of the behavioral research. But it *is* available, and appears, with a few exceptions, to show a fair consistency in obtaining positive effects. In fact, there is an increasing body of research showing that individuals who communicate high levels of empathy, warmth, and genuineness are also more effective in applying behavior modification, an interesting and potentially very important combination of interpersonal skills (relationship) and use of a structured technology (techniques) (Cairns, 1972; Dowling & Frantz, 1975; Harris & Lichenstein, 1971; Mickelson & Stevic, 1971; Morris & Suckerman, 1974a, 1974b; Namenek & Schuldt, 1971; Vitalo, 1970).

Now the point of this discussion is not to suggest that behavior modification and empathy, warmth, and genuineness are "the last word" as approaches for the helping professions. Rather, it is to emphasize that there are approaches such as these and others that increasingly are becoming available that auger very well for increasing the effectiveness of professionals based on research evidence of their success, and that the key job of every professional may simply be to be open to such new approaches as they are developed.

Toward Effective Practice: One Way or Another

The case against the overall effectiveness of practitioners in the helping professions included in this survey is a strong if not overwhelming one. Is it necessary, then, to admit defeat and crawl away from the scene of the battle? Or are there some options?

In fact there may be some ways to begin to address these issues and to bring about an increase in the general effectiveness of practice.

Perhaps the first step professionals may have to take is to rid themselves of the "rescue fantasy" that they can help everyone with everything. This may require the recognition that "personal care" may just be the best available "intervention" for a range of cases for which technical expertise simply is not sufficiently developed. At the same time, one major thrust of research may best be addressed to the question of variability of effects, specifically, attempting to determine which clients and problems really can be helped by professionals in their respective areas and then doing the best they can in those situations.

Second, professionals have to recognize their responsibility not only to treatment of individual clients but to changing social conditions, whether this means improving the humanity of our institutions, redistributing income, or eliminating discriminatory practices. There are several hundred thousand helping professionals in the groups included here. If all these people spent just 10% of their time working to improve social conditions, this could be one of the potentially more potent forces in the country involved in pressing for social change. The implications of this, of course, are that such social action also may have an important effect on reducing the incidence and prevalence of the problems with which many of the professionals included in this review are mainly concerned in their everyday practice—those problems that tend to call forth individualized rehabilitative or therapeutic efforts from professionals.

Third, helping professionals may just have to face the fact that some of their work is akin to that of the physician attempting to treat an incurable illness while continuing to hope for the best. In many instances, professionals simply do not know enough to affect significantly the problems with which they are dealing. Professionals just may have to recognize that many of their efforts and programs are based more on their values and philosophy than on anything else, content themselves with that fact, and attempt to educate the public about it.

Fourth, it may be that, in many instances, an outcome criterion of cost-efficiency will have to be substituted for one of effectiveness. In the absence of clear evidence that one or another approach is more effective, it may just be that the approach that is least expensive and does whatever it is supposed to do the quickest is the most desirable alternative. Thus, to the extent that the helping professions advocate for new programs or insist on the retention of old programs—whether these be of a therapeutic or educational nature—the value of these programs might best be judged by the criterion of what costs the least and/or does its job the fastest.

Finally, it seems crucial that helping professionals come to adopt more of an empirical model in both their training and practice endeavors. Although, as the options above are intended to suggest, improving the technological base of practice likely will not be sufficient to achieve success in all circumstances and with all problems, moving toward a more empirically based orientation may be a key to instituting a system for invigorating the practice of professionals in the direction of increased effectiveness in a substantial part of the areas of practice reviewed here. Although approaches with some degree of success are available, as reviewed previously, the approaches themselves are not the essence of the model. What is of particular importance is the model per se: emphasis on specifying inputs and outputs, development of technology, careful monitoring and evaluation of process and outcome and the relationship of process to outcome. Indeed, an emphasis on empiricism may mean that professionals are going to have to begin eschewing their cherished theories, moving toward an approach in the future that is composed largely of empirically derived and verified principles and procedures tied together by only one major proposition: Their application in practice leads to successful results with clients.

Such an orientation to practice actually has two main components. The first involves the use of approaches with evidence of effectiveness that may already be available, including the identification and weaving together of different threads in the research literature that hold the greatest degree of promise. (For an example from the field of education of the attempt to review research with the goal of developing an empirical approach to practice, see Dunkin & Biddle, 1974; for a similar attempt in the field of social work, see Fischer, 1978.) This is a massive undertaking requiring the commitment of researchers to identify and study such empirically grounded material, the commitment of educators to teach it, and the commitment of practitioners to practice it.

The second component of this orientation requires the development of *new* techniques and approaches to practice. This probably can best proceed by increased utilization of a new and rapidly developing technology of research investigation in which intensive study of single cases using a variety of rigorous case study research models is used in the development and evaluation of techniques as they are applied in actual practice. (For a detailed review of different models of intensive single case study designs, see Hersen & Barlow, 1976; see also Glass, Willson, & Gottman, 1972; Gottman, 1973; Gottman, McFall, & Burnett, 1969; Howe, 1974; Klein, Hapkiewicz, & Roden, 1973.) These designs provide immediate feedback to practitioners, necessitate the examination of variability and individualization of effects, and are carried out by practitioners themselves rather than by researchers who may be removed from practice, and whose efforts often are imposed on practitioners by administrative fiat. Such evaluations can be and already are being used with considerable success by some practitioners in all five areas of professional practice reviewed here, and their widespread use would auger well for an increase in the body of knowledge that can be applied with clients with some certainty that successful outcome would be achieved.

Another advantage to the use of rigorous single case study designs is that the results of numerous successful replications can be used to inform the more broadly based group experimental studies such as were reviewed in this article, which then can be conducted with a greater degree of certainty that effective results would ensue. Thus, these two types of research strategies—single case study designs and group experimental designs—can be used to complement each other. The point is that a moratorium on the use of group experimental designs, particularly to study traditional methods and programs, may be necessary. Such research already has provided invaluable information, although, with the exceptions noted above, largely about what does not work. But a more creative use of experimental design is called for: informed by the results of other research such as single case studies, comparing new and/or different practice methods with each other, and using more sophisticated forms of data analysis such as path analysis and Bayesian analysis to track down specific variables that may be related to success and failure in professional interventions (Jones & Borgatta, 1972, pp. 39–54).

This requires receptiveness on the part of professionals to new approaches if and when they become available. It means a willingness to maintain familiarity with the literature concerning the development of new approaches, and to use those approaches whether they were developed within the context of their own favorite theories or not, or even whether or not they were developed by members of one's own profession. And it means a willingness to be guided in practice by what is effective for clients with only one bias: to find out what will work and use it.

All of the above is predicated on the assumption that measures such as these—at least as starting points—will work, that is, will have some identifiable impact on improving the effectiveness of the services of the helping professions. But, these measures may, in fact, be too little and too late, and if they are, this presents a serious question as to whether or not the helping professions, in their present form at least, are obsolete, and should even endure.

But to the extent they do endure, the measures suggested above can be identified as a potential imperative for change from within the helping professions. That is, these changes would be based on the recognition by professionals that changes such as these, but certainly not limited to the specifics proposed above, are necessary, in fact, are unavoidable.

But there is another imperative for change. It is likely that unless the professionals in the several fields reviewed here can bring about such changes as described above—that is, changes geared to enhancing effectiveness and eventually demonstrating that effectiveness—such changes may be imposed on the helping professions from without. The public in general, and the government in particular, assuming that the helping professions do survive in a semblance of their present form, is unlikely to stand still in the face of continuing evidence of such a pervasive lack of effectiveness. Thus, failure to set standards *within* the helping professions is an open invitation for others to do so.

This could come in the form of federal standards for competence; regulations mandating periodic updating of knowledge and/or examinations; requirements for professionals to establish guidelines as to what they consider effective practice to be; the use of some system of peer, collegial, team, and/or consumer review; and the insistence on evaluation to determine whether those standards and guidelines have been achieved. All of this, initially at least, likely would be based on making funding contingent on implementation of these plans.

Is this taken from some Orwellian nightmare or from the regulations of some totalitarian nation? Not at all. In fact, such policies already have been approved and are beginning to be implemented with physicians in the United States through Public Law 92-603 passed in 1972 as an amendment to the Social Security Act. This law has mandated the establishment of Professional Standards Review Organizations charged with the development of programs to assure quality of care and cost-effectiveness and to ensure that physicians maintain their skills and have up-to-date knowledge. A main feature of this program involves peer review, but the law also makes provision for including nonphysician personnel in the review system (Decker & Bonner, 1975; Gosfield, 1975; Sullivan, 1974).

Although many physicians strongly protested this law, it is currently being implemented around the country, having passed the ultimate hurdle of the Supreme Court ("Review for Doctors," 1975). In fact, the law was hailed by many nonphysician professionals as an excellent way of ensuring more effective medical care. How different, then, is the case for just such legislation and the ensuing standards for any of the helping professions?

As mentioned previously, the human services professions never developed a tradition of basing even part of their practice on the results of research. In fact, many professionals appear to be so resistant to research findings—especially when they are negative but often even when they are positive—that major structural or institutional changes appear necessary in order to alter that pattern. Now, the point here is not to advocate for such a system of legislated and externally enforced accountability. Rather, it is that such changes would seem more desirable when initiated from within the helping professions rather than from without. But the point also is that, unless such changes *are* initiated, the public and government may not, indeed probably would be unwise to, wait much longer.

References

Anthony, W. A., Buell, G. J., Sharrat, S., & Altoff, M. E. Efficacy of psychiatric rehabilitation. *Psychological Bulletin*, 1972, *78*, 447–456.

Aspy, D. N., & Roebuck, F. N. From humane ideas to human technology and back again many times. *Education*, 1974, *95*, 163–171. (a)

Aspy, D. N., & Roebuck, F. N. *Research summary: Effects of training in interpersonal skills* Interim Report No. 4). National Institutes of Health, National Consortium for Humanizing Education, 1974. (b)

Astin, A. W. The functional autonomy of psychotherapy. *American Psychologist*, 1961, *16*, 75–79.

Averch, H. A., Carroll, S. J., Donaldson, T. S., Kiesling, H. J., & Pinvus, J. *How effective is schooling? A critical review and synthesis of research findings.* Santa Monica, Calif.: Rand Corporation, 1972.

Baekeland, F., & Lundwall, L. Dropping out of treatment: A critical review. *Psychological Bulletin*, 1975, *82*, 738–783.

Bergin, A. E. The evaluation of therapeutic outcomes. In A. E. Bergin & S. L. Garfield (Eds.), *Handbook of psychotherapy and behavior change: An empirical analysis.* New York: John Wiley, 1971.

Bergin, A. E., & Suinn, R. M. Individual psychotherapy and behavior therapy. In *Annual Review of Psychology.* Palo Alto, Calif.: Annual Reviews, 1975.

Bockoven, S., & Solomon, H. C. Comparison of two five-year follow-up studies: 1947 to 1952 and 1967–1972. *American Journal of Psychiatry*, 1975, *132*, 796–801.

Braukman, C. J., & Fixsen, D. L. Behavior modification with delinquents. In M. Hersen (Ed.), *Progress in behavior modification.* New York: Academic Press, 1975.

Briar, S. Family services. *Five fields of social services.* New York: National Association of Social Workers, 1966.

Briar, S. The age of accountability. *Social Work*, 1973, *18*.

Brody, N. *Personality: Research and theory.* New York: Academic Press, 1972.

Brown, G. E. (Ed.) *The multi-problem dilemma.* Metuchen, N.J.: Scarecrow Press, 1968.

Cairns, K. *Desensitization and relationship quality.* Unpublished master's thesis, University of Calgary, Alberta, Canada, 1972.

Carkhuff, R. R. *Helping and human relations* (2 vols.). New York: Holt, Rinehart & Winston, 1969.

Carkhuff, R. R. *The development of human resources.* New York: Holt, Rinehart & Winston, 1971.

Carkhuff, R. R., & Berenson, B. G. *Teaching as treatment.* Amherst, Mass.: Human Resource Development Press, 1976.

Carney, L. P. *Corrections and the community.* Englewood Cliffs, N.J.: Prentice-Hall, 1977.

Chu, F. D., & Trotter, S. *The madness establishment.* New York: Grossman, 1974.

Coleman, J. S. Methods and results in the I.E.A. studies of effects of school on learning. *Review of Educational Research,* 1975, *45,* 335–386.

Craighead, W. E., et al. *Behavior modification: Principles, issues, and applications.* Boston: Houghton Mifflin, 1976.

Davidson, W. S., & Seidman, E. Studies of behavior modification and juvenile delinquency: A review, methodological critique and social perspective. *Psychological Bulletin,* 1974, *81,* 998–1011.

Davis, A. E., Dinitz, S., & Pasamanick, B. *Schizophrenics in the new custodial community: Five years after the experiment.* Columbus: Ohio State University Press, 1974.

Decker, B. & Bonner, P. (Eds.) PSRO: *Organization for regional peer review.* Cambridge, Mass.: Ballinger, 1975.

Dowling, T. H., & Frantz, T. T. The influence of facilitative relationship on imitative learning. *Journal of Counseling Psychology,* 1975, *22,* 259–263.

Dunkin, M. J., & Biddle, B. J. *The study of teaching.* New York: Holt, Rinehart & Winston, 1974.

Dyck, G. The effect of a community mental health center upon state hospital utilization. *American Journal of Psychiatry,* 1974, *131,* 453–456.

Eiduson, B. T. Retreat from help. *American Journal of Orthopsychiatry,* 1968, *38,* 910–916.

Erickson, R. C. Outcome studies in mental hospitals: A review. *Psychological Bulletin,* 1975, *82,* 519–540.

Eysenck, H. J. The effects of psychotherapy: An evaluation. *Journal of Consulting Psychology,* 1952, *16,* 319–324.

Eysenck, H. J. *The effects of psychotherapy.* New York: International Science Press, 1966.

Fischer, J. *Analyzing research: A guide for social workers.* Honolulu: University of Hawaii, 1975(a).

Fischer, J. Training for effective therapeutic practice. *Psychotherapy: Theory, Research, and Practice,* 1975(b), *12,* 118–123.

Fischer, J. *The effectiveness of social casework.* Springfield, Ill.: Charles C. Thomas, 1976.

Fischer, J. *Effective casework practice: An eclectic approach.* New York: McGraw-Hill, 1978.

Forehand, R. & Atkeson, B. M. Generality of treatment effects with parents as therapists: A review of assessment and implementation procedures. *Behavior Therapy*, 1977, *8*, 575–593.

Friedson, E. *Professional dominance.* New York: Atherton Press, 1970.

Gage, N. L. *Teacher effectiveness and teacher education: The search for a scientific basis.* Palo Alto, Calif.: Pacific Books, 1972.

Gambrill, E. D. *Behavior modification: Handbook of assessment, intervention, and evaluation.* San Francisco: Jossey-Bass, 1977.

Garfield, S. L. Research on client variables in psychotherapy. In A. E. Bergin & S. L. Garfield (Eds.), *Handbook of psychotherapy and behavior change: An empirical analysis.* New York: John Wiley, 1971.

Glaser, D. (Ed.) *Handbook of criminology.* Chicago: Rand McNally, 1974.

Glass, G. V., Willson, V. L., & Gottman, J. M. *Design and analysis of time-series experiments.* Boulder: Laboratory of Educational Research, University of Colorado, 1972.

Glick, I. D., Hargreaves, W. A., & Goldfield, M. D. Short vs long hospitalization. A prospective controlled study: I. The preliminary results of a one-year follow-up of schizophrenics. *Archives of General Psychiatry*, 1974, *30*, 363–369.

Glick, I. D., Hargreaves, W. A., Raskin, M., & Kutner, S. J. Short versus long hospitalization: A prospective controlled study. II. Results for schizophrenic inpatients. *American Journal of Psychiatry*, 1975, *132*, 385–390.

Goffman, E. *Asylums.* New York: Doubleday, 1961.

Goffman, E. *Stigma.* Englewood Cliffs, N.J.: Prentice-Hall, 1963.

Gosfield, A. *PSROs: The law and the health consumer.* Cambridge, Mass.: Ballinger, 1975.

Gottman, J. M. N-of-one and N-of-two research in psychotherapy. *Psychological Bulletin*, 1973, *80*, 93–105.

Gottman, J. M., McFall, R. M., & Burnett, J. T. Design and analysis of research using time series. *Psychological Bulletin*, 1969, *72*, 299–306.

Graziano, A. M., & Fink, R. S. Second order effects in mental health treatment. *Journal of Consulting and Clinical Psychology*, 1973, *40*, 356–364.

Harris, D. E. & Lichenstein, E. *The contribution of non-specific social variables to a successful behavioral treatment of smoking.* Paper presented at the annual meeting of the Western Psychological Association, San Francisco, April, 1971.

Hersen, M., & Barlow, D. H. *Single case experimental designs.* New York: Pergamon Press, 1976.

Herz, M. I., Endicott, J., & Spitzer, R. L. Brief hospitalization of patients with families: Initial results. *American Journal of Psychiatry*, 1975, *132*, 413–418.

Hogarty, G. E., Goldberg, S. C., & the Collaborative Study Group, Baltimore.

Drug and sociotherapy in the aftercare of schizophrenic patients. *Archives of General Psychiatry*, 1973, *28*, 54–64.

Hogarty, G. E., Goldberg, S. C., Schooler, N. R., Ulrich, R. F., & the Collaborative Study Group. Drug and sociotherapy in the aftercare of schizophrenic patients. *Archives of General Psychiatry*, 1974, *31*, 603–618.

Howe, M. W. Casework self evaluation: A single subject approach. *Social Service Review*, 1974, *48*, 1–23.

Jamison, D., Suppes, P., & Wells, S. The effectiveness of alternative instructional media: A survey. *Review of Educational Research*, 1974, *44*, 1–67.

Jeffrey, C. R. *Crime prevention through environmental design.* Beverly Hills, Calif.: Sage Publications, 1971.

Jencks, C., et al. *Inequality: A reassessment of the effect of family and schooling in America.* New York: Basic Books, 1971.

Jones, W. C., & Borgatta, E. J. Methodology of evaluation. In E. J. Mullen & J. R. Dumpson (Eds.), *Evaluation of social intervention.* San Francisco: Jossey-Bass, 1972.

Kazdin, A. E. *Behavior modification in applied settings.* Homewood, Ill.: Dorsey Press, 1975.

Kazdin, A. E. *The token economy.* New York: Plenum, 1977.

Kirk, S. A., & Therrien, M. E. Community mental health myths and the fate of former hospitalized patients. *Psychiatry*, 1975, *28*, 209–217.

Klein, R. D., Hapkiewicz, W. G., & Roden, A. H. (Eds.) *Behavior modification in educational settings.* Springfield, Ill.: Charles C. Thomas, 1973.

Lambert, M. J., Bergin, A. E., & Collins, J. L. Therapist-induced deterioration in psychotherapy. In A. S. Gurman & A. M. Razin (Eds.), *Effective psychotherapy: A handbook.* New York: Pergamon, 1977, 452–481.

Letters to the editor, and Points and viewpoints. *Social Work*, March 1973, May 1973, July 1973, *18*.

Lipsius, S. H. Judgment of alternatives to hospitalizations. *American Journal of Psychiatry*, 1973, *130*, 892–896.

Lortie, D. The balance of control and autonomy in elementary school teaching. In A. Etzioni (Ed.), *The semi-professions and their organization.* New York: Free Press, 1969.

Luborsky, L. Another reply to Eysenck. *Psychological Bulletin*, 1972, *78*, 406–408.

Luborsky, L., Chandler, M., Auerbach, A. H., Cohen, J., & Bachrach, H. Factors influencing the outcome of psychotherapy: A review of quantitative research. *Psychological Bulletin*, 1971, *75*, 145–185.

Luborsky, L., Singer, B., & Luborsky, L. Comparative studies of psychotherapies: Is it true that everyone has won and all must have prizes? *Archives of General Psychiatry*, 1975, *32*, 995–1008.

Martinson, R. What works?—Questions and answers about prison reform. *Public Interest*, 1974, *35*, 22–54.

Meltzoff, J., & Kornreich, M. *Research in psychotherapy.* New York: Atherton Press, 1970.

Mickelson, D. J., & Stevic, R. R. Differential effects of facilitative and non-facilitative behavioral counselors. *Journal of Counseling Psychology*, 1971, *18*, 314–319.

Milan, M. A., & Mckee, J. M. Behavior modification: Principles and applications in corrections. In D. Glaser (Ed.), *Handbook of criminology*. Chicago: Rand McNally, 1974.

Milton, O. *Alternatives to the traditional*. San Francisco: Jossey-Bass, 1972.

Morris, R. J., & Suckerman, K. R. The importance of the therapeutic relationship in systematic desensitization. *Journal of Consulting and Clinical Psychology*, 1974, *42*, 148. (a)

Morris, R. J., & Suckerman, K. R. Therapist warmth as a factor in automated systematic desensitization. *Journal of Consulting and Clinical Psychology*, 1974, *42*, 244–250. (b)

Morrow, W. R. *Behavior therapy bibliography*. Columbia: University of Missouri Press, 1971.

Mosher, L. R., Menn, A., & Matthews, S. M. Soteria: Evaluation of a home-based treatment for schizophrenia. *American Journal of Orthopsychiatry*, 1975, *45*, 455–467.

Moynihan, D. F. Sources of resistance to the Coleman Report. *Harvard Educational Review*, Winter 1968.

Mullen, E. J., & Dumpson, J. R. (Eds.) *Evaluation of Social Intervention*, San Francisco: Jossey-Bass, 1972.

Namenek, A. A., & Schuldt, W. J. Differential effects of experimenters' personality and instructional sets on verbal conditioning. *Journal of Counseling Psychology*, 1971, *18*, 173–176.

O'Donnell, C. R. Behavior modification in community settings. In M. Hersen et al. (Eds.), *Progress in behavior modification* (Vol. 4). New York: Academic Press, 1977.

O'Leary, K. D., & Wilson, G. T. *Behavior therapy: Application and outcome*. Englewood Cliffs, N.J.: Prentice-Hall, 1975.

Paul, G. L. Chronic mental patient: Current status—Future directions. *Psychological Bulletin*, 1969, *71*, 81–94.

Rachman, S. *The effects of psychotherapy*. Oxford: Pergamon Press, 1971.

Raspberry, W. High cost of "Storing" prisoners. *Honolulu Advertiser*, January 12, 1976.

Review for doctors. *Time*, December 1, 1975, p. 63.

Rimm, D. C., & Masters, J. C. *Behavior therapy: Techniques and empirical findings*. New York: Academic Press, 1974.

Robin, A. L. Behavioral instruction in the college classroom. *Review of Educational Research*, 1976, *46*, 313–354.

Robison, J., & Smith, G. The effectiveness of correctional programs. *Crime and Delinquency*, 1971, *17*, 67–80.

Rosenshine, B., & Furst, N. F. Research on teacher performance criteria. In

B. O. Smith (Ed.), *Research in teacher education: A symposium.* Englewood Cliffs, N.J.: Prentice-Hall, 1971.

Scheer, N. B., & Gail, M. A comparison of patients discharged against medical advice with a matched control group. *American Journal of Psychiatry,* 1974, *131*, 1217–1220.

Shireman, C. H., Mann, K. B., Larsen, C., & Young, T. Findings from experiments in treatment in the correctional institution. *Social Service Review,* 1972, *46*, 38–59.

Shulman, L. (Ed.) *Review of research in education* (Vol. 4). Itasca, Ill.: F. E. Peacock, 1976.

Smith, W. G., Kaplan, J., & Siker, D. Community mental health and the seriously disturbed patient. *Archives of General Psychiatry,* 1974, *30*, 693–696.

Spitzer, S., & Denzin, N. K. *The mental patient: Studies in the sociology of deviance.* New York: McGraw-Hill, 1968.

Stein, L. I., Newton, J. R., & Bowman, R. S. Duration of hospitalization for alcoholism. *Archives of General Psychiatry,* 1975, *32*, 247–252.

Stein, L. I., Test, M., & Marx, A. J. Alternative to the hospital: A controlled study. *American Journal of Psychiatry,* 1975, *132*, 517–522.

Stephens, J. M. *The process of schooling.* New York: Holt, Rinehart & Winston, 1967.

Stone, A. A. *Mental health and the law: A system in transition.* National Institute of Mental Health, Center for Studies in Crime and Delinquency, 1975.

Strupp, H. H., Hadley, S. W., & Gomes-Schwartz, B. *Psychotherapy for better or worse.* New York: Aronson, 1977.

Stuart, R. B. *Trick or treatment.* Champaign, Ill.: Research Press, 1970.

Sullivan, F. S. Professional Standards Review Organizations: The current scene. *American Journal of Psychiatry,* 1974, *131*, 1354–1358.

These schools lower I.Q. *Honolulu Advertiser,* October 1977, Cl.

Travers, R. M. W. *Second handbook of research on teaching.* Chicago: Rand McNally, 1974.

Tropp, E. Expectation, performance and accountability. *Social Work,* 1974, *19*, 139–149.

Truax, C. B., & Carkhuff, R. R. *Toward effective counseling and psychotherapy.* Chicago: Aldine, 1967.

Truax, C. B., & Mitchell, K. Research on certain therapist interpersonal skills in relation to process and outcome. In A. E. Bergin & S. L. Garfield (Eds.), *Handbook of psychotherapy and behavior change.* New York: John Wiley, 1971.

Upton, D., Martinson, R., & Wilks, J. *The effectiveness of correctional treatment.* New York: Praeger, 1975.

Vitalo, R. L. Effects of facilitative interpersonal functioning in a conditioning paradigm. *Journal of Counseling Psychology,* 1970, *17*, 141–144.

Waldo, G. P., & Chiricos, T. G. Work release and recidivism: An empirical evaluation of a social policy. *Evaluation Quarterly,* 1977, *1*, 87–108.

Walker, DQ. F., & Schaffarzicu, J. Comparing curricula. *Review of Educational Research*, 1974, *44*, 83–111.

Wentworth, E. 23 Million U.S. adults can't cope. *Honolulu Advertiser*, November 2, 1975.

Wilder, J. F., Karasu, B., & Kligler, D. The hospital "dumping syndrome": Causes and treatment. *American Journal of Psychiatry*, 1972, *128*, 1446–1449.

Part 2

The 1980s: Building on Foundations

The difficulty lies, not in new ideas, but in escaping the old ones.
—John Maynard Keynes

False views, if supported by some evidence, do little harm, for everyone takes a salutary pleasure in proving their falseness; and when this is done, one path toward error is closed and the road to truth is often at the same time opened.
—Charles Darwin

As I stated in the preface, the organization of the book into decades is somewhat arbitrary, a device to impose some order on these chapters. Sometimes changes in professions and disciplines occur in fits and starts, sometimes they occur smoothly over time. However, one can see in this organization and in the flow of chapters why I subtitled the book, *Variations on a Theme*. The theme is the quest for increasingly more effective practice. The vocabulary changes over time; the latest vocabulary entry is Evidence-Based Practice (E-BP). I don't for a second believe that E-BP will be the end of this evolutionary development of social work vocabulary and social work knowledge. And perhaps that is the key here: Our changes over time have been more *evolutionary* than *revolutionary*! I realize that with that statement I am contradicting some of the work I will be presenting in this part, material I described as "revolutionary" at the time. But the hindsight that this book has necessitated has clarified a lot for me. I was criticized by some at the time for saying social work was in the midst of a revolution. I defended my position as more right than their position. In retrospect, just by looking at the trend of my own work, I can see that *they* probably were a little more right, at least about the notion that the changes were evolutionary, and it looks as though *I* was wrong . . . a little (so hard to admit!) However, I can provide *some* evidence, at least, that even at the time, I think I realized that the predominant issue was *not* whether the changes were revolutionary, but, rather, were they *real* changes; see "Revolution, Schmevolution: Is Social Work Changing or Not?" (Fischer, 1984).

Oh well; you live and learn.

It seemed to me, when reviewing work for this book, that this decade did have a predominant theme. If I were being melodramatic, I might call it "a profession in search of a knowledge base." However, I would prefer to eschew such fireworks, and instead suggest that our field was in a state of questioning: questioning the research and the researchers (see the epilogue, please), questioning our traditional knowledge base, questioning the need to look outside of social work for some answers (despite our obviously pluralistic knowledge base); and questioning how and whether our field could build on some of the issues raised in the prior decade to produce meaningful changes in finding more effective ways of conducting practice.

The work presented in this part was an attempt to address some of the issues raised in the 1970s as I, too, struggled with these very questions. In the 1980s, I attempted to propose some responses to the questions raised by the work in the 1970s. I hesitate today to use the word "answers" and prefer to call them "responses," though I was convinced at the time that these *were* answers that virtually were right in front of us.

So, what was some of the work that addressed these issues as I saw them at the time? And didn't this work really build on the foundations established in the prior decade? I think it did.

Chapters in Part 2

Chapter eight is titled, "Research and Knowledge-Building: The Case for Research Reviews." This chapter presents the notion that the increasing amount of research that was becoming available at the time may be too voluminous to master one study at a time (see also the introduction to part four). Therefore, the need to be diligent in conducting research *reviews* and being able to read and evaluate them seemed to me to be a paramount task for social workers. (I still agree with that principle, which is at the heart of Evidence-Based Practice, but as chapter fifteen shows, research reviews have changed dramatically over the years.) Research reviews also are placed in the context of an overall model for knowledge-building for effective intervention practices.

Chapter nine is titled "Increasing the Relevance of Research Education," by the late Walter Hudson and me. This chapter is the first of two (the second is chapter fourteen) that examine the research curricula in schools of social work and propose a structure for optimizing student experiences in research. Need I say that many social work students don't exactly take delight in their research courses? While our proposals may not exactly increase students' delight, they *were* intended to increase students' understanding of the various ways that research can affect *their* practice. After all, without our graduates having a sound foundation in understanding research, Evidence-Based Practice can never flourish.

Chapter ten is where I may, indeed, have been a little dramatic. This chapter and a companion piece (Fischer, 1981) are the first where I try to conduct a review of the changes that have occurred in our field over the past several years, and I call them "*revolutionary.*" The title of this chapter is "New and Emerging Methods of

Direct Practice: The Revolution in Social Work." In this chapter, I try to develop a theoretical perspective for understanding the changes, and then attempt to catalog them for both practitioners and scholars. My motivation at the time (I remember it clearly) was to try to introduce these changes in one place, and put them before the profession so that they could be considered and, hopefully, nurtured. I did not use the term "Evidence-Based Practice" because I am not even sure it had yet been created. But reading this chapter will give a clear indication about where I thought our profession was heading and should head.

Chapter eleven is called "A Framework for Evaluating Empirical Research Reports." Really rolls off the tongue, doesn't it? Here's my reasoning: If social workers are going to be called on to evaluate research so they can select the most effective interventions—later to be a key principle of Evidence-Based Practice—then we have to be *prepared* to do so. This chapter provides a comprehensive, structured framework for helping students and practitioners understand and evaluate individual studies and then to directly compare them with other studies. (I still use a variation of this framework in my research classes, to the great joy of my students.) You might also consider this a companion piece to chapter two, the framework for analyzing theories. With these two frameworks, I am hoping, even today, that social workers will be equipped for some of the more important and rigorous tasks facing practitioners: the analysis and selection of the material they use in practice.

Chapter twelve is another by Walter Hudson and me called, "Measurement of Client Problems for Improved Practice." In this chapter, Walter and I present an overview of a variety of ways practitioners can measure the problems and concerns with which they are working in practice. (As Walter would say, if you can't measure the client's problem, it doesn't exist!) Let me put it this way: Measurement of targets is the first and most important step on the road to evaluating one's practice. If practitioners don't measure the client's target problems, how is it possible to know whether one has accomplished one's goals? And if one doesn't know, more or less objectively, whether goals are accomplished, how would one know whether the problem has been resolved? These measurement procedures can be used with the designs described in chapter five.

Chapter thirteen is called "Eclectic Casework." It originally appeared in a book edited by John Norcross (1985) that was not addressed primarily to social workers but was more addressed to clinical psychologists, psychiatrists, and counselors. (I was the token social worker.) Some of the best-known authors in the new field of integrative and eclectic psychotherapy were represented in this book, and I was tickled pink to be invited to participate. I did my best to represent a strong and positive approach to clinical social work, including the results of the controlled studies that showed that social workers were as effective as psychiatrists and psychologists. This chapter presents an overview of what caseworkers do; reviews reasons and criteria for an eclectic practice; summarizes some available approaches that, given the evidence, would make reasonable choices for an eclectic practice; describes some possible common characteristics of effective interventions; and introduces the PRAISES model, a framework for integrating research and practice that I still use in some of my classes. The chapter also illustrates the flowcharts I use to teach intervention techniques. The entire package of flowcharts is available in the appendix. Feel free to copy the flowcharts and PRAISES model from this book.

Chapter fourteen, by Charles Glisson and me, is called "Statistical Training for Social Workers." This chapter can be viewed as the second part of the attempt in chapter nine to develop and present to the field a comprehensive approach to research education—in this case, the statistical training that would optimize students' understanding of that area. There is no question that "sadistics" is almost always one of the most challenging parts of the social work curriculum to teach and learn. Here, Charles and I lay out a rather assertive perspective on what an optimal statistics curriculum would be.

Chapter fifteen is the last in this part; it is titled, "Meta-Analysis: The Premise, the Promise, the Problems." Apart from my penchant for alliteration, the importance of meta-analysis cannot be understated. At the start of this part of the book, I emphasized the importance of research reviews. This chapter shows how in a short period of time, pretty much over the decade of the 1980s, the knowledge landscape can change. Meta-analyses are quantitative reviews of research. Meta-analyses appear now to be the predominant way of reporting research reviews in the literature. If a practitioner cannot understand meta-analyses, that practitioner simply cannot understand the literature. That is one heck of a handicap to have to bear if one is attempting to develop one's own evidence-based approach.

So this part concludes, in essence, with many challenges to becoming an effective practitioner, not the least of which is being able to master the literature of approaches that claim to be effective through an understanding of meta-analytic reviews.

References

Fischer, J. (1981). The social work revolution. *Social Work, 26,* 199–209.

Fischer, J. (1984). Revolution, schmevolution: Is social work changing or not? *Social Work, 29,* 71–74.

Norcross, J. C. (Ed.). (1985). *Handbook of eclectic psychotherapy.* New York: Brunner-Mazel.

Chapter 8

Research and Knowledge-building: The Case for Research Reviews

It is particularly important to point out right at the outset of this chapter that knowledge development, as a field, includes more than research (see, e.g., the Sage Publication journal, *Knowledge Creation, Diffusion, Utilization* [first issue, September 1979]). Perhaps the seminal work in social work in this arena has been Ed Thomas' attempts to conceptualize the knowledge development process in a series of articles (Thomas, 1978a, 1978b, 1978c). Thomas has proposed a systematic way of looking at a whole range of sources of basic information for social work. These sources include contributions from basic, applied, indigenous research; technology from science, allied technologies, social innovation, and practice; values and ideology; legal policy; and practice experience. Thomas translates each of these into five generation or transfer processes (the processes by which information from the basic source is converted for use by social workers) and spells out operational steps for the phases of the knowledge development process (the phases are analysis, development, evaluation, diffusion, and adaptation).

The point is that knowledge in social work has its roots in more than just research. In fact, Thomas' work—by going beyond research—offers us a tremendous mechanism for discussion with our colleagues who are somewhat suspicious of research. The key point of Thomas' work is that whatever the source—including values and "practice wisdom"—we can be systematic and rigorous in looking at the ways we develop knowledge.

I've already alluded to one of the problems in selecting a focus for this paper, and *that* is that the role of research in knowledge development really involves more than simply conducting a study. We can look at the role of research in knowledge development as a process that begins with an idea or felt need (as we used to say) and ends up as a concerted effort at dissemination for use in practice.

But I'd like to address another part of the process, or take another angle on the use of research for developing knowledge. Instead of focusing on the *conducting*

Fischer, J. (1980). Paper presented at the Group for the Advancement of Doctoral Education, Washington, D.C.

of research for knowledge development, which we often think of as the essence of knowledge development, the angle I would like to pursue involves the importance of research reviews—cumulating the results of research—for knowledge development in social work. The importance of this aspect was highlighted for me recently when reviewing the book *Social Service Research: Reviews of Studies* (Maas, 1978)—the latest in the National Association of Social Workers (NASW) series edited by Henry Maas. This series is potentially one of the most important resources in the field. The key ideas behind these volumes and behind the whole notion of the importance of research reviews is that they "assemble and make public critical reviews of research and resulting formulations that social workers will find helpful" on the grounds that "cumulative reviews of empirical research contribute to the growth and change of knowledge that is basic to informed practice" (Maas, 1978). Of course, not only do such reviews have great potential for making a direct impact on practice, but they, implicitly at least, form the basis for every *individual* study we undertake as we attempt to develop knowledge for our field. Each researcher presumably conducts a review of research in a given field before conducting his or her own study. Without doing that, of course, we have no idea as to where one study fits in the overall scheme of things.

Well, after reading the Maas book, I just wasn't sure what to make of it. I had real trouble trying to decide the extent to which the reviews in that book and many other reviews of research that I've read really did contribute to knowledge development. The main reason for this—in an oversimplified way—was that individual reviews vary considerably in the ways they apply basic principles for cumulating research findings. In fact, my sense is that we, as a field, really haven't decided on or developed *any* basic principles for cumulating findings.

So what I'd like to do in this chapter is present some preliminary ideas on some basic principles for cumulating the results of empirical research. No matter what type of perspective we take on the role of research in knowledge development, cumulating findings is key—either as a precursor to conducting an individual study or as an attempt to directly translate results of cumulated findings into practice. Incidentally, my own bias is that the latter—use of research reviews to cumulate findings to directly affect practice—is becoming one of the most important ways of changing knowledge in social work. This is largely because of the incredible knowledge explosion in social work and related fields that has occurred in the past several years. In just the clinical area alone, there are now several hundred controlled studies dealing with individuals, couples, and families showing effective methods of practice that are available for immediate utilization in social work (see e.g., Fischer, 1978). Reviews of research cumulating these findings and disseminating them to social workers—to practitioners for practice, teachers for teaching, and to researchers for further study—are the primary means for building them into the knowledge base and technology of the field. This, then, necessitates our taking an increased and sharper look at principles for cumulating findings.

These principles fall into two general categories—*selection principles* and *evaluation principles*.

Selection Principles

Simply stated—at the broadest level—whatever are the criteria for selection of studies for review, there should *be* some. The reviewer should clearly state his or her criteria and apply them consistently. Unless this occurs, a reader would never know the bases for selecting given reports, or especially, what was being omitted and why.

What I'd like to do now is suggest several criteria for selecting studies for reviews.

1.   A Focus for Reviews

The focus of research reviews should be taken from the primary mission of social work: to help people (individuals, families, groups, communities, etc.) enhance or restore their capacity for facilitative social functioning and to develop social conditions favorable to that goal. If helping is our mission, then finding out what methods of helping—or methods of intervention—do this best provides a clear definition of priorities for research and for selecting studies for review. This, then, is the key question: what methods of intervention, used by what kinds of practitioners, working with what problems, with what kinds of client/systems, in what kinds of situations, bring about the most effective results?

I would suggest, in other words, that the major priority for social work research should be on finding, developing, and evaluating the methods of intervention that best help us do our job. Accordingly, I would therefore suggest that the key selection criterion for reviews, and the one that would be most essential for developing knowledge for social work, be that such reviews be focused primarily on selecting studies that address this issue. Other questions—ranging from agency functioning to needs assessment—while important and addressable, should be given lower priorities.

It probably is obvious that no single individual—or group—sets the priorities for everyone else in the field. In fact, it may be impossible to establish priorities, especially in research, that meet with a very high consensus. We all have our vested interests. Yet, I believe that it may be possible (and probably critical to the profession's survival) to establish general acceptance of the notion that the establishment of effective methods of intervention is our primary concern, and then to encourage diversity of research pursuits (in terms of level of intervention, specific questions, methodologies, and field of interest) that in a variety of ways will address this superordinate concern.

2.   Exhaustiveness

If we are talking about reviews of research that cumulate findings, there is no excuse for a review not being exhaustive. This criterion is based on many social work reviews that simply do not adequately cover the field, omitting many studies.

Every study, including dissertations, that can be located must be included. Computer search systems and plain old legwork can handle this task. Without exhaustive reviews, a reader has no basis for understanding what has been selected and why. If the argument is that space limitations preclude exhaustive reviews, then reviewers are obliged to list all the available studies, summarize their findings, and analyze the trends contained in the data. One way of making this task more manageable is related to the previous criterion. The reviews can be exhaustive in the area of primary concern—interventions that work. Less exhaustive reviews can be reported for lower-priority areas.

3.   Avoid Theoretical Bias

It is incumbent on reviewers to include in their reviews work that focuses on theoretical orientations other than their own. For example, could one possibly review the state of the art with clinical populations and exclude the work on behavior modification, which includes several hundred controlled studies, the bulk of the clinical outcome research conducted in the past 10 to 15 years? Omission of theoretical orientations other than the reviewer's would give a peculiar slanted version to the true state of practice, and, in fact, considerably affect the value of a review.

4.   Avoid Professional Bias

Along the same lines as the previous criterion, a researcher must be exhaustive in reviewing work generated by members of professions other than social work. The issue is this: a profession such as social work cannot afford to ignore *any* research—no matter what the source—that deals with the phenomena of concern to that profession, especially when it involves effective methods of practice.

Evaluation Principles

The second major category of principles involve *evaluation principles*. All of the previous criteria pertained to *selection* guidelines. But what of studies that *are* included in a review?

The issues here are: can they be handled in such a way as to make reasonable conclusions about their results? Is it possible to get a clear sense of the cumulative nature of the results of these studies? Do we know which studies have conclusions in which we can place confidence, and which areas we must be dubious about? Unfortunately, the answers to these questions—in many reviews in the social work literature with which I am familiar—must be, not really.

In fact, the most crucial flaw in many reviews is that, with very few exceptions, reviewers do not *critically evaluate* the studies. They merely *describe* the findings. I am constantly struck, to paraphrase Kadushin (1978), by the way weakly supported or methodologically deficient conclusions and dubious assertions became established (facts) through citation in a review of research. The heart of the matter is that reviewers often do no more than report the findings (and sometimes the methodologies) of the studies they review. They don't evaluate the designs of the studies as to threats to internal and external validity or appropriate use of quantitative methods. In many instances, results of case studies are given as much credence as results of factorial designs. Many studies with which I am familiar that contain flaws absolutely negating their conclusions often are reported simply as factual; indeed, they are often ballyhooed.

Such a descriptive approach—merely *describing* the findings—simply has no place in scholarly reviews of research, and *may,* in fact, do more to set the field back than to advance it. It probably is obvious that such a review may actually be worthless; its value hinges on the extent to which the original pieces of research are totally free of any flaws that would affect their conclusions or generalizability. When a reviewer does not actually *evaluate* the research he or she reviews, we are left in a state of limbo: we know no more about results in which we can place confidence than we did when we started.

What I am suggesting, then, is that reviews must include rigorous methodological critiques of every study. At the minimum, threats to internal and external validity and analysis of the quantitative methods used must be reported. This provides the only basis for determining the amount of confidence one can place in a study's findings. Such evaluations also might help present additional guidelines for studies to emphasize in the review. There could be a methodological cut-off point: studies with the most serious methodological flaws might be summarized, while sounder studies could be emphasized because of their greater potential for knowledge development. In the absence of such evaluations, in the absence of knowing which of the studies have valid and generalizable conclusions, then, our conclusion must be: we have no way of knowing whether or not such reviews have at all advanced the state of knowledge, and the conclusions of such reviews must be treated with suspicion.

The Place of Research Reviews in a Model of Knowledge Development

So, then, given the importance of research reviews, what is their place in knowledge-development as a whole? I'd like to address that by examining a model for the development of intervention knowledge that incorporates research reviews.

It probably is obvious that no single individual—or group—sets the priorities for everyone else in the field. In fact, it may be impossible to establish priorities, especially in research, that meet with a very high consensus. We all have our vested interests. Yet, I believe that it may be possible (and probably critical to the profession's survival) to establish general acceptance of the notion that the establishment of effective methods of intervention is our primary concern, and then to encourage diversity of research pursuits (in terms of level of intervention, specific questions, methodologies, and field of interest) that in a variety of ways will address this superordinate concern.

In the research arena, social work researchers often have failed to use a variety of options available to them. Collaboration studies, for example, between agencies, schools, and so on, are few and far between. There have been very few actual uses of powerful factorial designs in social work research. And the use of the most sophisticated statistical procedures—for example, those derived from the General Linear Model such as multiple regression, are even rarer. The point here is not sophistication for the sake of sophistication or rigor for the sake of rigor. The point is that we simply can obtain more powerful and useful results from use of more sophisticated models of research.

Indeed, the field in some senses already has a great deal available to it that is not being utilized (Fischer, 1978). Some of the references presented earlier contain information on a variety of approaches, at least in work with individuals, couples, and families, that clearly have demonstrated their effectiveness. Moreover, systematic knowledge development processes have already been implemented in social work as can be seen, as just one example, in the work of Rothman (1974, 1976, 1978, 1980). Rothman and his colleagues used a basic research and development model to develop and disseminate empirically based principles and procedures geared toward social and organizational change. They first reviewed the literature from the social sciences; retrieved, codified, and generalized relevant principles; converted these into practice principles; pilot-tested and operationalized them; engaged in a series of field tests; elaborated the principles as actual practice techniques; then disseminated them in a variety of media.

Rothman's work, conducted over a period of years, clearly illustrates the steps and advantages of a systematic approach to knowledge development. It combines both empirical rigor and practical relevance and demonstrates the great potential that such a model has for enhancing practice effectiveness.

There are other movements afoot. A number of these were described by Edwin Thomas (1978d). These portend great improvements in the social work knowledge building process. For example, use of single-system designs (time series) can be integrated into the more traditional knowledge-building process in especially facilitative ways (Fischer, 1978). This process is illustrated in figure 8.1.

Social work can derive principles and procedures of intervention from behavioral theories and associated research (e.g., social psychology), from theories or systems of intervention, or, more inductively, from practice itself. These principles and procedures can be tested in practice using single-system designs involving planned replications. If such replications prove successful, they can form the basis for group experimental designs testing the effectiveness of those procedures in comparison to no treatment and/or groups with other treatments. If the interventions are not successful, they can be used as the basis for theory revisions, further testing, and so on. If the interventions appear to be effective in individual studies, then those studies should be replicated and their results can be cumulated in

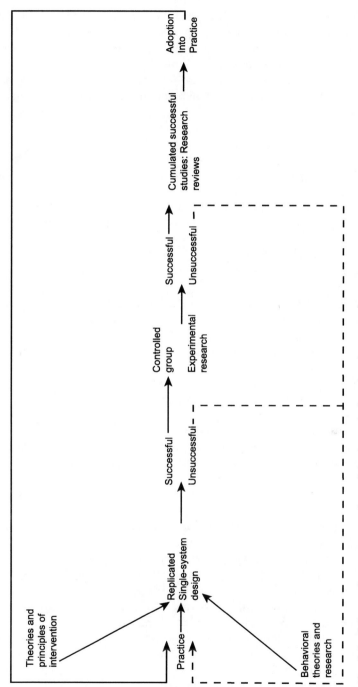

Fig. 8.1 Schematic representation of the knowledge development process

research reviews. Reviews that show replicated positive results for certain interventions then can be the impetus for adopting those interventions into practice, which, in turn, can provide a testing ground for the refinement and/or modification of interventions, say, with different client populations.

As suggested by the diagram in figure 8.1, the entire process is reciprocal as theory, research, and practice interact with and inform each other. It is also a long and arduous process. But in the end, can we really afford an alternative?

References

Fischer, J. (1978). *Effective casework practice: An eclectic approach.* New York: McGraw-Hill.

Glisson, C. (1980). Are social work doctoral program graduates quantitative illiterates? Paper presented at G.A.D.E. Conference, Washington, D.C., October.

Havelock, R. G. (1973). *Planning for innovation through dissemination and utilization of knowledge.* Ann Arbor, M.: Institute for Social Research, University of Michigan.

Human Interaction Research Institute. (1976). *Putting knowledge to use: A distillation of the literature regarding knowledge transfer and change.* Los Angeles: HIRI.

Kadushin, A. (1978). Children in foster families and institutions, in H. S. Maas (Ed.). *Social service research: Reviews of studies.* (pp. 90–148). New York: NASW.

Maas, H. S. (Ed.). (1978). *Social service research: Reviews of studies.* New York: NASW.

Rothman, J. (1974). *Planning and organizing for social change: Action principles from social science research.* New York: Columbia University Press.

Rothman, J. (1976). *Promoting innovation and change in organizations and communities.* New York: Wiley.

Rothman, J. (1978). Conversion and design in the research utilization process, *Journal of Social Service Research, 2,* 95–116.

Rothman, J. (1980). *Social R and D: Research and development in the human services.* Englewood Cliffs, NJ: Prentice-Hall.

Thomas, E. J. (1978a). Beyond knowledge utilization in generating human service technology. Paper presented at NASW Conference on "The Future of Social Work Research," San Antonio, Texas.

Thomas, E. J. (1978b). Generating innovation in social work: The paradigm of developmental research, *Journal of Social Service Research, 2,* 95–116.

Thomas, E. J. (1978c). Mousetraps, developmental research, and social work education, *Social Service Review, 52,* 468–483.

Thomas, E. (Ed.). (1978d). New models of social service research [Special issue]. *Journal of Social Service Research, 2(1).*

Chapter 9

Increasing the Relevance of Research Education: The University of Hawaii Research Program

There is substantial evidence that research training of graduate social work students has been less than successful. Research courses often are viewed by the students as the least helpful courses in the curriculum (1). After graduation, few practitioners either conduct research (2) or read, consult, utilize, or share research findings, especially when faced with difficult practice situations (3). And even when they do read research, it appears that social workers' judgments of the quality of the research and its implications for practice are strongly influenced by whether the findings support their own biases (4).

In response to this reaction to the place of research in practice, social work education as an institution seems to have shrugged its shoulders and given up. Over the past several years the proportion of the graduate curriculum devoted to research has been reduced, and many schools of social work have dropped any requirement for students to complete a research project in order to graduate (5). This trend persists despite the fact that the Council on Social Work Education, in its accreditation standards, recognizes the importance of research as a critical component of the curriculum (6), and despite indications of increasing need for mastering a variety of research skills in order to utilize practice methodologies found to be effective (7).

Analysis of the Problem

The purpose of this chapter is to develop some hypotheses regarding the nature of the problems confronting both training and utilization of research in the practice of social work, and to present a proposal, already implemented at one school of social work, for dealing with some of the instructional dynamics.

Numerous explanations have been offered regarding the present state of the art of education in social work research (8). Since the problems besetting the field appear to be institutional in nature, affecting social work education and practice

Fischer, J., & Hudson, W. W. (1980). In R. W. Weinbach & A. Rubin (Eds.), *Teaching Social Work Research* (pp. 23–29). New York: Council on Social Work Education (CSWE). Reprinted with permission of CSWE.

nationwide, we can reasonably rule out explanations that affect only one or two schools or limited geographic regions, for example, poor teachers in one locale, or negative attitudes in another. Instead, the source of the problem must be viewed in structural terms; specifically, how well does research training offered in schools of social work across the country mesh with the interests of students in graduate social work education (9)? Apparently not well at all. Much research training would seem to be relevant neither to student interests nor to the interests of graduates in their professional careers.

Two major goals for research training for all students in graduate social work education are prescribed by the Council on Social Work Education: to develop practitioners who will *utilize* research (research consumers), and to develop practitioners who will *conduct* research (research participants) (6). As suggested earlier, neither of these goals appear to have been attained, for two related reasons: (1) curriculum content of courses has traditionally focused on a body of knowledge that may not directly relate to achieving the most meaningful result for social work; and (2) too little attention has been paid the differing needs and career interests of students.

Divergent Practice Interests

The customary approach to research instruction in graduate social work education employs a course structure designed to teach students to *conduct* nomothetic research methodologies. These methods involve experimental design, field studies, and social surveys wherein data are collected on large samples or populations of people or events. As Hudson has noted, these methods depend on some form of data aggregation as a means of summarizing and describing obtained information (9), nearly always relying on such devices as the arithmetic mean, median, percentage distributions, and the like. Such aggregation of data obviously provides invaluable information about groups, information of great interest to social work students and practitioners with macro interests such as community work, planning, and administration, who deal with problems of collectivities, organizations, communities, and large systems.

Surveys and field studies may not be so interesting to the worker who is concerned with a single client, however. In essence we have ignored the students who are interested in micro social work—work with individuals, families, and groups as clinical treatment practitioners. Given the differences among micro and macro concerns, different types of research knowledge may be appropriate. Unfortunately, social work education has not distinguished between the two interest groups (9). It has been assumed that all students, regardless of practice interests, should be taught principles and methods of conducting nomothetic research.

Research Participation and Consumption

Even acknowledging the fact that nomothetic research is a prime tool for identifying effective programs and techniques of intervention in a large number of cases, instructing students in how to *conduct* such research does not necessarily speak to the second CSWE goal for research training—learning how to *utilize* it. Differing skills (with obvious overlap) are required for conducting and utilizing research. Traditional research curricula have focused on the former; thus, with more-or-less success, students have been taught to develop research questions, specify objectives, derive samples, develop questionnaires, analyze data (10), and write research reports. Far less attention has been paid to research consumerism; development of skills and attitudes regarding research analysis and evaluation often has not been part of research courses and projects (9).

Confluence of the Issues

As this analysis suggests, the focus on training for and conducting only one type of research has been dysfunctional for the profession. All students, regardless of practice interests, should be taught research that pertains to their career needs, both as research consumers and participants.

Recent developments in research make differentiation among the needs and interests of students not only more obvious, but more easily approached in the curriculum. The last twenty years have witnessed the development of an entirely new research technology. Variously called *idiographic research, single-system design,* or *time series design,* this research potentially can meet the previously ignored needs of by far the largest segment of graduate social work students—the clinicians (11). This methodology helps the clinician monitor and evaluate his or her progress, effectiveness, and efficiency with each and every case. It is the epitome of practice research, designed for use by the practitioner and client or client-group in a way that will produce more objective and clearer practice benefits in clinical or micro situations than more traditional methods of evaluation or research. In fact, the development and refinement of this technology makes possible the development of a curriculum that offers:

1. Courses on research analysis focused on research consumership for all students.
2. Courses on nomothetic methods for macro students.
3. Courses on idiographic methods for micro students.

Implementing the Proposed Program

The faculty of the University of Hawaii School of Social Work has recently completely revised its research curriculum in line with the preceding discussion. The key assumptions underlying these revisions are:

1. Traditional research training in social work has not been successful.
2. Research training should be directly relevant to the practice interests of students.

3. Research is a key part of the curriculum and its instruction should be relevant and complementary to other parts of the curriculum.

Based on these assumptions, the new program takes its goals from the faculty's perceptions of the two most important purposes of research training for social work practitioners:

1. To provide positive attitudes toward, and skills that can be used in, the analysis and consumption of available research to enhance development of an empirical orientation to practice.
2. To teach students research methods that will have direct impact on and relevance to their own practice.

Two programs of research were implemented for Fall semester 1977. One was a program for all students and the other a practice concentration in research for students whose goal was to become a social work researcher.

Curriculum for All Students

Based on the assumption that research is a critical component of the curriculum, students are required to take four semesters of research courses (ranging from eight to ten credits). However, considerable flexibility is built into the system so students are allowed several options to meet their own interests.

The First Year   All students are required to take the same introductory course. This course covers the following topics: (1) an introduction to scientific thinking; (2) brief overviews of the two types of research—nomothetic and idiographic— to familiarize students with the basic components; and (3) specific skill training and development of critical attitudes regarding the importance of analyzing and consuming research. The major focus of this introductory course is on learning to analyze and evaluate research as a guide to critical consumership. Much of this focus is on analysis of nomothetic research, to ensure that all students are familiar with its basic components.

In the second semester of the first year, students are given a choice between two courses focused on in-depth knowledge of research methods. The choice is made, depending on the student's practice interests, between: (1) nomothetic research methods, for students interested in macro social work methods, and (2) idiographic research methods, for students interested in micro social work methods. These courses represent a critical choice for the students. They are designed to fit special needs and interests and to be relevant to particular areas of practice specialty.

The Second Year   In the second year, students have several options for fulfilling the research requirement. (1) Students may complete a thesis (one student working with a committee of three graduate faculty). (2) Students may conduct a two-semester research project—one to six students working with one faculty member. It should be pointed out that most projects completed in this option consist of the students conducting the entire project from start to finish rather than simply assisting in some obscure part of a faculty member's research, with little reward in terms of understanding or participating in the entire research process. (3) Students can select two research courses from several available. Most of these courses focus on an advanced level of study of research analysis and consumption in specific, substantive fields, with the fields changing from semester to semester depending on student and faculty interests. (4) Students also can select a one-semester research course and a one-semester research project to be carried out under the supervision of a faculty member.

The basic design for the research curriculum can be diagrammed as in figure 9.1.

Research Concentration

For the small but growing number of students who wish research to be their major concentration, the school offers a specific research concentration. In the first semester, the same introductory research course that is taken by all students is taken by research concentration students. In the second semester, these students take a specially designed three-credit course focusing on an introduction to data analysis and nomothetic design, plus the two-credit idiographic research methods course. The third and fourth semesters involve two advanced courses, one of which is required to be on quantitative methods. The other course in the area of design or statistics is to be selected from a list of available courses. Students in the research concentration also are required to complete a thesis under the supervision of three members of the graduate faculty.

Conclusion

This curriculum is guided less by empirical evidence (what is demonstrated to work) than by the informed opinions of the faculty about what appears to be the best and most effective form of research education for students, especially in view of the problems in the traditional approach to teaching research. There is little or no evidence to indicate which of the teaching methods are best (12). Also, as yet there is no evidence that research learning such as that taught at Hawaii generalizes to practice and whether, if it does, it clearly adds an identifiable increment to effective practice. The school hopes to study the effects of this program on a longitudinal basis to determine its effectiveness. The first year's data are currently being analyzed. Preliminary results of an attitudinal survey show practically 100 percent agreement among students that the breakdown into nomothetic and idiographic research methods courses is relevant to their own practice interests. Thus, while in the faculty's opinion this curriculum seems to be the best being offered at this time, it is hoped that the development of the research curriculum will be

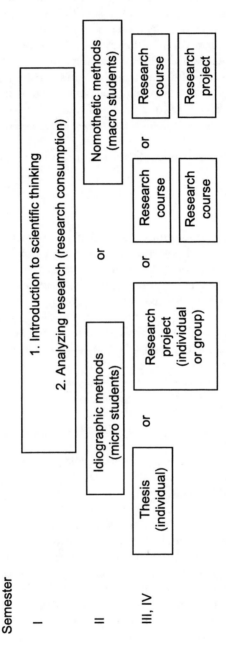

Fig. 9.1 Overview of 4-semester Research Curriculum

strongly affected by results from the evaluation of its impact, as well as by reports of similar research by other schools.

Since one of the goals of this research curriculum is to make research more relevant to practice, it should also be pointed out that there are other ways to approach this goal in developing a curriculum. One alternative to keeping practice and research courses separate is to teach both practice and research in the same courses, thereby eliminating the research course (e.g., the second semester research methods course at the University of Hawaii). This, perhaps, is the ultimate in integrating research and practice.

On the other hand, there are some problems in such a union. One problem is that in some schools, it simply may be politically impossible to accomplish. Another problem is that one or both of the content areas—research or practice—may suffer, since a given instructor may choose to emphasize one area over the other. Related to this problem is that some instructors, perhaps lacking expertise in one of the areas, may simply pay lip service to one (the research component) while focusing almost exclusively on the other (the practice component). Although any or all of these problems may be overcome, keeping the courses separate ensures that both practice and research components of the curriculum are adequately represented. The major integration can then occur through applications in the practicum, readings in relevant practice/research areas, and course assignments such as conducting actual case studies using appropriate practice/research methods to monitor and evaluate programs.

It should be noted that this or any other research curriculum has little or no control over a variety of factors that may be crucial in molding student attitudes toward research, including agency norms and supports, or other faculty opinions (8). However, awareness of these conditions (changes in which could form the basis for future investigation) should not preclude the attempt to make basic changes at the levels at which there is some control over both input and outcome.

This curriculum is not intended to work in isolation from other parts of the curriculum, where the utilization of research findings is encouraged as strongly as possible. Indeed, the specific research courses are intended to complement the other courses, both in helping students understand and utilize the results of research in those courses and in providing a base for truly integrating research and practice in the methods or practice courses and in the practicum.

References

1. Rosenblatt, A., The practitioner's use and evaluation of research. *Social Work,* 13 (January 1968), pp. 53–59; and B. Casselman, "On the Practitioner's Orientation Toward Research," *Smith College Studies in Social Work,* Vol. 42 (1972), pp. 211–233.
2. Kirk, S., M. J. Osmalov and Joel Fischer, "Social Workers' Involvement in Research," *Social Work,* Vol. 21 (March 1976), pp. 121–124.

3. Eaton, J. W., "Symbolic and Substantive Evaluation Research," *Administrative Science Quarterly,* Vol. 6 (1962), pp. 421–442.
4. Kirk, S., and Joel Fischer, "Do Social Workers Understand Research?" *Journal of Education for Social Work,* Vol. 12 (Winter 1976), pp. 63–67.
5. Zimbalist, S. E., "The Research Component of the Master's Degree Curriculum in Social Work: A Survey Summary," *Journal of Education for Social Work,* Vol. 10 (1974), pp. 118–123; and Allen Rubin and Sidney E. Zimbalist, "Trends in the MSW Research Curriculum: A Decade Later," (mimeographed, New York: Council on Social Work Education, 1979).
6. "Report from the Commission on Accreditation," *Social Work Education Reporter,* Vol. 16 (1968).
7. Fischer, Joel, *Effective Casework Practice: An Eclectic Approach* (New York: McGraw-Hill, 1978).
8. Kirk, S., and A. Rosenblatt, "Barriers to Students' Utilization of Research," (paper presented at the Annual Program Meeting of the Council on Social Work Education, Phoenix, Arizona, March 1977); J. L. Bushnell and G. M. O'Brien, "Strategies and Tactics for Increasing Research Production and Utilization in Social Work Education," in *Sourcebook on Research Utilization,* eds. Allen Rubin and Aaron Rosenblatt (New York: Council on Social Work Education, 1979), pp. 169–188.
9. Hudson, W. H., "Research Training in Professional Social Work Education: Issues and Problems," *Social Service Review,* Vol. 52 (March 1978), pp. 116–121.
10. Weed, P., and S. R. Greenwald, "The Mystics of Statistics," *Social Work,* Vol. 18 (March 1973), pp. 113–115.
11. Hersen, M., and D. Barlow, *Single Case Experimental Design* (New York: Pergamon, 1976).
12. Goldstein, H. K. *Maximizing Research Learning for Three Types of Social Work Students* (Tallahassee, Florida: Florida State University, 1972); H. K. Goldstein, *Evaluating Optimum Conditions for Learning in the Research Experience of Social Work Students* (Tallahassee, Florida: Florida State University, 1977); and F. W. Seidl, "Teaching Social Work Research: A Study in Teaching Method," *Journal of Education for Social Work,* Vol. 9 (Fall 1973), pp. 71–77.

Chapter 10

New and Emerging Methods of Direct Practice: The Revolution in Social Work

Social work is in the midst of a revolution. As revolutions go, it is a rather quiet revolution, but it is a revolution nevertheless. It is a revolution in the ways social workers are beginning to *view* knowledge and practice and in the ways social workers are beginning to *use* knowledge and *conduct* practice. It is a revolution that portends great improvements in the direct-practice branch of social work and one that bodes well for dramatically increasing the success of the profession in helping others.

The purpose of this chapter is to document the existence of this revolution by pulling together the evidence that can be gleaned from material presented at social work conferences, from the literature, and from less concrete sources of evidence, such as a new "spirit" or "world view" that seems to be emerging among many social workers. Accordingly, the first part of this chapter will provide both a framework for understanding the revolution and the evidence that such a revolution is indeed under way. This will be followed by overviews of each of the areas of knowledge and practice in which these changes are taking place. Major emphasis will be placed on one area—availability of a whole new range of specific practice procedures with supporting evidence of effectiveness. The chapter concludes with a review of some of the issues involved in these changes in addition to an evaluation of the prospects for the revolution being successfully completed.

The focus of this chapter is on what is called "direct practice" in social work. Unfortunately, the term "direct practice" does not communicate the same meaning to everybody. It has been used in a number of different ways in the literature for everything from "direct" work with individuals to "direct" work with communities. For purposes of this chapter, "direct practice" will be considered as the interpersonal helping branch of social work, the major defining characteristics of which are (1) provision of individualized and individualizing services, largely on a case-by-case basis; and (2) provision of these services mainly to individuals, families, and small groups. Although practitioners providing direct service may work with communities, this is not viewed as the primary focus of their activities when it occurs as part of their more general commitment—as social workers—to changing oppressive social conditions at broader levels of intervention.

The activities and methods grouped under the rubric direct service include those that have been called "social casework," "clinical social work," "social treatment," "social work practice with individuals, families, and groups," "group work," "interpersonal helping," and "social work practice with microsystems." This view of direct practice is not intended to be limited to (or confined by) any particular theoretical orientation, setting, or related conception of practice.

The most common role clusters used in providing direct services are the clinical-behavior change role, the consultant-educator role, and the broker-advocate role, each of which encompasses a number of specific activities.[1] Other social work roles (for example, lobbyist, agent of social change, organizer) may, of course, be used, but they are not viewed as the primary roles of the direct-service practitioner. Finally, although the focus of direct services is on individualizing problems and related intervention efforts, the assumption here is not necessarily that the problems are due to or intrinsic to the individual (for example, a result of "personality inadequacies" or "character deficits"). Instead, as shall be elaborated later in this chapter, the focus is on the individual *and* his or her environment and the transactions between them, the major idea being that regardless of causality, many problems can be resolved through provision of individualized services. Thus, intervention efforts may involve the individual (or family or small group), the impinging environment, or both.

The Revolution Can Be Now

Several years ago, Kuhn published *The Structure of Scientific Revolutions,* an essay on the mechanisms of control and change in science based on analysis of the historical changes in many branches of science.[2] Kuhn argued that, historically, sciences—and by extension, professions—tend to be governed by overriding models or paradigms that guide and structure scientific research and theorizing. These models prescribe the kinds of questions that scientists raise, provide rather rigid guidelines for the nature of solutions that are sought, bias scientists' perceptions of the phenomena with which they are concerned, and often ensure that research will not raise serious questions about the validity of the superordinate model. Thus, when anomalies, or deviations from the model (for example, inventions, new ideas) arise or are discovered in research, scientists attempt to account for these anomalies with the vocabulary and perceptions of the superordinate model.

---

[1] Joel Fischer, *Effective Casework Practice: An Eclectic Approach* (New York: McGraw-Hill, 1978).
[2] Thomas S. Kuhn, *The Structure of Scientific Revolutions,* International Encyclopedia of Unified Science. 2nd series, no. 2 (Chicago: University of Chicago Press, 1962).

However, over time, a series of anomalies appears, say, a number of studies with findings that diverge from the superordinate model. These lead to a "crisis" in that, while early negative results or new ideas are not accepted, scientists eventually begin to question the validity of the model that they are using to guide their thinking. This, in turn, leads to the examination and investigation of new models. Eventually, a new superordinate model is adopted that serves the same function as the old model, that is, to guide thought and practice. Kuhn terms this change in models a "paradigm shift."[3] The entire process is called a scientific revolution.

The Revolution in Social Work

Just how does this model of a scientific revolution fit with the history and current state of practice in social work?

In the first place, there is considerable evidence that, at least until the 1970s, the conceptions of most direct-service theoreticians and practitioners have been guided by a rather loosely structured superordinate model.[4] This model for the most part consisted of a foundation in use of common theoretical understandings, largely based on psychodynamic perspectives and their derivatives, in addition to shared professional conceptions of the most important characteristics of practice.[5] This "superordinate model" tended to control thought, particularly in social casework, but it also was viewed as important in many of the early social group work approaches, and in the family therapy approaches that social workers tended to adopt.[6] Although the knowledge base of practice expanded rapidly in the 1960s and 1970s, such as in the use of role theory, systems theory, and communication theory, these changes generally were not viewed as negating the use of traditional social work perspectives.[7]

Over many years, from the 1930s to the early 1970s, a series of controlled research investigations were conducted on the effectiveness of professional social work practice.[8] These studies provided discouraging results in that they failed to document the effectiveness of any form of the traditional practice of social work.

---

[3] Ibid.

[4] F. J. Turner, ed., *Social Work Treatment,* 2nd ed. (New York: Free Press, 1979); R. W. Roberts and R. Nee, eds., *Theories of Social Casework* (Chicago: University of Chicago Press, 1970).

[5] H. Bartlett, *The Common Base of Social Work Practice* (New York: NASW, 1970).

[6] R. W. Roberts and H. Northen, eds., *Theories of Social Work with Groups* (New York: Columbia University Press, 1976); F. H. Scherz, "Theory and Practice of Family Therapy," in *Theories of Social Casework,* eds. R. Roberts and R. Nee (Chicago: University of Chicago Press, 1970), pp. 219–264; S. N. Sherman, "Family Therapy," in *Social Work Treatment,* ed. F. J. Turner (New York: Free Press, 1974), pp. 457–494.

[7] H. S. Strean, *Social Casework: Theories in Action* (Metuchen, N.J.: Scarecrow Press, 1971); F. J. Turner, ed., *Social Work Treatment,* 2nd ed. (New York: Free Press, 1979).

[8] E. J. Mullen and J. R. Dumpson, eds., *Evaluation of Social Intervention* (San Francisco: Jossey-Bass, 1972); Joel Fischer, "Is Casework Effective? A Review," *Social Work,* 18 (1973a), 5–20; Joel Fischer, *The Effectiveness of Social Casework* (Springfield, Ill.: Chas. C Thomas, 1976).

Some of this research even suggested that some clients may be harmed or may deteriorate, possibly as a result of their contacts with professional social workers.

These consistently negative findings constituted, in Kuhn's terms, a clear set of anomalies or deviations from the superordinate model of thought in traditional practice.[9] The anomalies, also in fairly predictable fashion, led to a crisis, as manifested in part by the denouncement of the negative findings by many social workers.[10] The crisis was manifested also in increased examination and investigation by some social workers of new models of practice. Some of this investigation had been occurring for a considerable period of time but became increasingly obvious only in recent years through reports in the literature.

The next step, the final one, in Kuhn's model of scientific and professional revolutions, is the change from the old to the new superordinate model—the paradigm shift.[11] This too appears to be the case in social work.

What is the nature of this shift of paradigms in social work? In essence, the direct practice of social work appears to be moving away from vaguely defined, unvalidated, and haphazardly—or uncritically—derived knowledge for practice. In its most salient characteristics, the paradigm shift appears to involve a movement toward more systematic, rational, empirically oriented development and use of knowledge for practice. For want of a better phrase, this could be termed a movement toward scientifically based practice in social work.

There is evidence of at least three kinds that this part of the revolution is well under way in social work. These are (1) increasing work in systematizing the processes of knowledge development for social work practice; (2) increasing integration between research and practice; and (3) increasing availability of a wide range of intervention procedures of demonstrated effectiveness. Although there is considerable overlap among these developments, there is considerable advantage, for heuristic purposes, in reviewing them separately.

Changes in the Processes of Knowledge Development

One of the major signs of the paradigm shift toward scientifically based practice in social work is the development and refinement of new methods of generating knowledge for practice. Traditionally, social workers have tended to rely on a variety of vague, poorly defined criteria (or no criteria whatsoever) in selecting knowledge for practice. The main bases for selecting practice approaches—both for teaching in social work education and in actual practice—seemed to be faith, comfort with what already was known, the charisma of some theoretician or respected practitioner, or consensus among "experts" or peers. Such "criteria" tended to ignore use of systematic, rigorous, and rational selection of practice approaches.

[9] Kuhn, *Scientific Revolutions.*

[10] "Points and Viewpoints," *Social Work,* 18 (March, May, July, 1973); "Letters to the Editor," *Social Work,* 18 (March, May, July, 1973); Joel Fischer, "Has Mighty Casework Struck Out?" *Social Work,* 18 (1973b), 107–110.

[11] Kuhn, *Scientific Revolutions.*

Critical analysis of available approaches generally was precluded, such as analysis of research to determine the availability of evidence of effectiveness.

In distinction to these traditional selection methods, social workers increasingly are explicating new approaches to knowledge development and selection that are systematic, clear, and oriented to both the rigors of research evidence and the realities of practice. Perhaps the most sophisticated and comprehensive attempt to conceptualize the knowledge development process per se is the work of Thomas.[12] Thomas has proposed a framework for knowledge development which he calls Developmental Research and Utilization (DR and U). This framework includes, but goes beyond, other systematic methods of knowledge development such as the research and development approach characteristic of other fields, such as engineering and industry. Thomas suggests that there are at least ten sources of basic information for knowledge for social work. These sources are contributions from basic, applied, and indigenous research; technology from science, allied technologies, social innovation, and practice; values and ideology; legal policy; and practice experience. Each of these can be translated into five generation or transfer processes (that is, the processes by which information from the basic source is converted for use by social workers). These five processes include knowledge utilization, technological transfer, value realization, legal interpretation, and experiential synthesis. Each is explicated by Thomas along with examples of their transfer into a social technology (that is, applied knowledge relevant to social work).[13]

Finally, Thomas conceptualizes the whole DR and U process as having five phases: analysis, development, evaluation, diffusion, and adoption.[14] Thomas spells out the operational steps that comprise these phases.

The specificity of these methods of knowledge development has major implications for social work: Social workers can begin to harness the technologies of the social and physical sciences to build a greater degree of systematization, objectification, and precision into their selection of knowledge for practice. Social workers can use differentially a variety of methods to develop knowledge based on the needs and realities of practice; and, because as much certainty as possible is built into the process all along the line, the eventual use of this knowledge with clients is bound to increase social workers' potential for effective practice. Knowledge developed in this manner therefore should be more specifically relevant.

The conceptual framework for knowledge development proposed by Thomas is a useful schema for ordering and understanding the full range of knowledge development processes. In fact, some of these processes already have been applied in social work. Rothman's work is an excellent example of the potential use that can

[12] E. J. Thomas, "Beyond Knowledge Utilization in Generating Human Service Technology." Paper presented at NASW Conference on the Future of Social Work Research, San Antonio, Texas, October 15–18, 1978b; E. J. Thomas, "Generating Innovation in Social Work: The Paradigm of Developmental Research," *Journal of Social Service Research*, 2 (1978c), 95–116; E. J. Thomas, "Mousetraps, Developmental Research, and Social Work Education," *Social Service Review*, 52 (1978a), 468–483.

[13] Thomas, "Generating Innovation."

[14] Thomas, "Mousetraps, Developmental Research."

be made of a systematic approach to knowledge development for social work.[15] Rothman used a basic research and development model adapted from the physical sciences and industry to develop and disseminate empirically based principles and procedures geared to social and organizational change.

Rothman and his colleagues first reviewed the research literature from the social sciences bearing on social change. Relevant principles were retrieved, codified, and generalized. Next, they identified generalizations which were converted into more or less abstract practice principles (called "application concepts"). These abstract practice principles were then pilot-tested and developed as operational practice principles. Field testing and evaluation of the operational principles were made to determine their relationship to actual practice outcomes. The principles of practice were defined and "packaged" as actual practice techniques, and then widely disseminated in a variety of media (conferences, papers, articles, books, workshops), with the goal of encouraging their utilization in practice.

Rothman's work clearly identifies the steps and phases of the research and development process of research utilization: drawing on research from the social sciences to develop testable principles of practice leading to specific empirically based procedures, and then disseminating them for use by the profession. However, beyond illustrating the process per se, this work actually resulted in empirically demonstrated procedures for practice.[16] In combining both empirical rigor and practical relevance, Rothman's work demonstrates the great potential that use of a systematic model of knowledge development has for enhancing the effectiveness of practice.

Increasing interest in and work on the systematic development of knowledge for practice is likely to produce major long-term benefits for social work practice. The focus on careful and systematic selection and development of knowledge for practice will certainly affect the extent to which social work practice will be evaluated as effective.[17]

Integrating Research and Practice

One of the most important developments in direct practice in recent years is the increased potential for integrating research and practice. For many years the profession has paid lip service to this notion. Now, for several reasons, including

[15] J. Rothman, "Conversion and Design in the Research Utilization Process," *Journal of Social Service Research*, 2 (1978), 95–116; J. Rothman, *Planning and Organizing for Social Change: Action Principles from Social Science Research* (New York: Columbia University Press, 1974); J. Rothman, *Promoting Innovation and Change in Organizations and Communities* (New York: John Wiley, 1976); J. Rothman, *Social R & D: Research and Development in the Human Services* (Englewood Cliffs, N.J.: Prentice-Hall, 1980); J. Rothman and others, *Fostering Participation and Innovation: A Handbook for Human Service Professionals* (Itasca, Ill.: F. E. Peacock, 1978).

[16] Rothman and others, *Fostering Participation.*

[17] A helpful addition to the literature on knowledge development is the new Sage Publications Journal: *Knowledge: Creation, Diffusion, Utilization* (First issue, September 1979).

the availability of new research tools and changes in basic ideas about the place of research in social work education and practice, integration of research and practice is more of a reality than it was at any time in the past. There are two reasons for this closer integration: the development of new technology for building research into practice—the single-system design; and an increased interest in utilizing the results of research to guide practice.

Building Research Into Practice: The Single-System Design

For many years social workers have been urged to integrate research and practice, particularly by evaluating progress in their day-to-day practice. Unfortunately, such pleas were largely ignored because most social workers did not have the technological skills to conduct such evaluation. This is no longer the case. There is now a research technology available to social workers that can be utilized in practice which serves in a number of ways to enhance practice. In and of itself, this development may be the highlight of—and certainly is a key to—the revolution in social work practice.

Several terms have been used to describe this new technology: intensive or idiographic research; single N or N = 1 research; time-series designs; and experimental single-case study designs. The term used here—*single-system design*—was selected because it suggests that this form of research can be used with a variety of systems: individuals, families, groups, and organizations. All may be viewed as "single systems" for evaluation purposes.

The literature developed on this topic in the 1970s is quite extensive.[18] Recent social work conferences have featured numerous papers on this topic illustrating the potential utility of this type of research for social work practice.

In essence, single-system research has four key components, each of which is integrated in practice. The first component is the specification of a problem which the worker and client system agree to work upon together. The problem might be behavioral, cognitive, affective, environmental, or some combination of these. The next component is selecting a way to observe or measure the problem. A wide range of measurement procedures are available that can be used by practitioners of diverse theoretical orientations.[19]

The third component of the single-system research process is the systematic

---

[18] M. Bloom and J. Fischer, *Evaluating Practice: A Guide for the Accountable Professional* (Englewood Cliffs, N.J.: Prentice-Hall, Inc., 1982); S. Jayaratne and R. Levy, *Empirical Clinical Practice* (New York: Columbia University Press, 1979); M. Bloom and S. Block, "Evaluating Effectiveness and Efficiency in One's Own Practice," *Social Work*, 13 (1977), 130–136: W. J. Gingerich, "Procedure for Evaluating Clinical Practice," *Health and Social Work*, 4, no. 2 (1979), 105–130. M. Hersen and D. H. Barlow, *Single Case Experimental Designs* (New York: Pergamon, 1976); E. J. Thomas, "Uses of Research Methods in Interpersonal Practice," in *Social Work Research* (rev. ed.), ed. N. R. Polansky (Chicago: University of Chicago Press, 1975) pp. 254–283: M. W. Howe, "Casework Self-Evaluation: A Single-Subject Approach," *Social Service Review*, 48 (1974), 1–23.

[19] M. Bloom and J. Fischer, "Evaluating Practice."

collection of information about the problem on a regular basis over time, in terms of intensity, frequency of occurrence, and/or duration. Data collection can be carried out by the client, the worker, or others in the environment. It is begun before the intervention actually begins for periods of a few days or a week, or longer if necessary. The information collected before intervention begins is called the *baseline,* and it is used to aid in assessment and as a basis for evaluation because data that are collected after intervention can be compared with data collected prior to intervention.

The final component of single-system research is clearly identifying an intervention program (that is, one or more specific intervention techniques) and implementation of the program after the baseline assessment is completed. Of course, throughout the process the worker and client collect data on any changes that take place. This provides feedback to the worker and client system as to any changes in the problem that might be occurring and provides information on whether or not changes need to be made in the intervention program (for example, if the changes in the problem are in a negative direction).

Each of the four components of single-system research—specifying the problem, measuring it, collecting information about it over time, and specifying an intervention program—are essential components of effective practice.[20] Thus, integration between research and practice is more readily achieved, in fact, is practically automatic.

The data charted in Figure 10.1 are an example of a single-system design. In this case one of the problems of which the client complained was the feeling of being exploited on his job because he was not able to express his feelings to his employer and coworkers. Among other measures, the client and practitioner devised a self-anchored scale to measure the extent to which the client felt exploited, with a rating of "1" being "doesn't feel at all exploited" and "10" being "feels completely exploited by others." Data were collected for five days at work. On the basis of this information a specific intervention program was begun involving a combination of three procedures. The results of the entire process are shown in Figure 10.1.

The design pictured in Figure 10.1 is actually one of the most elementary of single-system designs. This is because it gives feedback on whether the problem changed, not necessarily on *why* the problem changed (that is, with this particular design, it is difficult to determine whether or not it was the practitioner's program, other factors, or combinations of these that produced the changes). However, a wide range of single-system designs is available (see the earlier references) that allow the practitioner to note, not only whether the problem has changed, but to draw a conclusion as to whether or not the techniques used were responsible for the change.

There has been the feeling expressed by some practitioners that practice will suffer if practitioners systematically monitor how well the intervention is going;

---

[20] E. J. Thomas, "The BESDAS Model for Effective Practice," *Social Work Research and Abstracts,* 13 (1977), 12–17.

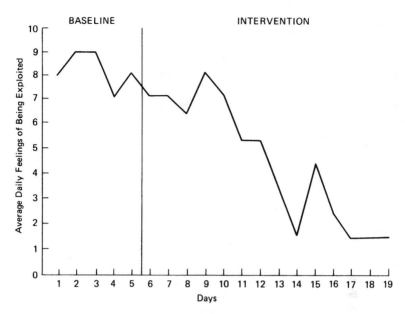

Fig. 10.1   Changes in the Client's Average Daily Ratings of Feeling Exploited at Work

their reservation seems to be that many problems cannot be measured, that this kind of research would be too demanding for the typical practitioner, and that this form of research might be too intrusive in practice.[21]

Yet, it seems that in most cases this kind of research does not intrude in a negative fashion; rather, practice is enhanced by its integration with research. Additional evidence for this is provided by practitioners in fields closely related to social work who have been evaluating their own practice for many years without negative results and with many positive effects.[22] It seems to be the case that building research into practice in the form of single-system designs has benefits that clearly outweigh some of the hypothetical problems. The advantages of single-system research can be summarized as follows:

1. It can be used by every practitioner with all cases.
2. It is designed by the practitioner to be used for the client's benefit.
3. It provides crucial information to help in assessing the case situation.
4. It allows the monitoring of progress with all cases.
5. It provides feedback as to whether the intervention program is working.

---

[21] E. J. Thomas, "Research and Service in Single-case Experimentation: Conflicts and Choices," *Social Work Research and Abstracts,* 14 (1978d), 20–31.

[22] M. B. Shapiro, "The Single Case in Clinical-Psychological Research," *Journal of General Psychology,* 74 (1966), 3–23; M. B. Shapiro, "The Single Case in Fundamental Clinical Psychological Research," *British Journal of Medical Psychology,* 34 (1961), 255–263; M. Hersen and D. H. Barlow, *Single Case Experimental Designs* (New York: Pergamon, 1976).

6. It enables the practitioner to make changes in the intervention program as the work progresses.

7. It focuses on a particular system and provides a means by which variations in effects can be seen from system to system.

The integration of research and practice by use of single-system designs is likely to be one of the major characteristics that distinguishes the practice of the past from that of the future.

Research Utilization

There is substantial evidence that social workers have been less than optimally prepared to utilize the results of research to help guide their practice.[23] Although the reasons for this are complicated and to some extent speculative, at least one possibility lies in the research education most professional social workers have received.[24] Despite recognition of the desirability of preparing students to utilize (or consume) research findings, most professional social work education programs have focused on teaching students how to *conduct* research. Thus, the skills and attitudes needed to critically *consume* research, which overlap with but are different from those needed to conduct it, have tended to receive short shrift.

Once again, though, there is evidence that this may be changing. At least two recent conferences have highlighted this change, the first being the "Conference on Research Utilization" sponsored by the Council on Social Work Education in New Orleans in October, 1977, and the second being the conference on the "Future of Social Work Research" sponsored by the National Association of Social Workers in San Antonio in October, 1978. At both of these conferences, a large part of the content focused on the desirability of preparing social work students and practitioners more adequately to use the results of empirical research to inform their practice.

The type of research discussed at these conferences is called extensive or nomothetic research (to distinguish it from the single-system designs discussed in the previous section), research based on experimental designs, field studies, and social surveys wherein data are collected on large cohorts (samples and/or populations) of people or events. This is the type of research that has been taught in most social work programs for decades. However, as mentioned previously, the focus has been on how to conduct it, rather than how to utilize it.[25]

---

[23] R. L. Simpson, "Is Research Utilization for Social Workers?" *Journal of Social Service Research,* 2 (1978), 143–157; S. A. Kirk, "Understanding the Utilization of Research in Social Work and Other Applied Professions." Paper presented at Conference on Research Utilization in Social Work Education, CSWE, New Orleans, October, 1977; J. Fischer and W. H. Hudson, "Increasing the Relevance of Research Education," in *Research Utilization in Social Work* (New York: CSWE, 1978).

[24] R. L. Simpson, "Is Research Utilization for Social Workers?" *Journal of Social Service Research,* 2 (1978), 143–157.

[25] S. E. Zimbalist, "The Research Component of the Master's Degree Curriculum in Social Work: A Survey Summary," *Journal of Education for Social Work,* 10 (1974) 118–123.

Evidence has accumulated that most social workers—certainly direct-service practitioners at any rate—do *not* conduct nomothetic research in their practice. Further, the development and accessibility of single-system designs and their obvious advantages for direct practice has made them the primary methods that direct-service practitioners are likely to use to conduct research into their own practice. Yet single-system designs cannot always be used to guide practice with regard to selecting techniques and programs of intervention based on clear evidence of effectiveness. This is because single-system designs, to a large extent, are not generalizable; at best, the rules for generalization to other workers, clients, and problems are rudimentary. The major advantage of nomothetic or large-group research is that the rules of evidence for generalization are clear.

Thus, differential roles for the two forms of research seem to be shaping up: single-system designs to monitor and evaluate progress with every case; nomothetic research to be used, when possible, as the basis for selecting intervention programs based on demonstrated evidence of effectiveness of the techniques and programs studied. These changes can be seen in the curricula of a number of schools of social work (for example, University of Hawaii, University of Michigan, University of Texas at Arlington, Rutgers, University of Wisconsin-Milwaukee, University of Chicago, University of Washington in Seattle) where research and practice courses are focusing both on preparing students to critically consume and utilize the results of nomothetic research to guide their selection of intervention techniques and programs and on teaching students to conduct single-system research to evaluate their own practice with each case or situation. (Of course, nomothetic research methods are relevant to practice for those students and practitioners involved in indirect methods such as administration and planning.)

All of this is not to say that nomothetic research should not be conducted by social workers. It must be, in the process of knowledge development for social work, precisely because of the potential for generalizing from such studies. However, there is a model of knowledge development that illustrates the way these two types of research can be used together. Several successful replications of single-system studies can be used to form the basis for a nomothetic study. Single-system designs can be used to provide the basic data for generating hypotheses for more elaborate nomothetic designs; the success of single-system designs would provide a reasonable basis for expecting successful outcomes from nomothetic research. Thus, nomothetic research, in turn, can be used to form a basis for practice more deeply rooted in empirical findings on effectiveness.

It may seem to be asking too much of social workers to require that they evaluate their practice with each case and also that they utilize research findings to guide their selection of techniques. In fact, though, this possibility may not be so remote from social work as can be seen in the work of Reid and Epstein regarding task-centered practice.[26] (This work could be cited also as another example of the

---

[26] W. J. Reid and L. Epstein, *Task-Centered Casework* (New York: Columbia University Press, 1972); W. J. Reid and L. Epstein, *Task-Centered Practice* (New York: Columbia University Press, 1977); W. J. Reid, *The Task-Centered System* (New York: Columbia University Press, 1978).

careful developmental work that currently is underway in building new practice approaches in social work.)

Task-centered practice involves an attempt to be oriented to research evidence in selection of techniques. Task-centered practitioners also are instructed in methods for monitoring and evaluating progress with their cases; thus, attention is paid to individual case evaluation. Finally, all of this has resulted in attempts to conduct nomothetic research and experimental evaluation of the entire approach.[27] Thus, despite the fact that task-centered practice is less than a decade old, it provides an interesting model—and one indigenous to social work—of the way practice and research can be integrated, both in education and in actual practice.

As can be seen, the increased focus on research utilization goes hand in hand with, and in fact may be one instance of, the work on knowledge development reviewed earlier in this chapter. As shall be illustrated in the following section, use of the results of research to inform practice is crucial in providing the field with empirically validated techniques of practice. Research utilization and single-system design also have clear overlap; indeed, it is precisely because of their interrelated but differential values that they are in combination a useful way to integrate practice—both in selecting empirically validated material and in evaluating progress. The increasing use of these approaches to developing knowledge for practice is a major indication that the revolution in practice is indeed here.

Use of Available Knowledge of Demonstrated Effectiveness

Although the results of research on direct practice in social work have been discouraging, the largely negative findings, while suggesting the need for change in the field, have not been sufficient to suggest a direction for change. However, there are other areas in the literature and in practice that not only suggest the need for change but which provide some clear direction for change. These are conceptual (rather than empirical or research-related) problems in the traditional knowledge base of direct practice in social work. Just a few of the most salient points will be reviewed here:[28] (1) Although social workers long have claimed to be agents of social-environmental change, specific knowledge regarding procedures for changing the environment has not been fully developed; (2) Traditional social work approaches do not make adequate use of those in the client's environment who may be available to help bring about change in the client and/or situation; (3) Most traditional approaches have overemphasized diagnostic knowledge (aimed at understanding and assessing the client situation) and paid insufficient attention to intervention knowledge, that is, what the worker actually *does* to bring about change); (4) Most of the technology in traditional practice has been vaguely defined; it has been difficult for social workers to define exactly *what* it is they do, *when* they do it, and *why* they do it; (5) There generally seems to be little rela-

---

[27] Reid, *The Task-Centered System.*

[28] Joel Fischer, *Effective Casework Practice: An Eclectic Approach* (New York: McGraw-Hill, 1978).

tionship between the assessment and intervention processes in traditional social work; and (6) Most traditional approaches have not spelled out specific techniques of practice, the actual procedures a practitioner must carry out in implementing intervention programs.

Now, it should be said that whether one agrees with this or not, or believes that social workers in the past have or have not been effective, the paramount concern of all professionals must be the discovery and use of the most promising methods of practice by which to provide help to clients.

The preceding analysis suggests the hypothesis that the vague knowledge base of practice has been inadequate and possibly is a major reason for the consistent lack of evidence of effectiveness in social work research. Just as assessment in practice leads to a specific intervention program, so this analysis suggests the major priority for practice. Essentially, this is the development of a potent practice technology, and more precisely, a body of specific intervention techniques that can be applied in each case, depending on the particular problem, with reasonable certainty that the techniques will be successful. This suggests the need for the development of an eclectic, empirically based approach to practice. The basic principle of such an approach is that when evidence exists that demonstrates the effectiveness of a technique that can be applied ethically and in accord with social work values, it should be used.

There are several key points in the utilization of such knowledge. The first is the importance of utilizing an empirical orientation to practice. That such an orientation to practice is indeed possible can be seen in several recent works. Mullen, for example, presented a method for utilizing research findings to guide social interventions which he calls "the construction of personal models for effective practice."[29]

The key point of this new thrust in the field is that social workers can use clear, specific, systematic, and rational criteria to select intervention methods. Traditionally, as noted earlier in this chapter in the section on new processes of knowledge development, social workers have tended to rely on vague, unsystematic criteria to select knowledge. Although this may have been a necessary step in the development of the profession, it no longer seems necessary or useful to continue to do so.

A second key point in use of such knowledge is that whether a practice approach or technique was developed by social workers or by practitioners from other fields, it is suitable for use in social work practice if it meets empirical criteria, if it is compatible with social work values, and if it can be demonstrated to be relevant to the problems and phenomena with which social work is concerned.

A third key point in utilizing knowledge is that new forms of practice must rely less on utilizing traditional *theories* than on developing and/or utilizing specific

---

[29] E. J. Mullen, "The Construction of Personal Models for Effective Practice: A Method for Utilizing Research Findings to Guide Social Intervention," *Journal of Social Service Research,* 2 (1978), 45–64; Fischer, *Effective Casework Practice;* E. J. Thomas, "The BESDAS Model for Effective Practice," *Social Work Research and Abstracts,* 13 (1977), pp. 12–17.

interventive *techniques*. That is, the necessity for basing practice on empirical knowledge and for utilizing a range of effective techniques that may be adopted from several different approaches to practice, bespeaks the need to reevaluate the conceptual basis of practice. The major alternative to traditional practice that is grounded in particular practice theories seems to be the development of an eclectic approach to practice comprised of a variety of empirically derived and validated principles and procedures. Such an approach uses careful, systematic criteria for selecting its components with the predominant criterion being evidence of effectiveness: the component leads to demonstrably successful results with clients (that is, if it works, it works).[30] Thus, practitioners can have available to them a body of specific techniques to apply with their clients, based on a careful assessment of the client, situation, and problem. The fact that the techniques of intervention are selected when possible because of their demonstrated effectiveness will increase probabilities that outcomes will be successful.

One of the strongest arguments for the development of an eclectic, empirically based approach is the fact that no single approach or theoretical orientation has a corner on effectiveness. Indeed, it seems counterproductive for practitioners to become overattached to any particular approaches to practice. First, this may keep them from objectively evaluating new approaches that become available. Second, the practitioner cannot afford to ignore the many procedures of documented effectiveness currently available, because of adherence to one approach, and thus end up using less-validated methods.

An eclectic approach does not include every principle or procedure under the sun, thrown together into some mushy super-approach. Rather, it is guided by the best the literature has to offer at any given point in time, using empirical evidence of effectiveness to determine just what *is* the best. This search for the best is a never-ending job, requiring social work educators and practitioners to evaluate the effectiveness of new approaches as they become available. Moreover, the possibility that new research may invalidate old research cannot be overlooked.

Finally, it is important to note that this empirically based model can be approached only as a goal. It is not likely that social workers will ever have every technique in their repertoire validated or a validated technique for every problem. Practice is much too complicated for that. Further, much of what has been described, certainly in terms of validated techniques, applies more to clinical and behavior-change social work functions than to the other social work functions noted earlier. Yet, the basic principles described here apply across the board: using research validated procedures when they are available, and attempting to use clear systematic criteria to select what is used. Thus, even when there is an absence of empirical research, there are several criteria that can be used in selecting procedures for practice.[31]

---

[30] Tony Tripodi, Personal Communication, October, 1978.
[31] Fischer, *Effective Casework Practice*.

Some Approaches with Evidence of Effectiveness

Using knowledge of documented effectiveness is the best means of integrating all three sources of evidence that have been described in this chapter regarding the revolution in social work practice. It is the best means by which new processes of knowledge development can come to fruition in the effort to improve the knowledge base of practice. It is in this way that utilization of the results of research can have its greatest payoff. And it is with these procedures that social workers conduct single-system research to monitor their continuing effect on clients.

It should be obvious that all of this material would be largely irrelevant if there were no approaches with evidence of effectiveness. In fact, in the clinical area alone, including work with individuals, couples, and families, several hundred controlled studies have been conducted. These studies have demonstrated effective practice using a wide range of currently available specific techniques that are already used by many social workers.

This section will describe the several approaches in which the bulk of this evidence of effectiveness seems to be concentrated. The four approaches were selected for two primary reasons: (1) Each approach has accumulated a substantial body of evidence of effectiveness (though not every technique used in each approach has been validated); and (2) each approach contains specific guidelines for implementation of procedures so that the practitioner knows what should be done given a particular client, problem, or situation. The four approaches to be reviewed include *structuring, behavior modification and therapy, cognitive change procedures,* and the *interpersonal skills of empathy, warmth, and genuineness.*[32]

Structuring   This approach is comprised of several dimensions, each adding some degree of structure to practice. The main reason for emphasizing the importance of structure for direct practice is that most research that has compared forms of structured practice with unstructured practice shows that structuring is as good or better.

Structuring involves a general orientation to practice, emphasizing careful planning and systematic use of variables designed to influence or change the problem. Beyond the general orientation, any number of specific procedures have been found either to be effective or to contribute to added structure in practice. Some of these include—

1. role induction interviews (that is, structuring the intervention process and clarifying expectations prior to the onset of intervention);
2. use of specific and precise goal setting;
3. use of contracts between worker and client;
4. use of time limits under certain conditions;

---

[32] Fischer, *Effective Casework Practice.*

5. use of several procedures to enhance client expectations;
6. use of homework assignments and tasks,[33]
7. use of a variety of findings from research in social psychology;[34]
8. use of a number of procedures to enhance generalization of effects (for example, from the office to the natural environment).[35]

Behavior Modification and Therapy   Behavior modification is an important addition to the direct-service practitioner's repertoire. Behavior modification is no longer meeting the resistance it met from some social workers in the 1960s because social workers are recognizing increasingly the compatibility of behavior modification and social work values and goals.

There are numerous important advantages for social workers in using behavior modification. Among the key advantages are—

1. availability of a wide range of specific intervention techniques, well over fifty in fact, including clear procedural guidelines for their implementation;
2. clear relationships between assessment and intervention (that is, the assessment provides a clear prescription regarding the techniques to use);
3. development of a number of principles and procedures focused specifically on social-environmental change, which is at the core of social work practice;
4. a number of procedures for training people in the natural environment;
5. consistent evidence of effectiveness—over 350 controlled experimental studies of behavior modification and therapy, including some seventy-five controlled studies comparing behavior modification with other approaches in almost every one of which behavior modification is shown to be as effective or more effective than the approach with which it was compared.[36]

It should be noted that the evidence on effectiveness of behavior modification varies from technique to technique. Thus, the greatest concentration of research evidence is around a core of techniques such as systematic desensitization (over

[33] W. J. Reid and L. Epstein, *Task-Centered Casework* (New York: Columbia University Press, 1972); Reid, *The Task-Centered System*.

[34] S. R. Strong, "Social Psychological Approach to Psychotherapy Research," in *Handbook of Psychotherapy and Behavior Change*, 2nd ed., eds. S. L. Garfield and A. E. Bergin (New York: John Wiley, 1978), 101–135; A. P. Goldstein, *Psychotherapeutic Attraction* (New York: Pergamon, 1971); A. P. Goldstein, "Relationship-Enhancement Methods," in *Helping People Change*, 2nd ed., eds. F. H. Kanfer and A. P. Goldstein (New York: Pergamon, 1980), 18–57; A. P. Goldstein and N. Simonson, "Social Psychological Approaches to Psychotherapy Research," in *Handbook of Psychotherapy and Behavior Change*, eds. A. E. Bergin and S. L. Garfield (New York: John Wiley, 1971) 154–196.

[35] A. P. Goldstein and F. H. Kanfer, *Maximizing Treatment Gains: Transfer Enhancement in Psychotherapy* (New York: Academic Press, 1979).

[36] A. E. Kazdin and G. T. Wilson, *Evaluation of Behavior Therapy: Issues, Evidence, and Research Strategies* (Cambridge Mass.: Ballinger, 1978).

100 controlled studies alone), assertive training, modeling, positive reinforcement (including shaping, token economies and differential reinforcement), contact desensitization (participant modeling), parent training procedures, and to a lesser extent, around such techniques as extinction, punishment (including response cost and time out), covert sensitization, behavior rehearsal, and so on.[37]

Thus, many behavioral procedures, though not supported by the level of evidence of the better documented behavior modification techniques, not only show beginning evidence of effectiveness, but are constructed to permit evaluation of their effectiveness.

Cognitive Change Procedures   The third approach to practice that is rapidly accumulating evidence of effectiveness and that is available for use by social work practitioners is comprised of a number of different procedures that have an important similarity: They focus on changing cognitive patterns or ways of thinking that are dysfunctional for the client and/or the client's environment. With the exception of the work of Ellis, Perlman, and Werner, this is a relatively new development.[38] Most of these procedures have been developed in the 1970s. Certainly almost all of the research on cognitive procedures has been conducted since 1970.

Because of the relative newness of the field, there is not common agreement about how it should be organized. Thus, the typology of procedures to be described is intended mainly to be heuristic; there is considerable overlap between each type. What is important in this description is that each set of procedures focuses on relatively different kinds of cognitive problems.

The first type of cognitive procedures are those devised to change misconceptions, unrealistic expectations, and other problematic ideas. Together, these procedures, some fifteen to twenty of them, can be called *cognitive restructuring*

---

[37] E. D. Gambrill, *Behavior Modification: Handbook of Assessment, Intervention, and Evaluation* (San Francisco: Jossey-Bass, 1977); J. Fischer and H. L. Gochros, *Planned Behavior Change: Behavior Modification in Social Work* (New York: Free Press, 1975); D. C. Rimm and J. C. Masters, *Behavior Therapy: Techniques and Empirical Findings,* 2nd ed. (New York: Academic Press, 1979): K. D. O'Leary and G. T. Wilson, *Behavior Therapy: Application and Outcome* (Englewood Cliffs, N.J.: Prentice-Hall, 1975); W. E. Craighead and others, *Behavior Modification: Principles, Issues, and Applications* (Boston: Houghton Mifflin, 1976); S. L. Garfield and A. E. Bergin, eds., *Handbook of Psychotherapy and Behavior Change,* 2nd ed. (New York: John Wiley, 1978); Kazdin and Wilson, *Evaluation of Behavior Therapy;* M. F. Goldfried and G. C. Davison, *Clinical Behavior Therapy* (New York: Holt, Rinehart & Winston, 1976); F. H. Kanger and A. P. Goldstein, eds., *Helping People Change,* 2nd ed. (New York: Pergamon, 1980); Neil S. Jacobson and Gayla Margolin, *Marital Therapy* (New York: Brunner/Mazel, 1979).

[38] A. Ellis, *Reason and Emotion in Psychotherapy* (New York: Lyle Stuart, 1962); A. Ellis, "Rational-Emotive Psychotherapy," in *Current Psychotherapies,* ed. R. Corsini (Itasca, Ill.: F. E. Peacock, 1973), 167–206; A. Ellis and R. A. Harper, *A New Guide to Rational Living* (North Hollywood, Calif.: Wilshire Book Co., 1975); H. H. Perlman, *Social Casework: A Problem-Solving Process* (Chicago: University of Chicago Press, 1957); H. D. Werner, *A Rational Approach to Social Casework* (New York: Association Press, 1964); H. D. Werner, "Cognitive Theory," in *Social Work Treatment,* ed. F. J. Turner (New York: Free Press, 1974); H. D. Werner, ed., *New Understandings of Human Behavior* (New York: Association Press, 1970).

techniques. Some of the prime movers in developing and conceptualizing cognitive restructuring techniques are Beck, Raimy, Lazarus, Mahoney, and Meichenbaum.[39]

The second type are methods for changing *irrational self-statements* (that is, changing from negative to positive the ways people label external events) to reduce distressed emotional reactions. The work of Ellis is of major importance here and has been instrumental in producing a body of several techniques.[40] Recent development of a procedure called *self-instruction* embodies many of Ellis' ideas systematically integrated with demonstrated behavior modification techniques.[41]

The third type of cognitive procedures involves systematic approaches to *problem solving and decision making.* Long considered an important area for social work practice, new developments in this area include making the problem-solving process more systematic and accumulating empirical evidence of effectiveness.[42]

The fourth type is what might be called *self-control*—teaching clients to change their own behaviors, thoughts, and feelings. The work in this area is expanding and includes procedures that incorporate both behavioral and cognitive features.[43]

There is, in fact, a trend in the therapeutic practices toward convergence of cognitive and behavioral procedures. This can be seen most clearly in the work of Meichenbaum (for example, the technique of *stress innoculation training)* and in the development of many other procedures as well.[44]

Overall, there has been an increase in the empirical findings on cognitive procedures, though nowhere near as impressive as the amount of evidence on behavior modification. Several dozen controlled studies have been conducted just since 1970.[45] This increase in the amount of research suggests that this field will continue to grow.

[39] A. T. Beck, *Cognitive Theory and the Emotional Disorders* (New York: International Universities Press, 1976); V. Raimy, *Misunderstanding of the Self* (San Francisco: Jossey-Bass, 1975); A. A. Lazarus, *Behavior Therapy and Beyond* (New York: McGraw-Hill, 1971); M. J. Mahoney, *Cognition and Behavior Modification* (Cambridge, Mass.: Ballinger, 1974); M. J. Mahoney, "Cognitive and Self-Control Therapies," in *Handbook of Psychotherapy and Behavior Change,* 2nd ed., eds. S. L. Garfield and A. E. Bergin (New York: John Wiley, 1978), 689–722; D. Meichenbaum, *Cognitive-Behavior Modification* (New York: Plenum, 1977).

[40] A. Ellis, *Reason and Emotion in Psychotherapy* (New York: Lyle Stuart, 1962); Ellis, "Rational-Emotive Psychotherapy"; A. Ellis and R. A. Harper, *A New Guide to Rational Living* (North Hollywood, Calif.: Wilshire Book Co., 1975); M. R. Goldfried and others, "Systematic Rational Restructuring as a Self-Control Technique," *Behavior Therapy,* 5 (1974), 247–254.

[41] D. Meichenbaum, *Cognitive-Behavior Modification* (New York: Plenum, 1977).

[42] I. L. Janis and L. Mann, *Decision-Making* (New York: Free Press, 1977).

[43] F. H. Kanfer, "Self Management Methods," in *Helping People Change,* eds. F. H. Kanfer and A. P. Goldstein, 2nd ed. (New York: Pergamon, 1980), 334–389; A. Ellis and R. A. Harper, *A New Guide to Rational Living;* M. J. Mahoney and C. E. Thoresen, *Self-Control: Power to the Person* (Monterey, Calif.: Brooks/Cole, 1974).

[44] Meichenbaum, *Cognitive-Behavior Modification;* Mahoney, "Cognitive and Self-Control Therapies;" J. P. Foreyt and D. P. Rathjen, eds., *Cognitive Behavior Therapy* (New York: Plenum, 1978); N. Huruitz, *Theory and Practice of Marital and Family Therapy* (New York: Macmillan, 1980); P. C. Kendall and S. D. Hollon, eds., *Cognitive-Behavioral Interventions: Theory, Research, and Procedures* (New York: Academic, 1979).

[45] Meichenbaum, *Cognitive Behavior Modification;* Mahoney, "Cognitive and Self-Control Therapies,"

Interpersonal Skills: Empathy, Warmth, and Genuineness   The fourth major practice approach that is based on a considerable amount of evidence of effectiveness
is the use of the *interpersonal skills* (or core conditions) of empathy, warmth, and
genuineness. Although the evidence here is neither as elegant nor as consistent as
in the other three approaches, it does seem to be sufficient to suggest that these
communication skills are critical for social work practice.[46]

Key to this approach is the development of scales to measure the communication of empathy, warmth, and genuineness (in addition to several other interpersonal dimensions). This allows for skills to be observed and their use to be evaluated. Further, development of these scales focuses attention on skill development
in education; there is increasing evidence that skills can be successfully learned in
courses focusing on structured, step-by-step experiential learning.[47]

These interpersonal skills are the essential skills needed in development of the
therapeutic relationship and in therapeutic interviewing skills. They are the foundation for the eclectic approach described here. Indeed, there are ten experimental
studies showing that practitioners who demonstrate mastery of these interpersonal
skills are more effective in their use of several behavioral procedures.[48]

Integrating an Eclectic Approach   The major value of an eclectic approach to
practice is that it encourages practitioner responses that are based on differential
assessments of needs and problems. Thus, skilled sensitive assessment of the person, problem, and situation is even more necessary using an eclectic approach than
a conventional one, where the range of techniques available to the practitioner is
more limited. Such an assessment is made more feasible by use of the BASIC ID
framework for assessment proposed by Lazarus.[49] Use of this framework assures
attention to assessment of a broad range of human functioning: Behavior, Affect,
Sensation, Imagery, Cognition, Interpersonal Relationships and Drugs (including
physical characteristics). (Another category of assessment that is useful to add to
this model for both intervention and assessment is Environment; see following section on the ecosystem perspective.) Implementation of this assessment framework
is made even more feasible by use of a systematic multimethod clinical assessment
package such as the one proposed by Nay.[50]

[46] C. B. Truax and K. M. Mitchell, "Research on Certain Therapist Interpersonal Skills in Relation to
Process and Outcome," in *Handbook of Psychotherapy and Behavior Change,* eds. A. E. Bergin and
S. L. Garfield (New York: John Wiley, 1971), 299–344; R. R. Carkhuff and B. Berenson, *Teaching As
Treatment* (Amherst, Mass.: Human Resources Development Press, 1976): M. B. Parloff and B. E. Wolfe,
"Research on Therapist Variables in Relation to Process and Outcome," in *Handbook of Psychotherapy,*
eds. Bergin and Garfield, 233–282: K. M. Mitchell and others, "A Reappraisal of the Therapeutic Effec-
tiveness of Accurate Empathy, Non-possessive Warmth, and Genuineness," in *Effective Psychotherapy:
A Handbook of Research,* eds. A. S. Gurman and A. M. Razin (New York: Pergamon, 1977) 482–502.

[47] J. Fischer, "Is Social Work Education Necessary?" (Paper presented at Annual Program Meeting of
the Council on Social Work Education, Boston, Mass., March, 1979.)

[48] Fischer, *Effective Casework Practice,* Chapter 8.

[49] A. A. Lazarus, *Multimodal Behavior Therapy* (New York: Springer, 1976).

[50] Ibid, p. 2; Robert Nay, *Multimethod Clinical Assessment* (New York: Gardner, 1979).

It appears to be possible to take a range of presumably diverse approaches and to integrate them into a meaningful whole.[51] At the broadest level, the approach can be integrated with professional values and with the criteria used to select them. Thus, for example, with use of empirical criteria, one has a ready-made typology involving the differential application of techniques based on the evidence of effectiveness with particular clients and problems.

At a middle-range level, an eclectic approach can be integrated through use of a conceptual model in which practice is conceived as a series of interrelated phases. Such a model is available in the work of Carkhuff, Carkhuff and Berenson, and Egan.[52] These authors have developed a conceptual model based on the major ingredients of successful helping and the stages in which they are employed. This model contains the following elements, each of which consists of a number of processes and techniques such as those from the eclectic approach described here:

1. Experiencing and Exploration
2. Understanding and Defining
3. Action
4. Goal Attainment and Evaluation

The third, and most "down-to-earth" level of integration which flows from the conceptual model is in the actual phases of practice developed as a specific framework that prescribes the ways assessment and intervention procedures are applied in an eclectic approach. Such a framework—comprised of fourteen phases—is described in Fischer.[53] The major purpose of this schema is to guide the implementation of the systematic, rigorous way of thinking that is characteristic of an eclectic approach and to provide detailed guidelines for practice. It is not intended to be a lock-step, rigid approach to integration but one that allows flexible utilization of procedures from different approaches in a systematic, meaningful way.

An Emerging Conceptual Framework for Practice

How do the eclectic approach and these new methods of practice fit in with what social work is all about? Although there are ways of integrating an eclectic approach in practice, it is necessary to place such an approach in a broader perspective, not only to aid in guiding practice, but so that the approach is consistent with social work values and goals, so that fragmentation is avoided, and so that the relationships between concrete parts of practice (for example, application of a technique) to the whole of social work can be understood and evaluated.

A conceptual framework of this kind may be available in recent work on an

[51] Fischer, *Effective Casework Practice.*

[52] R. R. Carkhuff and B. Berenson, *Teaching As Treatment* (Amherst, Mass.: Human Resources Development Press, 1976); R. R. Carkhuff, *Helping and Human Relations,* 2 vols. (New York: Holt, Rinehart & Winston, 1969); G. Egan, *The Skilled Helper* (Monterey, Calif.: Brooks/Cole, 1975).

[53] J. Fischer, *Effective Casework Practice.*

ecological perspective for social work practice, or what might be termed an "eco-systems model." This model of practice is in an early stage of development, but it appears to hold promise for social work, especially by providing a perspective by which to integrate ideas about the location, purpose, and function of social work practice.[54] A brief overview of this model will be presented here.

From an ecosystems perspective, people and their environment are viewed as complementary components of a system in which each continually shapes the other. Emphasis is placed on processes of mutual adaptation between persons and their environments. People are viewed as evolving and adapting by means of trans-actions with all elements of their environments. Thus, an ecosystems perspective demands that attention be given to the social and physical environments in which people function. This attention includes the quality and quantity of environmental resources available to support the individual.[55]

The focus of the ecosystems model is on the interface between people and their environments, and more particularly, on the transactions between them. This orientation recognizes the way people can mold their environment and the ways environments affect people, thus focusing attention on interventions that facili-tate person-environment transactions. Interventions are directed at environmental change and helping the individual cope with impinging environmental factors.

This approach provides a formulation for understanding the distinctive tasks and functions of social work: strengthening people's coping patterns and improv-ing environments to attain a better match between people's adaptive needs and potentials and their environments.[56] With this approach, social work practitioners focus on helping people and their environments overcome obstacles that limit and hamper adaptive capacities. Thus, assessment in practice requires an under-standing of the functions served by current transactions for the person and for the environment.[57]

The ecosystems approach allows practitioners to embrace established and emerging models of practice. As Germaine notes, the ecosystems perspective val-ues differential practice responses to differential definition of need. Thus, any par-ticular practice approach is important to the extent that it fits a particular problem definition.[58]

---

[54] C. B. Germaine, "An Ecological Perspective in Casework Practice," *Social Casework,* 54 (1973), 323–330; C. B. Germaine, "General Systems Theory and Ego Psychology: An Ecological Perspective," *Social Service Review,* 52 (1978), 535–550; C. B. Germaine, "Teaching An Ecological Perspective for Social Work Practice," in *Teaching for Competence in the Delivery of Direct Services* (New York: CSWE, 1976); C. B. Germaine, ed., *The Ecological Perspective in Social Work Practice: People and Environments* (New York: Columbia University Press, 1979); A. Gitterman and C. B. Germaine, "Social Work Practice: A Life Model," *Social Service Review,* 50 (1976), 601–610; C. B. Germaine and A. Gitterman, *The Life Model of Social Work Practice* (New York: Columbia, 1980); C. Meyer, *Social Work Practice: The Changing Landscape,* 2nd ed. (New York: The Free Press, 1976).

[55] Germaine, "Teaching An Ecological Perspective."

[56] Gitterman and Germaine, "Social Work Practice."

[57] Ibid.

[58] Germaine, "Teaching An Ecological Perspective."

Although this brief overview hardly does justice to the ecosystems model, it illustrates its potential utility for practice. It is consistent with social work tradition and philosophy, as well as with the most recent conceptions of the key, distinctive organizing principles of the profession.[59] The ecosystems model is both flexible and heuristic, providing an organizing, integrating framework that can be adapted to a variety of different uses. Further, it provides a focus and a locus for social work intervention.

The ecosystems model does not embrace any one system of practice; indeed, it does not prescribe any specific techniques of practice. In this respect, it is consistent with the eclectic approach described above. That is, the ecosystems model provides a conceptual framework for understanding social work practice at the broadest level and also provides a particular view of the problems with which social workers deal. An eclectic approach to practice adds flesh to the bones of the ecosystems model—the specific techniques of practice. The ecosystems model helps the practitioner understand the context of practice; the eclectic practitioner uses a repertoire of empirically demonstrated techniques to make use of understandings derived from an ecological perspective. Each perspective—ecosystems and eclectic approach—values differential practice responses that are based on differential assessments. As the ecosystems model continues to be developed and systematized, its values for organizing practice can be more clearly evaluated. Indeed, its continued development will necessitate empirical tests of its propositions. But as it stands now, the ecosystems model appears to offer a potentially fruitful perspective for understanding and organizing practice and for integrating an eclectic, empirically-based approach into a broader framework.

Prospects for the Revolution: Will It Succeed?

There is considerable overlap among the three major new developments discussed in this chapter: new processes of knowledge development, integrating research and practice, and use of available procedures of documented effectiveness. Each development points toward a "new social work," characterized by a higher degree of rigor and systematization than has been the case heretofore. Each points toward heavier reliance on the results of research—on an empirically oriented base for practice—than has been common in social work in the past; each calls for greater discrimination in the selection of the knowledge that social workers use, and for a higher degree of professional responsibility in trying to ensure that what we do does indeed work. With these three developments the basic values, ethics, and philosophy of social work—the profession's intrinsic humanistic orientation—are maintained while focusing increased attention on sharpening and refining the technology and the knowledge the practitioner utilizes in practice. In short, all of these new developments point to intensified focus on the outcome of social work practice and on increasing the extent to which social workers can be effective.

[59] NASW, "Specialization in the Social Work Profession," *NASW News,* 24 (1979), 20, 31.

What are the key characteristics of the "new breed" of social worker who makes use of these new developments? Thomas has suggested that the effective practitioner will focus on five component sets of activities, all of which are consistent with the developments described in this chapter: specifying behavioral problems and targets, using empirically based knowledge; guiding practice by use of data gathered by scientific procedures; providing accountable outcomes by determining the costs and benefits of intervention; and conducting practice in a self-correcting manner by using data that assists in determining the efficiency and effectiveness of practice.[60]

The formulation of practice described here along with others in the literature[61] suggests that the modern social worker could be described as the scientific practitioner. This is a social worker who—

1. systematically evaluates and monitors progress with each and every case;
2. grounds practice in empirically based knowledge, particularly the numerous available interventive techniques for which there is evidence of effectiveness, and uses those without such evidence only with due caution; and
3. has the skills, attitudes, and commitment to be able and willing to keep learning and searching for new and more effective approaches to intervention.

What are the chances that the revolution will come to fruition and that the practitioner-researcher will indeed be the new social worker? Whose responsibility is it to see that these changes come about?

It seems, first of all, that the logical entry point for new knowledge in the profession is through social work educators, the gatekeepers of the profession. If the revolution is to succeed, it is crucial that social work educators participate in the work of developing more effective intervention procedures. Social work educators should study these new approaches and disseminate them in their teaching, in workshops, and through publication.

Social work students, too, have the responsibility to learn these new methods of practice and to question the rationale for and empirical knowledge base of the material presented in class.

There are, too, clear responsibilities for social work practitioners. Ultimately, for the revolution to be successful, professional social workers must utilize the new knowledge in their day-to-day work with clients. Social work practitioners must be willing to give up old and more comfortable knowledge when new and more effective knowledge becomes available.

The key question in all of this is, perhaps, What are the alternatives? If the principles described in this chapter to inform selection of knowledge for social work

[60] Thomas, "The BESDAS Model."

[61] S. Briar, "Clinical Scientists in Social Work: Where Are They?" (Paper presented at University of Chicago, School of Social Service Administration Alumni Conference, May, 1974); S. Briar, "Toward the Integration of Practice and Research." (Paper presented at NASW Conference on the Future of Social Work Research, San Antonio, October, 1978); M. Bloom, *The Paradox of Helping: Introduction to the Philosophy of Scientific Practice* (New York: John Wiley, 1975).

education and practice are not used, what principles are used? If techniques for which there is empirical evidence of effectiveness are not used, what techniques are used?

The revolution can succeed. In fact, there is reason to believe that it is well under way. However, for the revolution to be uniformly successful, and for practice to become more effective, it appears to require that all members of the profession accept responsibility for encouraging these changes and implementing them in their own work. If no one will accept the responsibility, no one will act.

References

Bartlett, H., *The Common Base of Social Work Practice*. New York: NASW, 1970.

Beck, A. T., *Cognitive Theory and the Emotional Disorders*. New York: International Universities Press, 1976.

Bloom, M., *The Paradox of Helping: Introduction to the Philosophy of Scientific Practice*. New York: John Wiley, 1975.

Bloom, M., and S. Block, "Evaluating Effectiveness and Efficiency in One's Own Practice," *Social Work*, 13 (1977), 130–136.

Bloom, M., and J. Fischer, *Evaluating Practice: A Guide for the Accountable Professional*. Englewood Cliffs, N.J.: Prentice-Hall, Inc., 1982.

Briar, S., "Clinical Scientists in Social Work: Where Are They?" Paper presented at University of Chicago, School of Social Service Administration Alumni Conference, May, 1974.

Briar, S., "Toward the Integration of Practice and Research," Paper presented at NASW Conference on the Future of Social Work Research, San Antonio, October, 1978.

Carkhuff, R. R., *Helping and Human Relations. Vol. 1*. New York: Holt, Rinehart, and Winston, 1969a.

Carkhuff, R. R., *Helping and Human Relations. Vol. 2*. New York: Holt, Rinehart, and Winston, 1969b.

Carkhuff, R. R., and B. Berenson, *Teaching As Treatment*. Amherst, Mass.: Human Resources Development Press, 1976.

Craighead, W. E. and others, *Behavior Modification: Principles, Issues, and Applications*. Boston: Houghton Mifflin, 1976.

Egan, G., *The Skilled Helper*. Monterey, California: Brooks-Cole, 1975.

Ellis, A., *Reason and Emotion in Psychotherapy*. New York: Lyle Stuart, 1962.

Ellis, A., "Rational-Emotive Psychotherapy," in *Current Psychotherapies*, ed. R. Corsini Itasca, Ill.: F. E. Peacock, 1973, pp. 167–206.

Ellis, A., and R. A. Harper, *A New Guide to Rational Living*. North Hollywood, Calif.: Wilshire Book Co., 1975.

Fischer, J., *Effective Casework Practice: An Eclectic Approach*. New York: McGraw-Hill, 1978.

Fischer, J., "Has Mighty Casework Struck Out?" *Social Work*, 18 (1973b), 107–110.

Fischer, J., "Is Casework Effective? A Review," *Social Work*, 18 (1973a), 5–20.

Fischer, J., "Is Social Work Education Necessary?" Paper presented at Annual Program Meeting of the Council on Social Work Education, Boston, Mass., March, 1979.

Fischer, J., *The Effectiveness of Social Casework.* Springfield, Ill.: Chas. C Thomas, 1976.

Fischer, J., and H. L. Gochros, *Planned Behavior Change: Behavior Modification in Social Work.* New York: Free Press, 1975.

Fischer, J., and W. H. Hudson, "Increasing the Relevance of Research Education," in *Research Utilization in Social Work.* New York: CSWE, in press.

Foreyt, J. P., and D. P. Rathjen, eds., *Cognitive Behavior Therapy.* New York: Plenum, 1978.

Gambrill, E. D., *Behavior Modification: Handbook of Assessment, Intervention, and Evaluation.* San Francisco: Jossey-Bass, 1977.

Garfield, S. L., and A. E. Bergin, eds., *Handbook of Psychotherapy and Behavior Change* (2nd ed.). New York: John Wiley, 1978.

Germaine, C. B., "An Ecological Perspective in Casework Practice," *Social Casework,* 54 (1973), 323–330.

Germaine, C. B., "General Systems Theory and Ego Psychology: An Ecological Perspective," *Social Service Review,* 52 (1978), 535–550.

Germaine, C. B., "Teaching An Ecological Perspective for Social Work Practice," in *Teaching for Competence in The Delivery of Direct Services.* New York: CSWE, 1976.

Germaine, C. B. ed., *The Ecological Perspective in Social Work Practice: People and Environments.* New York: Columbia University Press, 1979.

Germaine, C. B., and A. Gitterman, *The Life Model of Social Work Practice.* New York: Columbia, 1980.

Gingerich, W. J., "Procedure for Evaluating Clinical Practice," *Health and Social Work,* 4, no. 2 (1979), 105–130.

Gitterman, A., and C. B. Germaine, "Social Work Practice: A Life Model," *Social Service Review,* 50 (1976), 601–610.

Goldfried, M. R., and others, "Systematic Rational Restructuring as a Self-Control Technique," *Behavior Therapy,* 5 (1974), 247–254.

Goldfried, M. R., and G. C. Davison, *Clinical Behavior Therapy.* New York: Holt, Rinehart and Winston, 1976.

Goldstein, A. P., *Psychotherapeutic Attraction.* New York: Pergamon, 1971.

Goldstein, A. P., "Relationship-Enhancement Methods," in *Helping People Change,* (2nd ed.), eds. F. H. Kanfer and A. P. Goldstein. New York: Pergamon, 1980, pp. 18–57.

Goldstein, A. P. and F. H. Kanfer, eds., *Maximizing Treatment Gains: Transfer Enhancement in Psychotherapy.* New York: Academic Press, 1979.

Goldstein, A. P., and N. Simonson, "Social Psychological Approaches to Psychotherapy Research," in *Handbook of Psychotherapy and Behavior Change,* eds. A. E. Bergin and S. L. Garfield. New York: John Wiley, 1971, pp. 154–196.

Hersen, M., and D. H. Barlow, *Single Case Experimental Designs*. New York: Pergamon, 1976.

Howe, M. W., "Casework Self-Evaluation: A Single-Subject Approach," *Social Service Review*, 48 (1974), 1–23.

Hurvitz, N., *Theory and Practice of Marital and Family Therapy*. New York: Macmillan, 1980.

Jacobson, Neil S., and Gayla Margolin, *Marital Therapy*. New York: Brunner/ Mazel, 1979.

Janis, I. L., and L. Mann, *Decision-Making*. New York: Free Press, 1977.

Jayaratne, S., and R. Levy, *Empirical Clinical Practice*. New York: Columbia University Press, 1979.

Kanfer, F. M., "Self-Management Methods," in *Helping People Change* (2nd ed.), eds. F. H. Kanfer and A. P. Goldstein. New York: Pergamon, 1980, pp. 334–389.

Kanfer, F. H., and A. P. Goldstein, eds., *Helping People Change* (2nd ed.). New York: Pergamon, 1980.

Kazdin, A. E., and G. T. Wilson, *Evaluation of Behavior Therapy: Issues, Evidence, and Research Strategies*. Cambridge, Mass.: Ballinger, 1978.

Kendall, P. C., and S. D. Hollon, eds., *Cognitive-Behavioral Interventions: Theory, Practice, and Procedures*. New York: Academic, 1979.

Kirk, S. A., "Understanding the Utilization of Research in Social Work and Other Applied Professions." Paper presented at Conference on Research Utilization in Social Work Education, CSWE, New Orleans, October, 1977.

Kuhn, T. S., *The Structure of Scientific Revolutions*. Chicago: University of Chicago Press, 1962.

Lazarus, A. A., *Behavior Therapy and Beyond*. New York: McGraw-Hill, 1971.

"Letters to the Editor," *Social Work*, 18 (March, May, July, 1973).

Mahoney, M. J., *Cognition and Behavior Modification*. Cambridge, Mass.: Ballinger, 1974.

Mahoney, M. J., "Cognitive and Self-Control Therapies," in *Handbook of Psychotherapy and Behavior Change* (2nd ed.), eds. S. L. Garfield and A. E. Bergin. New York: John Wiley, 1978, pp. 689–722.

Mahoney, M. J., and C. E. Thoresen, *Self Control: Power to the Person*. Monterey, Calif.: Brooks-Cole, 1974.

Meichenbaum, D., *Cognitive-Behavior Modification*. New York: Plenum, 1977.

Mitchell, K. M., and others, "A Reappraisal of the Therapeutic Effectiveness of Accurate Empathy, Non-possessive Warmth, and Genuineness," in *Effective Psychotherapy: A Handbook of Research*, eds. A. S. Gurman and A. M. Razin. New York: Pergamon, 1977, pp. 482–502.

Mullen, E. J., "The Construction of Personal Models for Effective Practice: A Method for Utilizing Research Findings to Guide Social Intervention," *Journal of Social Service Research*, 2 (1978), 45–64.

Mullen, E. J., and J. R. Dumpson, eds., *Evaluation of Social Intervention*. San Francisco: Jossey-Bass, 1972.

NASW, "Specialization in the Social Work Profession," *NASW News*, 24 (1979), pp. 20, 31.

O'Leary, K. D., and G. T. Wilson, *Behavior Therapy: Application and Outcome.* Englewood Cliffs, N.J.: Prentice-Hall Inc., 1975.

Parloff, M. B., and B. E. Wolfe, "Research on Therapist Variables in Relation to Process and Outcome," in *Handbook of Psychotherapy and Behavior Change* (2nd ed.), eds. S. L. Garfield and A. E. Bergin. New York: John Wiley, 1978, pp. 233–282.

Perlman, H. H., *Social Casework: A Problem-Solving Process.* Chicago: University of Chicago Press, 1957.

"Points and Viewpoints," *Social Work*, 18 (1973).

Raimy, V., *Misunderstandings of the Self.* San Francisco: Jossey-Bass, 1975.

Reid, W. J., "Needed: A New Science for Clinical Social Work," in J. Fischer, *The Effectiveness of Social Casework.* Springfield, Ill.: Chas. C Thomas, 1976, pp. 262–272.

Reid, W. J., *The Task-Centered System.* New York: Columbia University Press, 1978.

Reid, W. J., and L. Epstein, *Task-Centered Casework.* New York: Columbia University Press, 1972.

Reid, W. J., and L. Epstein, eds., *Task-Centered Practice.* New York: Columbia University Press, 1977.

Rimm, D. C., and J. C. Masters, *Behavior Therapy: Techniques and Empirical Findings* (2nd ed.). New York: Academic Press, 1979.

Roberts, R. W., and R. Nee, eds., *Theories of Social Casework.* Chicago: University of Chicago Press, 1970.

Roberts, R. W., and H. Northen, eds., *Theories of Social Work with Groups.* New York: Columbia University Press, 1976.

Rothman, J., "Conversion and Design in the Research Utilization Process," *Journal of Social Service Research*, 2 (1978), 95–116.

Rothman, J., and others, *Fostering Participation and Innovation: A Handbook for Human Service Professionals.* Itasca, Ill.: F. E. Peacock, 1978.

Rothman, J., *Planning and Organizing for Social Change: Action Principles from Social Science Research.* New York: Columbia University Press, 1974.

Rothman, J., *Promoting Innovation and Change in Organizations and Communities.* New York: John Wiley, 1976.

Rothman, J., *Research and Development in the Human Services.* Englewood Cliffs, N.J.: Prentice-Hall, 1978.

Scherz, F. H., "Theory and Practice of Family Therapy," in *Theories of Social Casework*, eds. R. Roberts and R. Nee. Chicago: University of Chicago Press, 1970, pp. 219–264.

Shapiro, M. B., "The Single Case in Clinical-Psychological Research," *Journal of General Psychology*, 74 (1966), 3–23.

Shapiro, M. B., "The Single Case in Fundamental Clinical Psychological Research," *British Journal of Medical Psychology*, 34 (1961), 255–263.

Sherman, S. N., "Family Therapy," in *Social Work Treatment,* ed. F. J. Turner. New York: Free Press, 1974, pp. 457–494.

Simpson, R. L., "Is Research Utilization for Social Workers?" *Journal of Social Service Research,* 2 (1978), 143–157.

Strean, H. S., *Social Casework: Theories in Action.* Metuchen, N.J.: Scarecrow Press, 1971.

Strong, S. R., "Social Psychological Approach to Psychotherapy Research," *Handbook of Psychotherapy and Behavior Change* (2nd ed.), eds. S. L. Garfield and A. E. Bergin. New York: John Wiley, 1978, pp. 101–135.

Thomas, E. J., "Uses of Research Methods in Interpersonal Practice," in *Social Work Research* (rev. ed.), ed. N. R. Polansky. Chicago: University of Chicago Press, 1975, pp. 254–283.

Thomas, E. J., "The BESDAS Model for Effective Practice," *Social Work Research and Abstracts,* 13 (1977), 12–17.

Thomas, E. J., "Beyond Knowledge Utilization in Generating Human Service Technology," Paper presented at NASW Conference on the Future of Social Work Research, San Antonio, Texas, Oct. 15–18, 1978b.

Thomas, E. J., "Generating Innovation in Social Work: The Paradigm of Developmental Research," *Journal of Social Service Research,* 2 (1978c), 95–116.

Thomas, E. J., "Mousetraps, Developmental Research, and Social Work Education," *Social Service Review,* 52 (1978a), 468–483.

Thomas, E. J., ed., "New Models of Social Service Research," Special Issue of *Journal of Social Service Research,* 2, no. 1 (1978).

Thomas, E. J., "Research and Service in Single-Case Experimentation: Conflicts and Choices," *Social Work Research and Abstracts,* 14 (1978d), 20–31.

Tripodi, T., Personal Communication, October, 1978.

Traux, C. B., and K. M. Mitchell, "Research on Certain Therapist Interpersonal Skills in Relation to Process and Outcome," in *Handbook of Psychotherapy and Behavior Change,* eds. A. E. Bergin and S. L. Garfield. New York: John Wiley, 1971, pp. 299–344.

Turner, F. J., ed., *Social Work Treatment* (2nd ed.). New York: Free Press, 1979.

Werner, H. D., *A Rational Approach to Social Casework.* New York: Association Press, 1964.

Werner, H. D., "Cognitive Theory," in *Social Work Treatment,* ed. F. J. Turner. New York: Free Press, 1974.

Werner, H. D., ed., *New Understandings of Human Behavior.* New York: Association Press, 1970.

Zimbalist, S. E., "The Research Component of the Master's Degree Curriculum in Social Work: A Survey Summary," *Journal of Education for Social Work,* 10 (1974), 118–123.

Chapter 11

A Framework for Evaluating Empirical Research Reports

Empirical research reports are defined in this chapter as published articles based on studies designed to contribute to the social work knowledge base through rigorous, replicable means. A methodology for evaluating the significance and validity of the knowledge derived from such reports is suggested in a framework whose value rests on answers to two basic questions:

1. Why is it important to analyze social work research?
2. Why is the framework presented in this chapter recommended?

The first question is addressed in the theme of this book: Research and evaluation should be applicable in social work practice situations, and the field of social work should not be dichotomized into practice and research orientations. These concepts are based on the belief that systematic, orderly procedures of empirical social work research and evaluation provide the most productive means to organize, understand, test, and develop social work knowledge. The capacity to perform competently in the social work profession, therefore, is based on the ability to analyze and utilize the results of social work research and evaluation.

The issue of competency in the profession was critically examined during the seventies.[1] This decade has been called the age of accountability because it emphasized social workers' responsibility to demonstrate their effectiveness. To demonstrate accountability, social work practice must be guided, as much as possible, by empirically validated principles and techniques.

Few (if any) empirical studies of social work research or evaluation are without flaws. Nevertheless, the social work practitioner/researcher must be able to analyze social work research and evaluation findings from reports and to make judgments as to their applicability. Otherwise, even minimum effectiveness in practice is unlikely.

Fischer, J. (1981). In R. Grinnell (Ed.), *Social Work Research and Evaluation*. Itasca, IL: F. E. Peacock. Reprinted with permission of Richard Grinnell & Oxford University Press.

[1] Scott Briar, "The Age of Accountability," *Social Work*, 18 (January 1973), pp. 2, 114.

The second question—why the framework presented in this chapter is recommended—relates to the accessibility and feasibility for use of this framework. The framework defines the key criteria for assessing research reports. It should aid social workers to develop the basic skills for analyzing reports and alert them to how these skills can be applied effectively and efficiently in conducting and writing up their own studies. The key evaluative criteria suggested for analyzing an empirical research study can be applied on a point-by-point basis in the analysis of a single study, or they can be used in comparing several studies. Each criterion in the framework is related to a specific aspect of the research process. Analyzing a study criterion by criterion should make it relatively easy to draw accurate conclusions about the study. As in all social work skills, however, the ease of using this framework increases with practice.

Figure 11.1 summarizes the framework for evaluating the strengths and weaknesses of empirical social work research studies. It is composed of 80 specific criteria which can be applied in the evaluation of any study. The criteria highlight specific analytic dimensions and indicate their importance in an evaluation. Each criterion is distinct, although there is a clear overlap among them.

The framework was developed by abstracting and synthesizing criteria for analysis from a number of different sources, both from within the field of social work and outside it.[2] The criteria are grouped into the four major categories of a research report discussed in the preceding chapter: problem, method, findings, and discussion.[3] The criteria in each category are described in the following sections.

Problem

The first category, the problem area under investigation, is concerned with the author's conceptualization of the phenomena to be tested. This segment of the framework can be used as an aid in understanding and evaluating the overall background and aims of the study.

Literature Review

Most studies are based on previous research or established theoretical conceptions. The study must demonstrate an adequate knowledge of the relevant literature and there should be references citing existing studies of similar phenomena. The evaluation should question how the author has related the present study to the literature, conceptually and methodologically.

The examination of the author's use of relevant literature should also assess the ways in which the problem area under investigation (the research question) has

---

[2] Tony Tripodi, Phillip A. Fellin, and Henry J. Meyer, *The Assessment of Social Research* (Itasca, Ill.: F. E. Peacock Publishers, 1969); Donald T. Campbell and Julian C. Stanley, *Experimental and Quasi-Experimental Designs for Research* (Chicago, Ill.: Rand McNally & Co., 1966); Elizabeth Herzogg, *Some Guidelines for Evaluative Research* (Washington, D.C.: United States Department of Health, Education, and Welfare, 1959).

[3] See Tripodi, Fellin, and Meyer, *Assessment of Social Research*.

FIGURE 11.1   Framework for Evaluating Empirical Research Reports

Criteria	Scale			
	Low		High	
A. PROBLEM				
1. Adequacy of the literature review	1	2	3	4
2. Clarity of the problem area (research question) under investigation	1	2	3	4
3. Clarity of the statement of the hypothesis	1	2	3	4
4. Clarity of the specification of the independent variable	1	2	3	4
5. Clarity of the specification of the dependent variable	1	2	3	4
6. Clarity of the definitions for major concepts	1	2	3	4
7. Clarity of the operational definitions	1	2	3	4
8. Reasonableness of assumption of relationship between the independent and dependent variables	1	2	3	4
9. Specification of confounding variables	1	2	3	4
10. Number of independent variables tested	1	2	3	4
11. Adequacy in the control of confounding variables	1	2	3	4
12. Clarity of author orientation	1	2	3	4
13. Clarity of the study's purpose	1	2	3	4
14. Clarity of the study's auspices	1	2	3	4
15. Reasonableness of the author's assumptions	1	2	3	4
B. METHOD				
16. Clarity of the specification of the kinds of changes desired	1	2	3	4
17. Clarity as to signs of client change	1	2	3	4
18. Appropriateness of the criterion measure in relation to the purpose of the study	1	2	3	4
19. Degree of validity of the criterion measure	1	2	3	4
20. Degree of reliability of the criterion measure	1	2	3	4
21. Degree of use of a variety of criterion measures (e.g., subjective and objective)	1	2	3	4
22. Clarity about how data were collected	1	2	3	4
23. Clarity about who collects data	1	2	3	4
24. Degree of avoidance of contamination in process of data collection	1	2	3	4
25. Clarity of the statement of the research design	1	2	3	4
26. Adequacy of the research design (re: purpose)	1	2	3	4
27. Clarity and adequacy of the time between pretests and posttests	1	2	3	4
28. Appropriateness in the use of control group(s)	1	2	3	4
29. Appropriateness in the use of random assignment procedures	1	2	3	4
30. Appropriateness in the use of matching procedures	1	2	3	4
31. Experimental and control group equivalency (at pretest)	1	2	3	4
32. Degree of control for effects of history	1	2	3	4
33. Degree of control for effects of maturation	1	2	3	4
34. Degree of control for effects of testing	1	2	3	4
35. Degree of control for effects of instrumentation	1	2	3	4
36. Degree of control for statistical regression	1	2	3	4
37. Degree of control for differential selection of clients	1	2	3	4
38. Degree of control for differential mortality	1	2	3	4
39. Degree of control for practitioner bias	1	2	3	4
40. Degree of control for temporal bias	1	2	3	4
41. Degree of control for selection-maturation interaction	1	2	3	4
42. Overall degree of success in maximizing internal validity (32–41)	1	2	3	4
43. Adequacy of sample size	1	2	3	4
44. Degree of adequacy in the representativeness of the client sample	1	2	3	4

FIGURE 11.1   Framework for Evaluating Empirical Research Reports (*continued*)

Criteria	Low		High	
		Scale		
45. Degree of adequacy in the representativeness of the practitioner sample	1	2	3	4
46. Degree of control for reactive effects of testing (interaction with independent variable)	1	2	3	4
47. Degree of control for special effects of experimental arrangements (e.g., Hawthorne effect, placebo effect)	1	2	3	4
48. Degree of control for multiple-treatment interference	1	2	3	4
49. Degree of control for interaction between selection and experimental variable	1	2	3	4
50. Overall degree of success in maximizing external validity (43–49)	1	2	3	4
C. FINDINGS				
51. Adequacy of the manipulation of the independent variable	1	2	3	4
52. Appropriateness in the use of follow-up measures	1	2	3	4
53. Adequacy of data to provide evidence for testing of hypotheses	1	2	3	4
54. Appropriateness in the use of statistical controls	1	2	3	4
55. Appropriateness of statistical procedures	1	2	3	4
56. Use of between-group statistical procedures	1	2	3	4
57. Degree to which data support the hypothesis	1	2	3	4
58. Extent to which author's conclusions are consistent with data	1	2	3	4
59. Degree of uniformity between tables and text	1	2	3	4
60. Degree of investigator (author) bias	1	2	3	4
61. Clarity as to cause of client changes	1	2	3	4
62. Degree to which alternative explanations were avoided in the design	1	2	3	4
63. Degree to which potential alternative explanations were dealt with	1	2	3	4
64. Degree of control of confounding effects of practitioners	1	2	3	4
65. Degree of control for confounding effects of clients	1	2	3	4
66. Degree of control for confounding effects of nonspecific treatment	1	2	3	4
67. Reasonableness of author's inferences	1	2	3	4
68. Clarity as to meaning of change(s)	1	2	3	4
69. Adequacy in relating findings to previous literature	1	2	3	4
70. Adequacy of conclusions in not generalizing beyond data	1	2	3	4
71. Extent to which the research design accomplished the purpose of the study	1	2	3	4
72. Appropriateness in the handling of unexpected consequences	1	2	3	4
D. DISCUSSION				
73. Degree of relevance to social work practice	1	2	3	4
74. Overall soundness of study	1	2	3	4
75. Degree of generalizability of the study's findings	1	2	3	4
76. Degree to which the independent variables are accessible to control by social workers	1	2	3	4
77. Extent to which a meaningful difference would occur if the independent variable were utilized in actual social work practice situations	1	2	3	4
78. Degree of economic feasibility of the independent variable if utilized in actual social work practice situations	1	2	3	4
79. Degree of ethical suitability of the manipulation of the independent variable	1	2	3	4
80. Extent to which the primary question is addressed (what methods, based on what theory, with what social workers, working with what clients, with what kinds of client problems, in what situations, are most successful?)	1	2	3	4

been derived from the general literature review. A research question might be: "Are the social work services in a given agency effective?" Identifying the question's origin and meaning permits comparison of similarities or differences between the study and others which address the same issues.

Hypothesis

A research question which is clearly formulated as a prediction comprises the study's hypothesis. An example of a hypothesis derived from the above research question might be: "Professional social work services in a given agency will produce significantly more positive changes in clients' images of themselves than will services provided by other professionals." A well-formulated hypothesis serves as a guide for the selection of data collection and analysis techniques.

In the evaluation, a clear hypothesis demonstrates the forethought put into the study's design. It also serves as a basis for the total evaluation. The analyses of the other three framework categories (method, findings, and discussion) rest on the study's purpose, as indicated by the author's hypothesis.

Independent and Dependent Variables

A testable hypothesis dictates a clear definition of the independent and dependent variables to be considered in the study. The independent variable is hypothesized to have some effect on the dependent variable; thus it is the assumed or predicted causal variable. The dependent variable is the one that the independent variable is assumed to affect.

The independent and dependent variables comprise the major concepts of the study. Since concepts are abstractions of ideas, the variables must be defined in terms of the general meaning they were intended to convey (nominal definitions). However, these concepts should also be defined in terms of the observable indicators (operational definitions) utilized in order to collect the data.

The greater the extent to which the variables are operationalized, the better. A study which simply suggests that "casework services" affect clients' self-esteem provides much less information than one which specifically defines the exact techniques that comprise the casework services. Unless the variables are clearly operationalized, the application of theory to social work practice is very difficult.

A study should be rated higher if it tests more than one kind of independent variable. This rating criterion can be explained in terms of the type and amount of information that can be generated from studies which test one independent variable, as compared to studies which test more than one. For example, if more than one form of social work intervention is tested, comparisons between the interventions can be derived.[4] Studies that have examined one social work intervention

---

[4] Gordon Paul, *Insight vs. Desensitization in Psychotherapy* (Stanford, Cal.: Stanford University Press, 1966).

technique provide valuable information. However, that information is increased tremendously if the effectiveness of an additional social work intervention technique can be simultaneously evaluated.

The evaluation of the study in terms of the independent and dependent variables should, therefore, address several issues. Is there clear specification of the independent and dependent variables? Is the anticipated cause-effect relationship stated clearly? Are the assumptions of the relationships between the two variables reasonable? Is more than one independent variable tested?

In addition to the independent and dependent variables, those variables that the author has designated as confounding should be identified. Confounding variables potentially qualify, modify, or explain any obtained relationship between the independent and dependent variables.[5] Attempts to control for the possible effects of the confounding variables through the study's design should be examined.

Author's Orientation

The next part of the evaluation of the problem formulation should seek to identify any biases of the author. What is the stated purpose or goal of the study? Why was it undertaken? How is the author's conceptualization of the problem area under investigation different from those in similar studies? What information is sought? How are the findings to be utilized, and who is to utilize them?[6]

In addition to a clearly stated purpose, the study's auspices and author orientation should also be clarified. Who is sponsoring the study? Where is it to be conducted? What is the orientation (theoretical and otherwise) of the author?

These questions are important in the identification of possible biasing effects. For example, an institution may want (or need) to prove that its program is effective, or an investigator may hope to prove that a particular social work intervention is worthwhile. Either one could intentionally or unintentionally become involved in the research or evaluation process, and this could have some effect on the outcome of the study. For example, the supervision of the social work intervention program or the collection of the data could influence or alter a study's results.[7] The author's presence in the intervention would emerge as a potential bias confounding the independent-dependent variable relationship.

In addition, the reasonableness of the author's assumptions about the study—both methodological and conceptual—should be assessed. These assumptions are propositions which are taken for granted ("given") in a study and which usually are not subject to empirical investigation. Such assumptions can be evaluated by reviewing other knowledge concerning the study's problem area, in terms of the purposes and method of the study.[8] An example of this would be a study of group therapy which assumed that group therapy is a uniform phenomenon,

---

[5] See Tripodi, Fellin, and Meyer, *Assessment of Social Research*.

[6] Ibid.

[7] See, for example, E. M. Goldberg, *Helping the Aged* (London: George Allen and Unwin, 1970).

[8] Tripodi, Fellin, and Meyer, *Assessment of Social Research*.

independent of profession, style of group therapist, and so on. In this example, group therapy was "whatever group therapists do." The reasonableness of this assumption is open to question, on the basis of information provided regarding the differential effects of the therapists' personality conditions.[9]

In summary, the problem formulation should be evaluated in terms of the author's conceptualization of the study itself and in terms of possible author biases. A study may be conceptualized very thoroughly and still be subject to question on theoretical or ideological grounds. In addition, author bias may help to explain or define methodological weaknesses or strengths of the research methods.

Method

This category is concerned with the basic foundation of the study—the research design and data collection techniques. This is the heart of the evaluation of any study.

Outcome Measures

Examination of the type of outcome measures adopted to indicate the presence or absence of the dependent variable is one of the most important steps in evaluation of the data collection techniques for a study. The statement of the problem area under investigation and the adoption of a research design should reflect the kinds of changes that have been hypothesized, or, at least, the kinds of changes or outcomes to be examined.[10] In this specification, the conceptual or empirical bases for selecting the desired types of changes should be identified. For example, if a study of casework intervention focuses on positive changes in family functioning, this section should clarify how these changes are to be identified. That is, the criterion or outcome measures utilized should be specified. The evaluation is concerned with whether the outcome measures selected are clearly defined and described in regard to how they are to be applied and their potential limitations.

In addition, the measures the author selects should be appropriate to the study's purpose. If the purpose of a study is to examine the effects of casework intervention on family interaction, individual psychological tests may not be appropriate to use as outcome measures. To verify the appropriateness of the measures, the validity and reliability of the measurements utilized should be clearly stated. The higher the validity and reliability of the measures, the better.

Use of a variety of outcome measures is preferable because client change tends to be multidimensional. Extensive examples in the literature examining the effects of social work intervention show that client change may surface in numerous different areas, which are often unrelated. For example, a major client change

---

[9] Ernest G. Poser, "The Effect of Therapists' Training on Group Therapeutic Outcome," *Journal of Consulting Psychology,* 30 (August 1966), pp. 283–289.

[10] Herzogg, *Guidelines for Evaluative Research.*

demonstrated in a projective test may not be reflected in actual behavioral change. And clients' subjective self-reports of improvement frequently are not reflected in other, more objective measures.[11]

Outcome measures should therefore involve both objective and subjective measurements whenever possible. Examples of objective measures are behavior ratings or physiological indicators. An example of a subjective measure is an opinion questionnaire. The criterion measures used should evaluate the effects of the independent variables on the actual functioning of individuals as closely as possible.

Data Collection

Evaluation of data collection calls for identifying how the data are collected, who collects them, and the steps taken to avoid contamination in the data collection process. This is primarily directed toward analysis of author objectivity and data reliability. Specifically, the controls for interviewer, test, and judgment biases in data collection should be examined.

One study which assessed casework effectiveness exemplifies such possible biases. In this study, social workers were requested to provide basic data on their clients' progress in the experimental group. Another group of "trained researchers" provided data on the control group.[12] Such a procedure presents an obvious potential source of bias.

Research Design

The method for collecting and analyzing data is usually specified in the research design. The design utilized, the methodological issues involved in using the design, and the way these issues can be handled in the design should be clearly stated. The general adequacy of the research design with regard to the purpose of the study should also be evaluated. If, for example, the purpose of the study is to evaluate the effectiveness of a specific casework technique, and a hypothetical-developmental design is chosen, the evaluation would be likely to conclude that the design is inappropriate to the purpose of the study.

If the research design involves a two-occasion (or more) design, the adequacy of the length of time between the testing sessions or test and follow-up should be examined. The question is whether the desired client changes could logically be expected to have taken place over the length of time allowed. If the period is fairly brief, a judgment must be made regarding the likelihood of contamination of the posttest by the pretest. For example, individuals may remember the answers from the pretest and answer the posttest accordingly. If there is no pretest, the

[11] See Allen E. Bergin and Michael J. Lambert, "The Evaluation of Therapeutic Outcomes," in Sol L. Garfield and Allen E. Bergin, eds., *Handbook of Psychotherapy and Behavior Change*, 2nd ed. (New York: John Wiley and Sons, 1978), pp. 139–190.

[12] Ludwig Geismar and Jane Krisberg, *The Forgotten Neighborhood* (Metuchen, N.J.: Scarecrow Press, 1967).

time allowed for the intervention should be evaluated to see if the effects of the intervention could emerge during the period.

Use of Control Groups and Group Assignment

Another consideration in analyzing a research design is whether control groups are utilized. If one or more control groups is used, the author should identify the type of control. Several varieties of control groups are available: untreated groups, waiting lists, terminations, placebo-effect groups, groups receiving other treatment, own controls, and combinations.[13] Probably the most desirable control group represents some combination, such as an untreated group whose characteristics are comparable to those of the experimental or treated group, plus a group which receives another form of social work treatment. The strengths and weaknesses of the type of control group selected must also be considered.

Because control groups are desirable in most social work investigations, it is important to evaluate how the members of the control (or comparison) and experimental groups are assigned. Some assignment is done on a haphazard, accidental, arbitrary, or post hoc basis. Three more scientific methods of group assignment are randomization, matching, and a combination of these two types.

Random assignment is the preferred method of group assignment. It should ensure that every individual has the same chance of being assigned to either group. Ideally and theoretically, the experimental and control groups should consist of individuals who differ only with regard to the group assignment. That is, some individuals are assigned to the experimental group and some are assigned to the control group. In this sense the term *random* is not synonymous with *arbitrary*. Rather, it refers to strict scientific procedures for the assignment of individuals to two or more groups.

In matching, group assignment is made on the basis of similarities among individuals on certain meaningful variables, particularly confounding variables which may be expected to affect the outcome of the study in some way. Matching may be done on the basis of pretest scores, age, sex, type of client problem, and so on. Matching is also initiated to ensure an equal distribution of any given variable in both groups, as opposed to a priori individual-by-individual matching.

One of the most desirable forms of group assignment combines matching and randomization procedures. For example, individuals can be screened in advance and matched according to meaningful variables, and then randomly assigned to either the experimental or control group. This procedure allows for equivalency between groups at the pretest occasion, although each individual still has an equal chance of being assigned to either the experimental or control group.

With any method of group assignment, it is important to determine whether the two groups are equivalent at the beginning of the intervention. Differences

[13] Julian Meltzoff and Melvin Kornreich, *Research in Psychotherapy* (New York: Atherton Press, 1970).

between the groups found at the beginning of the study could be responsible for differences at the conclusion. Within a certain probability level, pretest equivalence can be achieved through randomization. However, it should still be determined if group equivalency following assignment has been ascertained.

Internal Validity

The next key concern in evaluating a study is the extent to which internal validity has been maximized. Control of extraneous influences within the study (internal validity) allows for conclusions that the intervention did in fact make a difference. The appropriate use of control groups is the preferred method for handling problems of internal validity.

There are a number of extraneous variables however, which must be controlled for, or they could produce effects which otherwise would be attributed to the independent variable.[14] These include the effects of history, maturation, testing effects and instrumentation, statistical regression, differential selection and mortality, practitioner bias, temporal bias, and selection-maturation interaction.

The *effects of history* occur when any happening outside the experimental variable produces changes in the dependent variable. They are due to changes in the client's environment, such as getting a job or resolving family problems which produce changes in the client that cannot be attributed to the intervention. The effects of history are the most plausible rival hypothesis for explaining client changes when appropriate controls are not (or cannot be) used.

The second possible extraneous variable is the *effects of maturation*. This includes internal processes, both physiological or psychological, that may occur in individuals due to the passage of time. For example, maturation may occur as clients grow older or more tired.

The pretest also can contribute to poor internal validity by influencing scores on the posttest. These are the *effects of testing*. Testing can be controlled to some extent under one or both of the following conditions:

1. The time between the two tests is long enough to reduce memory of the first test.
2. Both experimental and control groups are subject to the same testing conditions.

Closely related to testing biases are the *effects of instrumentation,* or *instrument decay.* Instrument decay is due to a change either in the measuring instrument or in the users of the instrument (e.g., observers may become more sensitive).

A particularly important variable to control for is *statistical regression* (or regression to the mean). Statistical regression operates particularly within groups selected

---

[14] Campbell and Stanley, *Experimental and Quasi-Experimental Designs.*

on the basis of their extreme scores. It refers to the fact that extreme scores tend to change by moving toward the mean. Change of this type is predictable and is more likely to be due to statistical regression than to the intervention program.

For example, groups of individuals are often provided with treatment because they score poorly on certain psychological tests. Such groups tend to show evidence of later change regardless of whether they receive treatment. It is tempting to conclude that a group of such clients who receive treatment and show improvement at a later date change as a result of the treatment, when there is no control group for comparison purposes.

Another threat to internal validity is *differential selection,* or bias in the selection of clients for comparison groups. The principles of randomization aid in preventing this sort of design bias.

A related problem of client selection is *differential mortality.* This occurs when one group loses more or different types of members than the other group during the period of intervention. For example, in a study which compared the effectiveness of professional with nonprofessional practitioners, the author concluded that the nonprofessionals were favored on the outcome measures at the end of the treatment.[15] While the groups started with similar sample sizes, the nonprofessionals lost 33 percent of the clients in their groups. Thus the groups were no longer comparable at the end of the study. Perhaps the likeliest conclusion that could be drawn was that the professionals maintained a lower client dropout rate than the nonprofessionals.

Practitioner bias is also a threat to internal validity. This could operate in several ways. Social workers may not offer the treatment techniques that they agreed to provide prior to the study, or they may vary major aspects of their treatment methods from client to client. For example, they may use behavior therapy with one client, insight therapy with another client, and so on.

Control for *temporal bias* should also be assessed. All groups involved in the study should be measured at precisely the same time. Further, if two groups of social workers (e.g., professional versus nonprofessional) are being compared, for example, the frequency and length of the contacts with their respective clients should be similar.

One final threat to internal validity is a result of the interaction between two of the above variables—*selection* and *maturation.* This occurs when the selection of the experimental and control groups is not equivalent in terms of maturation. Comparing normal with distressed clients, or clients with extremely negative pretest scores to clients in another group with far more positive pretest scores, is an example. Independent of the treatment, the group with more negative scores ("distressed") would be expected to change far more than the other ("normal") group.

Once the study has been evaluated by all these criteria, an overall summary judgment as to the degree of success in maximizing internal validity is required.

[15] Poser, "Effect of Therapists' Training."

External Validity

Another key concern in evaluating a study has to do with its external validity. This refers to limitations on the extent to which findings can be generalized to clients, agencies, conditions, or measures other than those specifically involved in the study being evaluated.

In assessing generalizability, the first determination to make is the adequacy of the study's sample size. This is related to the description of the exact population for the study, or the aggregate of all individuals or elements that conform to some designated set of specifications. The sample consists of elements or members drawn from the population in order to find out something about the population.

If the study uses an extremely small sample as representative of a large population, the grounds for selecting such a sample should be clearly stated and justifiable. Few studies can claim a representative random sample drawn from either client or social work populations. Usually both of these populations are too large and complex. Nevertheless, every study must be evaluated in terms of the ways in which the author attempts to deal with this issue.

The degree to which the sample is representative of the population involves the study's external validity. The first and most obvious approach in dealing with *representativeness of the client or practitioner sample* lies with sampling restrictions. The relevant universes to which the generalizations are made must be clearly defined, and samples must be carefully drawn from them. Usually, this is very difficult. As a result, some restrictions occur. For example, a study might limit the sample in regard to size, time, place, type of client problem, and so on. Samples may also be restricted by stratification. A population can be divided into two or more strata, or classes, and samples can then be drawn from each stratum. Some examples of strata are sex, age, social class, race, and type of client problem.

The logic and adequacy of such restrictions and the adequacy of the sampling procedures utilized must be evaluated. Often there are genuine attempts to obtain representative samples of some client groups, but attempts to obtain representative samples of social workers are rare. In fact, a study may focus on social workers selected from one agency, or graduate social work students may be used as substitutes for experienced social workers. Generalizations from such studies must be constrained by failure to obtain a representative sample of experienced social workers.

The second major approach to ensuring representativeness is by testing or comparing the sample with other known samples from the same population. Samples of clients and social workers can be given tests or inventories, or demographic data can be used. These data can be compared with the known facts about the population of concern. For example, age, sex, and social class of the social workers studied can be compared with the demographic characteristics of other social workers at one or more agencies. Or social workers might complete inventories of therapeutic attitudes and preferences, which could then be compared to similar inventories completed by other workers. Thus comparisons with known facts about the general population can be used as one basis for determining a sample's representativeness.

Another threat to external validity is the possibility of *reactive or interactive effects of the testing with the experimental variable* (the treatment). The pretest may have made clients more sensitized to the treatment, so that changes in treatment effectiveness occur. This may mean that results would only be generalizable to clients who had been pretested and thereby sensitized. The best method to control for reactive effects lies in the choice of research design or in the choice of outcome measures not specifically related to the treatment, such as everyday performance or a behavioral criterion like number of reported juvenile offenses during the month prior to treatment.

The possibility of *special effects of experimental arrangements* is another threat to external validity. Knowledge of being in a study may have special meaning to some clients or workers, and their performance or reactions therefore may be atypical. An example of reactive effects would be an experimental group becoming more productive or more positive—the Hawthorne effect—as a result of client expectations. That is, the fact that the clients sought and obtained services may lead to a change in the outcome. Change is, therefore, independent of (or sometimes prior to) treatment.

Reactions to experimental arrangements could preclude generalizations regarding the effects of intervention to anyone who was not exposed to the treatment in experimental (research) situations. These reactive effects could pertain to both clients and social workers.

Lack of control for *multiple-treatment interference* also can threaten external validity, and caution in making generalizations is in order. Multiple treatment occurs when clients receive more than one treatment, such as medication in addition to one or more other types of intervention. In such cases, the effects of the prior treatment may either not be erasable or may have some sort of enhancing or depressing effect on the intervention. In either case, generalizations could pertain to only those groups that receive all the same treatments. This would also present a problem in attempting to determine which of the treatments has the major (or sole) effect on the client, if any is reported.

The last factor influencing external validity is the possible *interaction between selection of clients and the experimental variable* (the treatment). In these circumstances, special characteristics of the sample selected for treatment interact with the treatment to change its effects. For example, if a study shows that middle-class children respond well to verbal therapy, it cannot be assumed that all children, or children from low-income groups, will also respond well to this type of treatment. Rather, special characteristics of the sample tested—socioeconomic class rather than verbal therapy—could produce the results.

Once the analysis of all these criteria has been completed, a judgment as to the overall degree of control for external validity can be made. The adequacy of the sample size, adequacy of sample representativeness, degree of control for reactive effects of testing, control of experimental arrangements, control for multiple-treatment interference, and control for interaction between sample selection and the experimental variable all should be considered.

Findings

The findings section of the framework concentrates on assessing the ways in which the data are analyzed and how conclusions are derived from the data.

The first task is to determine whether or not there was a manipulation of the independent variable adequate to influence the dependent variable. In a sense, this is assessing the strength of the independent variable. It can be accomplished by examining the intensity of the independent variable, length of time over which the variable is presented, number of treatment sessions, and so forth.

Related to this factor is the persistence of the outcome, or change, over time. Evaluation of suitability of the length of time chosen for the follow-up should be based, at least in part, on the rationale for this decision presented in the study.

Data Collection and Statistical Procedures

Overall, the data collected must be adequate to provide evidence for the testing of the hypothesis. They also should be of sufficient quantity and quality, in both the experimental and control groups, to allow further evaluation.

If the data collection techniques are sound, some basic judgments about the statistics utilized in the study are next in order. First, the appropriateness of the use of statistical controls should be considered. Are statistical procedures used to control for variables that, if uncontrolled in the experimental situation, could affect the outcome? For example, if it is not possible to match the experimental and control groups on potentially meaningful variables, they should be controlled by statistical means such as with analysis of covariance.[16]

Next, the appropriateness of the statistics utilized must be assessed. This analysis depends on the type of data collected and the type of conclusions derived from the data. Every statistic assumes a particular level of measurement. This information should be the basis for determining whether the statistics used are appropriate for the conditions of study.

Another dimension to consider in the assessment of the appropriateness of statistics is the type of conclusions the author attempts to draw from the data. If the author is interested in conclusions regarding cause and effect, a statistic should be used which has been designed to test hypotheses where one group receives the treatment and the other does not. The statistic should also allow for a conclusion regarding whether or not observed differences between the groups are due to chance and are likely to reflect true differences in the populations from which the

[16] Tripodi, Fellin, and Meyer, *Assessment of Social Research*.

groups are drawn. Assuming the results are statistically significant, this provides a basis for drawing inferences about causality.

In an experimental study, for example, a *t* test between the groups or analysis of variance should be used rather than a correlational statistic, because these statistics provide information that allows inferences regarding cause and effect. However, the use of a given statistic cannot in itself generate causal conclusions, since the nature of the design and the problem being studied also enter in. Between-group measures are also needed for statistics used in inferring cause-effect relationships. One of the most common statistical errors is to compute two separate correlated *t* tests for the differences between pretest and posttest within the experimental group and within the control group. If the differences are statistically significant for the experimental group but not for the control group, the conclusion might be that the experimental treatment had an effect. Yet no direct statistical comparison between the two groups has been calculated. A more appropriate between-group measure, such as a group *t* test of the mean difference scores between groups or analysis of variance, might not find the differences statistically significant.

A recent study demonstrated this effect.[17] In a comparison of three groups to assess the effects of different methods of training, two groups showed statistically significant pretest-to-posttest mean changes within the groups on two different outcome variables. An overall analysis of variance, however, failed to show statistically significant differences between the three groups.

Similarly, one must understand whether multivariate statistics should have been used. This involves the number of outcomes measures in a study. For several reasons, when more than one outcome measure is used, and especially when those measures are correlated, repeated use of univariate statistics such as *t*-test and ANOVA or ANCOVA is inappropriate. These statistics are likely to produce Type I errors (significant when really not) when results are positive and Type II errors (not significant when really is) with negative results. The problems increase with the number of measures. In such cases, multivariate statistics should be used such as Hotelling's T^2 for two groups and MANOVA and MANCOVA for two or more groups.

The choice of univarite or multivariate statistics is complicated to assess. Multivariate statistics require a substantially larger sample than univariate statistics if they are to be used reliably. Both the use of univariate statistics with multiple outcome measures and multivariate statistics with a small sample can be reasons for decreased confidence in the reported results of a study.

Data Support of the Hypothesis

The next step in evaluating the author's conclusions is to determine whether or not the data support the hypothesis. The kinds of qualifications the author states

[17] Joel Fischer and Jules Greenberg, "An Investigation of Different Training Methods on Indigenous Non-Professionals from Diverse Minority Groups," paper presented at the National Association of Social Workers Conference on Social Justice, New Orleans, November 1972.

with regard to that support should also be examined. For example, the author may suggest that when additional variables were introduced (e.g., social class, sex), the strength of the findings was diminished. In fact, the findings may have been weakened when such contingent variables were introduced, or they may have been applicable in only certain very select circumstances.

An example is a study which assessed casework effectiveness.[18] The authors said "about seven of ten" clients and caseworkers reported global evaluations of "much better" or "somewhat better." They concluded, therefore, that the casework intervention was effective. However, when the clients were asked why they terminated (discontinued) treatment, only 30.6 percent said the "problem was solved or less stressful," and only 32 percent reported global evaluations of "much better." These figures may more accurately depict client sentiments regarding treatment than the authors' 7:10 ratio for both clients and caseworkers.

The author's consistency in using data should also be assessed. There should be uniformity between the data presented in the tables and the text, and the author's conclusions should be consistent with the data. This calls for a careful review of the author's description of the data. Biases may show up in the design or data analyses, or inadequate or erroneous interpretations or conclusions may be drawn from the data. How the author deals with results that do not support the hypothesis is also important, to ensure that such data are not simply ignored.

Conclusions About the Study

The remaining criteria in the findings section address the results and implications of the study, in terms of both the author's conclusions and one's own judgments. First to be assessed is the extent to which evidence is presented regarding the degree to which change is actually a function of the intervention. One consideration is the appropriate use of control groups. While a simple comparison between experimental and control groups may be adequate to establish the presence of change, it is insufficient to identify those aspects of treatment that actually cause effects.

The author's opinions about the implications of the study and judgments regarding the meaning of the changes found should also be assessed. The author should be clear as to the social, psychological, and professional meaning of the findings. The findings should be discussed in terms of existing norms or standards, cost effectiveness, efforts expended to obtain the effects in the study, efficiency, and so on. The author should relate the findings and conclusions to the literature and propose changes in theory or methodology suggested by the results. The adequacy of the author's conclusions should then be evaluated in terms of generalizability beyond the data in the study, such as applicability to different samples or populations of social workers or clients.

Finally, the extent to which the study accomplishes its purpose as developed

---

[18] Dorothy F. Beck and Mary A. Jones, *Progress on Family Problems* (New York: Family Service Association of America, 1973).

in the formulation of the problem should be evaluated. If there were unexpected consequences, the author should attempt to determine whether they were produced by some aspect of the research design or by the research methods or treatment utilized.

Discussion

The final part of the evaluation of an empirical research report consists of several criteria concerning the utilization of knowledge gained from the study. This calls for making judgments and decisions as to the possible ways in which the knowledge from the study could be applied in social work practice. Utilization is concerned with the relevance or meaningfulness of the study and the development of practical applications of the knowledge derived. In a sense, the discussion section of the analysis is a general summary of all the criteria presented in the framework. Decisions regarding utilization are based on the information gathered from analyzing the problem area, methods, and findings. The discussion is drawn from these analyses.

Relevance to Social Work Practice

The first aspect of utilization to consider is the meaningfulness of the study's findings in relation to social work practice. This can be determined by assessing the major implications of the study in terms of the dimensions of social work it addresses. These dimensions include clients, service delivery systems, methods and techniques of intervention, qualities of social workers, and levels of intervention—microsystem, mezzosystem, or macrosystem. Of course, a study need not be specifically conducted on social workers or their clients to be relevant to social work. Social work knowledge can be derived from numerous related fields such as anthropology, business, clinical psychology, and sociology.

Overall Soundness of the Study

The next step is an overall evaluation as to the soundness of the total study. This is a summary judgment based on preceding sections of the framework. For the sake of convenience, this judgment can be based on the extent to which threats to internal validity are avoided. It should consider the extent to which the independent variable clearly leads to the changes observed.

The generalizability of the study's findings, or the extent to which threats to external validity are avoided, must also be evaluated. Can similar treatment methods be applied for different goals or purposes? Is it reasonable to expect that positive results would ensue?

The greater the internal and external validity (soundness and generalizability) of the study, the greater value it will have. Potential use of the findings will therefore be widened.

Other Criteria for Assessing Utilization

There are several additional criteria for assessing utilization of social work research.[19] One is the extent to which the variables in the study are actually accessible to control by the social work practitioner/researcher. This means that they should be clearly identifiable (observable) and manipulable (within the power of the social worker to affect). If need be, as with a new technique developed in a study, they should also be teachable.

If a particular independent variable (intervention) is accessible, the difference it would make in social work practice if it were actually utilized is of interest. For example, a study might show that the use of a particular interventive technique successfully decreases the number of clients' eyeblinks per minute. Could this be evaluated as an important goal for professional social work practice? Or could the use of such a technique reasonably be expected to produce other more pervasive or more meaningful changes?

If the independent variable is accessible and would probably make a meaningful difference in social work practice, the economics of utilizing it then must be considered. Is it economically feasible to consider the use of such an independent variable in social work practice? Would the cost be within allowable limits?

Another criterion is whether it is ethically suitable to manipulate a given independent variable with clients. It is possible to demonstrate changes under laboratory conditions which would be entirely unethical in practice conditions. The intervention technique may also appear either professionally or personally unethical to other social workers. Therefore, it would be of limited value.

The final summary criterion is the extent to which the primary research question is answered. In other words, what kinds of social workers, working with what kind of clients, with what kind of client problems, in what practice situations, using what techniques, derived from what theory, produced what kinds of results?

Summary

The 80 criteria in the framework for evaluating empirical research reports are specified in Figure 11.1 at the beginning of this chapter. Obviously, some of these criteria are far more important than others. There is a considerable overlap among them, to the extent that some are actually subcategories. Examples are the various internal and external validity criteria listed in the method section.

Ideal research conditions are rarely possible, due to any number of economic, personal, or organizational constraints. Most authors are forced to compromise on some of these conditions. Therefore the overall impact of a study's deficiencies should be taken into account in judging the applicability of the knowledge derived from the study to social work practice.

As Figure 11.1 shows, each of the 80 criteria can be rated on a scale from 1 to

[19] See Tripodi, Fellin, and Meyer, *Assessment of Social Research*.

4. These ratings call for careful observation and personal judgment. In some instances, a study either meets a criterion or it does not. For example, on Criterion 28, a study which uses some type of control group would be rated with a 3 or 4, and a study which does not use a control group would be rated with a 1 or 2. In other situations, it is necessary to decide whether or not the study "adequately" meets a given criterion. An example is deciding whether there is a sufficiently clear specification of the independent variable. In other circumstances, the relative rating will be less judgmental. For example, a study using three independent criterion measures would be rated higher on Criterion 21, "Degree of use of a variety of criterion measures," than a study using only one.

Because there are clear differences in the importance of the various criteria, the overall rating given a study may be less important than ensuring that certain criteria are met. For example, it is more important for an experimental study to use a control group appropriately than to specify the theoretical orientation of the author. The implications for social work of research which meets the various criteria must always be considered.

In using this framework, one standard to consider is that if a study's results cannot be readily incorporated into the knowledge base of the social work profession, it is, for all intents and purposes, practically useless. A study may be designed and executed perfectly. Yet it will have only limited value to the profession if it does not address a meaningful problem area and if the results cannot be put into practice by social workers. Utilization of results is the ultimate outcome in social work research and evaluation.

Chapter 12

Measurement of Client Problems for Improved Practice

During the past few years, clinical social work practice and the way it is taught in the classroom have been changing in at least four important ways. First, social work practitioners are making greater efforts to be more specific in defining the problem to be treated and in identifying the specific treatment or intervention techniques to be employed. Second, they are becoming more eclectic in their use of theory, knowledge, and technique as a basis for planning and directing change efforts (Fischer, 1978). Third, they are making better use of some of the tools of science in order to monitor and evaluate intervention efforts and client problems for the purpose of increasing the likelihood of a more positive outcome for the client (Hudson, 1978b). Finally, as a consequence of these innovations, social work practitioners are increasingly using the tools of measurement as a basis for detecting, recording, and assessing the nature and degree of client problems and the extent of change or stability.

Whereas other chapters of this book present discussion, direction, and guidelines for understanding and using the first three practice innovations or directions, this chapter provides an introductory level of instruction and guidelines for the productive use of measurement for improving practice. It is intended to help social workers who want to practice more effectively to more accurately detect and report the consequences of their treatment or intervention efforts and to more accurately monitor, assess, and reflect the nature and degree of client problems and problem changes.

What Is Measurement?

What, then, is measurement? A good formal definition is that "measurement consists of rules for assigning numbers to objects in such a way as to represent quantities of attributes" (Nunnally, 1978, p. 3). In order to be useful, however, this definition requires some elaboration.

Fischer, J. & Hudson, W. W. (1982). In A. Rosenblatt & D. Waldfogel (Eds.). *Handbook of Clinical Social Work*. San Francisco: Jossey-Bass. Reprinted with permission of Aaron Rosenblatt.

The rules for assigning numbers to objects can be very simple or very complex, and a thorough understanding of their variety, scope, and effective use requires specialized study and training. Good sources for such training and study include Grinnell (1981, chaps. 7–9) Nunnally (1978), Helmstadter (1964), and Allen and Yen (1979). Although social workers do not have to become experts in psychometric theory, study in this area can be very helpful and is encouraged.

The essential point of Nunnally's definition of measurement is that numbers are assigned to objects in a consistent manner. For example, in measuring client problems, it is important to use the simple rule of assigning a large number to any problem the therapist or client considers serious and smaller numbers to problems considered less serious.

The mechanism used to apply the rule is called a measurement tool or instrument. If an expert is asked to rate the seriousness of a client's problem, the person doing the rating is the measurement instrument. If an orange is weighed on a balance scale, the balance is the tool of measurement. However, people rarely are regarded as measurement tools; more commonly, the tool is the device on which they record their measurement judgments. Therefore, the recording document used by an expert to rate the seriousness of a client's problem is considered the measurement tool, and such recording documents can be constructed in hundreds of different ways: single-item rating scales, open-ended questions, true-false items, forms for making behavioral observations, multiple-choice items, essay questions, category-partion scales (which include Likert-type scales, Osgood semantic differential scales, ladder scales, multi-item scales, unidimensional scales, multidimensional scales, and so forth).

Some of these different tools of measurement are described later in this chapter so that they can be used in practice, and several references are given to enable readers to locate, study, and then use various measurement devices.

Why Measure?

Many people complain about the use of measurement in social work practice. Some feel it dehumanizes the client, the worker, and the profession. Others feel that measurement in the "soft" sciences is generally so weak and flawed that it should not be used with clients or taken seriously as a guide for directing or even influencing the conduct of practice. Others feel that it is not necessary, because "good clinical judgment" is sufficient. Still others simply do not understand measurement, and some say that formal measurement is sometimes useful but is so complex and technical that it must be left in the hands of experts.

All of these arguments need to be addressed. Many of the things workers do can be dehumanizing, and measurement can be used in a dehumanizing way. However, it can also be used with intelligence and warmth for the purpose of better helping the client to cope with very serious problems. Some measurement tools are indeed quite crude and misleading and should not be used. However, many are highly accurate and dependable. One must never forget that, in all forms of measurement involving human judgment, the accuracy of the final measurement is a direct function of human discrimination and perceptual ability. In many cases, such abilities are nothing short of impressive. One must also never forget that "good clinical judgment" is an act of measurement. Those who claim that measurement must be left to experts are avoiding the issue. Some types of measurement do require specialized training, but a wide variety of measurement applications are available with very modest amounts of training and are well within the abilities of nearly all social work practitioners.

But why measure? The simplest answer is that we must and that we do so routinely, without knowing it. When a worker places a note in a client's record to indicate that the client's marital relationship has improved, the worker has performed a crude act of measurement. Anytime one observes progress, stability, or deterioration, acts of measurement are being performed. In short, the use of measurement in social work practice is inescapable and inevitable.

But, if workers are already using measurement, why formalize it? The answer is that the advance of any science or profession is clearly marked by its increased use of precision and control. Modern surgery has its roots in the barber shop, and, by analogy, workers must decide whether they will operate in the barber shop or in the modern surgical amphitheater. The use of measurement will be a major determinant in this choice.

If increased precision and control are basic to the improvement of social work practice, then the use of measurement must be a fundamental ingredient of such practice. If a client suffers from fear, anxiety, depression, or pain, it is important, for a number of reasons, to know how often and how much. Is the disorder frequent and severe enough to warrant treatment? Is the frequency or intensity of the problem great enough to imply one form of treatment or another? Does the problem occur at times and places that suggest either its cause or a possible solution? Once treatment or intervention begins, can the worker determine whether and at what rate the problem is abating or worsening? Can that knowledge be useful in making decisions about treatment: to retain or drop the treatment techniques being used or to add others? The extent to which such questions can be answered depends on the precision of the worker's information about the client's problem, and that level of precision has a marked impact on the extent to which the worker is able to control the problem.

What Can Be Measured?

Since anything that exists can be measured, all types of client characteristics can be measured. For example, measuring immaturity may be impossible because "immaturity" itself does not exist. But immaturity is manifested in behaviors that do exist (for example, a child not following instructions in a classroom), any of which could be measured as an indicator of immaturity. Thus, the way one defines the problem is crucial to whether or not it can be measured.

Of course, if workers do not set some limits of their own, they will be so busy measuring characteristics of the client that they will never get around to treatment, and the client will drop out in disgust or dismay. Therefore, a better question might be, What should be measured?

At a very minimum, the worker should measure two things: the problem to be changed and the change agent, or treatment. There are powerful advantages to measuring the client's problem and the treatment. By measuring the client's problem, workers can often determine what type of treatment and what types of resources are needed to deal with the problem; they can also make a prognosis concerning how long it will take to resolve the problem. Most important, by measuring the client's problem repeatedly over time on a regular basis, the worker can determine whether any progress is being made, information vital in helping to decide whether to continue or change the treatment.

Measurement is crucial for demonstrating whether treatment exists and whether it has the desired effect on the client's problem. Just as the problem that is not measurable does not exist and cannot be treated (Hudson, 1978a), the treatment that cannot be measured does not exist and cannot be administered (Gingerich, 1978).

Measurement for Single-System Designs

If some feel it is difficult enough to measure client problems, others will no doubt claim it is impossible to measure treatment. Actually, however, treatment is rather simple to measure. But, first, it is important to ask, What is treatment? Is it psychoanalysis, Gestalt therapy, supportive therapy, behavior modification, rational-emotive therapy? Decidedly not. These are theories of behavior and intervention. The treatment is the worker's behavior, what the worker does to create change in the client's problem.

If the behavior of the social worker is seen as the principal ingredient of treatment, that provides a simple basis for measuring treatment in a very useful way. Consider the total period of time during which the worker will have contact with a single client, and divide that period into two phases, or periods, *A* and *B*. During phase *A*, the worker will deliberately exhibit no treatment behavior and, during period *B*, the worker will exhibit professional behaviors specifically designed to have an impact on the client's problem. If the worker's behavior during period *A* is compared with that during period *B* and if one cannot detect any difference in those behaviors, it must be concluded that treatment does not exist. If, however, behavior during period *B* is distinctly different from behavior during period *A*, the worker has successfully measured treatment and, in the process, has demonstrated its existence.

The client's problem is the second factor that should be measured. If the client's problem is measured regularly during both time periods (*A* and *B*), the client problem measures taken during period *A* are called baseline measures, and those taken during period *B* are called treatment-phase measures. If treatment is really not present during the baseline period, one would expect the client's problem to be fairly stable—nothing is being done to change it. Also, if an effective set of treatment behaviors is selected, one would expect the client's problem measurements to change during the *B* period, or treatment phase—something is being done during that period that is intended to change the client's problem.

What has been described thus far is the simple *A-B* design. Many other designs are described elsewhere in this text, but the *A-B* design represents the fundamental design strategem used to help monitor and evaluate treatment: measure the treatment, and measure the client's problem on a regular or intermittent basis.

Basic Characteristics of Measurement

Although measurement applies to both the worker's treatment and the client's problem, the measurement of treatment is largely included in the research design. Because the issues of research design are discussed in detail elsewhere in this book, the remainder of this chapter will focus mainly on the task of measuring client problems.

Any strategem or device used to quantify a client's problem is called a measurement tool, and, if measurement tools are to have any utility in practice, they must possess several desirable characteristics. They must be reliable and valid; easy to administer, score, understand, and interpret; and brief. Clinical measurement tools should also be sensitive to change, and they should be fairly immune from reactivity (for those who want a more technical discussion of measurement characteristics, see Grinnell, 1981, chaps. 7–9).

If a measurement tool is not both reliable and valid, it is useless and should be discarded. Unfortunately, most practitioners are not in a position to make this determination for themselves. Even so, there are two good rules that can be followed: use specific measurement tools that have previously been shown to be reliable and valid, and use types or classes of measurement devices that have been shown to be reliable and valid. A number of these devices are described later in this chapter.

Often workers, in attempting to measure a client problem, will discover that little or no change can be observed. The problem could be that change does take place but the measurement tool is not sensitive enough to record it. For example, it is always possible to measure whether a client problem is present (a score of 1) or absent (a score of 0); in many cases, however, it is possible to do more. Suppose a problem of enuresis is defined as being present or absent (scored as 1 or 0). After working with the client, the worker notices real change taking place (the client has eighteen dry nights per month, as compared to only seven before treatment), but, because the problem is still present at some level, the client continues to obtain a score of 1. Insensitivity to change is often reflected in one or both of two ways: no change in obtained scores and low reliability. Clinician judgments concerning the amount of client change are notoriously unreliable (insensitive) and should be avoided.

Measurement tools vary considerably with respect to whether they are direct or indirect measures of some construct. At one extreme are the so-called projective tests, which are very indirect measures of some construct; at the other extreme are the behavioral measures, which are usually very direct measures of some construct. As a general rule, the more indirectly one measures some variable, the more one must depend on subjective interpretation of the results. In such cases, it is very difficult to establish the validity of the measure. The Rorschach, TAT, and Draw-a-Person tests are examples of indirect measures; after years of research, their validities are still in doubt (Hersen and Barlow, 1976).

Although behavioral measures are usually very direct measures of some construct, they can be abused. For example, temperature, respiration, pulse rate, and galvanic skin response are all excellent measures of the level of physiological activity, but do they also represent anxiety or fear? Sleeplessness is often associated with depression; nonetheless, some people who are not troubled with sleeplessness are very depressed.

As a general rule, the more directly a construct is measured, the more confidence the worker can have in the measurement results, and the easier it will be to establish the validity of those results. Consider, for example, the complex syndrome called depression. Depression can be measured in terms of behavioral symptoms, affects, relationship patterns, perceptions, and cognition. It can be measured directly by using a self-report, self-anchored scale, by behavioral observation, by self-reports of affects and cognitions, or by self-reports of behavioral symptoms. All of these measures tend to have very high validities.

Another desirable characteristic of measurement tools is that they be relatively nonreactive. A measurement tool that has high reactivity is one that causes the client's problem to change as a result of having the problem measured. One of the authors, for example, had a client who deliberately falsified her responses to the Generalized Contentment Scale (GCS) described later in this chapter. She candidly reported that, when she was honest with the scale, her score was higher and she felt worse. When she was dishonest, her scores were lower and she felt better. In other words, this client was deliberately manipulating her own reactivity to the measurement tool as a means of coping with and managing her own depression.

Reactivity is a serious problem for the scientist who is trying to isolate the true effects of experimental variables. In some cases, it may seem to be an aid to the clinician who is trying to help the client reduce or eliminate a personal or social problem. However, if observed improvement turns out to be purely reactive, it is doubtful that the gains will be sustained following termination of treatment. In assessing client problems and the effects of treatment, nonreactive gains are the most desirable and are more likely to be obtained when one uses measurement tools that are relatively nonreactive.

Defining Problems and Goals

In order to make good use of measurement in clinical practice, it is important to recognize that social work is a practice-based, problem-solving profession. In working with a client, one must define the problem to be solved in both measurable and treatable terms. In all of social work, social workers encounter and deal with only five broad classes of problems: (1) to provide concrete personal services (that is, clean the client's house); (2) to increase the capacity of the environment to provide positive supports for clients; (3) to decrease impediments and obstacles in the environment that retard or interfere with the client's functioning or welfare; (4) to increase or enhance client strengths and capacities for personal and social functioning; and (5) to decrease or eliminate client deficits in relation to personal and social functioning.

Although these broad classes of problems or goals describe the scope of all social work practice, they are of little use to the worker beyond the initial stage of case planning because they do not define any problem in either measurable or treatable terms. For example, a worker may initially decide that a specific client has clear deficits in social functioning, and the problem therefore becomes one of reducing or eliminating those deficits. But what are they, specifically? Suppose the worker further specifies the problem as an inability to get along with the boss at work. This description is more precise, but the problem is still not defined in sufficient detail to enable the worker to either measure or treat it.

Suppose the client is a technical writer for an advertising agency, and he resents the fact that his boss makes repeated changes in his work. He sees such changes as a criticism of his work; he feels the boss does not like him, and he feels resentment toward the boss, which he is now taking out on his wife through quarreling and irritability at home. The client feels that, if this situation continues, he will lose his job and possibly his marriage. Suppose it is the worker's diagnosis that the client severely misperceives his boss's attitudes and does not know how to discuss and negotiate conflict. The worker further decides that the best choice of treatment is cognitive restructuring or rational-emotive therapy. What needs to be measured? What needs to be changed? By the choice of treatment, the worker has decided what needs to change, and the measures that may reflect whether that change occurs certainly include (1) the number of times the boss makes changes in the client's work, (2) the number of times the client sees these as positive criticisms, (3) the number of times the client sees these as negative criticisms, (4) the number of times the client feels resentment, (5) the number of times the client quarrels with his wife, (6) the number of times he feels irritable at home, (7) the number of times he attempts to clarify with his boss the nature of and reason for the changes in his work, and so on.

Each of these measures can be defined as a problem for the client, and, by monitoring them at regular intervals, the worker can determine whether progress is being made in helping the client. However, the major point of this example is that the worker has progressed from a more general to a more specific and detailed definition of the problem. If the worker stops short of identifying one or more specific ways of measuring the client's problem, the worker will probably not be able to select an appropriate treatment technique. In other words, workers must select a specific intervention because they have good reason to believe that it will bring about change in the specific problems being measured. The definition and the measurement of the client's problems have a significant bearing upon finding a way to solve those problems.

Unfortunately, social workers are often taught in introductory research courses that it is difficult to prove one thing to be the cause of another. From a scientific point of view, the proof of causal relationships is indeed difficult, but that by no means dictates that causal thinking must be avoided. Quite the contrary, it is essential that social workers think, plan, and intervene from a strict causal frame of reference. If the client is anxious, what can the worker do to cause a reduction of anxiety? If the client is a thief, what can the worker do to cause him to stop stealing? If the client has a poor relationship with a spouse, what can the worker do to cause the marriage to improve? If a client is abused because of his passivity, what can the worker do to cause a reduction in that abuse?

These are difficult and, at the same time, extremely important questions that encourage the practitioner to consider what specific treatment techniques or services can be used to enhance the likelihood of a positive outcome. The chief merit of such causal thinking is that it is most productive when it is also very specific—specificity in planning and intervention is the hallmark of good practice. Specificity requires that workers address and at least tentatively answer several important questions: (1) What is the specific problem that should be changed? (2) What should not be changed? (3) What specific treatment techniques can be used that are known to be effective with this particular type of problem? (4) Who will use what technique with, to, or on behalf of whom?

In order to illustrate how these questions and ideas can and should be applied, let us consider a couple of examples. Suppose a diagnostic statement found in a case record says, "This is an inadequate mother who is trying to cope with three unruly children." Are any specific treatment techniques known to be effective in reducing "mother inadequacy"? Of course not. This diagnostic statement is inappropriate because it tells the worker nothing. Such statements should never be allowed in case records because labels such as "inadequate" provide no information about the problem or about what can or should be changed (Wodarski and Hudson, 1976). Who knows what the worker really meant? Perhaps the woman in question did not know how to use adult authority in the regulation of her children's behavior. Or perhaps the worker meant something entirely different.

The use of labels can be misleading or even dangerous. Many do not have real-world referents (Chase, 1938; Korzybski, 1933), and many represent a form of circular reasoning or illogic called reification (Hudson, 1976). If the mother in this example was referred to as inadequate because she was unsuccessful in coping with her children's unruliness, a more productive approach would be to focus on what specifically is meant by unruly and what specifically the mother was or was not doing in her efforts at parenting. If the worker can identify the specific ineffectual parenting behaviors, these can be partially or completely extinguished and then replaced by other behaviors that are more effective in controlling the children. Behavior can be treated but labels cannot; problems must be defined in measurable and treatable terms.

Suppose a client says he wants to experience everything he can—including killing someone. Calling this a "character disorder" does not tell the worker anything about the problem or how to go about solving it. Then why clutter up records with labels? Are there specific treatment techniques known to be effective in treating character disorders? Probably not, because the term is so broad that it can be used to describe a number of different problems. Suppose, on the other hand, that the worker has observed that the client's affective responses are cold, logical, and insensitive. Perhaps the client is starving for affection and for recognition of his real talent and is outraged at being treated by his mother as a fool, a child, and an incompetent. What can the worker do to help? The worker might give him an IQ test to discover how bright he really is. Or the worker might try to retrain the client and his mother to argue more productively and less destructively; teach the client to have and enjoy emotion; acknowledge that his boredom in school has a basis in reality; help the school to better assist the client with his education; and so on. The major point is that, the more specific one can be about the nature and cause of the problem, the more productively one can think about how to change it.

The forgoing discussions may seem rather removed from the issue of measurement, but the point is that, if the components of the client's problem are enumerated in considerable detail, an available measurement device can be selected to assess and monitor the client's problem or can be created on the spot to suit the client's unique situation. If the worker develops a treatment plan based on solid causal thinking ("What must I do to cause an improvement in each problem area?"), the worker will have automatically stated the goals of treatment, which can be used to guide the measurement and assessment of the client's problem.

Consider the case of the cold, logical, brilliant adolescent. The limited description of this case (a real one treated successfully by one of our students) provides enough details to enable the worker to construct an assessment scale. The worker, for example, could ask the client once every two weeks to give these ratings—1 = never, 2 = rarely, 3 = occasionally, 4 = frequently, and 5 = very frequently—to the items in the following chart:

1. I feel bored in school.   _____
2. My mother treats me like a child.   _____
3. Arguments with my mother seem to be rather destructive.   _____
4. I feel like I get a lot out of school.   _____
5. I feel strong emotion.   _____
6. I feel detached from my emotions.   _____
7. I would like to know what it feels like to kill someone.   _____
8. My mother has no respect for my intellectual ability.   _____
9. I feel affectionate and loving toward my mother.   _____
10. I prefer logic to emotion when I relate to others.   _____

If the worker reverse-scores items 4, 5, and 9 (by subtracting the client's rating from 6, so that 1 becomes 5, 2 becomes 4, and so on) and then adds up all ten item responses, the total score will provide a rough index of the magnitude of the client's problem. More important, the total score, plotted on a graph over time, will provide a relatively good description of the extent to which the client is or is not making progress in treatment.

Methods of Measurement

In comparison to social workers of the past, today's social workers increasingly have available to them a wide range of measurement tools that can aid in objectifying and systematizing practice. These tools are a major resource for operationalizing problems and goals, as described earlier, and, perhaps even more important, for monitoring and evaluating progress with every case. Not that some of these tools have not been available for several years (although some have been developed rather recently). Rather, social workers are becoming more aware of the need for such measurement tools, the clinical literature is increasingly reflecting their use, and more resources are being published (see References) that include collections of measurement procedures, thereby enhancing their accessibility to social workers.

This section of the chapter presents a review of the most basic available measures of clinical problems. These measures include: direct observation of behaviors, standardized measures, simple self-anchored scales that one can construct oneself, client logs, and unobtrusive measures (particularly the use of archival records). Of necessity, this chapter only reviews the use of these measures; in-depth discussions are available in Bloom and Fischer (1982), Jayaratne and Levy (1979), and in the other references cited.

A major set of measures—the electromechanical, or physiological, measures—has not been included here because they are generally expensive and complicated to use, require specialized training, are often unavailable to practitioners, and seem to have more narrow applicability than the other measures. Relatively few references examine in detail the use of such measures (see, for example, Pugh and Schwitzgebel, 1977; Lang, 1977; Epstein, 1976; Haynes, 1978). Such other devices as Goal Attainment Scaling (Kiresuk and Sherman, 1968; Kiresuk and Garwick, 1979) and Problem-Oriented Recording (Kane, 1974; Martens and Holmstrup, 1974) are not included here because, although they are extremely useful, they focus more on case planning, organization, and recording than on measurement per se.

Before proceeding with this section, try this exercise. Think of all the practice problems you have ever faced, or imagine some you might encounter one day. Write down those you think might not be measurable, and put that list aside until you have finished this chapter. At the conclusion of the chapter, there will be a suggestion as to how this list can be used.

The remainder of this section of the chapter consists of a review of the key measures available for use in clinical practice.

Direct Observation of Behavior

Direct observation refers to the counting and recording of behaviors as they actually occur. *Behavior,* as used in this context, refers to anything people do. Thus, a behavior could be overt (hitting, walking, crying) or covert (thinking, feeling). The key here is measurability. To be considered a behavior, it must be observable by someone—the client, the practitioner, a relevant other, or an independent observer. (Some good references on direct observation are Ciminero, Calhoun, and Adams, 1977; Haynes, 1978; Hersen and Bellack, 1976; Cone and Hawkins, 1977).

Observing behavior is one of the most important ways of evaluating whether problems really do change, because behavioral measures involve the actual functioning of the client. They can therefore provide at least as good a picture of real changes in the client or client-system as any other method of evaluation. That is, in line with the discussion earlier in the chapter, behavioral measures are often the most valid measures because they are the most direct expression of the problem to be solved. In addition, since behaviors lend themselves well to clear, specific definition, they can be recorded reliably. Finally, precisely because behaviors can be clearly pinpointed and the events affecting their occurrence detailed, use of behavioral measures add a great deal to the practitioner's assessment capabilities.

Instruments for Recording Behaviors   Questions that arise in deciding how to record behavior through direct observation include: Is the method portable enough to be used? Is it unobtrusive enough not to be distracting or embarrassing? Is the method likely to be used? Is the method pleasant or enjoyable to use?

Several different methods of direct observation are available. Some of the more complicated methods involve the use of codes—symbols or phrases used to represent specific categories of behavior (Haynes, 1978). Perhaps the simplest to use is a form—a prepared checklist with spaces or boxes for checking whether or not a behavior does occur. Other methods include small 3 in. × 5 in. cards to note when and where a behavior occurs; coins moved from pocket to pocket or from one compartment in a purse to another each time a behavior occurs; inexpensive wrist golf-score counters; necklaces or bracelets made of lanyards or rawhide with beads strung tightly on them and moved each time a behavior occurs; soap or a large rubber eraser kept in a pocket and an indentation made with a fingernail each time a behavior occurs. As you can see, the methods for recording behavior are limited only by the imagination of the practitioner.

Types of Behavior   There are two basic ways of recording behaviors: frequency counts and duration measures. (A third, interval recording, combines frequency and duration; measurement of intensity or magnitude will be described under self-anchored scales.)

Frequency measures involve simply counting how often a target behavior occurs during a given period of time. Frequency measures are used when the target problem occurs too often and has to be decreased or does not occur often enough and has to be increased. No special equipment is usually necessary. All that is required is that the behavior has a relatively clear beginning and end and that each occurrence takes a relatively constant amount of time.

Frequency counts, then, entail a simple tally of how many times a behavior occurs. A variety of behaviors can be assessed using frequency counts, including number of positive (or negative) thoughts, number of cigarettes smoked, number of mistakes, number of times a conversation is initiated, number of dates, number of times a child follows instructions, number of aggressive phrases used, and so on.

As with any measure, the behavior must be clearly and specifically defined. If the practitioner is not doing the recording, he or she will have to train someone else to do it, possibly the client or someone in the client's environment. To establish just how reliable these observations are, two observers are needed—for example, the primary observer and the practitioner or two people in the family. The two observers record the number of times a behavior occurs during a given time period. Then their observations are compared, and a percentage of agreement is determined— the interobserver reliability. Simply divide the larger number of behaviors into the smaller and multiply by 100. The result, in a percentage form, will tell the extent of agreement. For example, if observer 1 records ten behaviors as occurring and observer 2 records twelve behaviors, 10 would be divided by 12 and the result multiplied by 100 ($10/12 \times 100$), yielding 83 percent reliability. As a general guideline, 80 percent agreement or better is an indication of adequate reliability.

These reliability checks should be used frequently during training and occasionally once intervention has started just to be sure that the observers are being consistent. However, high reliability does not necessarily mean that two observers are recording the same behaviors all the time, only that they agree on total frequency. Thus, this figure should be interpreted cautiously.

Duration measures, the second key type of direct observation, are used when the problem concerns time: that is, when the problem or target behavior lasts too long or not long enough. The main logistical problem in using a duration measure is determining the length of time between the beginning and end of a behavior. Thus, some form of timepiece is necessary.

The main considerations in using duration measures are to be absolutely clear about defining when a behavior begins and ends and to be clear about the time period recorded. A wide range of behaviors can be recorded using duration measures, including studying, exercising, period of time of obsessive thoughts, insomnia, length of tantrums, periods of feeling depressed, and so on.

To establish interobserver reliability for duration measures, one would follow basically the same procedures as with frequency measures. Two observers record how long the behavior lasts over the same time period, and then the smaller duration is simply divided by the larger duration and multiplied by 100. It is important that the observers begin and end their total period of observation at the same time.

Standardized Measures

A standardized measure is one that has uniform procedures for scoring and administration and has certain types of information available about it (Anastasi, 1976). This information includes at least five areas: the purpose and interpretation of the measure; validity; reliability; administration and scoring; and norms (for comparison). All standardized measures do not address each of these areas equally well, but, to the extent that a measure does, one can be assured that it is standardized.

Standardized measures have a number of advantages. They are generally rather simple and inexpensive to use, take fairly little time or energy, are relatively available, and often provide a good deal of information about the problem of concern. Perhaps most important there is a standardized measure for just about any problem the practitioner might face.

However, there are certain disadvantages to the use of standardized measures. Some do not provide all the information needed to clearly evaluate them (for example, information on validity). Since most research on standardized measures is done on large groups, error is always possible when the measures are applied to an individual. Since standardized measures deal only with predetermined questions and problems, they may not be exactly suited to all the specific characteristics of the problems faced. In addition, most standardized measures, especially questionnaires, surveys, and nonbehavioral checklists, tend not to be very direct measures of a problem.

One of the advantages of standardized measures noted earlier—that so many are available that one can measure just about any clinical problem—could also prove to be a problem by making it difficult to choose among them. The following criteria, described in Anastasi (1976) and Bloom and Fischer (1982), are helpful in making such a choice: be sure the purpose of the measure relates to the problem with which you are dealing; try to select one that is as direct a measure of the problem as possible; look for data on reliability, validity (the more types of validity addressed, the better), and sensitivity to change; make sure the measure will be useful for your purposes (possible, practical, and so on); be sure the measure can be used repeatedly (high test-retest reliability indicating stability); and be sure it is short enough not to become aversive to the client.

Since there are so many standardized measures available—literally thousands, measuring most forms of human social functioning—it would be impossible to describe them all here. Therefore, the interested reader is referred to the following references, each of which reviews and evaluates a number of measures appropriate for particular uses: Levitt and Marsh, 1980; Comrey and others, 1973; Buros, 1972; Lake and others, 1973; Andrulis, 1977; Arkava and Snow, 1978.

One set of measures, the Clinical Measurement Package (CMP), will be described in this chapter, not only because it exemplifies what is available but also because it meets most of the criteria noted earlier, is suitable for use in single-system research (that is, as repeated measures), and forms an integrated package with the same format, scoring methods, and administration.

The CMP is a package of scales developed by Hudson and his coworkers (Hudson, 1977; Hudson and Glisson, 1976; Hudson and Procter, 1976a, 1976b; Giuli and Hudson, 1977; Hudson, Harrison, and Crosscup, 1980; Hudson, Acklin and Bartosh, 1980; Hudson, Wung, and Borges, 1980; Cheung and Hudson, 1980; Hudson and others, 1980). All of the work on these scales is available in a new volume entitled *The Clinical Measurement Package: A Field Manual* (Hudson, 1982).

The Clinical Measurement Package consists of nine twenty-five-item scales designed specifically for clinical practice and single-system research to monitor and evaluate the magnitude (extent, degree, intensity) of the client's problem through periodic administration of the same instrument. The first six scales are: (1) the Generalized Contentment Scale (GCS), a measure of the degree or magnitude of nonpsychotic depression, (2) the Index of Self-Esteem (ISE), which measures the degree or magnitude of the client's problem with the evaluative component of self-concept; (3) the Index of Marital Satisfaction (IMS), designed to measure the degree or magnitude of problems spouses have in their marital relationship; (4) the Index of Sexual Satisfaction (ISS), which is designed to measure the degree or magnitude of discord or dissatisfaction that partners experience with their sexual relationship; (5) the Index of Peer Relations (IPR), designed to measure the degree or intensity of a problem in the ability to relate to peers; and (6) the Index of Family Relations (IFR), designed to measure the degree or intensity of intrafamilial stress as seen by the client. Three other scales were designed to measure the degree or magnitude of parent–child relationship problems: (7) the Index of Parental Attitudes (IPA), completed by the parent, is designed to measure the degree of magnitude of a relationship problem a parent has with a child; (8) the Child's Attitude Toward Father (CAF) measures the degree or magnitude of relationship problems children have with their father; and (9) the Child's Attitude Toward Mother (CAM) measures the degree or magnitude of relationship problems children have with their mother. The latter two scales, CAF and CAM, are completed by the child. One of these instruments, the ISE, is reproduced as an example in Figure 12.1.

All of the scales have internal consistency reliabilities and test–retest reliabilities (stability) of 0.90 or better. They all have high content, concurrent, and construct validity. In addition, the scales appear to discriminate well between people known or admitting to have problems and people known or claiming not to have problems in each area. In other words, the scales clearly appear to be measuring what they are intended to measure.

All of the scales are scored in the same way, a distinct advantage when using several instruments. Following are the instructions for scoring; reverse-score every positively worded item. (The items to be reverse-scored are listed at the bottom of each scale.) For example, if the client scored one of these positively worded items as 1, rescore it as 5; 2 is rescored as 4; 3 is left unchanged; 4 is rescored as 2; and 5 is rescored as 1. After all the positively worded items have been rescored (all negatively worded items are left unchanged), add up all of the scores, then subtract 25 from the total. (Consult the references for scoring procedures to be used when clients fail to complete one or more items.) This method of scoring produces

Figure 12.1.   The Index of Self-Esteem (ISE)

INDEX OF SELF-ESTEEM (ISE)   Today's Date _____

NAME: _____

This questionnaire is designed to measure how you see yourself. It is not a test, so there are no right or wrong answers. Please answer each item as carefully and accurately as you can by placing a number by each one as follows:

1   Rarely or none of the time
2   A little of the time
3   Some of the time
4   A good part of the time
5   Most or all of the time

Please begin.
1. I feel that people would not like me if they really knew me well   _____
2. I feel that others get along much better than I do   _____
3. I feel that I am a beautiful person   _____
4. When I am with other people, I feel they are glad I am with them   _____
5. I feel that people really like to talk with me   _____
6. I feel that I am a very competent person   _____
7. I think I make a good impression on others   _____
8. I feel that I need more self-confidence   _____
9. When I am with strangers, I am very nervous   _____
10. I think that I am a dull person   _____
11. I feel ugly   _____
12. I feel that others have more fun than I do   _____
13. I feel that I bore people   _____
14. I think my friends find me interesting   _____
15. I think I have a good sense of humor   _____
16. I feel very self-conscious when I am with strangers   _____
17. I feel that, if I could be more like other people, I would have it made _____
18. I feel that people have a good time when they are with me   _____
19. I feel like a wallflower when I go out   _____
20. I feel I get pushed around more than others   _____
21. I think I am a rather nice person   _____
22. I feel that people really like me very much   _____
23. I feel that I am a likable person   _____
24. I am afraid I will appear foolish to others   _____
25. My friends think very highly of me   _____

a minimum score of 0 (lower scores are interpreted as absence of problems or minimal problems) and a maximum score of 100 (higher scores are interpreted as presence of problems).

On all scales, the higher the score, the greater the magnitude of the problem. Each of the scales has also been designed to have a "clinical cutting score" of 30, the idea being that people who score over 30 generally have been found to have clinically significant problems in the area being measured, whereas people who score below 30 do not. This guideline is potentially an important one for use in practice. However, this cutting point should be interpreted with caution, pending validation by further research. At present, it probably would be safe to view the 30 level as a very rough guide to the existence or absence of problems. A score of 29 does not mean complete absence of problems, and a score of 31 does not mean clinical intervention is obviously necessary. The point, though, is that higher scores deserve attention, and the goal of intervention is to reduce those scores to at least below 30.

Although these scales can be used to measure the severity, intensity, degree, or magnitude of a problem, they are not intended to be used to determine its source, locus, or origin. Thus, to that extent, they do not provide all the diagnostic or assessment information necessary prior to beginning an intervention program.

Further, it is assumed that, despite the high reliability of each scale, there will still be some measurement error. None of the scales is perfect. As a rough guide, then, assume that changes in score of five points or less over repeated administrations may be a result of this error, and that changes of more than five points in either direction probably reflect real changes in the client's problem or situation.

These scales are recommended for use approximately once per week both to evaluate change and to provide a basis for discussion between client and practitioner. Research by Hudson and his colleagues reveals that the scales do appear to be stable and reasonable measures of change when administered repeatedly over several weeks. Of course, if the client does express dissatisfaction with the use of these scales, they may have to be administered less frequently or dropped altogether and less aversive measures found.

Self-Anchored Scales

In some situations, direct observation of overt behaviors may be difficult or impossible, and standardized measures dealing with the problem of concern may not be available or practical. Does that mean that the client's problem can not be measured? Not at all. There is a type of measure that can be used in a range of situations and is so flexible that it has been called an "all-purpose measurement procedure" (Bloom, 1975). This procedure consists of actually developing one's own scale to measure whatever it is practitioner and client have decided to focus on. This do-it-yourself procedure is called a self-anchored scale (Bloom, 1975; Gingerich, 1979).

Self-anchored scales are simple self-report scales that can be constructed in an individualized fashion to measure a given problem. In essence, practitioner and client simply identify a particular problem area and establish a sliding scale—say, from zero to ten points—to measure that problem. These scales have numerous advantages. They are very flexible, and therefore can be used to tap a whole range of problems. Self-anchored scales can be used to measure the intensity of problems (for example, the intensity of pain in migraines) or the intensity of negative thoughts. Related to this, self-anchored scales can be used to measure internal thoughts and feelings—everything from fear to sexual excitement or self-esteem. Self-anchored scales are also very easy to construct and easy for the client to use; they therefore have the virtue of being highly efficient. Indeed, they can readily be used as repeated measures one or more times per day.

Self-anchored scales tend to have high face validity. That is, on the face of it, they appear to be measuring what they are intended to measure. That is, they can be used to measure things that only the client can report on and therefore often represent a fairly accurate portrayal of the client's circumstances, thoughts, or feelings. As self-reports, they may provide the primary focus for intervention—changing what a client thinks about himself or herself. Self-anchored scales can be used as primary or sole measures, if no other measures are available or appropriate, or as secondary measures to supplement other information (for example, data on overt behavior). Finally, the scores on self-anchored scales, like the scores on standardized measures or the frequency or duration data of behavioral measures, can be charted to provide a visual display of changes in the problem over time.

Several simple steps can be used to develop these scales:

1. Prepare the client. Help the client become as specific as possible about the problem. Help the client think of the need for a social or psychological thermometer (Bloom, 1975) with the high point the highest, best, most intense description of the problem and the low point the lowest description.
2. Select the number of points for the scale. Although these scales can run up to 100 points, for purposes of simplification, eleven-point scales are suggested. Thus, 5 (midpoint on the scale) could be neutral or moderate (compared with the two extreme poles); 0 would always be low and 10 always high. However, if the client has trouble discriminating between points on the scale, use fewer points.
3. Use equal intervals. Try to clarify that there is not a bigger jump between points 1 and 2 than between any other two points, say, 7 and 8.
4. Use only one scale per dimension, and try to limit each scale to measuring only one dimension. Instead of having two different dimensions at each pole (for example, happy on one end, depressed on the other), because people can and do experience contradictory feelings at the same time, it is clearer to use each scale to measure only one dimension at a time (for example, degree of sadness from low to high).
5. Anchor the scale points. The last step is attempting to use concrete examples to clearly define the points on your scale. At the most general level, you would want to identify the end points—for example, level 0, "Don't experience the problem at all," and level 10, "Feel the problem all the time." In addition, it is very helpful to try to develop examples of thoughts, feelings, and behaviors that might be occurring at those points to help the client recognize that level of intensity. Thus, the client might know to rate himself or herself

as severely depressed (level 10) when he or she cannot sleep or work and has suicidal thoughts.

An example of a scale measuring severity of feelings of anger would be:

0	1	2	3	4	5	6	7	8	9	10
Not at all angry					Moderately angry					Furious (want to scream and hit)

An example of a scale measuring intensity of cognitions of sadness would be:

0	1	2	3	4	5	6	7	8	9	10
No cognitions of sadness					Moderate sadness					Extremely intense sadness (crying most of the day)

Client Logs

The client log is essentially a journal kept by clients of events that they consider to be relevant to their problem situation. The use of the log helps the client take systematic and objective notes on such events in an attempt to avoid distortions when presenting information to the practitioner. The log, consisting of a more or less formal record of events that occur but may somehow be forgotten or overlooked, represents an attempt to help the client "tell it like it is" (Schwartz and Goldiamond, 1975; Bloom and Fischer, 1982).

The client log has two basic purposes or uses. The first and most important is an assessment device. Client logs help pinpoint target problems. They serve as sources of hypotheses for intervention and help in planning by allowing practitioner and client, in discussing the problem situation, to examine the log to determine which events appear to be related to the occurrence of the problem.

The second use is for evaluation purposes: the log provides an ongoing record of the client's activities in relation to the problems being worked on. The log often shows changes in these activities and problems as the client experiences them.

Overall, client logs are not to be construed as precise scientific instruments; their accuracy is based on the client's perceptions. Thus, questions of reliability and validity suggest that they probably should not be used as the primary source of assessment or evaluation information. On the other hand, logs do appear to be excellent sources of secondary or supplementary information. All client logs use basically the same format, a prepared form that lists across the top of the page the type of information to be collected. The information varies with the nature of the problem but, at the least, might include a brief description of some event or behavior that occurred and what the client did, thought, or felt about it. On the left-hand side of the page, the client lists the time each event occurred.

Client logs can be constructed according to two major variables, time and category of client problem. Clients can be asked to record any event that occurs that they consider to be important (critical-incident recording), or they can be asked to summarize, at preestablished intervals (for example, every hour or two), the key events that occurred during that interval (see Bloom and Fischer, 1982).

The categories of client problems can also vary in their specificity. The practitioner can leave the categories open and suggest that the client record any event that is "critical," or the categories can be highly specific—for example: Who did what to whom? What was your reaction? What events preceded and followed the problem situation? and so on. Examples of different types of client logs and forms are available in Schwartz and Goldiamond (1975) and Bloom and Fischer (1982).

Unobtrusive Measures

One of the concerns of many practitioners is that somehow the measurement process will affect practice in some presumably negative fashion. Indeed, that concern bears a grain of truth. Earlier in this chapter, we described the potential for one such effect, reactivity—changes in the problem due to the act of measurement itself. For many of the measurement procedures described thus far, however, reactivity can be either overcome or accounted for (see Nay, 1979; Bloom and Fischer, 1982).

But some methods of measurement, called unobtrusive measures, avoid the problem of reactivity: the client "is not aware of being [measured] and there is little danger that the act of measurement will itself serve as a force for change or elicit role playing that confounds the data" (Webb and others, 1966, p. 175).

Many of these unobtrusive measures are indirect ways of measuring problems and therefore should serve in most instances as secondary sources of data. These measures include physical traces (evidence left by an individual or group with no knowledge that it will be used for other purposes), behavior products (measurement of the effects of behaviors—for example, items left on a floor—rather than the behaviors themselves), and simple observations (where the observer observes a problem without being seen or noticed). All of these are described in detail in Webb and others (1966).

One type of unobtrusive measure that is often readily available to social workers is the archival record, data that are available from records kept for various purposes but not originally intended to be used in an intervention program. Because these records are often available from a variety of sources and can be used to measure the effects of an intervention program, they are probably the most important and useful type of unobtrusive measure.

In some instances, archival records may directly reflect the problem to be worked on and can therefore serve as primary measures. An example might be school records: attendance data, test scores, grades, and so on. Other forms of records, including agency record data, recidivism notes, actuarial data, and government data, may be used as primary or secondary sources, depending on the goals of a specific intervention program.

Of course, archival records do present some problems, including inflexibility, limited accessibility, incompleteness or inconsistency of available data, and systematic bias of content. However, since these data do overcome the effects of reactivity, they can prove to be a particularly valuable resource, especially in allowing evaluation of activities that otherwise might not be accessible to evaluation.

Selecting a Measure

Once familiar with the range of measures available, the practitioner needs to consider several factors in making a selection (see also Nay, 1979). The first involves the characteristics of the measure, in particular its reliability, validity, utility, and directness, as well as its suitability for single-system research. To the extent that a measure can be positively evaluated on each dimension, it should be considered as a prime candidate for use. The second factor to consider is the nature of the problem. Even though a measure is valid and reliable, it must accurately reflect the problem it is intended to measure. A behavioral measure would not be appropriate when the goal is to change an attitude, and vice versa. The third factor relates to the characteristics of the client and the resources available. Someone (the client or relevant other) must be willing and able to use the measure selected and be trained in its use, if necessary.

The last guideline for selecting measurement procedures is one of the most important: whenever possible, use more than one. Changes in clients are often multidimensional and often do not even correlate with each other. Not that several measures should be used merely in the hope that one will show change. Rather, systematic selection and use of more than one measure will increase the chances of identifying change if change really occurs. More specifically, use of more than one measure offers the opportunity to provide a balanced measurement package— that is, one that measures two different aspects of the same problem, taps internal and external change, uses both a direct and an indirect measure, or uses different vantage points to evaluate change (for example, client and practitioner).

Conclusion

Earlier in this chapter, it was suggested that you list some of the problems you have encountered in your practice that you consider to be immeasurable. In reviewing that list now, note whether any of those problems can in fact be measured by the procedures described in this chapter. Once you have clearly specified the problem, you should find it amenable to measurement by one or more of the instruments presented.

As noted earlier, measurement is at the very heart of the process of integrating research and practice and provides the opportunity for social workers to be clear about what they are doing and where they are going with every case or situation. Use of the measurement procedures described in this chapter provides the basis for assessment and evaluation processes that can be more systematic, more objective, and more helpful to clients and practitioners.

References

Allen, M. J., and Yen, W. M. *Introduction to Measurement Theory.* Monterey, Calif.: Brooks/Cole, 1979.

Anastasi, A. *Psychological Testing.* (4th ed.) New York: Macmillan, 1976.

Andrulis, R. S. *Adult Assessment.* Springfield, Ill.: Charles C Thomas, 1977.

Arkava, M. L., and Snow, M. *Psychological Tests and Social Work Practice.* Springfield, Ill.: Charles C Thomas, 1978.

Bloom, M. *The Paradox of Helping: Introduction to the Philosophy of Scientific Practice.* New York: Wiley, 1975.

Bloom, M., and Fischer, J. *Evaluating Practice: A Guide for the Helping Professional.* Englewood Cliffs, N.J.: Prentice-Hall, 1982.

Buros, O. K., (Ed.). *The Seventh Mental Measurements Yearbook.* (2 vols.) Highland Park, N.J.: Gryphon Press, 1972.

Chase, S. *The Tyranny of Words.* New York: Harcourt, Brace, 1938.

Cheung, P. P. L., and Hudson, W. W. "Assessing Marital Discord in Clinical Practice: A Revalidation of the Index of Marital Satisfaction." *Journal of Social Service Research,* 1982, 5 (1/2), 101–118.

Ciminero, A. R., Calhoun, K. S., and Adams, H. E. (Eds.). *Handbook of Behavioral Assessment.* New York: Wiley, 1977.

Comrey, A. L., and others. *A Sourcebook for Mental Health Measures.* Los Angeles: Human InterAction Research Institute, 1973.

Cone, J. D., and Hawkins, R. P., (Eds.). *Behavioral Assessment.* New York: Brunner/Mazel, 1977.

Epstein, L. H. "Psychophysiological Measurement in Assessment." In M. Hersen and A. S. Bellack (Eds.), *Behavioral Assessment: A Practical Handbook.* New York: Pergamon Press, 1976.

Fischer, J. *Effective Casework Practice: An Eclectic Approach.* New York: McGraw-Hill, 1978.

Gingerich, W. "Measuring the Process." *Social Work,* 1978, *23* (3), 251–252.

Gingerich, W. "Procedure for Evaluating Clinical Practice." *Health and Social Work,* 1979, *4,* 104–130.

Giuli, C. A., and Hudson, W. W. "Assessing Parent-Child Relationship Disorders in Clinical Practice." *Journal of Social Service Research,* 1977, *1* (1), 77–92.

Grinnell, R. M., Jr. (Ed.). *Social Work Research and Evaluation.* Springfield, Ill.: Peacock, 1981.

Haynes, S. N. *Principles of Behavioral Assessment.* New York: Gardner Press, 1978.

Helmstadter, G. C. *Principles of Psychological Measurement.* New York: Appleton-Century-Crofts, 1964.

Hersen, M., and Barlow, D. H. *Single Case Experimental Designs: Strategies for Studying Behavior Change.* Elmsford, N.Y.: Pergamon Press, 1976.

Hersen, M., and Bellack, A. S. (Eds.). *Behavioral Assessment: A Practical Handbook.* New York: Pergamon Press, 1976.

Hudson, W. W. "A Measurement Package for Clinical Workers." Paper presented at the 23rd annual program meeting of the Council on Social Work Education, Phoenix, Ariz., March 1977.

Hudson, W. W. "First Axioms of Treatment." *Social Work,* 1978a, *23* (1), 65–66.

Hudson, W. W. "Research Training in Professional Social Work Education." *Social Service Review,* 1978b, *52* (1), 116–121.

Hudson, W. W. *The Clinical Measurement Package: A Field Manual.* Homewood, Ill.: Dorsey, 1982.

Hudson, W. W. "Guidelines for Social Work Practice." School of Social Work, University of Hawaii, 1976. (Mimeographed.)

Hudson, W. W., Acklin, J., and Bartosh, J. C. "Assessing Discord in Family Relationships." *Social Work Research and Abstracts,* 1980, *16* (3), 21–29.

Hudson, W. W., and Glisson, D. H. "Assessment of Marital Discord in Family Relationships." *Social Service Review,* 1976, *50,* 293–311.

Hudson, W. W., Harrison, D. F., and Crosscup, P. "A Short-Form Scale to Measure Sexual Discord." *Journal of Sex Research,* 1981, *17,* 157–174.

Hudson, W. W., and Procter, E. K. "A Short-Form Scale for Measuring Self-Esteem." School of Social Work, University of Hawaii, 1976a. (Mimeographed.)

Hudson, W. W., and Procter, E. K. "The Assessment of Depressive Affect in Clinical Practice." School of Social Work, University of Hawaii, 1976b. (Mimeographed.)

Hudson, W. W., Wung, B., and Borges, M. "Parent-Child Relationship Disorders: The Parent's Point of View." *Journal of Social Service Research,* 1980, *3,* 283–294.

Hudson, W. W., and others. "A Comparison and Revalidation of Three Measures of Depression." School of Social Work, Florida State University, Tallahassee, 1980.

Jayaratne, S., and Levy, R. *Empirical Clinical Practice.* New York: Columbia, 1979.

Kane, R. A. "Look to the Record." *Social Work,* 1974, *17,* 412–119.

Kiresuk, T. J., and Sherman, R. E. "Goal Attainment Scaling: A General Method of Evaluating Comprehensive Community Mental Health Programs." *Community Mental Health Journal,* 1968, *4,* 443–453.

Kiresuk, T. J., and Garwick, G. "Basic Goal Attainment Scaling Procedures." In B. R. Compton and B. Gallaway (Eds.), *Social Work Processes.* (Rev. ed.) Homewood, Ill.: Dorsey Press, 1979.

Korzybski, A. *Science and Sanity: An Introduction to Non-Aristotelian Systems and General Semantics*. Lakeville, Conn.: The Institute of General Semantics, 1933.

Lake, D. G., and others. *Measuring Human Behavior: Tools for the Assessment of Social Functioning*. New York: Teachers College Press, Columbia University, 1973.

Lang, P. J. "Physiological Assessment of Anxiety and Fear." In J. D. Cone and R. P. Hawkins (Eds.), *Behavioral Assessment*. New York: Brunner/Mazel, 1977.

Levitt, J. L., and Marsh, J. "A Collection of Short-Form Repeated Measurement Instruments Suitable for Practice." Chicago: School of Social Service Administration, University of Chicago, 1980. (Mimeographed.)

Martens, W. M., and Holmstrup, W. "Problem-Oriented Recording." *Social Casework,* 1974, *55,* 554–561.

Nay, W. R. *Multimethod Clinical Assessment*. New York: Gardner, 1979.

Nunnally, J. C. *Psychometric Theory*. New York: McGraw-Hill, 1978.

Pugh, J. D., and Schwitzgebel, R. L. "Instrumentation for Behavioral Assessment." In A. R. Ciminero and others (Eds.), *Handbook of Behavioral Assessment*. New York: Wiley, 1977.

Schwartz, A., and Goldiamond, I. *Social Casework: A Behavioral Approach*. Chicago: University of Chicago Press, 1975.

Webb, E. J., and others. *Unobtrusive Measures: Nonreactive Research in the Social Sciences*. Chicago: Rand McNally, 1966.

Wodarski, J., Hudson, W. W., and Buckholdt, D. R. "Issues in Evaluative Research: Implications for Social Work." *Journal of Sociology and Social Welfare,* 1976, *4* (1), 81–113.

Chapter 13
Eclectic Casework

The winds of change are blowing on social casework. Since the earliest days of the profession, most caseworkers tended to approach knowledge development for practice in more or less unsystematic, haphazard, and uncritical ways. Criteria for knowledge selection were either vague, undefined, or, when they were available, unrelated to the empirical status of the knowledge. Such criteria included the comfort of the practitioner with new knowledge, the prestige of the proponent of new knowledge, or consensus among experts or peers. Part and parcel of this era was an inability of caseworkers to demonstrate their effectiveness in empirical research (Fischer, 1973, 1976).

But the last decade or so has seen major changes in the world view of many caseworkers, changes that have been described elsewhere as—in Kuhn's (1970) terms—revolutionary (Fischer, 1981). There appears to be a paradigm shift underway in casework involving a movement toward more systematic, rational, and empirically oriented development, selection, and use of knowledge for practice with a concomitant increase in practice effectiveness (Reid & Hanrahan, 1982). For want of better terminology, it appears as though casework is moving toward the development of a practice that could be called scientifically based. This development in social work, or at least its potential, is one that has also been noted by a number of other authors (Mullen, 1978; Thomas, 1977; Reid, 1978; Hepworth & Larsen, 1982; Gambrill, 1983; Wodarski, 1981; Bloom, 1975; Briar, 1978).

What Is Social Casework?

Casework is a branch of the social work profession, the branch that provides the individualized, individualizing, case-by-case services of social work. Caseworkers operate in a broad range of settings—from general and psychiatric hospitals to clinics, family service, and child care agencies to schools, rehabilitation centers

Fischer, J. (1985). In Norcross, J. C. (Ed.). *Handbook of Eclectic Psychotherapy.* New York: Brunner-Mazel, 320–352. Reprinted with permission.

and prisons. In fact, social workers provide the bulk of the clinical services in the mental health clinics in the United States (Goleman, 1985).

Often, caseworkers work in collaboration with other professionals, and in many instances, their assignments are identical (as in providing direct clinical services in outpatient clinics). Thus, there is often considerable overlap among the practices of caseworkers and other professionals, especially in the area of direct, therapeutic work with clients. Indeed, it is just such overlap, including the accumulated evidence showing no interprofessional differences in terms of views and attitudes toward clients or in outcome, that has led Giannetti and Wells (1985) to the suggestion that all of the psychotherapeutic professions may be engaged in a uniform enterprise (Henry, Sims, & Spray, 1971).

The commonalities among professions when engaged in providing a direct service or interpersonal influence role strongly suggest the need to be aware of knowledge from any source that can lead to greater effectiveness in practice, whether that knowledge is developed inside or outside a given profession. Thus, when practitioners from across the professions are engaged in common activities (e.g., therapeutic work with a depressed or highly anxious client), it is crucial for them to utilize the best, most effective knowledge available, no matter who has developed that knowledge.

On the other hand, this is not to say that there are not a number of differences among the professions with regard to training, interests, societal mandate, and spheres of functioning. Caseworkers operate from a far broader base than the field of psychotherapy provides. Caseworkers provide a wide range of services and function in a variety of roles other than the clinical or psychotherapeutic role. At the core of this functioning is a commitment not only to the individual, but also to the social and physical environments in which individuals function. It is this interaction between people and environments which is at the heart of social work concerns and provides a perspective for understanding the distinctive tasks and functions of social work: helping people cope with impinging environments and attempting to improve environments. Thus, in addition to a clinical or therapeutic role, caseworkers will provide concrete services, act as advocates for their clients, serve as brokers or mediators, and engage in social action to affect legislation and organizational or governmental policies.

However, since this book is concerned with psychotherapeutic services, this chapter will focus only on that role of caseworkers, with the understanding that many of the principles (e.g., of knowledge selection) apply to other casework roles even though some of the actual practice techniques may not.

Caseworkers and Eclecticism

Most caseworkers report that they are "eclectic," selecting that as their own description of their orientation, because they claim allegiance to more than one theory, or because their actual practice activities are not necessarily constrained by adherence to only one theoretical orientation (Jayaratne, 1978, 1982; Cocozzelli, in press). However, it is not at all clear that even those caseworkers who consider themselves to be eclectic use any systematic criteria to select their approaches in practice or that the use of two approaches of undemonstrated or questionable effectiveness is necessarily any better than use of just one approach of undemonstrated effectiveness. The real task of the eclectic practitioner is to be both systematic and empirically oriented in his/her selection of knowledge for practice, unhampered, to the extent possible, by the narrowness and biases of adherence to one particular school, cult, or theoretical orientation.

Background

Eclectic casework—to the extent that it is an increasing phenomenon in social work—arose out of a recognition in the early 1970s that traditional approaches to practice simply were not providing persuasive evidence of their helpfulness to clients. There were, as of the mid-1970s, no controlled studies providing a clear demonstration of the effectiveness of any form of social casework, regardless of the practice approach, or client population, or problem (Fischer, 1976). At the same time, an increasing number of studies were appearing in the literature of allied professions, particularly clinical psychology and counseling, suggesting that several techniques were available that had accumulated a considerable body of evidence of effectiveness. It was these two strands—lack of evidence of effectiveness from within casework and evidence of effectiveness from several other sources—that were the initial impetus to begin the process of trying to develop an approach that can integrate the best knowledge the clinical helping professions have to offer.

The Approach

The very nature of eclecticism—the fact that its components are selected from a variety of sources—mitigates against a tightly knit, integrated conceptual framework. It would be easy to see how some of the virtues of an eclectic approach—especially its potential effectiveness for practice—might be sacrificed for the sake of neatness, the attempt to fit all components into as nice a meta- or quasi-theoretical framework as possible. A key argument of this chapter, however, is that effectiveness in practice is the ultimate—in fact, the only—criterion for judging the success of an eclectic approach, and that a demonstrably effective technique cannot be ignored simply because it does not seem to fit within the "conceptual framework" of someone or other's brand of eclecticism. (It is not difficult to imagine "an eclectic approach" become just another cult.)

On the other hand, there are some areas, both conceptually and in practice, that suggest eclecticism need not be an unsystematic collection of a little bit of this and a little bit of that, but can become a rigorous, rational, and systematic approach to practice in its own right.

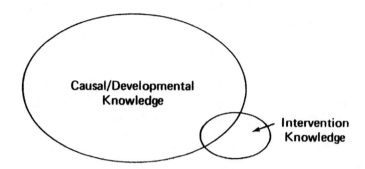

Fig. 13.1   Areas of knowledge and their relationships.

Knowledge Characteristics

There are two broad classes of knowledge potentially available to practitioners: causal/developmental knowledge and intervention knowledge (Fischer, 1978). Figure 13.1 illustrates the relationship between these two knowledge areas.

Causal/developmental knowledge is by far the largest area of knowledge in the social and behavioral sciences. This is the bulk of knowledge developed in anthropology, psychology, sociology, and much of psychiatry and social work. Causal/developmental knowledge essentially focuses on explanations geared toward understanding the development of human behavior (adaptive and maladaptive). To the extent that this knowledge has many implications for practice, it is in helping the practitioner understand *why* an individual (or other client system) developed as he or she did, providing at least part of the knowledge base of the assessment process.

The other area of knowledge, intervention knowledge, focuses on the question "What can be done to modify a given situation or problem?" Intervention knowledge is used to prescribe principles and procedures for inducing change.

As can be seen in Figure 13.1, there is some overlap between these areas, for example, in use of knowledge where understanding specific developmental considerations is a precondition (or provides specific guidelines) for intervention. But as Figure 13.1 also is intended to suggest, there are areas of intervention knowledge that are independent of causal/developmental knowledge. Perhaps even more important, there often is a lack of recognition of the real and important differences between these two areas of knowledge.

For many years in social work, caseworkers have attempted to use causal/developmental knowledge as a substitute for intervention knowledge, ignoring the fact that causal/developmental knowledge describes and explains only problem development. Thus, caseworkers became far more sophisticated in their diagnostic/assessment knowledge than in their intervention knowledge. This, in turn, led to a pervasive assumption in casework that understanding a problem somehow led almost automatically to the problem being changed.

But understanding is not helping. An entirely different set of principles and techniques is necessary in order to have specific guidelines for changing problems. Thus, major schools of casework developed with almost no attention to techniques: prescription of specific step-by-step procedures a practitioner could implement in practice (see, e.g., Roberts & Nee, 1970).

It seems clear from the plethora of research that will be cited later in this chapter that intervention knowledge can lead to effective practice independent of knowledge about the "cause" of problems. This does not mean, however, that intervention knowledge is applied haphazardly or unsystematically. It does mean that there are a variety of sources from which intervention knowledge may be derived ranging from theories or systems of psychotherapy or behavior change to techniques derived inductively from empirical research and/or clinical observation. The nature and extent of intervention knowledge can vary greatly, from elaborate principles explaining how behavior changes to comprehensive frameworks describing the therapeutic process.

But it appears as though there is one irreducible minimum, or *sine qua non,* for intervention knowledge, a minimal floor beyond which intervention knowledge cannot go without losing its identity as intervention knowledge. That minimum level is the need for specific *techniques*: step-by-step procedures for guiding and inducing change with clients. Techniques are the expression in action and in a precise form of what the practitioner should actually do in a given situation and with a given client or problem. It is these techniques that form the core of eclectic practice.

Intervention Knowledge and Theory

A key point of this chapter is that intervention knowledge for an eclectic approach can be derived from a variety of sources, including, but not limited to, theories, or systems, of intervention. Such systems can range from comprehensive and expansive general systems prescribing a whole range of techniques to mid-range and low-range theories focused on fewer phenomena. Indeed, it is tempting to consider limiting one's approach to techniques derived from only one system, especially if that system begins to accumulate a large number of positive research findings (e.g., behavior therapy). This is due to a variety of reasons including the facts that there is a certain security for the practitioner in the neatness of a more or less integrated system, and use of one system allows for the development of orderly and consistent ways of observing and explaining the relationships among a variety of events. A single system or theory can be useful, a clear way of observing, understanding, planning, implementing intervention, and predicting results.

On the other hand, there are several problems in devoting allegiance to particular systems:

1. Because of their more or less comprehensive nature, it is difficult to adhere to more than one or two theories at best.

2. Clinging to one theory may not only be not useful, it may lead to inaccurate or incorrect predictions and weak or ineffective interventions.

3. Clinging to the tenets of one system often channels the perceptions of adherents into narrow perspectives leading practitioners to try to force a number of significantly different people, problems, and events into an incompatible jell.

4. People and their problems are simply too complicated for the use of only one approach to resolve all problems.

5. No single perspective or theory has produced successful empirical results regarding all the problems that practitioners face. Indeed, as will be discussed later, empirical evidence appears to be scattered among several approaches.

6. Theories are too complicated to be validated in toto. At best, selected techniques can be validated.

7. The fact that there are so many competing casework, psychotherapy, and counseling theories—some estimate several hundred—suggests both that they all cannot be equally valid and that none has achieved sufficient documentation to stand alone as the only effective approach, thereby commanding universal acceptance by virtue of the weight of evidence.

8. There seem to be so many possibly valid principles from a range of different systems explaining behavior change that it seems as though " . . . the best strategy . . . would be to consider the hypothesis that different kinds of responses may be governed by different principles and may require different procedures for their modification" (Ford & Urban, 1963, p. 345).

9. Finally, relying exclusively on one or two theories as integrating bases for practice often precludes the systematic, objective examination of other approaches, even when positive evidence from these approaches becomes available. Theories become the master of the practitioner rather than the guide to practice, producing cults and schools and a faith in one's own theory that ignores rational decision making. Thus, the literature becomes filled with attacks and rejoinders as adherents of one approach attack adherents of other approaches while blissfully ignoring the deficiencies in their own approach. For example, now that the vituperation between psychoanalysts and behaviorists seems to have died down, a whole new generation of vituperation has developed involving advocates of behavior therapy, quasibehavior therapy, cognitive therapy, cognitive behavior therapy, multimodal therapy, and various eclectic therapies (see, e.g., Wilson, 1982). It is not infrequent to see these exchanges almost devoid of any reference to evidence of effectiveness.

In all, then, it appears not only unnecessary to think in terms of a unitary theoretical perspective as a guide to practice, it appears unwise as well. There is just too much evidence from too broad a range of approaches to make any other conclusion reasonable. Now this is not to say that there are not advantages to being guided by a theory in the *development* of techniques, nor is it to deny the possible value of knowledge about theoretical principles that might underlie techniques so they won't be applied blindly. But it is to say that for the *practitioner,* the evidence seems to point to the need to possess a framework for practice that utilizes the best knowledge available from a variety of different sources or, specifically, the development of an eclectic approach to practice.

Eclecticism Defined

The dictionary definition of eclecticism is " . . . not following any one system as of philosophy, medicine, etc., but selecting and using whatever is considered best in all systems" (*The American College Dictionary,* 1957, p. 381). Eclectic casework practice, then, consists of a variety of intervention techniques, derived from a number of different sources, including those that may appear to be incompatible on the surface, in large part on the basis of demonstrated effectiveness. These techniques would be applied with people and problems where the evidence indicates that such application has a substantial chance to produce successful outcome. The goal of this eclectic approach is to be outcome-oriented, and to be empirically based to the extent possible, and grounded in the use of interventive techniques that are developed and/or adapted through a process of rigorous and systematic testing, implementation, and retesting.

The eclectic approach is atheoretical for all the reasons described earlier. Rather than attempting to integrate a variety of presumably different intervention theories, or even principles derived from theories, the focus of integration is on techniques, with primary emphasis on those techniques that have been shown in empirical research to enhance the effectiveness of practice.

Essentially, eclecticism refers to a commitment to being guided in practice by what works, a commitment that takes precedence over devotion to any theoretical orientation. Thus, the practitioner can be divorced from any theoretical orientation currently in vague. But eclectic practice requires the ultimate in flexibility and open-mindness on the part of practitioners. They cannot afford to become complacent and satisfied with any one approach or any one technique no matter how efficient and effective it appears to be at a given time. This is because the knowledge used at any point in time will almost inevitably change as new research invalidates old. Thus, eclectic practice requires a continuing critical evaluative stance by practitioners and actually calls for far more work and a higher degree of competence than more narrowly or rigidly conceived practice.

It would be easy for practitioners to adopt systematic eclecticism as a slogan and to pay lip service to this rigorous form of practice, while at the same time continuing traditional practices. This does in fact appear to be happening in a large proportion of situations where caseworkers claim they are indeed eclectic and will use a variety of techniques based on whatever will help the client, as noted in the research on caseworkers' practice orientations reviewed earlier in this chapter. But the approach to eclecticism described here, rooted in empirical evidence whenever possible and requiring a large expenditure of time to become familiar with developments in the literature, goes beyond catch phrases and requires a restructuring of practice from its philosophical and epistemological bases to the nature of day-to-day contact with clients.

Eclecticism is not a disordered conglomeration of disparate methods thrown together into an expedient potpourri (Wolberg, 1966). Nor is eclecticism inevitably intellectually barren because there are no consistent rules to guide thoughts or action (Wolpe, 1969). Instead, eclecticism involves the selection from varied sources and studied amalgamation of intervention techniques of demonstrated effectiveness that can be used compatibly and in ways that support each other. These different techniques in implementation complement each other and serve to buttress weaknesses in the individual systems from which they were derived. Furthermore, even though the synthesis may seem harmonious at any given time, it is subject to constant study and reorganization as new techniques with evidence of effectiveness become available (Wolberg, 1966).

Now, the fact that there are literally hundreds of clinical approaches available poses some problems for eclectic practice. Is it possible to " . . . know all there is to be known about everything" (Thorne, 1973, p. 450)? Obviously, this is a patently impossible task. More important, it is not necessary. Eclecticism is not a camouflage for some mushy supertheory that attempts to integrate every approach merely because the approach exists. A wide variety of approaches do have to be studied, however, through systematic analysis to determine whether they do in fact offer the promise of adding effective techniques to the eclectic practitioner's repertoire. Furthermore, it is obvious that not all approaches have something to offer in terms of demonstrated success with particular problems. As will be demonstrated in the next section, the task of narrowing down the variety of available approaches is not only crucial, it becomes possible by using preselected criteria for evaluation, most particularly empirical evidence of the availability of effective techniques. In this way, several hundred approaches can quickly be narrowed down to only a handful that claim empirical evidence of effectiveness.

Eclectic practice is not a grab bag of procedures selected without a consistent underlying rationale. Nor does the eclectic practitioner utilize a "shotgun approach," blindly trying one technique, then another, until finally one "works." Nor is the eclectic practitioner a "Jack-of-all-trades, master-of-none," knowing a little about a good deal but a great deal about very little.

The fact is that an eclectic practitioner as described here uses specific principles to guide the selection of techniques for practice in a way that far exceeds the rigor that could be expected from adherents to any unitary practice orientation. Furthermore, the heart of eclectic practice is sensitive and accurate assessment of the individual case/situation with the goal of selecting the best possible techniques. These techniques are selected on the basis of familiarity with the practice and research literature with an eye to answering the following question: What technique is effective with what kind of problem with what client in what circumstances?

Indeed, the eclectic practitioner can and should be as highly trained in the use of a single technique as are practitioners whose training is *only* in that school *if* skill in use of that single technique is warranted by the evidence. The eclectic must have optimal levels of competence in the use of those techniques whose merit has been determined by other than blind faith or the fact that they are part of one's own theory. Eclectic practitioners can be judged not on how much they know of one approach but by a much more crucial criterion—how effective they are in helping clients.

Selecting and Integrating an Eclectic Approach

The most obvious questions that arise in considering the use of knowledge derived from a variety of divergent sources are, first, what guidelines are there for selection of that knowledge, and, second, how can this material be integrated for practice in a meaningful way?

Eclecticism is an attempt to bring order and systematization to the selection of approaches for practice. Clear, specific criteria are delineated against which any system can be evaluated. New approaches are carefully elaborated and assessed in relation to each other and to their potential use with clients. The criterion of effectiveness is given top priority. The special order and efficiency that is best produced by being systematic, and which is at a premium for the busy practitioner, is maintained and enhanced.

However, while the selection of knowledge for practice can appear relatively clear-cut, it could seem that practitioners would still have on their hands only a jumble of techniques without a real way of integrating them.

In fact, some form of integration of knowledge for practice is crucial so that the practitioner can systematically go about his or her business. Otherwise he or she would be left with a number of presumably contradictory techniques and an inability to figure out what technique to implement with what problem.

There are several ways in which practice is integrated in an eclectic approach. One is through a systematic client-problem-situation assessment, the purpose of which is to identify just what techniques to use in what situation. The second is through development of a systematic framework spelling out the process of practice in a way that adds a considerable amount of systematization. Both areas will be discussed in subsequent sections.

The third approach to integration is on a broader level and consists of the very guidelines used to select any given piece of knowledge for practice. This is an atheoretical integration grounded in certain values and propositions that cut across theoretical domains. Each criterion provides an aspect of philosophical, conceptual, or empirical evidence for use (or nonuse) of a given technique. It is these criteria that are used not only to evaluate and select different techniques, but also as principles of integration, producing a variety of techniques that all have been judged and can be compared on common dimensions.

There are several dozen criteria that actually can be used to evaluate any system of intervention (Fischer, 1971). The key ones will be summarized here.

At the broadest level, in making selections from among various options for practice and in integrating those options into a practice framework are preeminent ethical considerations. The first principle involves the extent to which use of a given technique is congruent with the values of social work: respect for the dignity and worth—or, more appropriately, the humanity—of every person. Second, in actual application, a technique can be evaluated as ethically suitable if its use does not demean (and, one hopes, enhances) the dignity and individuality of the persons involved and can be implemented in a way congruent with the values of clients and practitioners.

Another major dimension for use in both selection and integration is related to the area of concern of casework as described earlier: the interactions between people and their environments. This includes not only the behavior of individuals as they attempt to cope with life tasks and environmental demands, but the resources available in the environment that play a part in every person's development. Thus, a key dimension for selection and integration of knowledge for eclectic practice is the extent to which that knowledge is concerned with social functioning and the way people and systems interact.

Another criterion for selection and integration for practice lies in the extent to which knowledge deals with interventive practices (rather than purely casual/developmental understanding), either indirectly in presenting assessment guidelines that lead to selection of the appropriate technique with a given client, or directly in that the knowledge itself consists of a specific intervention technique.

These practice techniques are prescriptive guidelines—step-by-step procedures for implementation by the practitioner that allow him/her to induce change in the client or relevant environmental system. These techniques can deal with extinguishing or decreasing unwanted behavior, thoughts, feelings, or activities, or increasing desired behavior, thoughts, feelings, or activities. Either way, it is the specific techniques themselves which are at the heart of eclectic practice. (Indeed, without specific techniques to implement, it would be difficult to engage in *any* type of practice, let alone eclectic.)

The last, and perhaps most important, criterion for evaluating, selecting, and integrating knowledge for eclectic practice is the extent to which there is some degree of empirical validation of successful intervention with clients when techniques are implemented. When research establishes the efficacy of a technique, it must be a primary candidate for adoption, whatever its theoretical or professional point of origin.

A number of implications stem from major reliance on research. Obviously, there are numerous levels of research ranging from simple single-case designs to complex factorial designs with random assignment and controls. Thus, it is crucial to be able to evaluate the rigor and generalizability of a given study, as well as to be particularly concerned with the replication of results.

Second, even assuming two techniques have equivalent amounts and quality of evidence, there are other criteria by which to decide which techniques should be implemented in a given case. These criteria include: which is most efficient, is one less aversive to the client or practitioner, is the practitioner more competent at using one, does one have clearer guidelines for implementation, and is one more appropriate to (or designed for) this particular type of problem?

A third major implication arises from using research as a guide to selecting and integrating practice. Presumably, the studies upon which a judgment is made to select a technique also illustrate the conditions under which the technique is successfully used. This, in turn, has the makings of a very explicit client/problem typology which would demonstrate the kinds of problems and clients for whom a given technique has been and could be applied effectively. Thus, the practitioner in a sense "starts" with techniques (rather than any preset diagnostic categories), knowing the kinds of problems that respond to those techniques and developing a typology of techniques that are selected in practice according to evidence as to which problems respond best. Combination of several techniques, then, can supply not only a complementary range of intervention procedures, but a range of problem/situation configurations where the techniques can be most effectively applied. The goal, of course, is the maximum in technical flexibility for the practitioner in response to potential client problems.

It is important to note here that this empirically based model of eclectic practice is only a goal. It is unlikely that every technique in the practitioner's repertoire will be totally validated or that every problem faced in practice will have a validated technique. Practice is too complicated for that. And since no techniques claim 100% effectiveness in all cases, there will always be some clients who need new techniques or different combinations, or whom we simply do not have the knowledge to help. On the other hand, this empirical model seems a worthy goal to aim for, since the more closely we approach it, the better off our clients will be.

Now, absence of empirical validation does not automatically render a technique useless (unless, perhaps, it is being suggested as an alternative to a technique that does have empirical evidence of effectiveness). This is because a number of other criteria are available to assess knowledge for practice, particularly when empirical evidence is lacking. Thus, an approach might be assessed as to the clients and problems for which it is intended, the extent to which a technique is specified in step-by-step fashion, the internal consistency of a technique, the expected results, its ethical ramifications, and so on. In some situations and in the absence of research evidence to the contrary, such a technique might be the intervention of choice in a given situation. In the absence of research showing any other techniques to be effective with the problem, that technique might very well be the best for that problem at that time.

Ultimately, what is sought is a careful piecing together of a number of analytical dimensions. When a number of techniques can be evaluated as satisfactory by the variety of criteria described here, and can be seen to complement each other on the basis of some clearly defined prescriptive statements for use with a range of clients and problems, then some degree of integration for practice can be demonstrated to have occurred.

Treatment Applicability and Structure

Eclectic casework—and, for that matter, most eclectic approaches to therapeutic practice—is comprised of a range of techniques selected from a number of approaches that, on the surface at least, may seem somewhat disparate. For this very reason, it is difficult to concisely describe all dimensions of the approach such as those situations and clients for whom the approach is most relevant and the "typical" setting, frequency, and duration of the sessions. However, it is possible to say this: the components of this approach—as will be delineated in this chapter—have been used successfully with individuals, couples, and families along the full range of human functioning. Client problems with which some of these techniques have been successfully used range from the most severe dysfunctions, such as chronic mental illness, "autism," and "retardation," to moderate and mild problems, such as speech anxiety in college students. The only limits of an eclectic approach such as this one are the limits prescribed by the outcome research. These techniques are most appropriately used where there is evidence of effectiveness of their application.

Similarly, although many of these techniques have been used in relatively brief, 8-to-12-session contacts, no specific time limits or frequency of sessions that applies to all of them has been validated in research. The key here, perhaps, is that the eclectic approach described in this chapter is a highly structured one involving use of contracts; clear specification of goals, client tasks, and practitioner activities; and careful monitoring and evaluation of progress. This type of structure and feedback makes it less necessary to specify in advance how many sessions will be necessary since there is less danger than with more conventional, open-ended practice that client contacts will be interminable.

However, most eclectic caseworkers attempt to specify with their clients some time limits in advance, if only to emphasize the importance of hard work together and to enhance expectations of success and any possible goal gradient effect. These time limits can be renegotiated if more time is needed and there is a reasonable expectation that the extra time will lead to greater success.

Components of an Eclectic Approach

The essence of an eclectic approach to practice is *flexibility*. It is very possible, and even likely, that what appears to be a key ingredient of an eclectic approach at one time may be replaced at a later time because of new empirical evidence. Thus, not only might it be difficult to spell out every technique of an eclectic approach at a given time, but the relevance of such explication probably will be diminished in the future by shifts in the evidence generated by empirical research.

Nevertheless, an eclectic approach to practice that does not include a clear delineation of its components truly would be irrelevant lip service to a noble but unreachable goal. The purpose of this section is to examine some of the key components of an eclectic practice as of the mid-1980s, with the important caveat that the practitioner must not become wedded to any of these ingredients as though they were engraved in stone. What follows, then, is an attempt to provide an overview of what appears to be the best the literature has to offer at a particular time.

There seem to be four major "thrusts" in the clinical literature where the bulk of the evidence of effectiveness is contained. Brief overviews of these four areas will be presented. This will be followed by a delineation of several specific techniques and technique packages that have been derived from these four areas and that meet, in varying degrees, the criteria that were described earlier in this chapter.

Core Ingredients

The four major areas to be described here include: (1) the use of structure, (2) behavior therapy, (3) cognitive therapy, and (4) the interpersonal skills of empathy, warmth, and genuineness.

There are several reasons for selecting these four major areas as the core ingredients of an eclectic approach at this time. First, as noted previously, the bulk of the empirical evidence on clinical practice is concentrated in these four areas. This is not to say that all techniques in all four areas have been validated or even have been studied. Nor is it to say that there are not scattered findings throughout the literature about individual techniques from other areas that may be effective. But it is to say that all four of these areas have accumulated a fair to substantial amount of empirical evidence attesting to the effectiveness of some of their techniques. And it also appears that no other areas in the literature seem to come close to any of these four regarding the amount of evidence they have accumulated. Thus, these four areas appear to be the primary candidates from which judicious selection of techniques for practice can be made.

Second, all these areas contain specific guidelines for implementation of techniques or associated procedures so that it is clear what the practitioner should be doing when he or she is faced with a particular client, problem, or situation. The clarity of these techniques is also crucial for conducting evaluations of their effectiveness in empirical research.

Third, work in all these areas has been conducted with a wide variety of clientele, ranging from nonverbal, low-income clients to middle- and upper-class clients. Similarly, all four areas have been applied with a relatively wide range of problems. Thus, there seems to be a fair amount of generalizability across all four areas.

Structuring

Structuring is an umbrella term covering a variety of discrete principles and techniques that have appeared in the literature, but which do have one common thread: they all add some degree of "structure" to practice. Structuring is considered a critical variable for practice for one major reason: most research that has compared any form of structured with unstructured practice has concluded that structuring is as effective as and frequently more effective than unstructured practice. Indeed, the apparent potency of structuring has led some psychotherapy researchers to believe that structuring is the underlying reason for any approach to practice that demonstrates its effectiveness.

Structuring involves essentially two levels, a general orientation to practice and a range of specific techniques. At the most general level, structuring emphasizes careful planning, specificity, and systematic use of variables designed to influence or change the problem/situation. At a more specific level, a number of techniques or programs have been found either to enhance effectiveness or at least to contribute to added structure in practice. These include the following:

1. Role induction interviews: structuring and clarifying the intervention process and associated expectations prior to onset of intervention (Parloff and Wolfe, 1978).
2. Use of specific and precise goal setting.
3. Use of contracts between practitioner and client.
4. Use of time limits, particularly when no other major aspect of structuring is present (Reid & Shyne, 1969; Wattie, 1973; Shlien et al., 1962; Muench, 1964; Beck & Jones, 1973; Gordon & Gordon, 1966; Phillips & Wiener, 1966; Blenkner et al., 1964; Luborsky et al., 1975; Butcher & Koss, 1978).
5. Use of several techniques to enhance client expectations (Lick & Bootzin, 1975; Frank, 1972; Coe & Buckner, 1975; Fish, 1973; Murray & Jacobson, 1978).
6. Use of homework and task assignments (Reid, 1978; Martin & Worthington, 1982; Shelton & Levy, 1981).
7. Use of a variety of findings from social psychological research (Strong, 1978; Goldstein, 1980; Goldstein & Simonson, 1971; Feld & Radin, 1982).
8. Use of a number of techniques to enhance generalization or transfer of change and maintenance effects (Goldstein & Kanfer, 1979; Karoly & Steffen, 1980).

Behavior Therapy

Although social workers for some time were not convinced of the value of behavior therapy for their practice, there is some evidence that this no longer is the case (Thyer, 1983). Social workers increasingly are recognizing the compatibility of behavior therapy with social work philosophy and goals, particularly the shared view of the importance of the interactions between people and their environments.

Behavior therapy has a number of distinct advantages for eclectic practice, including:

1. Availability of several dozen specific intervention techniques, each of which includes clear procedural guidelines for implementation (Bellack & Hersen, 1985).

2. A clear relationship between assessment and intervention (that is, the end result of assessment is a clear prescription regarding which technique(s) should be selected).
3. Development of a number of techniques focused specifically on social-environmental change, a practice that is at the core of the social work perspective.
4. A number of specific techniques and programs for training caretakers in the natural environment (e.g., parents, teachers, etc.).
5. Consistent evidence of effectiveness–several hundred controlled, experimental studies, several hundred single case designs showing the relationship between application of a technique and client change, and a number of comparative studies showing that one or another technique of behavior therapy is as effective as or more effective than other approaches (Kazdin & Wilson, 1978; Rachman & Wilson, 1980; Rimm & Masters, 1979; Gambrill, 1977; Turner et al., 1981; Hersen et al., 1975–1984; Franks & Wilson, 1973–1984)

It is important to note here that evidence on effectiveness varies tremendously from technique to technique in behavior therapy, ranging from well over 125 controlled studies on one technique alone (systematic desensitization) to few, if any, controlled studies attesting to effectiveness of other techniques. On the other hand, many behavior therapy techniques do show limited evidence of effectiveness but, perhaps more important, are constructed in such a way as to permit evaluation of effectiveness.

Cognitive Change Techniques

The third area in which evidence of effectiveness is rapidly accumulating is comprised of several different techniques that have an important common dimension: they focus on changing cognitive patterns or ways of thinking that are dysfunctional for the client and/or the client's environment. This area illustrates the importance of practitioners being attuned to new developments: just about all the research on cognitive change has been conducted since 1970, a relatively recent period of time.

Cognitive change techniques are focused on a variety of areas of cognition and related affective and behavioral responses. These include changing misconceptions, unrealistic expectations, and dysfunctional self-statements; systematic approaches to problem solving and decision making; and applications in self-control or self-change approaches (Beck, 1976; Raimy, 1975; Mahoney, 1974, 1978; Meichenbaum, 1977; Emery et al., 1981; Janis, 1982; Beck et al., 1979; Ellis & Grieger, 1977). While the evidence on cognitive techniques is not nearly as impressive as the accumulated evidence on behavior therapy, the increase in studies and positive findings since the 1970s suggests that this is a field that will continue to grow in importance.

In fact, perhaps the major trend in clinical practice today is the convergence among cognitive and behavioral techniques (the techniques of self-instruction training and stress-inoculation training [Meichenbaum, 1977] are prime examples). This has produced what amounts to a new field: cognitive-behavior therapy (or cognitive-behavior modification), and a good deal of positive evidence has been generated from this confluence of two major streams of work in clinical practice (Meichenbaum, 1974; Foreyt & Rathjen, 1978; Kendall & Hollon, 1979; Franks et al., 1982; Wilson et al., 1984.)

Interpersonal Skills of Empathy, Warmth, and Genuineness

The fourth area for consideration for eclectic practice is directly related to the fact that the eclectic practitioner must be more than a technician or an automaton, blindly applying techniques without considering the important issues of the essential humanity of the relationship between practitioner and client. No school of therapy or theoretical orientation argues that practice is applied outside of an interview and relationship between practitioner and client. (As one group of noted behaviorists, after a careful examination of their own program, has stated, "Many clinical colleagues have told us all along that the 'relationship' is an essential component of any therapy. We are now convinced that they are right." Philips et al., 1973, p. 76). This points to the desirability of developing a relationship that will do as much as possible to enhance the interactions between client and practitioner.

To be optimally effective, it appears as though practitioners must succeed in at least two areas: (1) they must create those personal conditions which establish a relationship of trust, caring, and acceptance between themselves and their clients, and thereby increase their clients' amenability to therapeutic influence; and (2) in the context of these conditions, they must employ a technology or program involving a variety of techniques to influence their clients in desired directions (Bergin & Strupp, 1972). It is in this context that the interpersonal skills of empathy, warmth, and genuineness appear to be central.

Although the evidence here is neither as elegant nor as consistent as in the other areas, there does appear to be sufficient evidence to suggest that these communication skills are important for effective practice (Marshall et al., 1982; Truax & Mitchell, 1971; Carkhuff & Berenson, 1976; Parloff & Wolfe, 1978; Mitchell et al., 1977). The key to this approach is the development of scales to measure the communication of empathy, warmth, and genuineness (plus several other interpersonal dimensions; Carkhuff, 1969). This allows for these interpersonal skills to be observed, evaluated, and taught, with a fair amount of evidence now accumulated that they can be successfully learned in courses focusing on structured, step-by-step, experiential training (Marshall et al., 1982; Gantt et al., 1980).

These interpersonal skills can be viewed as the foundation of an eclectic approach, providing the crucial interviewing and relationship skills that influence the effective implementation of techniques. In fact, there is a body of several experimental studies showing that practitioners who demonstrate higher levels of one or more of these interpersonal skills are more effective than practitioners with lower levels in their use of a number of specific techniques (Dowling & Frantz,

1975; Morris & Suckerman, 1974a, 1974b; Cairns, 1972; Harris & Lichenstein, 1971; Mickelson & Stevic, 1971; Vitalo, 1970; Namenek & Schuldt, 1971; Naar, 1970; Bergin, 1969; Wandersman et al., 1976; Goldstein, 1976; Curtiss, 1976; Gold, 1976; Ricks et al., 1976).

Techniques for Eclectic Practice

The heart of eclectic practice is, of course, what the practitioner does. And the most important activity of the practitioner is the implementation of techniques. Techniques are step-by-step procedures used by the practitioner to induce and guide change. To the extent possible, the techniques are selected so as to be problem-specific and, one hopes, known to be the best possible intervention with a particular problem, client, and situation at that particular time.

There are several criteria that might be used in selecting a technique in practice to be used with a given problem:

1. Relative effectiveness compared to no treatment and/or other techniques—the paramount consideration.
2. Relative efficiency—the amount of time and energy required for use.
3. Resources available, including people who may be necessary to implement the procedures (e.g., in parent training), cost of implementation, and availability of time and materials.
4. Type of problem—if the practitioner's goal is to increase the occurrence of some behavior or activity, one would try to locate a technique designed to increase (and not decrease) that category of behavior or activities.
5. Design of the technique—some techniques are specifically designed to deal with the exact problem the practitioner is facing.
6. Clarity—wherein the operations to be used in implementing a technique are clearly spelled out.

In actual practice, it is rare for only one technique to be used with a particular problem. Most often, techniques are combined in programs or packages that have a broader effect than implementation of just one technique. Following, then, are several techniques and technique packages that were selected for two major reasons: (1) they have accumulated a substantial amount of empirical evidence of effectiveness with one or more problems; and/or (2) with a modicum of evidence, they are specifically designed to deal with certain problems that the other techniques listed do not successfully address.

Although this listing is not intended to be exhaustive, the techniques and technique packages that best appear to meet those criteria as of the mid-1980s are the following:

1. Assertion training and social skills training (Curran & Monti, 1982; Bellack & Hersen, 1979). These technique packages have been used successfully

with a wide range of skill deficits in populations that range from severely disturbed psychiatric patients to unhappy marital couples (Twentyman & Zimering, 1979).

2. Contingency management (Rimm & Masters, 1979). A "catchall" term for a whole variety of operant techniques to both strengthen or maintain desired behaviors and weaken or decrease undesired behaviors, these techniques and packages include reinforcement, punishment, extinction, time out, the token economy, overcorrection (Foxx & Bechtel, 1982), and others. Contingency management has been used successfully with almost all imaginable populations including children and adults, individuals, couples, and families, and with the most moderate to the most severe of problem behaviors (Bellack & Hersen, 1985).

3. Systematic desensitization (Wolpe, 1982). A technique for decreasing maladaptive anxiety, most successfully used when the anxiety is related to relatively specific stimuli, systematic desensitization has been the subject of more controlled investigations than any other therapeutic technique—well over 125—and has been found to be effective with a wide range of anxiety disorders (Walker et al., 1981).

4. Behavioral contracting (Kirschenbaum & Flanery, 1983). Although largely associated with contingency management, the use of contracting has received a fair amount of independent evidence of effectiveness in use with several problem populations and with individuals, families, and couples.

5. Problem solving (D'Zurilla & Nezu, 1982). Although the accumulated evidence is somewhat weak, and a number of problem-solving packages are available, the evidence is encouraging enough to suggest the importance of providing clients with an overall, step-by-step framework to aid in solving problems and making decisions. A framework that seems particularly useful is the one developed by Janis & Mann (1977).

6. Self-instruction training (Meichenbaum, 1977; Cormier & Cormier, 1985). A package essentially combining cognitive and behavioral techniques, self-instruction training has accumulated some 50 controlled studies showing it to be effective with several disorders including problems of impulsive children and public speaking and test anxiety (Rachman & Wilson, 1980).

7. Stress-inoculation training (Meichenbaum, 1977; Cormier & Cormier, 1985). Another combination of cognitive and behavioral techniques, stress-inoculation training, though not as extensively studied as self-instruction training, has been successfully used with problems involving interpersonal and general anxiety and stress and anger control (Novaco, 1979).

8. Cognitive restructuring (Goldfried, 1979; Ellis & Grieger, 1977). Although cognitive restructuring comes in a variety of packages (see Cormier & Cormier, 1985, for an excellent synthesis), it appears to be an important intervention for dealing with problems where the assessment suggests that unrealistic expectations, misconceptions, or dysfunctional self-statements may be at the root of those problems.

9. Modeling and participant modeling (contact desensitization) (Rimm & Masters, 1979; Cormier & Cormier, 1985; Walker et al., 1981). Modeling, and its many variations including contact desensitization, has been found to be an effective package in and of itself and in combination with other techniques for both increasing positive behaviors and activities and decreasing negative behaviors and activities. The population modeling has been applied with ranges from the slightly to severely impaired and includes behavioral, cognitive, and affective (decrease in anxiety) outcomes.

10. Covert sensitization (Cautela, 1967; Rimm & Masters, 1979). Although the evidence on covert sensitization is not extensive (Kazdin & Smith, 1979), there does seem to be enough to suggest that covert sensitization might be useful, in combination with other techniques, in decreasing unwanted sexual behaviors, alcohol abuse, smoking, and overeating. In particular, covert sensitization is one of the few techniques that addresses some of these problems without resort to electrical or mechanical devices or chemical aids.

11. Covert positive reinforcement (Kazdin & Smith, 1979; Walker et al., 1981). A limited amount of research suggests that covert reinforcement can be effective in modifying negative self-statements, test anxiety, weight control, certain specific animal phobias, and attitude change. This is a technique which is readily adaptable to use with other techniques in more broadly based intervention programs.

12. Covert modeling (Kazdin & Smith, 1979; Cormier & Cormier, 1985). Covert modeling has been shown in some studies to be as effective as live modeling, but with a very limited range of problems, essentially involving fear and lack of assertiveness. Once again, it is a technique that can readily be combined with others.

13. Exposure and response prevention (Mathews et al., 1981; Marshall et al., 1979). A relatively new technique package, exposure has been found to be effective in a number of studies with problems involving simple and social phobias, agoraphobia, and compulsive rituals (Foa & Steketee, 1979; Brehony & Geller, 1981).

14. Thought stopping (Rimm & Masters, 1979; Cormier & Cormier, 1985; Walker et al., 1981). Thought stopping is one of the few available techniques designed specifically to deal with problems involving obsessive thoughts that the client cannot control. Although the controlled evidence is insubstantial, there appears to be enough case study evidence to suggest that thought stopping might be included as one component in a broader intervention program.

15. Habit reversal (Azrin & Nunn, 1977, 1982; Turpin, 1983). This technique is specifically designed to overcome a variety of specific undesired habits such as tics, nail-biting, and hair pulling (trichotillomania). Although the number and quality of studies available are not impressive, habit reversal does appear to be a promising way of dealing with a variety of specific problems that most other techniques do not address.

It is probably obvious that just about all of the techniques described here have their roots in cognitive and/or behavioral formulations. The reason is simple: no other approaches or theoretical orientations have described their techniques in such specific fashion, allowing for clear evaluation, and then carried out the literally hundreds of studies that document the effectiveness of these techniques, especially in a way that they can be isolated and examined as independent entities. Indeed, some of the individual techniques described here have often been compared in controlled research to entire systems of therapy and found as effective or more effective (Kazdin & Wilson, 1978). Thus, this clarity and subsequent evaluation allow one to be able to distinguish between legitimate therapeutic procedures and fads.

Another advantage of this clarity of description involves ease of training. When step-by-step procedures are specified, learning how to use the techniques becomes a much easier task. The vagaries of trying to operationalize and implement complicated systems of intervention simply become unnecessary. Indeed, each one of the techniques and technique packages described here has been placed into a common format using step-by-step flowcharts. Two examples of these flowcharts are reproduced here as Figures 13.2 and 13.3, one of a technique with relatively few steps—self-instruction training—and the other of a more complicated technique—assertive training. Whenever possible, the flowcharts for these techniques were designed to follow the format in Cormier & Cormier (1985), a book that has been found to be the most useful in helping graduate students learn these techniques.[1]

Although only 15 techniques were described here, in fact, when the several techniques of contingency management and the variations of other techniques (e.g., different types of modeling) are explicated, the 15 techniques expand to over 25. Moreover, many of these techniques can and have been used not only with individual clients but with couples and families as well. Used together—and with a foundation in the interpersonal skills and structuring procedures described earlier—these techniques can provide an integrated and comprehensive approach to practice that at the present time appears to have the best chance of optimizing our effectiveness with our clients.

Common Characteristics of Techniques

Although the variety of techniques described here may appear disparate on the surface, it is possible that there are some characteristics that cut across many of them, thereby accounting for some degree of their success. Although this section is speculative, based on reviewing the research on techniques and attempting to categorize them regarding their commonalities and differences, it does seem that the most effective techniques have certain ingredients in common. These are described here mainly as hypotheses for future research on identifying the effective components of techniques. This scheme also has heuristic effects in that it serves as

[1] The whole package of flowcharts is reproduced in the Appendix of this book.

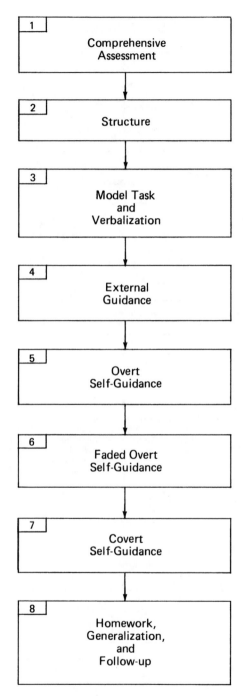

Fig. 13.2   Self-Instruction Training

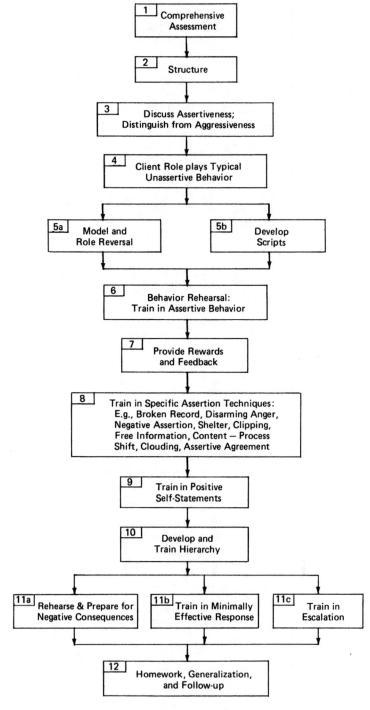

Fig. 13.3   Assertive Training

a handy vehicle for teaching practitioners. In essence, students are urged to examine their practice to ensure that as many of these ingredients as possible are present as they implement any given technique. Thus, the following is what might be proposed as some common characteristics of effective technique implementation:

1. Structure. Provide a verbal set including a rationale for use of the technique and an explanation of what is to be done, and enhance positive expectations of success.
2. Modeling. Demonstrate to the client what you want the client to do.
3. Extensive rehearsal and practice. It is almost impossible to expect a client to be successful at implementing the practitioner's ideas in real life unless he/she has practiced them—over and over again—with the practitioner.
4. Graduated steps. With few exceptions, it is better to move slowly rather than too quickly. This means, for example, moving from confronting low-anxiety-eliciting situations to increasingly higher-anxiety-eliciting situations. It also means use of shaping—moving from less to more complicated objectives.
5. Provide feedback. It is a good idea to try to provide your client with gentle and constructive suggestions on what to change or try next as you progress in your rehearsal.
6. Coping thoughts. Prepare the client with what to say to himself/herself when preparing for, confronting, or successfully completing an assignment.
7. Praise and positive reinforcement. Not only can the client's efforts be enhanced by praise from the practitioner, but praise and positive reinforcement from other sources (or self-reinforcement) should be built into the client's program whenever possible.
8. Homework and task assignments. It is crucial to give the client homework to try out in real life each part of what the practitioner and client have worked out in their contacts (Martin & Worthington, 1982).
9. Exposure. Increasing the time of the client's exposure to anxiety-producing events—in real life or in imagination—leads to optimal reduction in that anxiety.
10. Transfer of learning. It is absolutely critical that an entire phase of the intervention process be devoted to ensuring that therapeutic gains are maintained, both in direct practice with the client and in training others in the environment to support and reinforce those gains.

Assessment

The core of eclectic practice involves conducting an adequate assessment. It is through the assessment that the eclectic practitioner makes a judgment as to which technique to implement. As noted earlier in this chapter, one key factor in this assessment is being aware of what techniques work best with what problems (or, at least, were designed to be used with a given problem), so that the assessment can be clearly geared toward making that decision a rational one.

Although space limits the amount of detail that can be provided about assessment, some general principles can be described here. In essence, assessment for eclectic practice contains ingredients similar to those described across a broad range of theoretical orientations. The basic purpose is to provide detailed information that will lead to the establishment of specific goals, a strategy of intervention, and selection of specific intervention techniques. The purpose of assessment is not understanding for the sake of understanding; if the assessment does not lead the practitioner to select specific intervention techniques, the assessment probably has been inadequate.

The focus of assessment is on evaluating what is to be changed, what factors are maintaining or controlling the problem, what resources are necessary to bring about change, and what problems might result from bringing about change. Past factors need not be ignored, but the sole purpose of this information would be to shed light on current conditions (e.g., it would be important to know what efforts in the past have been made to deal with the problem). It is difficult, if not impossible, to take overt interventive action on past variables (Fischer, 1978). Similarly, the goal of assessment is not to assign diagnostic labels (although sometimes these are required by the system in which a practitioner works).

There are, at the broadest level, only a limited number of ways of collecting information for an assessment. For most situations, an eclectic practitioner will prepare an assessment package that would consist of all of these, using a multi-method approach such as that described by Nay (1979). The specifics (e.g., a questionnaire) may change depending on the problem, but if the practitioner uses several methods, he or she is more likely to produce well-rounded and informative assessments.

The major data collection methods include interviews, questionnaires and other structured instruments, and direct observations. A range of references are available describing all of these in great detail (Haynes & Wilson, 1979; Haynes, 1978; Kendall & Hollon, 1981; Cone & Hawkins, 1977; Barlow, 1981; Mash & Terdal, 1981; Hersen & Bellack, 1981; Ciminero, 1977; Sundberg, 1977).

Some general principles of assessment that can be used as guides are the following:

1. Use more than one data collection system.
2. Be sure to obtain a relevant sample of people, events, and activities.
3. Collect information on people and environments, assessing the way people interact with the various systems that affect them (families, peers, organizations, communities, and so on).
4. Conduct a force-field analysis in which you specifically delineate the forces that might aid or restrain change (Brager & Holloway, 1978).
5. Answer specific "what" questions (rather than "why" questions) (what is a person doing that is of concern, under what conditions does it occur, what are the effects of those activities, what does the client expect, and so on), being as specific as possible in identifying relevant variables.

6. Focus on variables that can be affected, rather than those that have only vague and perhaps inaccurate explanatory value.
7. Develop an integrative formulation (Siporin, 1975) that takes into account all of the above and that is written in terms relevant to selecting intervention techniques, specifically, pinpointing necessary areas of change and indicating the direction of these changes, whether they be to maintain, increase, or decrease some behavior, cognitions, activities, or other dimensions. Some eclectic practitioners also use additional guidelines to help in this process such as Lazarus' (1981) BASIC I.D. formulation to be sure that all aspects of functioning are covered and techniques are selected for each problem area.

Once all this is accomplished in a time period that, depending on the case, may run from less than an hour (with a client in crisis) to several sessions, it still remains for the practitioner to be able to select the correct techniques. Here is where knowledge of the available techniques is so crucial, and where the practitioner must formulate a typology linking specific problems to specific interventions. An assessment that concludes the problem is "anxiety" is not enough. The type of anxiety determines the choice of intervention technique based on prior evidence of effectiveness, and to some extent, the only way this can be done is if the practitioner knows what technique is effective with what type of anxiety (Goldfried & Davison, 1976). So, for example, if the anxiety can be traced to a specific stimulus situation, the technique of choice might be systematic desensitization or exposure (in the case of certain phobias). If the anxiety is a result of skill deficits, social skills or assertive training might be called for. If the anxiety is maintained by the client's dysfunctional verbalizations, cognitive restructuring might be the intervention of choice. If the anxiety seems to be a general, free-floating anxiety, then cognitive restructuring, or, secondarily, stress-inoculation training, might be called for. For problems due to speech and communication anxiety, the practitioner might choose systematic desensitization or self-instruction training. For stress and anger control, stress-inoculation training might be the intervention of choice. And if the anxiety appears to be the result of an untenable environment, the practitioner has the choice of helping the client cope with it using one of several techniques for decreasing anxiety as described previously, helping the client try to change that environment through social skills or assertive training, or attempting to change the situation himself or herself or help remove the client from it.

As can be seen, an adequate assessment requires a combination of assessment skills along with knowledge of the effects of a wide range of intervention techniques.

Research and Evaluation

It is difficult to see how eclectic practice or any other form of practice can be considered as sufficient without some form of systematic evaluation being considered part of the process. Although human service practitioners traditionally either have been reluctant to evaluate their practice or simply did not possess the requisite skills, there is now an evaluation technology available that can be built right into practice with each case and that can be used no matter what the theoretical orientation or types of techniques of the practitioner (Bloom & Fischer, 1982). This technology has important advantages for practice: it can be used by the practitioner with each case, it can be used to evaluate outcome, and it also allows the practitioner to monitor progress so that he or she can make changes in the intervention program if necessary.

There are several more or less interchangeable terms for this technology: single-case design, single-system design, time series research, idiographic research, single N and/or single-subject design, and so on. All of these names basically refer to a practice-oriented approach to evaluation wherein the individual, couple or family is viewed as a single unit and data are collected on client progress over time. Since the literature on this topic has developed extensively in recent years, it is not necessary to go into detail about this evaluation process here (Barlow et al., 1984; Kazdin, 1982; Bloom & Fischer, 1982; Jayaratne & Levy, 1979; Hersen & Barlow, 1976).

Boiled down to its essence, this form of evaluation has four key components:

1. Specification of the problems to be changed;
2. Finding a way to measure the problems;
3. Systematic collection of information on the problem over time, preferably including a baseline of information prior to intervention and using a planned format or design; and
4. Clearly identifying an intervention program, no matter what type of techniques the practitioner is using, that can be distinguished from the baseline/ assessment phase.

Although these steps seem rather simple, they *are* the core of this form of evaluation. Of course, each of these steps bears considerable elaboration such as the different types of measures available, how to use the measures, how to organize and implement the variety of designs, how to analyze the data, and so on. This type of information can be found in the references cited previously.

Obviously, the point here was not to review this methodology in depth, but to emphasize its importance to eclectic practice. If anything, eclectic practice can be characterized as an attempt to integrate research and practice. Use of systematic case evaluations is one of the key trademarks of practitioners who really are serious about enhancing the effectiveness of their practice.

A Framework for Practice

The framework presented here is an attempt to integrate, structure, and systematize the process of eclectic practice, and to highlight the interrelationship between practice and research in the overall process. A number of features characterize this framework, in the way they illustrate, or attempt to enhance, eclectic practice:

1. *Empirically based.* To the extent possible, this framework attempts to enhance development of an empirical base for practice. This actually has two meanings here. The first is the use of the results of research to inform practice, as in the selection of techniques. The second is in careful and systematic evaluations of the effects of intervention. This framework includes the specific steps of evaluation as parts of the steps of practice.
2. *Eclectic.* This framework is based on the assumption that the knowledge base of practice is both pluralistic and eclectic. It is pluralistic in the sense that the knowledge is derived from many sources. It is eclectic in that only the best available knowledge is selected from those sources. Eclecticism means using clear, precise, systematic criteria to select knowledge. In particular, this relates to the empirical base of practice in that, whenever possible, practice consists of a variety of techniques selected largely on the basis of evidence of effectiveness and applied with people and problems where the evidence indicates that such application has a good chance of producing a successful outcome. Of course, it is not always possible to achieve this ideal with every problem. But as an organizing principle of practice, it seems a worthwhile goal to shoot for. More concretely, this framework is intended to apply whatever the theoretical orientation, methods, or approach of the user.
3. *Systematic.* This framework is an attempt to systematize practice. This means clearly identifying the various phases of practice and organizing them into a step-by-step sequence that appears to offer a good chance of enhancing both effectiveness and efficiency. In fact, one of the most important characteristics of practice is being systematic: in how goals are identified, in how intervention techniques are selected, in how outcome is monitored. It also appears to make sense to try to organize the diverse activities of practice into a logical sequence that runs from initial contact to termination and follow-up.

    Although the process of practice is described here as a sequence of phases, this is not meant to prescribe a rigid, lock-step approach to practice. For example, depending on the problem or situation, the length of time for any phase could vary considerably, the phases could overlap, or a phase might not occur at all. Indeed, despite the fact that a number of phases are described, the essence of practice using this framework still must be flexibility: selecting what is done on the basis of a specific client-problem-situation configuration, individually tailored to the needs of a particular case. These are less formal steps in the process than aspects of the process that are likely to take place at some point. Thus, an attempt to organize that process may bring some order and direction into the subtleties and contradictions of real-life practice. Importantly, this framework has been found to be a very useful teaching device for new practitioners providing them with an anchor as they learn how to engage in practice.

4. *Accountable.* This framework is an attempt to add to our accountability as practitioners. It brings the entire process of practice out into the open for careful scrutiny by anyone concerned. It allows for an organized sequence of activities that can be specified and taught. It points out and builds into practice the necessity for carefully evaluating results with every case.

5. *Way of thinking.* This framework is intended to illustrate and/or enhance, perhaps more than anything else, a way of thinking about practice: systematic, data-based, outcome-oriented, flexible, depending on the needs of the client, empirically based, and up to date with the relevant literature. All of this is grounded in the ethics and values—the scientific humanism—which underlie the philosophy and practices of the helping professions.

The framework is comprised of five major phases and 18 steps, each of which is divided into component parts. The framework is called the PRAISES model, with PRAISES being an acronym for the five major phases (Table 13.1). Because of space limitations, only the outline and flowchart (Figure 13.4) of the framework can be presented here. Despite the fact that it looks like a General Motors wiring diagram at first glance, the flowchart on closer examination consists simply of the varied aspects that constitute the flow of eclectic practice.

Table 13.1   The PRAISES Model

Phase I. *PRe* Intervention
1. Evaluate the context
2. Process the referral
3. Initiate contact
4. Structure

Phase II. *Assessment*
5. Select problem
6. Conduct assessment
7. Collect baseline information
8. Establish goals

Phase III. *Intervention*
9. Develop intervention plan
10. Develop evaluation plan
11. Negotiate contract
12. Prepare for intervention
13. Implement intervention

Phase IV. *Systematic Evaluation*
14. Monitor and evaluate results
15. Assess and overcome barriers
16. Evaluate goal achievement

Phase V. *Stabilize*
17. Stabilize and generalize changes
18. Plan follow-up and termination

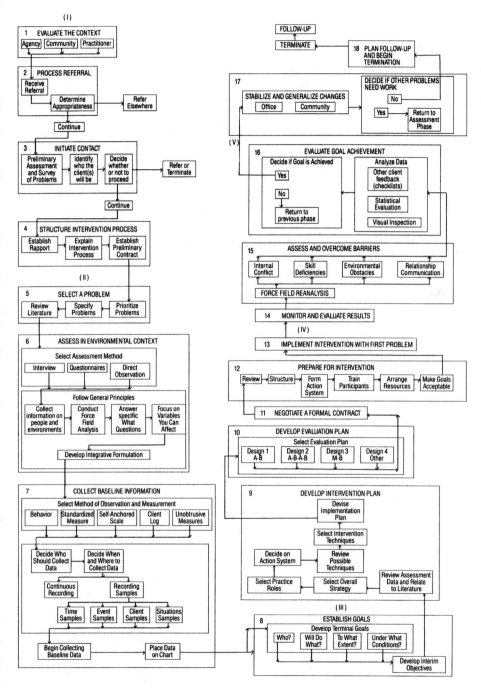

Fig. 13.4   PRAISES model: A framework for eclectic practice.

Case Example

The following case example (from Fischer, 1978) illustrates a number of aspects of eclectic practice. The entire process is grounded in the relationship—communication of empathy, warmth, and genuineness—and moves through several stages from initial exploration and structuring to selection and implementation of the technique to evaluation.

The client, Dean, 23 years old, has told the practitioner he wants to change his orientation from homosexual to heterosexual. Dean is obviously experiencing tremendous conflict over his homosexual orientation. He has been struggling with his problem over a year but has not sought any professional help until now. He begins hesitantly; he has let very few people in on the secret that he is "a homosexual." The practitioner recognizes Dean's tentativeness. He acknowledges how hard it must be for Dean to express himself about the problem, and how especially frightening it must be to do so with a stranger. The practitioner demonstrates to the client the kind of caring, respect, and nonjudgmentalness that Dean has not encountered before; the practitioner demonstrates also that he understands. Gradually, Dean realizes that this is a person who will not look with horror or shock at his behavior, and also that the practitioner is a person who will not plunge immediately into inappropriate advice giving ("So why don't you go out more with women?"). Gently the practitioner encourages Dean to explore the nature of the problem and his feelings about it.

Dean discloses numerous reasons for wanting to change: social pressure, the fear of being stigmatized as "abnormal," of being considered just a freak; the fear that his future employment possibilities will be limited; the fear of other people's reactions to learning he's gay; the fear of not being able to find personally meaningful, fulfilling, and lasting homosexual relationships.

The practitioner probes beneath the surface of these reasons. Dean is filled with anger at the lack of society's understanding of the homosexually oriented. Dean has tried dating women as a way of overcoming his attraction to men. That did not work: while he can be attracted to women, he says, he still is more attracted to men. His rage at his situation leaves him feeling hopeless and depressed, with feelings of being an unworthwhile person. He feels trapped in his situation—unable to "come out of the closet" except with a few of his closest friends, yet unable to change his own homosexual tendencies. The practitioner also acknowledges with Dean the pervasive fear Dean is experiencing over his situation, afraid to move in any direction, afraid of what might happen if he does. The early sessions are difficult ones for Dean, but as the practitioner moves with him, he increasingly realizes the practitioner is someone who cares and who can be trusted.

Gradually, and very tentatively, the practitioner begins to draw connections, to examine patterns in Dean's life. The practitioner notes, on the basis of what Dean has said, that in many situations in Dean's life he appears to be afraid to make changes, to take action. New situations particularly tend to paralyze Dean; the practitioner also helps Dean think about the possible analogy between other new situations and the newness of his relationship with the practitioner. As the practitioner probes at higher levels of empathy, and as Dean becomes more trusting and more comfortable, he helps Dean uncover and express some of his deepest fears about being homosexually oriented. He also confronts Dean on many apparent discrepancies. For example, a key discrepancy is that all the reasons Dean cites for wanting to change seem related to external pressures and that Dean may not have committed *himself* to the change. Dean has never said he really wants to change because it is what he truly and deeply desires. Most of his reasons for wanting to change are to avoid external pressures. But Dean actually views himself as, and deeply identifies with, being homosexually oriented.

Dean only gradually begins to deal with the fact that another alternative to changing his sexual orientation may be open to him. That alternative is to accept the fact of his homosexual orientation and to accept himself as he is. Part of this also is to learn to deal with the outside pressures that he experiences as overwhelming.

Gradually, always tentatively, the practitioner pushes Dean to deal with his situation—and with himself—in more honest terms. Dean finally admits that he really does not want to change his sexual orientation, but that, on the other hand, he does not know how to live with it either. But some of the anger—generated by the helplessness of being caught in what appeared to be a hopeless situation—already is diminishing as Dean increasingly reveals and understands more of himself. Dean begins to deal with himself in a more honest way than he ever has before.

The practitioner and Dean examine the alternatives: (1) stay in the closet and keep his homosexual preferences to himself; (2) come out of the closet and learn to deal with himself and his environment in constructive and comfortable ways; or (3) attempt to change his sexual orientation and become heterosexual. The practitioner promises his support and help no matter which of the three Dean selects.

Dean chooses. He wishes to remain homosexually oriented and despises the idea of keeping it secret. He therefore no longer wishes it to be a secret. The general goal Dean and the practitioner agree on, then, is to remain homosexually oriented and to learn to deal comfortably with it. Several subobjectives include learning how to tell people and handle their reactions comfortably, how to deal with current and future employers without undue anxiety, and how to develop better skills in relating to other homosexually oriented men.

Dean says that he finally realizes how tied up he has been over this decision and that finally deciding makes him feel as though a giant burden has been lifted from his shoulders. He feels less and less depressed as he begins to see that he is not helpless in the situation, that there is hope.

The practitioner strongly supports these changes. But he also cautions that while making the decision was a crucial step—more, that it added directionality to Dean's life and to Dean's efforts at helping himself—making the decision in the office is different from being able to carry out the consequences in real life. Dean readily acknowledges this; he knows there is much more work ahead.

The practitioner and Dean set up a multifaceted program. Indeed, one part of the action program is the deepening of the relationship between Dean and the practitioner, who unconditionally demonstrates caring and regard for Dean. Dean begins to learn that he is indeed a person deserving of high self-esteem.

The practitioner also consults community resources and locates at a clinic a group run specifically for homosexually oriented men struggling with crises similar to Dean's. This is offered as an additional support to Dean, and Dean readily accepts.

Dean has a variety of fears which the practitioner attacks in two ways: by setting up a program to deal specifically with the anxiety, and by setting up a program to deal specifically with the behaviors in which Dean must engage in the natural environment.

Together with Dean, the practitioner designs a systematic desensitization package focused around Dean's fear of criticism and ridicule. Items on the hierarchy, organized from lesser to greater fear stimuli, deal with many of the situations in which Dean would or could possibly find himself, including telling his employer about his homosexual activity.

At the same time as the desensitization program is being implemented, the practitioner and Dean implement a social skills and assertive training program. Using modeling, behavior rehearsal, feedback, and reinforcement, Dean is trained in a variety of behaviors needed to engage in satisfying interpersonal situations. These behaviors include revealing to others his homosexual orientation and dealing with a variety of reactions (positive and negative), and social skills training to compensate for Dean's discomfort with and apparent lack of knowledge about how to relate to other young adults, both men and women. Dean is given structured homework assignments on a graduated basis according to the amount of difficulty with which he is prepared to deal.

Throughout this stage, the program is carried out in the context of continuing communication of empathy, warmth, and genuineness from the practitioner. This includes social reinforcement, praise, and encouragement when progress is made or when efforts in the direction of progress (e.g., attempting new behaviors) are made. It includes support and help when Dean expresses fears or questions about the direction of the program. It includes being especially sensitive to Dean's behaviors and feelings during interview sessions and, at one point, temporary suspension of implementation of one of the techniques to discuss and deal with a crisis Dean was experiencing.

The practitioner has selected several measures to evaluate progress, including Dean's own reports of how he is doing—subjectively and in terms of behaviors accomplished. The measures include the Fear Survey Inventory (Wolpe, 1973), a measure of assertiveness (Rathus, 1973), and a measure of self-esteem (Hudson, 1982), which is administered to Dean once a week. In addition, behavioral measures are used including tape recordings of the number of Dean's positive self-references during randomly selected interview sessions and a self-report measure of actual approach behaviors with other young adults comparing baseline with intervention and postintervention frequencies.

After about three months, and at the conclusion of most of the action programs (Dean chose to remain in the group at the clinic), Dean's increasingly self-assured demeanor, his obvious behavioral changes in the environment, and his own pleasure in what he termed "the new me" indicated that the intensive stages of intervention could be terminated. Comparisons on all measures showed improvement; particularly dramatic was the improvement in Dean's overall self-assuredness and in the measure of self-esteem. He did, indeed, seem like a new man. Dean reported satisfactory social contacts and the ability to deal comfortably with others' reactions when he told them about his sexual orientation. Dean noted proudly that the surest sign that he was "ready" was that he had finally told his boss "his secret," prepared for the worst. The reaction of his boss was to shrug his shoulders and say, "Nobody's perfect!"

The practitioner and Dean planned some follow-up, with formal dates for contact over the next six months arranged in advance. It was an emotional leave-taking, as Dean, shaking his head when he left, commented, "I can't believe I'm the same person who sat here so tormented only three months ago."

Clinical Training

Because eclectic casework is essentially an evolving system, and because it has not been uniformly accepted as the optimal system in social work as a whole, it is difficult to specify all the parameters of effective clinical training. This is especially hampered by the fact that there is as yet no clear empirical evidence that caseworkers using this system are more effective than caseworkers using any other system.

However, it is possible to speculate about some aspects of training that would prepare practitioners to utilize an eclectic model. All of this must be viewed from the perspective that training for the degree of master of social work is essentially a two-year program, and that there are a number of competing (and legitimate) educational concerns within the MSW curriculum.

The typical MSW curriculum is comprised of five parts: courses in research, social policy, human behavior and the environment, social work practice, and two to three days of practicum experience for the entire two years. To produce the optimally functioning eclectic practitioner within that period of time would require the entire two years to be devoted to clinical training for eclectic practice. Since this essentially is impossible and may be undesirable as well (as mentioned earlier, social workers operate from a far broader base than therapeutic or clinical practice alone), the most efficient use of the time that is available in the two years would include the following:

1. Research courses including courses aimed at stimulating the practitioner's interest in and skill at assessing the research literature to form a basis for selecting empirically based techniques plus at least one course on single-system design teaching students how to monitor and evaluate their own practice.

2. Practice courses of three types. The first type would provide students with a conceptual model such as described in this chapter along with a practice framework such as the PRAISES model, including assessment skills. The second type would be courses devoted to reviewing major approaches to casework, counseling, and therapy. The third type would be courses organized around learning of specific techniques such as described here, with the understanding that students will need to keep abreast of the literature and new developments in the field.
3. Practicum experience where students are guaranteed the opportunity to implement a range of the techniques learned in class with actual clients.

In fact, such a curriculum is available at the University of Hawaii and a few other schools of social work in the United States. It is hoped that future research will validate the effectiveness of both this type of training and its impact on clients.

Future Directions

Eclectic casework practice is a development geared toward enhancing the overall effectiveness of practice. Although there is no evidence as yet as to the effectiveness of eclectic caseworkers versus any other type of practitioners, the indirect evidence on effectiveness can be derived from the fact that the bulk of eclectic practice is comprised of use of a variety of techniques that, in their own right, have been shown to be effective. Moreover, eclectic practice is an attempt to systematize and objectify practice and calls for greater discrimination in the selection of knowledge than was true in the past and for a higher degree of professional responsibility in trying to ensure that what we do does indeed work. Eclectic casework practice maintains the profession's intrinsic humanistic orientation while focusing increased attention on sharpening and refining the technology the practitioner uses.

The eclectic caseworker is someone who might be considered the new breed of social worker, the scientific practitioner. This is a social worker who: (1) systematically evaluates and monitors progress with each case; (2) grounds practice to the extent possible in empirically based knowledge, particularly the numerous available intervention techniques for which there is evidence of effectiveness, and uses those without such evidence only with due caution; and (3) has the skills and attitudes to be able and willing to keep learning and searching for new and more effective approaches to intervention.

The future of eclectic practice promises to be an exciting one. There is some evidence from informal contacts among social work faculty that the core ingredients of eclectic casework are being taught at an increasing number of universities. But a number of largely empirical issues need to be addressed:

1. What is the optimal training arrangement for eclectic caseworkers and can generalization to actual practice after graduation be attained?
2. Is the PRAISES model or any other integrative framework essential to the success of eclectic practice?

3. Is there a need—and can it be empirically assessed—for developing a more unified theoretical framework for integrating the variety of techniques of which eclectic casework is comprised?
4. And, most important, does eclectic casework really make a difference? Will future research clearly establish that practitioners using eclectic casework are more effective than practitioners using any other form of practice?

References

Azrin, N. H., & Nunn, R. C. (1977). *Habit control.* New York: Simon & Shuster.

Azrin, N. H., & Nunn, R. C. (1982). Habit reversal: A method of eliminating nervous habits and tics. *Behaviour Research and Therapy, 11,* 619–628.

Barlow, D. H. (Ed.) (1981). *Behavioral assessment of adult disorders.* New York: Guilford.

Barlow, D. H., et al. (1984). *The scientist practitioner.* New York: Pergamon.

Beck, A. T. (1976). *Cognitive therapy and the emotional disorders.* New York: International Universities Press.

Beck, A. T., Rush, A. J., Shaw, B. F., & Emery, G. (1979). *Cognitive therapy of depression.* New York: Guilford.

Beck, D. F., & Jones, M. A. (1973). *Progress on family problems.* New York: Family Service Association of America.

Bellack, A. S., & Hersen, M. (Eds.). (1979). *Research and practice in social skills training.* New York: Plenum.

Bellack, A. S., & Hersen, M. (Eds.). (1985). *Dictionary of behavior therapy techniques.* New York: Pergamon.

Bergin, A. E. (1969). A technique for improving desensitization via warmth, empathy and emotional re-experiencing of the hierarchy event. In R. Rubin & C. Franks (Eds.). *Advances in behavior therapy, 1968* (pp. 117–130). New York: Academic.

Bergin, A. E., & Strupp, H. H. (1972). *Changing frontiers in the science of psychotherapy.* Chicago: Aldine-Atherton.

Blenkner, M., et al. (1964). *Serving the aging: An experiment in social work and public health nursing.* New York: Community Service Society.

Bloom, M. (1975). *The paradox of helping: Introduction to the philosophy of scientific practice.* New York: Wiley.

Bloom, M., & Fischer, J. (1982). *Evaluating practice: Guidelines for the accountable professional.* Englewood Cliffs, NJ: Prentice Hall.

Brager, G., & Holloway, S. (1978). *Changing human service organizations: Politics and practice.* New York: Free Press.

Brehony, K. A., & Geller, E. S. (1981). Agoraphobia: Appraisal of research and a proposal for an integrative model. In M. Hersen et al. (Eds.), *Progress in behavior modification,* Vol. 12 (pp. 1–66). New York: Academic Press.

Briar, S. (1978). Toward the integration of practice and research. Paper presented at NASW Conference on the Future of Social Work Research, San Antonio, October, 1978.

Butcher, J. N., & Koss, M. P. (1978). Research on brief and crisis-oriented psychotherapies. In S. L. Garfield & A. E. Bergin (Eds.), *Handbook of psychotherapy and behavior change* (2nd ed.) (pp. 725–768). New York: Wiley.

Cairns, K. (1972). Desensitization and relationship quality. Unpublished master's
thesis, University of Calgary, Alberta, Canada.

Carkhuff, R. R. (1969). *Helping and human relations,* Vol. 2. New York: Holt,
Rinehart, & Winston.

Carkhuff, R. R., & Berenson, B. (1976). *Teaching as treatment.* Amherst, MA:
Human Resources Development Press.

Cautela, J. R. (1967). Covert sensitization. *Psychological Reports, 20,* 459–468.

Ciminero, A. R. (Ed.). (1977). *Handbook of behavioral assessment.* New York:
Wiley.

Cocozzelli, C. L. (In Press). The theoretical orientation of clinical social workers:
Ideology or pragmatism? *Journal of Social Service Research.*

Coe, W. C., & Buckner, C. G. (1975). Expectation, hypnosis, and suggestion
methods. In F. H. Kanfer & A. P. Goldstein (Eds.), *Helping people change*
(pp. 393–432). New York: Pergamon.

Cone, J. D., & Hawkins, R. P. (Eds.). (1977). *Behavioral assessment.* New York:
Brunner/Mazel.

Cormier, W. H., & Cormier, S. L. (1985). *Interviewing strategies for helpers* (2nd
ed.). Monterey, CA: Brooks/Cole.

Curran, J. P., & Monti, P. M. (Eds.). (1982). *Social skills training.* New York:
Guilford.

Curtiss, S. (1976). The compatibility of humanistic and behavioristic approaches
in a state mental hospital. In A. Wandersman et al. (Eds.), *Humanism and
behaviorism: Dialogue and growth* (pp. 235–252). New York: Pergamon.

Dowling, T. H., & Frantz, T. T. (1975). The influence of facilitative relationship on
imitative learning. *Journal of Counseling Psychology, 22,* 259–263.

D'Zurilla, T. J., & Nezu, A. (1982). Social problem solving in adults. In P. C. Kendall (Ed.), *Advances in cognitive-behavioral research and therapy,* Vol. 1
(pp. 201–274). New York: Academic Press.

Ellis, A., & Grieger, R. (Eds.). (1977). *Handbook of rational-emotive therapy.* New
York: Springer.

Emery, G., Hollon, S. D., & Bedrosian, R. C. (Eds.). (1981). *New directions in cognitive therapy.* New York: Guilford.

Feld, S., & Radin, N. (1982). *Social psychology for social work and the mental
health professions.* New York: Columbia.

Fischer, J. (1971). A framework for the analysis of clinical theories of induced
change. *Social Service Review, 45,* 440–454.

Fischer, J. (1973). Is casework effective? A review. *Social Work, 18,* 5–20.

Fischer, J. (1976). *The effectiveness of social casework.* Springfield, IL: Charles C
Thomas.

Fischer, J. (1978). *Effective casework practice: An eclectic approach.* New York:
McGraw-Hill.

Fischer, J. (1981). The social work revolution. *Social Work, 26,* 199–207.

Fish, J. M. (1973). *Placebo therapy.* San Francisco: Jossey-Bass.

Foa, E. B., & Steketee, G. S. (1979). Obsessive-compulsives: Conceptual issues and treatment considerations. In M. Hersen et al. (Eds.), *Progress in behavior modification,* Vol. 8 (pp. 1–53). New York: Academic Press.

Ford, D., & Urban, H. (1963). *Systems of psychotherapy.* New York: Wiley.

Foreyt, J. P., & Rathjen, D. P. (Eds.). (1978). *Cognitive behavior therapy.* New York: Plenum.

Foxx, R. M., & Bechtel, D. R. (1982). Overcorrection. In M. Hersen et al. (Eds.). *Progress in behavior modification,* Vol. 13 (pp. 227–288). New York: Academic Press.

Frank, J. D. (1972). *Persuasion and healing* (2nd ed.). Baltimore: Johns Hopkins.

Franks, C. M., & Wilson, G. T. (Eds.). (1973–1984). *Annual review of behavior therapy,* Vol. 1–9. New York: Guilford.

Franks, C. M., Wilson, C. M., Kendall, P. C., & Brownell, K. D. (Eds.). (1982). *Annual review of behavior therapy,* Vol. 8. New York: Guilford.

Gambrill, E. D. (1977). *Behavior modification: Handbook of assessment, intervention, and evaluation.* San Francisco: Jossey-Bass.

Gambrill, E. (1983). *Casework: A competency-based approach.* Englewood Cliffs, NJ: Prentice-Hall.

Gantt, S. et al. (1980). Paraprofessional skills: Maintenance of empathic sensitivity after training. *Journal of Counseling Psychology, 27,* 374–379.

Gianetti, V. J., & Wells, R. A. (1985). Psychotherapeutic outcome and professional affiliation. *Social Service Review, 59,* 32–43.

Gold, G. H. (1976). Affective behaviorism: A synthesis of humanism and behaviorism with children. In A. Wandersman et al. (Eds.), *Humanism and behaviorism: Dialogue and growth* (pp. 253–264). New York: Pergamon.

Goldfried, M. R. (1979). Anxiety reduction through cognitive-behavioral intervention. In P. C. Kendall & S. D. Hollon (Eds.), *Cognitive-behavioral interventions* (pp. 117–152). New York: Academic Press.

Goldfried, M. R., & Davison, G. C. (1976). *Clinical behavior therapy.* New York: Holt, Rinehart and Winston.

Goldstein, A. (1976). Appropriate expression training—humanistic behavior therapy. In A. Wandersman et al. (Eds.), *Humanism and behaviorism: Dialogue and growth* (pp. 223–234). New York: Pergamon.

Goldstein, A. P. (1980). Relationship-enhancement methods. In F. H. Kanfer & A. P. Goldstein (Eds.), *Helping people change* (2nd ed.) (pp. 18–57). New York: Pergamon.

Goldstein, A. P., & Kanfer, F. H. (Eds.). (1979). *Maximizing treatment gains: Transfer enhancement in psychotherapy.* New York: Academic Press.

Goldstein, A. P., & Simonson, N. (1971). Social psychological approaches to psychotherapy research. In A. E. Bergin & S. L. Garfield (Eds.), *Handbook of psychotherapy and behavior change* (pp. 154–196). New York: John Wiley.

Goleman, D. (1985, April 30). Social workers vault into a leading role in psychotherapy. *The New York Times,* pp. C1, C9.

Gordon, R., & Gordon, K. (1966). Is short-term psychotherapy enough? *Journal of the Medical Society of New Jersey, 63,* 41–44.

Harris, D. E., & Lichenstein, E. (1971). The contribution of non-specific social variables to a successful behavioral treatment of smoking. Paper presented at the Annual Meeting of the Western Psychological Association, San Francisco, April 1971.

Haynes, S. N. (1978). *Principles of behavioral assessment.* New York: Gardner.

Haynes, S. N., & Wilson, C. C. (1979). *Behavioral assessment.* San Francisco: Jossey-Bass.

Henry, W. E., Sims, J. H., & Spray, S. C. (1971). *The fifth profession.* San Francisco: Jossey-Bass.

Hepworth, D. H., & Larsen, J. (1982). *Direct social work practice.* Homewood, IL: Dorsey.

Hersen, M., & Barlow, D. H. (1976). *Single case experimental designs.* New York: Pergamon.

Hersen, M., & Bellack, A. S. (Eds.). (1981). *Behavioral assessment: A practical handbook* (2nd ed.). New York: Pergamon.

Hersen, M., et al. (Eds.). (1975–1984). *Progress in behavior modification,* Vol. 1–16. New York: Academic Press.

Hudson, W. W. (1982). *The clinical measurement package.* Homewood, IL: Dorsey.

Janis, I. L. (Ed.). (1982). *Counseling on personal decisions.* New Haven: Yale.

Janis, I. L., & Mann, L. (1977). *Decision-making.* New York: Free Press.

Jayaratne, S. (1978). A study of clinical eclecticism. *Social Service Review, 52,* 621–631.

Jayaratne, S. (1982). Characteristics and theoretical orientations of clinical social workers: A survey. *Journal of Social Service Research, 4,* 17–30.

Jayaratne, S., & Levy, R. (1979). *Empirical clinical practice.* New York: Columbia University Press.

Karoly, P., & Steffen, J. J. (Eds.). (1980). *Improving the long-term effects of psychotherapy.* New York: Gardner.

Kazdin, A. E. (1982). *Single-case research designs.* New York: Oxford.

Kazdin, A. E., & Smith, G. A. (1979). Covert conditioning: A review. *Advances in Behavior Research and Therapy, 2,* 57–98.

Kazdin, A. E., & Wilson, G. T. (1978). *Evaluation of behavior therapy: Issues, evidence, and research strategies.* Cambridge, MA: Ballinger.

Kendall, P. C., & Hollon, S. D. (Eds.). (1979). *Cognitive-behavioral interventions: Theory, practice, and procedures.* New York: Academic Press.

Kendall, P. C., & Hollon, S. D. (1981). *Assessment strategies for cognitive-behavioral interventions.* New York: Academic Press.

Kirschenbaum, D. S., & Flanery, R. C. (1983). Behavioral contracting: Outcomes and elements. In M. Hersen et al. (Eds.), *Progress in behavior modification*, Vol. 15 (pp. 217–275). New York: Academic Press.

Kuhn, T. S. (1970). *The structure of scientific revolutions* (2nd ed.). Chicago: University of Chicago Press.

Lazarus, A. A. (1981). *The practice of multi-modal therapy*. New York: McGraw-Hill.

Lick, J., & Bootzin, R. (1975). Expectancy factors in the treatment of fear: Methodology and theoretical issues. *Psychological Bulletin, 82,* 917–931.

Luborsky, L., Singer, B., & Luborsky, L. (1975). Comparative studies of psychotherapy. *Archives of General Psychiatry, 32,* 995–1008.

Mahoney, M. J. (1974). *Cognition and behavior modification*. Cambridge, MA: Ballinger.

Mahoney, M. J. (1978). Cognitive and self-control therapies. In S. L. Garfield & A. E. Bergin (Eds.), *Handbook of psychotherapy and behavior change* (pp. 689–722). New York: Wiley.

Marshall, E. K., Kurtz, P. D., et al. (Eds.). (1982). *Interpersonal helping skills.* San Francisco: Jossey-Bass.

Marshall, W. L., et al. (1979). The current status of flooding therapy. In M. Hersen et al. (Eds.), *Progress in behavior modification,* Vol. 7 (pp. 205–275). New York: Academic Press.

Martin, G. A., & Worthington, E. L. (1982). Behavioral homework. In M. Hersen et al. (Eds.), *Progress in behavior modification,* Vol. 13 (pp. 197–226). New York: Academic Press.

Mash, E., & Terdal, L. (1981). *Behavioral assessment of childhood disorders.* New York: Guilford.

Mathews, A. M., et al. (1981). *Agoraphobia: Nature and treatment.* New York: Guilford.

Meichenbaum, D. (1977). *Cognitive-behavior modification.* New York: Plenum.

Mickelson, D., & Stevic, R. (1971). The differential effects of facilitative and non-facilitative behavioral counselors. *Journal of Counseling Psychology, 18*(4), 314–319.

Mitchell, K. M., Bozarth, J. D., & Krauft, C. C. (1977). A reappraisal of the therapeutic effectiveness of accurate empathy, non-possessive warmth, and genuineness. In A. S. Gurman & A. M. Razin (Eds.), *Effective psychotherapy: A handbook of research* (pp. 482–502). New York: Pergamon.

Morris, R. J., & Suckerman, K. R. (1974a). The importance of the therapeutic relationship in systematic desensitization. *Journal of Consulting and Clinical Psychology, 42,* 148.

Morris, R. J., & Suckerman, K. R. (1974b). Therapist warmth as a factor in automated systematic desensitization. *Journal of Consulting and Clinical Psychology, 42,* 244–250.

Muench, G. (1964). An investigation of time-limited psychotherapy. *American Psychologist, 19* (abstract).

Mullen, E. J. (1978). The construction of personal models for effective practice: A method for utilizing research findings to guide social intervention. *Journal of Social Service Research, 2,* 45–64.

Murray, E. J., & Jacobson, L. I. (1978). Cognition and learning in traditional and behavioral therapy. In S. L. Garfield & A. E. Bergin (Eds.), *Handbook of psychotherapy and behavior change* (2nd ed.) (pp. 661–688). New York: Wiley.

Naar, R. (1970). Client-centered and behavior therapies: Their peaceful coexistence: A case study. *Journal of Abnormal Psychology, 76,* 155–160.

Nameneck, A. A., & Schuldt, W. J. (1971). Differential effects of experimenters' personality and instructional sets on verbal conditioning. *Journal of Counseling Psychology, 18,* 173–176.

Nay, W. R. (1979). *Multimethod clinical assessment.* New York: Halsted.

Novaco, R. W. (1979). Cognitive regulation of anger and stress. In P. C. Kendall & S. D. Hollon (Eds.), *Cognitive-behavioral interventions* (pp. 241–286). New York: Academic Press.

Parloff, M. B., & Wolfe, B. E. (1978). Research on therapist variables in relation to process and outcome. In S. L. Garfield & A. E. Bergin (Eds.), *Handbook of psychotherapy and behavior change* (2nd ed.) (pp. 233–282). New York: John Wiley.

Phillips, E. L., et al. (1973). Behavior shaping works for delinquents. *Psychology Today, 7,* 75–79.

Phillips, E. L., & Wiener, D. (1966). *Short-term psychotherapy and structured behavior change.* New York: McGraw-Hill.

Rachman, S. J., & Wilson, G. T. (1980). *The effects of psychological therapy* (2nd ed.). New York: Pergamon Press.

Raimy, V. (1975). *Misunderstandings of the self.* San Francisco: Jossey-Bass.

Rathus, S. A. (1973). A 30-item schedule for assessing assertive behavior. *Behavior Therapy, 4,* 398–406.

Reid, W. J. (1978). *The task-centered system.* New York: Columbia University Press.

Reid, W. J., & Hanrahan, P. (1982). Recent evaluations of social work: Grounds for optimism. *Social Work, 27,* 328–340.

Reid, W., & Shyne, A. (1969). *Brief and extended casework.* New York: Columbia.

Ricks, D. F., Wandersman, A., & Poppen, P. J. (1976). Humanism and behaviorism: Toward new syntheses. In A. Wandersman et al. (Eds.), *Humanism and behaviorism: Dialogue and growth.* (pp. 383–402). New York: Pergamon.

Rimm, D. C., & Masters, J. C. (1979). *Behavior therapy: Techniques and empirical findings* (2nd ed.). New York: Academic Press.

Roberts, R. W., & Nee, R. (Eds.). (1970). *Theories of social casework.* Chicago: University of Chicago Press.

Shelton, J. L., & Levy, R. L. (1981). *Behavioral assignments and treatment compliance.* Champaign, IL: Research Press.

Shlien, J., et al. (1962). Effects of time limits: A comparison of two psychothera-pies. *Journal of Counseling Psychology, 9,* 31–34.

Siporin, M. (1975). *Introduction to social work practice.* New York: Macmillan.

Strong, S. R. (1978). Social psychological approach to psychotherapy research. In S. L. Garfield & A. E. Bergin (Eds.), *Handbook of psychotherapy and behavior change* (pp. 101–135). New York: John Wiley.

Sundberg, N. D. (1977). *Assessment of persons.* Englewood Cliffs, NJ: Prentice-Hall.

Thomas, E. J. (1977). The BESDAS model for effective practice. *Social Work Research and Abstracts, 13,* 12–17.

Thorne, F. C. (1973). Eclectic psychotherapy. In R. Corsini (Ed.), *Current psycho-therapies* (pp. 445–486). Itasca, IL: F. E. Peacock.

Thyer, B. A. (1983). Behavior modification in social work practice. In M. Hersen et al. (Eds.), *Progress in behavior modification,* Vol. 15. New York: Aca-demic Press.

Truax, C. B., & Mitchell, K. M. (1971). Research on certain therapist interpersonal skills in relation to process and outcome. In A. E. Bergin & S. L. Garfield (Eds.), *Handbook of psychotherapy and behavior change* (pp. 299–344). New York: Wiley.

Turner, S. M., Calhoun, K. S., & Adams, H. E. (Eds.). (1981). *Handbook of clinical behavior therapy.* New York: Wiley.

Turpin, G. (1983). The behavioral management of tic disorders: A critical review. *Advances in Behavior Research and Therapy, 5,* 203–245.

Twentyman, C. T., & Zimering, R. T. (1979). Behavioral training of social skills: A critical review. In M. Hersen et al. (Eds.), *Progress in behavior modifica-tion,* Vol. 7 (pp. 319–400). New York: Academic Press.

Vitalo, R. (1970). Effects of facilitative interpersonal functioning in a verbal con-ditioning paradigm. *Journal of Counseling Psychology, 17,* 141–144.

Walker, C. E., Hedberg, A., Clement, P. W., & Wright, L. (1981). *Clinical proce-dures for behavior therapy.* Englewood Cliffs, NJ: Prentice-Hall.

Wandersman, A., Poppen, P., & Ricks, D. (Eds.). (1976). *Humanism and behav-iorism: Dialogue and growth.* New York: Pergamon.

Wattie, B. (1973). Evaluating short-term casework in a family agency. *Social Casework, 54,* 609–616.

Wilson, G. T. (1982). Clinical issues and strategies in the practice of behavior therapy. In C. M. Franks et al. (Eds.), *Annual review of behavior therapy: Theory and practice,* Vol. 8. New York: Guilford.

Wilson, G. T., Franks, C. M., Brownell, K. D., & Kendall, P. C. (Eds.). (1984). *Annual review of behavior therapy,* Vol. 9. New York: Guilford.

Wodarski, J. S. (1981). *The role of research in clinical practice.* Baltimore: Univer-sity Park Press.

Wolberg, L. (1966). *Psychotherapy and the behavioral sciences.* New York: Grune & Stratton.

Wolpe, J. (1969). Presidential address, second annual meeting of the Association for the Advancement of Behavior of Therapy. In R. Rubin and C. Franks (Eds.), *Advances in behavior therapy, 1968*. New York: Academic Press.
Wolpe, J. (1973). *The practice of behavior therapy*. New York: Pergamon Press.
Wolpe, J. (1982). *The practice of behavior therapy* (3rd ed.). New York: Pergamon.

Chapter 14
Statistical Training for Social Workers

The increased emphasis on research methods in social work education has prompted a great deal of confusion and disagreement over the extent and type of research content to be included in curricula (Austin, 1978; Heineman, 1981; Hudson, 1982; Glisson, 1982; Karger, 1983). The debate has been particularly intensive over the extent to which social workers should be trained in statistics (Cowger, 1984; Glisson, 1985; Pieper, 1985). Currently, there is considerable disagreement about the value of statistical training and an enormous variation among social workers in their ability to either understand or undertake statistical analyses.

This article has four objectives related to statistical training: 1) to establish the value of statistical training for social workers; 2) to assess current levels of training provided to social workers; 3) to present general, educational principles for statistical training in social work; and 4) to provide specific objectives and curricula for bachelor's, master's, and doctoral social work programs covering the continuum of statistical methodologies in the three programs.

The Value of Statistical Training for Social Workers

Because research in the social sciences relies heavily upon statistical analysis, statistical training is vital to the enhancement of practice: First, it allows social workers to read more critically social and behavioral science research related to their areas of practice, and second, they can conduct research related to their areas of practice that will be integrated into the larger body of social science research.

Without statistical training, one must depend solely on authors' interpretations of a study and, more importantly, on their critiques of results. Again, the majority of published research in social and behavioral sciences, whether in sociology, psychology, political science, social work, etc., depend on statistical analyses. The statistically naive consumer of this research becomes a victim of the authors' errors

Glisson, C. & Fischer, J. (1987). *Journal of Social Work Education, 23,* 50–58. Reprinted with permission of the Council on Social Work Education.

because such a consumer must blindly accept conclusions without having the ability to critique statistical methodology.

Perhaps even more serious, social workers without statistical training must rely on other professions for research related to their own areas of expertise. Legislators, judges, administrators, and other decision-makers, must also rely on this information in making decisions that impinge upon areas traditionally involving social workers.

Ironically, at a time when social work has just begun to include research in its literature and curricula, some argue that social work should abandon research and thereby abolish the need for statistical training. For example, Pieper argues that other social sciences have abandoned empirical research and that social work has benefited little from what she calls its "long history" of empirical research (Heineman, 1981; Pieper, 1985). These assertions are combined with the erection of several "straw men": researchers are not objective, statistical significance is not substantive significance, and researchers formulate questions to fit a specific research method. These issues have been addressed thoroughly in the social science research literature for over three decades. Pieper, however, makes serious errors in interpreting this literature.

For example, Pieper (1985:5) uses Cronbach's suggestion that social science depends on correlative research as support for her anti-empirical stance. Cronbach never advocated the abandonment of empirical research. This, and that the majority of social work empirical research *is* correlative research (Glisson, 1983), suggests that Pieper misunderstood the source and the issue.

Similarly, Pieper (1985:7) uses Nunnally's distinction between statistical significance and inferences regarding substance and casualty as support for rejecting inferential statistics. Like Cronbach, Nunnally never advocated the abandonment of either research or inferential statistical analyses but was recommending changes and improvements in existing practices.

Although Pieper's errors are numerous, further comment will be addressed specifically to her assertion that social work has clung to empirical research long after other social sciences have abandoned it. Following Hudson (1982), research articles rely on data generated by systematic measurements of observable entities for the purpose of describing relationships among variables.

A recent review of all articles published over a six year period in five social work journals, *Social Work, Social Service Review, Journal of Social Work Education, Journal of Social Service Research,* and *Social Work Research and Abstracts,* found that 44% of the articles reported or summarized the results of empirical research (Glisson, 1983). Other analyses of social work journals have reported even lower percentages of articles that report empirical research (Jayaratne, 1979; Simpson, 1978; Weinberger & Tripiodi, 1969).

Recent issues of the journals of the American Psychological Association were reviewed to determine if, as Pieper claims, psychology has abandoned empirical research. Each article in the first issue published in 1986 of *Psychological Bulletin, American Psychologist, Journal of Personality and Social Psychology, Journal of Consulting and Clinical Psychology* and *Journal of Abnormal Psychology* was included in the review. Although two of the journals have as specific editorial policies the publishing of issue-oriented articles and review articles, over 90% of the articles published in these five APA journals reported or summarized the results of empirical research (82 out of 90 articles), over twice the percentage found in the five social work journals of which two (*JSSR* and *SWRA*) have an editorial policy of specifically publishing empirical research. A similar review of the first 1986 issues of journals of the American Sociological Association (*American Sociological Review, Journal of Health and Social Behavior, Social Psychology Quarterly* and *Sociology of Education*) indicate 90% (36/40) of recent ASA Sociology articles reported or summarized the results of empirical research, again over twice that found in the social work journals.

Moreover, given that the first empirically-based psychological research laboratory was established in 1867 by Wilhelm Wundt, Pieper's (1985:6) claim that social work has engaged in empirical research "longer than have the other social sciences," is clearly incorrect. Those who argue that social work has fully developed an empirically-based literature, or argue that other social sciences have abandoned empirical research, ignore the evidence presented here.

Another common theme is that social workers do "qualitative" research, not quantitative research, and therefore do not need training in statistics. However, of more than one thousand articles in five major social work journals published over a six-year period only ninety-five (2%) attempted qualitative analysis (Glisson, 1983).

The definition of qualitative varies; however, if it means research that incorporates one or more qualitative variables, then social workers, as well as psychologists and sociologists, engage in qualitative research. Most social work research (90%) incorporates at last one qualitative variable (Glisson, 1983). These variables are found, however, in the same research studies that incorporate quantitative variables and are subjected to the same statistical analyses as the quantitative variables. If, on the other hand, qualitative research refers to articles that incorporate no statistical analyses, then social work journals, like newspapers, have plenty of these. These articles also have no hypotheses, no variables, and no analyses of any sort, qualitative or quantitative, i.e. no systematic approach that could be called research.

Systematic qualitative social science research methodology does exist although it is rarely used. Unfortunately, social workers know as little about qualitative methods of analyses as about quantitative methods of analyses. Most published social science research depends on the latter, however, thereby placing it out of the conceptual reach of many social workers.

The Current Levels of Statistical Expertise Among Social Workers

Two recent studies provide evidence that the current level of statistical expertise among social workers ensures their inability to either critique existing social science research or to contribute meaningfully to it.

The first study examined the research curricula of all social work doctoral programs in the U.S. and categorized each program by the level of training the students receive in statistics (Glisson, 1982). On the basis of course outlines, the majority of the doctoral programs were found to be teaching statistics at an undergraduate level.

The second study, mentioned earlier, was based upon a thorough reading of all articles published in five journals over a six year period (Glisson, 1983). Articles were categorized according to the applied statistical techniques reported in them. The results corroborated findings of the first study. Although 90% of the authors were educated at the doctoral level, the majority of the articles incorporate statistical analyses taught in undergraduate psychology and sociology courses.

The elementary level of statistical training found in doctoral curricula and statistical analyses reported in social work journals indicate that research efforts are hampered by an overall lack of knowledge of intermediate and advanced analytic techniques. This lack of knowledge limits the types of questions and variables that can be addressed by social work researchers and results in a misapplication or misinterpretation of statistical analyses, as described in several recent articles (Glisson & Hudson, 1981; Glisson & Fischer, 1982; Cowger, 1984; Glisson, 1985; Hudson, Thyer & Stocks, 1985; Orme & Tolman, 1986; Orme & Combs—Orme, 1986). More advanced training in statistical techniques at the BSW, MSW, and DSW/Ph.D. levels is mandatory if the limitations and errors found in published social work research are to be eliminated in the future.

General Educational Principles for Statistical Training in Social Work

Social work educational programs have systematically ignored the importance of adequate statistical preparation for social workers, yet the profession appears to be moving toward a far more empirically-based stance about its knowledge. For example, the social worker as "scientist-practitioner" described by Hopps (1985) in *Social Work,* and the scientific approach to social work described by Gambrill (1985) in *Social Work Research and Abstracts,* appear to be increasingly dominant themes. Yet without adequate statistical training, those themes have a hollow sound, paying only lip service to an important, but unattainable ideal. In order to implement either model, students must be prepared to understand, both in their reading of the social science research literature and in their own conducting of empirical research, the range of statistical practices commonly applied in the social and behavioral sciences. The teaching of statistics in social work could be based on the following educational principles:

1. All social workers do not do all things. The objectives and curricula that follow are based on the obvious notion that different levels of the educational continuum have different goals. Thus, a continuum of statistical expertise is presented with objectives established for each level of social work education: the BSW, the MSW, and the Ph.D.

2. There are two major tasks related to the teaching and learning of statistics. First, be able to read and understand statistical analyses in order to understand adequately social science research articles. Second, be able to actually compute statistics in the conduct of one's own research. Separate objectives have been developed for each area.

3. Computer literacy is an integral part of statistical training. Basic statistics can and should be calculated by hand to provide more insight into their application and interpretation, but the complexity of advanced statistics and the need to master computer applications point to building in the use of computer-based analyses.

4. It is assumed that students will be taking other research courses, particularly in research design and measurement and that the burden of helping students understand and evaluate the overall research process is shared with other courses. In addition, it is important that statistics not be taught in a vacuum. Intrinsic to the conception of the statistical curriculum presented here is the importance of teaching the applicability of statistics to social problem areas throughout the entire continuum. Students have to know the where, when and why, as well as the how of statistical analysis.

5. The teaching of statistics as a continuum is based on the idea that a foundation of specific principles dominates as a core of learning. For many years in the social and behavioral sciences (as well as the physical sciences), that foundation has been the general linear model, or GLM, which serves as a set of organizing concepts and principles out of which most commonly used statistics are derived (Cohen & Cohen, 1983; Pedhazur, 1982). It has only been since the early sixties, however, that the proponents of various popular analytic techniques, such as the t-test for comparing means, analysis of variance, correlation, multiple regression, and trend analysis, have explicitly recognized and developed the underlying relationships that unite these and other commonly used analytic methods that were developed, in some instances, quite independently of each other. In fact, it is still not unusual to find social work statistics curricula that present, for example, analysis of variance and multiple regression as two distinct, unrelated approaches to the analysis of data derived from experiments and surveys, respectively. The importance of the GLM is highlighted throughout most of the suggested courses as a conceptual base, which makes it easier for the student to grasp the relationships among the various commonly used statistics. We fully recognize the ongoing development of analytic methods (i.e., Breiman & Friedman, 1985), and are not advocating the exclusive dependence on traditional GLM-based methodologies in the analysis of research data. However, because of their current dominance in social and behavioral research, these techniques must form the core of the curriculum.

6. The statistical methods are organized on a continuum from the simplest procedures to the most sophisticated, suggesting the importance of cumulative learning, in that each semester's work builds on the previous semesters. This

also suggests the importance of beginning each semester with a review of prior work, especially if there is a time lapse between statistical courses. It also suggests the importance of the use of statistical prerequisites for admission to the advanced social work degrees or, at least, the availability of remedial courses for students not mastering the content from earlier semesters.

7. Finally, the importance of the teacher and the teaching method are emphasized to make statistics courses palatable. These courses, no matter how elementary, have always been a major hurdle for most social work students. That social work graduate students have the lowest quantitative GRE score of any academic group plays no small role in the creation of this hurdle. In teaching these statistics courses, we therefore urge instructors to forego the "turn your back on the students and derive formulas on the blackboard" approach, but try to encompass a sense of the wonder of explaining what, for the students, will be essentially a new approach to conceptualizing and understanding the variation in the world around them and a new language to discuss that variation. This teaching should also include many examples that are described with the help of concrete analogies and geometric explanations, along with the algebraic expressions. We recommend that the teacher move back and forth among the analogies, the geometry, and the algebra in explaining any statistical concept so that those students needing more explanation, for example, an analogy or a geometric explanation, will have it.

Objectives and Curriculum for the Three Social Work Degrees

The continuum for the teaching of statistics is organized according to the knowledge necessary for the BSW, MSW, and DSW in social work. The specific educational objectives and the statistical content for each program are described in Table 14.1. The curricula are intentionally specific, because the current deficit in statistical training for social workers is so acute that any vagueness would invite misinterpretation. It is also recognized, however, that a certain unintended rigidity might be suggested, an unfortunate byproduct of the intentional specificity.

Bachelor's Degree   The objectives for the bachelor's degree will be met with one course. The first objective is that the student acquire an understanding of and competence in computing descriptive statistics and simple univariate, inferential statistics that incorporate a single independent and a single dependent variable. These would include the t-test for means, one-way ANOVA, chi-square analysis, simple correlation and simple regression.

A second objective is that the student acquire the ability to read with understanding more advanced, univariate, inferential statistics that include multiple independent variables, as they are reported in research articles. These statistical techniques would include factorial analyses of variance, analyses of covariance and multiple regression.

Master's Degree   The first objective for the master's degree is that the student understand and be able to compute multifactor, univariate statistics using the GLM approach. This would include those statistical techniques that incorporate multiple independent, or predictor, variables and a single dependent, or criterion, variable. The second objective is for the student to be able to read with understanding multivariate statistical analyses, those analyses that incorporate multiple dependent, or criterion, variables. These would include factor analysis, canonical analysis, and discriminant function analysis.

There is a good deal to be accomplished in the master's program, for which we recommend two semesters of statistics. Upon completion of the MSW program, a graduate would have good reading knowledge of most commonly used statistics, and be able to apply a good many of the statistical techniques that he or she might use in conducting research.

The Doctoral Degree   Given the focus of most social work doctorates as preparation for teaching and research, graduates should be prepared for a range of tasks involving the understanding of and ability to calculate most statistical techniques used in the social and behavioral sciences. In addition to a doctoral graduate's ability to understand, critique and compute the statistics taught in the BSW and MSW programs, there are three additional objectives. The first is that the student be able to critique and compute most advanced applications of univariate statistics to complex designs and problems. The second is the ability to critique and compute a range of multivariate statistical procedures. Finally, the student should be competent in computer applications to the solution of both univariate and multivariate statistical problems.

Because of the central position played by research in doctoral education, three statistics courses are required. In the first course, the focus is on advanced univariate applications of the general linear model. The second focuses on the most commonly used multivariate statistics in the family of procedures generally known as canonical analysis.

The third course covers a variety of additional multivariate methods currently applied in social and behavioral science research. Although all of the methods in this third course could not be explored in depth, the preparation in statistics received by the students in previous courses would allow an efficient use of time. With the exception of factor analysis, the techniques listed here are used less than those covered in previous courses, but their increasing application in published research make their inclusion prudent in doctoral level programs. Given these suggestions, it should be made clear that this last course is conceptualized as a special topics course that reviews a variety of techniques not included in the earlier general linear model content. Therefore, these topics might fluctuate from semester to semester, depending on current interest and professional trends.

Upon completion of the doctorate, the graduate should be able to correctly analyze data from most studies, and independently continue his or her study of

Table 14.1 Course Content for Statistical Training in Social Work

	BSW	MSW	DSW/Ph.D.
Objectives	1. Understanding and computing simple descriptive statistics and univariate inferential statistics that incorporate one IV and one DV.	1. Understanding and computing multi-factor univariate inferential statistics using GLM approach, and computer applications.	1. Understanding and computing advanced applications of univariate statistics.
	2. Ability to read univariate statistical analyses that incorporate more than one IV.	2. Ability to read multivariate analyses, including factor analysis, canonical analysis and discriminant function analysis.	2. Understanding and computing multivariate statistics.
			3. Competence in computer applications to the solutions of both univariate and multivariate procedures.
First Semester	1. Introduction to variable and measurement.	1. Review of BSW course material.	1. Review of MSW course material.
	2. Introduction to frequency distributions and probability.	2. Introduction to concept of GLM foundation of t-tests, ANOVA, regression.	2. Foundation of GLM in matrix algebra, geometry and calculus.
	3. Introduction to central tendency, variability and correlation.	3. Introduction to computation of factorial ANOVA and multiple regression.	3. Advanced GLM techniques for partitioning variation in unbalanced designs.
	4. Introduction to t-tests for means, one-way ANOVA, simple correlation and regression, chi-square analysis.	4. Introduction to post hoc comparisons and interaction.	4. Advanced repeated measures designs.
	5. Computer applications for above.	5. Introduction to computation of ANCOVA.	5. Advanced trend analysis.
	6. Introduction to reading factorial ANOVA, ANCOVA and multiple regression.	6. Computer applications for above.	6. Computer applications for above.

Second
Semester

1. Application of matrix algebra in GLM solutions.
2. Introduction to partitioning of variation in unbalanced designs.
3. ANCOVA with multiple covariates.
4. Introduction to repeated measures.
5. Introduction to trend analysis.
6. Complex interactions and simple main effects.
7. Computer applications for above.
8. Introduction to reading multivariate analyses.

1. Matrix foundations of multivariate analysis.
2. Introduction to computing canonical analyses.
3. Introduction to computing Hotelling's t-squared.
4. Introduction to computing multivariate ANOVA.
5. Introduction to computing discriminant function analyses.
6. Computer applications for above.

Third
Semester

1. Special topics multivariate course to include a variety of multivariate procedures.
2. Factor analysis.
3. Cluster analysis.
4. Smallest space analysis.
5. Log linear analysis.
6. Computer applications for above.

statistics as new techniques emerge. This is essential if the profession is to retain any position in research expertise that it gains from the implementation of more advanced statistics curricula.

Conclusion

Without adequate training in statistical methods, social work practitioners are unable to utilize existing social science research findings in making intervention decisions that directly affect their clients, and they are poorly equipped to contribute to research efforts that determine policy and program decisions that indirectly affect clients.

The lack of training in statistical methodologies affects social work scholarship as well. The elementary level of statistical applications found in much published social work research places limitations on the types of research questions addressed, and renders results to a secondary position of influence among the social sciences generally.

The described curricula propose more sophisticated levels of training than that found in many social work educational programs. The objectives of these statistical curricula are to enable social workers to consume and critique completed social science research relevant to their substantive area of practice; to influence the design and application of policy and program research that impacts target groups and service systems for which the practitioner intends to advocate, and; to conduct independent research that will contribute to existing levels of knowledge among the social sciences.

It is important to note again that the proposed curricula depend on content that is not unique across either the social or physical sciences. The intentionally specific arrangement of the content presented here meets specific objectives for the three levels of social work training. More importantly, a case has been made for the necessity of such content if social workers are to be able to critique and assimilate existing social science research, to contribute to policy and program research affecting decision-making at community, state, and federal levels, and to assume leadership roles in the development of the larger body of social science literature.

References

Austin, D. M. (1978). Research and social work: Education paradoxes and possibilities. *Journal of Social Service Research,* 2 (Winter), 159–76.

Breiman, L. and Friedman, J. (1985). Estimating optimal transformations for multiple regression and correlation, *Journal of the American Statistical Association,* 80, (September), 580–619.

Cohen, J. and Cohen, P. (1983). *Applied multiple regression/correlation analysis for the behavioral sciences.* Hillsdale, N.J.: Lawrence Erlbaum Associates.

Cowger, C. (1984). Statistical significance tests: Scientific ritualism or scientific method? *Social Service Review,* 58 (September), 358–372.

Gambrill, E. D. (1985). Evaluating approaches to the development of knowledge, *Social Work Research and Abstracts,* 21 (4), 2.

Glisson, C. (1982). Research teaching in social work doctoral programs, *Social Service Review,* 56 (December), 629–639.

Glisson, C. (1983). Trends in social work research. Advancement of Doctoral Education, at the University of Alabama, Tuscaloosa.

Glisson, C. (1985). In defense of statistical tests of significance. *Social Service Review,* 59 (3), 377–386.

Glisson, C., & Fischer, J. (1982). Use and nonuse of multivariate statistics. *Social Work Research and Abstracts,* 18 (1), 42–44.

Glisson, C. & Hudson, W. (1981). Applied statistical misuse in educational research: An admissions criteria example. *Journal of Education for Social Work,* 17 (2), 35–41.

Heineman, M. (1981). The obsolete scientific imperative in social work research. *Social Service Review,* 55 (September), 371–397.

Hopps, J. (1985). Effectiveness and human worth. *Social Work,* 30 (6), 467.

Hudson, W. W. (1982). Scientific imperatives in social work research and practice. *Social Service Review,* 56 (2), 246–258.

Hudson, W. W., Thyer, B. A. & Stocks, J. T. (1986). Assessing the importance of experimental outcomes. *Journal of Social Service Research,* 8 (4), 87–98.

Jayaratne, S. (1979). Analysis of selected social work research journals and productivity rankings among schools of social work. *Journal of Education for Social Work,* 15 (3), 72–80.

Karger, H. J. (1983). Science, research, and social work: Who controls the profession? *Social Work,* 28 (3) 200–205.

Orme, J. G., & Combs-Orme, T. D. (1986). Statistical power and Type II errors in social work research. *Social Work Research and Abstracts,* 22 (3), 3–10.

Orme, J. G., & Tolman, R. M. (1986). The statistical power of a decade of social work education research. *Social Service Review* 60 (4), 619–633.

Pedhazur, E. J. (1982). *Multiple regression in behavioral research.* New York: Holt, Rinehart and Winston.

Pieper, M. H. (1985). The future of social work research. *Social Work Research and Abstracts,* 21 (4), 3–11.

Simpson, R. L. (1978). Is research utilization for social workers? *Journal of Social Service Research,* 2 (2), 143–158.

Weinberger, R. and Tripodi, T. (1969). Trends in types of research reported in selected social work journals. *Social Service Review,* 43 (4), 439–447.

Chapter 15

Meta-analysis: The Premise, the Problems, the Promise

What responsibilities do social workers have when new tools or technologies became available? The possibilities range from uncritical and total adoption of the new technology, to uncritical and total rejection of the new technology. Somewhere in between lies the critical evaluation and assessment of the potentialities of the new technology, and adoption or adaptation of those components that both can withstand careful scrutiny and appear to offer benefits for some aspects of the social work enterprise.

With the fairly recent advent of the methods of meta-analysis, social work has the perfect opportunity to engage in this process of careful and critical evaluation of a new technology that may have important implications for the field.

Meta-analysis is actually a generic term for a number of different empirical literature review or data synthesis methods. As distinct from primary analysis (the original analysis of data in a study) and secondary analysis (reanalysis of data from a given study using better statistical procedures or answering new questions), the term meta-analysis (or analysis of analyses) was coined by Glass (1976) to refer to a method of statistical analysis of the findings of a number of empirical studies. Since 1976, the method developed by Glass has been refined and modified by Glass as well as others; at the same time, a number of other meta-analytic methods have been developed. It is in this broader sense, then, of any method of aggregation and statistical analysis of the findings of several studies, that the term meta-analysis will be used in this chapter.

Meta-analysis arose in part out of dissatisfaction with the traditional, narrative, research review, which is the most common form of research review in social work (e.g., Maas, 1966, 1971, 1978; Mullen, Dumpson et al., 1972; Fischer, 1973, 1976; Wood, 1978; Reid and Hanrahan, 1982; Rubin, 1985). In traditional narrative reviews, the reviewer assembles a group of studies on a particular topic and attempts to organize a series of possibly diverse outcomes to produce a reasonably consistent overall conclusion. While this organization may use some quantitative

Fischer, J. (1988). Paper Presented at Conference on "Empiricism in Clinical Practice," American Institute for Economic Research, Great Barrington, Mass., August, 1988.

methods (e.g., totaling up the number of positive outcomes and comparing it with the number of negative outcomes, sometimes called the "box score" approach), the narrative review, to distinguish it from meta-analysis, does not attempt to statistically aggregate findings across studies in order to provide a standardized numerical estimate of the magnitude of the independent variable or effect size. Thus, narrative reviews have been criticized as subjective (few if any formal rules), scientifically unsound (ignoring good statistical practices), and an inefficient way of extracting useful information (especially when a large number of studies is being reviewed) (Light and Pillemer, 1982).

In the last ten years, meta-analysis practically has been a growth industry unto itself. This is particularly in the fields of education and psychology, of special relevance to social work because of a major emphasis on meta-analysis of clinical or therapeutic services. The basic methodology has been developed and debated in dozens of books and articles (e.g., Hedges and Olkin, 1985; Rosenthal, 1984; Hunter, Schmidt, and Jackson, 1982; Glass, McGaw, and Smith, 1981; Walberg and Haertel, 1980, section one; Michelson, 1985; *Journal of Consulting and Clinical Psychology,* 1983; Green and Hall, 1984; Light, 1983, part one).

At the same time, any number of substantive areas in the social and behavioral sciences and human services have been evaluated through meta-analytic techniques, with over 300 meta-analyses having been conducted by 1983 (Kulik, 1984, cited in Bangert-Drowns, 1986), and many more since then. A few examples of topics of recent meta-analyses are: psychotherapy in general (Smith, Glass, and Miller, 1980), psychotherapy versus placebos (Prioleau, Murdock, and Brody, 1983), cognitive therapy versus systematic desensitization (Berman, Miller, and Massman, 1985), family therapy (Hazelrigg, Cooper, and Borduin, 1987), psychotherapy with children (Casey and Berman, 1985), effects of professional versus nonprofessional training (Berman and Norton, 1985), deinstitutionalization in mental health (Straw, 1983), preventive child health care (Shadish, 1982), psychotherapy versus drug therapy (Steinbrueck, Maxwell, and Howard, 1983), sex roles and mental health (Bassoff and Glass, 1982), cognitive coping strategies (Mullen and Suls, 1982), numerous reviews of specific disorders and specific treatments (Shapiro, 1985), and in education, dozens of examples ranging from curriculum and instruction to programmatic research investigation around such issues as the effects of home environment, peer influences, and socioeconomic status on academic achievement (Walberg and Haertel, 1980).

Despite the hundreds of meta-analyses in related fields, very few articles on meta-analysis in social work could be located. These include Videka-Sherman's (1985, 1988) report on practice effectiveness, Tobler's (1986) report on adolescent drug prevention programs, two reviews of meta-analysis (Nurius, 1984; Nurius and Yeaton, 1987), and two interesting and creative applications of meta-analysis to single system designs (Gingerich, 1984 and Corcoran, 1985). It is not at all clear why social work has been so slow to move into the use of meta-analysis procedures, although two possibilities include a paucity of studies on which to perform meta-analysis, and our traditional reluctance to explore and adapt new technologies.

Nevertheless, since social work as a profession uses a pluralistic knowledge base, a continuing awareness of new knowledge developments as they occur is obviously required. This should be combined with evaluation of their relevance to social work. This, in turn, requires awareness of tools that can aid us in making decisions about new knowledge. With allegiance to the scientific method as a superordinate value in social work, and the use of empirical or research-related criteria for selection of knowledge as one way of operationalizing that allegiance, it would appear that any new tool that may be of value in objectively assessing the empirical status of a given body of knowledge—as meta-analysis purportedly does—would be a potential candidate for utilization by social work.

Thus, the relatively recent origins of meta-analysis, and our relative slowness at examining it, presents an excellent opportunity for critical evaluation and possible dissemination to the field before we become too outdated in our approach to the assessment of empirical research. The potential benefits of meta-analysis for social work—helping us evaluate our own efforts and helping us evaluate the efforts of others in related disciplines to avoid unsound or irrational adaptation of their work—appear too great to wait much longer.

To further that goal, then, the purpose of this chapter is to evaluate both the potential of meta-analysis for social work and the problems associated with its use. In the following section, an overview of several methods of meta-analysis is presented. This is followed by a critique of those methods—the problems and issues. The final section presents some conclusions about the utility of meta-analysis and its potential value to the field as compared and in some instances, combined, with more traditional approaches to research integration.

The Premise

The very newness of meta-analysis suggests the importance of reviewing some of its major methods and basic characteristics before moving any further in this discussion. Accordingly, this section first provides an overview of several of the major approaches to meta-analysis in as nontechnical a way as possible. This is followed by an attempt to synthesize these approaches into a model of the basic processes of meta-analysis. The section concludes with a review of the key benefits of meta-analysis.

Major Methods of Meta-Analysis

Several approaches to meta-analysis have been developed since the mid-seventies. Actually, there is some overlap among many of them in that most either combine significance levels or effect sizes or both. Though significance level and effect size usually are correlated, they do provide different information. When combined across studies, the significance level approach provides information about whether the results for the set of studies likely was due to chance, while the effect size approach examines the magnitude of the effect (how meaningful it is) across studies.

Indeed, because of the basic similarities, some of the differences among meta-analytic approaches may appear somewhat trivial (e.g., use of different statistics to compute effect sizes or combine significance levels). In fact, many researchers actually do combine more than one method in a single meta-analysis. However, for purposes of introduction to this topic, the differences are probably sufficient to justify a brief, separate discussion of several of them. Unfortunately, there is no generally accepted taxonomy of meta-analytic methods. Thus, in an effort to be somewhat consistent with one recent attempt to categorize these approaches, this discussion will follow the categories and explication presented by Bangert-Drowns (1986), who describes five basic methods of meta-analysis.

The Glass Approach   This method of meta-analysis is by far the best known and most frequently used (and criticized) approach; it is described most thoroughly in Glass, McGaw, and Smith (1981). It proceeds through three basic steps. The first is to collect as many studies as possible on the topic area, including those with wide variation in methodological quality. The second key step is to transform the outcomes of each study into a common metric—the core idea of meta-analysis; this allows the results of studies to be compared across studies and outcome measures. This is done by computing an effect size (ES), which is sometimes denoted as delta (Δ). Glass's ES is computed by subtracting the mean of the control group from the mean of the experimental group and then dividing that by the standard deviation of the control group:

$$ES = \frac{\overline{X}_E - \overline{X}_C}{S_C}$$

A related method for determining ES is to use the same formula but to divide by the pooled, within-group standard deviation, ES = $(\overline{X}_E - \overline{X}_C)/S$ this sometimes is called Cohen's d (Cohen, 1977; Hedges, 1981). These two formulas are discussed in more detail later in this chapter.

$$d = \frac{\overline{X}_E - \overline{X}_C}{\sqrt{\dfrac{\left[(n_e - 1)(S_e)^2\right] + \left[(n_c - 1)(S_c)^2\right]}{n_e + n_c - 2}}}$$

The theory underlying Glass's ES is based on the assumption that outcomes are normally distributed so that a Z-table can be used to determine the percentile rank of the average person in the experimental group. The interpretation of ES, then, is the standardized mean difference between two groups or the mean difference in standard deviation units. Effect size (ES) is constructed to show the overlap in the distributions of scores for the groups so that a positive effect size means the experimental group did better on the average than the control group and a negative effect size indicates the control group did better. Thus, an ES of +1 suggests that the average person in the experimental group (assuming pretest comparability of scores between the E and C group) is about 1 standard deviation above the average person in the control group. Stated another way, the experimental conditions (i.e., treatment) presumably moved the typical client in the experimental group from the 50th percentile, where both groups are equal, to the 84th percentile of the control group; thus, the average experimental group client exceeded 84 percent of the control group clients on the particular outcome measure evaluated.

So, as further examples, an ES of 1.41 means the average E group client scored above 92 percent of C group members, an ES of .23 means the average E group client scored above 59 percent of the C group members, an ES of −1 means the average E group member scored higher than only 16 percent of the C group (i.e., the C group did better), and an ES of 0 means both groups were equal (the average E group client scored better than 50 percent of the C group).

In Glass's approach, the unit of analysis is each outcome measure in each study, that is, the study's findings. Thus, if a study has several outcome measures, it will have several ES's and it will be represented more frequently in the overall meta-analysis. To get an overall ES for all the measures in all the studies in a meta-analysis, Glass simply takes the mean of all ES's. Because different samples from the same population do not produce exactly the same mean, Glass also calculates the standard error of the mean to reflect how variable the different sample means might be. Small standard errors are viewed as better than larger ones; thus, if the standard error of the mean for the ES's of one type of therapy (Type A) is .05 and for another (Type B) is .25, it could be said that the mean for Type A is nearer its true mean that is Type B's since the standard error of Type B is five times greater. Glass also uses the standard error to look at the mean difference between ES's, so that a mean difference equal to two standard errors is used as a guideline to interpret nonrandom differences between two ES's (Smith, Glass, and Miller, 1980, pp. 89–90).

Since many individual studies do not report means and standard deviations, Glass and his colleagues have developed a number of creative ways of transforming scores to derive ES's. These methods include a range of procedures for solving equations from different parametric and nonparametric statistics,[1] plus probit transformations for dichotomous variables (percentages, etc.) (described in Glass, McGaw, and Smith, 1981).

The third step in Glass's approach is to examine the data for possible relationships among a number of potential independent variables and the overall effect sizes. This is accomplished by coding any number of variables that could have affected overall ES and using such parametric statistics as multiple regression to

---

[1] For two groups only:

$$t \text{ to } d : d = \frac{2t}{\sqrt{df(n_1 + n_2 - 2)}}$$

$$F \text{ to } d : d = \frac{2\sqrt{F}}{\sqrt{df \text{ (error)}}}$$

df (error) = subtract 1 from each group and sum up

examine the relationship. Thus, size of study, differences in setting, number of sessions, type of outcome measure, and so on are examined to see if they affect the variability in the findings of the meta-analysis.

Study Effect Meta-Analysis The second type of meta-analysis is called study effect meta analysis (SEM) by Bangert-Drowns (1986). This approach was developed by Mansfield and Busse (1977), and carried out in a number of examples by Kulik and his colleagues, largely on educational outcomes (e.g., Bangert-Drowns, Kulik, and Kulik, 1983; Kulik and Bangert-Drowns, 1983/1984; Kulik, Kulik, and Cohen, 1979; Landman and Dawes, 1982).

This approach was conceived, in part, to overcome what were seen as problems in Glass's approach. Rather than focusing on the study finding as the unit of analysis as Glass does, SEM uses the study per se as the focus. Thus, if a given study has more than one outcome measure, the effect sizes related to each separate dependent variable are combined. For example, a study with two dependent variables—say, self-esteem and marital satisfaction—could use several measures of each. The SEM would combine the outcome measures for each dependent variable by averaging them to form a single ES. If more than one dependent variable is present, the average effect size is combined to form a single ES for each study. No matter how many outcome measures are used in a study, that study would yield only one ES, suggesting that the study itself rather than the individual findings is the unit of analysis.

The rationale for this approach is in part based on the attempt to keep the overall results of a meta-analysis from being biased by a few studies that could each produce numerous outcomes compared to other studies that have only one outcome measure. Similarly, by not using ES's from each outcome measure, SEM purports to avoid the possibility of one type of nonindependence of the resulting data. This in turn allows the use of statistical procedures with greater confidence.

It generally appears as though SEM is more rigorous in selecting studies for inclusion than Glass's approach. Typically, if threats to internal validity are present in a study, SEM would tend to exclude that study, where Glass, perhaps, might include it but try to control for methodological rigor by a coding scheme that allows a regression analysis to look at the effect of methodological rigor on ES.

On the other hand, since only one ES is calculated per study and strict inclusion standards are used, this could yield rather small samples that would limit further analyses and conclusions. It also suggests the importance of rigorous, consistent standards in judging studies to avoid bias in selection, although the same criticism applies not only to Glass's coding scheme for assessing rigor, but to other reviewers' selection criteria as well.

In many ways, however, SEM is similar to the Glass approach. Both use similar procedures to determine ES, both attempt to code a variety of features and analyze them as independent variables to determine their impact on overall ES, and both attempt to evaluate what the literature says about the effectiveness of one or more interventions.

Combined Probability Method   Over the last decade, Rosenthal and his colleagues have developed some meta-analytic methods that not only examine ES, but examine statistical significance by combining probabilities (Rosenthal, 1976, 1978, 1983; Rosenthal and Rubin, 1982a, 1982b, 1986). These methods have been used to review a number of areas, particularly in the field of social psychology and education (e.g., Rosenthal and Rubin, 1978; Cooper 1979; Arkin, Cooper, and Kolditz, 1980; Dusek and Joseph, 1983). Rosenthal's approach is continuously evolving, incorporating the work of others on methodological refinements of certain aspects of meta-analysis as they become available. Thus, the overview here will touch on only certain key characteristics.

In one of his earliest reports, Rosenthal (1978) reviewed a number of methods for combining probabilities. These probabilities are obtained from independent studies in order to develop an overall level of significance for the results of several studies examining the same hypothesis. These methods were: adding logs, adding probabilities, adding t's, adding Z's, adding weighted Z's, testing the mean p, testing the mean Z, counting, and blocking (combining into an overall ANOVA with the studies as a blocking variable). While Rosenthal argued that different techniques have different advantages under special circumstances, he generally favored the method of adding Z's (with the caveat that with a small number of studies, at least two other methods should also be reported; Rosenthal, 1978). Rosenthal suggests use of this method largely because it is rather simple and routinely applicable.

Counting Z's, also known as Stouffer's Z, is computed by calculating a one-tailed probability level for each study, and then listing its corresponding standard normal deviate or Z. If more than one outcome measure is used, the average Z score associated with the p levels of each outcome measure can be used. The Z scores can then be summed across studies and divided by the square root of the number of studies to produce an overall Z score that reflects the overall probability that the combined results of the studies could have occurred by chance (Hazelrigg, Cooper, and Borduin, 1987). As a simple example (Rosenthal, 1983), suppose in two studies with significant results, study A has a one-tailed p of .05 and study B has a one-tailed p of .0000001, but in the opposite direction. The Z's that correspond to these p's in a table of the normal curve are -1.64 and 5.20. The computations then would be

$$\frac{Z_1 + Z_2}{\sqrt{2}} \text{ or } \frac{(-1.64) + (5.20)}{1.41} = 2.52.$$

The p value associated with a Z of 2.52 is .006 (one-tailed), supporting the results of the more significant of the two outcomes.[2] The overall Stouffer's Z, then, defines the probability that the pooled subjects would be distributed among treatments as they are in the collected studies (Bangert-Drowns, 1986).

To make this Stouffer's Z somewhat more intuitively understandable, a "fail-safe

---

[2] That is, a significant Z shows that the combined effect of all studies is significant.

N" can be calculated based on an extension of Stouffer's Z (Rosenthal, 1979; Cooper, 1979). The fail-safe N refers to the number of studies of no (null) effect that would have to be added to the known studies to raise the combined probability to nonsignificance. (This refers to studies of null effect, not negative effect, a smaller number of which could have the same impact—overall nonsignificance). This fail-safe N can be seen as a measure of stability of the findings of the meta-analysis in relation to possibly unretrieved studies (Hazelrigg, Cooper, and Borduin, 1987).

Rosenthal also routinely recommends computation of an ES. He uses either Cohen's d (described earlier) or Pearson's r and the coefficient of determination (r^2, the proportion of variance in one variable associated with or accounted for by the other variable). When using r (the correlation between the independent variable, say intervention, and the study outcome), Rosenthal computes r and the associated Z, then adds the Z's and divides by the number of studies to form a mean Z ($\bar{Z}$) that corresponds to the mean r. Then, an r to Z or Z to r table is used to look up the r associated with the mean Z.

Because there often seems to be a problem with interpretation of r and r^2, Rosenthal and Rubin (1982c) developed what they call the Binomial Effect Size Display (BESD). The BESD is an effect size display that purports to show the effect on success rate of the implementation of a particular intervention. The BESD is based on the binomial distribution, but Rosenthal and Rubin (1983) present evidence to show it is useful for both dichotomized or continuous variables that can be dichotomized. The BESD shows that what might be considered a negligible r of .32 that would account for "only 10 percent of the variance" (r^2), is actually equivalent to increasing the success rate from 34 percent to 66 percent by means of a given intervention. An ES such as d or Δ can be converted to r (Rosenthal and Rubin, 1986; Glass, McGaw, and Smith, 1981; Hedges, 1982a, 1982c), and then examined in the BESD to aid in interpretation of ES. The general purpose BESD is abbreviated in table 15.1 (Rosenthal and Rubin, 1986):

All of the previously mentioned procedures are integrated into what might be seen as a typical format, illustrated most recently by the meta-analysis of family therapy outcome by Hazelrigg, Cooper, and Borduin (1987). First, all the relevant studies in a particular area are collected. Next, the one-tailed p values and their corresponding Z values are calculated. If more than one outcome measure is used in a study, the average of these Z scores is used, thereby ensuring that each study

Table 15.1 Binomial effect size display

		Success rate increased		Differences in
r	r^2	From	To	success rates
.10	.01	.45	.55	.10
.20	.04	.40	.60	.20
1.00	1.00	.00	1.00	1.00

contributes equally to the combined p. Next, the ES for each study is calculated, using either r or, more frequently, Cohen's d. (An additional advantage of d is that it is associated with a measure of distribution overlap, called U_3. The U_3 presents the percentage of people in the group with the lower mean score who are surpassed by the average person in the group with the higher mean scores. Thus, with a d of .25 indicating the E group was one quarter of a standard deviation better than the C group, U_3 would be equal to .60, meaning that the average person in the E group did better than 60 percent of the C group; Hazelrigg, Cooper, and Borduin, 1987.)

Once the d's and Z's for the individual studies are computed, the mean ES and combined probabilities are calculated as described above. The d's simply are averaged to obtain the mean ES, and Stouffer's Z is calculated to examine the probability that the combined results from all the studies was due to chance. The BESD may be used to enhance understanding of the ES, and the fail-safe N would be calculated to enhance understanding of the combined Z.

It would also be possible to compute a measure of the homogeneity of effect sizes in the group of studies (Rosenthal, 1984). However, this procedure will be discussed in the subsequent section. In addition, if there are multiple effect sizes in the individual studies due to multiple dependent variables, a new set of procedures described by Rosenthal and Rubin (1986) can be used. These procedures, requiring in addition to the individual ES or p levels only the degrees of freedom in the study and the typical intercorrelation among the variables, can be used to obtain a single summary ES from multiple ES's. They can also be used to test the significance of this summary ES, and to compute the ES for a contrast and its significance level among the multiple ES's of a single study.

Overall, Rosenthal's approach focuses on two units of analysis: the study, with computation of the average d, and the individual subject in combining probabilities because the individual Z's are already sensitive to sample size. As Bangert-Drowns (1986) suggests, there does not seem to be rigorous attention to differences in methodology in the individual studies selected, nor is there any attempt to use parametric statistics to examine relationships among specific characteristics of the studies and overall ES's or combined probabilities. Thus, more subtle analyses of the studies are not undertaken. Indeed, it may be that Rosenthal's methods lead to increasing focus on conclusions about large samples of subjects, which are similar to the purposes of the next two methods of meta-analysis.

Data Pooling with Tests of Homogeneity   This approach to meta-analysis, exemplified in work by Hedges (1982a; 1982b; Hedges and Olkin, 1985) and Rosenthal and Rubin (1982a; Rosenthal, 1984), is an attempt to use a study's statistics to approximate the pooling of all the subjects from all the studies in a single, large comparison. In other words, this use of meta-analysis is an attempt to approximate data pooling (Bangert-Drowns, 1986).

This perspective suggests the importance of certain methodological implications (Bangert-Drowns, 1986). First, given the focus on pooling across studies, not only must the researcher be concerned with variability across studies but with variability associated with the ES in each study. Second, since independent and dependent variables as well as sampling units are not the same across studies, the researcher must be concerned with whether or not the group of effect sizes is homogeneous to determine whether variation among effect sizes is due merely to sampling error or to nonchance variables. Then, if the effect sizes as a group are found to be homogeneous, they can be averaged without undue concern.

In order to examine homogeneity of effect sizes, Hedges (1982a; Hedges and Olkin, 1985) has developed a test for the homogeneity of effect sizes. Designated as H, Hedges' (1982a) test of homogeneity represents the variability among study outcomes as the sum of squared differences between each ES and the weighted average ES. The ratio (H) of this sum of squared differences to the sum of sampling variances in all the ES's is shown to be distributed as chi square. This chi square test of homogeneity is accomplished by combining ES measures across studies and testing the homogeneity of variance for each class of dependent variables. If H is not significant, suggesting the data are homogeneous and come from a common population, then no further breakdown is necessary and effect sizes can be pooled across studies and a mean ES can be reported and tested statistically to see if it is significantly different from zero. If, on the other hand, H is significant, suggesting the effect sizes are heterogeneous, then they should not be pooled because the ES's are not estimating the same parameter. Instead, possible moderator variables can be tested individually using ES's associated with each variable. The analogy here might be to analysis of variance (ANOVA) in that post hoc tests are not performed unless the primary test is significant.

Related to Hedges' test of homogeneity is the formula proposed by Rosenthal and Rubin (1982a; Rosenthal, 1984) for testing for significant differences among ES's in a heterogeneous group. In essence, this approach is analogous to contrasts in ANOVA in that the sum of normally weighted ES's is distributed as a standard normal deviate. Then, this Z simply is tested for statistical significance.

The unit of analysis for these tests of homogeneity appears to be the subject, with the overall focus being on average ES's for homogeneous groups. There appears to be a general willingness to include in these meta-analyses a wide range of studies with substantial variations in methodology and experimental variables. Then, the test of homogeneity is used to determine whether or not this diverse group of studies produces homogeneous or heterogeneous outcomes. The approach is not recommended when the outcome measures are not related, and its reliability is uncertain when the samples under consideration are small or nonnormal. Nevertheless, tests of homogeneity do address one aspect of meta-analytic method that other approaches have not fully explored.

Data Pooling with Sampling Error Correction (Psychometric Approach)   The last approach to meta-analysis is one developed by Hunter and Schmidt (1978; Hunter, Schmidt, and Jackson, 1982). Their meta-analysis approach basically is an attempt to examine certain artifacts that they say account for the largest part of variation in findings across studies. These artifacts are sampling error, variation in criterion reliability, variation in test reliability, and variation in range restriction.

The approach of Hunter and Schmidt is similar to the previous one (data pooling with tests of homogeneity), although Hunter and Schmidt do not use specific tests of homogeneity. Hunter and Schmidt first collect as many studies as possible on the question of interest, including a wide range of studies of varying methodological adequacy. They develop one ES for each study, attempting to correct the ES's for un- reliability or other artifacts when the necessary information is available in a study.

They next use calculations that are similar to those used by the previous method of data pooling with tests of homogeneity to determine the overall variability of ES's. They calculate the sum of squared differences between each ES and the estimated population effect that is then weighted by proportional sample sizes. Their calculation of variation attributable to sampling error is next and is similar to Hedges', though Hunter and Schmidt do not test specifically for homogeneity, at least in the same way. Instead, they take the total variation and subtract variation due to sampling error. If this removes roughly 75 percent of the overall variation, Hunter and Schmidt assume the ES's are homogeneous (i.e., the effect sizes esti- mate one parameter), and mediating variables need not be examined.

However, if after correcting for sampling error the variation is still large, Hunter and Schmidt recommend examination of mediating variables. This is done by cod- ing possible independent variables such as study and experimental conditions, in a way similar to Glass's approach, so that the effect of those variables can be in- vestigated. Two methods of doing this are available. The first is to divide ES's into groups based on these categories. If the variable really does exert an influence on outcome, the means of the categories should be different and their variation less than the variation for the combined group. The second possibility is to develop correlations between these variables and ES's to look at their possible relationship (Bangert-Drowns, 1986).

An important by-product of this approach is to use the overall mean and stan- dard deviation, corrected for statistical artifacts, and the identified mediating vari- ables in a multiple regression analysis, again along the same lines as recommended by Glass. This will provide more detailed information about experimental effects.

This approach to meta-analysis combines certain aspects of several others. It focuses on development of conclusions based on large groups of subjects as do the approaches of data pooling with tests of homogeneity of Hedges and of Rosenthal and Rubin. Rather than testing for statistical significance, though, it focuses on real measures of variation, sampling error, and artifactual or mediating variables. It also allows for use of regression models to examine possible effects of a range of study and experimental (treatment) variables.

A Generic Model of Meta-Analysis

Despite a number of distinctions among the different methods of meta-analysis, it is possible to distill out from these approaches some salient features that can be incorporated into a kind of model of the meta-analytic process. This model is an attempt to simplify and integrate what may have appeared as rather diverse options in the preceding section. Each of the steps of the model is developed in more detail in earlier reviews by Jackson (1980) and Cooper (1982).

Stage 1. Formulate the Problem   In this stage, the purpose of the review is developed, and the questions and hypotheses are formulated. Such issues as the types of evidence that should be included in the review are addressed. Definitions and operational definitions that distinguish relevant from irrelevant studies for inclusion in the review are developed.

Stage 2. Collect Data   The researcher decides what population of studies will be selected and the procedures to be used to locate relevant studies. It is best at this stage to collect as many studies as possible—both published and unpublished—to protect against a nonrepresentative group of studies.

Stage 3. Evaluate the Studies   In this stage, the reviewer establishes the criteria for including and excluding studies in the review. As in the stages above, this decision can radically affect the nature and conclusions of the review. These quality criteria are then applied to select the actual studies upon which the meta-analysis will be carried out. Obviously, stages two and three have the key effect on the extent to which the studies reviewed are representative.

Stage 4. Analyze the Studies   The first part of stage four is to develop and apply a coding scheme to identify salient characteristics of the studies for analysis. The next step is to select and apply one or more of the methods of meta-analysis described in the previous section, synthesizing the (usually) large amounts of data available.

Stage 5. Interpreting the Results   In this stage, the reviewer interprets the results of the meta-analysis. Because of the relative newness of meta-analytic methods, it would be especially helpful for reviewers to try to establish in advance the criteria and rules of evidence they will be using to interpret their results. This would permit others to more objectively evaluate the results.

Stage 6. Report the Review   The reviewer reports the results of his or her analysis in journal articles and public presentations. Like any other piece of research, it is incumbent upon the reviewer to present enough detailed information about the methodology used in the review to make it possible for others to not only thoroughly understand the entire review process, but to replicate it if they so desire.

As can be readily seen from examining those six stages, the meta-analytic process is really no different from—and should be no more nor less mysterious than—any other research project. The main apparent difference is in stage four, the analysis of data. In fact, while this meta-analytic aggregation of data across studies is somewhat unique, it is in reality only a variation of other forms of statistical analyses of primary data. Thus, as Jackson (1982) points out, it is incumbent upon the meta-analyst to pay the same attention to rigorous methodology and reporting standards as those that should be adhered to by other researchers.

Benefits of Meta-Analysis

As can be inferred from all of the preceding discussion, there are numerous potential benefits that can accrue to both the research and practice enterprises in social work from use of meta-analysis. Some of these benefits are:

1. Meta-analysis efficiently summarizes large bodies of literature. With the huge outpouring of research in the social and behavioral sciences and the helping professions, it is extremely difficult to develop a traditional, narrative review that succinctly and cogently summarizes those data. Meta-analysis is precisely designed to do just that, integrating scores of study outcomes and processes in a manageable format.
2. Meta-analysis is able to develop a common metric for transforming disparate data from a number of different studies into a format for easy comparison.
3. Meta-analysis adds to the potential rigor and objectification of research reviews by providing quantitative, rigorous analyses of outcomes. These analyses can overcome the more subjective analyses of traditional, narrative reviews. Further, meta-analysis can increase statistical power by combining results from several studies into a single analysis.
4. Meta-analysis can examine relationships and trends that are too subtle to be otherwise located (Green and Hall, 1984). Statistical analysis of the data across studies allows the meta-analyst to discover what factors, substantive or methodological, may be associated with various outcomes.
5. Meta-analysis not only allows general, overall conclusions to be reached about a body of research, but also the study of interactions among studies, testing hypotheses that individual studies and traditional reviews cannot, such as the effect of different theoretical orientations on a range of outcomes.
6. Meta-analysis, because of its focus on quantification of variables, pressures researchers, theoreticians, and practitioners to conceptualize more sharply and to examine the empirical evaluation of interventions more critically (Fiske, 1983). By requiring clear specification of variables, ordered classification of varying categories (types of client problems, treatments, etc.), and clear explication in the primary research report, meta-analysis focuses attention on continuing problems of vagueness and obtuse reporting in the social and behavioral sciences and human services.
7. Meta-analysis can specifically point to gaps in the literature, thereby leading to selection of more focused and meaningful new directions for research.
8. Meta-analysis can contribute to the quality of subsequent research by high-

lighting criteria for quality of research and by illustrating research methods that appear to have been most successful in earlier investigations.

These benefits of meta-analysis are far from trivial and constitute major advances in the art and science of research reviewing. However, the benefits of meta-analysis do make an important assumption: that meta-analysis will be applied properly and in error-free ways so that conclusions are untainted by inappropriate assumptions and/or methodological flaws in the meta-analysis itself. That this may not always be possible is discussed in the following section.

The Problems

The many potential contributions of meta-analysis to research reviewing and the relative newness of the meta-analysis enterprise make it absolutely crucial that potential problems in implementation of meta-analysis are openly debated. This can lead to a clearer evaluation of the prospects for social work of utilization of one or more of the meta-analytic methods available.

Unfortunately, there are a plethora of problems that are associated with meta-analysis. These range from questions about the basic assumptions of meta-analysis to issues regarding the statistical properties of some of the computations involved in meta-analysis. This section will describe a number of those potential problems, in the hope that highlighting them here will have a positive impact on the adaptation and use of meta-analytic procedures in social work. Since there are several major methods of meta-analysis as well as minor variants of some of them, each of the problems being discussed does not necessarily apply to all the methods. Where possible, these distinctions will be pointed out.

Much of the literature cited earlier in this chapter contains discussions of problems of meta-analysis; indeed, the number of problems or potential problems is large enough to be prohibitive of an exhaustive discussion of them all here. Thus, this section consists essentially of a summary of some of the major problems. More detailed discussion is available in references such as Glass, McGaw, and Smith (1981); Rosenthal (1984); Hunter, Schmidt, and Jackson (1982); Michelson (1985); Green and Hall (1984); Wortman (1983); *Journal of Consulting and Clinical Psychology* (1983); Light (1983a, 1983b); Searles (1985); Strube and Hartmann (1982, 1983); Strube, Gardner, and Hartman (1985); Wilson and Rachman (1983); and Wilson (1985). Because many of these criticisms have been debated back and forth in the literature—with this debate often rising (or lowering) to the level of invective—no attempt will be made to present every minute aspect of all sides of each debate. Instead, the purpose here simply is to establish the range of possible problems that could impede a meta-analytic review.

The problems will be grouped into four categories for discussion: (1) selecting a method of meta-analysis; (2) selecting studies for review; (3) meta-analytic statistics; and (4) interpretation of the results of meta-analysis. The purpose of such categorization is partly for convenience and partly heuristic. It allows grouping of issues with some conceptual similarities, although certainly some overlap exists among the categories. Thus, this categorization is less than definitive but somewhat more than arbitrary.

Selecting a Method of Meta-Analysis

Given the availability of several methods of meta-analysis, the obvious—key—question is: Which is the best method to use? Stated another way, how should one go about selecting a method of meta-analysis?

If selection of a method of meta-analysis is similar to the way scientists, researchers, and practitioners select their methods in other areas, then the answer to this question for most meta-analysts probably is that they will choose on the basis of the one they are first exposed to, feel most comfortable with, or other even vaguer criteria. And, in fact, given the recent origins of meta-analysis and the rather formidable defenses about the value of each by its originators, such criteria may be the only available at this time.

In an effort to overcome such problems, however, Bangert-Drowns (1986) has proposed some general guidelines for making the number of decisions that must be made in conducting a meta-analysis. These guidelines are summarized here.

Purpose.   The reviewer first decides on the purpose of his or her review. If the purpose is largely to describe a body of literature, then perhaps the Glass or SEM method might be best. If the purpose is to approximate an increased sample size in order to test a specific hypothesis and to determine a generalizable treatment effect, then the methods of data pooling with tests of homogeneity may be best.

Treatment of Study Variation.   There are three kinds of data variation to consider. The first is differences in research quality, with Glass's method being the most liberal and SEM being among the most strict. The second is a consideration of whether to mix both independent variables (e.g., including studies that test different approaches to clinical practice) and dependent variables. Again, Glass appears to be the most liberal of the meta-analysts in including a range of theoretical orientations and outcome measures, while SEM attempts to analyze different dependent variables separately. The third issue regarding variation is management of outcome variance. This can be handled by one of two ways. The first is by treating each study or study finding as a single data point and using statistics to relate characteristics of the studies to outcomes (Glass and SEM). The second way to handle this is to consider each ES as a summary statistic with its own sampling error and to account for it, as in data pooling with or without tests of homogeneity.

Unit of Analysis.   Here the reviewer has to decide whether the focus will be on the study itself, or the study finding, or the subject, with Glass using the study finding, SEM using the study, the combined probability method using the study for ES and the subject for combined probability, and the data pooling methods using the subject as the unit of analysis.

Outcomes of Analysis.   The outcomes of analyses are obviously a function of the method used. All methods of meta-analysis produce an ES. But in addition, the different methods offer: comparison of effect sizes in preestablished categories (Glass and SEM); combined probabilities and fail-safe N (combined probability method); use of regression models to establish predictors of outcome (Glass, SEM, and data pooling with sampling error correction); effect sizes for homogeneous groups (data pooling with tests of homogeneity); and variation attributable to sampling error and evaluation of mediating variables (data pooling with sampling error correction).

As can be readily seen from the above listing, these guidelines are both complicated and not absolute. Decisions have to be made by reviewers at several levels, and in fact, a given meta-analysis could end up using procedures from more than one method. Even the use of such guidelines does not prevent subjectivity in selection of a method. Thus, selection of a method is viewed here as a considerable problem for meta-analysis reviewers, accounting for its inclusion in this section.

Selecting Studies for Review

Several issues are included in this category. They are: combining divergent studies, methodological quality of the primary research, sampling bias due to unpublished studies, the effects of deficient reporting, and other limitations imposed by the primary studies.

Combining Divergent Studies   Although the main purpose of meta-analysis is to synthesize results from a number of different studies, this has been criticized as being inappropriate conceptually and/or methodologically. Called the apples and oranges problem, this criticism cuts to the heart of meta-analysis, arguing at the most basic level that it makes no sense to integrate (like apples and oranges) the findings of different studies (Glass, McGaw, and Smith, 1981).

Broken down into its component parts, the apples and oranges problem has at least three aspects, involving issues regarding: (1) combining studies of divergent methodological adequacy (because of its significance this will be discussed in a separate section); (2) combining different independent variables; and (3) combining different dependent variables.

The issue regarding combining of independent variables is one of construct validity in that the question can be raised that when more than one independent variable (say, theoretical orientation) is examined in a single meta-analysis, it could obscure differences among subcategories (Presby, 1978). For example, eighteen (nineteen, including placebo) therapy types were examined by Smith, Glass, and Miller (1980); this was made even more problematic by collapsing them into superclasses of therapies called behavioral, verbal, and developmental. Thus, the question of whether such categories represent true, underlying constructs possibly blurs distinctions and diminishes the practical and theoretical relevance of such an analysis. Similarly, the constraints on external validity would be considerable. In other words, of what importance is it that the average ES for verbal therapies is .85 and for developmental therapies is .42?

Perhaps, as suggested by Glass, McGaw, and Smith (1981), the answer to these questions lies in the purpose of the reviewer. If the reviewer wishes to make broad, global statements about the effectiveness of some set of interventions as a way of informing policy decisions, or even simply wishes to summarize a body of literature in a fairly global fashion, then the issue of construct validity can be assessed against that reviewer's purpose and hypotheses to establish the validity of the categories selected. In addition, subsequent analyses can be conducted breaking down the overall ES into ES's related to the specific categories.

The main dangers of this approach are that such global answers to problems could lead to an unwarranted laxity and decreased motivation for critical thinking on the part of practitioners in a field of study if they hear that, overall, some global intervention (e.g., psychotherapy) is effective. It is all too easy to attempt inappropriately to transfer such global conclusions to one's specific approach to practice. Furthermore, such broad conceptualizations could lead to development of poorly formulated hypotheses in future research in which a range of independent variables are targeted for analysis. Thus, questions that are particularly relevant to particular groups of problems or clients may get overlooked.

The second part of this problem, combining different dependent variables, has been dealt with in two major ways. The first is to use a separate ES for each outcome measure (as in Glass's approach) and the second is to combine or pool related outcome measures. The consequences of this decision are significant. If one calculates an ES for each outcome measure, then it is difficult to interpret their combined effect. What is it that would be measured if the conclusion of meta-analysis on 565 separate effect sizes (one for each outcome measure) was that therapy X produces an overall ES of 1.29 on. . . . ? It is difficult to know just what is being affected.

Indeed, a study by Burns (1981; cited in Bangert-Drowns, 1986) showed that some individual studies can seriously distort the overall meta-analysis when an ES is calculated for each measure. Burns (1981) found a total of 413 ES's from thirty-three studies, but the range of ES's per study was from 1 to 120. Thus, a given study that uses several outcome measures can exert undue influence on the overall meta-analysis by virtue of the number of measures it uses.

This contributes to what might be called the problem of inflated n's. Since a single study can be overrepresented because of its many outcome measures, it can affect the external validity of a meta-analysis. That is, it is difficult to know what the target population is because the sample is so distorted.

To make this even more complicated, since the mean ES is used (average of all the ES's in a review), and the mean is affected by extreme scores, a study that contributes disproportionately large or small effect sizes can also distort the results. Thus, one study with ten large effect sizes can produce an overall moderate ES when averaged with ten very low ES's from ten studies. This would give a false impression of moderate effectiveness when, in fact, in this example, only one study showed effectiveness and ten did not.

Similarly, the use of a separate ES for each outcome measure violates the statistical principle of the assumption of independence, thereby producing possibly unreliable results (this is discussed in more detail elsewhere in this section).

On the other hand, averaging different measures into a single ES also presents problems (Wilson, 1985). Since different measures often respond differentially to the same treatment, pooling the measures may distort or destroy such differential effects. Thus, failure to attend to the conceptual relevance of individual measures produces possibly meaningless averages.

In a similar vein, Paul (1985) has illustrated how averaging measures into a single ES can destroy important differences. Using data from an earlier study (Paul, 1966), he demonstrated that the mean ES showing the advantage of systematic desensitization over placebo treatment on two key scales was .45. However, the mean of all measures was .04, illustrating perhaps the problem for interpretation as well as calculation of pooling outcome measures into a single ES.

One possibility when considering pooling of effect sizes is to examine the pooled effects in comparison with the studies with the best designs that are included in the sample. If the results appear to diverge substantially, perhaps pooling is not the best choice. Similarly, if the range of measures and effects is diverse, pooling is probably not recommended. It is also possible to test for heterogeneity of the pooling by using the procedures recommended by Hedges and Olkin (1985) for testing sets of effect sizes for homogeneity to see if pooling is appropriate.

While the choices here between using separate effect sizes for each measure or pooling measures may leave the reviewer feeling "damned if you do and damned if you don't," the reality of such constraints must be addressed by each reviewer whose rationale for a method can then be appropriately evaluated.

Methodological Quality of Primary Research   One of the most serious problems of all in meta-analysis—among several serious problems—is the issue of limitations due to variations in the methodological adequacy of the primary studies. Most basically, what this means is that inclusion of primary studies with methodological flaws can produce meta-analytic conclusions that also are flawed. In other words, "garbage in, garbage out." This is such a crucial problem that many of the critiques of meta-analysis previously cited spend a considerable portion of their space attempting to deal with it (see also Erwin, 1984).

The two major issues involved in this problem are the definition of quality and deciding what to do about studies of varying quality (Strube, Gardner, and Hartmann, 1985). The first issue is more or less subjective. That is, one might define high quality as any study that has random assignment and a control group. Someone else might argue that even those two conditions are insufficient without the addition of a placebo group. Others might argue that the lower limit of quality would include rigorous (say, matched but not randomly assigned) quasi-experiments. Of course, even if the most rigorous standards are applied (randomly assigned experiment with control and placebo groups), it is obvious that implementation of the design could pose numerous other problems, such as measurement or provision of treatments at different time intervals. This opens up the design to several other threats to internal validity: differential mortality; nonintegrity of treatment (lack of comparability among practitioners in implementation of treatments); differential times of exposure to treatments and/or placebos; differential levels of enthusiasm, warmth, empathy, or other interpersonal skills among practitioners; and so on. The flaws that could result from these problems range from mild to severe and could result in any number of threats to the internal validity of a study. It is also quite clear that different reviewers will have different criteria and that few will expend the time and energy in analyzing the primary studies that are required to ferret out all of these possible flaws, any of which could seriously affect the conclusions of a meta-analysis.

Be that as it may, the next decision a meta-analyst has to make is what to do about these variations in quality. Two general decisions have been made in the meta-analysis literature. The first is to attempt to exclude studies with methodological deficiencies and the second is to attempt to code them and analyze the impact of study quality on overall outcome.

The first approach—to exclude studies of poor quality—is best represented by the SEM method, which attempts to be as rigorous as possible in inclusion criteria. Unfortunately, while methodological inadequacies such as no random assignment, control, or placebo group can be rather easily detected and studies without them excluded, it is virtually impossible to find a meta-analysis that has been thorough enough to rule out studies that contain some of the other flaws previously described. On top of that, ruling out some studies that appear methodologically inferior (at least to a particular reviewer) could lead to omission of very important information that will affect the overall conclusion of the review. Among other reasons, this is because methodological flaws do not necessarily invalidate a study's conclusions; they only diminish the confidence one can have in such conclusions.

The second approach, coding of quality and examining the impact of quality on outcome through a regression model, is exemplified by Glass's approach. Recognizing that internal validity can affect a study's findings, Glass, McGaw, and Smith (1981) argue that this is an empirical question and that meta-analysis can handle the problem by analyzing the effect of threats to internal validity on ES. Thus, studies may be coded as high, medium, or low on internal validity and then this is examined as an independent variable. Indeed, Glass, McGaw, and Smith (1981) argue that this method supports a conclusion that "many weak studies can add up to a strong conclusion" (p. 221).

The problem is, can a coding system such as Glass's really handle the issue? In the first place, such a coding system is likely to be as subjective as the inclusion criteria discussed earlier, so that it may not reliably (or validly) capture the range of threats to internal validity. Second, such a system is a rather global and indirect way of dealing with the variety of specific threats to internal validity, and as such, cannot properly eliminate such threats. Third, an overabundance of studies with methodological flaws in a given sample of studies (as is likely to be the case upon close examination in many areas of research) will not provide an adequate basis for comparison of studies of varying quality. Fourth, the results of such an analysis only reveal whether there is a difference among studies of varying methodological adequacy; it does not even address the issue of whether the reported results in a study are valid. And finally, it is likely that no amount of massaging of the data can turn a deficient database into a useful meta-analytic conclusion.

In all, whatever approach the meta-analyst chooses in this arena is likely to produce problems. It may be that one possibility is to attempt to use rigorous criteria of inclusion and then to also code for minor methodological inadequacies to determine their impact on ES. It would also be possible to do a separate meta-analysis of the excluded studies to examine their impact on outcome. Whatever the meta-analyst does decide, the criteria should be made clear and explicit and the method of research analysis thoroughly described. The bottom line, though, is that the field of meta-analysis has yet to convincingly demonstrate methods of analysis that can overcome basic limitations in the database of primary studies.

Sampling Bias Due to Unpublished or Undiscovered Studies A key limitation in conducting any research review (meta-analysis or otherwise) is the fact that studies in the review may or may not (but probably not) be representative of all the studies conducted in a given area. This is a result of two problems: (1) the reviewer may not have done an adequate job in finding all the published research; and (2) there is a potentially huge body of research on any given topic that was conducted but never published. The latter problem has been dubbed the "file drawer problem" (Rosenthal, 1979) in that many studies that were never published were said to be tucked away in file drawers. Overall, this potential sample bias could operate in two ways: (1) the magnitude of effects and significance levels may not be representative; and (2) the direction of effects may not be representative (Strube, Gardner, and Hartmann, 1985).

The first problem—not discovering the total number of published studies—might be illustrated by the Smith, Glass, and Miller (1980) report which claimed that "all controlled studies of the effectiveness of any form of psychotherapy formed the population of interest for this project" (p. 55). While the authors did place some minimal limitations on their definitions (p. 57), subsequent analysis found that possibly hundreds of controlled studies that were available at the time and that met their definition were omitted (Searles, 1985).

The second problem—unpublished studies—is at least in part a function of well-established evidence that publication policy is biased toward the reporting of statistically significant findings, and may also discriminate against studies that use novel methods or include novel theoretical variables (Strube, Gardner, and Hartmann, 1985). Those problems are so severe as to possibly exclude from most meta-analyses studies that have not reached statistical significance, seriously skewing the sample and hence the results. This is one possible reason for the results of so many meta-analyses to be positive, or positively biased (as discussed later in this chapter).

There have been some attempts to deal with this problem. Rosenthal's (1979) fail-safe N, which calculates the number of hypothetical no-effect studies that are needed to make an overall significant p nonsignificant, has been developed to be used when combining probabilities is the method of meta-analysis. More recently, Orwin (1983) developed a similar procedure for use in effect size analysis.

Both of these are a step forward in the attempt to deal with this problem. But neither is a substitute for an exhaustive search that produces all published and unpublished work. However, such efforts are extremely difficult and time-consuming. But if they are not demonstrably successful, it is more than likely that any given meta-analysis is reporting the results of a biased sample and is, therefore, in its conclusions, also biased.

Deficient Reporting   One of the key steps in meta-analysis is the coding of study characteristics so that the meta-analysis proper can be undertaken. The success of this coding depends on three variables: the customary reporting practices of the research area being integrated, the individual differences among the area's researchers (Orwin and Cordray, 1985), and the training (or effectiveness) of the coders. All of these problems become exaggerated when the primary information needed is missing or incomplete and is either estimated or transformed.

A recent study (Orwin and Cordray, 1985) examined part of this problem by examining just two sources of information that could influence reporting quality: interrater reliabilities and confidence judgments. Their study showed that both reliabilities and confidence judgments varied greatly across individual coding items and studies. Reanalysis incorporating reliability corrections and confidence judgments suggested that "deficient reporting injects considerable noise into meta-analytic data, which can lead to spurious conclusions regarding causes of effect sizes, adequacy of models, and related matters" (p. 144). In other words, just two of several potential sources of deficient reporting could seriously affect the overall conclusions of a meta-analysis.

Orwin and Cordray (1985) suggested ways in which meta-analysts can counter effects of deficient recording: (1) take coder reliability more seriously; (2) rate data quality and incorporate data quality information into analyses; and (3) consider alternate sources of information such as contacting the original investigators.

While any and all of these methods may be helpful, the extent to which they can and will be implemented by meta-analysts is unknown. Yet such coding problems are at the heart of a successful meta-analysis. Indeed, the training of coders for meta-analysis and the extent to which such phenomena as observer drift occur in meta-analytic reviews typically is unreported. If this, in fact, means it also is not attended to with special care, then the problems for the actual statistical analysis of data in a meta-analysis could be tremendous.

Limitations Imposed by Primary Studies   A number of other factors related to the primary studies can impose restrictions or lead to variations in interpretation of meta-analysis. Strube, Gardner, and Hartmann (1985) summarize these as limitations due to psychometric, methodological, and theoretical characteristics of the original studies.

Psychometric factors include such problems as measurement error (a concern specifically addressed by Hunter, Schmidt, and Jackson [1982] in their data pooling with sampling error correction approach) and validity of measurement. Variations in reliability and/or validity of variables in the primary studies can produce corresponding variation and resulting confused interpretation in the meta-analysis.

A second set of limitations on meta-analysis is imposed by methodological characteristics of the original study (other than quality, which was discussed previously). Thus, the goals of the primary researcher, the type of design (between versus within subject, experimental versus correlational), types of comparison conditions, nature of the control, and method of data analysis all will vary among studies. These variations are bound to have an influence on the meta-analysis, and can be significant contributors to variability in meta-analytic outcome.

The third characteristic of the primary research that can have an effect on meta-analysis is the theories that are used to inform the research. Theory typically guides selection of variables, both independent and dependent. This obviously means that a wide range of variables could be omitted from a substantial portion of the primary research, thus imposing potentially serious limitations on what can be concluded from that research.

The point of all this is that the final calculation and interpretation of a meta-analysis is not necessarily guided by the actual importance of the intervention (Strube, Gardner, and Hartmann, 1985). Although some of the other variables discussed here may be treated as artifacts and statistically analyzed (as in the meta-analysis approach of Hunter, Schmidt, and Jackson, 1982), the fact that so many of them are in operation imposes considerable constraints on what can be determined by a meta-analysis, especially of a broad range of psychometrically, methodologically, and theoretically different studies.

Meta-Analytic Statistics

The problems reviewed in this section are: the calculation of effect size, problems due to nonindependence of data, the issue of potential positive bias in meta-analysis, and the problem of using aggregated versus unaggregated data.

Calculation of Effect Size   The most commonly recommended procedures for estimating ES are Δ (Glass, McGaw, and Smith, 1981) and d (Cohen, 1977). This presents a problem as to which of those two is the best estimate. In fact, there is not uniform agreement among meta-analysts as to this issue. The basic differences are that Δ uses the standard deviation of the control group to scale the differences between group means, while d uses the pooled standard deviation. Glass, McGaw, and Smith (1981) argue that the standard deviation of the control group is the best choice because it has the advantage of assigning equal effect sizes to equal means since pooling could lead to different standardized values of identical mean differences in a study where several treatments are compared to a control. This is because sample standard deviations for different treatment groups will be different. Also, the computations for Δ are clear and easily calculated.

On the other hand, Hedges (1981, 1982a) argues that pooling of standard deviations is a more precise estimate since the assumption of homogeneity of variances for *populations* is reasonable, especially since two groups per experiment with equal population variances is typical in meta-analysis (Hedges and Olkin, 1985). Hedges (1981) also obtained a distribution for Δ, showing that it is positively biased; he developed a correction factor (K) that, when multiplied by the effect size, d, produces an unbiased ES. However, this correction factor is most important for smaller samples, so that when the sample size exceeds ten, the ES's with and without K virtually are identical (Hedges, 1982a).

If studies largely use correlational procedures such as r then these correlations can be used as the direct measure of ES. And, of course, t and F values can be readily transformed into r, though they also can be transformed into the other measures of ES. Similarly, Green and Hall (1984) suggest that when outcome measures are clearly identifiable and comparable across studies (e.g., the Stanford-Binet I.Q.), these measures can be used directly rather than resorting to an ES such as Δ or d.

A more serious complication arising from this problem has been demonstrated by Paul (1985). He has shown how using different methods to calculate ES on the same set of data results in vastly different findings. On one set of measures, Paul (1985) calculated ES's that ranged from 1.93 to 3.06 depending on whether pooled standard deviations or the standard deviation of the control group were used and depending also on whether the data were posttest only, prepost change data, or improvement scores. Not only might this be one factor accounting for the increasingly common phenomenon of divergent results of different meta-analyses applied to the same studies (Searles, 1985), but at best it leads to serious questions of over- or under-interpretation, depending solely on the meta-analytic method used.

In all then, at least with regard to the dispute between use of Δ and d, it appears as though d, with the correction factor K, for small samples is viewed by many meta-analysts outside of the Glass camp as the best estimate of ES. Again, however, there is still substantial disagreement among meta-analysts on this issue. Since Δ and d essentially are similar, the choice of which estimate of ES to be used—at least until further statistical analysis and proofs are available and become widely accepted—may depend more on the personal preferences of the individual meta-analyst and the type of estimates he or she wishes to discuss than on precise statistical theory.

Nonindependence of Data   Meta-analysis typically is carried out on large data sets deriving multiple results from the same study. This can produce the problem of nonindependence of data, throwing in jeopardy the reliability of estimates and raising serious questions about use of statistics that assume independence, such as the parametric statistics. In fact, Landman and Dawes (1982) describe five possible sources of nonindependence: (1) nonindependent samples across studies; (2) multiple measurement of the same subjects across time; (3) use of several measures with the same subjects; (4) nonindependence of scores in a single outcome measure (e.g., use of both a global outcome plus several subsets of items that comprise the global measure); and (5) nonindependence of studies (say, multiple experiments) within a given article.

The problem of nonindependence is recognized by Glass, McGaw, and Smith (1981) as particularly difficult to resolve. A number of solutions have been suggested, ranging from Tukey's jackknife procedure (Mosteller and Tukey, 1968), to averaging of effect sizes or significance levels to produce one per study (though this obscures within-study analyses), to simply ignoring the problem. In actual practice, the last solution, ignoring the problem, is by far the most frequently used. Apart from simply ignoring the problem, none of the proposed solutions adequately deals with the total range of nonindependence problems.

The problem can be immense. Glass, McGaw, and Smith (1981) showed that after taking nonindependence into account, a confidence interval ranged from .002 to .371, whereas a confidence interval when independence is just assumed ranged from –.10 to +.50, a difference of well over 300 percent.

Thus, this continues to be a most serious problem for meta-analysis. Indeed, the expected lack of reliability due to the inappropriate use of statistics that assume independence could be one of the factors responsible for the frequently discrepant findings of different meta-analyses on the same body of research. Meta-analysts will have to develop statistical procedures to more readily deal with this problem or, at the least, as Strube, Gardner, and Hartmann (1985) suggest, warn readers of the possible distortions in their conclusions.

Positive Bias   Meta-analyses may be positively biased. Across the wide range of meta-analytic reviews, especially in the area of psychotherapy, a vast majority of reviews have found positive effects. This is especially striking when those results are compared with more traditional, narrative reviews of similar research (Green and Hall, 1984).

This issue was particularly illuminated by a study by Cooper and Rosenthal (1980) in which graduate students and faculty members were randomly assigned to two methods of research review: traditional (narrative) and statistical (meta-analysis). Each group summarized the same seven studies on a single hypothesis. In essence, the meta-analytic reviewers found significantly more support for the hypothesis and estimated a significantly larger magnitude of effect than did traditional reviewers. Those conclusions were upheld across academic status and gender.

One possible reason for the existence of positive bias in meta-analysis lies in the construction of the meta-analytic effect size statistics such as Δ and d. It is easy to demonstrate how positive bias occurs: any difference between the experimental and control group where the experimental group mean is larger than the control group mean will yield a positive ES, even when the statistics in the primary analysis show that difference to be nonsignificant. When the standard deviation is relatively small, this ES can be of very large magnitude. For example, a nonsignificant mean difference of .5 between the experimental and control groups with a control group standard deviation of .25 would yield an ES of 2.0 using Glass's Δ. Thus, any sample of null studies is likely to produce a substantial number of positive effect sizes.

This is somewhat analogous to the power of conventional statistics in that, with everything else being equal, the larger the difference between the means and the smaller the variability, the greater the ES (although even a large standard deviation will produce a positive, albeit relatively small, ES when the experimental group mean is larger than the control group mean). The basic issue here, though, is that when the statistics in the primary analysis show the difference to be nonsignificant and thereby likely due to chance, and the ES statistics show a positive ES, this built-in positive bias in calculating ES (of what value is a positive ES when it may be due to chance?) typically leads to similarly inflated and possibly spurious meta-analytic conclusions.

This process is additionally complicated by the practice of combining several effect sizes. As Green and Hall (1984) point out, a string of weak or conflicting results might be discounted by a traditional reviewer, but might add up to a credible pattern for the meta-analytic reviewer. This could operate somewhat like the nonparametric sign test where a number of positive but nonsignificant findings could add up to an overall significant effect.

Of course, in addition to these reasons, the positive bias in meta-analysis—especially in comparison to traditional narrative reviews—could be a result of any of the problems reviewed in this section, acting alone or in interaction with the others to inflate the real relationship among the variables studied. But to the extent that such positive bias does exist in meta-analysis, it obviously could influence a field's perception of the strength of findings in that field, thus undermining support for future research. A complacency factor could set in. In addition, such bias may seriously undercut the major raison d'etre for meta-analysis: that it produces more objective results than traditional narrative reviews. Thus, the jury is still out on that issue.

Aggregated Versus Unaggregated Data   There are serious problems involved in aggregating data from individual studies when trying to draw conclusions about unaggregated phenomena. Stated another way, aggregating individual data to determine relationships at the group level can lead to error—or at least different conclusions. In part, this may be because there could be difference in error variance (discrepancies between individual and group covariation) when group data are used. Indeed, the use of aggregate data has been shown to produce a number of hazards, even in an individual study (Borgatta and Jackson, 1980). While problems of variation, including sampling error, have been addressed by Hunter, Schmidt, and Jackson (1982) in their method of data pooling with sampling error correction, their focus has not been on exactly this problem, or at least conceptualized in this way.

An example from a different area might illuminate this issue. Glisson (1986), examining the relationship between leadership and commitment in a number of organizations, found that when individual responses were the unit of analysis, the relationship was positive, but when individual responses were aggregated and group data were analyzed, the relationship was negative. This discrepancy probably was caused by the fact that there is greater within-group variation than between-group variation; that is, the characteristics of the individual have more influence on individual responses than do the characteristics of the group.

The question for meta-analysis is: are there similar systematic—or even unsystematic—changes introduced when one moves from analyzing a single study to aggregating the results of those individual studies?

Interpretation of the Results of Meta-Analysis

The final problems to be discussed are the interpretation of effect size and issues regarding causality in meta-analysis.

Interpretation of ES Since effect size, such as Δ or d, is so crucial to most meta-analysis, it may seem somewhat surprising that there is no real consensus about how to actually interpret the meaning of ES. This is especially true when only one, overall ES is reported and there is no test of statistical significance. Thus, while there is consensus about the conclusion that an ES of .25 means that the typical experimental group client exceeded the score of 59 percent of control group clients, the meaning beyond that is unclear. Of course, many meta-analysts would be comfortable in stopping with that demonstration. Others, though, might wonder just how meaningful an ES of .25 (or .10 or .97) actually is.

In an early work, Cohen (1962) suggested some rough guidelines for interpreting effect sizes as small, medium, or large; his rules of thumb were that a .2 ES was small, a .5 ES was medium, and a .8 ES was large. These suggestions recently were supported by Light (1983b).

Glass, McGaw, and Smith (1981) disagree with this reasoning. They propose instead more individualized interpretation. Thus, they argue some effect sizes are meaningful without comparison to anything else (such as a zero ES). Others can be interpreted by comparing them with known and familiar effects (e.g., by referencing them to effects of well-known interventions). They argue that as experience accumulates, particular magnitudes of ES will gain meaning by reference to what is typical in similar circumstances. Thus, if a certain drug is known to consistently produce effect sizes of .50 on standardized measures, then a new drug that consistently produces effect sizes of 1.00 is particularly meaningful.

The essence of this argument is that there is no inherent value to an ES of any given size because every ES must be validated in the context of what is typical, what is expected, and what is desired.

Unfortunately, this begs the question somewhat, and actually seems to undermine the elaborate statistical calculations that form the basis for ES. In other words, why go through all the complicated procedures if, when one finally calculates an ES, the final interpretation is subjective? This may even negate the benefits of meta-analysis over more traditional, narrative reviews.

It is perhaps too obvious an issue to wonder what should be done when there are no commonly accepted, standard, or typical bases, such as the effect sizes collected over time from several reviews of the same phenomenon. Indeed, it is as likely that the results of different independent meta-analyses of the same material could provide discrepant results (e.g., Smith, Glass, and Miller [1980] versus Andrews and Harvey [1981] versus Landman and Dawes [1982]).

Beyond that, the question becomes even more complicated when effect sizes within a single study are compared. Some authors routinely use parametric statistics such as ANOVA to compare mean differences between two or more ES's for statistical significance. Others, especially the Glass group, essentially use the criteria described previously (i.e., nonstatistical comparisons). This leads to several problems, such as use of qualifiers like relatively larger (ES), about equally effective, somewhat smaller (ES), and so on, with the reader left to interpret the meaning of those statements (e.g., Smith, Glass, and Miller, 1980). It also can lead to different interpretations of similar ES's within the same study. Thus, Smith, Glass, and Miller (1980) define the ES of .98 (S.E. of .05) for behavior therapy as "clearly superior" (p. 98) to the ES of .85 (S.E. of .04) for verbal therapies. But in other places in the same study, the same or even larger differences in ES are interpreted as not different. Thus, an ES of .69 (S.E. of .05) for psychodynamic therapy with neurotics was considered to be "the same magnitude of effect" (p. 90) as an ES of .90 (S.E. of .16) for psychodynamic therapy with psychotics. They also violated in both cases their rule that "a mean difference equal to two standard errors was used as a guideline for interpreting nonrandom differences between two effects" (p. 90). Such discrepant interpretations appear throughout this study.

The BESD table developed by Rosenthal and Rubin (1982c) is one way of attempting to standardize interpretation of effect sizes, and it is indeed useful. But it too still falls short of a way of judging the real or perhaps more accurately, statistical, significance of any given effect size.

The whole issue is made even more complicated by the fact that the same ES can be interpreted in a number of different ways. As Strube, Gardner, and Hartmann (1985) point out, a d of 1.0 can be interpreted in several ways: (1) the treated group has a mean outcome exceeding an untreated group by one standard deviation; (2) the treatment accounts for 20 percent of the variance in outcome; (3) 84.1 percent of the treated subjects can be expected to exceed the average untreated subject on the outcome measure (U_3); and (4) treatment increases the success rate for subjects by 44.7 percent (BESD). Since all of these descriptions really reflect the same underlying effect, it is crucial that meta-analysts not attempt to inflate or deflate their results according to their own biases by selecting a particular ES estimate. At the least, such a variety of interpretations can contribute to the confusion of journal readers trying to understand the complications of a meta-analysis.

In all, then, this crucial issue of substantive interpretation of effect size is one that must be addressed and clarified in subsequent research on, and refinement of, meta-analysis.

Issues Regarding Causality   Meta-analysts typically misinterpret their work, claiming that it is able to establish causal relationships among variables. This simply is not the case. As Cooper (1982) suggests, a review contains two different sources of evidence about the relations among variables. The first is from the individual studies where, in experiments, the researcher manipulates the independent variable to examine causality. The second is from the review itself, where the meta-analyst uses a variety of statistical methods to look for associations among variables.

The essence here is manipulation of variables. The only way to establish causality is to systematically manipulate independent variables to establish their relationship to dependent variables. Even if a meta-analytic review is based on rigorous experiments, since it does not systematically manipulate variables nor order them temporally, there is no basis for inferring which characteristics of studies reviewed actually cause different outcomes. In other words, even a large ES or significant combined probability does not provide conclusive evidence as to *why* such results were obtained. A whole range of other variables that simply cannot be eliminated are potential alternative explanations for most meta-analytic results.

The Promise

Although the number of pages in this chapter devoted to the problems of meta-analysis far exceeded the discussion of the benefits of meta-analysis, the point is not that the problems, therefore, so outweigh the benefits that meta-analysis properly can be ignored. Rather, the issue is that many of these problems place limitations on what can be expected from meta-analysis at this stage in its development. Further, categorizing problems in such a manner will hopefully lead to a research agenda designed to address them in some way (e.g., the development and refinement of appropriate meta-analytic statistical procedures). Indeed, it is based on the assumption that some of those problems will be successfully addressed that allows the promise of meta-analysis to be elaborated upon here. Thus, this section discusses some of the implications and potential contributions of meta-analysis for social work that have not yet been addressed in this chapter.

Narrative Review Versus Meta-Analysis: The Debate

At the heart of any type of research review is the logic, rigor, and training of the reviewer. There simply is no substitute for these qualities, whether the review is a traditional, narrative one or a meta-analysis. The success of the review depends on the extent to which the reviewer is aware of and adequately deals with problems in his or her method of review.

The above principles can be viewed as bridging the gap between the somewhat arbitrarily constructed camps of narrative review advocates and meta-analysis advocates. Indeed, Cook and Leviton (1980) and Leviton and Cook (1981) point out a number of factors that make a harsh distinction between these methods seem unnecessary. These include the fact that all literature reviews share both qualitative judgments and quantitative techniques, that there are no inherent weaknesses in traditional reviews, that many criticisms of narrative reviews were aimed at poor practices of reviewers rather than any inherent methodological problems, and that both meta-analytic and narrative reviews can provide important and even complementary information.

As if to second these ideas, Light and Pillemer (1982), supporters of meta-analysis, argue that qualitative information is as important as quantitative information for explaining conflicting and puzzling outcomes. They discuss six ways in which qualitative information is essential for literature reviews. They also describe three broad strategies for combining different types of information in a review: quantifying descriptive reports, presenting quantitative outcomes narratively, and allying statistical and descriptive evidence while maintaining the integrity of each. The main point of Light and Pillemer (1982) is that reviews organized to utilize both types of information will ultimately maximize knowledge about the complexities of program evaluation.

A very interesting recent development along these very lines is the work of Slavin (1986) on best-evidence synthesis. Best-evidence synthesis (BES) combines the quantification of effect sizes and systematic, exhaustive study selection of the best of the meta-analyses with the attention to methodological and substantive issues and individual studies characterizing the best narrative reviews. Rigorous inclusion criteria are at the heart of BES so that it focuses on the studies in a substantive area that have the best internal and external validity using clearly specified criteria for inclusion. Effect size data are used in a complementary way to a thorough discussion of the literature being reviewed. Thus, the literature synthesis section might look like the analogous section in a narrative review, with the addition of a table describing the study characteristics and effect sizes. Basically, the effect sizes act as a point of departure for the critical discussion and evaluation of the literature.

In essence, then, the debate over meta-analysis versus narrative reviews may be somewhat illusory, akin to debates among adherents of competing theoretical orientations in clinical practice. The goal of research reviewing is to make possible the best judgments about what problems, treated by what methods, informed by what theory, affecting what clients, in what situations, will be best. Strategies for handling such questions through the review process could then involve:

1. A narrative review alone. This essentially might be when the number of primary studies is relatively small, say under twenty, and/or when the outcomes are clearly in the same direction rendering quantitative aggregation less necessary.
2. A meta-analysis alone, especially when the opposite of the conditions above pertain (i.e., more than twenty primary studies and particularly when the re-

sults are not consistently in one direction), and perhaps incorporating a combination of methods including effect size calculation, combined probabilities (both with fail-safe procedures), testing for heterogeneity, and sampling error corrections.
3. A combination of methods along the lines suggested by Light and Pillemer (1982) or Slavin (1986).

The basic point of this discussion is perhaps that review methods should be utilized in the same way one uses primary research methods: by first developing a research question, and then by selecting a method of analysis that appears to be the best for that particular question.

Meta-Analysis and Social Policy

One of the areas where meta-analysis can have a particular impact is on social policy. This is in large part because the results of meta-analysis can be easily communicated to nonprofessional policymakers, especially when they are in an early stage of policy analysis and different policy options are being evaluated regarding what is known about them.

A recent article by Kiesler (1985) discusses a number of potential contributions of meta-analysis to policy formulation. He suggests that meta-analysis can be useful in: (1) providing a preliminary, overall look at a potential policy problem; (2) examining the effects of interventions across a broad array of problems (from health and mental health to child welfare); and (3) focusing attention on studies that do not exist when they are needed to answer serious policy questions.

A number of problems affecting the use of meta-analysis for policy development also are described by Kiesler (1985). When added to the problems reviewed in the previous section, these problems span the full range, from questions about statistics to oversimplifying and overgeneralizing conclusions ("psychotherapy is effective"). Yet, the use of meta-analysis for policy formulation remains an interesting and relatively unexplored arena.

Some interesting suggestions were made by Nurius (1984) for using meta-analysis to inform both policy development and other areas of practice. She emphasizes the importance of translating research findings (meta-analytic or otherwise) into understandable form and providing generalizations to be converted into guidelines for action. Nurius (1984) suggests that meta-analytic methods and findings can be incorporated into already existing research-utilization frameworks in social work such as Rothman's Social Research and Development (Rothman, 1980a, 1980b) or the developmental research paradigm of Thomas (1978, 1984). Not only could meta-analysis be useful in the context of knowledge development within these systems (i.e., by aggregating and analyzing the data), but the research utilization systems provide a series of steps and procedures for transforming meta-analytic results into practice principles and then disseminating them to the professional audience.

Single System Designs

One of the least explored areas for use of meta-analytic procedures is the area of single system or single case designs (Bloom, Orme, and Fischer, 1988). Such applications have been described in social work by Gingerich (1984) and Corcoran (1985), and in clinical psychology by Hartmann and Gardner (1982; cited in Strube, Gardner, and Hartmann, 1985). Meta-analytic procedures have potential for both analysis of outcomes within a study (a perennial problem in single system designs), as well as aggregating and evaluating data across single system designs.

Unfortunately, characteristics of some complex single system designs, such as the alternating treatment design, pose still unresolved problems about how the within-phase standard deviation should be determined. Of even more concern is the fact that the data in a substantial portion of single system designs are auto-correlated and thus nonindependent, thereby once again imposing limitations on the use of statistics that can be used when the assumption of independence is violated.

In addition to the use of parametric statistics such as described in this chapter, Hartmann and Gardner (1982; cited in Strube, Gardner, and Hartmann, 1985) discuss the possibilities of using nonparametric statistics such as the sign test and log-linear techniques to analyze data from single system designs. Although still assuming independence, nonparametric statistics may be useful when precise parametric information is not available or cannot be estimated with confidence. It is even possible to estimate effect sizes from nonparametric statistics (Strube, Gardner, and Hartmann, 1985; Glass, McGaw, and Smith, 1981).

There are still a number of problems that need to be resolved in the application of meta-analysis to single system designs, including the different procedures and interpretations that may be necessary for analyzing one study (within-subject) versus aggregating the results of several studies (between-subject; Strube, Gardner, and Hartmann [1985]). Nevertheless, as a new technology applied to what is also a relatively new technology, it appears as though integration of meta-analysis with single system designs may have an interesting future.

The Future of Meta-Analysis

Like any development in research or in practice, the future of meta-analysis depends on the ways its advocates can develop and refine the methodology to overcome reasonable criticisms of its applications. If the past ten years provides any hint about the next ten years, those refinements and developments are on the horizon. The fast and furious pace of new developments in meta-analysis over the past ten years, then, augurs well for the future.

It is likely that meta-analysis is not a fad, although as an enterprise, it may be some time before it is uniformly accepted as a legitimate contribution to research in the social and behavioral sciences. But since the potential benefits of meta-analysis can be seen as crucial to the ongoing success of social work, its viability will hopefully be enhanced rather than only challenged. This is because what meta-analysis attempts to do is develop an empirical base that can be used to inform our practice. Again, that is the main mandate generated from adherence to the scientific method as an orienting value of social work. Indeed, the research review is a key way of cumulating, interpreting, and disseminating knowledge about effective interventions and other major domains of practice. The results of rigorous research reviews, in other words, make a central contribution to the empirical base of practice and, ultimately, to helping evaluate and establish the effectiveness of our profession. Whether meta-analysis will be the major contributor in that effort or just one of several contributors remains to be seen. But, at the very least, meta-analysis can generate a great deal of renewed interest in the research review process, per se, and if that alone were to be its contribution, it would be evaluated by future generations of social workers as very worthy indeed.

References

Andrews, G. and Harvey, R. (1981). "Does Psychotherapy Benefit Neurotic Patients?" *Archives of General Psychotherapy, 38,* 1203–1208.

Arkin, R., Cooper, H. M., and Kolditz, T. (1980). "A Statistical Review of the Literature Concerning the Self-Serving Bias in Interpersonal Influence Situations." *Journal of Personality, 48,* 435–448.

Bangert-Drowns, R. L. (1986). "Review of Developments in Meta-Analytic Methods." *Psychological Bulletin, 99,* 388–399.

Bangert-Drowns, R. L., Kulik, J. A., and Kulik, C.-L. C. (1983). "Effects of Coaching Programs on Achievement Test Performance." *Review of Educational Research, 53,* 571–585.

Bassoff, E. S. and Glass, G. V. (1982). "The Relationship Between Sex Roles and Mental Health: A Meta-Analysis of Twenty Six Studies." *The Counseling Psychologist, 10,* 105–112.

Berman, J. S., Miller, C. R., and Massman, P. J. (1985). "Cognitive Therapy Versus Systematic Desensitization: Is One-Treatment Superior?" *Psychological Bulletin, 97,* 451–461.

Berman, J. S. and Norton, H. C. (1985). "Does Professional Training Make a Therapist More Effective?" *Psychological Bulletin, 98,* 401–407.

Bloom, M., Orne, J. and Fischer, J. (1988). *Evaluating Practice: Guidelines for the Accountable Professional* (2nd ed.). Englewood Cliffs, N.J.: Prentice-Hall.

Borgatta, E. F. and Jackson, D. J. (Eds.). (1980). *Aggregate Data: Analysis and Interpretation.* Beverly Hills, CA.: Sage.

Casey, R. J. and Berman, J. S. (1985). "The outcome of Psychotherapy with Children." *Psychological Bulletin, 98,* 388–400.

Cohen, J. (1962). "The Statistical Power of Abnormal-Social Psychological Research: A Review." *Journal of Abnormal and Social Psychology, 65,* 145–153.

Cohen, J. (1977). *Statistical Power Analysis for the Behavioral Sciences.* New York: Academic Press.

Cook, T. D. and Leviton, L. C. (1980). "Reviewing the Literature: A Comparison of Traditional Methods with Meta-Analysis." *Journal of Personality, 48,* 449–472.

Cooper, H. M. (1979). "Statistically Combining Independent Studies: A Meta-Analysis of Sex Differences in Conformity Research." *Journal of Personality and Social Psychology, 37,* 131–146.

Cooper, H. M. (1982). "Scientific Guidelines for Conducting Integrative Reviews." *Review of Educational Research, 52,* 291–302.

Cooper, H. M. and Rosenthal, R. (1980). "Statistical Versus Traditional Procedures for Summarizing Research Findings." *Psychological Bulletin, 87,* 442–449.

Corcoran, K. J. (1985). "Aggregating the Idiographic Data of Single-Subject Research." *Social Work Research and Abstracts, 21,* 9–12.

Dusek, J. B. and Joseph, G. (1983). "The Bases of Teacher Expectancies: A Meta-Analysis." *Journal of Educational Psychology, 75,* 327–346.

Erwin, E. (1984). "Establishing Causal Connections: Meta-Analysis and Psychotherapy." *Midwest Studies in Philosophy, 9,* 421–436.

Fischer, J. (1976). *The Effectiveness of Social Casework.* Springfield, Ill.: Charles C. Thomas.

Fischer, J. (1973). "Is Casework Effective? A Review." *Social Casework, 18,* 5–21.

Fiske, D. W. (1983). "The Meta-Analytic Revolution in Outcome Research." *Journal of Consulting and Clinical Psychology, 51,* 65–70.

Gingerich, W. J. (1984). "Meta-Analysis of Applied Time-Series Data." *Journal of Applied Behavioral Science, 20,* 71–79.

Glass, G. V. (1976). "Primary, Secondary, and Meta-Analysis of Research." *Educational Researcher, 5,* 3–8.

Glass, G. V., McGaw, B. and Smith, M. L. (1981). *Meta-Analysis in Social Research.* Beverly Hills, CA.: Sage.

Green, B. F. and Hall, J. A. (1984). "Quantitative Methods for Literature Reviews." *Annual Review of Psychology, 35,* 37–53.

Glisson, C. A. (1986). "The Group Versus the Individual as the Unit of Analysis in Small Group Research." *Social Work with Groups, 7,* 15–30.

Hazelrigg, M. D., Cooper, H. M. and Borduin, C. M. (1987). "Evaluating the Effectiveness of Family Therapies: An Integrative Review and Analysis." *Psychological Bulletin, 101,* 428–442.

Hedges, L. V. (1981). "Distribution Theory for Glass's Estimates of Effect Size and Related Estimators." *Journal of Educational Statistics, 6,* 107–128.

Hedges, L. V. (1982a). "Estimation of Effect Size from a Series of Independent Experiments." *Psychological Bulletin, 92,* 490–499.

Hedges, L. V. (1982b). "Fitting Categorical Models to Effect Sizes From a Series of Experiments." *Journal of Educational Statistics, 7,* 119–137.

Hedges, L. V. (1982c). "Fitting Continuous Models to Effect Size Data." *Journal of Educational Statistics, 7,* 245–270.

Hedges, L. V. and Olkin, I. (1985). *Statistical Methods for Meta-Analysis*. New York: Academic Press.

Hunter, J. E. and Schmidt, F. L. (1978). "Differential and Single-Group Validity of Employment Tests by Race: A Critical Analysis of Three Recent Studies." *Journal of Applied Psychology, 63,* 1–11.

Hunter, J. E., Schmidt, F. L., and Jackson, G. B. (1982). *Meta-Analysis: Cumulating Research Findings Across Studies*. Beverly Hills, CA.: Sage.

Jackson, G. B. (1980). "Methods for Integrative Reviews." *Review of Educational Research, 50,* 438–460.

Journal of Consulting and Clinical Psychology, (1983), *5,* No. 1, whole issue.

Kiesler, C. A. (1985). "Meta-Analysis, Clinical Psychology, and Social Policy." *Clinical Psychology Review, 5,* 3–12.

Kulik, J. A. and Bangert-Drowns, R. L. (1983/1984). "Effectiveness of Technology in Precollege Mathematics and Science Teaching." *Journal of Educational Technology Systems, 12,* 137–158.

Kulik, J. A., Kulik, C.-L. C. and Cohen, P. A. (1979). "A Meta-Analysis of Outcome Studies of Keller's Personalized System of Instructions." *American Psychologist, 34,* 307–318.

Landman, J., and Dawes, R. M. (1982). "Psychotherapy Outcome." *American Psychologist, 37,* 504–516.

Leviton, L. C. and Cook, T. D. (1981). "What Differentiates Meta-Analysis From Other Forms of Review?" *Journal of Personality, 49,* 231–236.

Light, R. J. (1983b). "Introduction." In R. J. Light (Ed.), *Evaluation Studies Review Annual. Vol. 8.* Beverly Hills, CA.: Sage, 13–23.

Light, R. J. (Ed.). (1983a). *Evaluation Studies Review Annual. Vol 8.* Beverly Hills, CA.: Sage.

Light, R. J. and Pillemer, D. B. (1982). "Numbers and Narrative: Combining their Strengths in Research Reviews." *Harvard Educational Review, 52,* 1–26.

Maas, H. S. (Ed.). (1966). *Five Fields of Social Service: Reviews of Research*. New York: N.A.S.W.

Maas, H. S. (Ed.). (1971). *Research in the Social Services: A Five Year Review*. New York: N.A.S.W.

Maas, H. S. (Ed.). (1978). *Social Service Research: Reviews of Studies*. Washington, D. C.: N.A.S.W.

Mansfield, R. S. and Busse, T. V. (1977). "Meta-Analysis of Research: A Rejoinder to Glass." *Educational Researcher, 6.*

Michelson, L. (Ed.). (1985). "Meta-Analysis and Clinical Psychology." *Clinical Psychology Review, 5,* 1–89.

Mosteller, F. M. and Tukey, J. W. (1968). "Data Analysis, Including Statistics." In G. Lindzey and F. Aronson (Eds.), *Handbook of Social Psychology*. Reading, MA.: Addison-Wesley.

Mullen, B. and Suls, J. (1982). "The Effectiveness of Attention and Rejection as Coping Styles: A Meta-Analysis of Temporal Differences." *Journal of Psychosomatic Research, 26,* 43–49.

Mullen, E. J., Dumpson, J. R. et al. (Eds.). (1972). *Evaluation of Social Intervention*. San Francisco, CA.: Jossey-Bass.

Nurius, P. S. and Yeaton, W. H. (1987). "Research Synthesis Reviews: An Illustrated Critique of 'Hidden' Judgments, Choices and Compromises." *Clinical Psychology Review, 7,* 695–714.

Nurius, P. S. (1984). "Utility of Data Synthesis for Social Work." *Social Work Research and Abstracts, 20,* 23–32.

Orwin, R. G. (1983). "A Fail-Safe N for Effect Size." *Journal of Educational Statistics, 8,* 157–159.

Orwin, R. G. and Cordray, D. S. (1985). "Effects of Deficient Reporting on Meta-Analysis: A Conceptual Framework and Reanalysis." *Psychological Bulletin, 97,* 134–147.

Paul, G. L. (1966). *Insight Versus Desensitization in Psychotherapy*. Stanford, CA.: Stanford University Press.

Paul, G. L. (1985). "Can Pregnancy be a Placebo Effect? Terminology, Designs, and Conclusions in the Study of Psychosocial and Pharmacological Treatments of Behavioral Disorders." In L. White, B. Tursky, and G. Schwartz (Eds.), *Placebo: Clinical Phenomenon and New Insights*. New York: Guilford, 137–163.

Presby, S. (1978). "Overly Broad Categories Obscure Important Differences Between Therapies." *American Psychologist, 33,* 514–515.

Prioleau, L., Murdock, M., and Brody, N. (1983). "An Analysis of Psychotherapy Versus Placebo Studies." *Behavioral and Brain Sciences, 6,* 275–310.

Reid, W. J. and Hanrahan, P. (1982). "Recent Evaluations of Social Work: Grounds for Optimism." *Social Work, 27,* 328–340.

Rosenthal, R. (1976). "Interpersonal Expectancy Effects: A Follow-Up." In R. Rosenthal, *Experimental Effects in Behavioral Research*. New York: Irvington, 440–471.

Rosenthal, R. (1978). "Combining Results of Independent Studies." *Psychological Bulletin, 85,* 185–193.

Rosenthal, R. (1979). "The File Drawer Problem and Tolerance for Null Results." *Psychological Bulletin, 86,* 638–641.

Rosenthal, R. (1983). "Assessing the Statistical and Social Importance of the Effects of Psychotherapy." *Journal of Consulting and Clinical Psychology, 51,* 4–13.

Rosenthal, R. (1984). *Meta-Analytic Procedures for Social Research*. Beverly Hills, CA.: Sage.

Rosenthal, R. and Rubin, D. B. (1978). "Interpersonal Expectancy Effects: The First 345 Studies." *Behavioral and Brain Sciences, 1,* 377–386.

Rosenthal, R. and Rubin, D. B. (1982a). "Comparing Effect Sizes of Independent Studies." *Psychological Bulletin, 92,* 500–504.

Rosenthal, R. and Rubin, D. B. (1982b). "Further Meta-Analytic Procedures for Assessing Cognitive Gender Differences." *Journal of Educational Psychology, 74,* 708–712.

Rosenthal, R. and Rubin, D. B. (1982c). "A Simple, General Purpose Display of Magnitude of Experimental Effect." *Journal of Educational Psychology,* 74, 166–169.

Rosenthal, R. and Rubin, D. B. (1986). "Meta-Analytic Procedures for Combining Studies with Multiple Effect Sizes." *Psychological Bulletin,* 99, 400–406.

Rothman, J. (1980a). *Social R and D: Research and Development in the Human Services.* Englewood Cliffs, NJ.: Prentice-Hall.

Rothman, J. (1980b). *Using Research in Organizations: A Guide to Successful Application.* Beverly Hills, CA.: Sage.

Rubin, A. (1985). "Practice Effectiveness: More Grounds for Optimism." *Social Work,* 30, 469–476.

Searles, J. S. (1985). "A Methodological and Empirical Critique of Psychotherapy Outcome Meta-Analysis." *Behavior Research and Therapy,* 23, 453–463.

Shadish, W. R. (1982). "A Review and Critique of Controlled Studies of the Effectiveness of Preventive Child Health Care." *Health Policy Quarterly,* 2, 24–52.

Shapiro, David A. (1985). "Recent Applications of Meta-Analysis in Clinical Research." *Clinical Psychology Review,* 5, 13–34.

Slavin, R. E. (1986). "Best-Evidence Synthesis: An Alternative to Meta-Analytic and Traditional Reviews." *Educational Researcher,* 15, 5–11.

Smith, M. L., Glass, G. V., and Miller, T. I. (1980). *The Benefits of Psychotherapy.* Baltimore, MD.: Johns Hopkins University Press.

Steinbrueck, S. M., Maxwell, S. E., and Howard, G. S. (1983). "A Meta-Analysis of Psychotherapy and Drug Therapy in the Treatment of Unipolar Depression with Adults." *Journal of Consulting and Clinical Psychology,* 51, 856–863.

Straw, R. B. (1983). "Deinstitutionalization in Mental Health: A Meta-Analysis." In R. J. Light (Ed.), *Evaluation Studies Review Annual. Vol. 8.* Beverly Hills, CA.: Sage, 253–278.

Strube, M. J. and Hartmann, D. P. (1982). "A Critical Appraisal of Meta-Analysis." *British Journal of Clinical Psychology,* 21, 129–139.

Strube, M. J. and Hartmann, D. P. (1983). "Meta-Analysis: Techniques, Applications, and Functions." *Journal of Consulting and Clinical Psychology,* 51, 14–27.

Strube, M. J., Gardner, W. and Hartmann, D. P. (1985). "Limitations, Liabilities, and Obstacles in Reviews of the Literature: The Current Status of Meta-Analysis." *Clinical Psychology Review,* 5, 63–78.

Thomas, E. J. (1978). "Generating Innovation and Social Work: The Paradigm of Developmental Research." *Journal of Social Service Research,* 2, 95–115.

Thomas, E. J. (1984). *Designing Interventions for the Helping Professions.* Beverly Hills, CA.: Sage.

Tobler, N. S. (1986). "Meta-Analysis of 143 Adolescent Drug Prevention Programs: Quantitative Outcome Results of Program Participants Compared to a Control or Comparison Group." *The Journal of Drug Issues,* 4, 537–567.

Videka-Sherman, L. (1988). "Meta-Analysis of Research on Social Work Practice in Mental Health," *Social Work, 33,* 325–338.

Videka-Sherman, L. (1985). *Harriett M. Bartlett Practice Effectiveness Project.* Silver Spring, MD.: N.A.S.W. (mimeo).

Walberg, H. J. and Haertel, E. H. (Eds.). (1980). "Research Integration: The State of the Art," *Evaluation in Education, 4,* whole issue.

Wilson, G. T. and Rachman, S. (1983). "Meta-Analysis and the Evaluation of Psychotherapy Outcome: Limitations and Liabilities." *Journal of Consulting and Clinical Psychology, 51,* 54–64.

Wilson, G. T. (1985). "Limitations of Meta-Analysis in the Evaluation of the Effects of Psychological Therapy." *Clinical Psychology Review, 5,* 35–47.

Wood, K. M. (1978). "Casework Effectiveness: A New Look at the Research Evidence." *Social Work, 23,* 437–458.

Wortman, P. M. (1983). "Evaluation Research: A Methodological Perspective." *Annual Review of Psychology, 34,* 223–260.

Part 3

The 1990s: Connecting the Past with the Future

Do not think of knocking out another person's brains because he differs in opinion from you. It would be as rational to knock yourself on the head because you differ from yourself ten years ago.
—Horace Mann

I can feel guilty about the past, apprehensive about the future, but only in the present can I act.
—Abraham Maslow

It seems to me, in retrospect, that the 1990s weren't quite as, uh, roarin' as the 70s and 80s may have been. The previous two decades really had seen quite a bit of change in some of the substance of knowledge for practice, research, and evaluation. I call the decade of the 1990s, "Connecting the Past with the Future," because I believe social work was, if not in a holding pattern, then in an era of consolidation. This consolidation was in the area of knowledge development for practice, at the very least.

Perusing the journals, though, it seemed clear to me that our field was kind of on the verge of taking off in some direction; could it be in the direction of Evidence-Based Practice? I say that change seemed imminent because one could see a higher level of rigor in published research, a broader selection of more sophisticated topics and designs, and certainly more sophisticated analyses. All of this, I expected, was the new foundation for further changes in social work.

Perhaps these developments were a result of the increasing number of doctoral graduates in social work. More doctoral programs, more doctorate faculty, more doctoral graduates and, of course, more doctoral and post-doctoral research all added up to the potential changes I was sensing. That is just my own hypothesis, of course.

Chapters in Part 3

This part of the book has three chapters. Two of them were not written primarily for social work; however, the topics parallel some of the discussion that was occurring within our field. Therefore, I believe these chapters are equally relevant for social work as they were to the field of psychotherapy for which they originally were intended.

The first chapter, chapter 16, is called "Whatever Happened to Eclecticism? An Analysis of Psychotherapy Integration, the Latest Psychotherapeutic Fad." This chapter contains an analysis of several questions relating to the possibility, desirability, and necessity of trying to integrate a variety of different theoretical approaches to practice into some kind of super theory or meta-theory. (That this is still an important topic might be seen in the recent request I received from a publisher, just one month before writing these words, to review a book prospectus proposing just such a meta-theoretical, integrative approach for social work.) This paper has some practical and practice-oriented conclusions that are consistent with some of the earlier material in this book.

Chapter 17 is titled "Empirically Based Practice: The End of Ideology?" Borrowing a part of this title from a famous political essay, this chapter, published in 1993, was an update of developments in social work practice since the 1981 publication of my work on the social work "revolution" (see chapter 10). This chapter reveals many of the new developments in practice, particularly those associated with research-backed activities. In looking back at this chapter, particularly in the context of the developments of the 1980s, I am still convinced that the field was moving in important new directions, perhaps different enough to justify considering the changes in social work to be a "paradigm shift" (Kuhn 1970). In other words, I think, in retrospect, that this chapter suggests social work really was on the path toward Evidence-Based Practice.

The final chapter in part 3, chapter 18, is called "Uniformity Myths in Eclectic and Integrative Psychotherapy." In this chapter, I address what I considered three important myths that pervade a good deal of the thinking in direct practice. The first is that all approaches have equivalent outcomes. The second is that all approaches/ theories of direct practice are equally sound. And the third myth this chapter addresses is that cultural homogeneity exists for all practitioners and clients, encouraging the dissemination of instantly obsolete Western theories to practitioners from other traditions and cultures. Each of these myths and its implications for practice are discussed, and I offer some suggestions for dealing with each myth. Although the literature on evidence-based practice largely seems to have supplanted the literature on eclecticism, the principles discussed in this chapter apply, I believe, to both eclectic *and* evidence-based practice.

Reference

Kuhn, T. S. (1970). *The structure of scientific revolutions* (2nd ed.). Chicago: University of Chicago Press.

Chapter 16

Whatever Happened to Eclecticism? An Analysis of Psychotherapy Integration, the Latest Psychotherapeutic Fad

Is psychotherapy integration possible?
Is psychotherapy integration desirable?
Is psychotherapy integration necessary?

These three questions are at the heart of my attempt in this chapter to provide an analysis of the state of development of psychotherapy integration. The analysis is organized into five parts.

Part one examines issues in the definition of psychotherapy integration. Part two examines the proposition that we *should* have psychotherapy integration. Part three examines the proposition that we *can* have psychotherapy integration. Part four examines the empirical evidence—developed especially through use of meta-analysis—that some argue provides an empirical foundation for psychotherapy integration. Finally, part five proposes some directions regarding what appears to be the most feasible approach to psychotherapy integration at the present time.

Defining Psychotherapy Integration

Shakespeare's line that "a rose by any other name would smell as sweet" is a maxim that obviously does not apply to the psychotherapy integration movement. "Psychotherapy integration" comes in all different shapes and forms, and therein lies the problem. How is it possible to have—let alone research—a field called psychotherapy integration if most of us cannot even agree what the field will include?

Many integrationists (e.g., Arkowitz, 1989; Norcross and Grencavage, 1989) have dealt—or not dealt, actually—with this issue by using the broadest definition possible of what psychotherapy integration is. They generally include as approaches to psychotherapy integration three broad areas: (1) technical (or systematic or procedureal or prescriptive) eclecticism; (2) the common factors approach; and (3) theoretical integration. For these authors, just about any approach or perspective

Fischer, J. (1992). Keynote Address Presented at the First International Congress on Integrative and Eclectic Psychotherapy, Mazatlan, Mexico, June 1992.

that is not considered to be a unitary school, theory, or method is considered to be integrative.

But this view is so broad as to be virtually meaningless. Few of the major schools of psychotherapy are so insular, so removed from the views, theories, and research of others, that they can be considered nonintegrative. The cognitive therapies were never only cognitive, the behavioral therapies never only behavioral; even the most orthodox of Freudian analysts entertain—dare I say, use—concepts derived from latter-day ego psychology.

So, if virtually everything is included in the definition of a term, the term—in this case, psychotherapy integration—literally means nothing. This lack of clarity, precision, and specificity (or, put more positively, openness and flexibility) in defining psychotherapy integration is perhaps one of the reasons that most therapists in one study preferred integration over eclecticism as self-descriptors (Norcross and Prochasaka, 1988). Indirect support for the position that lack of clarity rather than systematic thinking is a defining characteristic of most therapists' view of integration, can be found in the same study of therapists cited previously. The question of what therapists are integrating was answered in one word: everything, including "techniques, theories, and formats from every theory ever promulgated" (Norcross and Grencavage, 1989, p. 235).

This definitional vagueness presents a huge challenge—perhaps the major challenge to advocates of the integrationist perspective. In fact, it also presents a challenge in analyzing or critiquing psychotherapy integration if so much of the field is included and so little excluded. Therefore, some constraints are necessary, certainly for this chapter, and probably for the field as a whole if it is to progress in a meaningful way.

One clue to this delimitation of terms (or increased specificity of terms) can be derived from the three approaches to integration described previously. Only one of those approaches—theoretical integration—actually uses the word integration in its title. More importantly, theoretical integration, as compared to other possible forms of integration, can be viewed as the ultimate type of integrationism, the result of the most complex and difficult of the integrationist processes.

It seems, then, reasonable to argue that true integrationism implies going beyond combining approaches (as in eclecticism) and identifying commonalities (such as in the common factors perspective). Indeed, one may even make the case that theoretical integration—the conceptual or theoretical synthesis of diverse theoretical systems—stands apart from the other two perspectives (eclecticism and common factorism) on at least two dimensions. The first is a theoretical or conceptual dimension in which it can be said that theoretical integration, more than the other two perspectives, is concerned with, or more focused on, constructs and concepts, the basic building blocks of theory. The second dimension is empirical evidence, about which it can be argued that systematic or technical eclecticism, and to some extent common factorism, are more concerned with what the research evidence reveals than is the theoretical integration perspective.

I hope to avoid the problem of setting up theoretical integration as a straw man—easy to knock down. For example, it is obvious that theoretical integration cannot be successful without ultimate recourse to empirical evidence (and it is also obvious that eclecticism and common factorism are also concerned with concepts, not just research). Nevertheless, the focus of the subsequent sections of this chapter will be on problems and issues in the theoretical integration movement.

Should We Have Theoretical Integration?

What is the point of attempting to develop theoretical integration in the field of psychotherapy? What is the goal? What will it accomplish? Surprisingly, these issues do not seem to be adequately examined in the literature, if they are examined at all.

A review of factors that appear to have fostered the psychotherapy integration movement described five such factors (Norcross and Grencavage, 1989):

1. The proliferation of therapies
2. The inadequacy of single theories
3. The equality of outcomes (a topic to which I will return in a subsequent section)
4. The search for common components
5. Socioeconomic contingencies (ranging from the growth in the therapy industry to demands by third-party payers and insurance companies)

How and why should these factors—singly or in combination—lead to integrationism, particularly theoretical integration?

For example, does the fact that individual theories appear inadequate mean they will be more adequate when integrated? And how does a cause—the search for common components—become an effect—the search for common components as one type of integrationism?

But these points beg what seems to me to be the core issue for evaluating any new development in our field: How will it produce more effective change procedures, and how will it benefit our clients?

Without paying paramount attention to outcomes, our efforts can easily get sidetracked. The analogy to the therapy process is an obvious one: Without clear goals, it is impossible to know where we are going or what things will be like when we get there. Indeed, theoretical integration actually seems to me to be like a process goal in psychotherapy: We may achieve it, but what difference will it make; how will it really help?

So the issue of why we should have theoretical integration, and how it will help our clients, seems to me unanswered. This observation is bolstered by perusal of the two most prominent journals in the integrationist movement—the *Journal of Integrative and Eclectic Psychotherapy* and the *Journal of Psychotherapy Integration*. First, one notes an obvious lack of evidence of, and even reference to, effectiveness data. One would be hard-pressed to look through those journals or other literature on theoretical integration and see major attention given to the ultimate outcomes of psychotherapy.

Second, one will see a preponderance of articles written by, and references to, a relatively small circle of authors who are in the forefront of the integration movement.

This suggests another possibility: that psychotherapy integration is more the product of a small group of ideologically-committed authors, then a genuine movement in the field. This cadre of authors is productive and influential; two journals devoted to this topic are impressive at this relatively early state in the development of integrationism. But, as yet, the movement does not appear to have widespread support, if the lack of diversity of authors on these topics is any criterion at all.

In short, I do not think the field has yet moved to the point where theoretical integration, and perhaps the whole integrationist movement, can be considered as a legitimate therapeutic trend. The absence of attention to evidence of effectiveness, and the relatively small cadre of supporters, suggest that the psychotherapy integration movement may still be accurately characterized as a fad.

Can We Have A Theoretical Integration?

There are times in the development of most fields when even fads have the potential for evolving into legitimate trends. Is this one of them? Is it likely that there will be a time in the relatively near future when we may see some well-developed and empirically useful theoretical integration?

It appears to me to be unlikely.

There, of course, have been some well-known attempts to develop theoretical integration: Dollard and Miller's (1950) attempt to translate psychodynamics into S-R terms, Ford and Urban's (1963) effort at utilizing a common language to compare and analyze ten different psychotherapy theories, and Wachtel's (1977) well-known synthesis of psychoanalysis and behavior therapy are but a few early examples. But, obviously, these efforts really have not caught on.

There are good reasons, too. How does one decide which theories to integrate, or even which concepts of which theories? There are so many different concepts within each theory, and so many different theories—even under common rubrics like psychoanalysis or behavior therapy—that it seems almost impossible to select which ones to integrate. What criteria does one use to select concepts or constructs for integration? How does one integrate concepts that are poorly defined and/or totally unverified, and why would one want to do so in the first place?

The basic epistemologies of theories—and their proponents—vary to such an extent that any effort to integrate would necessitate ignoring most crucial assumptions, propositions, and worldviews. Differences between a logical-positivistic and a naturalistic or qualitative perspective are not easy to overcome, let alone integrate.

And, as any therapist knows, we apply *techniques* with our clients, not theories. The reality is that even a successful effort at theoretical integration may not actually impinge on the techniques we use to affect our clients. Thus, integration may, in point of fact, have no effect on what we actually *do,* anyway. If the realities of our practice do not change even with theoretical integration, what is the point?

Further, review of the articles published in our two integrationist journals shows a bewildering variety of concepts proposed as grist for the integrationist mill. Cognitive schemas, self-confirmation, levels of emotional awareness, the therapeutic alliance, self-experiencing, behavioral enactment . . . the list goes on and on.

Yet there are certain commonalities among these concepts. First, few, if any, of them even approximate the loftier ideals of theoretical integration (conceptual integration may be a more accurate term), and in fact, many of these ideas smack more of common factorism rather than integration in any meaningful sense.

Second, many of these concepts are derived from causal or developmental theory rather than intervention theory. Thus, their real contribution in influencing change efforts—specific techniques or what we actually do with our clients—has yet to be demonstrated.

Third, none of these efforts have as yet provided acceptable empirical evidence that their integration produces more effective service to clients than any other approach.

And fourth, this proliferation of integration efforts seems not only not to have produced greater clarity in the field, but it seems to be moving toward accomplishing the opposite effect—greater confusion and uncertainty—perhaps even chaos (Lazarus and Messer, 1991). We may be moving away from the major empirical advances of the last two decades and toward a conceptual fuzziness reminiscent of the early years of psychotherapy.

It simply appears to me that the field is not yet at a place where we are so effective that we can afford the luxury of theoretical integration. Indeed, my hypothesis is that, to the extent that theory is necessary at all, the field is better served by apartness or theoretical *specialization.* Certainly, most of our most productive techniques have been developed by implementation of principles derived from individual theories.

Does the Evidence Justify Integration?

A key argument justifying theoretical integration (and, to some extent, the common factors approach) is that research on psychotherapy has produced roughly equivalent outcomes across approaches (Norcross and Grencavage, 1989; Stiles, Shapiro, and Elliott, 1986). Surprisingly, most references on this topic cite as a basis for this conclusion the results of a number of meta-analytic reviews (such as Smith, Glass, and Miller, 1980) or the review by Lambert and Bergin (1986), which in itself is mainly a review of meta-analyses on the outcomes of psychotherapy.

So the answers to this question—does the evidence justify integrationism—largely hinge on an understanding of the meta-analytic literature and the methodologies of meta-analysis itself.

Unfortunately, such an undertaking requires considerably more space than is available for this chapter. (However, appendix A is a brief overview of some of the major methods of meta-analysis as well as some of the major problems and issues in its use; see also chapter 15 for a detailed discussion of problems with meta-analysis.) Yet without such an undertaking, one is tempted simply to accept the word of others who report that meta-analysis shows that all therapies have roughly equivalent outcomes. This leads me to conclude that we are faced with a new homogeneity assumption, with even more misleading implications ("it doesn't matter what therapy one uses; they are all the same") than those described by Kiesler (1966) regarding psychotherapy research in general.

There are two problems with this conclusion. The first is that this is not uniformly the case, even in the Smith, Glass, and Miller (1980) review, which is widely cited as drawing such a conclusion. Part of the problem depends on how one interprets roughly equivalent. For example, Smith, Glass, and Miller (1980) conclude that an effect size (ES) of .98 for behavior therapy was "clearly superior" to the ES of .85 for verbal therapies (p. 98). This conclusion and others like it often are ignored. Is this difference roughly equivalent or not? (The difference would be interpreted in this way: the typical behavior therapy client scored .13 standard deviations better than typical verbal therapy clients, the typical behavior therapy client exceeded 84 percent of clients in the control group, and the typical verbal therapy client exceeded 80 percent of control group clients.)

Even more importantly, the second problem with the equivalent outcome conclusion is that the methods of meta-analysis are beset by so many problems and issues (summarized in Appendix A) that serious limitations have to be placed on what can be expected from meta-analytic conclusions. It may in fact be true that different therapies produce roughly equivalent results, but it may in fact not be true. And if meta-analysis is to be the arbiter, it is clear that we have a long way to go before clear conclusions about the differential effectiveness of the therapies can be reached. It appears that we often readily accept—without critical examination—assertions that fit with our belief systems. My argument is that the methods and conclusions of meta-analysis cry out for just such a critical examination before those conclusions can be accepted.

Some Directions for the Future

It seems to me that the evidence—conceptual and empirical—to date points in the direction of concluding that theoretical integration is, at best, in the very earliest stage of development, or, at worst, a fad. Either way, I believe the future for theoretical integration looks rather gloomy. Some amazing breakthroughs will be necessary before I can be convinced that this is a useful—or even possible—direction for the field.

On the other hand, some very creative people are doing their best to develop the literature in this area, and the next decade may just bear witness to those breakthroughs.

But what does that leave us for the present? What does the field of integrationism have to offer today to the broader field of psychotherapy?

At the start of this chapter, I distinguished between theoretical or conceptual integration and empirical integration; it is the latter area—empirical integration, including systematic eclecticism and the common factor approach—that seems to have the most to offer.

So, in the spirit of integrationism, but certainly not *theoretical* integration of course, I would like to propose for the debate (or, more accurately in some cases, second the proposals of others) three additions to the integrationist knowledge base.

Empirically-Based Eclecticism

It seems almost impossible for the field of psychotherapy integration, let alone psychotherapy in general, to progress much further without paying paramount attention to the field's prime directive: *first, find and use what works.* In order to do this one has to shed one's theoretical (and perhaps even some integrationist) biases and allegiances, and make a personal and professional commitment to use empirically-demonstrated methods wherever that is possible. Of course, it is obvious to all of us that a comprehensive, empirically-based practice is a goal for the future rather than a reality for today. (It also may be a little less obvious to some of us as to what constitutes adequate empirical evidence.) Our practice and our clients are simply too complex and complicated to think that we can have an empirically-validated technique for each and every problem and situation. Nevertheless, empirically-based, eclectic practice provides an important model for the practice of today, and a goal for the practice of tomorrow.

Empirically-based eclecticism is a term that is intended to encompass all forms of eclecticism where the superordinate goal is to find what works and use it. Thus, approaches like the technical eclecticism of Lazarus (1986, 1989; Lazarus and Messer, 1991) and the systematic eclecticism of Beutler (1986) are included under the rubric. Similarly, the rationale, mechanisms, and problems with eclecticism are also reviewed in more detail than is possible here in those publications as well as in Fischer (1986).

Suffice it to say that the ultimate goal of the empirically-based eclectic practitioner is to have at his or her disposal a variety of intervention techniques of more or less demonstrated effectiveness. This increasingly is possible.

In the 1970s, when the movement toward empirically-based practice began to crystallize, it was possible to identify four areas where the bulk of the evidence of effectiveness seemed to be accumulating. Those areas were: (1) procedures that added structure to the intervention process (e.g., time limits, contracts, homework); (2) behavior therapy; (3) cognitive changes techniques; and (4) interpersonal skills such as empathy, warmth, and genuineness (Fischer, 1981). Indeed, research in most of these areas has continued to accumulate, with the fourth area broadened to include a number of other process variables involving client-practitioner interactions that may enhance outcome, such as therapist well-being (Beutler, Crago, and Arizmendi, 1986; Orlinsky and Howard, 1986; Lambert, 1989).

One important feature of this research is that it almost always focused on specification of the actual interventions involved. That is, the broad approach or theory—say, behavior therapy—was not being studied. Rather, it was individual techniques derived from those approaches that were being investigated. Not only is this additional reason for not devoting oneself to a single practice theory (an entire school of thought is usually not subject to investigation nor is one likely to be validated even if it were somehow possible to study), but it provides the special service to practitioners of identifying specific techniques that can be applied differentially depending on the specific circumstances of the case.

A number of such techniques can be identified (Fischer, 1986). They were selected for two basic reasons:

1. They have accumulated a substantial amount of empirical evidence of effectiveness with one or more problems; and/or
2. With a modicum of evidence, they are specifically designed to deal with certain problems that the other techniques listed do not successfully address.

Although this listing is not intended to be exhaustive, the techniques and technique packages that best appear to meet those criteria at the beginning of the 1990s are the ones described in Appendix B of this chapter.

It is probably obvious that most of these techniques have their roots in cognitive and/or behavioral formulations. The reason is simple: No other approaches or theoretical orientations have described their techniques in such specific fashion, allowing for their clear evaluation, and then carried out the literally hundreds of studies that document the effectiveness of those techniques, especially in a way that they can be isolated and examined as independent entities. Thus, this clarity and subsequent evaluation allows us to be able to distinguish between legitimate therapeutic procedures and fads.

Another advantage of this clarity of description involves ease of training. When step-by-step procedures are specified, learning how to use the techniques becomes a much easier task. The vagaries of trying to operationalize and implement complicated systems of intervention simply become unnecessary. Indeed, each one of the techniques and technique packages described in Appendix B has been placed into a common format using step-by-step flowcharts. An example of these flowcharts using the technique of stress inoculation training is included here as Appendix C. Wherever possible, the flowcharts for these techniques were designed to follow the format in Cormier and Cormier (1991), an excellent book that I have found to be by far the most useful book for helping students and practitioners learn these techniques.

Although only sixteen techniques are described, when the several techniques (e.g., different techniques of contingency management) are explicated, the sixteen techniques expand to over thirty. Moreover, many of these techniques can and have been used not only with individual clients but in groups, and with couples and families as well. Further, these techniques form the basis for any number of combined, complex intervention programs, such as communication and skill training programs, child management programs, and conflict resolution programs.

All of this is not to say that these techniques form the whole of therapeutic practice. Our everyday experience plus a huge body of empirical and theoretical literature makes that quite clear. Rather, the point is that techniques with evidence of effectiveness serve as a floor of effective therapy, a crucial part of the foundation. Combined with such dimensions as structuring procedures, interpersonal skills, and the like, these techniques at the present time appear to have an excellent chance of enhancing our effectiveness with our clients.

Common Characteristics of Techniques

Although the variety of techniques described here may appear disparate on the surface, it is possible that there are some characteristics that cut across many of them, thereby accounting for some degree of their success. Although this is speculative, based on reviewing the research on techniques and attempting to categorize them regarding their commonalities and differences, it does appear as though the most effective techniques may have certain ingredients in common. These common ingredients are described here mainly as hypotheses for future research on identifying the effective components of techniques. This scheme also has heuristic effects in that it serves as a handy vehicle for teaching practitioners. In essence, students can be encouraged to examine their practice to ensure that as many of these ingredients as possible are present as they implement any given technique. Thus, following is what might be proposed as some common characteristics of effective technique implementation:

1. Structure: Provide a verbal set including: a rationale for use of the technique, an explanation of what is to be done, and enhancing positive expectations of success.
2. Modeling: Demonstrate to the client what you want the client to do.
3. Extensive rehearsal and practice: It is almost impossible to expect a client to be successful at implementing the practitioner's ideas in real life unless he or she has practiced them—over and over again—with the practitioner.
4. Graduated steps: With few exceptions, it appears as though it is better to move slowly rather than too quickly. This means, for example, moving from confronting low anxiety-eliciting situations to increasingly higher anxiety-eliciting situations. It also means use of shaping—moving from less to more complicated objectives.
5. Provide feedback: It seems to be a good idea to try and provide your clients with gentle and constructive suggestions on what to change or try next as they progress in their rehearsal.
6. Coping thoughts: Prepare the client with what to say to himself or herself when preparing for, confronting, or successfully completing an assignment.
7. Praise and positive reinforcement: Not only can the client's efforts be

enhanced by praise from the practitioner, but praise and positive reinforcement from other sources (or self-reinforcement) should be built into the client's program whenever possible.

8. Homework and task assignments: It seems crucial to give the client homework to try out in real life each part of what the practitioner and client have worked out in their contacts.

9. Exposure: It appears as though increasing the time of the client's exposure to anxiety-producing events—in real life or in imagination—leads to optimal reduction in that anxiety.

10. Transfer of learning: It is absolutely critical that an entire phase of the intervention process be devoted to ensuring that therapeutic gains are maintained, both in direct practice with the client and in training others in the environment to support and reinforce those gains.

11. Interpersonal skills: All therapeutic interventions take place in an interpersonal context. It seems clear that provision of quality interpersonal skills—such as empathy, warmth, and genuineness—forms the matrix out of which effective interventions occur.

Process Integration

Since the heart of eclectic practice is the use of a variety of intervention techniques selected systematically, it is particularly important to develop some method for integrating what otherwise might be viewed as a messy hodge-podge of interventions. One framework that was developed to enhance this type of integration is called the PRAISES Model (Fischer, 1986).

The PRAISES Model is a framework developed to integrate, structure, and systematize the process of eclectic practice. It is comprised of five main phases divided into a total of eighteen steps, with the term PRAISES being an acronym for the five major phases (see table 16.1).

The phases and steps of the model have been placed on a flowchart to aid in guiding the process of practice (see Appendix D). As can be seen from the flowchart, each of the major steps is subdivided into the tasks and activities that together comprise the process of practice.

This framework is intended to illustrate a number of characteristics of this approach to practice:

1. Empirically-based: To the extent possible, it utilizes the results of research to inform practice. This ranges from findings on the importance of interpersonal skills, to structuring, to the use of techniques of demonstrated effectiveness (Garfield and Bergin, 1986; Fischer, 1986).

2. Eclectic: The framework is based on the assumption that no single approach to practice has unequivocal evidence of effectiveness, and that the best approach to practice is the one that systematically incorporates the most effective ingredients available.

Table 16.1   The PRAISES Model

Phase I. *PR*e-Intervention
   1. Evaluate the context
   2. Process the referral
   3. Initiate contact
   4. Structure
Phase II. *A*ssessment
   5. Select problem
   6. Conduct assessment
   7. Collect baseline information
   8. Establish goals
Phase III. *I*ntervention
   9. Develop intervention plan
  10. Develop evaluation plan
  11. Negotiate contract
  12. Prepare for intervention
  13. Implement intervention
Phase IV. *S*ystematic *E*valuation
  14. Monitor and evaluate results
  15. Assess and overcome barriers
  16. Evaluate goal achievement
Phase V. *S*tabilize
  17. Stabilize and generalize changes
  18. Plan follow-up and termination

3. Systematic: The framework is an attempt to clearly identify the various phases of practice and organize them into a step-by-step sequence that could vary for the individual client or problem, but that overall appears to be a minimal set of important practice activities.

4. Accountable: Use of a framework such as this is an attempt to add to our accountability as practitioners by bringing the entire process of practice out into the open for scrutiny by anyone interested.

5. Integrating Research and Practice: The specific evaluation and practice steps are integrated in this framework in such a way that makes no artificial distinction between the two.

6. A Way of Thinking: Perhaps more than anything else, this framework is intended to illustrate a way of thinking about practice: systematic, structured, oriented to client outcomes, empirically-based, and up-to-date with relevant literature.

This framework is designed to be especially useful by serving as an anchor for practitioners, especially new practitioners, as they wend their way through the trials and tribulations of the treatment process. Its clarity should add to our ability to teach the otherwise vague psychotherapy process. Further, the framework can be flexibly adapted to the needs of just about any case; it highlights important practice activities at any stage of treatment so even if some activities are performed in different sequences, the practitioner can always check back to see that he or she has covered activities that might otherwise have been skipped. The framework also is theory-free; no matter what approach to practice the practitioner prefers, it can be incorporated in the PRAISES Model. Finally, the essence of empirically-based eclecticism is the use of a variety of different interventions. Obviously, they cannot be applied in an arbitrary or helter-skelter fashion. The PRAISES Model offers the potential of helping the practitioner organize and sequence the necessary interventions in a way that hopefully will add to both overall efficiency and overall effectiveness.

Conclusion

This chapter has examined the integrative movement with particular emphasis on theoretical integration. For a variety of reasons—including definitional vagueness, lack of clarity in the reasons for and goals of theoretical integration, and problems in actually constructing a theoretically integrated approach—the tentative conclusion is that theoretical integration is more of a fad than a legitimate therapeutic trend.

As an alternative to theoretical integration, I have proposed empirically-based eclecticism and *process* integration as a way of emphasizing the most important priorities of our field—finding the best ways of helping our clients and using them.

But it is clear to me that the area of integration—however one defines it—is perhaps the most exciting area in the field of psychotherapy today. With so many productive minds engaged in integrationist work, I would not be at all surprised if the conclusions of this chapter are very short-lived. In fact, I look forward to that possibility.

References

Arkowitz, H. (1989). "The Role of Theory in Psychotherapy Integration," *Journal of Eclectic and Integrative Therapy, 8,* 8–16.

Beutler, L. E. (1986). "Systematic Eclectic Psychotherapy," in J. C. Norcross (ed.). *Handbook of Eclectic Psychotherapy.* New York: Brunner/Mazel, 94–131.

Beutler, L. E., Crago, M., and Arizmendi, T. G. (1986). "Research on Therapist Variables in Psychotherapy," in S. L. Garfield and A. E. Bergin (eds.) *Handbook of Psychotherapy and Behavior Change,* 3rd Ed. New York: Wiley, 257–310.

Cormier, W. H. and Cormier, L. S. (1991). *Interviewing Strategies for Helpers.* 3rd Ed. Monterey, CA: Brooks/Cole.

Dollard, J. and Miller, N. E. (1950). *Personality and Psychotherapy: An Analysis in Terms of Learning, Thinking and Culture.* New York: McGraw-Hill.

Fischer, J. (1986). "Eclectic Casework," in J. C. Norcross (ed.). *Handbook of Eclectic Psychotherapy.* New York: Brunner/Mazel, 320–392.

Fischer, J. (1981). "The Social Work Revolution," *Social Work, 26,* 199–207.

Ford, D. H. and Urban, H. B. (1963). *Systems of Psychotherapy: A Comparative Study.* New York: John Wiley.

Garfield, S. L. and Bergin, A. E. (1986). *Handbook of Psychotherapy and Behavior Change,* 3rd Ed. New York: Wiley.

Kiesler, D. J. (1966). "Some Myths of Psychotherapy Research and the Search for a Paradigm," *Psychological Bulletin, 65,* 110–136.

Lambert, M. J. (1989). "The Individual Therapist's Contribution to Psychotherapy Process and Outcome," *Clinical Psychology Review, 9,* 469–485.

Lambert, M. J., and Bergin, A. E. (1986). "The Effectiveness of Psychotherapy," in S. L. Garfield and A. E. Bergin (eds.). *Handbook of Psychotherapy and Behavior Change,* 3rd Ed. New York: Wiley, 157–212.

Lazarus, A. A. (1989). "Why I Am An Eclectic (Not An Integrationist)," *British Journal of Guidance and Counseling, 17,* 248–258.

Lazarus, A. A. (1986). "Multimodal Therapy," in J. C. Norcross (ed.) *Handbook of Eclectic Psychotherapy.* New York: Brunner/Mazel, 65–93.

Lazarus, A. A. and Messer, S. B. (1991). "Does Chaos Prevail? An Exchange on Technical Eclecticism and Assimilative Integration," *Journal of Psychotherapy Integration, 1,* 143–158.

Norcross, J. C. and Grencavage, L. M. (1989). "Eclecticism and Integration in Counseling and Psychotherapy: Major Themes and Obstacles," *British Journal of Guidance and Counseling, 17,* 227–247.

Norcross, J. C. and Prochaska, J. O. (1988). "A Study of Eclectic (and Integrative) Views Revisited." *Professional Psychology: Research and Practice, 19,* 170–174.

Orlinsky, D. E. and Howard, K. I. (1986). "Process and Outcome in Psychotherapy," in S. L. Garfield and A. E. Bergin (eds.). *Handbook of Psychotherapy and Behavior Change,* 3rd Ed. New York: Wiley, 311–381.

Smith, M. L., Glass, G. V. and Miller, T. I. (1980). *The Benefits of Psychotherapy.* Baltimore, MD: John Hopkins University Press.

Stiles, W. B., Shapiro, D. A., and Elliott, R. (1986). "Are All Psychotherapies Equivalent?" *American Psychologist, 41,* 165–180.

Wachtel, P. L. (1977). *Psychoanalysis and Behavior Therapy: Toward an Integration.* New York: Basic Books.

Appendix A. Meta-Analysis

Summary of Major Approaches*

Common Ingredients: All transform the outcomes of individual studies into a common metric using effect sizes (ES), combined significance levels, or both, plus other statistics to quantitatively analyze the results of several studies.

---

* Bangert-Drowns, R. L. (1986). Review of Developments in Meta-Analytic Methods. *Psychological Bulletin, 99,* 388–99.

1. *The Glass Approach* (Δ).   Subtracts for each outcome measure mean of control group from mean of experiment group and divides by standard deviation of control group ES = $(\bar{X}_E - \bar{X}_C)/S_C$. Uses Z-table to determine percentile rank of average person in the E group compared to the C group. Uses regression to examine relationship of other variables to ES. Most widely used method.

2. *Study Effect M-A* (Mansfield and Busse).   ES's related to each dependent variable are averaged and combined into one ES per study. Somewhat more rigorous in selection of studies than #1. Uses same ES formula as #1; both methods might also use Cohen's d (same formula as #1 but with pooled SD as denominator).

3. *Combined Probability Method* (Rosenthal).   Probability level for each study is calculated along with corresponding standard normal deviate (Z). Average Z scores used if more than one outcome measure. Z scores summed across studies to produce overall Z, reflecting probability that combined results could have occurred by chance. Called "counting Z's" or Stouffer's Z. Also uses ES (Cohen's d) and Binomial Effect Size Display (showing effect of a given intervention on success rate).

4. *Data Pooling with Tests of Homogeneity* (Hedges).   Uses statistic H to test for homogeneity of ES's. H represents variability among study outcomes as the sum of squared differences between each ES and the weighted average ES. The ratio of this to the sum of sampling variances in all the ES's is distributed as chi square. Each class of dependent variables across studies is tested for homogeneity. If H is not significant, data are homogeneous and ES's across studies are pooled and tested statistically. If H is significant, ES's should not be pooled and moderator variables are examined. Can also test for significant differences among heterogeneous ES's.

5. *Data Pooling with Sampling Error Correction* (Hunter and Schmidt).   Examines artifacts that may explain variation across studies: sampling error, variation in criteria reliability, variation in test reliability, variation in range restriction. Uses several different statistics including tests of homogeneity, ES's, correlations, and regression. (also called Psychometric M–A).

Problems and Issues

1. Selecting A Method of Meta-Analysis
   No definitive guidelines exist for which method is best. Judgments usually subjective. Reviewers often combine several.
2. Selecting Studies for Review
   a. *Combining Divergent Studies.* Includes issues re: combining independent variables (this could obscure differences among types of interventions), combining dependent variables (combining can produce distortion due to extreme scores in one study; separate ES's for each measure may violate principle of assumption of independence); and methodological quality

of primary studies (G.I., G.O.; some M.-A.'s exclude poor quality studies, others code and analyze; both ways are subjective).

b. *Sampling Bias.* Reviewer may not locate all studies, or some conducted studies may not be published. Could distort magnitude or direction of effects.

c. *Deficient Reporting and Limitations of Primary Studies.* Judgments of M-A coders, lack of information in primary studies, and variations in primary studies all can affect results of M-A.

3. Meta-Analysis Statistics

a. *Calculation of ES.* No uniform agreement between use of Δ and d; use of one versus the other can result in vastly different findings.

b. *Nonindependence of Data.* Several different sources of nonindependence can lead to lack of reliability and raise questions about use of most statistics. Can produce huge differences in results when nonindependence taken into account.

c. *Positive Bias.* M-A reviewers typically find more positive results than qualitative reviewers. ES statistics always positive when E group $\bar{X}$ is larger than C group, even if difference is not significant in primary study. For example, using Δ to calculate ES with a nonsignificant difference between E group ($\bar{X}$ – 2.5) and C group ($\bar{X}$ – 2.0) and S_c – .25 – ES of 2.0, implying average E group client scored above 97.7 percent of C group.

d. *Aggregated versus Unaggregated Data.* Aggregating individual data to determine conclusions about unaggregated data, especially at the group level, can lead to distorted conclusions.

4. Interpretation of Results of M-A

a. *Interpretation of ES.* No real consensus about how to interpret meaning of ES, especially when one overall ES is reported and no test of statistical significance. Interpretation often subjective or interpreted in different ways by different reviewers.

b. *Issues Regarding Causality.* No basis for establishing causal relationships among variables since variables are not manipulated or temporally ordered.

Appendix B.

Techniques and Technique Packages

Techniques and References	Population	Problem
1. Assertion training and social skills training[7,10,23]	Full range of clients from severely disturbed psychiatric patients to unhappy couples	Wide range of skill/behavior: deficits ranging from self-care and assertion skills to communication training
2. Contingency management (including positive reinforcement, token economy, etc.)[3]	Almost all populations including children and adults; individuals, couples, families	Full range of problems from mild to severe
3. Systematic Desensitization[4,24]	Mainly adults, moderate disorders	Decreasing maladaptive anxiety, especially related to specific stimuli
4. (Behavioral) Contracting[17]	Individuals, families, couples	Weight loss, marital and family problems, academic behaviors, medication compliance
5. Problem-solving[11,15]	Adults, moderate to severe problems	Problem-solving skills in a variety of contexts; decrease in some specific problem behaviors
6. Self-instruction training[2,20]	Children and adults, moderate disorders	Impulsive children, public speaking, and test anxiety
7. Stress-inoculation training[2,20,21]	Adults, moderate disorders	Interpersonal and general anxiety, stress and anger control
8. Cognitive restructuring[12,14,2]	Adults, mild to moderate disorders	Unrealistic expectations, misconceptions, dysfunctional self-statements
9. Modeling and participant modeling[2,3,4]	Children and adults; individuals, groups, couples, and families, slight to severe impairment	Decrease in anxiety, increase in social skills
10. Covert sensitization[3,9,16]	Adults	Unwanted sexual behaviors, alcohol abuse, smoking, and overeating
11. Covert positive reinforcement[4,16]	Adults, mild to moderate disorders	Negative self-statements, test anxiety, weight control, animal phobias
12. Covert modeling[2,16]	Adults, mild to moderate disorders	Phobias, lack of assertiveness, mild fears
13. Exposure and response prevention[3,13,18,19]	Adults, mild to moderate disorders	Simple and social phobias, agoraphobia, compulsive rituals

Techniques and References	Population	Problem
14. Thought stopping[2,3,4]	Adults, mild to moderate thoughts	Obsessive thoughts
15. Habit reversal[5,6,22]	Adults and children	Tics, nailbiting, trichotillomania
16. Paradoxical instruction[25]	Adults, mild to moderate disorders	Procrastination, depression, anxiety, sleep disorders

General
[1] Bellack, A. S. & Hersen, M. (eds.). *Dictionary of Behavior Therapy Techniques.* New York: Pergamon, 1985.
[2] Cormier, W. H. & Cormier, L. S. *Interviewing Strategies for Helpers* (2nd edition). Monterey, California: Brooks/Cole, 1985.
[3] Rimm, D. C. & Masters, J. C. *Behavior Therapy: Techniques and Empirical Findings* (2nd edition). New York: Academic Press, 1979.
[4] Walker, C. E. et al. *Clinical Procedures for Behavior Therapy.* Englewood Cliffs, N.J.: Prentice-Hall, 1981.

Specific Techniques
[5] Azrin, N. H. & Nunn, R. C. *Habit Control.* New York: Simon & Shuster, 1977.
[6] Azrin, N. H. & Nunn, R. C., "Habit Reversal: A Method of Eliminating Nervous Habits and Tics," *Behavior Research and Therapy,* Vol. 11, 1982, 619–628.
[7] Bellack, A. S. & Hersen, M. (eds.). *Research and Practice in Social Skills Training.* New York: Plenum, 1979.
[8] Brehony, K. A. & Celler, E. S., "Agoraphobia: Appraisal of Research and a Proposal for an Integrative Model," in M. Hersen et al. (eds.). *Progress in Behavior Modification,* Vol. 12. New York: Academic Press, 1981, 1–66.
[9] Cautela, J. R., "Covert Sensitization." *Psychological Reports,* Vol. 20, 1967, 459–468.
[10] Curran, J. P. & Monti, P. M. (eds.). *Social Skills Training.* New York: Guilford, 1982.
[11] D'Zurilla, T. J. & Nezu, A., "Social Problem Solving in Adults," in Kendall P. C. (ed.). *Advances in Cognitive-Behavioral Research and Therapy,* Vol. 1. New York: Academic Press, 1982, 201–274.
[12] Ellis, A. & Greiger, R. (eds.). *Handbook of Rational-Emotive Therapy.* New York: Springer, 1977.
[13] Foa, E. B. & Steketee, G. S., "Obsessive Compulsives: Conceptual Issues and Treatment Considerations," in M. Hersen et al. (eds.). *Progress in Behavior Modification,* Vol. 8. New York: Academic Press, 1979, 1–53.
[14] Goldfried, M. R., "Anxiety Reduction Through Cognitive-Behavioral Intervention," in P. C. Kendall & S. D. Hollon (eds.). *Cognitive-Behavioral Interventions.* New York: Academic Press, 1979, 117–152.
[15] Janis, I. L. & Mann, L. *Decision-Making.* New York: Free Press, 1977.
[16] Kadzin, A. E. & Smith, G. A., "Covert Conditioning: A Review." *Advances in Behavior Research and Therapy,* Vol. 2, 57–98, 1979.
[17] Kirschenbaum, D. S. & Flannery, R. C., "Behavioral Contracting: Outcomes and Elements," in M. Hersen et al. (eds.). *Progress in Behavior Modification,* Vol. 15, New York: Academic Press, 1983, 217–275.
[18] Marshall, W. L. et al., "The Current Status of Flooding Therapy," in M. Hersen et al. (eds.). *Progress in Behavior Modification,* Vol. 7. New York: Academic Press, 1979, 205–275.
[19] Matthews, A. M. et al. *Agoraphobia: Nature and Treatment.* New York: Guilford, 1981.
[20] Meichenbaum, D. *Cognitive-Behavior Modification.* New York: Plenum, 1977.
[21] Novaco, R. W., "The Cognitive Regulation of Anger and Stress," in P. C. Kendall and S. D. Hollon (eds.). *Cognitive-Behavioral Interventions.* New York: Academic, 1979, pp. 241–286.
[22] Turpin, G., "The Behavioral Management of Tic Disorders: A Critical Review." *Advances in Behavior Research and Therapy,* Vol. 5, 1983, 203–245.
[23] Twentyman, C. T. & Zimering, R. T., "Behavioral Training of Social Skills: A Critical Review." In M. Hersen et al. (eds.). *Progress in Behavior Modification,* Vol. 7, New York: Academic Press, 1979, 319–400.
[24] Wolpe, J. *The Practice of Behavior Therapy,* 3rd edition. New York: Pergamon, 1982.
[25] Dowd, E. T. and Trutt, S. D., "Paradoxical Interventions in Behavior Modification," in M. Hersen et al. (eds.). *Progress in Behavior Modification,* Vol. 23. New York: Academic Press, 1988, 96–130.

Appendix C.

Flowchart of Self-Instruction Training

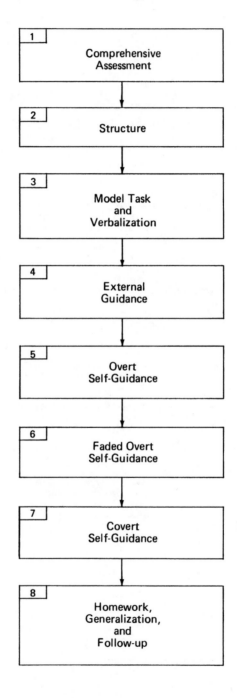

Appendix D.

PRAISES Model: A Framework for Eclectic Practice.

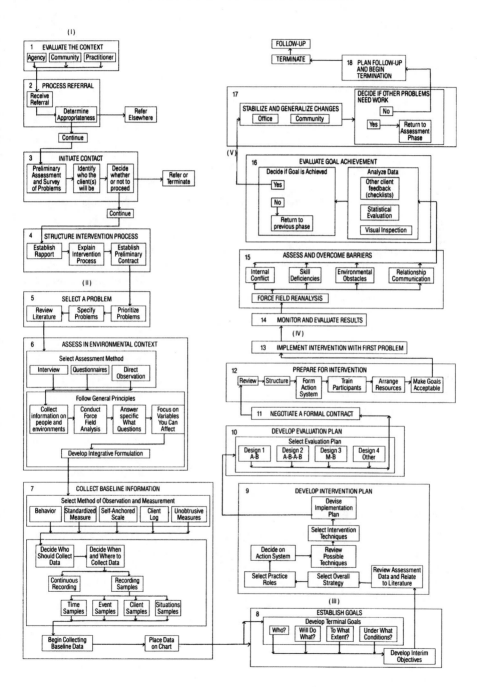

Chapter 17
Empirically Based Practice: The End of Ideology

It has been a full decade since a series of changes that were occurring in social work were dubbed a "quiet revolution" (Fischer, 1981). The revolution was viewed essentially as a move away from vague, unvalidated, and haphazardly derived knowledge traditionally used in social work toward more systematic, rational, and empirically oriented development and use of knowledge for practice. The changes in the field that were seen as some of the components of the revolution were: (1) work on systematizing the processes of knowledge development in social work; (2) increasing integration between research and practice; and (3) increasing availability of intervention techniques with evidence of effectiveness. In its entirety, the revolution appeared to be a movement toward scientifically based practice in social work.

The purpose of this chapter is to examine whether these changes have indeed become more pronounced in social work over the past decade. Each of the areas mentioned above will be reexamined for evidence regarding their salience in the social work practice of today and as a basis for future changes. In addition, some new developments with important portents for the future of social work will also be reviewed. Because of the enormous explosion of knowledge and literature in social work in recent years, most of the focus of this chapter will be on the clinical or direct practice function of social work, although it is hoped that the implications of these developments will pertain to other social work activities as well.

The Model of Practice

While there has not been uniform agreement that recent decades have borne witness to an actual revolution in social work, it seems fairly clear that there have been substantial changes in many social workers' perspectives on practice. This is best illustrated by the major conference sponsored by the School of Social Welfare,

Fischer, J. (1993). *Journal of Social Service Research, 16*, 9–64. Reprinted with permission of The Haworth Press.

SUNY-Albany, in August, 1988, called "Empiricism in Clinical Practice: Present and Future." At this conference, social work practitioners, educators, and researchers from North America met to discuss the ways in which research and practice are increasingly intertwined. A book based on the conference, *Advances in Clinical Social Work* (Videka-Sherman and Reid, 1990) will serve to describe a number of facets of this emerging model of practice.

And just what is this emerging model? Several terms have been used to describe this model of practice: scientific practice, empirically based practice, empirical practice, and empirical-clinical practice (Jayaratne & Levy, 1979; Bloom & Fischer, 1982; Siegel, 1984; Blythe & Briar, 1985; Ivanov, Blythe, & Briar, 1987). At its heart, this model of practice focuses on integrating research and practice in at least two basic ways: attempting to use the results of research to inform practice (e.g., in the selection of intervention techniques), and using research methods to monitor and evaluate progress and outcome with each and every case. At a broader level, this empirical practice model views practice and research as virtually the same phenomenon in the clear and consistent way one views client problems, formulates hypotheses, collects information, resolves problems.

This empirical model can be seen as the matrix for the changes that have appeared in social work over the past two decades. Indeed, the presence of an empirical focus increasingly linking up the theory, research, and practice endeavors in social work can be detected in all of the areas that will be examined here: epistemology and knowledge development in social work; increasing integration of research and practice; availability of more precise frameworks for practice and evidence of effectiveness of many clinical techniques; and newer developments in research and computers that have the potential for having a major impact on social work practice.

Epistemology and Knowledge Development in Social Work

Developments in this area have been among the most interesting of the past decade. Indeed, some of the most persistent and strident challenges to empirically based practice, including advocacy of alternative routes for development of the field, were part of an epistemological debate in social work in the 1980s. Since a profession's view of epistemology and its methods of knowledge development can form the basis for any changes in its practice, it seems appropriate to examine these issues before any other developments are explored.

Unfortunately, the scope of this chapter and space limitations preclude the kind of in-depth examination that these issues actually require. On the other hand, there are a number of references available that do provide such an examination (Heineman, 1981; Karger, 1983; Geismar, 1982; Hudson, 1982; Schuerman, 1982; Haworth, 1984; Heineman Pieper, 1985; Mullen, 1985; Glisson & Fischer, 1987; Ivanov, Blythe & Briar, 1987; Brekke, 1986; Peile, 1988; Wood, 1988; Bloom, 1988; Dean & Fenby, 1989; Thyer, 1989; Ivanov & Blythe, 1989.

The Epistemological Debate

The importance of epistemology—the theory of knowledge or, more broadly, philosophy of knowledge—for a profession can be easily summarized: a profession's epistemology hypothetically determines the methods of knowledge development used by the profession, the types of knowledge developed, and, ultimately, the actual practice of the profession. Viewed in this light, it is easy to see why discussions of epistemology potentially are so important and actually generate so much controversy.

This great epistemological debate largely has taken place during the decade of the eighties, and, at the risk of oversimplification, can be boiled down to three arguments: logical positivism versus other philosophies of knowledge development, quantitative versus qualitative research methodologies, and good guys versus bad guys.

Logical Positivism Versus Other Philosophies   At the most basic level, this debate concerns the core philosophy and belief that drive the knowledge-development enterprise in social work. One side of the argument is that social work has been captive to a philosophy of logical positivism (or "logical empiricism"). This point of view argues that such a philosophy—with emphasis on prediction, objectivity, and control of variables—is logically inadequate, inappropriate for social work, insensitive to both the context and nuances of variables, glorifies research method and especially quantification to the detriment of other ways of knowing, and tends to discourage both contribution and utilization by practitioners.

Proponents of this argument have offered alternative epistemological philosophies under a variety of rubrics, including the heuristic approach (Heineman Pieper, 1985), existentialism, subjectivism and phenomenological epistemologies, and normative inquiry (Peile, 1988), critical theory, and deconstructionism (Dean & Fenby, 1989). While these perspectives vary along several dimensions, they tend to emphasize the value of subjective experience, the value of the context of research and interactions among researchers and those being studied, recognition of the subjectivity and inherent biases in all measurement and data collection, focus on process, removing the binds and blinders of experimental-type designs in favor of informed judgments of researchers, and support the use of insight, intuition, and involvement by both researchers and practitioners.

The opposing camp—those arguing either for empirically oriented perspectives or simply against nonempirically oriented perspectives—argue that the debate is actually a red herring. This point of view is that logical positivism is a distortion or misnomer for what passes as the research and knowledge development enterprise in social work, since many methods are rooted in principles that predate the philosophies of logical positivism. Further, most of the literature in social work, it is argued, does not even involve empirical research (Glisson & Fischer, 1987); the relative handful of experiments dealing with social work effectiveness (Mullen & Dumpson, 1972; Fischer, 1973, 1976; Wood, 1978; Reid & Hanrahan, 1982; Rubin,

1985; Videka-Sherman, 1988) compared to other professions, such as clinical psychology, are seen as mute testimony to social work's traditional lack of allegiance to logical positivism or rigorous research methodologies as a priority for knowledge development in the field.

Proponents of an empirical orientation argue that parts of the world around us are indeed knowable and measurable, and that important knowledge for the field can be derived through systematic measurement, observation, and experimentation. Thus, the canons of research are seen as providing extremely useful guidelines to accurately observe reality; they rule out spurious, confounding, and alternative explanations for observed phenomena; and, in fact, help provide the cleanest possible answers (though certainly not "the truth") about the best available way to help the clients and consumers of social work services.

Finally, proponents of this point of view challenge the critics to provide examples of nonempirical research that can in fact be used to make clear, informed decisions about the ultimate research-and-practice questions: which techniques, used by which practitioners, are most successful with which clients with what types of problems in what settings? Since it appears as though only a tiny percentage of studies in social work—possibly less than 10 percent—attempt qualitative analyses anyway (Glisson, 1983), it may be that the rhetoric about their value is not in proportion to the availability of such studies to be used to make critical decisions about practice.

Qualitative versus Quantitative Methodologies   A logical outgrowth of the epistemological debate is the debate about research methodologies and the relative value of qualitative and quantitative research. Indeed, this debate is most accurately described as a specific, but very important, instance of epistemological differences as they can affect actual research practice. In other words, the quantitative-qualitative controversy may be viewed as one way of operationalizing some of the issues described in the previous section.

The quantitative-qualitative argument to some extent duplicates the epistemological issues. Since quantitative methodologies have in fact been the more-or-less predominant form of research in social work, qualitatively oriented methodologists often attack them as obsolete and irrelevant for practice. They argue that qualitative methods are more compatible with the mission and style of social work and are more likely to be utilized by practitioners.

Quantitative researchers respond by arguing that quantitative methods allow far greater clarity about causal phenomena and generalization, since well-established procedures can rule out threats to internal and external validity. Thus, quantitative studies actually can have the greatest potential for furthering progress in the profession, since guidelines for utilizing their results are clearly formulated. Further, these researchers point out that qualitative methods often are unsystematic, vague, and not really focused on the problems of most concern to social workers: developing the most effective ways of helping clients.

The debate can be put into perspective by describing some basic characteristics of both types of research, following the discussion by Epstein (1988). Quantitative designs by and large are used to test and validate predictive and cause-and-effect hypotheses while qualitative designs are used to assemble descriptions of the world around us, either as ends in themselves or as a basis for future hypotheses. Quantitative methodologies tend to use deductive logic, applying theory to the circumstances under investigation, while qualitative studies most often use inductive logic, deriving concepts and even theory from the circumstances being studied.

Research that is described as quantitative attempts to use objective methods, striving to control for biases involved in measurement and design procedures, while qualitative studies attempt to describe social reality from the subjective point of view of participants. Quantitative studies attempt to translate concepts into operational indicators and numerical indices to test hypotheses using statistical procedures in order to validate predictions. Qualitative studies typically eschew such methods, focusing more on detailed observation of events and discussion of their meaning with the people targeted for study, validating concepts by comparing similarities among individual cases and making generalizations inductively.

Finally, the designs used by the two types of methods vary a great deal. Quantitative studies use surveys, correlational and experimental designs, standardized methods of observation when possible, and focus on attempting to control alternative explanations for the events being observed. Qualitative designs typically use participant observation, purposeful conversation, and ethnomethodological approaches to attempt to minimize intrusiveness of the design. The major thrust of quantitative designs is toward quantitative/descriptive or explanatory studies, while qualitative designs are more geared toward exploratory research.

These differences clearly can be related to their epistemological roots as well as to the individual proclivities of the researchers who use them. There are indeed distinct differences in the perspectives and methods used by the two camps. On the other hand, as Epstein (1988) points out, both approaches are planned, attempt to be systematic, and both certainly are empirical in the sense that they rely on experience and observation. In addition, most advocates for both points of view generally agree that both approaches are necessary for knowledge development, disagreeing more strenuously on the extent to which they should be used in social work. Thus, in the seeds of these similarities may come some possibilities for rapprochement.

Good Guys versus Bad Guys   At times, the level of acrimony between the opposing camps has created siege mentalities, where the substance of the arguments—and the potentials for improvement of the social work enterprise—have become secondary issues. Researchers and practitioners often aligned themselves with one or another group, precluding careful examination of the issues. Thus, while the debate degenerated into bad guys versus good guys warfare, bad and good (as usual) depended solely on whose side one was on. Thus, the quantitative camp viewed themselves as tough minded and the qualitative camp as tender minded. The qualitative researchers viewed themselves as politically progressive and oriented to practitioners' real needs and the quantitative camps as politically conservative, caring only about research for the sake of research. Qualitative researchers are portrayed as being opposed to quantitative research because they don't know anything about statistics, while quantitative researchers are portrayed as automatons, uncaring about people.

Indeed, the politics of these issues was an important factor in the debate, with qualitative researchers arguing that quantitative researchers, who are in the majority in social work, control all the positions of influence. Thus, the type of research that is taught in schools of social work, funded, and published is controlled by quantitative researchers. The reward system in social work was seen as punishing qualitative researchers while rewarding quantitative researchers. In fact, the political basis of the argument was extended by Davis (1985), who argued that the major knowledge development enterprise in social work—essentially comprised of quantitative researchers—was dominated by the "male voice," while the "female voice" of the profession—essentially embodied in social work practitioners—has been suppressed.

Is Resolution Possible?   Perhaps the best way to address this question is to reframe it: are there legitimate ways in which a variety of points of view about research methodology and knowledge development can be accommodated in social work? The answer to this question is a resounding yes. At the very least, the debates on these issues have produced a far clearer understanding about some of the potential contributions that can be made by qualitative research. As Reid (1987c) has pointed out, there are many areas of inquiry for which qualitative methodologies are simply more appropriate than traditional quantitative methods. Thus, the question should not be which is the best philosophy, method, or perspective for social work, but given a particular research question, what is the best method and design for addressing that question. Epstein (1989) has described a number of utilization guidelines for making just such a determination.

Thus, one can envision a research enterprise where the highest priority is placed on a multimethod perspective with a profession-wide commitment not to advocate for one's own perspective, but to develop the best methods for answering the variety of questions important to social work. Several models for synthesis of these conflicts were recently described by Peile (1988), including the critical, new paradigm, and creative paradigms. Each of these models offers a paradigm for synthesis that could contain some basis for resolution of conflicting epistemological views.

A second priority involves the need for broader dissemination of studies using nontraditional methods, both in social work education and in the profession's publication outlets. Such dissemination necessarily would include clearer statements by nontraditional methodologists of not only the potentialities for their designs but the limitations imposed by the peculiarities of observation, measurement, design, and analysis. It is also important for students and practitioners to be exposed to these designs and the implications for practice that can be derived from them; thus, the number of such studies made available to the field must be expanded, using as many forms of dissemination as possible, including books, journals, and conference presentations.

Finally, it behooves all social workers to be able to evaluate a variety of approaches to knowledge development, and to be able to critically analyze debates such as those described here. To that end, it is crucial that social workers utilize some type of framework with guidelines that will help them review competing claims. Just such a framework has been proposed by Gambrill (1985), and includes a number of criteria that can enhance real learning of differences among approaches by focusing on the soundness of arguments while dismissing distracting appeals to emotionality and buzz words.

Advances in Knowledge Development

Compared to the issues regarding epistemology, the past decade has seen only modest development and dissemination of new technology in the area of knowledge development, that is, the basic methods for generating new knowledge for practice. While the focus still is on clear and systematic operationalization of the processes of knowledge development, recent years have witnessed attempts at continuation and refinement of changes that had begun in the 1970s and earlier (Fischer, 1981). Indeed, if one of the hallmarks of the movement toward empirically based practice is increasing clarity and refinement of knowledge development for practice, then these changes need to be given far broader attention in the profession and their dissemination enhanced. Some examples of these advances include work on developmental research, social R & D (research and development), and work on evaluating and transferring technology from other fields.

Developmental Research   Major work in this area is best exemplified by contributions by Thomas (1984, 1985, 1988) and Reid (1983, 1987a, 1988). Developmental research is not devoted to the traditional development of knowledge in general, but instead may be defined as strategies directed toward the analysis, design, development, and evaluation of innovations in human services (Thomas, 1985). A major focus of developmental research, then, is the development of empirically based intervention technology. This is at the heart of the changes that have been occurring in social work over the past two decades.

One might argue that developmental research offers a unique research paradigm in and of itself. Research is used in a variety of different ways, including reviewing existing research literature, assessing practitioners' current modes of practice, designing intervention programs, evaluating their implementation, using these evaluations to revise the model, and again systematically evaluating its implementation and effectiveness.

This model of research features close cooperation between the practice and research enterprises in social work; in fact, it illustrates how they can be one and the same. As Reid (1987c) notes, developmental research overcomes a number of obstacles of conventional research by using the self-corrective powers of research, avoiding inherent obstacles between practitioners and researchers involving utilization of findings from external research, and by applying products that are joint creations of the service/research endeavor.

One of the major contributions of the past decades, in fact, is the book by Thomas (1984) describing in detail the process of designing interventions for the human services. This book goes into more detail than any other in social work about the elaborate process of designing interventions, and could be viewed as a major building block for empirically based practice. Indeed, as Thomas (1984) points out, it is paradoxical to think that with intervention methods being the major way social work achieves its objectives, the prior lack of a methodology of intervention design is both shocking and an acute problem. This book, and the other contributions of developmental research, address this deficiency.

Unfortunately, there are still many problems to be overcome. While there may be hope that some of the newer outcome studies in social work may be focused on evaluation of interventions that were in part designed by the practitioners and evaluation team in the project (Reid, 1987c), the main contributions of developmental research have yet to be thoroughly disseminated and well integrated into the profession. Further, some of the concepts, designs, vocabulary, and processes of developmental research are complex and perhaps overelaborate for ready use by most practitioners. And finally, there are no guarantees that the product of a developmental research effort, once disseminated, will be appropriately used or even effective once it is integrated into everyday practice.

Nevertheless, advances in developmental research provide great potential for enhancing empirically based practice once some of these problems are more thoroughly addressed.

Social R & D   In some ways, social R & D is simply another term for developmental research. However, work on social R & D, as exemplified particularly by the work of Rothman (1988; Rothman & Lubben, 1988; Rothman et al., 1981; Rothman, Erlich, & Teresa, 1983), takes on special importance because of a somewhat broader purview than the developmental research tradition in social work. Rothman has moved his work from Michigan to the U.C.L.A. Center for Child and Family Policy, where he has focused not only on clinical, empirically based practice, but on attempting first to identify a social problem or issue of concern to social work and then on developing an intervention approach for dealing with it. The interventions may be clinical but they may also have a broader focus. Once a problem has been identified in discourse with an agency, a series of ten steps follow (Rothman, 1986).

The ten steps actually involve transferring the technology of industrial R & D into social service-related work, integrating and synthesizing currently available research into policy and intervention proposals. The steps of Rothman's social R & D are: (1) searching the relevant literature to retrieve pertinent existing literature; (2) synthesis of existing literature; (3) translating this general literature into action guidelines—a practical form suggesting a direction for intervention; (4) obtaining practical or professional knowledge of the subject to supplement the existing research synthesis; (5) designing specific intervention programs based on the above; (6) field testing of these programs in pilot studies in community agencies, and establishing a working model to implement programs; (7) evaluation of pilot programs; (8) conducting and evaluating a broader main field test or development project; (9) packaging of successfully tested programs in easily understood forms; and (10) the use of marketing techniques to diffuse the programs to agencies and practitioners in as wide a geographic area as possible (Rothman, 1986).

An example of recent application of most of these principles is available in Rothman (1988), involving runaway and homeless youths. It illustrates the way social R & D, though involving considerable effort and commitment by participants in the process, can systematically adapt research to serve practice.

Transferring Technology from Other Fields   Social work traditionally has identified itself as a profession using a pluralistic knowledge base—that is, one that utilizes knowledge derived from many sources. A corollary of this tradition, and one that is especially important for empirically based practice, is that only the best knowledge should be derived. Although there may be many criteria for deciding what is best, a critical factor is research evidence about that knowledge, especially research evidence that application of the knowledge leads to demonstrably improved services and outcomes for clients. In fact, this is the basis for development of the eclectic, empirically based approach that is at the heart of changes in the practice of social work (Fischer, 1978, 1986).

In order to develop a broad, effective knowledge base for social work, in addition to efforts such as developmental research and social R & D within the field, it is critical for social workers to be aware of developments from outside our field that have potential for improving our practice. This in turn requires the development of frameworks for systematically evaluating such knowledge to avoid haphazard, uncritical selection. Fortunately, such frameworks are available both for evaluating research (Mullen, 1983, 1988; Fischer, 1993; Tripodi, Fellin, & Meyer, 1969) and for evaluation of theory (Nugent, 1987; Fischer, 1978). Thus, the process of systematic knowledge selection can proceed apace, requiring only identification of areas external to the field for evaluation.

There are numerous areas available for possible adaptation for social work, including literally all of the behavioral and social sciences and the frequently familiar work of related helping professions like clinical psychology, counseling, and psychiatry. But one area that often is overlooked has led to development of a major contribution regarding transfer of technology to social work, and that is the area of social psychology. Although typically viewed as more of a basic than applied science, theory and research in social psychology contains numerous important implications for social work.

The major work by Feld and Radin (1982; see also Brehm & Smith, 1986) on use of social psychology for social work and the mental health professions is an important example of the way technology from other fields can be evaluated and translated into useful principles for practice. Feld and Radin (1982) provide an extensive review of the results of research in social psychology, and link that information to service delivery strategies in social work. They take such social psychological concepts as interpersonal attraction, altruism, social roles, attribution, social influence, attitude change, and a variety of findings on groups and demonstrate the ways these research findings can have a significant influence on direct practice. It is systematic work on knowledge transfer such as this, combined with the results of developmental research within social work, that ultimately can produce important advances in the development of empirically based practice.

Integrating Research and Practice

There seems little question that the heart of the development of an empirically based approach to practice is the extent to which theory, research, and practice can be integrated. As indicated earlier in this article, this integration occurs in at least two ways: (1) using the results of research to inform practice, and (2) monitoring and evaluating one's own practice. While the major developments in these two areas occurred during the 1970s (Fischer, 1981), the decade of the 1980s witnessed continuing development in both areas with increasing sophistication and elaboration of models of both research utilization and evaluation of practice. For example, two recent publications clearly illustrate the way data-gathering techniques typically thought of as research can be used in everyday practice and how research findings, concepts, and logic can be integrated into practice (Siegel, 1988; Siegel & Reamer, 1988).

Developments in these and any other areas are particularly enhanced when supported by institutional structures. Two recent structural modifications that are likely to affect the integration of research and practice are, first, the adoption of a new accreditation policy by the Council on Social Work Education (1982) that calls for content on research to include systematic evaluation of the student's own practice, and, second, development of a new journal called *Research on Social Work Practice,* edited by Bruce Thyer. This new journal focuses on both group (nomothetic) and single-system (idiographic) designs evaluating the outcomes of practice, empirical reports on assessment procedures in practice, reviews of empirically based practice research literature, and other work that might advance the scope of practice. Due to begin publication in January, 1991, this journal, along with *Journal of Social Service Research* and *Social Work Research and Abstracts,* is certain to add a new dimension to the fostering of developments in empirically based practice.

Research Utilization

If social work is to move toward greater use of empirically based practice, there is no substitute for practitioners being able to utilize the research produced by others. Unfortunately, it is well documented that a number of barriers exist to utilization of research by practitioners. Many of these factors have been described by Rosen (1983) and include factors related to: (1) the knowledge to be used, (2) the practice situation and setting, (3) characteristics of the practitioner, (4) the medium through which knowledge is being communicated, and (5) the social context. In other words, to what extent is knowledge likely to be utilized when the knowledge is not perceived as relevant to practice, is seen as requiring too much time away from practice to find and master, is published only in journals that are not accessible and then only in obtuse language, and is not supported by peers and supervisors?

A recent comprehensive review by Kirk (1988) summarizes much of the work on research utilization in social work over the past several years. He concludes that while the barriers are indeed formidable, some progress is occurring. There are signs that researchers increasingly are sensitive to beginning where the practitioner is, that qualitative studies may be able to provide information of more immediate relevance to practice, that technology needs to be and can be modified to meet more adequately the needs of practitioners, and that work on developmental research and social R & D, such as reviewed in a previous section, has great potential for increasing the use of research-derived modes of practice.

Another comprehensive review on the use of evaluation results in education, mental health, and social services offers some additional empirically derived guidelines that can enhance utilization (Cousins & Leithwood, 1986). Twelve factors influencing utilization were isolated. Six were concerned with implementation of evaluations and included evaluation quality, credibility, relevance, communication, the findings themselves, and timelines of evaluation for users. Six others were concerned with features of the decision or policy setting: information needs of users, decision characteristics, political climate, competing information, personal characteristics of users, and user commitment and receptiveness to evaluation information. Cousins and Leithwood (1986) also developed a preliminary framework suggesting relationships among these variables. Overall, use of research findings appeared to be strongest when: (1) evaluations were perceived as appropriate in approach, methodological sophistication, and intensity; (2) the decisions to be made were significant to users and of a sort considered appropriate for the application of formally collected data; (3) evaluation findings were consistent with the beliefs and expectations of the users; (4) users were involved in the evaluation process and had a prior commitment to the benefits of the evaluation; (5) users considered the data reported in the evaluation to be relevant to their problems; and (6) when a minimum amount of information from other sources conflicted with the results of the evaluation.

Findings such as these by Cousins and Leithwood (1986) and Kirk (1988) are challenges to those in the field eager to advance the profession's use of the empirically based practice model. They provide fertile suggestions not only for ways of enhancing adoption of research findings in practice, but for further research on the utilization process itself (such as the moderately successful project on agency-based research utilization in a residential child care setting by Grasso, Epstein, & Tripodi, 1988).

An important way of enhancing the process of utilization of research findings lies in the work on construction of personal practice models by Mullen (1983, 1988). Using an open systems framework that incorporates cognizance of societal, agency, client, and practitioner factors, Mullen specifies a series of steps that can be used by the individual practitioner to apply research findings to develop his or her own practice model. The steps include: (1) identification of substantive findings concerning intervention variables and their effects on clients; (2) identification of the quality of the evidence; (3) development of summary generalizations; (4) deduction of practice guidelines; and (5) specification of an evaluation plan (Mullen, 1978).

The importance of Mullen's work is that it provides a series of steps that a practitioner can actually implement. This removes the work on research utilization from abstract conceptualizations to specific ways a practitioner can begin to enhance his or her own practice through the use of empirically derived interventions.

Single-System Designs

No other phenomenon is more a trademark of the move toward empirically based practice than the area of clinical evaluation, particularly use of single-system designs (SSDs). These designs essentially involve any number of variations on a series of four basic steps: (1) identifying a problem to be changed and finding ways to measure it; (2) collecting information on the problem on a repeated basis prior to the onset of intervention; (3) identifying a specific intervention, implementing it, and continuing to collect information on the problem; and (4) analyzing the data by evaluating any changes in the problem over the course of the entire process. These designs are so central to empirically based practice because they involve the practitioner taking charge of designing and implementing his or her own evaluations of the effectiveness of practice and using the results of those evaluations to improve practice. While SSDs may not be the only way for practitioners to monitor and evaluate their own practice, they certainly offer a major advance compared to traditional practices of subjective evaluation or nonevaluation. They appear to be the primary method of evaluation recommended by advocates of empirically based practice.

Recent work on SSDs has exploded in social work. A bibliography compiled by Thyer and Boynton (1989) dealing with publications completely or partially concerned with SSDs has identified over 220 publications in social work alone on this topic. For example, a recent book by Blythe and Tripodi (1989), though not solely concerned with single-system designs, has focused on measurement in direct practice. Actually the book has a broader purview than just measurement, since it basically is concerned with integration of basic research concepts in a problem-solving model of direct clinical practice. In particular, Blythe and Tripodi

(1989) make important contributions to illustrating the way measurement and other research methods can be used to aid in: specifying intervention objectives, selecting interventions, proceduralizing interventions, ensuring that interventions are implemented as intended, and examining termination and follow-up with clients. Since one of the weak points in previous work on SSDs is a deemphasis on specification of interventions in favor of greater emphasis on measurement and design elements, the Blythe and Tripodi (1989) book makes a major contribution toward redressing this problem.

One of the more interesting recent contributions to the literature in social work is a book that unfortunately has not been widely disseminated. Based on a conference at the University of Washington in 1985, the publication of the proceedings, *Perspectives on Direct Practice Evaluations* (Gottlieb et al, 1987), contains a number of innovative gems. They include works on using a new concept, theoretical significance, to evaluate outcome (Bloom); use of qualitative methods in SSD (Reid & Davis); training social work administrators to use evaluation in daily practice (Wodarski & Lindsey); and a number of other contributions. These works show social workers looking well beyond the basic steps of the SSD process and developing a creative literature around the issues and problems faced by practitioners confronted with the task of evaluating their own practice.

Outside of social work, the field has moved toward increasing sophistication about the processes of SSD as well as refinement of many of the procedures. For example, Barlow, Hayes, & Nelson (1984) have proposed a new conceptualization of SSD that varies from but includes traditional formulations (Bloom, Fischer, & Orme, 1993; Barlow & Hersen 1984). They have devised a three-level model of designs including within-series elements (such as the standard A-B design), between-series elements (such as alternating intervention designs), and combined series elements (such as multiple baseline and reversal designs).

Other developments have focused particularly on some thorny statistical issues in SSD, such as the problem of autocorrelation (*Behavioral Assessment,* 1988a, 1988b; Edgington, 1984), or on increasingly sophisticated strategies for addressing problems in SSDs such as the capability to examine joint effects of treatment components and generalization and maintenance effects (Barrios, 1984; Barrios & Hartmann, 1988).

A major criticism of SSDs, particularly in social work, has been that these designs appear most useful for behavioral types of practice that allow for easier specification of variables, but that nonbehavioral practice with more of a tradition of considering complex whole situations cannot be so easily evaluated. An increasing body of literature, however, is available with both conceptualizations and actual examples of practice integrating nonbehavioral practice with SSDs (Nelsen, 1981); for example, psychodynamic practice (Dean & Reinherz, 1986; Broxmeyer, 1978); paradoxical instruction (Kolko & Milan, 1983) and communication theory (Nelsen, 1978). These and numerous other examples serve to illustrate the diverse application of SSDs and bolster the idea that they are essentially nontheoretical in the range of approaches to which they might be applied. This work also illustrates the idea that empirically based practice has potential for practitioners from a variety of theoretical orientations, with the overarching organizing principle being the search for more effective modes of practice.

While SSDs do appear to be making an important impact on the field and certainly in professional education, there still are questions about the extent to which these designs are being utilized in social work practice, even when they are learned during the education experience. A few studies have been conducted evaluating the extent to which practitioners use all or part of the clinical evaluation technology they have been taught (Welch, 1983; Mutschler, 1984; Gingerich, 1984a; Richey, Blythe, & Berlin, 1987). The results ranged from total nonuse to use of at least one single system design by 40 percent of respondents (Gingerich, 1984a), to use of a number of components of single-system evaluation by respondents with minimal use (11 percent) of the total clinical evaluation package (Richey, Blythe, & Berlin, 1987). These results, of course, are affected by methodological considerations and response rates but on the whole, they do not add up to overwhelming endorsement by practitioners of the actual use of clinical evaluation procedures. This is true even though it appears as though clients tend to find SSD procedures more acceptable than just the practitioner's opinion (Campbell, 1988). Of course, another way to look at these data is to recognize that even some use is better than no attempt at specification and objectification, and better than what would be expected without training. Indeed, as Bloom (personal communication, August, 1990) points out, when one compares the extent to which SSDs are used by social workers after graduation with the extent to which experimental/control designs are used, SSDs look very good. This may indicate considerable progress in the teaching of research to social workers.

One constructive way of approaching this issue is to use already existing literature to begin systematic programming for enhanced utilization. Just such an analysis was developed by Robinson, Bronson, & Blythe (1988), who applied the literature on implementation of human service innovations to adoption of SSDs. They provide a number of suggestions that can be used as guidelines for enhancing utilization of SSDs. (1) The technology itself needs more work to enhance its relevance and applicability to specific settings. (Indeed, the increasing sophistication of the work on these designs as described earlier may just make them even more inaccessible to practitioners.) Thus, work on increasing the relevance of these designs can be marketed to agencies in handbooks, manuals, and videotapes for training and implementation. (2) Practitioners need to be convinced of the value of SSDs, and more evidence on their benefits needs to be supplied. (3) It is crucial to increase organizational supports for using SSDs. (4) More evidence of the applicability of these designs across different practice models is needed, with subsequent alteration of evaluation procedures to make them more compatible with those models. (5) The processes by which practitioners adopt new practice methods need to be more clearly identified and utilized in implementation efforts.

(6) Greater effort has to be made to reach practitioners through workshops and training materials, using evaluation of different implementation efforts to produce more successful implementation models.

In connection with these suggestions, a new book by Reid (1987) addresses the whole range of issues involved in developing a research program in human service agencies. While the guidelines contained in this book pertain to just about any of the areas described in this article, they are perhaps most germane to implementation of evaluation designs by practitioners. The book provides a number of thoughtful, workable strategies for successfully conducting research while simultaneously providing services to clients. The topics covered range from synthesizing research into daily job responsibilities to making research fun. This book is important reading for practitioners and researchers who are attempting to integrate research and evaluation procedures in agency practice.

As if these issues were not enough, the area of SSDs has also seen its version of the "great epistemological debate." A number of authors have described the conflict between research and practice objectives, questioned the applicability of SSDs to different practice approaches, criticized the overemphasis on quantitative methods in SSDs, and questioned the pragmatics of applicability (Thomas, 1978; Ruckdeschel & Farris, 1986, 1982; Crane, 1985; see also Thomas, 1984). Of course, there also have been a number of responses to these issues (Gambrill & Barth, 1980; Levy, 1985; Geismar & Wood, 1982; Ivanov, Blythe, & Briar, 1987; see also Gingerich, 1988, for a comprehensive review of the issues).

As with the broader epistemological issues, this "mini-epistemological debate" has not necessarily won converts to one side or another. What it has helped to do, though, is sensitize advocates of clinical evaluation to the actual needs of practitioners. Even advocates for SSDs are calling for the need to deemphasize the research role of SSDs while emphasizing the assessment of client change, develop designs more systematically related to the practice context in which they will be used, develop ways to measure client progress that are more consistent with practice constraints, acknowledge the designs practitioners prefer to use when given free choice, and find ways to develop stronger systems of agency supports (Levy, 1981; Gingerich, 1988). It is suggestions like these—that emphasize reality, practicality, and relevance—that may have the greatest chance of maximizing use of systematic evaluation procedures by practitioners, as the entire empirically based model continues to evolve.

Practice Techniques with Evidence of Effectiveness

If the trademark of the empirically based practitioner is the use of single-system designs, than certainly the hallmark of this perspective is the attempt to identify intervention approaches that are clear, systematic, precise, and, above all, effective. The corollary of this effort is that empirically based practitioners cannot be bound by allegiance to any single theoretical orientation, but only by the commitment to finding the interventions that most successfully provide help to clients (Fischer,

1981). While most social work practitioners do, in fact, report themselves as "eclec-tic" (Jayarantne, 1978, 1982; Cocozzelli, 1987), it is not clear that such practitioners use systematic criteria to select their approaches or even necessarily attend at all to evidence of effectiveness in making those selections.

The last decade has seen an outpouring of work on eclectic and integrative approaches, both in practice with individuals and families, including a journal, *Journal of Integrative and Eclectic Psychotherapy,* devoted solely to those topics (Norcross, 1986, 1987; Liddle, 1982; Lebow, 1987; Reid, 1987b). These works have called attention to a number of issues involved in developing an eclectic practice. More importantly, they have provided a variety of different frameworks that can be used by practitioners in developing an eclectic practice as well as providing examples of eclectic practice in action (see especially Norcross, 1986).

Practice Areas for Attention

An eclectic, empirically based approach to practice perhaps is the most demand-ing approach to practice. This is because the practitioner never can be satisfied with what he or she already knows; new approaches with even broader applicability and/or greater evidence of effectiveness may become available at any time. Thus, a guiding principle of this type of practice is to attempt to keep informed of new developments in the field as they occur. Fortunately, the enormity of the task is made somewhat manageable by the presence of a number of annuals and journals that do a good job of synthesizing recent developments (e.g., *Review of Behavior Therapy: Theory and Practice,* Guilford Press, 12 volumes; *Progress in Behavior Modification,* Academic Press, 25 volumes; *Annual Review of Psychology,* Annual Reviews, Inc., 40 volumes; and the journal *Clinical Psychology Review*).

In addition to these publications, several recent books have provided step-by-step accounts of the application of many empirically derived techniques to a vari-ety of common practice problems (e.g., Corcoran, 2000; Bellack & Hersen, 1990; Barlow, 1985; Hersen & Bellack, 1985). These books are particularly important because they translate research on many of the most effective clinical techniques into actual practice strategies that practitioners can use with their clients. The problems addressed in these books range from substance abuse to anxiety and stress to depression to sexual difficulties. Typically included in these works are a rationale for the interventions selected, description of the specific techniques, and summaries of actual case records or interventions.

Another area related to empirically based practice that has received consider-able attention is problem assessment (McReynolds, 1989). The essence of effective, empirically based practice is a proper assessment; it is through the assessment that the practitioner makes the decision about just what intervention techniques will be applied to which problems. Comprehensive works on assessment, including not only new measurements but strategies of assessment, make the task of the empiri-cally based practitioner somewhat easier in being able to focus on only relatively few sources (e.g., Hersen & Bellack, 1988; Mash & Terdal, 1988; Barlow, 1981;

Corcoran & Fischer, 1987; Goldstein & Hersen, 1984). There have been major advances in the technology of assessment over the past decade and these advances promise to enhance empirically based practice by providing a higher degree of precision in assessment. This, in turn, allows more systematic and sensitive selection of intervention procedures.

Frameworks for Practice

The complexities of implementing an eclectic, empirically based approach to practice require paying special attention to the intervention process. That is, compared to traditional, unitheoretical intervention approaches, empirically based practice emphasizes application of techniques of assessment and intervention derived from several sources. Haphazard application of these techniques not only is the opposite of what empirically based practice is all about, but more importantly, would probably doom the chance for the enhanced outcomes that empirically based practice promises.

During the past decade, several publications have presented systematic frameworks that can guide the integration and implementation of techniques derived from various sources. Within social work, just a sampling of these include publications by Rose and Edleson (1987), Hepworth and Larsen (1990), Simons and Aigner (1985), and Gambrill (1983). Each of these books incorporates a step-by-step framework for intervention as well as a discussion of specific intervention techniques for implementation.

Outside of social work, a few recent books have focused specifically on the decisions that are an explicit part of the treatment process and frameworks for integrating them. In addition to the groundbreaking eclectic work by Lazarus (1986), these works are by Beutler and Clarkin (1990), Nezu and Nezu (1990), and Kanfer and Schefft (1988). In particular, the work of Beutler and Clarkin (1990) attempts to provide a guide to prescriptive selection of psychosocial interventions. Though not relying solely on empirically based intervention techniques, this book does attempt to use a research-based model that sequentially considers client dimensions, environments, settings, practitioners, and approaches to practice. Thus, it attempts to systematize and integrate the process of treatment selection that ordinarily may be engaged in intuitively.

Specific Available Techniques

The ultimate goal of the empirically based practitioner is to have at his or her disposal a variety of intervention techniques of more-or-less demonstrated effectiveness. This increasingly is possible.

A decade ago, when the movement toward empirically based practice began to crystallize, it was possible to identify four areas where the bulk of the evidence of effectiveness seemed to be accumulating. Those areas were: (1) procedures that added structure to the intervention process, (2) behavior therapy, (3) cognitive change procedures, and (4) the interpersonal skills of empathy, warmth and genuineness (Fischer, 1981). Indeed, research in these areas has accumulated at an astounding rate, with the fourth area broadened to include a number of other process variables involving client-practitioner interactions that have been shown to enhance outcome (Garfield & Bergin, 1986; Beutler, Crago, & Arizmendi, 1986; Orlinsky & Haward, 1986; Marshall & Kurts, 1982; Lambert, 1989).

One important feature of this research is that it almost always focused on specification of the actual interventions involved. That is, the broad approach or theory—say, behavior therapy—was not being studied. Rather, it was individual techniques derived from those approaches that were being investigated. Not only is this additional reason for not devoting oneself to a single practice theory (an entire school of thought is usually not subject to investigation nor is one likely to be validated even if it were somehow possible to study), but it provides the special service to practitioners of identifying specific techniques that can be applied differentially depending on the specific circumstances of the case.

A number of such techniques can be identified (Fischer, 1986). They were selected for inclusion here for two basic reasons:

1. They have accumulated a substantial amount of empirical evidence of effectiveness with one or more problems; and/or
2. With a modicum of evidence, they are specifically designed to deal with certain problems that the other techniques listed do not successfully address.

Although this listing is not intended to be exhaustive, the techniques and technique packages that best appear to meet those criteria as of the beginning of the 1990s are the following:

1. Assertion Training and Social Skills Training (Donahoe & Driesenga, 1988; Curran & Monti, 1982; Bellack & Hersen, 1979). These technique packages have been used successfully with a wide range of skill deficits in populations that range from severely disturbed psychiatric patients to unhappy marital couples (Twentyman & Zimering, 1979).
2. Contingency Management (Rimm & Masters, 1979). A catch-all term for a whole variety of operant techniques to both strengthen or maintain desired behaviors and weaken or decreased undesired behaviors, these techniques and packages include reinforcement, punishment, extinction, time out, the token economy, overcorrection (Foxx & Bechte, 1982), and so on. Contingency management has been used successfully with almost all imaginable populations, including children and adults, individuals, couples, and families, and with the most moderate to the most severe of problem behaviors.
3. Systematic Desensitization (Wolpe, 1982). A technique for decreasing maladaptive anxiety, most successfully used when the anxiety is related to relatively specific stimuli, systematic desensitization has been the subject of more controlled investigations than any other therapeutic technique—well

over 250—and has been found to be effective with a wide range of anxiety disorders (Walker et al., 1981).

4. Behavioral Contracting (Kirschenbaum & Flanery, 1983). Although largely associated with contingency management, the use of contracting has received a fair amount of independent evidence of effectiveness in use with several problem populations and with individuals, families, and couples.

5. Problem-solving (D'zurilla & Nezu, 1982). Although the accumulated evidence is somewhat weak, and a number of problem-solving packages are available, the evidence is encouraging enough to suggest the importance of providing clients with an overall, step-by-step framework to aid in solving problems and making decisions. One framework that seems particularly useful is the one developed by Janis and Mann (1977).

6. Self-instruction Training (Meichenbaum, 1977; Cormier & Cormier, 1985). A package essentially combining cognitive and behavioral techniques, self-instruction training has accumulated several dozen controlled studies showing it to be effective with several disorders, including problems of impulsive children and public speaking and test anxiety (Rachman & Wilson, 1980).

7. Stress-inoculation Training (Meichenbaum, 1977; Cormier & Cormier, 1984). Another combination of cognitive and behavioral techniques, stress-inoculation training, though not as extensively studied as self-instruction training, has been successfully used with problems involving interpersonal and general anxiety and stress and anger control (Novaco, 1979).

8. Cognitive Restructuring (Goldfried, 1979); Ellis & Grieger, 1977; Cormier and Cormier, 1985). Although cognitive restructuring comes in a variety of packages (see Cormier & Cormier, 1985, for an excellent synthesis), it appears to be an important intervention for dealing with problems where the assessment reveals unrealistic expectations, misconceptions, or dysfunctional self-statements may be at the root of those problems.

9. Modeling and Participant Modeling (contact desensitization) (Rimm & Masters, 1979; Cormier & Cormier, 1985; Walker et al., 1981). Modeling—and its many variations, including contact desensitization—has been found to be an effective package in and of itself and in combination with other techniques for both increasing positive behaviors and activities and decreasing negative behaviors and activities. The populations to which modeling has been applied range from the slightly to severely impaired and include behavioral, cognitive, and affective (decrease in anxiety) outcomes.

10. Covert Sensitization (Cautela & Kearny, 1986; Kazdin & Smith, 1979). Although the evidence on covert sensitization is not extensive, there does seem to be enough to suggest that covert sensitization might be useful, in combination with other techniques, in decreasing unwanted sexual behaviors, alcohol abuse, smoking, and overeating. In particular, covert sensitization is one of the few techniques that addresses some of these problems without resort to electrical or mechanical devices or chemical aids.

11. Covert Positive Reinforcement (Cautela & Kearny, 1986; Kazdin & Smith,

1979; Walker et al., 1981). A limited amount of research suggests that covert reinforcement can be effective in modifying negative self-statements, test anxiety, weight control, certain specific animal phobias, and attitude change. This is a technique that is readily adaptable to use with other techniques in more broadly based intervention programs.

12. Covert Modeling (Cautela & Kearny, 1986; Kazdin & Smith, 1979; Cormier & Cormier, 1985). Covert modeling has been shown in some studies to be as effective as live modeling, but with a very limited range of problems, essentially involving fear and lack of assertiveness. Once again, a technique that readily can be combined with others.

13. Exposure and Response Prevention (Marshall et al., 1979). A relatively new technique package, exposure has been found to be effective in a number of studies with problems involving simple and social phobias, agoraphobia, and compulsive rituals (Barlow, 1988; Foa & Steketee, 1979; Brehony & Geller, 1981).

14. Thought Stopping (Rimm & Masters, 1979; Cormier & Cormier, 1985; Walker et al., 1981). Thought stopping is one of the few available techniques designed specifically to deal with problems involving obsessive thoughts which the client cannot control. Although the controlled evidence is insubstantial, there appears to be enough case study evidence to suggest that thought stopping might be included as one component in a broader intervention program.

15. Habit Reversal (Azrin & Nunn, 1973; Turpin, 1983). This technique is specifically designed to overcome a variety of specific undesired habits such as tics, nailbiting, and trichotillomania. Although the number and quality of studies available are not impressive, habit reversal does appear to be a promising way of dealing with a variety of specific problems that most other techniques do not address.

16. Paradoxical Instruction (Dowd & Trutt, 1988). This technique has several variations, including symptom prescription, reframing, restraining, and positioning. There is some evidence that these techniques can be useful with problems involving procrastination, depression, anxiety, and sleep disorders.

It is probably obvious that most of the techniques described here have their roots in cognitive and/or behavioral formulations. The reason is simple: no other approaches or theoretical orientations have described their techniques in such specific fashion, allowing for their clear evaluation, and then carried out the literally hundreds of studies that document the effectiveness of those techniques, especially in a way that they can be isolated and examined as independent entities. Indeed, some of the individual techniques described here have often been compared in controlled research to entire systems of therapy and found to be as effective or more effective (Kazdin & Wilson, 1978). Thus, this clarity and subsequent evaluation allows one to be able to distinguish between legitimate therapeutic procedures and fads.

Another advantage of this clarity of description involves ease of training. When step-by-step procedures are specified, learning how to use the techniques becomes a much easier task. The vagaries of trying to operationalize and implement complicated systems of intervention simply become unnecessary. Indeed, each one of the techniques and technique packages described here has been placed into a common format using step-by-step flowcharts. An example of these flowcharts, using the technique of self-instruction training, is reproduced here as figure 17.1. Wherever possible, the flowcharts for these techniques were designed to follow the format in Cormier & Cormier (1985), an excellent book that has been found to be by far the most useful in helping students and practitioners learn these techniques.

Although only sixteen techniques were described here, in fact, when the several techniques of contingency management and the variations of other techniques (e.g., different types of modeling) are explicated, the sixteen techniques expand to over thirty. Moreover, many of these techniques can and have been used not only with individual clients but in groups and with couples and families as well. Further, these techniques form the basis for any number of combined, complex intervention packages, such as communication and skill training programs, child management programs, and conflict resolution programs. With this increasing sophistication comes the corresponding mandate that these techniques—not to mention this entire model of practice—be systematically applied to areas of special importance to social work that currently are under-researched—such as family violence, including child and partner abuse (Saunders & Azar, 1989; Eisikovits & Edleson, 1989). Such application and investigation in outcome research is a crucial next step in enhancing the relevance of this material for practitioners. In the meantime, used together—and with a foundation in the interpersonal skills and structuring procedures described as other approaches with evidence of effectiveness (Fischer, 1981)—these techniques can provide an integrated and comprehensive approach to practice that at the present time appears to have the best chance of optimizing our effectiveness with our clients.

Recent Developments

Although there are a number of innovations on the horizon that ultimately could have an impact on the direction of empirically based practice, two developments in particular seem to be of special significance. These are the areas of meta-analysis and the integration of expert systems and computers into practice.

Meta-Analysis

Meta-analysis is a generic term for a number of methods for aggregating and statistically analyzing the results of several studies. Traditionally, most reviews of research in social work have been of the narrative type, in which the reviewer assembles and then analyzes a number of studies on a particular topic, drawing

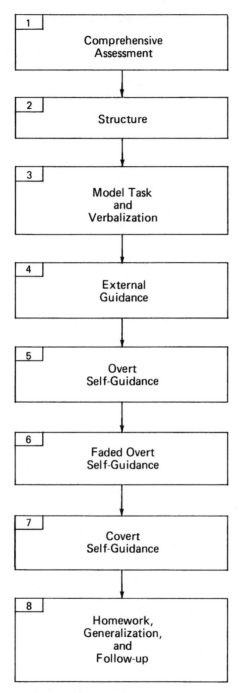

Fig. 17.1 Self-Instruction Training

conclusions by pointing out strengths and weaknesses of the studies and perhaps by using the box score approach, totaling up the number of positive outcomes and comparing it with the number of negative outcomes. Such conclusions frequently are tempered by references to the rigor or soundness of individual studies.

In contrast to this method, meta-analysis uses any one of a number of statistical techniques, usually involving calculation of one or several effect sizes, or combining significance levels or both. This allows the reviewer to conclude whether the results for the set of studies likely was due to chance (combined significance levels) or what the magnitude of the effect for the set of studies was (effect sizes).

A huge body of literature has developed regarding the basic methodology of meta-analysis (e.g., Hedges & Okin, 1985; Shapiro, 1985; Rosenthal, 1984; Hunter, Schmidt & Jackson, 1982; Glass, McGaw & Smith, 1981; Green & Hall, 1984; Walberg & Haertel, 1980). In addition, literally hundreds of meta-analyses have been conducted in areas of interest to social work in the past ten years, including, as just a few examples, psychotherapy (Smith, Glass, & Miller, 1980), family therapy (Hazelrigg, Cooper, & Borduin, 1987), psychotherapy with children (Casey & Berman, 1987), marital therapy (Hahlweq & Markmen, 1988), and deinstitutionalization in mental health (Straw, 1983). In social work, the main attempt at meta-analysis of social work research was the review by Videka-Sherman (1988) of research on social work practice in mental health (with a critique by Hogarty, 1989).

The onslaught of meta-analytic reviews has the making of a revolution in and of itself. As just anecdotal evidence of the increasing availability of meta-analytic reviews, until three years ago, in an advanced research seminar taught by the author, not a single student found and utilized a meta-analysis as the basis for their course assignment. In the spring semester, 1990, 80 percent of the reviews identified by students were meta-analyses.

And why not?

Since social work as a whole uses a pluralistic knowledge base, and empirically based practice in particular is focused on objectively assessing the empirical status of the interventions used, any new technique that appears to add to our capabilities for making sound judgments about the knowledge we utilize must be welcome. This is just what meta-analysis purports to do, by objectively analyzing large bodies of research and presenting results in manageable and, hence, accessible form.

On the other hand, there are a number of serious issues involved in the use of meta-analysis. These recently were summarized by Fischer (1988) as issues in four areas:

1. Selecting a method of meta-analysis. There are no clear guidelines about how to evaluate which is the best method to use and, hence, no clear selection criteria.
2. Selecting studies for a meta-analytic review. These issues include problems with combining divergent studies, varying methodological quality of the primary studies, sampling bias due to unpublished studies, the effects of deficient reporting, and other limitations imposed by the primary studies.

3. Problems with meta-analytic statistics. These include basic problems with the calculation of effect size, problems due to nonindependence of data, potential positive bias, and issues regarding the use of aggregated and non-aggregated data.
4. Interpretation of the results of meta-analysis. These issues include problems in interpreting the meaning of the effect size and issues regarding interpretation of causality.

Although these problems are far too numerous to describe in detail here, just a single example might suffice. It is possible to conduct a review using a meta-analytic effect size and find a positive effect size (meaning the average client in the experimental group did better than most clients in the control group to a specified degree) even though anywhere from one to all of the primary studies in the review showed no statistically significant difference between the groups. Thus, the reviewer will conclude that the treatment that is the subject of the review had an effect when, in fact, the primary studies revealed no such effect at all. This and other factors produces a consistent positive bias in meta-analytic findings (let alone a conflict between the meaning of established statistical procedures and meta-analytic statistics) to the extent that most meta-analyses find that just about all approaches "work" just about all of the time. Such findings do little to advance the field, producing more confusion, and perhaps apathy, than anything else.

Some of the issues surrounding meta-analysis are so serious that they may undercut the attempt of meta-analytic reviewers to really achieve consensus on the value of this approach. On the other hand, the developments and modifications in meta-analysis are proceeding at a furious pace. For example, a number of researchers have suggested use of meta-analytic techniques for analysis of data from single-system designs (Gingerich, 1984b; Gorcoran, 1985; Videka-Sherman, 1986). Thus, some of the problems may eventually be resolved so that the results of meta-analysis can be incorporated into practice with greater confidence.

There does appear to be considerable work necessary before the potential value of meta-analysis can come to fruition. Meta-analysis is more than a fad; it is an attempt by researchers to add to the empirical base that informs practice. Thus, it is crucial for all social workers at least to be able to understand basic meta-analytic methods so that they can intelligently analyze, critique, and consume results. Certainly, the next decade will witness an even greater outpouring of meta-analyses along with modifications in method that may add to the overall reliability and validity of meta-analysis and hence to its utility.

Computers and Expert Systems

It is possible that the next generation of social workers will be using computers as an integral part of their practice. Indeed, in some ways, computers already have arrived as important adjuncts to practice. This has produced a major thrust regarding the need for computer literacy for social work students (Cnaan, 1989).

A new journal on computers for human service workers allows researchers and practitioners to keep abreast of developments in the field (*Computers in Human Services,* Haworth Press).

Some of the already traditional (!) uses of computers, such as word processing and assisting in the management of large data sets for organizations, are already well established in social work. But, in addition to these, there are at least two other ways in which computers may be able to add to practitioners' capabilities: as support for ongoing tasks in practice and as expert systems.

On-Going Support in Practice   A number of innovative programs have been developed for use by practitioners to aid in various activities of the practice process, including assessment (e.g., Butcher, 1987, on computerized assessment), record-keeping, monitoring of treatment, evaluation, and even direct counseling (see Cnaan, 1989, for a brief review). These developments really provide an opportunity for all practitioners, let alone empirically based ones, to enhance and systematize their work. Although there are numerous examples of such programs, brief review of two will serve to exemplify the capabilities of others.

One common use of computers is to aid in single-system design evaluation of practice. A program developed by Bronson and Blythe (1987), called CAPE, is designed to aid practitioners in storing and graphing clinical data and providing simple statistical tests to analyze those data. This program was developed to be relatively easy for novices to use and to be clinically relevant. It handles only baseline-intervention designs (A-B) so far, though these designs are the ones most preferred by practitioners. CAPE does require use of the LOTUS 1-2-3 spreadsheet program, which, because of its special features, makes it a good tool for analyzing client data. The CAPE program is described in the Bronson & Blythe (1987) article and is available from the authors.

A second program with wider ranging capabilities is the Computer Assisted Social Services Program (CASS) developed by Hudson (1988). This program, which requires a hard disk microcomputer, is one of the most powerful general purpose assessment systems available for use with microcomputers. This program stores a number of different clinical assessment scales, allows employment of a variety of other assessment devices, administers and scores assessment tools, interprets assessment scales, prepares graphs, accommodates an unlimited number of social histories and questionnaires, can provide tests and examinations, and incorporates a number of other file and case management functions. The CASS comes with a massive manual of instructions; more information can be obtained in Hudson (1988) or from the WALMYR Publishing Company, Tempe, Arizona.

There are, of course, a number of obstacles to using computers in practice. If students are not computer literate at graduation, then they probably will be unlikely even to pursue this area. Further, many practitioners see use of computers as increasing dehumanization of the practice process and resist computerization on ethical grounds. And, of course, inherent limitations in any computer program—

ranging from difficulty in operations to lack of flexibility in choice of operations—pose severe constraints.

On the other hand, it is not just a cliche to say that the computer age is upon us. It is a reality that the social work enterprise must address in order to maintain currency and relevance in today's world.

Expert Systems A particularly unique and intriguing application of computers is the work on expert systems (Mullen & Schuerman, 1988; Schuerman, 1987; Gingerich, 1990). Expert systems are derived from work on artificial intelligence in such a way that they attempt to capture the knowledge and skill of human experts in order to provide help to others on real world problems. While the technology is still rather basic and in a developing stage, it is likely that the decade of the 1990s will witness an explosion in new technology and availability of expert systems to social work practitioners.

Expert systems function by allowing the user to ask a series of questions about a case. The computer applies the rules with which it has been programmed, deduces the nature of the problem, and arrives at a recommendation. The computer then presents the recommendation to the user along with some supporting explanations if they are requested. Though development of expert systems in social work certainly has not yet lived up to its potential, Mullen & Schuerman (1988) estimate that expert systems in social work are capable of being developed in such areas as needs assessment, problem assessments, classification, intervention, and evaluation—virtually the whole range of social work practice endeavors.

Several potential uses of experts systems in social work, described by Gingerich (1990), are: to make scarce expertise on important problems more available, to train practitioners in new intervention methods, to enhance the consistency with which interventions are applied, to mine and refine practice wisdom, and to develop and test practice theory. These are, indeed, crucial areas for improving practice and would be most significant services. The decade of the nineties is likely to see a proliferation of computer and expert system services available to practitioners. Only time will tell if these services can be made accessible and relevant to clinical practice, whether practitioners will use them, and whether their use is justified in terms of enhancing the outcomes of practice (see also Mutschler & Jayaratne, 1993).

Conclusions

The developments described in this article are not only the achievements of the past decade, they also represent the basis for developments in the future. Like all developments, their eventual success and institutionalization depend on their modification and adaptation to enhance their relevance for practice and thus their intrinsic interest for practitioners. Indeed, because of the increasing sophistication of many of these developments and their remoteness from actual clinical practice, it is important to keep the zeal of the revolutionaries from running away with—and sabotaging—the revolution. In addition, continuing research is needed to examine many of the trends described in this article. For example, there is little or no evidence at this time that the empirically based practitioner is more effective than the nonempirically based practitioner. At this phase of development of the model, effectiveness is in part assumed because of the priority given to use of intervention techniques that already have been more or less validated in independent research, and because the empirically based practitioner is committed to monitoring his or her own practice. But these assumptions must eventually be tested in rigorous outcome research.

There is an unfortunate and somewhat illogical, vicious circle implied in examining the successful establishment of empirically based practice as the model of choice. Institutionalization of this model means acceptance of the model at all levels of the social work enterprise—student, faculty, practitioner. But such institutionalization implies a prior acceptance of the model at those levels, which cannot occur without some degree of institutionalization.

The success of any new model—or new paradigm (Kuhn, 1970)—in a profession or science is probably best assured when adherents of other models leave the field and are replaced by advocates of the new. Thus, new students in the field are taught only the new model and the old model gradually dies out. This seems to be an increasingly possible scenario in social work, as the proliferation of research-oriented doctoral graduates come to replace educators from a different tradition. By the year 2000, the new social work may be the norm, or well on the way to becoming so.

References

Azrin, N. H., & Nunn, R. C. (1982). Habit reversal: A method of eliminating nervous habits and tics, *Behavior Research and Therapy, 11,* 619–628.

Barlow, D. H. (1988). *Anxiety and its disorders: The nature and treatment of anxiety and panic.* New York: Guilford.

Barlow, D. H. (Ed.), (1985). *Clinical handbook of psychological disorders.* New York: Guilford.

Barlow, D. H. (Ed.) (1981). *Behavioral assessment of adult disorders.* New York: Guilford.

Barlow, D. H., Hayes, S. C., & Nelson, R. O. (1984). *The scientist practitioner.* New York: Pergamon.

Barlow, D. H., & Hersen, M. (1984). *Single-case experimental designs,* (2nd ed.). New York: Pergamon.

Barrios, B. A. (1984). Single-subject strategies for examining joint effects: A critical evaluation. *Behavioral Assessment, 6,* 103–120.

Barrios, B. A., & Hartmann, D. P. (1988). Recent developments in single subject methodology: Methods for analyzing generalization, maintenance, and multicomponent treatments. In M. Hersen et al. (eds.), *Progress in Behavior Modification, 22,* 11–47. New York: Academic Press.

Behavioral Assessment (1988a). Whole issue, *10,* 131–223.

Behavioral Assessment (1988b). Whole issue, *10,* 227–297.

Bellack, A. S., & Hersen, M. (Eds.) (1979). *Research and practice in social skills training.* New York: Plenum.

Bellack, A. S., & Hersen, M. (Eds.) (1990). *Comparative treatment for adult disorders.* New York: Wiley.

Beutler, L. E., & Clarkin, J. F. (1990). *Systematic treatment selection: Toward targeted therapeutic interventions.* New York: Brunner/Mazel.

Beutler, L. E., Crago, M., & Arizmendi, T. G. (1986). Research on therapist variables in psychotherapy. In S. L. Garfield & A. E. Bergin, (eds.). *Handbook of psychotherapy and behavior change,* (3rd ed.), 257–310. New York: Wiley.

Bloom, M. (1988). On the epistemology of social work practice knowledge. Invited paper. Empiricism in clinical practice: Present and future, American Institute for Economic Research, Great Barrington, MA, August, 1988.

Bloom, M., Fischer, J., & Orme, J. (1993). *Evaluating practice: Guidelines for the accountable professional* (2nd ed.). Englewood Cliffs, NJ: Prentice-Hall.

Blythe, B. J., & Briar, S. (1985). Developing empirically based models of practice. *Social Work, 30,* 483–488.

Blythe, B. J., & Tripodi, T. (1989). *Measurement in direct practice.* Newbury Park, CA: Sage.

Brehm, S. S., & Smith, T. (1986). Social psychological approaches to psychotherapy and behavior change. In S. L. Garfield and A. E. Bergin (eds.), *Handbook of psychotherapy and behavior change,* (3rd ed.), 69–115. New York: Wiley.

Brekke, J. S. (1986). Scientific imperatives in social work research. *Social Service Review, 60,* 538–554.

Bronson, D. E., & Blythe, B. J. (1987). Computer support for single case evaluation of practice. *Social Work Research and Abstracts, 23,* 10–13.

Broxmeyer, N. (1978). Practitioner-research in treating a borderline child. *Social Work Research and Abstracts, 14,* 5–11.

Butcher, J. N. (1987). *Computerized psychological assessment: A practitioner's guide.* New York: Basic Books.

Campbell, J. A. (1988). Client acceptance of single-system evaluation procedures. *Social Work Research and Abstracts, 24,* 21–22.

Casey, R. J., & Berman, J. S. (1985). The outcome of psychotherapy with children. *Psychological Bulletin, 98,* 388–400.

Cautela, J. R., & Kearney, A. J. (1986). *The covert conditioning handbook.* New York: Springer.

Cnaan, R. A. (1989). Social work education and direct practice in the computer age. *Journal of Social Work Education, 25,* 235–243.

Cocozzelli, C. (1987). A psychometric study of the theoretical orientations of clinical social workers. *Journal of Social Service Research, 9,* 47–70.

Cormier, W. H., & Cormier, L. S. (1985). *Interviewing strategies for helpers* (2nd ed.). Monterey, CA: Brooks/Cole.

Corcoran, K. J. (1985). Aggregating the idiographic data of single-subject research. *Social Work Research and Abstracts, 21,* 9–12.

Corcoran, K. (2000). *Structuring change* (2nd ed.) Chicago: Lyceum.

Corcoran, K., & Fischer, J. (1987). *Measures for clinical practice: A sourcebook.* New York: Free Press.

Council on Social Work Education (CSWE). (1982). *Handbook of accreditation standards and procedures.* New York: CSWE.

Cousins, J. B., & Leithwood, K. A. (1986). Current empirical research on evaluation utilization. *Review of Educational Research, 56,* 331–364.

Crane, D. R. (1985). Single-case experimental designs in family therapy research: Limitations and considerations. *Family Process, 24,* 69–77.

Curran, J. P., & Monti, P. M. (Eds.) (1982). *Social skills training.* New York: Guilford.

Davis, L. V. (1985). Female and male voices in social work. *Social Work, 30,* 106–115.

Dean, R. G., & Fenby, B. L. (1989). Exploring epistemologies: Social work action as a reflection of philosophical assumptions. *Journal of Social Work Education, 25,* 46–54.

Donahoe, C. P., & Driesenga, S. A. (1988). A review of social skills training with chronic mental patients. In M. Hersen et al. (eds.), pp. 131–164. *Progress in Behavior Modification, 23.* New York: Academic Press, 1988.

Dowd, E. T., & Trutt, S. D. (1988). Paradoxical interventions in behavior modification. In M. Hersen et al. (eds.), pp. 96–130. *Progress in Behavior Modification, 23.* New York: Academic Press.

D'Zurilla, T. J., & Nezu, A. (1982). Social problem solving in adults. In P. C. Kendall, (ed.), pp. 201–274. *Advances in Cognitive-Behavioral Research and Therapy,* Vol. 1. New York: Academic Press.

Edgington, E. S. (1984). Statistics and single case analysis. In M. Hersen et al. (eds.), pp. 83–19. *Progress in Behavior Modification, 16.* New York: Academic Press.

Eisikovits, Z. C., & Edleson, J. L. (1989). Intervening with men who batter: A critical review of the literature. *Social Service Review, 63,* 384–414.

Ellis, A., & Grieger, R. (Eds.) (1977). *Handbook of rational-emotive therapy.* New York: Springer.

Epstein, I. (1988). Quantitative and qualitative methods. In R. M. Grinnel (ed.), pp. 178–184. *Social Work Research and Evaluation,* (3rd. ed.) Itasca, IL: F. E. Peacock.

Feld, S. & Radin, N. (1982). *Social Psychology for Social Work and the Mental Health Professions.* New York: Columbia.

Fischer, J. (1973). Is casework effective? A review. *Social Work, 18,* 5–21.

Fischer, J. (1976). *The effectiveness of social casework.* Springfield, IL: Charles C Thomas.

Fischer, J. (1978). *Effective casework practice: An eclectic approach.* New York: McGraw-Hill.

Fischer, J. (1981). The social work revolution. *Social Work, 26,* 199–207.

Fischer, J. (1986). Eclectic casework. In J. C. Norcross (ed.), pp. 320–352. *Handbook of eclectic psychotherapy.* New York: Brunner/Mazel.

Fischer, J. (1988). Meta-analysis: The premise, the problems, the promise. Invited paper, Empiricism in clinical practice: Present and future, American Institute for Economic Research. Great Barrington, MA, August, 1988.

Fischer, J. (1993). Framework for analysis of empirical research. In R. M. Grinnel (ed.), *Social Work Research and Evaluation,* 2nd ed. Itasca, Ill. F. E. Peacock.

Foa, E. B., & Steketee, G. S. (1979). Obsessive-compulsives: Conceptual issues and treatment considerations. In M. Hersen et al. (eds.), pp. 1–53. *Progress in Behavior Modification,* Vol. 8. New York: Academic Press.

Foxx, R. M., & Bechtel, D. R. (1982). Overcorrection. In M. Hersen et al. (eds.), pp. 227–288. *Progress in Behavior Modification,* Vol. 13. New York: Academic Press.

Gambrill, E. D. (1983). *Casework: A competency-based approach.* Englewood Cliffs, NJ: Prentice-Hall.

Gambrill, E. D. (1985). Editorial. *Social Work Research and Abstracts, 21,* 2.

Gambrill, E. D., & Barth, R. P. (1980). Single-case study designs revisited. *Social Work Research and Abstracts, 16,* 15–20.

Garfield, S. L., & Bergin, A. E. (Eds.). (1986). *Handbook of psychotherapy and behavior change,* (3rd. ed.) New York: Wiley.

Geismar, L. L. (1982). Comments on the obsolete scientific imperative in social work research. *Social Service Review, 56,* 311–312.

Geismar, L. L., & Wood, K. M. (1982). Evaluating practice: Science as faith. *Social Casework, 63,* 266–272.

Gingerich, W. J. (1984a). Generalizing single-case evaluation from classroom to practice setting. *Journal of Education for Social Work, 20,* 74–82.

Gingerich, W. J. (1984b). Meta-analysis of applied time-series data. *Journal of Applied Behavioral Science, 20,* 71–79.

Gingerich, W. J. (1988). Rethinking single-case evaluation. Invited paper, Empiricism in clinical practice: Present and future, American Institute for Economic Research, Great Barrington, MA: August, 1988.

Gingerich, W. J. (1990). Expert systems and their potential uses in social work. *Social Casework, 71.*

Glass, G. V., McGraw, B. & Smith, M. L. (1981). *Meta-analysis in social research.* Beverly Hills, CA: Sage.

Glisson, C. A. (1983). Trends in social work research. Paper presented to Annual Meeting of Group for the Advancement of Doctoral Education, University of Alabama, Tuscaloosa, AL.

Glisson, C. A., & Fischer, J. (1987). Statistical training for social workers. *Journal of Social Work Education, 23,* 50–58.

Goldstein, G., & Hersen, M. (Eds.) (1984). *Handbook of psychological assessment.* New York: Pergamon.

Gottlieb, N. et al. (Eds.) (1987). *Perspectives on direct practice evaluation.* Seattle: University of Washington.

Grasso, A. J., Epstein, I., & Tripodi, T. (1988). Agency-based research utilization in a residential child care setting, *12,* 61–80.

Green, B. F., & Hall, J. A. (1984). Quantitative methods for literature reviews. *Annual Review of Psychology, 35,* 37–53.

Hahlweq, K., & Markman, H. J. (1988). Effectiveness of behavioral marital therapy: Empirical status of behavior techniques in preventing and alleviating marital distress. *Journal of Consulting and Clinical Psychology, 56,* 440–447.

Haworth, G. O. (1984). Social work research: Practice and paradigms. *Social Service Review, 58,* 343–357.

Hazelrigg, M. D., Cooper, H. M., & Borduin, C. M. (1987). Evaluating the effectiveness of family therapies: An integrative review and analysis. *Psychological Bulletin, 101,* 428–442.

Hedges, L. V., & Olkin, I. (1985). *Statistical methods for meta-analysis.* New York: Academic Press.

Heineman, M. B. (1981). The obsolete scientific imperative in social work research and practice. *Social Service Review, 57,* 371–397.

Heineman Peiper, M. (1985). The future of social work research. *Social Work Research and Abstracts, 21,* 3–11.

Hepworth, D. H., & Larsen, J. (1990). *Direct social work practice: Theory and skills,* (3rd ed.) Chicago: Dorsey.

Hersen, M., & Bellack, A. S. (Eds.) (1985). *Handbook of clinical behavior therapy with adults.* New York: Plenum.

Hersen, M., & Bellack, A. S. (Eds.) (1988). *Dictionary of behavioral assessment techniques.* New York: Pergamon.

Hogarty, G. E. (1989). Meta-analysis of the effects of practice with the chronically mental ill: A critique and reappraisal of the literature. *Social Work, 34,* 363–373.

Hudson, W. H. (1988). Computer-based clinical practice: Present status and future possibilities. Invited paper, Empiricism in clinical practice: Present and future. American Institute for Economic Research, Great Barrington, MA: August, 1988.

Hudson, W. H. (1982). Scientific imperatives in social work research and practice. *Social Service Review, 56,* 242–258.

Ivanov, A., & Blythe, B. J. (1989). Response to 'exploring epistemologies.' *Journal of Social Work Education, 25,* 176–177.

Ivanov, A., Blythe, B. J., & Briar, S. (1987). The empirical clinical practice debate. *Social Casework, 68,* 290–298.

Janis, I. L., & L. Mann. (1977). *Decision-making*. New York: Free Press.

Jayaratne, S. (1978). A study of clinical eclecticism. *Social Service Review, 52,* 621–631.

Jayaratne, S. (1982). Characteristics and theoretical orientations of clinical social workers: A survey, *Journal of Social Service Research, 4,* 17–30.

Jayaratne, S., & R. Levy. (1979). *Empirical clinical practice*. New York: Columbia University Press.

Jayaratne, S., Tripodi, T. & Talsma, E. (1988). The comparative analysis and aggregation of single-case data. *Journal of Applied Behavioral Science, 24,* 119–128.

Kanfer, F. H., & Schefft, B. K. (1988). *Guiding the process of therapeutic change*. Champaign, IL: Research Press.

Karger, H. J. (1983). Science, research and social work: Who controls the profession? *Social Work, 28,* 200–205.

Kazdin, A. E., & Smith, G. A. (1979). Covert conditioning: A review. *Advances in Behavior Research and Therapy,* Vol. 2, 57–98.

Kazdin, A. E., & G. T. Wilson. (1978). *Evaluation of behavior therapy: Issues, evidence, and research strategies*. Cambridge, MA: Ballinger.

Kirk, S. A. (1988). Research utilization: A friendly revisit. Invitational paper, Empiricism in clinical practice, American Institute for Economic Research, Great Barrington, MA: August, 1988.

Kirschenbaum, D. S., & Flanery, R. C. (1983). Behavioral contracting: Outcomes and elements. In M. Hersen et al. (eds.), pp. 217–275. *Progress in Behavior Modification,* Vol. 15, New York: Academic Press.

Kolko, D. J., & Milan, M. A. (1983). Reframing and paradoxical instruction to overcome resistance in the treatment of delinquent youths: A multiple baseline analysis. *Journal of Consulting and Clinical Psychology, 51,* 655–660.

Krug, S. E. (1988). *Psychware sourcebook,* (3rd ed.) Kansas City, MO.: Test Corporation of America.

Kuhn, T. S. (1970). *The structure of scientific revolutions* (2nd ed.). Chicago: University of Chicago Press.

Lambert, M. J. (1989). The individual therapist's contribution to psychotherapy process and outcome. *Clinical Psychology Review, 9,* 469–485.

Lazarus, A. A. (1981). *The practice of multi-modal therapy*. New York: McGraw-Hill.

Lazarus, A. A. (1986). Multi-modal therapy. In J. C. Norcross (Ed.), pp. 65–93. *Handbook of eclectic psychotherapy*. New York: Brunner/Mazel.

Lebow, J. L. (1987). Developing a personal integration in family therapy: Principles for model construction and practice. *Journal of Marital and Family Therapy, 13,* 1–14.

Levy, R. A. (1981). On the nature of the clinical-research gap: The problems with some solutions. *Behavioral Assessment, 3,* 235–242.

Marshall, E. K., & Kurtz, P. D. (Eds.). (1982). *Interpersonal helping skills*. San Francisco: Jossey-Bass.

Marshall, W. L., et al. (1979). The current status of flooding therapy. In M. Hersen et al. (eds.), pp. 205–275. *Progress in behavior modification,* Vol. 7. New York: Academic Press.

Martin, G. A., & Worthington, E. L. (1982). "Behavioral Homework," in M. Hersen et al. (eds.), pp. 197–226. *Progress in behavior modification,* Vol. 13. New York: Academic Press.

Mash, E. J., & Terdal, L. G. (Eds.) (1988). *Behavioral assessment of childhood disorders,* (2nd ed.) New York: Guilford.

McCullough, L., Farrell, A. D., & Longabaugh, R. (1986). The development of a microcomputer-based mental health information system. *American Psychologist, 41,* 207–214.

McReynolds, P. (1989). Diagnosis and clinical assessment: Current status and major issues. *Annual Review of Psychology, 40,* 83–108.

Mullen, E. J. (1978). The construction of personal models for effective practice: A method for utilizing research findings to guide social interventions. *Journal of Social Service Research, 2,* 45–65.

Mullen, E. J. (1983). Personal practice models. In A. Rosenblatt & D. Waldfogel (eds.), pp. 603–622. *Handbook of clinical social work.* San Francisco: Jossey-Bass.

Mullen, E. J. (1985). Methodological dilemmas in social work research. *Social Work Research and Abstracts, 21,* 12–20.

Mullen, E. J. (1988). Constructing personal practice models. In R. M. Grinnel (ed.), pp. 503–534. *Social work research and evaluation,* (3rd ed.) Itasca, IL: F. E. Peacock.

Mullen, E. J., et al. (Eds.). (1972). *Evaluation of social intervention.* San Francisco, CA: Jossey-Bass.

Mullen, E. J., & Schuerman, J. R. (1988). Expert systems and the development of knowledge in social welfare. Invited paper, Empiricism in clinical practice: Present and future, American Institute for Economic Research, Great Barrington, MA: August, 1988.

Mutschler, E. (1984). Evaluating practice: A study of research utilization by practitioners. *Social Work Research and Abstracts, 20,* 332–337.

Nelsen, J. C. (1978). Use of communication theory in single-subject research. *Social Work Research and Abstracts, 14,* 12–19.

Nelsen, J. C. (1981). Issues in single-subject research for nonbehaviorists. *Social Work Research and Abstracts, 17,* 31–37.

Nezu, A. M., & Nezu, C. M. (Eds.). (1990). *Clinical decision making in behavior therapy.* Champaign, IL: Research Press.

Norcross, J. C. (Ed.). (1986). *Handbook of eclectic psychotherapy.* New York: Brunner/Mazel.

Norcross, J. C. (Ed.). (1987). *Casebook of eclectic psychotherapy.* New York: Brunner/Mazel.

Novaco, R. W. (1979). The cognitive regulation of anger and stress. In P. C. Kendall & S. D. Hollon (eds.), pp. 241–286. *Cognitive-behavioral interventions: Theory, research, and procedures.* New York: Academic Press.

Nugent, W. R. (1987). Use and evaluation of theories. *Social Work Research and Abstracts, 23,* 14–19.

Orlinsky, D. E., & Howard, K. I. (1986). Process and outcome in psychotherapy. In S. L. Garfield and A. E. Bergin (eds.), pp. 311–381. *Handbook of Psychotherapy and Behavior Change.* New York: Wiley.

Peile, C. (1988). Research paradigms in social work: From statement to creative synthesis, *Social Service Review, 62,* 1–19.

Rachman, S. J., & Wilson, G. T. (1980). *The effects of psychological therapy,* (2nd ed.) New York: Pergamon.

Reid, D. H. (1987). *Developing a research program in human service agencies.* Springfield, IL: Charles C Thomas.

Reid, W. J. (1983). Developing intervention methods through experimental designs. In A. Rosenblatt and D. Waldfogel (eds.), pp. 650–672. *Handbook of clinical social work.* San Francisco: Jossey-Bass.

Reid, W. J. (1987a). Evaluating an intervention in developmental research. *Journal of Social Service Research, 11,* 17–38.

Reid, W. J. (1987b). The family problem-solving sequences. *Family Therapy, 14,* 135–146.

Reid, W. J. (1987c). Research in social work. In A. Minahan et al. (eds.), pp. 474–487. *Encyclopedia of social work,* (18th ed.) Silver Spring, MD: NASW.

Reid, W. J. (1988). Change process research: A new paradigm? Invited paper, Empiricism and clinical practice: Present and future, American Institute for Economic Research, Great Barrington, MA: August, 1988.

Reid, W. J., & Hanrahan, P. (1982). Recent evaluations of social work: Grounds for optimism. *Social Work, 27,* 328–340.

Richey, C., Blythe, B. J. and Berlin, S. B. (1987). "Do Social Workers Evaluate Their Practice?" *Social Work Research and Abstracts, 23,* 14–20.

Rimm, D. C., & Masters, J. C. (1979). *Behavior therapy: Techniques and empirical findings,* (2nd ed.) New York: Academic Press.

Robinson, E. A. R., Bronson, D. E., & Blythe, B. J. (1988). An analysis of the implementation of single-case evaluation By practitioners. *Social Service Review, 62,* 286–301.

Rose, S. D., and Edleson, J. L. (1987). *Working with children and adolescents in group.* San Francisco: Jossey-Bass.

Rosen, A. (1983). Barriers to utilization of research by social work practitioners. *Journal of Social Service Research, 6,* 1–15.

Rosenthal, R. (1984). *Meta-analytic procedures for social research.* Beverly Hills, CA: SAGE.

Rothman, J. (1986). Supplying the missing link. *Social Welfare, 2,* 23.

Rothman, J. (1989). Intervention research: Application to runaway and homeless youths. *Social Work Research and Abstracts, 25,* 13–18.

Rothman, J., Erlich, J. L., & Teresa, J. G. (1981). *Changing organizations and community programs.* Newbury Park, CA: SAGE.

Rothman, J. & Lubben, J. E. (1988). The partialization strategy: An empirical re-formulation of demonstration project planning. *Administration in Social Work, 12,* 45–60.

Rothman, J. et al. (1983). *Marketing human service organizations.* Newbury Park, CA: SAGE.

Ruckdeschel, R. A., & Farris, B. E. (1981). Assessing practice: A critical look at the single-case design. *Social Casework, 62,* 413–419.

Saunders, D. G., & Azar, S. T. (1989). Treatment programs for family violence. In L. Ohlin and M. Tonry (eds.). *Family violence, crime and justice: A review of research, 11.* Chicago: University of Chicago Press.

Scheurman, J. R. (1982). The obsolete imperative in social work research. *Social Service Review, 56,* 144–148.

Scheurman, J. R. (1987). Expert consulting systems in social welfare. *Social Work Research and Abstracts, 23,* 14–18.

Shapiro, David A. (1985). Recent applications of meta-analysis in clinical re-search. *Clinical Psychology Review, 5,* 13–34.

Siegel, D. H. (1988). Integrating data-gathering techniques and practice activities. In R. M. Grinnel (ed.), pp. 465–482. *Social work research and evaluation,* (3rd ed.) Itasca, IL: F. E. Peacock.

Siegel, D. H. (1984). Defining empirically based practice. *Social Work, 29,* 3 25–331.

Siegel, D. H., & Reamer, F. G. (1988). Integrating research findings, concepts and logic into practice. In R. M. Grinnel (ed.), pp. 483–502. *Social work re-search and evaluation,* (3rd ed.) Itasca, IL: F. E. Peacock.

Simons, R. L., & Aigner, S. M. (1985). *Practice principles: A problem-solving ap-proach to social work.* New York: MacMillan.

Thomas, E. J. (1978). Research and service in single-case experimentation: Con-flicts and choices, *Social Work Research and Abstracts, 14,* 20–30.

Thomas, E. J. (1984). *Designing interventions for the helping professions.* Beverly Hills, CA: SAGE.

Thomas, E. J. (1985). The validity of design and development and related con-cepts in developmental research. *Social Work Research and Evaluation, 21,* 50–57.

Thomas, E. J. (1988). Modes of practice in developmental research. Invited pa-per, Empiricism in clinical practice: Present and future, American Institute for Economic Research, Great Barrington, MA: August, 1988.

Thomas, E. J., et al. (1987). Assessing procedural descriptiveness: Rationale and illustrative study. *Behavioral Assessment, 9,* 43–56.

Thyer, B. A. (1989). Exploring epistemologies: The debate continues. *Journal of Social Work Education, 25,* 174–176.

Thyer, B. A., & Boynton, K. E. (1989). Single-subject research designs in social work practice: A bibliography, Unpublished paper.

Tripodi, T., Fellin, P., & Meyer, H. S. (1969). *Assessment of social research*. Itasca, IL: F. E. Peacock.

Turpin, G. (1983). The behavioral management of tic disorders: A critical review. *Advances in Behavior Research and Therapy*, Vol. 5, 203–245.

Twentyman, C. T., & Zimering, R. T. (1979). Behavioral training of social skills: A critical review. In M. Hersen et al. (eds.), pp. 319–400. *Progress in behavior modification*, Vol. 7. New York: Academic Press.

Videka-Sherman, L. (1986). Alternative approaches to aggregating the results of single-subject studies. *Social Work Research and Abstracts, 22,* 22–23.

Videka-Sherman, L. (1988). Meta-analysis of research on social work practice in mental health. *Social Work, 33,* 325–338.

Videka-Sherman, L., & Reid, W. R. (Eds.). (1990). *Advances in clinical social work research*. Washington, DC: NASW.

Walberg, H. J., & Haertel, E. H. (Eds.). (1980). Research integration: The state of the art. *Evaluation in Education, 4,* whole issue.

Walker, C. E., Hedberg, A., Clement, P. W., & Wright, L. (1981). *Clinical procedures for behavior therapy*. Englewood Cliffs, NJ: Prentice-Hall.

Welch, G. (1983). Will graduates use single-subject designs to evaluate their casework practice? *Journal of Education for Social Work, 19,* 42–47.

Wood, K. M. (1988). Epistemological issues in the development of social work practice knowledge. Invitational paper, Empiricism in clinical practice: Present and future, American Institute for Economic Research, Great Barrington, MA: August, 1988.

Chapter 18

Uniformity Myths in Eclectic and Integrative Psychotherapy

Almost thirty years ago, Kiesler (1966) described a number of "uniformity assumption myths" that he believed were impeding progress in psychotherapy research. His argument was that nearly all domains of variables in psychotherapy and psychotherapy research are considerably more heterogeneous than the then-current descriptive labels implied. Thus, lack of progress in psychotherapy research was based partly on assuming that those variables (e.g., clients, problems, psychotherapists) were homogeneous and thereby asking the wrong questions.

While it is not clear that Kiesler's concerns have been adequately addressed, even today, it does appear as though a new class of uniformity myths may be affecting the newest developments in the field of psychotherapy. These myths are assumptions underlying some of the key foundations of the fields of integrative and eclectic psychotherapy. In sum, these myths are: (1) that all psychotherapies have equivalent outcomes; (2) that all theories (or systems) of psychotherapy are equally sound; and (3) that cultural homogeneity exists for all eclectic and integrative clients and psychotherapists, encouraging the uncritical dissemination of Western approaches to psychotherapists from other traditions and cultures.

Based upon observations from the First and Second International Congresses on Integrative and Eclectic Psychotherapies as well as upon a review of the literature, including key books and journals in the field (e.g., *Journal of Integrative and Eclectic Psychotherapy: Journal of Psychotherapy Integration;* Stricker & Gold, 1993; Norcross & Goldfried, 1992), this article will discuss each of these myths in turn, including implications of each for the field of eclectic and integrative psychotherapy.

Myth One: All Psychotherapies Have Equivalent Outcomes

No proposition is a more important undergirding to the integrative movement than this one. In fact, this belief is a main rationale for efforts to synthesize useful

Fischer, J. (1994). Keynote Address Presented at The Second International Congress on Integrative and Eclectic Psychotherapy, Lyon, France, June, 1994.

concepts and methods from different therapeutic approaches and attempts to specify factors common to successful psychotherapy (Norcross & Newman, 1992).

Virtually every account of the development and current state of integrative and eclectic psychotherapy states that research has found few differences or none at all among psychotherapies regarding effectiveness (most recently, e.g., Norcross & Newman, 1992; Lambert, 1992; Gold, 1993; Glass, Victor, & Arnkoff, 1993; Arnkoff, Victor, & Glass, 1993). In fact, this belief has been stated so frequently and in so many ways in recent years that it has become an article of faith in the integrationist movement: State it often enough and everyone will come to believe it.

But is the equivalence proposition true? That is, does it reflect the actual results of research, and, if so, where is the research that documents it?

Of course, the debate about equivalence of outcomes has been present in the literature for a number of years (see, e.g., Luborsky, Singer, & Luborsky, 1975; Giles, 1983; Stiles, Shapiro, & Elliott, 1986; and, up to the present, Giles, Neims, & Prial, 1993; Elliott, Stiles, & Shapiro, 1993). Therefore, the purpose here is not to reproduce all aspects of the debate, but to illustrate—at the least—that the issue is far from settled. Indeed, it is precisely because the issue is not settled, because there is substantial evidence supporting nonequivalence, and because the integrationist literature deals with this debate as though it were settled in favor of equivalence to allow the basis for integration, that this myth is particularly pernicious.

A recent review of research (Lambert, 1992) states that there are three possible explanations for this finding of equivalence: (1) different therapies achieve similar goals through different processes; (2) different outcomes do occur but are not detected by past research methods; and (3) different therapies embody common factors that lead to common rates of change. But there is a fourth possibility: research has not, in fact, documented the equivalence of outcome hypothesis.

It is important to note that in the same review by Lambert (1992), that concludes that there is no evidence that different schools or techniques have superior evidence, another part of the article concludes that techniques do, in fact, make a demonstrable difference (Lambert, 1992). In addition, the second possibility mentioned previously (that research methods are inadequate to discover differences) does not substantiate a conclusion that all psychotherapies—in reality—have equivalent outcomes. It is, instead, a commentary on the state of research, not of practice.

More importantly, it is crucial to understand that the bulk of the conclusions about equivalence appear to come from interpreting (and misinterpreting) results of meta-analysis. There are two crucial points to make about meta-analysis. The first is that the methodology of meta-analysis has so many serious flaws that it may be impossible to draw definitive conclusions about comparative therapeutic effectiveness. The heart of the matter was stated by London (1988): "Meta-analytic research shows charity for all treatments and malice towards none."

Part of the problem in understanding the results of meta-analysis may be due to methodological and/or conceptual problems with many of the procedures. A recent review by Fischer (1990; also see Wilson & Rachman, 1983; Searles, 1983) describes many of the problems and issues with meta-analysis. They can be summarized as follows:

1. Selecting a method of meta-analysis. There are no clear guidelines about how to evaluate which is the best method to use and, hence, no clear selection criteria.

2. Selecting studies for a meta-analytic review. These issues include problems with combining divergent studies, varying methodological quality of the primary studies, sampling bias due to unpublished studies, and the effects of deficient reporting and other limitations imposed by the primary studies.

3. Problems with meta-analytic statistics. These include basic problems with the calculation of the effect size, problems due to nonindependence of data, potential positive bias, and issues regarding the use of aggregated and nonaggregated data.

4. Interpretation of the results of meta-analysis. These issues include problems in interpreting the meaning of the effect size and issues regarding the interpretation of causality.

Although these problems are too numerous (and often rather technical) to describe in detail here, just a single example might suffice. It is possible to conduct a review using a meta-analytic effect size and find a positive effect size (meaning the average client in the experimental group did better than most clients in the control group, to a specified degree) even though anywhere from one to all of the primary studies in the review showed no statistically significant difference between the groups. Thus, the reviewer will conclude that the treatment that is the subject of the review had an effect when, in fact, the primary studies revealed no such effect at all. This and other factors produces a consistent positive bias in meta-analytic findings (let alone a conflict between the meaning of established statistical procedures and meta-analytic statistics) to the extent that most meta-analyses find that just about all approaches "work" just about all of the time.

Given the problem in interpreting the results of meta-analysis, and thereby in comparing different effect sizes, it is very difficult to draw a clear conclusion about equivalence.

Thus, while meta-analytic procedures are not necessarily biased toward finding equivalence, the relatively early stage of development of these procedures suggests the need for caution in drawing definitive conclusions—about equivalence or any other type of research—at this time.

The second crucial point about the results of meta-analysis that questions conclusions about the equivalence of psychotherapies is that meta-analyses do *not* uniformly support those conclusions. In fact, in one of the first—the largest and the most influential meta-analysis—one of over 400 controlled studies by Smith, Glass, and Miller (1980), the conclusion was that behavior therapy was "clearly superior" to the verbal therapies. Differential results also have been found in several subsequent meta-analytic reviews (Shapiro & Shapiro, 1982; Casey & Berman, 1985; Weisz et al., 1987; Searles, 1983; Dobson, 1989, and Svartberge & Stiles, 1991).

Based on these results, then, at best the issue of equivalence of outcomes across schools of psychotherapy is an open one. The facts are that the data from meta-analysis do not seem to provide evidence clearly substantiating one conclusion or another. But it may be that the strategy for answering this question needs to be addressed. If meta-analysis cannot supply a clear answer, what can?

In large part, the only way to definitively answer this question is the strategy of comparative studies. Unless one therapy is directly compared to another in the same study, any conclusion is speculative. There have, in fact, been scores of such studies. Often the results were mixed; however, since the 1970s, comparative research has revealed that behavioral and cognitive-behavioral methods, that is, directive approaches, have rarely if ever been found to be inferior to the alternative treatment, and in most cases were superior (Kazdin & Wilson, 1978; Lambert, 1992). Indeed, Giles, Neims, & Prial (1993) have noted over 100 controlled studies comparing different psychotherapy approaches that support directive over traditional psychotherapies.

In areas of practice where results from comparative research are not compelling, a secondary, less direct strategy involves generalizability from cumulated results. What competent therapist would select a technique that has been studied (and even found effective) five to ten times over a technique successfully studied hundreds of times? Using this guideline, once again behavioral and cognitive-behavioral techniques appear to offer the greatest empirical support in many areas of concern to psychotherapists. However, only time and the continued production of research can contribute to conclusions about effectiveness with this research strategy (Giles, Neims, & Prial, 1993; Hersen & Ammerman, 1994).

In all, then, the equivalence of outcomes conclusion appears to be more myth than substance. To push the point to the extreme, if therapy X has hundreds of studies attesting to its effectiveness and therapy Y had none or even just a few, why would one want to integrate these two approaches? (That this may not be such an extreme example can be seen in the work of Wachtel, 1977). Indeed, integration of two such therapies might even hamper the effectiveness of therapy X, producing an overall lower level of effectiveness than was the case prior to integration.

On the other hand, when examined carefully, if equivalence of outcomes *were* true, it would seem to remove the basis for most integrative and eclectic endeavors. If all therapies are the same, why bother to integrate? It wouldn't matter what the components of an integrative approach would be. Equivalent outcomes would be even more problematic for true eclectic approaches. If the meaning of eclecticism is the attempt to use the best techniques available from a range of sources—and best defined as most effective—then there would be no basis at all for selection: all techniques would produce the same results, removing the basis for selecting one over the others.

Myth Two: All Theories of Psychotherapy Are Equally Sound

If all theories of psychotherapy were equally sound, that is, met the requirements of science for good theory (see, for example, Marx, 1963; Dubin, 1969), integration and perhaps eclecticism could proceed apace. There would be no barriers to integration because it would be possible, even appropriate, to combine divergent theories or concepts without undue concern about their formal status as theories (or concepts). That is, all theories would be equal grist for the integrationist mill.

This perspective seems ludicrous on the face of it, but review of the literature on theoretical integration reveals that this myth does, in fact, appear to be a basic assumption of most attempts at integration (Stricker & Gold, 1993; Norcross & Goldfried, 1992; Norcross & Newman, 1992). This review revealed at best a rather casual attitude toward theory construction and analysis; at worst, a potential for developing psychotherapeutic approaches that are based on very shaky foundations. An integrated approach based on synthesis of weak theories may be weaker yet than the theories upon which it is based. Hence, its interventions may be less successful (or do more harm) than the interventions based on the original theories.

This is a subtle but widely prevalent myth. It can be seen throughout the literature and in conference presentations in one or more of three guises.

The first is the lack of formal critical analysis of intervention theories. In general, there are two basic approaches to studying theory. The first is to step within the bounds of the theory itself, learn what the theorist has to say, and then accept or reject it on the basis of ambiguous, poorly defined, or (often) no criteria. This might be called the *descriptive* approach because, after considerable study, the reader generally is prepared only to describe what the theory states. This is the prevailing method in the literature. The second approach to studying theories involves developing a number of criteria—external to any specific theory—that a theory could or should address or around which it might be constructed, and then stepping outside the boundaries of the theory and assessing the theory against those criteria (Ford & Urban, 1963; Fischer, 1978). This is the approach that largely is missing from the integrative literature. The main advantages of this approach lie in its utilization of standardized guidelines for studying diverse theories and in its objectivity: all theories are evaluated against the same criteria.

The myth of theoretical uniformity holds that all theories of psychotherapy are equally sound, so that none have to be studied objectively. However, there are frameworks for conducting analyses of psychotherapy theories. For example, Fischer (1971, 1978) presents an eighty-item framework for evaluating clinical theories in terms of structural characteristics of theories (using such criteria as internal consistency, clarity, parsimony, comprehensiveness, etc.); characteristics as a clinical theory (for example, articulation with theory of development, prescription of procedures, etc.); empirical status (for example, success in validating effectiveness, emphasis on testable propositions), and assumptions about the nature of humans (for example, view of the nature of human beings); and moral implications (for example, attention to value issues); (see also Nugent, 1987, and Ford & Urban, 1963, for other frameworks). Such analysis not only can help destroy the myth of theoretical homogeneity, but can also help produce a stronger basis for constructing integrative and eclectic therapies.

The second form of the myth of theoretical uniformity can be seen in the lack of critical analysis of what theories (or aspects of theories) are to be integrated (or included in an eclectic approach). Throughout the literature, authors seem to be selecting theories, or concepts or techniques from theories, for integration in a haphazard, unsystematic way, using mainly their own biases or preferences as a guide.

How can this result in useful—helpful—approaches to intervention? There are numerous clinical theories available, and each is composed of a myriad of concepts. How does one integrate concepts or constructs that are poorly defined or totally unverified, and why would one want to (Fischer, 1992)? Moreover, the epistemologies of theories vary tremendously, so integration and perhaps even eclecticism would necessitate ignoring the crucial assumptions, propositions, and worldviews of each of the original theories.

Not only does the task of deciding what theories to integrate (let alone actually proceeding to attempt to integrate them) seem at best suspiciously subjective and at worst mind-boggling, but when one considers the vast array of potential concepts derived from those theories that are available for consideration for integration, the task literally appears to be impossible. Numerous concepts have only recently been proposed as possible key concepts for integration: cognitive schemas, assimilation, balance, self-confirmation, levels of emotional awareness, the therapeutic alliance, self-experiencing, behavioral enactment, and many other concepts.

Integrative proposals such as these would be possible only in an uncritical atmosphere that suggests all theories and all concepts are of equal value—the myth of theoretical uniformity.

The third guise of this myth is the apparent assumption in the field that research supporting the effectiveness of a therapeutic technique also supports the theory upon which the technique is based. While this assumption is a less direct and less prevalent form of the myth of theoretical uniformity, its role in this process is to *appear* to provide empirical support for the soundness of a theory, and, hence, enhance the formal status of a theory, to facilitate integration. Thus, according to this myth, such research would appear to be validating underlying theories, thereby allowing for easier integration. In its most popular form, this can be seen in authors' confusing descriptions and explanations of their theories with *validation* of their concepts, propositions, and predictions. Thus, for example, the original respondent theory (reciprocal inhibition) underlying Wolpe's technique of systematic desensitization (Wolpe, 1958), would be considered validated when the technique of systematic desensitization provided a large body of research attesting to its effectiveness. Or, in a similar vein, positive results in psychotherapy research regarding Beck's cognitive theory would appear to be validating Beck's theory of cognition (Beck, 1991; Alford & Norcross, 1991).

Of course, this supposed connection would be more apparent than real. Because an author believes an underlying theory explains the success of a technique or even offers a cogent explanation of the presumed process underlying the technique does not *validate* those processes. This requires an entirely different program of research that may or may not produce the hoped-for results.

Thus, acceptance of this third form of the myth of theoretical equivalence can produce a superficially satisfying yet conceptually inadequate—and perhaps, invalid—effort at integration.

These three forms of the myth of theoretical equivalence, in any or all guises, add up to a potential for producing integrated theories of such weak formal status that deriving successful intervention principles and procedures would be virtually impossible. The need to more closely and critically conduct formal theoretical and empirical analyses to address these problems is obvious. The time, energy, and work required to do so, however, present major hurdles in accomplishing such a task.

Myth Three: Cultural Homogeneity Exists for All Eclectic and Integrative Psychotherapists and Their Clients

This may be one of the most detrimental and prevalent myths of all. Its ubiquitousness can be seen in perusal just of the programs for the first and second International Congresses on Integrative and Eclectic Psychotherapy, as well as the contents of the integrative journals mentioned earlier. How else can one explain the widespread appearance of papers describing the implementation of Western, largely English-originated, psychotherapies in so many countries around the world? Either these Western psychotherapies have been empirically demonstrated to be effective among different ethnic, cultural, or national groups, which warrants their widespread diffusion and adoption, or there is a widespread belief in the myth of cultural homogeneity: the differences among cultures of both the psychotherapist and the client are so trivial that psychotherapeutic approaches from one culture readily can be adopted by another.

The area of psychotherapy integration is not only an intellectual development in the field, but also a movement, as witness the two main societies concerned with integrationism, the Society for the Exploration of Psychotherapy Integration and the International Academy of Eclectic Psychotherapists. Indeed, both organizations have branches in many countries around the world. Given this international perspective, one might expect to find a considerable literature dealing with the topic of transfer of knowledge from one culture to another. Surprisingly, through, review of the integration literature revealed virtually no articles dealing with this topic.

The problem across countries is only an exaggerated version of the problem within countries. In the situation within countries, especially in the United States, majority-group psychotherapists typically attempt to apply, with little or no sensitivity, psychotherapies that are poorly suited (or not suited at all) to their clients from minority or oppressed groups (Baruth & Manning, 1991). How much greater may the gap be when the psychotherapies are imported completely from a *different* culture with different language, beliefs, customs, and traditions, even though the importers (the therapists) themselves speak the language and share (many of) the traditions of their clients in the country that imports the knowledge?

Actually, the general literature on psychotherapy has addressed the issue of cross-cultural or multicultural counseling and psychotherapy in a number of works (Baruth & Manning, 1991; Sue 1981; Pedersen et al., 1981; Christensen, 1985). For example, Sue (1981) has described many of the basic competencies for culturally skilled practitioners, including beliefs and attitudes (e.g., the culturally skilled practitioner is comfortable with differences that may exist between the therapist and the client in terms of race, ethnicity, and beliefs), knowledge (e.g., the culturally skilled practitioner possesses specific knowledge and information about the particular group with which he or she is working), and skills (e.g., the culturally skilled practitioner is able to send and receive both verbal and nonverbal messages accurately and appropriately with clients who may differ in terms of race, ethnicity, or values and beliefs).

However, virtually all of this literature is concerned with working with clients from within one's own country (e.g., clients from minority or oppressed groups). No literature could be located in psychotherapy that focused on the problem of *transfer of knowledge* from one nation, with its unique language, beliefs, values, and cultural practices, to another nation with a different language, beliefs, values, and cultural practices. While many of the guidelines developed for use within one's own nation may indeed be applicable in other cultures, the lack of a body of knowledge to facilitate such transfer is a major deficit in the psychotherapy literature in general, and in the integration literature in particular.

Part of the problem may be that in many countries, psychotherapists appear to ignore basic truths about their own cultures, as well as basic, useful, indigenous problem-solving methods (for a number of examples of such indigenous problem-solving methods, especially among Asian and Pacific Island cultures, see Mokuau, 1991). Instead, they appear to favor the adoption of Western methods, largely derived from English-speaking countries. The widespread adoption of integrative and eclectic approaches seems only the latest manifestation of this problem in the history of the field of psychotherapy. Indeed, the common occurrence of this phenomenon of assuming cultural homogeneity actually facilitates importation and adoption of knowledge and may only reflect aspirations to what appears to be the most highly developed conceptually and hence the most professional-appearing knowledge. Thus, the desire to import and adopt Western knowledge may be part of the drive for increased professional status among psychotherapists all around the world.

Now the point of this argument is not that importation of knowledge from another culture is always and totally inappropriate. Nor is it to simply plead that we must all be more sensitive to this problem, whether applying psychotherapeutic techniques across the board to all clients from all different groups within our own countries, or when attempting to import knowledge from other cultures for consideration in one's own.

Rather, in a way that is consistent with the earlier arguments in this chapter, the point here is that for knowledge to be imported from one culture to another, a systematic process of careful study needs to be undertaken, examining specific characteristics of the knowledge to be imported, characteristics of the importing culture, and ways to make changes—adaptations—in the knowledge when those characteristics are not congruent.

The key here may be the difference between *adoption* and *adaptation*. Adoption means more-or-less total importation and use of ideas without critical examination of their equivalence and utility across cultures (Berry 1969; Frijda & Jahoda, 1966). Adaptation implies a process whereby equivalence is examined to determine whether knowledge from one culture has the same function in the originating culture as in others. Moreover, adaptation suggests careful consideration of cultural similarities and dissimilarities and a *modification* of the original knowledge to fit the circumstances of other cultures.

There are several types of equivalence one needs to assess before considering transfer of knowledge from one culture to another (Lonner, 1981). The first and perhaps most important type of equivalence is *functional* equivalence. Functional equivalence refers to the notion that similar activities may have different functions in different societies (Frijda & Jahoda, 1966); if this is so, transfer is either impossible—or at the least, more difficult. Functional equivalence of activities or behaviors exists when those activities or behaviors develop in response to a problem shared by two or more cultural groups (Berry, 1966). The task becomes one of finding common ground among culturally different activities and behaviors. Without such equivalence, it is likely that knowledge transfer cannot occur. Thus, a therapy designed to treat depression would be a poor candidate for transfer if the depression itself (its manifestations, signs, symptoms, etc.) does not have functional equivalence in the two cultures under consideration.

A second form of equivalence, operating more on the individual than group level, is *conceptual* equivalence (Lonner, 1981). This type of equivalence refers to the meaning that people attach to specific stimuli, which could range from test items to types of comments, suggestions, or directives offered by therapists to their clients. Unless stimuli are conceptually equivalent and also are relevant to functionally equivalent cultural indicators, interpretation of responses across cultures could be largely guesswork (Lonner, 1981).

Two more specific forms of equivalence are *linguistic* and *metric* equivalence (Lonner, 1981). Linguistic equivalence means determining that specific phrases and terms that have one set of meanings in the original culture also have the same meaning in another. Asking a client to keep track of his or her negative self-statements may make perfect sense in middle-class America but may have no real context in another culture.

Metric equivalence is mainly related to use of tests and measures, many of which have been transferred from one culture to another in the field of psychotherapy. The key point here is that it must be ascertained that those tests and measures measure the same phenomena in both cultures and, moreover, that the scores mean the same thing (or that any systematic differences across cultures are clarified).

Once these forms of equivalence are assessed, and at the least, functional and conceptual equivalence are ascertained, it may be possible to move forward with a more precise examination of characteristics of the originating culture, the importing

Table 18.1 Framework for Cross Cultural Knowledge Transfer

Assumptions/characteristics of the knowledge	Assumptions/characteristics of the importing culture
1. What are the key assumptions of the knowledge re nature of human beings?	1. What are the key assumptions of the culture re nature of human beings?
2. What model of human behavior does the knowledge purport to use?	2. Does the culture accept a common model of human behavior?
3. How culturally specific is the knowledge?	3. What mechanisms are available in the culture for modification of extracultural knowledge?
4. Are there assumptions or practices in the knowledge that will conflict with different cultural values and traditions?	4. Does the culture provide mechanisms for integrating or adapting knowledge that conflicts with basic cultural traditions or values?
5. Does the knowledge have equivalence?	5. Does the imported knowledge have the same meaning in the new culture?
6. Has the new knowledge been shown to be effective in *both* cultures in controlled research utilizing placebo, alternative treatment, and, perhaps, traditional problem-solving groups?	

culture, and the knowledge that is to be transferred. To that end, a framework has been developed to examine a number of issues in transfer of knowledge from one culture to another. The framework, summarized in table 18.1, is only suggestive of some of the questions that can be addressed. In the table, a number of questions are posed to critically examine assumptions and characteristics of knowledge that is being considered for transfer to a different culture (or ethnic group). Each of these questions then leads to a corresponding question about characteristics of the culture that may import the knowledge, thus providing clues as to the need for knowledge adaptation mechanisms. Once answers to questions like those in table 18.1 are ascertained, the critical step of knowledge modification—to make it more culturally appropriate—must be undertaken.

Some examples may help in clarifying use of the framework. The first question has to do with cultural assumptions regarding the nature of human beings. All cultures have embedded in them a view about the nature of people that hypothetically could range from the idea that people essentially are "ugly," seething cauldrons of primordial drives, to a view of people as intrinsically creative, self-actualizing beings. Transfer of therapies based on one view to cultures with radically different views may be inappropriate; indeed, the whole focus of such a therapy might be viewed as an inappropriate transfer from one culture to another.

The second question requires analysis of the models of human behavior underlying the knowledge and the ways in which those models may or may not be reflected in a second culture. Transfer of knowledge that is based on a highly individualistic model of human behavior, such as predominates in the United States, may be quite inappropriate to a culture such as in Japan, where the prevailing model focuses on the group as the superordinate criterion for acceptable behavior.

The third question requires analysis of the level of cultural specificity of the knowledge to be transferred. For example, direct eye contact is the preferred mode of behavior between therapist and client in most Western psychotherapies. In many Asian cultures, however, direct eye contact is seen as intrusive, impolite, and/or threatening. Understanding this, and then examining the imported knowledge for ways of modifying such guidelines regarding the therapist's behaviors, could dramatically ease problems of transfer of knowledge.

The fourth question requires analysis of the potential conflict in cultural values between cultures. This could be a key to successful knowledge transfer. For example, a recent paper discussed the use of cognitive restructuring in the conversion of homosexuality in Syria (Hajjar, 1994). Within at least the professional subculture of psychotherapy in the United States, this use of cognitive restructuring may be unethical, whereas it may not only not be unethical in Syria, it may be highly desirable to convert homosexuals. Transfer of knowledge when there are two competing value systems can prove awkward at best, and ineffective and seriously detrimental to clients at the worst.

The fifth question calls for a summary analysis of the levels of equivalence of meaning of the knowledge in assessing its potential for transfer. Thus, in group assertion training among YAVIS clients in the United States, the broken record technique (repeated presentations of one's request or response when the client believes his or her rights are being ignored) is a commonly used procedure. In another culture, however, such an approach could be seen as inappropriate, insulting, or threatening, and sabotage the therapeutic process, or worse. For example, among native Hawaiians, a group problem-solving process called *ho'oponopono* requires prayer, a sense of being safe, honest confession to god and to family members for wrong doing, and genuine forgiveness and respect for elders and authorities (Kauahi, 1992). Direct verbal challenges are not sanctioned in this atmosphere, and importation of group therapy ideas, where such challenges are acceptable, would be viewed with considerable alarm.

Finally, the last question is key: to what extent is there research available that provides a firm empirical foundation for wanting to transfer knowledge in the first place?

While the entire process from assessment of knowledge to its modification for transfer may appear laborious, without such a process, the myth of cultural homogeneity would go unchecked, as would the likely worldwide propagation of culturally insensitive, inappropriate, and, hence, potentially ineffective psychotherapeutic knowledge.

Conclusion

The three myths described in this chapter appear to be serious barriers to the development of effective psychotherapeutic methods, both within and across cultures. As a relatively new development, the field of integrative and eclectic psychotherapy has the opportunity to address these myths through systematic analysis and critique of current knowledge and practices. The goal of such an endeavor, as is the goal of this chapter and the goal of all psychotherapists, is to develop and implement the most sensitive and effective psychotherapeutic approaches, those that will benefit not just a small number of clients, but can prove useful for the bulk of people with whom therapists work.

References

Alford, B. A. & Norcross, J. C. (1991). Cognitive therapy as integrative therapy. *Journal of Psychotherapy Integration, 1,* 175–190.

Arnkoff, D. B., Victor, B. J., & Glass, C. R. (1993). Empirical research on factors in psychotherapeutic change, in G. Stricker & J. R. Gold (Eds.), *Comprehensive handbook of psychotherapy integration.* (pp. 27–42). New York: Plenum.

Baruth, L. G. & Manning, M. L. (1991). *Multicultural counseling and psychotherapy: A lifespan perspective.* New York: Merrill.

Beck, A. T. (1991). Cognitive therapy as *the* integrative therapy. *Journal of Psychotherapy Integration, 1,* 191–198.

Berry, J. W. (1969). On cross-cultural comparability. *International Journal of Psychology, 4,* 119–128.

Casey, R. & Berman, J. (1985). The outcome of psychotherapy with children. *Psychological Bulletin, 98,* 388–400.

Christensen, C. P. (1985). A perceptual approach to cross-cultural counseling. *Canadian Counsellor, 19,* 63–81.

Dobson, K. (1989). A meta-analysis of the efficacy of cognitive therapy for depression. *Journal of Counseling and Clinical Psychology, 57,* 414–419.

Dubin, R. (1969). *Theory building.* New York: Free Press.

Elliott, R., Stiles, W. B. & Shapiro, D. A. (1983). Are some therapies more equivalent than others? In T. R. Giles (Ed.), *Handbook of effective psychotherapy* (pp. 455–480). New York: Plenum.

Fischer, J. (1971). A framework for the analysis of clinical theories of induced change. *Social Service Review, 45,* 440–454.

Fischer, J. (1978). *Effective casework practice: An eclectic approach.* New York: McGraw Hill.

Fischer, J. (1990). Problems and issues in meta-analysis. In L. Videka-Sherman & W. J. Reid (eds.), *Advances in clinical social work* (pp. 297–325). Silver Springs, MD: NASW.

Fischer, J. (1992). *What ever happened to eclecticism? An analysis of psychotherapy integration, the latest psychotherapeutic fad.* Keynote address presented at the First International Congress on Integrative and Eclectic Psychotherapy, Mazatlan, Mexico, June, 1992.

Ford, D. H. & Urban, H. B. (1963). *Systems of psychotherapy.* New York: Wiley.

Frijda, N. & Jahoda, G. (1966). On the scope and methods of cross-cultural research. *International Journal of Psychology, 1,* 109–127.

Giles, T. R. (1983). Probable superiority of behavioral interventions-II: Empirical status of the equivalence of therapies hypothesis. *Journal of Behavioral Therapy and Experimental Psychiatry, 14,* 189–196.

Giles, T. R., Neims, D. M., and Prial, E. M. (1993). The Relative Efficacy of Prescriptive Techniques, in T. R. Giles (Ed.), *Handbook of Effective Psychotherapy* (pp. 21–39). New York: Plenum.

Glass, C. G., Victor, B. J., & Arnkoff, D. B. Empirical research on integrative and eclectic psychotherapies. In G. Stricker & J. R. Gold (Eds.), *Comprehensive handbook of psychotherapy integration* (pp. 9–26). New York: Plenum.

Hajjar, M. (1994). *Could the cognitive behavioral restructuring interventions be a real help in the conversion of certain patterns of homosexuality?* Paper presented at the Second International Congress on Integrative and Eclectic Psychotherapy, Lyon, France, June, 1994.

Hersen, M. & Ammerman, R. T. (1994) (Eds). *Handbook of prescriptive treatments for adults.* New York: Plenum.

Kauahi, D. (1992). The Hawaiian community: Cultural concepts and perspectives. In J. Fischer (Ed), *East-west directions: Social work practice, tradition and change* (pp. 49–58). Honolulu, HI: University of Hawaii.

Kazdin, A. E. & Wilson, G. T. (1978). *Evaluation of behavior therapy: Issues, evidence and research strategies.* Cambridge, Mass.: Ballinger.

Kiesler, D. J. (1966). Some myths of psychotherapy research and the search for a paradigm. *Psychological Bulletin, 65,* 110–136.

Lambert, M. J. (1992). Psychotherapy outcome research: Implications for integrative and eclectic therapists. In J. C. Norcross & M. R. Goldfried (Eds.), *Handbook of psychotherapy integration* (pp. 94–129). New York: Basic Books.

London, P. (1988). Metamorphosis in psychotherapy: Slouching toward integration, *Journal of Integrative and Eclectic Psychotherapy, 7,* 3–12.

Lonner, W. J. (1981). Psychological tests and intercultural counseling. In Pedersen, P. P., Draguns, J. G., Lonner, W. J. & Trimble, J. E. (Eds.), *Counseling across cultures* (pp. 275–303). Honolulu, HI: University of Hawaii Press.

Luborsky, L., Singer, B. & Luborsky, L. (1975). Comparative studies of psychotherapies. *Archives of General Psychiatry, 32,* 995–1008.

Marx, M. H. (1963). The general nature of theory construction. In M. H. Marx (Ed.) *Theories in contemporary psychology* (pp. 4–46). New York: MacMillan.

Mokuau, N. (Ed.). (1991). *Handbook of social services for Asian and pacific islanders.* New York: Greenwood.

Norcross, J. C. & Goldfried, M. R. (Eds.) (1992). *Handbook of psychotherapy integration.* New York: Basic Books.

Norcross, J. C. & Newman, C. F. (1992). Psychotherapy integration: Setting the context. In J. C. Norcross & M. R. Goldfried (Eds.), *Handbook of psychotherapy integration* (pp. 3–45). New York: Basic Books.

Nugent, W. R. (1987). Use and evaluation of theories. *Social work research and abstracts, 23,* 14–19.

Pedersen, P. P., Draguns, J. G., Lonner, W. J. & Trimble, J. E. (Eds.). (1981). *Counseling across cultures.* Honolulu, HI: University of Hawaii Press.

Searles, J. (1983). A methodological critique of psychotherapy outcome meta-analysis. *Behavior research and therapy, 23,* 453–463.

Shapiro, D. A. & Shapiro, D. (1982). Meta-analysis of comparative therapy outcome studies: A replication and refinement. *Psychological Bulletin, 92,* 581–604.

Smith, M. L., Glass, G. V., & Miller, T. I. (1980). *The benefits of psychotherapy.* Baltimore, MD: Johns Hopkins University Press.

Stiles, W., Shapiro, D. & Elliott, R. (1986). Are all psychotherapies equivalent? *American Psychologist, 41,* 165–180.

Stricker, G. & Gold, J. R. (Eds.) (1993). *Comprehensive handbook of psychotherapy integration.* New York: Plenum.

Sue, D. W. (1981). *Counseling the culturally different: Theory and practice.* New York: Wiley.

Svartberg, M. & Stiles, T. (1991). Comparative efficacy of short-term psychodynamic psychotherapy: A meta-analysis. *Journal of Counseling and Clinical Psychology, 59,* 704–714.

Wachtel, P. (1977). *Psychoanalysis and behavior therapy.* New York: Basic Books.

Weisz, J., Weiss, B., Alicke, M., & Klotz, M. (1987). Effectiveness of psychotherapy with children and adolescents: A meta-analysis for clinicians. *Journal of Consulting and Clinical Psychology, 55,* 542–549.

Wilson, G. & Rachman, S. (1983). Meta-analysis and the evaluation of psychotherapy outcome: Limitations and liabilities. *Journal of Consulting and Clinical Psychology, 51,* 54–64.

Wolpe, J. (1958). *Psychotherapy by reciprocal inhibition.* Palo Alto, CA: Stanford University Press.

Part 4

The Twenty-first Century: Toward Evidence-Based Practice

You will observe with concern how long a useful truth may be known, and exist, before it is generally received and practiced.
  —Benjamin Franklin

Without leaps of imagination, or dreaming, we lose the excitement of possibilities. Dreaming, after all, is a form of planning.
  —Gloria Steinem

The Ben Franklin quote at the head of this part could have two meanings. I hope that the first one is wrong. I hope it is not another sign of the truth of Max Planck's warning that I cited in part 1 that for any real change to occur, the old guard must die out and the new guard be taught the new ways from the start of their education.

I really *want* to believe the second meaning, that the saying is perhaps, in a sense, symbolic of what this book illustrates. And that is that the newest truths—say, about Evidence-Based Practice (EBP)—may have been with us all along, but in different guises, different variations on a theme. I have called these earlier versions "eclectic practice," "empirically based practice," "scientific practice" and even just plain old "effective practice." Maybe, just maybe, EBP is just the latest iteration of a particular theme after all.

Or maybe EBP is really different.

I don't think I can resolve this issue even to my own satisfaction, because there are excellent arguments on both sides. For example, the increased rigor required for an approach to be called EBP may take the idea of "empirically based" so far from what it appeared to mean twenty years ago that one could argue EBP is a new animal. On the other hand, one could just as logically argue that EBP is the evolutionary result of many decades of the move toward incorporating more empirical results, more research, in our view of what is important information for practice.

Indeed, although the term "Evidence-Based Practice" can be seen increasingly in the literature, that appearance does not *automatically* grant it the status of a legitimate professional development. After all, like many other apparently legitimate developments in social work, EBP may just turn out to be the latest professional buzzword, maybe the latest in a string of social work fads. This could turn out to be the case even though the National Institute of Mental Health (NIMH) recently has devoted funds to developing and pilot testing a social work curriculum—called REACH-SW (Research and Empirical Applications for Curriculum Enhancement in Social Work)—that is designed to help social work educators teach students about evidence-based practice approaches. It couldn't be even remotely possible that NIMH is wrong, could it?

(Some recent evidence of the "buzzword" idea: I recently received five reviews for a new edition of an evaluation book I am working on with Martin Bloom and John Orme. In four out of the five reviews, the reviewers wanted much more on evidence-based *practice,* though our book is not a practice book: it is an *evaluation* book, or more precisely, a book on *evaluation-based practice.*)

The basic assumption of EBP is that the greater the amount of rigorous, empirical research supporting an intervention particularly (but, actually, *any* aspect of practice such as assessment and evaluation), with everything else being equal, the greater the likelihood of success with subsequent clients with similar target issues. Indeed, EBP logically means that an exhaustive review of the research literature must be done for *all* points of contact with the client, from the first interview (such as techniques of structuring and engagement) all the way through termination and follow-up. In my own teaching, I use the PRAISES model, discussed in earlier chapters of this book, to identify each of the areas where contacts with clients and relevant others takes place. I then attempt to review the research evidence on each of those aspects of practice. This is very time consuming, of course; luckily, professors have all the time in the world to conduct these reviews of research. So, it is my opinion that any attempt to limit the meaning of Evidence-Based Practice to only a few of these points of intervention—for example, assessment, or evaluation, or even the major intervention techniques or programs that are used—degrades the concept and meaning of Evidence-Based Practice.

As you will see in chapter 21, where EBP is discussed, and from this introduction, EBP places many heavy demands on social workers to review essentially *all* the research/evaluation literature on the problems with which we work. These demands go substantially beyond the demands of what we in the past called "empirically based practice," advocates of which considered interventions as empirically based with as few as two well-designed studies available. Thus, with a key principle of Evidence-Based Practice being that all research on a relevant topic be reviewed and analyzed by practitioners, EBP takes the field further in the direction of comprehensive and rigorous evaluation of the literature than we ever have been before. And precisely because of these increased demands on practitioners, both Evidence-Based Practice itself and *manuals* describing the methodology of EBP, no matter how well and clearly written, can be pretty intimidating (Gibbs, 2003; Cournoyer, 2003; Rubin, 2008).

In fact, the methodology of EBP contains, in my opinion, a few inherent problems for social work that we must consider as we think about adopting that approach (see Gibbs and Gambrill [2002] for an extensive discussion of the pros and cons of EBP).

First, there is no generally accepted criterion defining how many studies or what percent of studies must be positive to deserve being established as evidence based. This criterion problem appears in many other areas of research as well, so it is not unique to EBP. Yet, it has not been solved. Some EBP advocates would argue, say, that when the *preponderance* of the evidence is in a positive direction, an intervention may be termed evidence based. This may be acceptable to some, but "preponderance" also can be taken to mean "majority," as in one over 50 percent. That would be a pretty slim margin to consider an intervention as evidence based. This issue will not be easily resolved, nor is it likely to easily disappear. So, some conventions will have to be established whereby practitioners can make decisions on what is evidence based and what, given the state of the literature at any given time, is not. This issue is made even more complicated by recent assertions by Io-anndis (2005a, 2005b) that most published, positive research findings—particularly individual studies but also many meta-analyses—may be false!

Here is where the methods of meta-analysis, described in chapter 15, might help, the comments of Ioanndis notwithstanding. Using meta-analysis to review research produces a single number, called an *effect size* (ES), which can summarize the effects of an intervention across any number of studies. Perhaps there will be increasing agreement over time as to just how large that effect size must be to justify a decision on the status of a given body of research as evidence based.

My recommendation would be to recognize an ES of .80 as a minimum ES for considering a procedure as evidence based. The magnitude of an ES of .80 or larger generally is regarded as a fairly large ES, and also is relatively rare. This recommendation to use .80 as the minimum ES for evidence-based decision-making is consistent with Cohen's (1988) recommendation that .80 can be considered as a large ES. It also is consistent with the review by Lipsey and Wilson (1993) that an ES of .80 is, indeed, relatively rare in the intervention literature. Since a decision about what is and what is not evidence based could have very important implications for our practice with clients, would it not make sense to be especially cautious by using larger and less common ESs to attempt to ensure that such a decision is well grounded in the evidence? (Ioanndis' argument about effect sizes basically is that the smaller the effect size, the more likely are the results of a meta-analysis to be false. This argument actually supports the idea about the importance of agreement on using relatively large effect sizes.)

As a corollary to the effect-size recommendation, for published reviews of literature that are not meta-analyses or are conducted by practitioners themselves, I recommend that a minimum of 80 percent of collected and reviewed studies provide clear, positive results before a procedure can be considered as evidence based. I recognize that this 80 percent criterion is somewhat arbitrary. But I recommend 80 percent because it is the rough cut-off point that we use in research to indicate good reliability for a measure. Since reliability refers to *consistency*, it seems to me to be reasonable to expect the same level of consistency across studies examining the effectiveness of some procedure before we consider that procedure as evidence based. And, like the recommended ES of .80, this 80 percent criterion is relatively high, a conservative figure for attempting to make a decision about what to do to help our clients improve their lives.

In both cases of meta-analyses and traditional, published reviews, in accord with what I discussed in chapter 8, I would suggest one additional criterion. My argument also would be that those reviews that contain critiques of the *methods* of the studies reviewed (or in the case of meta-analyses, quantitative analyses of the effect of studies' methodologies on the overall ES), and then use those critiques for making decisions about the overall effectiveness of a given procedure, should be given the highest priorities for our consideration of what is evidence based. For reviews that do not critically analyze the studies they review but only *report* them, far less confidence should be placed in their conclusions.

A second problem in EBP is that many of the specific problems with which we work in real practice simply either have not accumulated much research or haven't been rigorously studied at all. I am continuously beset by that problem many times a semester when I try to help my students find reviews of the literature. It is very frustrating and unfortunately common.

As someone who was in practice, full and part time, for many years, and who reviews the literature periodically with my students, I cannot imagine, given the current state of our knowledge, that the knowledge about all problems and all interventions, let alone even *most* problems and interventions, could be considered to be evidence based. Every social worker who has ever practiced knows how complicated our cases can be. Many (dare I say, most?) of our cases contain problems, strengths, and issues that the evaluation literature doesn't even address, let alone contain evidence about what works.

All this seems to me to be the case, unless we accept a somewhat refined meaning of the word *evidence*. If our sole understanding of "evidence" is some body of knowledge that has been rigorously, empirically verified in a large number of studies, then it seems to me that we, as a profession, will be empirically *challenged,* not empirically *based*. If, however, we recognize that "evidence" means using the best information available at any time *including* the results of evaluation when only modest amounts of, or no, empirical data are available, then perhaps EBP is indeed a currently viable approach. There are many criteria available to evaluate knowledge, particularly when there is little or no empirical evidence. Many of these criteria were reviewed in chapter five. These criteria were presented with the idea that they are not *substitutes* for rigorous empirical evidence, but as complementary and supplementary to empirical criteria. Thus, there is some potential for EBP in the understanding that "evidence" is not *only* the results of the most rigorous form of empirical research, but includes other forms of information as well. However, this perspective always assumes that there will be a rigorous review of the research literature before these other criteria are implemented.

Third, and finally, is a problem with EBP that is at the heart of my own caution about a full embrace of EBP. That problem is one of understanding what we might call consumerism: will social workers actually *use* Evidence-Based Practice? Any one who has participated with practitioners in case reviews and other everyday practices knows the pressure under which most social workers work. Recent headlines in the newspapers of Hawai'i about a child who was severely abused after being discharged from the care of Child Protective Services shows just how great that pressure can be. Will line workers have the time, willingness, knowledge, and enthusiasm to embark on this new(ish) adventure, even for a *portion* of their cases? Are EBP advocates actually expecting practitioners to engage in the activities described in chapter 21, including exhaustive reviews of research for all or even some points of intervention, analyze all the data, then make unspecified and unknown changes in evidence-based procedures to accommodate their specific clients and contexts, and then implement those procedures?

I don't actually know the answer to these questions, and even if there were data to examine, I believe the results would vary by geographic location, by agency, by ethnicity and culture of the client, by *the individual practitioner.* Indeed, at the heart of all this, my take on learning about all forms of effective practice is that learning about them is an *individual responsibility,* and that the most motivated, best trained, most highly committed practitioners most often will rise to the challenge.

But since most social workers work in agencies, I see effective practice, and particularly Evidence-Based Practice, as an *organizational responsibility* as well as an individual one. I believe agencies can contribute to developing EBP as the standard of practice for their organizations. Some of the ways of doing that, in general, were described in chapter four. Here, however, is how the agency, per se, could function to promote EBP in particular: every month, one social worker can volunteer or be designated to review the literature to find and examine a particular intervention that is relevant to that agency's area of concern to see if the data allow a determination that it is an effective, evidence-based intervention. That social worker will be given sufficient time and resources to implement the methodology of EBP, including the literature search and the evaluation of the information. Once a month, the agency can schedule a meeting for the social worker to present to the rest of the staff results on his or her conclusions about a particular intervention. That would include possible variations that might need to be addressed, given that agency's particular clients and other issues. For those interventions deemed to be evidence based, handouts describing how the intervention is conducted and on what problems can be provided. The agency might even want to consider scheduling follow-up role-play sessions so that all the practitioners in that agency can become knowledgeable about that evidence-based intervention.

Within a year, an agency committed to this approach could potentially provide for its practitioners up to twelve evidence-based interventions, and, I hope, the positive results for their clients that Evidence-Based Practice promises.

So, ultimately, what will distinguish EBP as a legitimate development for our profession, and not a fad or pipe dream of ivory tower professors (like me), is the extent to which it is embraced and *utilized on a regular basis* by practitioners.

I really do believe that EBP, as imperfect as it may seem, can bring a higher degree of effectiveness to the practice of social workers than we may have enjoyed in the past. But I am not (totally) naive. In many ways, I see EBP as a *goal* for practice rather than as an approach that can be immediately implemented for all social workers in all practices with all clients and all problems. That goal may never be attainable across the board. I look at it this way: When I go to see a physician, I hope that physician has done as much as possible to implement EBP in his or her practice so that any condition I may present is treated with the best available interventions. Don't the clients of social workers deserve the same?

Chapters in Part 4

Chapter 19 is titled, "An Eclectic Approach for Persons with Substance-Related Disorders." In this chapter, I describe a comprehensive approach—from definition to assessment to intervention to evaluation—for dealing with problems related to substance use/abuse. What I tried to produce in this material is a perspective and a program that was as close to Evidence-Based Practice—especially regarding the interventions—as I could make it. Of course, I didn't use the term "evidence-based practice." That term was, at the time, not widely disseminated in the social work literature. Nevertheless, as you will see, the focus in many parts of this chapter was on trying to use the results of research and evaluation wherever possible to inform the development of practice methods. That is about as close to EBP as one could get at the time, I suppose, without actually using those words.

Chapter 20 contains some brief ideas about a part of the future of social work practice, a future that contains the "Use of Computers in Evaluation and Practice." Written with Martin Bloom and John Orme, this chapter contains an overview of some very practical uses of computers. Originally written for our book, *Evaluating Practice* (Bloom, Fischer, & Orme, 2009), this chapter covers some general ideas about how computers might be advantageous. It also looks at the way computers can be used to develop explicit aides for practice and evaluation, including programs to manage data, do your analyses for you, and a variety of other, dare I say it, clever ideas. I have included our discussion of the contents of a CD-ROM that contains MS Word and other programs that can be used to creatively develop practical tools for learning about and actually keeping track of our own evaluation and practice efforts. Since this chapter was written specifically for our book, I hope you will forgive the numerous references to it. Thanks.

The final chapter in this book, chapter 21, is called "Evidence-Based Practice." As with chapter 20, this chapter also was cowritten by Bloom and Orme. Short though it may be, especially compared with some of the other chapters, in chapter 21 you will find numerous references to books and sites on the Web that can help you develop an approach to practice that takes advantage of many of the works that cover the research and evaluation literature on Evidence-Based Practice. In this chapter, at last, you will see an overview of Evidence-Based Practice. This overview will provide a definition of EBP, some important references to the EBP literature, and a discussion of the implications of EBP for practice evaluation. I can only hope the wait was worth it. The path toward Evidence-Based Practice, for this book at least, is now complete.

References

Bloom, M., Fischer, J., & Orme, J. (2006). *Evaluating practice: Guidelines for the accountable professional (6th Ed.)*. Boston: Allyn & Bacon.

Cohen, J. (1988). *Statistical power analysis for the behavioral sciences* (2nd ed.). New York: Academic Press.

Cournoyer, B. R. (2003). *The evidence-based social work skills book*. Boston: Allyn & Bacon.

Gibbs, L. E. (2003). *Evidence-based practice for the helping professions: A practical guide with integrated multi-media*. Pacific Grove, CA: Brooks/Cole.

Gibbs, L. E., & Gambrill, E. (2002). Evidence-based practice: Counterarguments to objections. *Research on Social Work Practice, 12,* 452–476.

Ioanndis, J. (2005a). Contradicted and initially stronger effects in highly cited clinical research, *JAMA,* 218–228.

Ioanndis, J. (2005b). Why most published research findings are false. *PLoS Med, 2(8):* e124, 696–701. Retrieved from www.plosmedicine.org

Lipsey, M. W., & Wilson, D. B. (1993). The efficacy of psychological, educational and behavioral treatment. *American Psychologist, 48,* 1181–1209.

Rubin, A. (2008). *Practitioner's guide to using research evidence*. New York: Wiley.

Chapter 19

An Eclectic Approach for Persons with Substance-related Disorders

Introduction

There is little question that substance abuse is one of the hot topics from the 1980s up until today. Both the lay and the professional literature are rife with references to the problems and dangers associated with substance use and abuse—and rightly so. The direct and indirect costs of substance abuse—in terms of dollars and lives—are enormous.

However, the real issues involved sometimes are lost in the virtual national hysteria that has arisen since the days of the Reagan administration. The hysteria regarding drug usage in the United States has been well documented by Abbie Hoffman (1987) in his book *Steal This Urine Test.* Hysteria also can be seen, perhaps, in the statement of a graduate social work student who announced in class that an alcoholism expert in a lecture had asserted that 80 percent of human service professionals either have problems with alcohol themselves or come from families where at least one member does. Finally, the national preoccupation with substance abuse can be seen in President Bush's declaration in September of 1989 that "the gravest domestic threat facing our nation today is drugs" (*Honolulu Advertiser,* September 6, 1989, p. A-4).

Obviously, then, there is a great need for social work practitioners to get some kind of handle on the enormous range of problems associated with substance abuse and perhaps to carve out some area of special understanding (or expertise) as a way of addressing some of these problems.

This chapter provides the basis for doing just that. Because of the complexity of and enormous literature on substance abuse problems, and the space limitations inherent in a book such as this, this chapter will not be a general treatise on the nature of substance abuse. Thus, many important and fascinating issues will not be explored, such as,

Fischer, J. (2000). In H. Briggs & K. Corcoran (Eds.). *Social Work Practice: Treating Common Client Problems.* Chicago: Lyceum Books. Reprinted with permission of Lyceum Books, Inc.

1. Theories and research about the etiology and maintenance or continuation of substance abuse.
2. The existence of the addictive personality.
3. The concept of addiction, per se (Peele, 1989).
4. Total abstinence versus limited use of some substance for those recovering from abuse.
5. The pros and cons of twelve-step programs (Herman, 1988).
6. The disease model controversy (Fingarette, 1988).
7. Substance abuse prevention (Nathan & Gorman, 1998) and education (Milgram, 1987) programs.
8. Public policy issues (Fraser & Kohlert, 1988).

Many of the references cited in this chapter, however, do address these issues, especially such recent books as Donovan and Marlatt (1988); Miller and Heather (1986); Lewis, Dana, and Blevins (1988); Bratter and Forrest (1985); McCrady and Sher (1985); Galatner (1983); and Nirenberg and Maisto (1987).

Instead of addressing the issues listed above, the focus of this chapter (in keeping with the purposes of this book) is on clinical implications of substance abuse. Substance-related disorders will be viewed essentially as a variety of problems in living that are manifested in biological/physiological, social, and psychological realms of human functioning. The use of the term "problems in living" is not intended to deny the powerful and significant effects of substance abuse. Rather, it is an attempt to destigmatize and delabel the problem and is linked to the approach to intervention that will be described later in this chapter, especially in regard to the need for development of individualized goals and interventions.

Subsequent sections of this chapter describe some dimensions of the problems of substance abuse, both epidemiologically and clinically; present some assessment and evaluation guidelines; and focus most intensively on describing a program for clinical intervention with the problems of, and problems associated with, substance abuse.

Problem Identification

Several substances typically are considered to have the potential to be abused, including alcohol, licit and illicit drugs, food, caffeine, and the nicotine in smoking and smokeless products. There are a number of commonalities among all these substances: all can be used by some people without any problems, whereas other people experience serious problems with their use; all involve short-term pleasurable activities with potential for long-term negative consequences; all involve biosociopsychological phenomena; and all, when abuse is most extreme, seem to involve some aspect of compulsiveness on the part of the abuser in his or her attachment or involvement with the substance (see Miller, 1987).

This chapter focuses mainly on just two of the substances—alcohol and drugs. This is largely because of space limitations, but it is also because the assessment and intervention strategies for alcohol and drug abuse are relatively similar, and because social work practitioners apparently see more instances of alcohol and drug abuse—as identified problems, at any rate—than the other forms of substance abuse. However, it should be pointed out that the intervention techniques to be discussed in this chapter can also be applied to abuse of other substances and that simply because they are not covered here, the problems associated with abuse of these substances are not viewed as less serious than those associated with alcohol and drug abuse.

Definition of Substance Abuse

Perhaps the most widely used definition of disorders associated with use of substances such as those described above is the one contained in the *Diagnostic and Statistical Manual* (DSM-IV) of the American Psychiatric Association (APA, 1994; see also Maxman, 1986). This definition distinguishes between two major conditions associated with dysfunctional use of substances: substance dependence and (the more commonly used term) substance abuse. The DSM-IV also identifies certain substance-induced disorders, including substance intoxication, substance withdrawal, substance-induced mental disorders included elsewhere in the DSM-IV, and a variety of disorders related to each of the specific substances (e.g., alcohol, amphetamines, etc.). This chapter focuses mainly on the overarching categories of substance dependence and substance abuse.

Substance dependence refers essentially to a cluster of cognitive, behavioral, and physiological symptoms that indicate that a person has impaired control in the use of one or more substances and continues use of the substance despite adverse consequences (APA, 1994). The primary symptoms of dependence, according to the DSM-IV, include, but are not limited to, physiological tolerance and withdrawal. Tolerance refers to either the diminishing effects over time of a fixed amount of a substance or the need to increase amounts of a substance in order to maintain the same effect. Withdrawal refers to the symptoms that occur when use of the substance is reduced or stopped. The symptoms of tolerance and withdrawal vary according to the specific substance and the frequency, amount, and chronicity of its use.

Substance dependence can show up in a variety of ways. The DSM-IV lists seven symptoms, three of which must be present for at least a month or have occurred repeatedly over a longer period for substance dependence to be present.

Substance abuse is referred to in the DSM-IV as a residual category in that maladaptive patterns of substance use are present that do not meet the criteria for dependence. These criteria, one of which must be present for one month or occur repeatedly for a longer period, are 1) failure to fulfill major role obligations; 2) use of the substance in hazardous situations (e.g., driving while intoxicated); 3) legal problems; and 4) persistent social or interpersonal problems.

There are at least two problems with the DSM-IV view of substance abuse. One is that it focuses mainly on the abuse, per se, and not on the myriad problems that could be associated with it. Thus, it implies that substance abuse is a more or less homogeneous problem, and, correspondingly, that treatment can be a more or less homogeneous activity (focused only on the abuse). The second problem is that the seven diagnostic criteria for substance dependence (of which at least three must be present) and the four for abuse all are indicative of very severe problems of substance use. By no stretch of the imagination can the presence of any of those criteria be construed as mild (e.g., the main criterion for evaluating both dependence and abuse is "a maladaptive pattern of substance use, leading to clinically significant impairment or distress . . ." (APA, 1994, pp. 181, 182).

It is especially important to recognize that substance abuse and the problems associated with it vary tremendously in severity from person to person. It would be overly simplistic to say that a person does or does not abuse some substance. A far more useful perspective—for both assessment and intervention—would be to view the use of substances on a continuum from nonproblematic to extremely problematic. In other words, deciding who has or does not have a problem with substance use depends on a variety of factors related not only to use (or misuse) of the substance, but also to the ways in which that misuse affects total functioning. Just such a continuum regarding problems with substance use has been proposed by Lewis et al. (1988), who conceptualize disorders associated with substance abuse as ranging along the following continuum:

1. Nonuse
2. Moderate, nonproblematic use
3. Heavy, nonproblematic use
4. Heavy use; moderate problems
5. Heavy use; serious problems
6. Dependence; life and health problems

This continuum allows for greater individualization in goals and techniques of intervention and avoids overgeneralized or stereotypical thinking about the supposed homogeneity of substance abusers.

The complexities of all of the above, then, necessitate some working definition of substance abuse that can help guide practitioners' activities. Such a working definition might be as follows: when use of alcohol or drugs (or, for that matter, any substance) affects an individual's biological/medical, social, behavioral, or psychological functioning, that problem can be viewed as one of substance abuse. This definition allows for the wide variety of problems typically associated with substance abuse to be viewed on the continuum described above. Thus, at one end of the continuum, few if any problems are associated with substance use, while at the other end of the continuum, serious problems exist in one or more areas of the individual's life. These problems could include dependence and/or abuse (as defined by the DSM-IV) and could also include the pattern that often brings people to the attention of professional helpers (voluntarily or involuntarily) and the overwhelming involvement or attachment to the substance—the compulsiveness and inability to control its use that was mentioned earlier as a common characteristic of serious abuse of all substances.

In line with the DSM-IV, this chapter focuses on the following classes of substances, individually or in combination: alcohol; amphetamines (e.g., speed and certain appetite suppressants); caffeine; cannabis (e.g., marijuana, hashish); cocaine; hallucinogens (e.g., LSD); inhalants (e.g., glue sniffing); opioids (e.g., heroin); phencyclidine (PCP); and sedatives, hypnotics, and aniolytics. Throughout this chapter, the term "substance abuse" will be used in the general sense of problems associated with the use of any of the above substances, rather than the more narrow use described in the DSM-IV. Perhaps an even more appropriate general term might be "substance misuse," although this typically is taken to mean a less severe set of problems than substance abuse.

Prevalence of Substance Abuse

The United States is a society of alcohol and drug users: some 90 million adults use alcohol on a regular basis (Miller, 1987). By the time they reach their mid-twenties, up to 80 percent of Americans have tried an illicit drug, and at any given time some 37 percent of high school seniors have had five or more drinks in one sitting within the preceding two weeks (Johnston, O'Malley, & Bachman, 1986). In other words, alcohol and drugs seem to be as American as apple pie and ice cream.

It is difficult to know precisely how many of the users of these substances actually have problems of abuse or dependence or misuse. Some estimates are available, however, from a community survey of three metropolitan areas that was conducted in the early 1980s (Robins et al., 1984; see also Helzer, 1987). This survey examined lifetime prevalence of fifteen DSM-III psychiatric disorders, with lifetime prevalence being the proportion of people in a representative sample who had ever experienced the disorder up to the time of assessment. Of all the disorders, by far the most prevalent was substance abuse, with 15 to 18.1 percent of the population being diagnosed. Of these, alcohol abuse ranged from 11.5 to 15.7 percent of the population, and drug abuse from 5.5 to 5.8 percent. These percentages translate into hefty numbers of the American population; with 1987 census figures showing roughly 185 million adult Americans, these data suggest that some 3 million or more adult Americans, at some time in their lives, may have been affected by alcohol and/or drug abuse. Given that the 1987 census figures show roughly 89 million households, this means that up to 37 percent of American households may be affected.

The prevalence of alcohol and drug abuse appears to be substantially higher for whites than other racial and ethnic groups, despite the common perception that substance abuse is mainly a "minority problem" (Smith, 1993). There are few differences related to education regarding prevalence of substance abuse (again with one exception in one city that showed higher rates of alcohol abuse among non–college graduates). There are clearer differences according to gender: most data show higher rates of substance abuse for men than women, with this difference being greatest for alcohol abuse (a ratio of up to 5 to 1).

Although these data are startling, their true meaning becomes clear when examining the implications of these problems for everyday life. The direct and indirect costs—both in health terms and financially—of alcohol and drug abuse are immense. One of the leading experts on the topic, J. Danforth Quayle (1983), estimated, perhaps conservatively, that the price paid for health care, days away from work, and lost productivity amounts to approximately $70 billion per year. The medical risks are even more frightening, with a huge variety of illnesses associated with alcohol and drug abuse (Wartenberg & Liepman, 1987; Segal & Sisson, 1985). More importantly, estimates are that drug and alcohol abuse are related to the deaths of up to 130,000 people per year, including the many innocent victims of people who drive while under the influence of some substance (Hoffman, 1987; Wartenberg & Liepman, 1987).

Add to all this the incalculable toll of substance abuse on individual functioning, family life, and employment, and it can be clearly seen that substance abuse is indeed one of the major problems of the era. Indeed, when the categories of substance abuse are expanded to include nicotine and food, with some 50 million smokers and 40 million overweight Americans (Miller, 1987), the enormity of the problem becomes even more apparent, with countless billions of dollars added to the nation's costs and hundreds of thousands of deaths added every year to the number of deaths associated with alcohol and drugs alone (Wartenberg & Liepman, 1987; *Honolulu Advertiser,* April 4, 1989, p. D2).

Clinical Manifestations of Substance Abuse

Despite the many myths about the "typical alcoholic" or "typical drug addict," it would be inappropriate to try to characterize the clinical manifestations of substance use as though they apply to all people with substance abuse problems. The dangers here are stereotyping and overgeneralizing; it is perhaps better to err by individualizing than by assuming that all people are alike. This is not to say that there are not some commonalities among the manifestations of substance abuse. Rather, it is to say that the range of possibilities of clinical manifestations of substance abuse is so great that the real need for assessment and intervention is to be able to precisely pinpoint areas for change that are specific for each individual. This is one more rationale for use of the continuum of abuse—ranging from nonuse to misuse to serious abuse—described earlier.

Problems related to substance abuse can show up in all realms of human functioning. As mentioned earlier, the DSM-IV describes seven possible diagnostic criteria (or patterns of behavior) related to dependence (e.g., a great deal of time spent in trying to get, use, or recover from the substance; persistent desire or one or more unsuccessful attempts to cut down or control substance use), and four criteria or patterns related to abuse. Not all of these need to be present either for the formal diagnosis to be made or for serious problems as a result of substance use to be present.

Similarly, the DSM-IV lists several categories of disorders caused by the direct effect of various substances on the nervous system that could be present in any given case of substance misuse. These include intoxication, withdrawal, delirium, withdrawal delirium, delusional disorder, mood disorder, and other syndromes. Thus, the clinical manifestations of abuse could include one or more of these disorders as well.

In addition, any individual who misuses or abuses some substance could be suffering from any one of a number of medical problems associated with the abuse (Wartenberg & Liepman, 1987). These problems run the gamut from malnutrition to cancer to respiratory and cardiovascular problems to a variety of infections, such as hepatitis or even AIDS.

Finally, Lewis et al. (1988) list numerous problems that typically, but not uniformly, are associated with substance abuse. These include employment problems; problems with friends or neighbors; problems with spouse, children, parents, or other relatives; problems with arrests and the criminal justice system; financial problems; problems of belligerence, depression, anxiety, and so on. These numerous problems all are ways in which the clinical manifestations of substance abuse can be seen.

Practitioners who work exclusively with individuals who abuse only one substance may see more commonalities among presented problems than those who work with abuse of a range of different substances. However, when substance abuse as a whole is examined, it is obvious that it can manifest itself in so many ways, and in so many realms of human functioning, that it requires the practitioner to be especially sensitive and to be able to carefully assess each individual for the unique ways in which the problems may be manifested. The next section presents some guidelines and tools that emphasize the importance of such individualized assessment.

Assessment and Evaluation

This chapter emphasizes the idea that problems associated with substance use should be viewed as problems in living, leading to the necessity of individualizing goals and interventions. It is, therefore, probably not an overstatement to say that the assessment of the client is the most important phase of the clinical process. This is because the assessment identifies the specific problems of each client, sets specific goals for each case, selects specific interventions tailored to the problems and goals, and develops a plan to monitor and evaluate the success of the intervention. Even though initial goals and interventions are selected, however, the assessment does not stop there; substance abuse involves such a complicated set of problems that goals and interventions may have to be reformulated constantly on the basis of new or better evidence, changes in the problems, or the appearance of new problems. Indeed, the very complexity of the assessment process requires mastery of a great deal of material, much of which can be obtained from comprehensive guides to the assessment process (e.g., Donovan & Marlatt, 1988; Lewis et al., 1988; Baker & Cannon, 1988; Miller, 1981; McCrady & Sher, 1985; Sobell, Sobell, & Nirenberg, 1988; Nirenberg & Maisto, 1987; Bratter & Forrest, 1985).

Assessment in this chapter is used for the purposes described above rather than for diagnosis. Diagnosis serves important purposes, including agency or insurance requirements. However, for reasons described earlier regarding problems with the DSM-IV categories, the diagnosis, per se, is downplayed here in order to focus on the broader perspective of clinical assessment of not only the substance abuse itself, but also of the context and problems associated with that abuse.

Basic Principles

A number of basic principles underlie the assessment methodologies discussed here.

1. Substance abuse is a biopsychosocial problem that is very complicated and requires a multivariate assessment process to properly understand it. Thus, a variety of assessment methods must be utilized.
2. The problems of, and associated with, substance use occur on a continuum, from nonproblematic to severely problematic. Thus, the purpose of assessment is not to make a simplistic determination of whether or not an individual abuses some substance, but to examine the problem in all its manifestations.
3. There are a variety of interventions available to deal with the diverse problems associated with substance abuse. It is crucial for the practitioner to be aware of these interventions so that the best interventions available can be selected for each component of the problem.
4. The focus of assessment for substance abuse is largely on the present, especially on factors that might be maintaining the abuse. This is because factors that might be associated with the original development of abuse may not be the ones maintaining it; in fact, they may no longer be present at all.
5. The practitioner must be aware of the importance of socioeconomic, ethnic, and cultural variables in conducting an assessment. The basic principle is, the greater the difference between the practitioner and client (in values, attitudes, socioeconomic status, etc.), the greater the sensitivity required of the practitioner to properly understand the client's situation (see Lum, 1986; Schare & Milburn, 1996) for frameworks for conducting assessments that are attuned to sociocultural issues).
6. Assessment for substance abuse is very complex. Misconceptions associated with abuse, poor professional education in this area, difficulty of gaining cooperation from some clients, variability of problems associated with abuse, need to understand prior treatments with relapsed clients, and the covert

nature of some problems of abuse all have been cited as reasons why assessment for substance abuse is especially difficult (Sobell et al., 1988). Thus, the practitioner must take even more care than with other problem areas to ensure that he or she has done as thorough and sensitive a job as possible.

7. Despite the need to know as much as possible about the problem so that one can make a rational decision about the best available intervention, reality suggests that this must be balanced with the amount of time available to the practitioner, i.e., the cost efficiency of the assessment process (Donovan & Marlatt, 1988). In order to avoid practitioners becoming overwhelmed with assessing each case, Donovan & Marlatt (1988) describe the use of clinical hypothesis testing (generating hypotheses based on data collected) and segmented assessment strategies (funneling from very broad to increasingly specific foci in the assessment).

8. The practitioner who works with substance abuse needs an extensive body of knowledge to aid in understanding the variety of factors associated with the abuse. This includes not only knowledge that all practitioners might have about dealing with social and psychological problems (employment difficulties, depression, cognitive distortions, anxiety, and so on), but also knowledge about the specific substance of concern, including biophysiological factors, behavioral factors, cognitive-expectational factors, and social factors (Donovan & Marlatt, 1988).

Areas for Collection of Information

There are a number of areas about which practitioners should collect information to help in goal formulation and treatment planning. These have been hinted at above but will be described in a little more detail here. Although the most common focus of assessment for substance abuse is the pattern of the abuse itself, the other elements described here are viewed as no less important in developing a comprehensive understanding of the client and the client's problems.

Medical Information   Because of the numerous possible medical complications that could be associated with substance abuse, it is crucial for every client to have a thorough medical evaluation. In addition, it is important for practitioners to solicit information from clients about any physical problems as early in their contacts as possible in the event that referral to a physician is necessary.

Presence of Related Social/Psychological Disorders   In addition to the several substance abuse—related disorders described in the DSM-IV mentioned earlier, there are a number of problems about which practitioners must be aware. These include the behaviors, thoughts, and feelings associated with disorders involving depression, anxiety, sleep, eating, sex, and impulse control. Problems in any of these areas pose serious complications in the lives of clients who abuse some substance and will need attention if a comprehensive treatment program is to be developed.

Life Stresses   In addition to the above, there are any number of events that could complicate substance abuse patterns and, indeed, could even be associated with maintaining the abuse. These life stresses must be carefully assessed. They include problems with family, income, housing, and peer relationships.

Prior Treatment History   The practitioner must be informed about the client's attempts to receive treatment for any of the problems described above, or for the substance abuse itself. The practitioner then should determine the reasons for the success or failure of those programs and try to build on the successes and not duplicate the failures.

Client Motivation and Expectations   The client may have a number of preconceived notions of what treatment may be like. These expectations can have a serious impact on the success or failure of treatment, and it is crucial for the practitioner to elicit these expectations from the client and to create positive expectations of success as part of treatment. Similarly, it is important to know and understand the client's motivation for seeking treatment. Obviously, the client's commitment to the process could be influenced by any number of factors, ranging from genuine desire for change to the desire to avoid some legal problems or dissolution of a marriage. This information allows the practitioner to make judgments about the extent to which he or she will need to emphasize enhancing the client's motivation as a major or minor part of the intervention.

Availability of Social Supports   In making decisions about the type of treatment that will be recommended, the practitioner will have to understand the client's social support system, if indeed he or she has one (McCrady & Sher, 1985). The presence or extent of social support could have a bearing on the type of treatment (i.e., in- or outpatient), types of tasks and homework assigned the client, type of maintenance program, and so on.

Functional Analysis of the Pattern of Substance Abuse   Ultimately, of course, the practitioner will have to do a careful assessment of the pattern of substance use and factors that may be associated with it, including antecedents that may be eliciting substance abuse and consequences that could be maintaining it. Sobell et al. (1988) have provided a comprehensive list of areas to be examined in such an assessment, including the following:

1. Specific quantities and frequency of use of the substance.
2. Usual and unusual substance-use circumstances and patterns.
3. Predominant mood states and situations antecedent and consequent to substance use.

4. History of withdrawal symptoms.
5. Identification of possible difficulties the client might encounter in refraining from substance use.
6. Extent and severity of previous substance use.
7. Multiple substance use.
8. Reports of frequent thoughts or urges to use substances.
9. Review of positive consequences of substance abuse.
10. Risks associated with nonabstinence treatment goal.

Other Areas   In addition to the areas described above, Shaffer and Kauffman (1985) offer a number of hypotheses to be tested in assessing substance abuse. These hypotheses—actually partial formulations—include biological hypotheses (e.g., can the substance use be understood as an attempt to reduce dysphoria?), sociological hypotheses (e.g., does the substance use occur in limited or varied environmental contexts?), and behavior hypotheses (e.g., can the problems be understood as contingent upon the reinforcing properties of the substance?).

Methods of Data Collection

In order to collect information on the wide range of activities, behaviors, patterns, thoughts, and feelings described above, a number of different methods of data collection must be employed. These methods include interviews with clients and others, self-report measures, direct observation (including analogue measures), biochemical measures, and records.

Interviews   The interview is, of course, the major medium for the collection of the information described in the previous section. This is as much the case in the area of substance abuse as it is in any other clinical area. Thus, standard social work intervention strategies are used to elicit and analyze this information. However, there are some specifics that differentiate interviews in this area from those in other areas (see, e.g., Shaffer & Kauffman, 1985). A summary of interviewing conditions that provide the most useful information in the area of substance abuse has been provided by Sobell et al. (1988, pp. 29–30) and includes the following: 1) when the client is alcohol and drug free; 2) when rapport is developed both by the practitioner's style and by stressing confidentiality and the importance of the information; 3) when the terminology used is clearly understood by both parties; 4) when the focus of the interview is information gathering rather than social labeling; 5) when the client's self-reports are checked out against other sources; and 6) when data are gathered, to the extent possible, in a clinical research setting.

The interview typically contains both structured and unstructured portions. A very useful guide for the initial interview was developed by Lewis et al. (1988), along with a psychosocial and substance-use history form and a behavioral assessment and functional analysis interview form. A widely used structured interview format for assessment of alcohol abuse is the Comprehensive Drinking

Profile (Marlatt, 1976), and a structured interview format for drug abuse, called the G-DATS, has been described by Boudin et al. (1977). Another structured interview format for both drug and alcohol abuse is the Addiction Severity Index (McClellan et al., 1980

Self-Report Measures   Especially important areas for the collection of data on substance abuse are self-report measures and self-monitoring. These measures range from simple oral reports the client might make during the interview to the use of standardized questionnaires. For the purposes of this chapter, these two types of self-report measures will be divided into two categories: standardized scales and self-monitoring.

Standardized Scales   One of the fastest growing areas of assessment for substance abuse is that of standardized scales. Many of these measures have reported fairly good reliability and validity data. Standardized measures cover not only problems of abuse, but also problems that could be related to, abuse, such as depression, anxiety, and cognitive distortions (see Corcoran & Fischer, 2000a, 2000b, for a collection of over 400 short-form measures for clinical practice; and *see* Hersen & Bellack, 1988, for a dictionary of well over 400 assessment procedures). Some of the most useful standardized self-report scales developed for assessing substance abuse are the Substance Abuse Problem Checklist (Carroll, 1984), the Michigan Alcohol Screening Test (Selzer, 1971), the Drug Abuse Screening Test (Skinner, 1982), the Hilton Drinking Behavior Questionnaire (Hilton & Lokane, 1978), and the Callner-Ross Assertion Questionnaire (Ammerman & Van Hasselt, 1988).

Self-Monitoring   The second major type of self-report measure is called self-monitoring. Self-monitoring refers essentially to the client routinely recording, via diaries or logs, problems and behaviors related to abuse. This includes recording not only actual use patterns, but also problems associated with use and the urges and consequences related to use. Essentially, the process of self-monitoring involves training the client to record a variety of factors related to abuse, including some or all of the following: time, date, and amount of the substance; antecedents and consequences, including thoughts, feelings, and behaviors of self and others; and activities associated with substance use. These data are collected before, during, and after treatment and can be used as a basis not only for assessment, but also for evaluation. Of course, the practitioner's response to the client's efforts at self-monitoring can play a major role in how useful and accurate these data are (Sobell et al., 1988).

Reliability and Validity of Self-Report Data   A major concern about self-report data in the area of substance abuse is their reliability and validity. The prevailing myth is that such data are almost always suspect. In fact, a substantial amount of research shows that self-reports in the area of substance abuse can be both reliable and valid (Sobell et al., 1988; Ridley & Kordinak, 1988), including good agreement between self-reports and reports by collaterals (Sobell et al., 1988). The main cautions about these conclusions are that they apply mainly when the client is interviewed under the following conditions: he or she is substance free, he or she is in a clinical/research setting, and he or she is assured of confidentiality.

Direct Observation   Although rather difficult to implement in clinical settings, direct observation has been used in some instances to provide information on use of some substances (Foy, Cline, & Laasi, 1987). One type of direct observation involves the use of analogue measures, in which tasks are developed that are considered analogous to the natural environment in which a person must work to obtain a substance (typically alcohol). Another type of direct observation is where the client is placed in a simulated bar or living room environment and provided with the substance (again, typically alcohol), and then observed as to the patterns and amounts ingested.

Biochemical Measures   A wide range of biochemical measures typically are used in comprehensive substance abuse programs. Although many of these are not available to the individual clinician (especially without research/medical supervision), they nevertheless add an important dimension to understanding the patterns of clients' substance use. These measures have been reviewed by Sobell et al. (1988); Foy et al. (1987); and Wells, Hawkins, and Catalano (1988a, 1988b) and include blood-alcohol level analysis, liver function tests, Antabuse monitoring, urinalysis, breath alcohol tests, alcohol dipstick (for ethanol concentrations), and the sweat patch. Some of these tests are used for assessing recent use (e.g., breath and urine tests), and others for extended use (e.g., liver function tests).

Records   A final source of data is official records (Sobell et al., 1988). These records could include police, hospital, and school reports. Of course, these data may be incomplete or even biased (e.g., member of a minority group may be picked up by police for apparent illegal behaviors far more frequently than members of the majority group or upper-income people displaying the same behaviors). Nevertheless, official records can form part of the basis for a comprehensive assessment, especially when used in context as only one source of data about the problem as a whole.

Integrative Formulation

The last part of the assessment process is to develop an "integrative formulation" (Siporin, 1975). The integrative formulation consists of a summary of the information collected by the practitioner, plus the practitioner's analysis of that information. The integrative formulation pulls together disparate pieces of information collected during the assessment, allowing the practitioner to reflect on that information and decide what it all means. If the practitioner is required to make a formal diagnosis, say, based on the DSM-IV, this is where he or she would do it, adding to that diagnosis, ideally, the concept of the continuum described earlier in this chapter. The integrative formulation would then be used as the basis for goal setting and for the development of treatment plans.

Goal Setting   Goal setting is a particularly sensitive area for substance abuse treatment because it raises a number of difficult issues, foremost among them the issue of abstinence versus controlled use (especially of alcohol). Although the literature is too extensive to be covered thoroughly here (see recent reviews by Lewis et al., 1988; Maisto & Carey, 1987; Foreyt, 1987; Brownell, 1984), there does appear to be sufficient evidence to suggest that controlled use may be an appropriate goal for a small percentage of clients under very select circumstances.

Be that as it may, the setting of goals in the area of substance abuse should

1. Reflect the broad ranges of problems identified in the assessment (not just the substance abuse, per se).
2. Be clear and precise.
3. Allow evaluations.
4. Include long- and short-term goals.
5. Add to specificity by identifying *who* is to change, what will be changed, *to what extent,* and under what *conditions* (Gottman & Leiblum, 1974; Brown & Brown, 1977). This will allow the practitioner to be as specific as possible in identifying specific areas of change.

Treatment Plan   The final part of the assessment process is developing a treatment plan that will address each of the problem areas and goals that have been identified. (One model of a treatment plan for substance abuse—including some very useful forms—is presented by Lewis et al., 1988.) The idea here is to select those intervention techniques that have the best evidence of effectiveness and apply them in a systematic way to each of the problems identified in the assessment. Although this may not always be possible, it is this effort to link previous research on effectiveness with a given client's individualized problems that is a hallmark of the eclectic approach.

Obviously, a number of factors in addition to previous research play a part in developing a treatment plan for substance abuse. These include issues such as, Will the treatment be in- or outpatient? How motivated is the client? To what extent are environmental factors involved? How extensive are the abuse and the problems associated with it? How familiar is the practitioner with the techniques recommended by the research, and does he or she have the commitment to learn them?

The final step in the assessment process is putting everything into a written contract with the client. Not only will the contract itself be a positive force in structuring the treatment, but it also will clarify goals, time limits, mutual tasks and responsibilities, monitoring and evaluation activities, and precisely how and by whom the treatment will be implemented.

Interventions for substance abuse can be evaluated with every client using a type of evaluation approach called single-system designs (Bloom, Fischer, & Orme, 1999). These designs rely on the use of repeated measures on target problems/ behaviors, stretching from a baseline/assessment (nonintervention) phase through the intervention and maintenance phases. Any of the measures discussed in the section on methods of data collection, above, can be used to track changes in the target, whether these measures are collected by the client, practitioner, or relevant other. These designs allow for monitoring of change on a daily basis so that the intervention program can be changed if the results are less than optimal. All single-system designs allow for a clear determination of whether the practitioner's interventions might have produced those changes. A comprehensive yet practical approach to these designs is in the book by Bloom et al. which discusses how to conceptualize and identify problems and goals, as well as how to measure client problems. The book also discusses the designs themselves and methods for analyzing the data collected with single-system designs, including easy-to-construct charts for visual analysis of changes over time.

Eclectic Intervention

This section focuses on specific intervention techniques that could be incorporated in a comprehensive treatment program for substance abuse. There is, in fact, no single specific treatment (or theory) of choice; rather, a number of different interventions can be applied, depending on the individual client, problem, and situation.

Research and Practice Support

Unfortunately, in the area of substance abuse there is no single intervention program with unequivocal support, nor is there a single source of literature that one can turn to that clearly illustrates empirical support for one or more intervention programs. Indeed, the interventions described in this section are derived from several sources, including recent research.

1. Review of evaluation research on substance abuse (Matuscha, 1985; Merbaum & Rosenbaum, 1984; Nathan & Gorman, 1998; APA, 1995; Thyer & Wodarski, 1998, chs. 9–11; Hester & Miller, 1989; Miller & Hester, 1986; Maisto & Carey, 1987; Stitzer, Bigelow, & McCaul, 1983; Ingram & Salzberg, 1988; Cox, 1987; Miller, 1985; Colletti & Brownell, 1982; McCrady & Sher, 1985). The upshot of all this research is that there are several techniques that have been effective with some substance abuse clients under some circumstances, but no techniques that are effective with all clients under all circumstances. Further, although it appears that (with alcohol abuse at least) some treatment is better than no treatment, the type of treatment is not always crucial. However,

there are many commonalities regarding treatment techniques in some of the most successful programs. The recommendations in this chapter will focus mainly on techniques that have been used successfully in several programs.

2. Less rigorous research, case studies, and practice experience. The literature on substance abuse is replete with hundreds of references to innovative programs, new techniques, small-group studies, and case studies, many of which can be found in the references cited throughout this chapter. Although this literature is too immense to be reviewed comprehensively here, some of those reports are incorporated in the recommendations later in this chapter (see, e.g., *Social Casework,* 1989).

3. Adaptations of effective techniques. There are a number of techniques with substantial evidence of effectiveness in areas other than substance abuse (see Fischer, 1978; Nathan & Gorman, 1998; Pikoff, 1996; Roth & Foragy, 1996; and Chambless et al., 1998, for reviews of some of these techniques). Because the perspective of this chapter is that problems associated with substance abuse can be as serious as the abuse itself, and a number of these related problems have been treated successfully independent of treatment for substance abuse (e.g., problems of anxiety, depression), a number of these treatment techniques are incorporated in the recommendations here.

Basic Principles of Intervention

There are a number of basic principles of intervention that underlie the treatment recommendations here.

1. Treat the whole person. It is crucial to remember, first of all, that substance abuse is usually not an independent problem—many other problems typically are associated with it; and second, that substance abuse rarely occurs in a vacuum. People exist in environments, and the successful treatment of substance abuse requires attention to the environmental context.

2. There is no single best treatment. The treatment always must be tailored to the individual client and problem. This matching of treatment to client is perhaps the key ingredient of an effective program.

3. Be prepared for failure. Work in the area of substance abuse is usually difficult and frequently unrewarding for the practitioner. On the one hand, it is easy to begin blaming clients and/or feeling burned out, especially when clients are uncooperative or even disruptive. On the other hand, the intrinsic rewards of success are so great that they may make all the effort worthwhile. Typically, practitioners working in the area of substance abuse are unusually committed and have abandoned the rescue fantasy of being able to help everyone with everything. Indeed, sometimes they can reframe the difficulties as challenges, thus leading to a more positive, self-reinforcing outlook.

4. Attend to diversity in clients. In addition to the variations in client problems in this area, there is a tremendous diversity in other characteristics: race, gen-

der, ethnicity, socioeconomic status, sexual orientation, and the like. Many of these variations can become barriers to successful interventions, especially if the practitioner views the client as an alcoholic or a drug addict and does not take into account his or her other human characteristics. This individualizing includes being aware of the client's world views; being sensitive to his or her culture, values, and norms; working to understand different patterns of communication; and using all this knowledge and awareness to create more individualized and sensitive intervention programs.

5. Use a variety of roles. One of the great strengths of social work is the wide variety of roles that can be employed on the client's behalf. If the practitioner views intervention as taking place solely in the clinical role, he or she could be undercutting the effectiveness of the program. Problems associated with substance abuse often involve the need for intervention with significant others and in the environment in such practitioner roles as consultant, advocate, and broker. Case management is an important option for clients with multiple needs (Brindis et al., 1995).

6. Attend to client motivation. Although poor client motivation frequently is used as an explanation (and sometimes as an excuse) for treatment failures, motivating the client to continue in treatment can be viewed as just one more challenge to the expertise of the practitioner. Indeed a number of successful strategies for enhancing client commitment in the area of substance abuse have been reviewed by Miller (1985), who describes several techniques that have been successfully used to enhance client motivation. These include giving advice, providing feedback, setting specific goals, role playing and modeling, maintaining continuity of contact, manipulating external contingencies, providing choice, and decreasing the attractiveness of the problem behavior. (A number of other procedures for enhancing client commitment are described by Meichenbaum & Turk, 1987; and Shelton & Levy, 1981.)

7. Focus on a positive relationship. Any intervention program should be grounded in the core interpersonal skills of effective practice. Empathy, warmth, respect, and genuineness—ingredients of a positive relationship—are the heart of all practice, but are especially important when working in the area of substance abuse. First, practitioners will find that the clients are more willing to work and cooperate with practitioners who communicate high levels of these skills (Meichenbaum & Turk, 1987). This is particularly critical in the area of substance abuse. Second, there is clear evidence that the effectiveness of many intervention techniques will be increased when the practitioner implements them with high levels of interpersonal skills (Fischer, 1978). Thus, interpersonal skills—the relationship—and techniques bolster each other in enhancing overall practice effectiveness.

8. Use clinical guidelines. Clinical guidelines involve recommendations for clinical intervention based on the results of research and the consensus of experienced practitioners. Just such a set of guidelines has been developed by the APA (1995). These guidelines discuss choices regarding treatment settings as

well as both pharmacological and psychosocial interventions. The strength of the evidence for each recommendation is provided. Guidelines such as these can indicate what the state of the art is at any given time and can be used to optimize the effectiveness of our interventions.

Intervention Techniques

The interventions described here, none of which rely on electrical or chemical interventions and thus can be used by social workers, have been synthesized from a variety of sources, as described earlier. Although, of course, these are not the only successful treatments, it is likely that combinations of these techniques, systematically applied to individualized components of clients' problems, constitute some of the more effective strategies available as of the early 1990s. Indeed, some of these treatments, when combined, have been called "ideal services" (Nathan & Gorman, 1998). Obviously, because this is a multidimensional treatment program, not all of the techniques will be applied with all clients. Thus, the key, once again, is judicious matching of individual intervention components with client problems.

The individual components of this program are divided into twelve separate categories: detoxification and motivation enhancement, self-regulation and self-control, contingency contracting, stress-control training, aversive treatment, cognitive coping strategies, coping and social skills training, education about the substance, lifestyle intervention, marital and family counseling, community reinforcement, and group support and self-help groups.

Detoxification and Motivation Enhancement   One of the axioms of treatment is that clients cannot be using or abusing substances if treatment is to be successful. Thus, a first step in treatment is to help the client withdraw from the substance he or she is using. This is usually a short-term process, but the period may also be an intense one, as the client may be experiencing some discomfort. There are several options for detoxification, depending on the extent of use, level of dependence on the substance, degree of social support, and resources available (McCrady & Sher, 1985; Lewis et al., 1988). The detoxification process could occur on an outpatient basis without involvement of a detoxification center, or in either a nonmedical (social) or a medical detoxification center, with both types of centers involving either partial or full hospitalization. Detoxification is the first step in a comprehensive treatment effort; however, a substantial part of the assessment, goal setting, and treatment planning could take place during this first step, and the detoxification effort can be coordinated with subsequent treatment to produce a more comprehensive and integrated approach for the client.

To the extent that the client becomes able to participate, this early stage begins the process of assessing and enhancing the client's motivation for treatment, using some of the techniques described in the previous section. In addition, if the client appears to be uncooperative, perhaps denying that he or she has a problem, specific intervention strategies to overcome this denial should be considered.

Frequently, these strategies involve planned confrontations by family members, friends, or perhaps other group members in a detoxification program. These confrontations should be carefully planned and supervised, and could involve such techniques as family members making a list of specific incidents in which they were hurt by the client's substance abuse and then rehearsing how to present these to the client. Other, more recent, variations of planned family confrontations include programmed confrontation and programmed request by the client's spouse, as described by Thomas and Yoshioka (1989).

Self-Regulation and Self-Control   There is little question that after termination of the formal substance abuse program, the client will have to take control of his or her own program. The self-regulation, self-control component not only is intended to prepare the client to do just that, but also provides in-treatment benefits.

The very terms self-control and self-regulation imply that it is actually the client who generates and designs a unique self-improvement program, although this is not typically the case (Merbaum & Rosenbaum, 1984). In fact, the self-control package really is just one component of an overall comprehensive program in which the client learns certain techniques that he or she will continue to apply once the formal part of the program is completed.

A number of techniques for self-control components have been suggested by Nathan & Gorman (1998), Merbaum and Rosenbaum (1984), and Kanfer (1986). Some of these techniques are

1. Self-monitoring. Clients are taught to keep track of any substance-related thoughts, behaviors, or feelings, as well as amounts and circumstances of any substance use. The goal here is to increase awareness of patterns and urges so that the client can eventually engage in some change activity. It also may be that the recording itself will have a (positive) reactive effect.
2. Self-evaluation. Although related to self-monitoring, the focus here is on setting goals and encouraging self-evaluation of adherence to these goals.
3. Self-reinforcement. A crucial component of any intervention program, self-reinforcement involves teaching clients to reinforce themselves—covertly (through thoughts) and overtly (through desired activities) for successful adherence to goals, successful completion of tasks, or even partial successes.
4. Self-control manual. Clients are given training manuals that help them develop comprehensive self-control programs.

Contingency Contracting   The use of contracts is increasingly a part of everyday practice in many social work organizations. Contracts have numerous advantages, including ensuring explicitness, adding to structure, enhancing the client's commitment, clarifying goals, and clarifying client and practitioner responsibilities. Contingency contracts, per se, go a step further by actually spelling out relationships between desired behaviors and reinforcement for those behaviors (see Epstein & Wing, 1984). They provide for reinforcement of desired activities, such as self-monitoring or adhering to a program of abstinence, and sometimes punishment for undesired activities or behaviors, such as nonadherence.

Contingency contracts for health and substance abuse problems were recently reviewed by Epstein and Wing (1984). They describe numerous characteristics of these contracts, including the variety of potential patterns of reinforcement, their use with several substance abuse problems, inclusion of third parties in these contracts, and the use of behaviors that are incompatible with substance use. Contingency contracts can be used in a variety of ways to deal with problems of abuse, per se (e.g., adherence), as well as those only indirectly related to abuse (e.g., relationship problems). As such, they are a flexible and important part of the practitioner's armamentarium.

Stress-Control Training   A key factor in helping clients overcome problems of substance abuse is training them to deal with anxiety and stress. It is not uncommon for practitioners to hear clients who have abused alcohol or drugs for many years state that they never experienced any anxiety in all that time; the alcohol and drugs prevented the anxiety from occurring or killed it quickly when it did occur. Indeed, a major theory of the etiology of substance abuse is that it serves a tension-reducing function.

The goal here, however, is to help clients deal with tension and stress once they have stopped using alcohol and drugs. Many Americans think nothing of using a glass or two of wine or a tranquilizer to help them navigate through a stormy emotional period. However, people with problems of substance abuse, once they complete treatment, usually have to control stress and anxiety without resorting to drugs and alcohol.

In these circumstances, clients can be taught to use a variety of relaxation and stress-control techniques. Many of these have been spelled out by Cormier and Cormier (1985). They include meditation and muscle relaxation, systematic desensitization, stress inoculation training, and emotive imagery. All of these techniques focus on providing the client with a variety of ways of dealing with stress and anxiety reactions, with stress inoculation training providing the broadest range of potential responses. In addition, all of these techniques can be taught by the practitioner during the treatment program and can then be used as self-control techniques by the client once the formal treatment program is completed.

Aversive Treatment   Aversive treatments have a long and substantial history in the treatment of substance abuse. Some degree of success in at least limiting consumption has been found for both chemical (the drug Antabuse) and electrical aversion therapies. A technique called covert sensitization (Cautela, 1967) produces an effect similar to other aversive therapies, but does so without the use of chemical or electrical aversion.

Covert sensitization pairs aversive images with images involving substance use. Clients are instructed to imagine a scene in which they are about to use alcohol or drugs, and to incorporate realistic, unpleasant information about the antecedents, location, and so on, in the scene. In this way, clients are taught to imagine another scene—one of disgusting or repugnant responses, such as vomiting all over oneself—that, through repeated practice, becomes paired with the first scene. Clients also are instructed to imagine feeling total relief upon leaving the first scene and refraining from substance use.

Covert sensitization appears to be a moderately successful way of helping clients reduce urges to consume and levels of consumption. The research, however, is neither rigorous nor extensive enough to suggest that this should be more than one technique in a more comprehensive program.

Cognitive Coping Strategies   The way people think about their problems is often strongly related to what they do about them. Thus, clients' self-statements, expectations, and beliefs may be critical factors in maintaining patterns of substance abuse. A number of cognitive techniques are available to help clients develop ways of coping with both life problems and urges to use some substance.

Cognitive Restructuring   Cognitive restructuring is a complex technique (some might say an entire approach to therapy) that focuses on identifying and altering clients' dysfunctional beliefs and negative self-statements or thoughts (Cormier & Cormier, 1985). Often a number of such dysfunctional beliefs and self-statements are uncovered in the assessment process (e.g., "I can never stop using"; "I need [substance X] to keep functioning"), and cognitive restructuring can be directed to altering those beliefs. This not only is beneficial in and of itself, but also can ease the way in other areas of the program by reducing resistance.

Guided Imagery   The focus of guided imagery techniques, such as covert modeling (Cormier & Cormier, 1985), is on helping the client rehearse adaptive rather than maladaptive (using the substance) responses to problem situations. Guided imagery can also be used to rehearse any task or activity that the practitioner suggests as a homework assignment.

Thought Stopping   The key components in a pattern of substance abuse often are the thought processes, which include obsessive thinking about the need and desire for a substance. This obsessive thinking typically takes place in the interval between the last use of the substance and the possible next use and is one of the features of compulsiveness in substance abuse that was discussed earlier. Thought stopping is a fairly simple technique to implement and works to control unproductive, obsessive, or self-defeating thoughts by suppressing or eliminating them and teaching the client to switch to productive or reinforcing thoughts (Cormier & Cormier, 1985).

Coping and Social Skills Training   One of the keystones of effective treatment of substance abuse is a broad-based coping and social skills training program. Such programs foster a greater sense of self-efficacy (Bandura, 1977) or perceived control in clients by teaching them to cope more effectively with everyday problems in living (Marlatt, 1979). There are any number of social skills that might be the focus of such a program, and the determination of which skills are missing from the client's repertoire is based on information obtained from the assessment.

A number of skills have been the target in substance abuse programs: assertiveness, communication skills, job-hunting and interview skills, refusing the invitation to use a substance, and so on.

Most social skills programs incorporate similar techniques: modeling, coaching, rehearsal, reinforcement, and feedback. These techniques are applied in various ways and to varying degrees in developing an overall social skills training program that best meets the needs and aptitudes of individual clients. Social skills training is particularly amenable to implementation in groups, because groups provide greater potential for rehearsal opportunities. As such, social skills training has been a major focus of intervention in both residential and outpatient treatment centers (Monti, Abrams, Kadden, & Cooney, 1989; Ingram & Salzberg, 1988).

Education   One component of a comprehensive substance abuse program typically is education about the substance itself and especially about the negative health and social effects of use of the substance. This education usually takes place through films, readings, lectures, and group discussions. Educational programs operate on two assumptions: 1) that the substance user may not know about the negative effects of substance use; and 2) that even if the client does know about such effects, it is a good idea to reinforce or update that knowledge.

Actually, evidence of the effectiveness of education as a sole or even just one component of a treatment program is rather skimpy. One way of bolstering its effectiveness is through the use of emotional role play, a technique with some evidence of effectiveness with smokers (Janis & Mann, 1977). In emotional role play, the client role plays some emotionally devastating scene (e.g., telling relatives that he or she has cancer of the liver brought on by too much drinking and will die in two months) as a way of breaking down defenses about use of a harmful substance. Such an experience can produce a change in the client's feelings of personal vulnerability, thereby opening the door for more serious consideration of the educational content.

Lifestyle Intervention   This is a catch-all phrase for using a number of interventions that focus on other problems in the client's life, whether or not they are related directly to the substance abuse (Marlatt, 1979). The idea here is that bringing these other elements of the client's life into balance (or within tolerable levels for the client) cannot help but have an overall impact on the client's level of well-being and self-efficacy. Lifestyle intervention can consist of a number of components, including the following:

1. Supplementary counseling. This would include using any or all of the techniques discussed here plus others to deal with problems in the client's life.

Such problems could include depression, anxiety, problems at work, money problems (perhaps calling for a referral for income supplementation programs), and so on. This also could include supportive counseling to help the client as he or she proceeds through the treatment program.

2. Exercise and hobby programs. Once the client is cleared by a physician for participation, an exercise program can be a particularly useful antidote to substance use. Similarly, a hobby can occupy time that a client might otherwise spend thinking about or engaging in substance use.

3. Substitution. The client can be taught to substitute desired alternative activities (e.g., jogging) for substance use.

Marital and Family Counseling   For those clients who are married or living with a family, consideration of that context is a major priority in a comprehensive program. As Lewis et al. (1988) state, "No substance abuser—in fact, no client—can be treated effectively unless his or her social interactions are taken into account" (p. 157). Attention to the client's social support system can be a major factor in attaining optimal effectiveness.

A focus on the marriage and family has numerous benefits: it can reduce pressures on the client so that he or she can be more successful in the program; it provides support to family members, who also may be suffering through the treatment program; it enhances follow-up and maintenance by teaching the spouse and family how best to deal with the client once he or she is discharged; and it enhances overall family functioning.

Because marital and family therapies and attention to environmental supports are trademarks of social work, there is little need to expand on this topic here except to note that there are several intervention programs available that focus on marital and family therapy in the area of substance abuse, per se (e.g., Lewis et al., 1988; Schlesinger, 1988; O'Farrell, 1987; McCrady & Sher, 1985). Recent research shows family therapy is particularly useful for adolescent substance abuse (Waldron, 1997).

Community Reinforcement   Because all clients operate in an environmental context, community reinforcement has shown particular promise as a way of enhancing the client's social support system. Although there is more than one variation of the program, community reinforcement is designed to restructure family, social, and vocational reinforcers in a manner that reinforces nonuse of the substance while discouraging further use (Miller & Hester, 1986). The components of community reinforcement programs range from buddy systems to family training to attendance at social clubs where the problematic substance is not available. But in all such programs, the focus is on reinforcing nonuse and helping clients avoid or deal successfully with situations that could result in use of the substance.

Self-Help Groups   One of the more controversial but most widely used interventions is the self-help group support operation, such as Alcoholics or Narcotics

Anonymous. These organizations often are called twelve-step groups because they typically follow the twelve-step program outlined by the founders of Alcoholics Anonymous.

The controversy about these groups runs the gamut from scattered accusations of lack of evidence of effectiveness, to criticism from professionals who do not like to be out of control of treatment, to complaints from group members who do not approve of the philosophy and methods, and so on. But there are few professionals in the field of substance abuse who do not know numerous clients who say, "A.A. (or N.A.) saved my life."

Thus, it seems reasonable to consider such programs as important adjuncts to professional treatment programs. In the first place, they provide group support, not only during treatment but also on a permanent basis, long after the formal treatment program has been terminated. Second, they operate on a twenty-four-hour basis, with the client being able to phone a sponsor at any time of the day or night. And third, the absence of evidence does not automatically mean that such programs are not effective. The task of research (which is particularly complicated with such groups) may be to attempt to discover the characteristics of clients and twelve-step programs that are most optimally matched and to make referrals on that basis.

Maintenance and Generalization

Of what use is an intervention program that is successful during the formal treatment, but is unsuccessful once that treatment is terminated? That key question is addressed by maintenance programs in the area of substance abuse. Indeed, relapse—an uncontrolled return to drug or alcohol use—is perhaps the most important issue that the substance abuse practitioner must confront.

One report stated that almost 90 percent of clients treated for substance abuse relapsed within one year after termination of formal treatment (Polich, Armor, & Braiker, 1981). Although rates of relapse vary by substance, program, and other characteristics, it is almost a cliché to say that substance abuse remains one of the problems that is most refractory to successful treatment. Thus, it becomes the task of the practitioner to work into the client's treatment program a comprehensive antirelapse program that is geared toward maintaining treatment gains and generalizing them into the client's everyday life.

A Relapse Model

Much of the work on relapse has been pioneered by Marlatt (1979; Marlatt & Gordon, 1985; see also Lewis et al., 1988). Among his contributions are the identification of determinants of relapse and the development of a model of relapse that leads to specific intervention strategies.

Relapse episodes were classified by Marlatt and Gordon (1985) into two categories. The first is intrapersonal/environmental determinants, which is subdivided into categories of coping with negative emotional states (e.g., frustration or anger), coping with negative physical/physiological states, enhancement of positive emotional states, testing personal control, and giving in to temptations or urges.

The second major category is interpersonal determinants. This is subdivided into coping with interpersonal conflict, social pressure, and enhancing a positive emotional state (in an interpersonal situation).

In a study of these factors as determinants of relapse for alcohol, smoking, and heroin, Marlatt and Gordon (1985) found that 76 percent of all relapse episodes fall into just three categories: coping with negative emotional states (37 percent), social pressure (24 percent), and coping with interpersonal conflict (24 percent). The remaining 24 percent of all relapses fell in increments of from 3 to 7 percent into the other five categories.

These and other data led Marlatt to develop a model of the relapse process (Marlatt & Gordon, 1985). The model is based on the notions of self-efficacy and personal control in that it assumes that a client who is refraining from using a substance experiences a sense of personal control that leads to a sense of self-efficacy. This perception continues until the person meets a high-risk situation, one that poses a threat to the client's sense of control and increases the risk of potential relapse. This high-risk situation is affected by covert antecedents, beginning with a possible lifestyle imbalance leading to the desire for indulgences or immediate gratification. This can lead either to urges or cravings mediated by expectancies for immediate effects of the substance, or to rationalization, denial, and apparently irrelevant decisions (choices that enhance the probability of a relapse).

Once the high-risk situation exists, if the client is prepared with a coping response, the result will be increased self-efficacy and lower probability of relapse. However, if no coping response is available, the result will be decreased self-efficacy plus positive outcome expectancies for the effects of the substance. This will lead to initial use of the substance followed by an abstinence violation effect (AVE) that would include dissonance, conflict, guilt, and perceived loss of control. All of this then results in the increased probability of a relapse.

The whole model, then, from start to finish, follows the following steps:

1. Lifestyle imbalance
2. Desire for indulgence or immediate gratification
3. Urges or cravings
4. Rationalization, denial, and apparently irrelevant decisions
5. High-risk situation
6. No coping response
7. Decreased self-efficacy
8. Initial use of substance
9. AVE
10. Increased probability of relapse

Use of this model in understanding determinants of relapse can be aided by the use of four new instruments that were developed to help predict clients' relapse potential. The first is the Relapse Precipitants Inventory (Litman, 1986), a twenty-five—item measure that appears to distinguish between relapses and nonrelapses. The second is the Coping Behaviors Inventory (Litman, 1986), a thirty-six—item inventory that evaluates a person's ability to develop coping strategies. The third is the Inventory of Similar Situations (Annis, 1986), a 100-item questionnaire designed to assess situations in which a client drank heavily over the past year. The last is the Situational Confidence Questionnaire (Annis, 1986), a 100-item instrument designed to assess self-efficacy in relation to a client's perceived ability to cope effectively with alcohol.

One of the major contributions of this generic relapse model is that it suggests a number of points for intervention that lead to several of the maintenance strategies discussed below.

Maintenance and Generalization Strategies

The literature increasingly reflects a good deal of concern about ensuring maintenance and generalization of interventions in all problem areas (Goldstein & Kanfer, 1979; Karoly & Steffen, 1980). This literature has produced a number of general principles regarding maintenance of therapeutic gains, including the following:

1. Make sure that the behavior or activity is being performed at the desired level prior to termination.
2. Try to approximate as much as possible the conditions of real life in your intervention program.
3. Use more than one intervention agent (e.g., have the client rehearse with other practitioners, clients, etc.).
4. Try to find events in everyday life that will help maintain the desired activity and build these into the program.
5. Decrease the program gradually (do not end it all at once).
6. Train the client to continue the activities in real life by having him or her practice them in advance of termination.
7. Use real-life homework assignments throughout the intervention process.
8. Gradually decrease the similarity between the artificial and real situations.
9. Train others in the client's environment to maintain the desired behavior or activities (e.g., train in the use of contingency management). This is an especially important strategy for ensuring generalization.

In addition to these general principles, a number of maintenance strategies, have been developed specifically in the area of substance abuse. A recent review of the outcome research for aftercare in the treatment of alcohol abuse shows that such programs contribute significantly to overall positive outcome (Ito & Donovan, 1986). Although several different aftercare or maintenance strategies were evaluated, the findings were consistent and substantial enough to suggest that such maintenance strategies be made a major part of every intervention program with substance abuse.

Several of these maintenance strategies have been described succinctly by Lewis et al. (1988, ch. 6; see also Daley, 1986). Many of them consist of continuing parts of the intervention program described in the previous section, so they need only be mentioned here. In addition, many also fit the specific stages of Marlatt's relapse model and will be briefly described.

Strategies Related to Relapse Model   These strategies can, of course be used at any time, but there is a particularly neat fit between the stages of the model and selection of an intervention. The idea here is to prepare the client in advance for dealing with any of the situations indicated in the model.

1. Lifestyle imbalance requires development of a balanced daily lifestyle, including jogging, hobbies, meditation, and so on.
2. Desire for indulgence requires substituting positive indulgences, such as recreational activities.
3. Urges and cravings can be countered by preparing the client with coping imagery and stimulus control techniques.
4. Rationalization, denial, and apparently irrelevant decisions can be countered by labeling these phenomena as warning signals and by teaching the client to use a decision matrix in which he or she lists immediate positive and negative consequences for using or not using the substance.
5. High-risk situations can be dealt with by having the client use self-monitoring and self-evaluation skills that teach him or her to recognize those situations and by teaching a variety of avoidance strategies.
6. The absence of a coping response is dealt with by the use of skill training plus a technique called relapse rehearsal. Relapse rehearsal teaches clients to imagine a relapse situation in which they successfully use a coping technique to avoid using the substance.
7. To counter decreased self-efficacy and positive outcome expectancies for using the substance, the client can be taught to use relaxation training, stress management, and efficacy-enhancing imagery. In addition, the client can be educated about immediate versus delayed use of the substance.
8. To avoid initial unplanned use of the substance, clients can be taught the techniques of programmed relapse. This is a fairly tricky technique to use and is not recommended for most cases because it involves programming the first relapse (e.g., the first drink of alcohol) under the supervision of the practitioner. Other techniques include a contract to limit the extent of use plus a reminder card for what the client should do if he or she has a slip.
9. For AVE, with its risk of relapse, clients can be taught through cognitive restructuring that a slip is actually a mistake to be learned from and does not have to lead to a complete relapse.

General Maintenance Strategies   In addition to the strategies above that fit the Marlatt model, a number of other strategies and techniques could be considered, including the following:

1. Use of booster sessions and follow-ups. These should be scheduled in incrementally increasing intervals following termination (e.g., at two weeks, one month, three months, six months, one year).
2. Use of problem-solving training to help clients deal with life problems in a functional way without having to turn to substance use.
3. Use of exercise programs to maintain the benefits of physical health.
4. Continued membership in a self-help group with periodic follow-ups from the social worker (phone calls will do) to encourage the client's attendance.

Conclusion

As this chapter has illustrated, the problem of substance abuse and its modification is very complex. The essence of successful treatment is two-pronged: 1) critical use of the available literature to be informed about what works (with the awareness that new developments are appearing daily); and 2) careful individualizing of clients and problems so that specific treatment programs can be developed. It is hoped that the assessment and intervention guidelines presented here will be of use to students and practitioners who have made a commitment to working in this area. In the long run, it is this commitment that will lead to the greatest satisfaction and increasingly more effective treatment.

References

American Psychiatric Association (1994). *Diagnostic and statistical manual of mental disorders*. (4th Ed.). Washington, DC: APA.

American Psychiatric Association (1995). Practice guidelines for the treatment of patients with substance use disorders: Alcohol, cocaine, opioids. *American Journal of Psychiatry, 152,* 3–50.

Ammerman, R. T., & Van Hasselt, V. B. (1988). The Callner-Ross Assertion Questionnaire. In M. Hersen & A. S. Bellack (Eds.), *Dictionary of behavioral assessment techniques.* New York: Pergamon.

Baker, T. B., & Cannon, D. S. (Eds.). (1988). *Assessment and treatment of addictive disorders.* New York: Praeger.

Bandura, A. (1977). Self-efficacy: Toward a theory of behavior change. *Psychological Review, 84,* 191–215.

Bloom, M., Fischer, J., & Orme, J. G. (1999). *Evaluating practice: Guidelines for the accountable professional.* (3rd Ed.). Boston: Allyn and Bacon.

Boudin, H. M., et al. (1977). Contingency contracting with drug abusers in the natural environment. *International Journal of the Addictions, 12,* 1–16.

Bratter, T. E., & Forrest, G. G. (Eds.). (1985). *Alcoholism and substance abuse: strategies for clinical intervention.* New York: Free Press.

Brindis, et al. (1995). A case management program for chemically dependent clients with multiple needs. *Journal of Case Management, 4,* 22–28.

Brown, J. A., & Brown, C. S. (1977). *Systematic counseling: A guide for the practitioner.* Champaign, IL: Research Press.

Brownell, K. D. (1984). The addictive disorders. In C. M. Franks (Ed.), *Annual Review of behavior therapy* (Vol. 10). New York: Guilford Press.

Carroll, J. F. X. (1984). Substance abuse problem checklist: A new clinical aid for drug and/or alcohol dependency. *Journal of Substance Abuse Treatment, 1,* 31–36.

Cautela, J. R. (1967). Covert sensitization. *Psychological Record, 20,* 459–468.

Chambless, D., Snderson, W., Shoham, V., Johnson, S., Pope, K., Crits-Cristoph, P., Baker, M., Johnson, B., Woody, S., Sue, S., Beutler, L., Williams, D., & McCurry, S. (1998). Update on empirically validated theories II. *The Clinical Psychologist, 51,* 3–16.

Colletti, G., & Brownell, K. D. (1982). The physical and emotional benefits of social support: Application to obesity, smoking and alcoholism. In M. Hersen (Ed.), *Progress in behavior modification, Vol. 13.* New York: Academic Press, 109–178.

Corcoran, K., & Fischer, J. (2000a). *Measures for clinical practice: A sourcebook.* (3rd ed.). (Vol. 1, Couples, families and children). New York: Free Press.

Corcoran, K., & Fischer, J. (2000b). *Measures for clinical practice: A sourcebook.* (3rd Ed.). (Vol. 2, Adults). New York: Free Press.

Cormier, W. H., & Cormier, L. S. (1985). *Interviewing strategies for helpers.* (2nd Ed.). Belmont, CA: Brooks/Cole.

Cox, W. M. (Ed.). (1987). *Treatment and prevention of alcohol problems: A resource manual.* New York: Academic Press.

Daley, D. C. (1986). *Relapse prevention workbook.* Holmes Beach, FL: Learning Publications, Inc.

Donovan, B. M., & Marlatt, G. A. (1988). Assessment of addictive behaviors: Implications of an emerging biopsychosocial model. In B. M. Donovan & G. A. Marlatt (Eds.), *Assessment of addictive behaviors: Behavioral, cognitive, and physiological procedures.* New York: Guilford Press.

Epstein, L. H., & Wing, R. R. (1984). Behavioral contracting: Health behaviors. In C. M. Franks (Ed.), *New developments in behavior therapy.* New York: Haworth Press.

Fingarett, H. (1988). Alcoholism: The mythical disease. *Utne Reader, 30,* 64–68.

Fischer, J. (1978). *Effective casework practice: An eclectic approach.* New York: McGraw-Hill.

Foreyt, J. P. (1987). The addictive disorders. In G. T. Wilson (Ed.), *Review of Behavior Therapy* (Vol. 10). New York: Guilford Press.

Foy, D. W., Cline, K. A., & Laasi, N. (1987). Assessment of alcohol and drug abuse. In T. D. Nirenberg & S. A. Maisto (Eds.), *Developments in the assessment and treatment of addictive behaviors*. Norwood, NJ: Ablex.

Galatner, M. (1983). *Recent developments in alcoholism*. (Vols. I and II). New York: Plenum.

Goldstein, A. P., & Kanfer, F. H. (1979). *Maximizing treatment gains: Transfer enhancement in psychotherapy*. New York: Academic Press.

Gottman, J. M., & Leiblum, S. R. (1974). *How to do psychotherapy and how to evaluate it*. New York: Holt, Rinehart and Winston.

Hersen, M., & Bellack, A. S. (Eds.). (1988). *Dictionary of behavioral assessment techniques*. New York: Pergamon.

Hester, R. K., & Miller, W. R. (1989). *Handbook of alcoholism treatment approaches*. New York: Pergamon.

Hilton, M. R., & Lokane, V. G. (1978). The evaluation of a questionnaire measuring severity of alcohol dependence. *British Journal of Psychiatry, 132,* 42–48.

Hoffman, A. (1987). *Steal this urine test*. New York: Penguin.

Ingram, J. A., & Salzberg, H. C. (1988). Cognitive-behavioral approaches to the treatment of alcoholic behavior. In M. Hersen (Ed.), *Progress in behavior modification*. New York: Academic Press.

Ito, J. K., & Donovan, D. (1986). Aftercare in alcoholism treatment: A review. In W. R. Miller & N. Heather (Eds.), *Treating addictive behaviors*. New York: Plenum.

Janis, I. L., & Mann, L. (1977). *Decision-making*. New York: Free Press.

Johnston, L. D., O'Malley, P. M., & Bachman, J. G. (1986). *Drug use among American high school students, college students, and other young adults*. Rockville, MD: National Institute on Drug Abuse.

Kanfer, F. H. (1986). Implications of a self-regulation model of therapy for treatment of addictive behaviors. In W. R. Miller & N. Heather (Eds.), *Treating addictive behavior*. New York: Plenum.

Karoly, P., & Steffen, J. J. (Eds.). (1980). *Improving the long-term effects of psychotherapy*. New York: Gardner.

Lewis, J. A., Dana, R. O., & Blevins, G. A. (1988). *Substance abuse counseling: An individualized approach*. Pacific Grove, CA: Brooks/Cole.

Litman, G. K. (1986). Alcoholism survival: The prevention of relapse. In W. R. Miller & N. Heather (Eds.), *Treating addictive behaviors*. New York: Plenum.

Lum, D. (1986). *Social work practice and people of color*. Pacific Grove, CA: Brooks/Cole.

Maisto, S. A., & Carey, K. B. (1987). Treatment of alcohol abuse. In T. D. Nirenberg & S. A. Maisto (Eds.), *Developments in the assessment and treatment of addictive behaviors*. Norwood, NJ: Ablex.

Marlatt, G. A. (1976). The drinking profile: A questionnaire for the behavioral assessment of alcoholism. In E. J. Mash & L. G. Terdal (Eds.), *Behavioral therapy assessment: Diagnosis, design and evaluation*. New York: Springer.

Marlatt, G. A. (1979). Alcohol use and problem drinking: A cognitive-behavioral analysis. In P. C. Kendall & S. D. Hollon (Eds.), *Cognitive-behavioral interventions*. New York: Academic Press.

Marlatt, G. A., & Gordon, J. R. (1985). Determinants of relapse: Implications of the maintenance of behavior change. In P. O. Davidson & S. M. Davidson (Eds.), *Behavioral medicine: Changing health lifestyles*. New York: Brunner/Mazel.

Matusha, P. R. (1985). The psychopharmacology of addiction. In T. E. Bratter & G. G. Forrest (Eds.), *Alcoholism and substance abuse*. New York: Free Press.

Maxman, J. S. (1986). *Essential psychopathology*. New York: W.W. Norton.

McClellan, A. T., et al. (1980). An improved evaluation instrument for substance abuse patients: The addiction severity index. *Journal of Nervous and Mental Disorders, 168,* 26–33.

McCrady, B. S., & Sher, K. (1985). Treatment variables. In B. S. McCrady, N. E. Noel, & T. D. Nirenberg (Eds.), *Future directions in alcohol abuse treatment research*. Washington, DC: US Department of Health and Human Services.

Meichenbaum, D., & Turk, D. C. (1987). *Facilitating treatment adherence: A practitioner's guidebook*. New York: Plenum Press.

Merbaum, M., & Rosenbaum, M. (1984). Self-control theory and technique in the modification of smoking, obesity, and alcohol abuse. In C. M. Franks (Ed.), *New developments in behavior therapy*. New York: Haworth Press.

Milgram, G. G. (1987). Alcohol and drug education programs. *Journal of Drug Education, 17,* 43–57.

Miller, P. M. (1981). Assessment of alcohol abuse. In D. H. Barlow (Ed.), *Behavioral assessment of adult disorders* (pp. 271–300). New York: Guilford Press.

Miller, P. M. (1987). Commonalities of addictive behaviors. In T. D. Nirenberg & S. A. Maisto (Eds.), *Developments in the assessment and treatment of addictive behaviors*. Norwood, NJ: Ablex.

Miller, W. R. (1985). Motivation for treatment: A review with special emphasis on alcoholism. *Psychological Bulletin, 98,* 84–107.

Miller, W. R., & Heather, N. (Eds.). (1986). *Treating addictive behaviors*. New York: Plenum.

Miller, W. R., & Hester, R. K. (1986). The effectiveness of alcoholism treatment: What research reveals. In W. R. Miller & N. Heather (Eds.), *Treating addictive behaviors*. New York: Plenum.

Monti, P. M., Abrams, D. R., Kadden, R. M., & Cooney, N. L. (1989). *Treating alcohol dependence: A coping skills guide*. New York: Guilford Press.

Nathan, P. E., & Gorman, J. M. (Eds.). (1998). *A guide to treatments that work*. New York: Oxford University Press.

Nirenberg, T. D., & Maisto, S. A. (1987). *Developments in the assessment and treatment of addictive behavior*. Norwood, NJ: Ablex.

O'Farrell, T. J. (1987). Marital and family therapy for alcohol problems. In W. M. Cox (Ed.), *Treatment and prevention of alcohol problems.* New York: Academic Press.

Peele, S. (1989). *The diseasing of America: How the addiction industry captured our soul.* Cambridge, MA: Lexington.

Pikoff, H. B. (1996). *Treatment effectiveness handbook: A reference guide to the key research reviews in mental health and substance abuse.* Buffalo, NY: Data for Decisions.

Polich, J. M., Armor, D. M., & Braiker, H. B. (1981). *The course of alcoholism: Four years after treatment.* New York: Wiley.

Ridley, T. D., & Kordinak, S. T. (1988). Reliability and validity of the Quantitative Inventory of Alcohol Disorders (QIAD) and the veracity of self-report by alcoholics. *American Journal of Drug and Alcohol Abuse, 14,* 263–292.

Robins, L. N., et al. (1984). Lifetime prevalence of specific psychiatric disorders in three sites. *Archives of General Psychiatry, 41,* 949–958.

Roth, A., & Foragy, P. (1996). *What works for whom? A critical review of psychotherapy research.* New York: Guilford Press.

Schare, M. L., & Milburn, N. G. (1996). Multicultural assessment of alcohol and other drug use. In L. A. Suzuki (Ed.). *Handbook of multicultural assessment.* San Francisco, CA: Jossey-Bass, 453–473.

Schlesinger, S. E. (1988). Cognitive-behavioral approaches to family treatment of addictions. In N. Epstein, S. E. Schlesinger, & W. Dryden (Eds.), *Cognitive behavioral therapy with families.* New York: Brunner/Mazel.

Segal, R., & Sisson, B. V. (1985). Medical complications associated with alcohol use and the assessment of risk of physical damage. In T. E. Bratter & G. G. Forrest (Eds.), *Alcoholism and substance abuse.* New York: Free Press, 137–175.

Shaffer, H., & Kauffman, J. (1985). The clinical assessment and diagnosis of addiction: Hypothesis testing. In T. E. Bratter & G. G. Forrest (Eds.), *Alcoholism and substance abuse.* New York: Free Press, 225–258.

Shelton, J. L., & Levy, R. L. (1981). *Behavioral assignments and treatment compliance.* Champaign, IL: Research Press.

Siporin, M. (1975). *Introduction to social work practice.* New York: Macmillan.

Skinner, H. A. (1982). The drug abuse screening test. *Addictive Behaviors, 7,* 363–371.

Sobell, L. C., Sobell, M. B., & Nirenberg, T. D. (1988). Behavioral assessment and treatment planning with alcohol and drug abusers: A review with an emphasis on clinical application. *Clinical Psychology Review, 8,* 19–54.

Social Casework. (1989). *Social Casework, 70* (6), Entire issue.

Stitzer, M. L., Bigelow, G. E., & McCaul, M. E. (1983). Behavioral approaches to drug abuse. In M. Hersen (Ed.), *Progress in behavior modification* (Vol. 14.). New York: Academic Press.

Thomas, E. J., & Yoshioka, M. R. (1989). Spouse interventive confrontation in unilateral family therapy for alcohol abuse. *Social Casework, 70,* 340–347.

Thyer, B. A., & Wodarski, J. S. (Eds.). (1998). *Handbook of empirical social work practice.* (Vol. 1, Mental Disorders). New York: Wiley.

Waldron, H. B. (1997). Adolescent substance abuse and family therapy outcome: A review of randomized trials. *Advances in Clinical Child Psychology, 19,* 199–234.

Wartenberg, A. A., & Liepman, M. R. (1987). Medical consequences of addictive behaviors. In T. D. Nirenberg & S. A. Maisto (Eds.), *Developments in the assessment and treatment of addictive behaviors.* Norwood, NJ: Ablex.

Wells, E. A., Hawkins, J. D., & Catalano, R. F. (1988a). Choosing drug use measures for treatment outcome studies, I: The influence of measurement approach on treatment results. *The International Journal of the Addictions, 23,* 851–873.

Wells, E. A., Hawkins, J. D., & Catalano, R. F. (1988b). Choosing drug use measures for treatment outcome studies, II: Timing baseline and follow-up measurement. *The International Journal of the Addictions, 23,* 851–873.

Chapter 20
Use of Computers in Evaluation and Practice

As the prices of personal computers continue to drop, and programs for their use become more accessible and easy to use, it is inevitable that practitioners in the human services will come to rely on personal computers to help manage and enhance their practice. Computers increasingly are becoming a crucial part of evaluation and practice. In fact, one might argue that recent advances in computer technology have revolutionized the way practitioners engage in practice and evaluation. This development has been hastened by three major phenomena: (1) the increasing sophistication of users of computers–computers are available at home and at work, and more and more people are becoming familiar with their use; (2) the incredible drop in prices of personal computers, making them more accessible to people than ever before; and (3) recognition by practitioners of the value of computers for evaluation and practice. Indeed, some practitioners feel completely hampered in their practice and evaluation activities if they are denied access to their computers for even a short time. (You can include the authors in this latter group.)

Recent reviews of computer technology for practice by Petrucci et al. (2004), Newman (2003), and Taylor & Luce (2003) illustrate the wide range of activities for which computers currently are being used in practice. These activities include computer-assisted assessment; computer-assisted interviews; treatment programs of surprising effectiveness; online support; e-therapy; virtual reality treatment programs; single-system evaluation, the topic of this book; decision support systems; and expert systems. And of course, we would add that computers are at the heart of finding and analyzing information for evidence-based practice (see, e.g., http://www.evidencebrookscole.com/index.html).

We want to encourage you to explore the World Wide Web and to take advantage of the vast resources available there. To begin, open the Internet browser program on your computer, such as Netscape or Microsoft Internet Explorer, and type in the following address in the top window: http://www.ablongman.com/

Bloom, M., Fischer, J., & Orme, J. (2009). *Evaluating Practice: Guidelines for the Accountable Professional* (6th ed.). Boston: Allyn & Bacon.

bloom and then hit "Enter". This will bring you to the website for this book. It will provide you with an overview of the book, allow you to connect directly with sites devoted to CASS and CAAP, provide you with links to other interesting sites, and if you click on "Technical Support," will provide you with technical information about SINGWIN and an e-mail address where you can get technical support for this program.

Personal computer programs are available not only to graph the results of single-system designs but also to easily store, retrieve, organize, communicate, disseminate, and analyze recorded information for practitioners, supervisors, and administrators (Baskin, 1990; Benbenishty, 1989; Corcoran & Gingerich, 1994; Mutschler, 1987; Newman, Consoli, & Taylor, 1997; Patterson, 2000; Patterson & Basham, 2006). However, because there are so many, it's impossible to describe all the different computer programs for the management of client data. (A recent review of the use of computers in assessment and treatment of clinical disorders is available in Newman et al., 1997). This is a rapidly growing area, so you should also look for current developments in journals such as *Journal of Technology in Human Services, Social Science Computer Review,* and *Computers in Psychiatry/Psychology;* in reference books such as *Personal Computer Applications in the Social Services* (Patterson, 2000), *Data Analysis with Spreadsheets* (Patterson & Basham, 2005), *Computer Use in Psychology: A Directory of Software* (Stoloff & Couch, 1992), *Psychware Sourcebook* (Krug, 1993), and *The 125th Mental Measurements Yearbook* (Plake, Impara, & Spies, 2003); and on the Web in such places as CUSSnet (http://www.uta.edu/cussn/cussn.html), General Psychiatric Rating Scales (http://www.neurotransmitter.net/generalscales.html); and in software review sections of professional journals. However, to provide you with a concrete example of one of the best, most versatile, and well-developed assessment systems, we've included detailed instructions for installing and using the Computer Assisted Social Services Program CD-ROM included with this book (CASS; Hudson, 1996a, 1996b; Nugent, Sieppert, & Hudson, 2001; Nurius & Hudson, 1993).

Another tremendous resource on the Internet is called *Information for Practice* developed by Gary Holden. An archive that is updated monthly, this site contains information pertinent to all human service professionals on topics including government, measurement, psychology, social science, and many more. All you have to do is type the following address into your browser and hit "Enter" and you'll be there: http://www.nyu.edu/socialwork/ip. You can subscribe to this free, Internet-based information service for human service professionals by sending a blank e-mail message to join-information-for-practice@forums.nyu.edu.

Finally, there are several recent books that are excellent resources for finding sites on the Internet that can be helpful to professionals: *Research Navigator Guide: The Helping Professions* (Kjosness et al., 2004), *Information Technology for Social Work* (Schiller, 2005), *The Insider's Guide to Mental Health Resources Online* (Grohol, 2004), *Social Work and the Web* (Vernon & Lynch, 2000), and *A Quick Guide to the Internet for Social Workers* (Yaffe & Gotthoffer, 2000). These books describe sites that provide everything from information on new interventions to self-help and consumer/client education. For online updates to the Grohol book, visit the site http://www.insidemh.com.

Some Advantages and Disadvantages of Using Computers

There are some concerns raised by the use of personal computers to manage client data (e.g., Moreland, 1987; Siegel, 1990). Computers require start-up time in learning the operation of the computer and the particular software program. They also require a financial investment in the computer equipment and software. In addition, eliciting information via computer may seem intimidating and impersonal to some clients, and there are some clients who won't be able to use some of these systems (e.g., those who can't read). Extra care needs to be taken to ensure that clients understand the task at hand and are able to respond appropriately.

The personal computer management of client data does have some important benefits, as suggested by the following description of CASS and other related personal computer software (see also Butcher, 1987; Hudson, 1990b; Nurius & Hudson, 1993). Computers can increase the speed and efficiency with which information is managed, and this can free up time to deliver services. They also can increase the accuracy with which measures are administered and scored. Even the most conscientious practitioner can make mistakes in scoring measures, and these mistakes can lead to incorrect practice and evaluation decisions; computers don't make such errors if properly used. Finally, there's some evidence that clients are more willing to reveal sensitive personal information (e.g., alcohol abuse, sexual behaviors) to a computer than to a practitioner or on a pencil-and-paper questionnaire (e.g., Malcolm, Sturgis, Anton, & Williams, 1989; Millstein & Irwin, 1983). Therefore, in some cases using the personal computer to elicit information directly from clients might provide more valid client information.

Computer Analysis of Data for Single-System Designs

Personal computers can increase the speed, efficiency, and accuracy with which single-system data are analyzed. Personal computers also increase the range of statistical procedures that can be used because they can do certain mathematical procedures that would be too cumbersome to do by hand or with a calculator (autocorrelation and some tests of statistical significance come to mind). However, the use of personal computers to analyze single-system data requires an investment of time and money, especially initially. On the other hand, computer programs are becoming more and more user friendly, and computers are increasingly available to practitioners in the workplace (Schoech, 2008). Therefore, they can be important tools for the analysis of single-system data.

You could use a wide variety of computer programs to compute particular statistics for the analysis of single-system design data. There are several broad categories of such programs. First, there are commercial programs designed primarily for the analysis of group designs. These programs compute some of the statistics we discuss in this book. They include SPSS and SAS, two programs widely used by social science researchers.

Second, any search of the Internet for shareware programs will turn up a number of diverse personal computer programs that will compute some relevant statistics and charts. These programs are distributed free or for a small fee.

Third, spreadsheet programs such as Microsoft Excel can compute some relevant statistics, and are especially useful for constructing line charts. For example, Excel can be customized to compute statistics for the analysis of single-system designs (e.g., Fisher, Kelley, & Lomas, 2003; Orme & Cox, 2001; Patterson & Basham, 2006; Todman & Dugard, 2001). It also can be used easily to graph the results of single-system designs (Carr & Burkholder, 1998; Grehan & Moran, 2005; Hillman & Miller, 2004; Lo & Konrad, 2007; Moran & Hirschbine, 2002; Patterson & Basham, 2006). (Grehan & Moran, 2005, Hillman & Miller, 2004, and Moran & Hirschbine, 2002, can be downloaded for free from "The Behavior Analyst Today" website located at: http://www.behavior-analyst-online.org/newBAT/index.html. See the "Interactive Exercises" document in the "Word Documents" folder on your CD-ROM, and the Workbooks in the "Excel Workbooks" folder on your CD-ROM.)

Finally, there are programs designed for specific limited types of analysis of single-system design data. For example, Crosbie (1993, 1995; Crosbie & Sharpley, 1991) developed a personal computer program named ITSACORR designed specifically to conduct time-series analyses of single-system data, although questions have been raised about the accuracy of this and other time-series analyses proposed for the analysis of single-system design data (Huitema, 2004). McKnight, McKean, and Huitema (2000) developed an alternative to ITSACORR for the analysis of time- series data (www.stat.wmich.edu/slab/Software/Timeseries.html). Van Damme and Onghena (Onghena & Edgington, 1994; Onghena & Van Damme, 1994) developed SCRT, a personal computer program designed specifically to conduct randomization tests for single-system designs, and other programs for randomization tests are summarized in Todman and Dugard (2001). Other specific programs have been discussed in Franklin, Allison, and Gorman (1997).

Many of the programs mentioned here are very useful and sophisticated computer programs, but most of the things they do are not relevant to the analysis of single-system designs, or they don't do some of the things needed in the analysis of single-system design data. Also, some, but not all, of these programs are quite expensive. In any case, personal computer-based data analysis is a rapidly growing area, so you should look for current developments in such journals as *Journal of Technology in Human Services, Social Science Computer Review,* and *Computers in Psychiatry/Psychology;* in reference books such as *Data Analysis with Spreadsheets* (Patterson & Basham, 2006); on the Web in such places as HUSITA (http://www3.uta.edu/sswtech/husita/); and in software review sections of professional journals.

SINGWIN: A Personal Computer Program for the Analysis of Single-System Design Data

We are pleased to include with this book what we think is the most comprehensive program for the analysis of single-system design data. This program is named SINGWIN, and it is a Windows-based program designed by Charles Auerbach, David Schnall, and Heidi Heft Laporte specifically for this book.

SINGWIN computes most of the statistics we discuss, and generates most of the graphs and charts. Furthermore, as you'll see in Chapter 23, SINGWIN is a program that we think you'll find very user-friendly and it only will take a small investment of your time to learn. It's menu-driven, and we believe that after a small amount of practice you won't even need the instructions provided in Chapter 23.

All computer programs—no matter how carefully constructed, tested, and explained—pose problems and questions for users. Also, most computer programs grow over time to encompass new features. To address these issues, you can go to the web page for this book: www.ablongman.com/html/bloom/. There is a button marked "Technical Support." You also can request technical support for SINGWIN by sending email to singwin@ymail.yu.edu. Finally, "Frequently Asked Questions" concerning SINGWIN, and answers to these questions, are contained on the CD-ROM that comes with the book (see the "SINGWIN Frequently Asked Questions" document in the "Word Documents" folder on your CD-ROM.). Also, the web site for this book contains the most recent updates for SINGWIN available to users who purchased the program with the book.

CD-ROM Resources

This section illustrates many possibilities for computer-based additions to evaluation and practice (from Bloom, Fischer, & Orme, 2009).

One of the major features of this book is the material we have included on the CD-ROM that comes with the book. First, we have three programs using the Windows operating system, including step-by-step guidelines for their installation and use. Knowledge about and use of computers is increasingly a priority in the helping professions, and we hope the inclusion of this material will be a boon to readers. One of the programs is called SINGWIN; it was developed specifically for this book, and it is our hope that it will make calculation of some of the analytic methods less dreary and time consuming. The other included programs, Computer Assisted Social Services (CASS) and Computer Assisted Assessment Package (CAAP), will help you manage caseloads, administer measures, and even graph your results. These programs can help simplify the occasionally tedious part of evaluation practice and enhance your efficiency overall. We believe it will be well worth your while to learn how to use these new tools for evaluation, not just for this book but for the whole of your professional career in the twenty-first century.

In addition to SINGWIN, CASS, and CAAP, the CD contains a number of other materials in a Student Manual that we hope you will find useful in learning and using single-system designs to evaluate your practice. There are four folders in the Student Manual: *an Excel Workbook, PDF Files, PowerPoint Presentations, and Word documents.* To see how to open these folders and the exciting files contained in them, see the following.

Websites

We invite you to visit the *Evaluating Practice* website created by John Orme and Mary Ellen Cox (http://utemhsrc.csw.utk.edu/evaluatingpractice/). This site contains a list of Frequently Asked Questions (FAQ), PowerPoint presentations that cover most of this book and that can be viewed or downloaded, links to related sites, a discussion of problems with the use of the computer programs accompanying this book, and numerous other features. The site will act as a clearinghouse for information about evaluating practice. Those readers willing to share course syllabi, data, exercises, and so on, can send them to John Orme (jorme@utk.edu) to be posted on the web page.

The main website of the publisher for this book is http://www.ablongman .com/bloom. On this site you can find information on downloading the programs included with this book, technical support, links to other sites, and other information related to the book.

When all is said and done, more than anything else, we hope this book will provide some stimulating ideas for you, will challenge you to do your best in your practice efforts with clients and consumers, and will help you to meet the challenges of accountable practice in the twenty-first century.

Student Manual

This CD is loaded with a number of resources and activities. It is our hope that these resources will make the process of learning about the topics in this book easier, more interesting, and dare we say it, fun.

The resources include the computer programs CASS, CAAP, and SINGWIN that you'll be reading about and using throughout this edition of *Evaluating Practice.*

In addition to SINGWIN, CASS, and CAAP, this CD contains a number of other materials that we hope you'll find useful in learning and using single-system designs to evaluate your practice. These include Microsoft Word documents, Excel workbooks, PowerPoint presentations, and Adobe pdf files, and this document describes these materials.

Accessing Resources on the CD

Insert your CD, click "Exit" and you'll see the following:

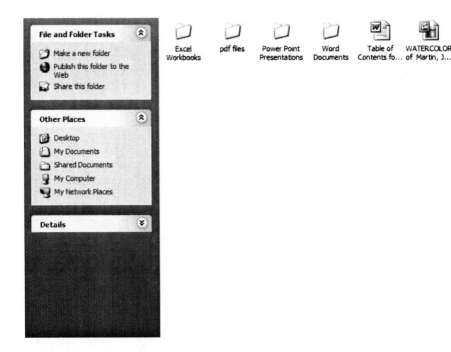

Notice the four folders:

1. Excel Workbooks
2. PDF files
3. Power Point Presentations
4. Word Documents

We describe the contents of these folders in more detail below. Each of these folders contain multiple files. To find the files, simply click on the folder it is in, then scroll down until you find the file in which you're interested. Click on it to review the contents.

Also, notice the Word document, "Table of Contents fo . . ."; this is the document you're reading now. Finally, notice the "Watercolor of Martin, J . . ."; click on this file if you want to view a little piece of artwork.

The Word documents, Excel workbooks, and PowerPoint presentations were developed and tested on Microsoft Office 2003. They probably work on other versions of Microsoft Office, but they haven't been tested on other versions. We apologize in advance if they don't. Please email John Orme to report any problems (jorme@utk.edu).

Now, let's turn to a description of the files contained in each of the four folders.

Word Documents

All of the Word documents described in this section are contained in the "Word Documents" folder. Just click on this folder and you'll see a list of the Word files described in this section. Then, just click on the file you want to open and, where needed, the file contains instructions for its use. (You need to have Microsoft Office installed on your computer to open these documents.)

Behavioral Observation Forms
This is a Word document that contains copies of the behavioral observation forms described and illustrated in chapter 5. Feel free to use and modify as needed.

Bibliography
This is a Word document that contains a bibliography of published single-system designs. It's not exhaustive by any means, but we hope that it gives you a place to start reading some of the interesting ways in which these have been used.

Client Consent Form
This is a Word document that contains the client consent form discussed in chapter 25.

Goal Attainment Scaling Form (GAS)
This is a Word document that contains a blank Goal Attainment Scaling Form (GAS). Feel free to use it and modify as needed.

Interactive Exercises
This is a Word document that contains interactive exercises designed to dynamically illustrate the relationship between single-system design data, statistics computed from these data, the interrelationships among different statistics, and the graphical representation of these data. This file contains instructions for its use. When you open this file you can scroll to the table of contents contained in this file, click on a section, and go right to that section.

These exercises are dynamic in the sense that you can change the SSD data in this document and, when you change them, related numbers and associated charts will be updated and changed automatically. In each example, data, statistics, and charts are together on one screen. So, you can examine a wide variety of *what if* scenarios and immediately see what happens.

These exercises were created by first constructing the Excel workbooks described following, and then embedding these workbooks in this Word document. However, you don't have to know anything at all about Excel to do these exercises, and you don't need to use these workbooks unless you want to look at them and see how they're constructed.

Intervention Plan

This is a Word document that contains a form that will help you practice what we preach. It was developed to parallel the suggested activities in the book, starting with chapter 3 and the discussion of identifying objectives and goals, through developing a measurement plan and measures of your target to developing interventions and techniques, an evaluation plan, and finally, your analysis of your results. We urge you to use this Intervention Plan with a real or even hypothetical client or on a self-change program as you read through the book. This will provide you with the real life learning that is such an essential element of comprehensive learning of any topic. Simply fill in the places on the Intervention Plan that correspond to where you are in moving through the book.

The Intervention Plan is designed to be used on your computer in Word. Simply click on "File" then "Save As" and you can save it in Word as "Intervention Plan" or any other designation that would remind you where to find it among your Word files. Then, you can just keep a running record of everything you do with your "client." (Remember that the bottom "Drawing" toolbar in Word allows you to draw lines and other figures in all possible directions, so that you can create the phases of your single-system design, described in the next chapter. Just right-click on the toolbar at the top and then click on "Drawing.")

Another way to use the Intervention Plan is simply to copy it and have it available as a regular paper form. If you use it this way, we'd suggest that before you copy it, you use your "enter" button to provide more space between categories. That is because when the form is used on your computer, Word automatically creates more space when you need it (see the appendix to this chapter for a copy of the Intervention Plan).

Statistical Computations

This is a Word document that shows you how to calculate the statistics discussed in the sixth edition of *Evaluating Practice*. When you open this file you can scroll to the table of contents contained in this file, click on a section, and go right to that section.

Statistical Process Control Charts (SPC)

This is a Word document that contains information about Statistical Process Control (SPC) charts beyond that discussed in chapter 22 of the sixth edition of *Evaluating Practice*.

SINGWIN Frequently Asked Questions

This is a Word document that contains questions we have been asked about SINGWIN, and our answers to these questions.

Walmyr Assessment Scales

This is a Word document that contains eighteen of the Walmyr Assessment Scales (WAS) discussed in chapter 7 of the sixth edition of *Evaluating Practice* and in previous editions. When you open this file you can scroll to the table of contents contained in this file, click on the name of a measure, and go right to that measure. Note that the Walmyr Assessment Scales are copyrighted and should not be used without purchasing them or otherwise obtaining permission to use them. These scales are reproduced for illustrative purposes only. If you want to use these scales you can order copies for a very nominal fee from http://walmyr.com.

WALMYR RC

This is a Word document containing a table listing coefficient alpha, clinical cutoff, and standard error of measurement (SEM) for many of the WALMYR scales (Hudson, 1997, p. 7). Also, for each of these scales it reports *Reliable Change* (RC), which is discussed in chapter 7. Reliable Change indicates minimum change indicating reliable change (RC). So, for example, for the Generalized Contentment Scale a change of 12 points would indicate reliable change, but a change of 10 points would not.

Orme's Course Syllabus

This is a Word document that contains John Orme's practice evaluation course syllabus. Feel free to use and modify it for educational purposes.

Fischer's Course Syllabus

This is a Word document that contains Joel Fischer's practice evaluation course syllabus. Feel free to use and modify it for educational purposes.

Excel Workbooks

All of the Excel workbooks described in this section are contained in the "Excel Workbooks" folder. Just click on this folder and you'll see a list of the Excel files described in this section. Then, just click on the file you want to open and, where needed, the file contains instructions for its use. (You need to have Microsoft Office installed on your computer to open these workbooks.)

Running Case

This is an Excel workbook that was developed to dynamically illustrate contextualized, response-guided, single-system design practice using a running case. The name of this workbook is *Running Case.xls*. This file contains instructions for its use.

Excel Scoring Program for Walmyr Assessment Scales

This is an Excel workbook designed to compute total scores for the Walmyr Assessment Scales. The name of this workbook is *Walmyr Scoring.xls*. After specifying items that should be reverse scored enter data from any of the Walmyr Assessment Scales and the total score will be computed automatically.

Excel Scoring Program for the Center for Epidemiological Studies Depression Scale (CES-D)

This is an Excel workbook that contains the CES-D scale and it can be used to compute a total score for the CES-D. The name of this workbook is *CES-D.xls*.

Visual Analysis

This is an Excel workbook that ws developed to dynamically illustrate the visual analysis of SSD data. The name of this workbook is *Visual Analysis.xls*. This file contains instructions for its use.

Excel Workbooks

This is a folder that contains multiple Excel workbooks. We designed these workbooks primarily to be used in the *Interactive Exercises* document described previously. To a limited extent they can be used to chart and analyze single-system design data. For example, most of these workbooks are limited to the situation where you have an A-B design with 15 or fewer data points total for baseline and intervention. The SINGWIN is a much more integrated, comprehensive, and versatile program for analyzing single-system data, but you might find these workbooks useful under some circumstances. Also, we realize that many readers of this book use Excel, and these workbooks provide examples of how Excel can be used to chart and analyze single-system design data.

The *Excel Workbooks* folder contains the following workbooks, the workbook names correspond to statistics and charts discussed in this book, and each workbook contains instructions for its use:

- autocorrelation.xls
- binomial.xls
- boxplot.xls
- c-chart.xls
- CES-D.xls
- cdc.xls
- chi-square.xls
- descriptives.xls
- moving average.xls
- p-chart.xls
- Running Case.xls
- t-test.xls
- Visual Analysis.xls
- Walmyr Scoring.xls
- X-Bar-R-chart.xls (also creates the R-chart)
- X-mR-chart.xls

PDF Files

All of the Adobe PDF files described in this section are contained in the "PDF files" folder. Just click on this folder and you'll see a list of the PDF files described in this section. To open a file just click on it. (You need to have Adobe reader installed on you computer to open the PDF files.)

Prologue from Evaluating Practice (5th ed.)

This is a single PDF file that contains the prologue from the fifth edition of *Evaluating Practice*. This prologue presents an integrated perspective on practice methods, theories and research studies, ethics, and evaluation of your own practice. It provides a holistic experience by telling a story in which you can imagine that you're one of the principal actors in the evaluation process that takes place over time. The story is a very detailed adventure story of three students with one client in common, as well as other clients. They have to do an evaluation of this case, and proceed by steps through all of the stages we discuss in the book. We try to present some realistic "stumbles" as well as some good recoveries to a reasonable evaluation product.

Probability Tables

There are four probability tables and these are described in chapter 19.

PowerPoint Presentations

This folder contains PowerPoint presentations for teaching and learning practice evaluation. These presentations correspond to Orme's course syllabi in the "Word Documents" folder. Feel free to use and modify these in any way you like for educational purposes.

Just click on the PowerPoint Presentations folder and you'll see a list of presentations. To open a PowerPoint presentation just click on it. (You need to have Microsoft Office installed on your computer to open these presentations.)

References

Benbenishty, R. (1989). Combining the single-system and group approaches to evaluate treatment effectiveness on the agency level. *Journal of Social Service Research, 12,* 31–47.

Butcher, J. N. (Ed.). (1987). *Computerized psychological assessment: A practitioner's guide.* New York: Basic Books.

Corcoran, K., & Gingerich, W. J. (1994). Practice evaluation in the context of managed care: Case-recording methods for quality assurance reviews. *Research on Social work Practice, 4*(3), 326–327.

Grohol, J. M. (2004) (rev. ed.). *The Insider's Guide to Mental Health Resources Online.* New York: Guilford Press.

Hudson, W. W. (1990B). Computer-based clinical practice: Present status and future possibilities. In L. Videka-Sherman & W. H. Reid (Eds.), *Advances in clinical social work research*. Silver Spring, MD: National Association of Social Workers Press, 105–117.

Hudson, W. W. (1996A). *Computer-assisted social services*. Tallahassee, FL: WALMYR.

Hudson, W. W. (1996B). *Computer-assisted assessment package*. Tallahassee, FL: WALMYR.

Kjosness, J. Y., Barr, L. R., & Rettman, S. (2004). *Research navigator guide: The helping professions*. Boston: Allyn & Bacon.

Krug, S. E. (1993). *Psychware sourcebook* (4th ed.). Kansas City, MO: Test Corporation of America.

Malcolm, R., Sturgis, E. T., Anton, R. F., & Williams, L. (1989). Computer-assisted diagnosis of alcoholism. *Computers in Human Services, 5,* 163–170.

Millstein, S. G., & Irwin, C. E., JR. (1983). Acceptability of computer acquired sexual histories in adolescent girls. *Journal of Pediatrics, 103,* 815–819.

Moreland, K. L. (1987). Computerized psychological assessment: What's available. In J. N. Butcher (Ed.), *Computerized psychological assessment: A practitioner's guide*. New York: Basic Books.

Mutschler, E. (1987). Computer utilization. In *Encyclopedia of social work* (18th Ed.). Silver Spring, MD: National Association of Social Workers Press.

Newman, M. G. (2004). Technology in psychotherapy: An introduction. *Journal of Clinical Psychology, 60,* 141–145.

Newman, M. G., Consoli, A., & Taylor, C. B. (1997). Computers in assessment and cognitive behavioral treatment of clinical disorders: Anxiety as a case in point. *Behavior Therapy, 28,* 211–235.

Nugent, W. R., Sieppert, J. D., & Hudson, W. W. (2001). *Practice Evaluation for the 21st Century*. Belmont, CA: Brooks/Cole.

Nurius, P. S., & Hudson, W. W. (1988). Computers and social diagnosis: The client's perspective. *Computers in Human Services, 5,* 21–36.

Nurius, P. S., & Hudson, W. W. (1993). *Human services: Practice, evaluation & computers*. Pacific Grove, CA: Brooks/Cole.

Patterson, D. A. (2000). *Personal computer applications in the social services*. Boston: Allyn & Bacon.

Patterson, D. A., & Basham, R. E. (in press). A data visualization procedure for the evaluation of group treatment outcomes across units of analysis. *Small Group Research*.

Petrucci, C. J., Kirk, S. A., & Reid, W. J. (2004). Computer technology and social work. In A. R. Roberts & K. R. Yeager (Eds.), *Evidence-based practice manual*. New York: Oxford University Press, 85–94.

Plake, B. S., Impara, J. C., & Spies, R. A. (2003). *The fifteenth mental measurements yearbook*. Lincoln, NE: Buros Institute, University of Nebraska.

Schiller, P. (2005). *Information technology for social work: Practice skills for the 21st century*. Boston: Allyn & Bacon.

Siegel, D. H. (1990). Computer-based clinical practice: An asset or pie in the sky? In L. Videka-Sherman & W. J. Reid (Eds.), *Advances in clinical social work research*. Silver Spring, MD: National Association of Social Workers Press, 118–122.

Stoloff, M. L., & Couch, J. V. (1988). *Computer use in psychology: A directory of software* (2nd ed.). Washington, DC: American Psychological Association.

Taylor, C. B., & Luce, K. H. (2003). Computer and internet-based psychotherapy interventions. *Current Directions in Psychological Science, 12,* 18–22.

Vernon, R., & Lynch, D. (2000). *Social Work and the Web*. Belmont, CA: Wadsworth.

Yaffe, J., & Gotthoffer, D. (2000). *A quick guide to the internet for social workers*. Boston: Allyn & Bacon.

Appendix

Intervention Plan

Practitioner:
Supervisor:
Setting:

Part 1: Targets

Target (first priority)
Client's view:
Practitioner's view:
  Clarity:
  Countability:
  Verifying sources:
  Dereification:
  Increase or decrease:
  Specific statement of measurable problem:
  References you've consulted on problem (theoretical and empirical):

Objectives and Goals

Objective (short-term)	Goal (long-term)
Who?	Who?
Will do what?	Will do what?
To what extent?	To what extent?
Under what conditions?	Under what conditions?
Statistical goals	Statistical goals

Specific statement of measurable objective(s):
Specific statement of measurable goal(s):
Date on which client and practitioner agreed on goal(s):
    Goal 1:
    Goal 2:
    Goal 3:

Measures (two per target)
    Objective/Goal 1:
      Reliability:
      Validity:
      References on measures:

    Objective/Goal 2:
      Reliability:
      Validity:
      References on measures:

Summary

Target	Goal	Objective	Measures
1.			
2.			
3.			

Part II: Design

Plan for Collecting Data and Monitoring Outcomes
    Who?
    When?
    Where?
    How often?
    Who will chart?

Baseline
    Type (concurrent and/or reconstructed):
    Baseline plan:
    Estimate of length of baseline:

Design
    Type of design:
    Chart of design (include baseline data if available) (NOTE: you can double-click
      on the chart to revise it and insert your own data):

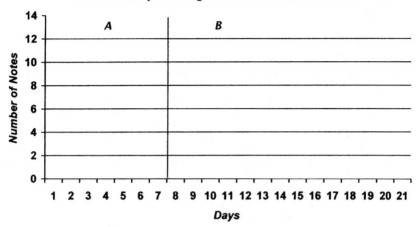

Number of Early Warning Notes After Student Suicide

Date you and your data collector agreed on data collection procedures and data collection checklist completed:

Part III: Intervention & Maintenance

Intervention

Specific intervention program or technique(s):

Specific components of the program described above (e. g., the techniques that make up the program):

Intervention program or techniques described in the following professional references:

Effectiveness (outcome data) of intervention described in the following professional references:

Possible negative effects of these interventions:

Individuals (and their organizations) with whom you have consulted re: use of these interventions:

Ethical issues considered:

Date informed consent signed by client:

Date you and supervisor agree on intervention program:

Date you and client agreed on intervention program:

Date you expect to begin intervention:

Expected length of time before target problem begins to change (based on literature):

Expected length of time for problem(s) to be resolved:

Maintenance Program

Type of maintenance program:

Techniques to be used for maintenance and generalization:

Modifications to design due to maintenance program:
Type of design with maintenance phase added:

Part IV: Results

Graph (Double-click on chart to revise and insert your own data):

Number of Early Warning Notes After Student Suicide

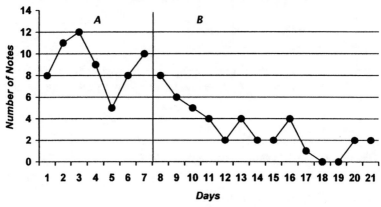

Autocorrelation:
Visual analyses:
Appropriate-to-data statistics:

Part IV: Discussion

Full-page interpretation of results; what happened, why intervention worked or did not work; how intervention program could be improved.

Chapter 21

Evidence-Based Practice

*It is not enough to do your best; you first have to know **what** to do and **then** do your best.*
—W. Edwards Deming

Evidence-based practice (EBP) is one of the most important developments in decades for the helping professions—including medicine, nursing, social work, psychology, public health, counseling, and all the other health and human service professions (Briggs & Rzepnicki, 2004; Brownson et al., 2002; Dawes et al., 1999; Dobson & Craig, 1998a, 1998b; Gilgun, 2005; Roberts & Yeager, 2004; Sackett et al., 2000). That is because evidence-based practice holds out the hope for practitioners that we can be at least as successful in helping our clients as the current available information on helping allows us to be. Both the importance and the multidisciplinary nature of EBP can be seen in the Roberts and Yeager (2004) compendium, *Evidence-Based Practice Manual,* a collection of chapters describing the meaning, methods, and examples of EBP.

Evidence-based practice represents both an ideology and a method. The *ideology* springs from the ethical principle that clients deserve to be provided with the most effective interventions possible. The *method* of EBP is the way we go about finding and then implementing those interventions (see, e.g., manuals on EBP methods by Gibbs, 2003; Cournoyer, 2003; and Rubin, 2007; see also http://www.evidence.brookscole.com/index.html). *Evidence-based practice represents the practitioner's commitment to use all means possible to locate the* best *(most effective) evidence for any given problem at* all *points of planning and contacts with clients.* This pursuit of the best knowledge includes extensive computer searches, as described in the following (Gibbs & Gambrill, 2002).

Evidence-based practice is an enormous challenge to practitioners because the methods of locating the most effective interventions go beyond, or are more rigorous than, even those of *empirically-based practice.* Thus, for example, where a

From Bloom, M, Fischer, J. & Orme, J. (2009), *Evaluating practice: Guidelines for the accountable professional (6th Ed.).* Boston: Allyn and Bacon.

practitioner using empirically-based practice might be satisfied with locating two or three controlled studies as evidence of effectiveness (Chambless et al., 1996, 1998), practitioners using EBP will do whatever it takes to locate *all* studies of effectiveness on a particular problem, typically using *reviews* of research on intervention effectiveness, and then critically assessing the studies in those reviews for evidence of validity and utility for practice. The emphasis in EBP is on the comprehensiveness of the search and critical evaluation of the results, all in as close collaboration with clients as possible, including sensitivity to socially and culturally relevant approaches to intervention (Ancis, 2003; Mio & Iwamasa, 2003; Sue & Sue, 2004).

The EBP model has spawned a huge literature, including methods of education and critical thinking for this rigorous form of practice (Crisp, 2004; Gambrill, 2005; Gira et al., 2004; Howard et al., 2003); EBP skill-training manuals (Rubin, 2008; Bisman & Hardcastle, 1999; Cournoyer, 2003; Gibbs, 2003; Weisz & Hawley, 1998); issues and challenges regarding EBP (Norcross et al., 2005; Gibbs & Gambrill, 2002); *principles* of change that work (Castonguay & Beutler, 2006); manuals presenting procedural guidelines for applying intervention techniques (Cormier et al., 2009; Lecroy, 2008; Van Hasselt & Hersen, 1996); evidence-based assessment (Hunsley, Crabb, & Mash, 2004; Mash & Barkley, 2007); evidence for an empirical foundation for the most effective relationship factors (Norcross, 2002; Norcross & Hill, 2004); EBP for groups (Macgowan, 2008); EBP with families (Corcoran 2002, 2003); evidence-based internships (Thomlison & Corcoran, 2008); and methods for intervention planning and assessment (Beutler & Groth-Marnat, 2003; Beutler & Mailik, 2002; Haynes & O'Brien, 2000; Hersen, 2004; Hunsley, Crabb, & Mash, 2004; Lopez & Snyder, 2003; Seligman, 2004; Vance & Pumariega, 2001; Woody et al., 2003).

Most importantly, the EBP movement has produced an outpouring of literature on the most effective procedures for prevention and intervention (Abramovitz, 2006; Antony et al., 2005; Antony & Barlow, 2001; Barlow, 2001a, 2001b; Barrett & Ollendick, 2004; Bellack, 2006; Bloomquist & Schnell, 2002; Carr, 2000; Corcoran, 2003, 2004; Cormier et al., 2009; Dobson & Craig, 1998a, 1998b; Dugus & Robichaud, 2006; Dulmus & Rapp-Paglicci, 2005; D'Zurilla & Nezu, 2006; Emmelkamp and Vedel, 2006; Fisher & O'Donohue, 2006; Fisher, Hayes, & O'Donohue, 2003; Fonagy et al., 2002; Freeman & Power, 2006; Gambrill, 2006; Gullotta & Blau, 2007; Gullotta & Bloom, 2003; Hersen & Bellack, 1999; Hoffman & Otto, 2007; Hoffman & Tompson, 2002; Kazantzis & L'Abate, 2006; Kazdin, 2005; Kazdin & Weisz, 2003; Kendall, 2005; Lambert, 2004; Liddle et al., 2002; Levkoff, 2006; Lyddon & Jones, 2001; MacDonald, 2001; Marlatt & Gorman, 2005; Marlatt and Donovan, 2005; Nathan & Gorman, 2007; O'Donohue & Ferguson, 2003; O'Hare, 2005; Reiser & Thompson, 2005; Roberts & Yeager, 2006; Roberts & Yeager, 2004; Rosqvist, 2005; Roth & Fonagy, 2004; Rygh & Sanderson, 2004; Silverstein et al., 2006; Stout & Hayes, 2004; Thyer & Wodarski, 1998; Wedding et al., 2005; and Wodarkski & Thyer, 1998).

Our view of evidence-based practice is that it depends on the successful integration of the two primary types of research: single system designs as the heart of evaluation-informed practice and experimental and quasi-experimental controlled group designs that form the basis for practitioners' decisions about what procedures are the most effective for a particular case. Indeed, the importance of systematic evaluation with each and every case, once you have selected the best available program, can be seen in one compelling fact: The evidence is clear that even interventions selected on the basis of several randomized, controlled studies cannot be assumed to be effective with each and every client. The research clearly shows that both characteristics of clients (Clarkin & Levy, 2004) and characteristics of practitioners (Beutler et al., 2004) can have profound effects on outcomes. Cultural, socioeconomic, ethnic, and a host of other demographic and interpersonal variables can keep what seems like the perfect intervention from doing what one might expect given the reported results in the literature.

We believe the *evidence*-based practice model and the *evaluation*-informed practice approach, in a sense, complete each other. The one uses a systematic and comprehensive search of the empirical literature to find what works best, the other provides methods for ongoing monitoring, guiding, and evaluating client progress. People and their situations are complex. So many things can go wrong during an intervention, even given the best of relationships, that the evidence-based practitioner always monitors and evaluates progress with every case and situation so as to be able to tell how well the intervention is—or is not—progressing. Thus, to be a well-rounded evidence-based practitioner, we strongly recommend the use of single system designs to allow you, the practitioner, to receive regular feedback on how well your clients are doing and to make changes accordingly. This is particularly so given the recent evidence that routine monitoring and receipt of feedback that is characteristic of evaluation-informed practice can reduce deterioration and improve overall outcome (Faul et al., 2001; Lambert et al., 2002, 2003). In other words, the evidence seems to support the idea that evaluation-informed practice fits the bill as an integral partner of evidence-based practice.

The essence of successful practice is to help resolve client problems and to attain client objectives, without creating problems for others or new problems for the client. Probably the most clear and socially accountable way of determining whether our practice is successful is through systematized, relatively objective evaluation methods that can be replicated (repeated) by others. This is part of the science of practice—professional action that is informed by the best available information, guided by techniques of demonstrated effectiveness, and combined with objective evaluation components, all within the context of professional values.

Yet this focus on the science of evidence-based and evaluation-informed practice is not intended to rule out other crucial aspects of practice. The art and creativity of (and the values and philosophy undergirding) practice that make it humane and caring we believe can be combined with the empirical/scientific orientation to produce what we call the *scientific practitioner*. Here, then, is our definition of the scientific practitioner. Such a practitioner combines the following elements in his or her practice:

1. Using the results of research and evaluation to the extent possible to select intervention techniques and other procedures that have evidence of effectiveness, and use of techniques without such evidence, only with caution; this is the heart of evidence-based practice.
2. Systematic monitoring and evaluation of his or her practice with each and every case, particularly through use of single system designs; this is the heart of evaluation-informed practice.
3. Having the skills and attitudes—the commitment—to keep learning, to keep searching for new and more effective ways to serve consumers.
4. Above all, maintaining a commitment in words and deeds to the ethics and values of the helping professions; a sensitivity, caring, and concern for the well-being, rights, and dignity of clients and consumers.

In other words, the scientific practitioner is a person who is strongly concerned with humane helping that is provided in the most effective manner possible. Each element—the scientific, the ethical, and the practice—clarifies and reinforces each other. None can be minimized in favor of the other without detriment to the whole.

As you can probably guess, we believe that thinking about evaluation during the course of practice will help to sharpen the thinking of practitioners and offer insights that cannot easily be attained in other ways. However, we want to emphasize that if ever occasions arise when the procedures of evaluation interfere with some specific interventive practice, our ethics tell us there is no choice but to put those intervention concerns first. We should do nothing (in the name of research or evaluation) that harms clients or their chances for successful service. Since the primary goal of evaluation is to improve practice, we do not believe in sacrificing the meaning and relevance of practice on the altar of scientific rigor. We believe, however, that occasions involving serious conflicts between practice and evaluation are rare. As we will try to show, in the great majority of situations, evaluation will help us to think clearly and act effectively and humanely on behalf of our clients.

Steps in Evidence-Based Practice

While this book is about evaluation-based practice, the importance of evidence-based practice suggests to us that we should present a brief overview of the actual procedures involved in conducting evidence-based practice. Therefore, we will summarize in this section some of the far more detailed information on conducting evidence-based practice that you can find in skill-training manuals (e.g., Rubin, 2007; Gibbs, 2003; Cournoyer, 2003). We present these procedures as a series of steps.

Before we present these steps, however, we want to recognize with you the enormous challenge to most practitioners presented by this approach, and the large amount of time and stress that can be involved in applying these steps in a conscientious fashion. We hope you will remember, then, two possibilities in applying evidence-based practice that may help mitigate some of that pressure. First, one possibility is that you begin your pursuit of EBP gradually. You might want to start, sort of in an exploratory way, with just one case to try using evidence-based practice. Assess for yourself the time and effort that applying these evidence-based practice steps takes in that case. This way, you can properly judge the costs and benefits of EBP. (Of course, we hope you will reap a huge amount of benefits in applying evidence-based practice with that first case in that you will see demonstrable, positive changes for your client.) Then, you can gauge just what resources you will need to apply EBP with subsequent cases. We are certain that each application will become easier as you gain experience, as with any new approach, including using single system designs.

The second possibility to keep in mind actually depends on the kinds of services you provide in your organization. In many organizations, the caseloads include similar problems, admittedly with variations among individual clients. This may mean that review of the literature to ascertain what will be useful for evidence-based practice with one client/problem configuration may be generalizable to many of your cases. That is a huge savings in your time and energy in conducting these steps. In fact, as you will see, there inevitably will be client problems and situations where the literature is only minimally helpful, and in which inspiration for the best approach will come from your own experiences and those of your colleagues.

So, keeping those possibilities in mind, following are the steps involved in evidence-based practice.

Step 1. Develop A Question.   This is not as easy as it may first appear. The question may be as complicated as, what are the key factors affecting homelessness, or as focused as, what intervention works best with a given problem? For example, we may be working with clients with overwhelming anxiety. We would want to ask questions such as, what are the best methods for assessing anxiety, and what interventions work best with what different types of anxiety? We also want to be aware in seeking answers to our practice questions that characteristics of the client, practitioner, setting, and other environmental variables play an important part in getting the clearest and best answers to our questions. An intervention that cannot be adjusted to account for cultural differences among clients may not be the best answer to your question.

Step 2. Find the Evidence.   The heart of evidence-based practice is in the search process, trying to find the best answers to the questions we ask. The largest part of the manuals available on EBP is devoted to this search process. Here, we can only provide a brief summary of search procedures.

There are three ways of finding evidence, all of them connected to the way we use the literature. Further, all of them also are connected to our use of the internet, one of the trademarks of the evidence-based practitioner. The first two methods consist of finding published reviews of the research literature, while the third method involves do-it-yourself reviews.

The first method of finding the evidence is to find a meta-analytic review. *Meta-analyses* are quantitative reviews of the literature. A meta-analysis seeks to find all published (and sometimes unpublished) studies on a topic and synthesizes the results by finding a common metric to report the results of all the studies. That common metric is called an effect size, symbolized by a single statistic, most typically, *d*. The higher the effect size, the greater is assumed to be the impact of the intervention. Because of the importance of the decision for our clients about what is and what is not evidence-based, we recommend that practitioners be especially cautious in making that decision by using larger and less common effect sizes to try to ensure that such a decision is well grounded in the evidence. To that end, we recommend that an effect size of *.80* be the minimum one that practitioners use as a guideline for deciding what is evidence-based and what may not be. An effect size of .80 is regarded by many as large (Cohen, 1988), and also is relatively uncommon in the meta-analytic literature (Lipsey & Wilson, 1993). For meta-analyses with effect sizes lower than .80, we recommend that you use extra diligence and caution in applying the results. This is not to say that meta-analyses with effect sizes lower than .80 are not useful. There simply may not be available a meta-analysis with an overall effect size that large. In such situations, meta-analyses with lower effect sizes may be the best evidence available. (For an excellent introduction to both meta-analyses and systematic reviews, described following, see Littel, Corcoran, and Pillai, [2008].)

The second method of finding evidence is to find a published traditional or narrative review of the literature. In their more rigorous forms, these are called *systematic reviews* because they follow a specific protocol in conducting all aspects of the review. These reviews also attempt to collect all available studies, but rather than conducting a *quantitative* analysis, either present only the *results* of several studies or add to that by analyzing the methodologies of those studies. Then, a conclusion about effectiveness is drawn by *logical* (rather than quantitative) means. This is sometimes called the box-score method because the reviewer often just adds up the total of positive studies and negative studies and presents a conclusion.

For these reviews, too, we recommend a great deal of caution in accepting a conclusion about what is evidence-based. We recommend that unless *80 percent* or more of the published studies are positive, caution be used in making a conclusion that a procedure is evidence-based. (That 80 percent is the same percentage we use for accepting a measure as reliable, that is, consistent. The same principle applies here.) For reviews with a lower percentage of positive studies, once again we advise due caution in applying the results.

Here are a couple of hints about using the results of these traditional reviews. First, if the reviewer does not *analyze* the studies but only *describes* the results presented by the original authors of the studies, your confidence in accepting the conclusions should be decreased because there would be no way of knowing from the review whether the methods of the studies affected the results.

Second, if the reviewer only presents the results of the studies with positive outcomes, this may mean he or she has not done a comprehensive search. Thus, your confidence in the conclusions of that review should be greatly decreased. (Presentation of only positive results is actually a very common practice in book chapters on the effectiveness of different intervention techniques.) Obviously, an incomplete search can be a sign that the reviewer was selectively looking only for results that corroborate the reviewer's opinions.

The third method is to conduct a review of all the available evidence yourself. This method clearly is the most time-consuming and difficult of the three methods. But you will find, unfortunately, that many of the questions you pose in your search for the evidence simply have not been reviewed by others, or that the reviews are out-of-date. We define out-of-date reviews as those roughly three or more years old, an admittedly stringent criterion. This does not mean that older reviews are worthless. All it really means is that over time, things change. Some of those things may be the evidence on the effectiveness of a given procedure. Therefore, all we are saying is that you may have to do some additional work yourself, either by supplementing older reviews with newer findings or by deciding to find all of the evidence yourself, using the older review as a source for references. (From our own experience in attempting to find evidence-based interventions, we know exactly how frustrating this process can be.) The key challenge in conducting your own review is to try to ensure the review is comprehensive enough to incorporate all the literature. To that end, you may have to use different databases and multiple search terms to ensure that all possible search options were pursued.

To help in this type of search and the searches for published reviews, we present in table 21.1 a number of the prime internet sources for conducting such searches.

Although most if not all searches for evidence-based procedures will involve searches on the internet, that does not, by any means, rule out use of other resources. For example, mental health practitioners might choose to turn to the collection of "treatments that work" by Nathan and Gorman (2007). This excellent book contains descriptions and reviews of the research for twenty-five mental health problems where the accumulated evidence points to interventions that appear to be effective. All of the evidence for each treatment is presented on a graded hierarchy of rigor, starting with "Type I Studies" that are rigorous, experimental clinical trials, and ending with "Type VI Studies," such as case studies and opinion papers. While the chapters vary somewhat in the extent of the evidence presented, this book is an excellent starting point for reviewing what others consider to be effective interventions.

Step 3. Analyze the Evidence.   As if it is not enough to *find* the evidence, now you have to *analyze* it. For analysis of individual studies, this means having more than just a passing understanding of research design and methodology as well as the commitment to putting in the time to apply your understanding to the analysis of studies. This means knowing about, let's say, the difference between experimental and quasi-experimental designs (hint: it's random assignment); understanding that there is a hierarchy of evidence from which one might make inferences about effectiveness, ranging from experimental designs to uncontrolled case studies (see

Table 21.1   Internet Sites for Evidence-Based Practice Searches

1. We recommend that two of the first sites you visit are the Campbell Collaboration at http://www .campbellcollaboration.org [go to C2 and scroll down for reviews] for complete reviews of the effects of social and behavioral interventions; as of early 2008, this relatively new site had completed five reviews in education, ten in crime and justice and seventeen in social welfare. Go to www.cochrane.org for the Cochrane Collaboration and detailed summaries of systematic reviews of the effects of health care interventions, including many reviews of psychosocial interventions. You can find a complete list of all the Cochrane Collaboration reviews at the top of their page where it says "A-Z."

2. If you still have connections with your university, such as maintaining your university e-mail address, you may still be able to use their databases at no charge. If that is so, we highly recommend that you locate the database called EBSCOHost. This database contains over twenty databases, including *Academic Search Primer,* which has full text (complete for downloading) articles from over 4,500 journals. For example, one of the data bases in EBSCOHost is *Psychology and Behavioral Sciences Collection* that alone has 575 full text journals available; this database is particularly useful for members of the helping professions (your library may have a different version called *PsycINFO*).

3. Most readers probably are aware of Google for everyday searches. Google has a specialized feature called Google Scholar that is free and can be used to find research and other publications on many of the topics of interest for evidence-based practice. You can enter just one or two words as your search term (e.g., "meta-analysis and depression") or you may even enter an entire question to ensure broader coverage (e.g., "What are the most effective interventions for depression?").

Rubin [2007] for an extensive description of this hierarchy and what can be gleaned from each level of evidence); understanding whether the statistics used in a study are appropriate or inappropriate; and so on. This is called research consumerism, and it is one of the reasons all education programs in the helping professions place so much emphasis on research methods classes. How can one be a good consumer of research and hence, evidence-based, if one cannot properly analyze the studies that will guide decisions?

We understand that in the hard reality of everyday work in an organization, we simply are not going to be able to find rigorous empirical research to provide the evidence for all of our questions. Therefore, we recognize that some evidence may be considered weak by some standards. Thus, when we discuss evidence, we simply mean the best evidence that is available, starting with rigorous empirical research, of course, but including other sources when such research is not available. The decision to apply the available evidence is made with the understanding that the decision is the best one that could be made under the circumstances, and that careful evaluation of each case will reveal the wisdom of that choice. (Again, we highly recommend the new book by Rubin [2007] as an excellent introduction to analyzing research for evidence-based practice.)

Step 4. Combine the Evidence with Your Understanding of the Client and Situation.   Although the process of arriving at an evidence-based practice decision is complex, it becomes even more interesting when we consider how to adapt it to the current client/problem/situation configuration. If all the evidence that is accumulated is based on a population that is different from the client with whom you are working, then you will have to find the best way to adapt what you found in the literature to the context in which you are working. The number of such contextual variables that could affect your decision are numerous, including ethnic and cultural differences, income level and income security, housing, family situation, and so on. We suggest that you take each piece of the evidence from your information search, and ask: How specifically will this fit with my client? What can I do to make it more suitable to my client? (Clarkin & Levy [2004] and Beutler et al. [2004] go into detail about making suitable adaptations from the research literature to your own specific case, especially with regard to the effects of different client and practitioner characteristics.) For example, using interventions originally used with preschoolers may be modified to assume more cognitive sophistication in elementary school students; dealing with views of unmarried mothers as suitable caretakers of their children may differ by ethnicity; different cultures may permit more or less child tending by older siblings. Your conceptual mapping of the situation will have to take into consideration these kinds of perspectives.

Step 5. Application to Practice. In a sense, this might be the easiest part of evidence-based practice. Once the decision is made to implement the material you have identified as evidence-based, all that is left to do is to implement that material. Of course, a practitioner might find that he or she does not have sufficient knowledge to immediately implement that material; therefore, a period of familiarization will be necessary. This can be greatly eased by maintaining in one's possession some of the books described previously that present the intervention techniques that have been found to be effective in proceduralized manuals (e.g., Cormier et al., 2009; Lecroy, 2008; Van Hasselt & Hersen, 1996).

Step 6. Monitor and Evaluate Results. Even with interventions that have the soundest base of evidence, evaluation of the application in practice is necessary. Perfect results are never guaranteed, and that is how and why evaluation-informed practice is so crucial to evidence-based practice. We, as practitioners, must always be accountable for our efforts. And the primary way we demonstrate that accountability, once an evidence-based decision is implemented, is through our systematic and careful monitoring and evaluation of that application.

Integrating Evaluation-Informed and Evidence-Based Practice: The PRAISES Model

Although we have argued that it is critically important to integrate evaluation and practice, it still remains for us to provide examples of precisely how that integration might occur. We have described evidence-based practice as using the best evidence at *all* points of planning and contact with the clients. And it is exactly these points that have to be operationalized clearly in order for you to understand not only how evaluation-informed and evidence-based practice can be integrated, but identifying every point in the overall intervention process—from first contact to follow-up—where they *can* and *should* be integrated.

To that end, we present in figure 21.1, the PRAISES Model, a framework for integrating evaluation-informed and evidence-based practice (Fischer, 1986). We understand that at first glance this framework can be somewhat intimidating, as it may look more like a General Motors wiring diagram than a flowchart for use by helping professionals. But we want to assure you, on the basis of well over two decades of teaching using the PRAISES Model, that this framework is very useful and quite adaptable. Here's why: A careful look at the flowchart will show that the flowchart actually is a compilation of virtually all the steps many practitioners go through anyway, but in this case, they are systematized in a flowchart that is intended to add a more structured approach to those steps.

Indeed, to that end, the PRAISES Model is an attempt to integrate, structure, and systematize the process of evidence-based practice, while highlighting the inter-relationships among interventive practices and evaluation in the overall process. Let's just briefly describe some of the characteristics of this framework and the ways in which they illustrate and enhance evidence-based practice.

1. *Empirically-based.*   To the extent possible, this framework attempts to en-hance development of the empirical base for evidence-based practice. As we have pointed out, the empirical base of evidence-based practice has two meanings. The first is the use of the results of classical evaluation research to guide selec-tion of interventions that have demonstrated effectiveness. The second meaning is in the careful and systematic evaluation of the effects of our interventions. This framework highlights the points of planning and contact with the clients where evaluation-informed and evidence-based decisions need to be made. In other words, every time the practitioner plans to see the client, he or she should have a handle on what the empirical evidence says about that contact (e.g., the very first interview; the very last interview or the termination contact).

2. *Integrative.*   The PRAISES Model flowchart attempts to integrate all prac-tice and evaluation activities. This is the basis for our earlier assertions that good practice incorporates good evaluation. There are no distinctions made between evaluation and practice in the flowchart. Only the different activities required at each step are described.

3. *Eclectic.*   This framework is based on the assumption that the knowledge base of practice in the helping professions is both pluralistic and eclectic. It is plu-ralistic in the sense that knowledge is derived from many sources. It is eclectic in that only the best available knowledge is derived from those sources. Eclecticism refers to the use of clear, precise, systematic criteria to select knowledge. In particu-lar, this relates to the empirical base of evidence-based practice in that, whenever possible, evidence-based practice is comprised of a variety of procedures and techniques selected largely on the basis of evidence of effectiveness and applied with people and situations where the evidence indicates that such application has a good chance of producing a successful outcome. Of course, it is not always possible to achieve this ideal with each and every problem/situation. But as an

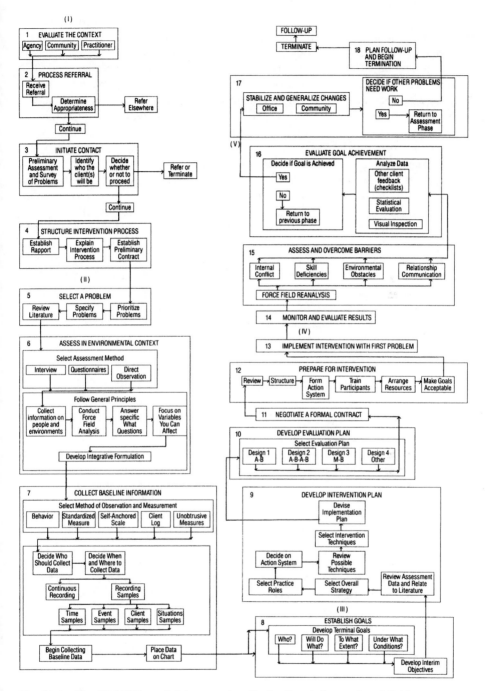

Fig. 21.1   The PRAISES model: Integrating Evaluation-Informed and Evidence-Based Practice

organizing principle of evidence-based practice, it seems like a worthwhile goal to shoot for. More concretely, this framework is intended to apply whatever the theoretical orientation, methods, or approach of the user are.

4. *Systematic.*   This framework is an attempt to systematize practice. This means clearly identifying the various phases of practice and organizing them in a step-by-step sequence. In fact, one of the most important characteristics of practice is being systematic: in how goals are defined, in how intervention techniques are selected, in how outcome is monitored, and so on. It also appears to make sense to try to organize the diverse activities of practice into a logical sequence that runs from initial contact to termination and follow-up.

Although we describe the process of practice in the flowchart as a sequence of steps within phases, we do not intend to prescribe a rigid, lock-step approach to practice. For example, depending on the problem or situation, the length of time for any step could vary considerably, the steps could overlap, or a particular step might even not occur at all. Indeed, despite the fact that a number of steps are described, the essence of professional practice using this framework must be flexibility: That is, selecting what is done on the basis of a specific client/problem/situation configuration. This attempt to organize that process is intended to bring some order and structure into the subtleties and contradictions of real-life practice. Importantly, this framework has been found to be a very useful device for newer practitioners, providing them with an anchor as they learn how to engage in evidence-based practice.

5. *Accountable.*   This framework is an attempt to add to our professional accountability as practitioners. It brings the entire process of practice out into the open for scrutiny by others. It points out and builds into practice the necessity for carefully evaluating results with every case, and this is the very *heart* of accountability.

6. *Way of Thinking.*   The PRAISES Model is intended, perhaps more than anything else, to illustrate and enhance a way of thinking about practice: systematic, data-based, outcome-oriented, structured, flexible depending on the needs of the client, evidence-based, informed by ongoing evaluation, and up-to-date with the relevant literature. All of this is grounded in the ethics and values—the scientific humanism—that underlie the philosophy and practices of the helping professions.

The PRAISES Model is comprised of five major phases and eighteen steps, each of which is divided into component parts. The term PRAISES is an acronym for the five phases. Following is a summary of the phases, and the eighteen steps.

PHASE I. *PRe*-Intervention
1. Evaluate the context
2. Process the referral
3. Initiate contact
4. Structure

PHASE II. *Assessment*
  5. Select problem
  6. Conduct assessment
  7. Collect baseline information
  8. Establish goals

PHASE III. *Intervention*
  9. Develop intervention plan
  10. Develop evaluation plan
  11. Negotiate contract
  12. Prepare for intervention
  13. Implement intervention

PHASE IV. *Systematic Evaluation*
  14. Monitor and evaluate results
  15. Assess and overcome barriers
  16. Evaluate goal achievement

PHASE V. *Stabilize*
  17. Stabilize and generalize changes
  18. Plan and implement termination and follow-up

References

Abramovitz, J. S. (2006). *Obsessive-Compulsive disorder: Advances in psycho-therapy—an evidence-based practice.* Ashland, OH: Hogrefe & Huber.

Ancis, J. R. (Ed.). (2003). *Culturally responsive interventions: Innovative approaches to working with diverse populations.* New York: Brunner-Routledge.

Antony, M. M., et al. (Eds.). (2005). *Improving outcomes and preventing relapse in cognitive-behavior therapy.* New York: Guilford.

Antony, M. M., & Barlow, D. H. (2001). *Handbook of assessment and treatment planning for psychological disorders.* New York: Guilford Press.

Barlow, D. H. (2001a). *Anxiety and its disorders* (2nd ed.). New York: Guilford Press.

Barlow, D. H. (Ed.). (2001b). *Clinical handbook of psychological disorders* (3rd ed.). New York: Guilford Press.

Barrett, P. M., & Ollendick, T. H. (Eds.). (2004). *Handbook of interventions that work with children and adolescents.* New York: Wiley.

Bellack, A. S. (Ed.). (2006). *Behavioral treatment for substance abuse in people with serious and persistent mental illness.* New York: Brunner-Routledge.

Beutler, L. E., & Mailik, M. L. (Eds.). (2002). *Rethinking the DSM: A psychological perspective.* Washington, DC: APA.

Beutler, L. E., & Groth-Mamat, G. (2003). *Integrative assessment of adult personality* (2nd ed.). New York: Guilford Press.

Beutler, L. E., Malik, M., Alimohamed, S., Harwood, T. M., Talebi, H., Noble, S., & Wong, E. (2004). Therapist variables. In M. Lambert (Ed.), *Bergin and Garfield's handbook of psychotherapy and behavior change* (5th ed.), (pp. 227–306). New York: Wiley.

Bisman, C. D., & Hardcastle, D. A. (1999). *Integrating research into practice.* Belmont, CA: Wadsworth.

Bloomquist, M., & Schnell, S. V. (2002). *Helping children with aggression and conduct problems: Best practices for interventions.* New York: Guilford Press.

Briggs, H. E., & Rzepnicki, T. L. (Eds.). (2004). *Using evidence in social work practice: Behavioral perspectives.* Chicago: Lyceum Books.

Brownson, R. C., Baker, E. A., Leet, T. L., and Gillespie, K. N. (2002). *Evidence-based public health.* New York: Oxford.

Carr, A. (Ed.). (2000). *What works with children and adolescents?* London: Brunner Routledge.

Castonguay, L. G., & Beutler, L. E. (Eds.). (2006). *Principles of therapeutic change that work.* New York: Oxford University Press.

Chambless, D. L., et al. (1996). An update on empirically validated techniques. *The Clinical Psychologist, 49,* 5–18.

Chambless, D. L., et al. (1998). Update on empirically validated techniques, 11. *The Clinical Psychologist, 51,* 8–16.

Cohen, J. (1988). *Statistical power analysis for the behavioral sciences* (2nd ed.). Hillsdale, NJ: Erlebaum.

Clarkin, J. F., & Levy, K. N. (2004). The influence of client variables in psychotherapy. In M. L. Lambert (Ed.), *Bergin and Garfield's handbook of psychotherapy and behavior change* (5th ed.), (pp. 194–226). New York: Wiley.

Corcoran, J. (2002). *Evidence-based family approaches: Clinical and social applications.* New York: Oxford University Press.

Corcoran, J. (2003). *Clinical applications of evidence-based interventions.* New York: Oxford.

Cormier, S., & Nurius, P. S. (2003). *Interviewing and change strategies for helpers: Fundamental skills and cognitive behavioral interventions* (5th ed.). Pacific Grove, CA: Brooks/Cole.

Cormier, S., Nurius, P. S., & Osborn, C. J. (2009). *Interviewing and change strategies for helpers: Fundamental skills and cognitive-behavioral interventions* (6th ed.). Pacific Grove, CA: Brooks/Cole.

Cournoyer, B. R. (2003). *The evidence-based social work skills book.* Boston: Allyn & Bacon.

Crisp, B. R. (2004). Evidence-based practice and the borders of data in the global information era. *Journal of Social Work Education, 40,* 73–86.

Dawes, M., et al. (1999). *Evidence-based practice: A primer for healthcare professionals.* Edinburgh, UK: Churchill Livingstone.

Dobson, K. S., & Craig, K. D. (Eds.). (1998a). *Best practice: Developing and promoting empirically supported interventions.* Newbury Park, CA: SAGE.

Dobson, K. S., & Craig, K. D. (Eds.). (1998b). *Empirically supported therapies: Best practice in professional psychology.* Thousand Oaks, CA: SAGE.

Dugus, M. J., & Robichaud, M. (2006). *Cognitive-behavioral treatment for generalized anxiety disorder: From science to practice.* New York: Brunner-Routledge.

Dulmus, C. N., & Rapp-Paglicci, L. A. (Eds.). (2005). *Handbook of preventive intervention for adults.* New York: Wiley.

D'Zurilla, T. J., & Nezu, A. M. (2006). *Problem-solving therapy* (3rd ed.). New York: Springer.

Emmelkamp, P., & Vedel, E. (2006). *Evidence-based treatment for alcohol and drug abuse.* New York: Brunner-Routledge.

Faul, A. C., McMurty, S. L., & Hudson, W. W. (2001). Can empirical clinical practice techniques improve social work outcomes? *Research on social work practice, 11,* 277–299.

Fischer, J. E., & O'Donohue, W. T. (Eds.). (2006). *Practitioner's guide to evidence-based psychotherapy.* New York: Springer.

Fisher, L., Hayes, S., & O'Donohue, W. T. (Eds.). (2003). *Empirically supported techniques of cognitive-behavioral therapy: A step-by-step guide.* New York: Wiley.

Fonagy, P., Target, M., Cottrell, D., Phillips, J., & Kurtz, Z. (2002). *What works for whom: A critical review of treatments for children and adolescents.* New York: Guilford Press.

Freeman, C., & Power, M. (Eds.). (2006). *Handbook of evidence-based psychotherapies.* New York: Wiley.

Gambrill, E. (2006). *Critical thinking in clinical practice* (2nd ed.). New York: Wiley.

Gibbs, L. E., & Gambrill, E. (2002). Evidence-based practice: Counterarguments to objections. *Research on Social Work Practice, 12,* 452–476.

Gibbs, L. E. (2003). *Evidence-based practice for the helping professions: A practical guide with integrated multimedia.* Pacific Grove, CA: Brooks/Cole.

Gilgun, J. F. (2005). The four cornerstones of evidence-based practice in social work. *Research on Social Work Practice, 15,* 52–61.

Gira, E. C., Kessler, M. L., & Poertner, J. (2004). Influencing social workers to use research in practice: Lessons from medicine and the allied health professions. *Research on Social Work Practice, 14,* 68–80.

Gullota, T. P., & Blau, G. M. (2007). *Handbook of child behavioral issues: Evidence-based approaches to prevention and treatment.* New York: Routledge.

Gullota, T. P., & Bloom, M. (Eds.). (2003) *Encyclopedia of primary prevention and health promotion.* New York: Kluwer/Plenum.

Haynes, S. N., & O'Brien, W. H. (2000). *Principles and practice of behavioral assessment.* New York: Kluwer/Plenum.

Hersen, M. (2004). *Psychological assessment in clinical practice: A pragmatic guide.* New York: Brunner Routledge.

Hersen, M., & Bellack, A. S. (Eds.). (1999). *Comparative interventions for adult disorders.* Somerset, NJ: Wiley.

Hofmann, S. G., & Otto, M. W. (2007). *Cognitive-behavior therapy of social phobia: evidence-based and disorder specific treatment techniques.* New York: Routledge.

Hofmann, S. G., & Tompson, M. C. (Eds.). (2002). *Treating chronic and severe mental disorders: A handbook of empirically supported interventions.* New York: Guilford Press.

Howard, M. O., McMillen, C. J., & Pollio, D. E. (2003). Teaching evidence-based practice: Toward a new paradigm for social work education. *Research on Social Work Practice, 13,* 234–259.

Hunsley, J., Crabb, R., & Mash, E. J. (2004). Evidence-based clinical assessment. *Clinical Psychologist, 57,* 25–32.

Kazantis, N., & L'Abate, L. (Eds.). (2006). *Handbook of homework assignments in psychotherapy.* New York: Springer.

Kazdin, A. E. (2005). *Parent management training: Treatment for oppositional, aggressive, and antisocial behavior in children and adolescents.* New York: Oxford University Press.

Kazdin, A. E., & Weisz, J. R. (Eds.). (2003). *Evidence-based psychotherapies for children and adolescents.* New York: Guilford Press.

Kendall, P. C. (Ed.). (2005). *Child and adolescent therapy: Cognitive-behavioral procedures* (3rd ed.). New York: Guilford Publications.

Lambert, M. L. (Ed.). (2004). *Bergin and Garfield's handbook of psychotherapy and behavior change* (5th ed.). New York: Wiley.

Lambert, M. L., Whipple, J. L., Hawkins, E. J., Vermeersch, D. A., Nielson, S. L., & Smart, D. W. (2003). Is it time for clinicians to routinely track patient outcome? A meta-analysis. *Clinical Psychology: Science and Practice, 10,* 288–301.

Lambert, M. L., Whipple, J. L., Vermeersch, D. A., Smart, D. W., Hawkins, E. J., Nielson, S. L., & Goates, M. (2002). Enhancing psychotherapy outcomes via providing feedback on client progress: A replication. *Clinical Psychology and Psychotherapy, 9,* 91–103.

Lecroy, C. W. (Ed.). (2008). *Handbook of evidence-based treatment manuals for children and adolescents* (92nd ed.). New York: Oxford.

Levkoff, S. E.,et al. (2006). *Evidence-based behavioral health practices for older adults.* New York: Springer.

Liddle, H. A., Santisteban, D. A., Levant, R. F., & Bray, J. H. (Eds.). (2002). *Family psychology: Science-based interventions.* Washington, DC: APA.

Lipsey, M. W., & Wilson, D. B. (1993). The efficacy of psychological, educational, and behavioral treatment. *American Psychologist, 48,* 1181–1209.

Littel, J., Corcoran, J., & Pillai, V. (2008). *Systematic reviews and meta-analysis.* New York: Oxford.

Lopez, S. J., & Snyder, C. R. (Eds.). (2003). *Positive psychological assessment. A handbook of models and measures.* Washington, DC: APA.

Lyddon, W. J., & Jones, J. V. (Eds.). (2001). *Empirically supported cognitive therapies: Current and future applications.* New York: Springer.

Macdonald, G. (2001). *Effective interventions for child abuse and neglect: An evidence-based approach to planning and evaluating interventions.* New York: Wiley.

Macgowan, M. J. (2008). *A guide to evidence-based group work.* New York: Oxford.

Marlatt, G. A., & Donovan, D. M. (Eds.). (2005). *Relapse prevention: Maintenance strategies in the treatment of addictive behaviors* (2nd ed.). New York: Guilford.

Mash, E., & Barkeley, R. A. (Eds.). (2007). *Assessment of childhood disorders* (4th ed.). New York: Guilford.

Mash, E. J., & Barkeley, R. A. (2006). *Treatment of childhood disorders* (3rd ed.). New York: Guilford.

Mio, J. S., & Iwamasa, G. Y. (2003). *Culturally diverse mental health: The challenges of research and resistance.* New York: Brunner-Routledge.

Nathan, P. E., & Gorman, J. M. (Eds.). (2007). *A guide to treatments that work* (3rd ed.). New York: Oxford.

Norcross, J. C. (Ed.). (2002). *Psychotherapy relationships that work.* New York: Oxford University Press.

Norcross, J. C., et al. (2005). *Evidence-based practices in mental health: Debate and dialogue on the fundamental questions.* Washington, DC: American Psychological Association.

Norcross, J. C., & Hill, C. E. (2004). Empirically-supported therapy relationships. *Clinical Psychologist, 57,* 19–24.

O'Donohue, W., & Ferguson, K. E. (Eds.). (2003). *Handbook of professional ethics for psychologists: Issues, questions, and controversies.* Thousand Oaks, CA: SAGE.

O'Hare, T. (2005). *Evidence-based practices for social workers: An interdisciplinary approach.* Chicago: Lyceum Books.

Reiser, R. P., & Thompson, L. W. (2005). *Bipolar disorder: Advances in psychotherapy—evidence-based practice.* New York: Hogrefe & Huber.

Roberts, A. R., & Yeager, K. R. (Eds.). (2006). *Foundations of evidence-based practice in social work.* New York: Oxford.

Roberts, A. R., & Yeager, K. R. (Eds.). (2004). *Evidence-based practice manual: Research and outcome measures in health and human services.* New York: Oxford.

Rosqvist, J. (2005). *Exposure treatment for anxiety disorders: A practitioner's guide to concepts, methods, and evidence-based practice.* New York: Routledge.

Roth, A., & Fonagy, P. (Eds.). (2004). *What works for whom? A critical review of the psychotherapy research.* New York: Guilford.

Rubin, A. (2007). *Practitioner's guide to using research for evidence-based practice.* New York: Wiley.

Rygh, J. L., & Sanderson, W. C. (2004). *Treating generalized anxiety disorder: Evidence-based strategies, tools, and techniques.* New York: Guilford.

Sackett, D. L., Strays, S. E., Richardson, W. S., Rosenberg, W., & Haynes, R. B. (2000). *Evidence-based medicine: How to practice and teach EPB* (2nd ed.). New York: Churchill Livingstone.

Seligman, L. (2004). *Diagnosis and treatment planning in counseling* (3rd ed.). New York: Plenum.

Silverstein, S. M., et al. (2006). *Schizophrenia advances in psychotherapy—Evidence-based practice.* Ashland, OH: Hogrefe & Huber.

Stout, C. E., & Hayes, R. A. (Eds.). (2004). *The evidence-based practice: Methods, models, and tools for mental health professionals.* New York: Wiley.

Sue, D. W., & Sue, D. (2004). *Counseling the culturally diverse: Theory and practice.* New York: Wiley.

Thomlison, B., & Corcoran, K. (2008). *The evidence-based internship: A field manual.* New York: Oxford.

Thyer, B. A., & Wodarski, J. S. (Eds.). (1998). *Handbook of empirical social work practice: Mental disorders.* New York: Wiley.

Vance, H. B., & Pumariega, A. (Eds.) (2001). *Clinical assessment of child and adolescent behavior.* New York: Wiley.

VanHasselt, V., & Hersen, M. (Eds.) (1996). *Sourcebook of psychological treatment manuals for adult disorders.* New York: Plenum.

Wedding, D., et al. (Eds.). (2005). *Advances in psychotherapy: Evidence-based Practice.* (Book series.) Ashland, OH: Hogrefe & Huber.

Weisz, J. R., & Hawley, K. M. (1998). Finding, evaluating, refining, and applying empirically supported treatments for children and adolescents. *Journal of Clinical Child Psychology, 27,* 206–216.

Wodarski, J. S., & Thyer, B. A. (Eds.). (1998). *Handbook of empirical social work practice. Social problems and practice issues.* New York: Wiley.

Woody, S. A., Detweiler-Bedell, J., Teachman, B. A., & O'Hearn, T. (2003). *Treatment planning in psychotherapy: Taking the guesswork out of clinical care.* New York: Guilford.

Epilogue

Remember that schools and professions are subject to the same deadening forces that affect all other human institutions—an attachment to time-honored ways, reverence for established procedures, a preoccupation with one's own vested interests, and an excessively narrow definition of what is relevant and important. . . .
The peaks lie ahead of you, but whether you scale them depends on your own vision and boldness.
—John W. Gardner

The future ain't what it used to be.
—Yogi Berra

I hope when you read this epilogue you will understand what I meant in my introduction to the prologue when I said the article reprinted there, "Is Casework Effective?" was dear to my heart. Was it ever!

Reflections on Destroying Social Work

Ubi explorari vera non possunt,
Falsa per metum augentur.[1]
  —Quintus Curtius Rufus
  De Rebus Gestis Aleandri Magni

How naïve could I be? When I wrote "Is Casework Effective?" (Fischer, 1973a), I had no idea what I was doing.

O.K., that's not completely accurate. I *was* just a kid of thirty-two, fresh out of Berkeley a few years earlier with my social welfare doctorate. But I did know a little bit about research. And I did know that my goal in writing that article was to call the profession's attention to the issue of what were, to say the least, questionable, outcomes of research on the effectiveness of social work practice. And I was pretty sure that social work had yet to deliver any sound evaluations that reasonably could be used to provide evidence of effective practice.

But, hell, lots of social workers knew something about research. And others also had raised the issues of questionable outcomes (e.g., Mullen and Dumpson et al., 1972). And others before me also had stated that social work wasn't delivering, in a demonstrable way, on implicit and explicit promises to provide effective services (Briar, 1967). Why, around that time, Scott Briar, then of Berkeley, and soon to be dean at the University of Washington, even had dubbed that era "The Age of Accountability" (Briar, 1973). So, what, I reasoned, could possibly be *that* big of a deal about *my* review?

What I didn't know, though (and therefore hadn't counted on), was just how much and how many social workers *cared* about those issues. What I never would have believed, but perhaps should have known, was how personally my professional colleagues would take even hints that the field had not produced a single

Fischer, J. (2004). *Reflections, Winter,* 50–58. Reprinted with permission of *Reflections*.

[1] "When the truth cannot be clearly made out, what is false is increased through fear." I used this quote on the front page of *The Effectiveness of Social Casework* (Fischer, 1976). No one ever asked me what it meant.

study providing sound evidence of effectiveness. And what I was certainly unprepared for was the number of new, but refreshingly delightful, enemies I made just by publishing a review of research. Ah, those were the days, my friends. Those were the days.

Planting the Seeds (of Destruction?)

Then take him to develop, if you can
And hew the block off, and get out the man.
  —Alexander Pope
  Dunciad IV

I started my doctoral program at Berkeley as a twenty-seven-year-old, scared and quaky clinical social worker. I moved, in one day, from a V.A. clinical social work position in San Francisco with a staff of twenty-five women and one man (me) to the Berkeley doctoral program with a faculty of twenty-five men and one woman (Lydia Rapoport). It was for me, perhaps, simultaneously culture and gender shock. But I was exposed to great minds at Berkeley, talking about their books and other publications, and whose wealth of knowledge I thought I could never even *hope* to acquire; people like Scott Briar, Henry Miller, Henry Maas, Harry Specht, Neil Gilbert, Lydia Rapoport, and a bunch of others. (Intimidating, these folks, especially to a practitioner; no wonder I was so scared.)

I graduated three years later as a scared (and maybe scarred) DSW, scared because I wasn't sure if I knew as much as I hoped I knew. (I'm still scared about that because I found out I didn't and still don't!) But what I thought I *had* learned was a whole new way of approaching and thinking about my field: more analytic than simply accepting what the so-called experts said, more willing to ask tough questions and to try to find the answers to those questions. Somehow during that experience, I also started wondering, are we really doing everything we can in my beloved social work to provide the best possible help for our clients?

I'm not sure where that idea came from, but I spent my whole second year at Berkeley studying for the comprehensive exam at the end of the year (thinking at the same time that I was getting a brain tumor). No formal classes, just get ready for the exam! I started reading outside the literature of social work, primarily in clinical psychology and counseling (mental health and theories of psychotherapy were two of my three areas of specialization; the third was casework), and I was floored by the differences in the contents of our two fields. In clinical psychology and counseling, I was exposed to the work and research of Carl Rogers and his disciples, Truax and Carkhuff (1967). I read about the burgeoning behavior therapy/behavior modification movement and about cognitive therapy. I read Joseph Wolpe's (1969) book on systematic desensitization and assertion training. I read so many books, in fact, that my head was swimming. Most of all, I read study after study that showed that some interventions demonstrably were helping clients and that some interventions, especially the ones we used in social work, were not.

And I read social work literature, too. But where was the research on effectiveness? And where was the literature on the newest intervention approaches? I could find only Harold Werner's (1965) groundbreaking book on cognitive therapy and Ed Thomas' (1967) work at the University of Michigan on behavior modification, and only a tiny handful—actually, maybe just one, as I recall—of published articles at the time in the entire social work literature on behavior modification. How could that be? I couldn't understand why there was such a huge information gap between those fields and ours, especially since many of our clients were suffering from the same problems that other fields seemed to be successfully addressing. Where the heck was the social work research and literature on all these issues?

When I graduated from Berkeley, I really scored. The University of Hawaii, a little-known program floating out in the middle of the Pacific, made me an offer I couldn't refuse: an associate professorship right out of my doctoral program, after having taught only one course (a one-year casework class at Berkeley), and with my three years of clinical practice background. (I later learned it wasn't such a big honor. The University of Hawaii in those days really was hard up!)

I spent about a year wondering what I had gotten myself into, and then, serendipity hit. A colleague mentioned to me that a publisher's rep was in town and asked if I would like to meet with him to present any ideas I might have. Quickly, I decided I did, indeed, have an idea. I met with the publisher and told him that our field sorely needed an introduction to the literature of other fields that appeared to be having more success in dealing with client problems than we social workers were. We agreed that I would edit a book on those approaches, and for the next year I worked almost nonstop (no student assistants in those days) assembling material for that book, copying literally hundreds of articles from the literature for consideration (Fischer, 1973b).

I also wanted to see whether my assumptions about the lack of effectiveness research in social work were correct. So, as a sidelight, and with the help of a group of students, I went about trying to identify all the controlled studies I could find on the effectiveness of social work intervention. Again, this was purely a sidelight to what I really was concerned with: finding evidence of the most effective approaches to dealing with the problems with which we deal in social work, no matter what the professional source of that literature.

The Harvest

They have sown the wind,
And they shall reap the whirlwind.
   —Hosea VIII 7

My students and I found eleven controlled studies that evaluated the effectiveness of *any* form of social work, though they all referred to casework as the main intervention. (I later learned we missed a couple of studies; there weren't any online searches in those days.) We analyzed those studies to death. When I thought the results were worth publishing, I asked each of the students if they would like to work on publishing an article with me. They all said no; they were sick of the whole business, having worked on this project for a whole year. So, I set out to publish these results myself.

Here's what I concluded in the article "Is Casework Effective?" (Fischer, 1973a): there was not a single study of social work intervention available at the time that provided sound evidence of the effectiveness of any form of social work practice. Perhaps even more striking, I also found that in almost 50 percent of the studies, clients in experimental groups, all of whom were treated by MSW-level practitioners, actually did worse or changed more slowly on at least one measure than clients receiving no treatment or treatment by nonprofessionals. I called this the deterioration effect, in line with the same term used in the psychotherapy literature (Bergin, 1971).

So, what's such a big deal about that?

Reactions

The central finding of a social research study has a disturbing effect when at variance with commonly accepted values. For some, the finding then becomes a challenge to be disputed phrase by phrase; for others, a challenge to reexamine assumptions on which the values rest.
    —Gordon Brown
    The Multi-Problem Dilemma

"Their" Responses

You might've thought I had announced the end of the social work world! Indeed, I was told by some social workers many years later that that is exactly how they perceived it. One noted practitioner from the East Coast, who eventually became a good friend and actually ended up setting up a series of workshops for me in the 1980s, told me that she threw the journal across the room, yelling an unprintable "s-word" when she read the article. Another person, a social work professor at Columbia, after meeting me at a Council on Social Work Education (CSWE) Annual Program Meeting, invited me to do a presentation in her class. She told the class that she used to hate me. I received some delightful hate mail informing me that legislators in some states were using my article to justify the hiring of nonprofessionals rather than professional social workers since professionals do no better with their clients than nonprofessionals, "according to Fischer." Why not get the same terrible effects for less money? I guess this was the reasoning.

Most startling to me, though, were the *published* responses, such as in the letters to the editor in our most important journal, *Social Work*. Some were supportive, but most were, shall we say, unsupportive. These latter responses ranged from condemnations of me to condemnations of the research, from blatant defensiveness to outright hostility. Some were thoughtful, but many were ridiculous ("Other professions don't evaluate *their* practice, why should we evaluate ours?" "Social work doesn't have to be evaluated; we *know* it works!"). After the first shock of seeing all those responses in print, and knowing those authors were dead serious, I have to admit I started seeing the whole thing as almost a game, and a pretty hilarious one at that.

A few years later, while working on another review of research on the effectiveness of interventions in five fields—social work, corrections, psychotherapy and counseling, elementary and secondary education, and psychiatric hospitalization—I found that the results, with a few prominent exceptions, were similar across the board: replicated evidence of effectiveness was sorely lacking (Fischer, 1978a). More to the point, I also found that practitioners' reactions to reviews with negative findings were strikingly similar to the ones I had seen in social work. I could have removed the term social worker from all those responses and substituted teachers or psychologists and we wouldn't have missed a beat. I guess people are people, no matter what the professional label.

Several years after the "Is Casework Effective?" flap, Harvey Gochros, my friend and colleague at the University of Hawaii, who was the pioneer in bringing human sexuality content into the social work curriculum, said to me, "Well, anyone who knows about the University of Hawaii School of Social Work probably thinks that all we do is teach about sex and *how to destroy social work.*"

I'm not sure that some people *ever* forgave me for that paper. I was doing a keynote address at a conference in 1980; my paper was about the way social workers were addressing, and addressing positively in theory, research and practice, what many of us viewed as a crisis of confidence in the old intervention methods. (This paper was published later as "The Social Work Revolution" [Fischer, 1981, 1993]). I had provided a discussant with a copy of the paper in advance. When I finished, she stood up and spent thirty minutes denouncing me for "Is Casework Effective?"!

My Responses

> *Est proprium stultitiae aliorum vitia cernere, oblivisci suorum*[2]
> —Cicero
> *Tusculanarum Disputationum*

Continuing the "Destruction"   I couldn't resist. After reading those letters to the editor in *Social Work,* I wanted to write a response. But I wanted to do it a different way. I chose parody as the type of response that seemed to fit most readily with my perceptions of the whole experience. Remember, it was the early 1970s. Baseball was the national sport. Nixon was in trouble in the White House. So, I relied on both phenomena to write my favorite article of all time, including those written by everyone else, "Has Mighty Casework Struck Out?" (Fischer, 1973c). I

[2] "It is the peculiar quality of a fool to perceive the faults of others, and to forget his own."

can still remember sitting in my office in the oldest building of the University of Hawaii, trying to think up humorous ways to react to all the furor. I actually had an unindicted, coconspirator in there with me, a promising young faculty member named Stuart Kirk, now comfortably ensconced in a policy chair at UCLA. The two of us were howling as we put together, among other things, a list of sports-related depictions of some of the critical responses, for example, "The Manager's Motto" (Evaluations of Won-Lost records aren't necessary. Everyone knows the Players always Win. So why study the Game?). I even threw in a few veiled references to Nixon's troubles, talking about a "select committee of groundskeepers" (which was supposed to be a metaphor—or whatever you call it—for the Select Committee of U.S. senators that was investigating Nixon). Ha ha.

The editor of *Social Work,* my former professor Scott Briar, phoned to tell me that the journal was publishing my entire response, but that, and these were his exact words, "They're gonna kill you!" This was the first known threat on my life from my social work colleagues!

I must have thought at the time that this evaluation stuff was a productive side-line, so I decided to pursue it even further. Over the next couple of years, I found six more controlled studies, and thought that this whole issue might be worth a book. Publisher Charles C. Thomas thought so, too. So, I wrote one. While writing this piece, I went back and took a look at that book, *The Effectiveness of Social Casework* (Fischer, 1976). That book, in retrospect, was surprisingly good, if I do say so myself. And I do. The book reanalyzed—in depth—what turned out at that time to be seventeen controlled evaluations of social work effectiveness. The conclusions I drew were essentially the same as in the article: As of 1976, after conducting seventeen controlled evaluations of social work practice, there still were no studies—in the *history* of social work—that provided sound evidence of the effectiveness of any type of practice, and, now, *three quarters* of the studies, unfortunately, contained evidence of the deterioration of clients of professional social workers! I also explored a number of possible reasons for these results, including what I was convinced at the time and still am convinced today was a primary reason: the weak, vague, impotent, primarily psychodynamically-based interventions—if they even could be called interventions—that were the basis for almost all direct practice up to that time.

But that, in retrospect, wasn't what excited me most about that book. There were two *real* highlights of the book that I was most excited about. The first was that I sent the manuscript to some of the most prominent social work researchers, theorists, and practitioners of the time, each of whom wrote a chapter in response to my analyses. Some social work kids sadly may not recognize all of these names; they included William Berleman, Jerome Cohen, Harvey Gochros, Walter Hudson, Ed Mullen, Bernice Polemis, William Reid, Herb Strean, Eugene Talsma, Francis Turner, and Harold Werner. These were thoughtful, smart, and committed social workers; their responses, which varied across the entire range on the scale of agreement with my conclusions, are worth reading even today.

The most important long-term effect this book had on me was that many of those authors became my lifelong friends.

The second highlight of the book was one of those once-in-a-lifetime experiences. I decided to write the person whom I thought was the most prominent psychologist in the world, the best-known proponent of evaluation in the social sciences, and the person who, literally, started the accountability ball rolling by publishing the very first reviews on the effectiveness of psychotherapy, and ask him if he would write a foreword for my book. And he agreed! Hans J. Eysenck wrote a terrific four-page foreword; he and I even corresponded for a while on some of the issues in evaluation. This was new-social-work-faculty heaven for me.

That book received quite the reception from our field. There was a clause in the contract with the publisher that said that if the book didn't sell 2,000 copies in three years, I would not receive royalties. Three years and one month after publication, I got a letter from the publisher saying the book had sold 1,878 copies, thank you very much, so I would not be receiving any royalties. If only I had known; I would have bought those last, lousy 122 copies just to get the damn royalties.

Some years later, I came across the book in our university library when I was looking for something else. I pulled it from its hallowed slot and found that, in ten years, only two people had borrowed it.

Even More Constructive   I really took those negative findings from the evaluations of social work practice to heart. I essentially spent the biggest chunk of the rest of my career—and still focus on this issue in my teaching and writing—working on finding more effective and useful methods of evaluation and intervention compared to the largely ineffective methods of the past. And I think that, along with several hundred of my closest friends, I found an awful lot of them.

I view myself in a way that might be different from how some folks may view me based on my research publications. I really see myself as a practitioner who uses research to bolster practice rather than as a researcher interested in studying practice. Even today, when I teach research, I teach it from the perspective of practice. After all, what else is research for but to enhance practice?

So, since writing "Is Casework Effective?", my perhaps heavy-handed attempt to provide a wake-up call to the profession, virtually everything I've worked on has focused on ways to make life better for practitioners—and, ultimately, of course, for clients—whether the focus was on research/evaluation methods or intervention techniques of demonstrated effectiveness.

Since publication of that first edited book, calling attention to the literature from outside of social work (Fischer, 1973b), I have written books about behavior therapy (Fischer and Gochros, 1975), an eclectic approach to practice (Fischer, 1978b), a number of books with Harvey Gochros on intervention with problems involving human sexuality (e.g., Gochros and Fischer, 1980), a series of books with Martin Bloom and John Orme focused on teaching practitioners ways to evaluate their practice (e.g., Bloom, Fischer, and Orme, 2003), and a series with Kevin Corcoran on standardized measures that clinicians can use to aid in evaluating their practice (e.g., Corcoran and Fischer, 2000a, 2000b).[3]

I've also made numerous conference presentations around the United States and in other countries and conducted a number of workshops, all focused on new, more effective evaluation and intervention methods for social work practice.

All of this work has been geared toward finding empirically-based answers to the questions raised by the negative findings in "Is Casework Effective?"

But being asked to write an article by *Reflections* editor, Alex Gitterman, has raised a nagging question in my mind: If I were to croak tomorrow, would I still be largely remembered—if I'm remembered at all—as the guy who tried to destroy social work? Was it a mistake for me to write that article?

What's It All About, Joey?

The Moving Finger writes; and having writ,
Moves on; nor all your Piety nor Wit
  Shall lure it back to cancel half a Line,
Nor all your Tears wash out a word of it.
  —Omar Khayyam
  Rubaiyat

It's not how much you learn in life,
But how much of what you learn you understand.
  —J. Arthur
  Traveling Friends

After all these years, if I had it to do over again, would I change anything in "Is Casework Effective?" In general, I guess my answer is no. I believe it was the right, the *important,* thing to do at the time. I believed then, and I still believe now, that it is as important to know what *doesn't* work—so that we don't apply interventions to our clients that don't help, and may hurt—as it is to know what *does* work, so we can do in practice what we are supposed to do: *help.*

Oh, I might make a change or two in the contents of the article. For example, I know much more about research now then I did then, so I believe I could do better analyses of the studies than I did thirty years ago. And I *would* change one small part in the article that has bothered me, lo, these thirty years. In the article, I said that five out of eleven of the studies, just under 50 percent, showed evidence of the deterioration effect. In fact, I miscounted in the original article. (Are research teachers supposed to be able to count, too?) Actually *six* out of eleven, just *over* 50

---

[3] I hope readers will forgive all the self-referencing. First of all, I'm old, and old guys like to reminisce about what they've done. Second, I wanted to include citations to only the literature that wouldn't be critical of my work.

percent, showed evidence of the deterioration effect. (There, it's out. If this article did nothing else for me, it allowed me finally to correct that error.)

Publishing "Is Casework Effective?" and my response to the responses, "Has Mighty Casework Struck Out?" produced some heat all right, but I believe it opened up some incredible opportunities for me that never might have been available. Over the course of my career, I have been able to meet, and publish with, some of the most fantastic people and social work scholars that the field has ever seen. I'd like to drop a few names here (drum roll please): Stuart Kirk, Bob Weinbach, Henry Miller, Harvey Gochros, Jean Gochros, Oscar Kurren, the late Dan Sanders, Velma Kameoka, Chuck Mueller, Martin Bloom, John Orme, Walter Hudson (whose recent death is a huge loss for me personally and for social work), Charles Glisson, and the irrepressible Kevin Corcoran.

I want to tell you two things about these people. First, writing with them not only did not create any break-ups among us (not uncommon among people who write, work, or live together), but I count all of these people as truly good friends.

The second thing about these authors that I want you to know is that I taught them everything they know. This may account for any shoddiness that may creep into their work on very rare occasions.

I also want to acknowledge a number of other friends whom I believe writing "Is Casework Effective?" helped me meet. Unfortunately, I haven't actually written with these social work scholars, but I *have* freely plagiarized their work over the years, and I guess it's time to 'fess up: Tony Tripodi, Ed Mullen, Alex Gitterman, the late Scott Briar, Bruce Thyer, Allen Rubin, Frank Turner, and the late, great Bill Reid.

I've been incredibly lucky. Publishing that article thirty years ago has been very good to me; I only hope it was good for our profession, as well.

I believe the field of social work practice is in far sounder condition today than it was thirty years ago. In those days, we could point to the *problems* in the field, but we hadn't discovered, and certainly had not institutionalized, very many of the answers. Today, social work practitioners have the opportunity to learn evidence-based practice, with many of our interventions soundly based in empirical evidence. This has been a momentous, perhaps paradigmatic, change for the field.

I'm not sure about the extent to which "Is Casework Effective?" played a part in the changes in social work practice. I believe that, in life, timing is everything. Maybe I just rode the crest of a new wave that would have crashed on our professional shore anyway. But what a ride! What a rush!

Whether these changes would have occurred evolutionarily without a nudge from me is not for me to say. But changes for the better (helping clients more effectively) *have* occurred in our field, and I'm just happy to be a part of them. I certainly can say now, thirty years later, that to the best of my knowledge, social work was not destroyed by publication of that article.

Actually, one of the nicest compliments I ever received came recently from one of social work's most prolific scholars. Bruce Thyer recently told me that when he read "Is Casework Effective?" back in 1973, he experienced an epiphany. Could an author ask for anything more?

References

Bergin, A. E. (1971). The evaluation of therapeutic outcomes. In A. E. Bergin & S. L. Garfield (Eds.), *Handbook of psychotherapy and behavior change: An empirical analysis*. New York: Wiley.

Bloom, M., Fischer, J., & Orme, J. (2003). *Evaluating practice: Guidelines for the accountable professional*. Boston: Allyn and Bacon.

Briar, S. (1967). The current crisis in social casework. In *Social Work Practice*. New York: Columbia.

Briar, S. (1973). The age of accountability. *Social Work, 8,* 2–14.

Corcoran, K. and Fischer, J. (2000a). *Measures for clinical practice. Vol. 1: Couples, families, and children*. New York: Free Press.

Corcoran, K., and Fischer, J. (2000b). *Measures for clinical practice. Vol. 2: Adults*. New York: Free Press.

Fischer, J. (1973a). Is casework effective? A review. *Social Work, 18,* 5–21.

Fischer, J. (1973b). *Interpersonal helping: Emerging approaches for social work practice*. Springfield, IL: Charles C Thomas.

Fischer, J. (1973c). Has mighty casework struck out? *Social Work, 18,* 107–110.

Fischer, J. (1976). *The effectiveness of social casework*. Springfield, IL: Charles C Thomas.

Fischer, J. (1978a). Does anything work? *Journal of Social Service Research, 1,* 215–243.

Fischer, J. (1978b). *Effective casework practice: An eclectic approach*. New York: McGraw-Hill.

Fischer, J. (1981). The social work revolution. *Social Work, 26,* 199–209.

Fischer, J. (1993). Empirically-based practice: The end of ideology? *Journal of Social Service Research, 15,* 19–64.

Fischer, J., & Gochros, H. (1975). *Planned behavior change: Behavior modification in social work*. New York: Free Press.

Gochros, H., & Fischer, J. (1980). *Treat yourself to a better sex life*. Englewood Cliffs, NJ: Prentice-Hall.

Mullen, E., & Dumpson, J., et al. (1972). *Evaluation of social interventions*. San Francisco: Jossey-Bass.

Thomas, E. J. (1967). *The socio-behavioral approach and applications to social work*. New York: CSWE.

Truax, C. B., & Carkhuff, R. R. (1967). *Toward effective counseling and psychotherapy*. Chicago: Aldine.

Werner, H. D. (1965). *A rational approach to social casework*. New York: Association Press.

Wolpe, J. (1969). *The practice of behavior therapy*. New York: Pergamon.

Appendices

Those are my principles. If you don't like them . . . well, I have others.
—Groucho Marx

The two Appendices contain some material that I hope will be useful for you, whether you are faculty, students, or practitioners. These appendices focus very specifically on learning some of the most important skills for practice.

Appendix A is titled "A Model for Learning the Core Conditions." In this material, I present a course/workshop that I developed to be used for teaching students and practitioners how to communicate higher levels of empathy, warmth, and genuineness. Research on lab courses such as this probably produces the most consistent positive outcomes in social work education (Wodarski, 1986). The exercises are quite explicit, and the overall results that lead to practitioners being able to communicate higher levels of these conditions are very encouraging in attempting to build an evidence-based approach in social work education.

The second appendix contains a number of flowcharts that I developed to help in my teaching of specific intervention techniques. I briefly introduced these flowcharts and described their use and advantages in chapter 13, "Eclectic Casework." These flowcharts of specific intervention techniques and programs mainly were developed to be consistent with the book I was using at the time to teach practice, *Interviewing Strategies for Helpers* (Cormier & Cormier, 1985), although some of the flowcharts were not addressed in that book. I sincerely hope, once again, that these techniques will prove useful to those readers who are committed to developing evidence-based practice as part of their personal approach and commitment to practice.

References

Cormier, W. H., & Cormier, S. (1985). *Interviewing strategies for helpers* (2nd ed.). Monterey, CA: Brooks/Cole.

Wodarski, J. S. (1986). *An introduction to social work education.* Springfield, IL: Charles C. Thomas.

Appendix A
A Model for Training and Learning the Core Conditions

Most approaches to therapeutic practice are rather interesting. They may be well written, even poetic; they may use abstract, flowing concepts that sound important; they may even, on rare occasions, offer something that the practitioner can actually do. There almost always appears to be "something" in every approach that seems worthy of consideration for adoption into practice by someone, even if that "something" resides only in the reputation of a theorist.

The approach involving the core conditions, however, offers substantially more than an "interesting" perspective on practice. It contains, in the first place, one of the two key elements essential for adoption in practice: its use demonstrably leads to effectiveness in work with clients.

But without the second key element, such an approach still might be only of minimal value. The second element is presentation of the approach in such a way that it can be successfully learned by practitioners. There would be little utility, except perhaps in the *selection* of candidates for professional degrees, in knowing that high levels of the core conditions lead to effective practice if there were no way to train practitioners to achieve higher levels. Otherwise, the vast majority of the profession would be condemned to watching those few individuals fortunate enough to have been exposed to positive developmental circumstances conduct all or most of the profession's most important business—helping our clients.

This appendix presents part of the basis for the second key factor in considering adoption of the core conditions for practice—a methodology and principles and procedures for training and learning the core conditions. The purposes of this appendix are threefold:

1. This description, it is hoped, can serve as a stimulus for adapting such a training model to the curricula of schools of social work. By providing some educational principles and concrete procedures, the model can be considered illustrative of a particular approach to education in one area of practice

Fischer, J. (1978). *Effective Casework Practice: An Eclectic Approach*. New York: McGraw-Hill. Reprinted with permission of McGraw-Hill.

and may be used in whole or in a revised form to serve the particular needs of a given instructor, school, or group of students.

2. This model may prove helpful in the stimulation of ideas and content for the development and presentation of continuing education workshops and in-service training programs to enhance the interpersonal skills of social workers already in practice.

3. Finally, because the model is a training and *learning* model, it is intended to provide some guidelines or checkpoints for practitioners or students not involved in courses focused on the core conditions as a means of helping them evaluate and enhance their own interpersonal skills. To this end, following each section of the training model, per se, a summary of objectives is presented regarding what one should know in relation to the training material covered in that section. These summaries are provided as much as possible in practice-oriented terms to provide additional and specific guidelines for self-instruction. (One approach to self-instruction utilizing this model would be to make audiotapes of role playing or actual interviews and then to evaluate them against the specific objectives described in this appendix.)

The approach described here is modified from the work of several authors concerned with teaching the core conditions (Truax & Carkhuff, 1967; Carkhuff, 1969a, 1971; Sydnor et al., 1972, 1973, combined and integrated with the work called "microcounseling" by Ivey, 1971). This approach has been utilized in a number of different ways by the author: as part of a graduate course in general social work practice, as part of an advanced graduate course in social casework, by itself as an elective graduate course in the social work curriculum, as a continuing education course, and as a short-term workshop in a variety of settings. The length of time for this training approach has varied from eighteen to sixty hours. While the complete experience is designed for a sixty-hour period (four hours per week in a fifteen-week academic semester), the time variations of necessity have produced variations in the content of training. Hence, what is presented in this appendix really is the model—the guide or standard against which adaptations are made. Finally, this training approach has been used with nonprofessionals, workers with and without bachelor degrees, undergraduate students, graduate social work students, graduate students from other fields (e.g., educational psychology), and practicing professionals including M.S.W. social workers, nurses, psychologists, and psychiatrists.

Again, it is important to emphasize that the approach is not presented here as the last word in training. Instead, it is intended as a model, a plan that can be modified or adapted as the situation demands. However, it should be pointed out that the model described here does incorporate most of the basic aspects of training for the core conditions derived in as systematic and logical a way as possible from previous work, including research, on this subject. It does not sacrifice arbitrarily what previous research and experience have suggested might be important segments of the training. On the other hand, if this model were to be applied or adopted indiscriminately by others whose style and/or knowledge is considerably at variance with some of the material described here, the training experience would likely be less effective. In these cases, one hopes that at least part of the material can be adapted perhaps to fit in with training in related areas that already is ongoing. However, it should also be noted that other approaches to this type of training are available (e.g., Bullmer, 1975; Danish & Hauer, 1973; Egan, 1975a, 1975b), some of which the learner or teacher may find more compatible.

Basic Principles of Effective Training and Learning

Several basic principles underlie and provide direction for the actual training activities. These principles cut across all aspects and phases of the experience, and their implementation, through the training procedures, furnishes the core of the educational experience (see also Carkhuff, 1969a, 1969b).

Principle 1: Effective Training and Learning Operate Through a Focus on the Scales Measuring Empathy, Warmth, and Genuineness

The scales measuring the core conditions made possible the extensive research on effectiveness and also are the central focus of training. This might seem an obvious principle, but actually, at times, it is difficult to maintain. Students (or trainees or participants) often want to explore the use of a variety of techniques for helping people, e.g., interpretation, clarification, ventilation. However, as noted in the Introduction, there is little or no evidence that differential use of such verbal techniques is related to effectiveness. Thus, what is focused on in the training is not so much specific use of given techniques, or even any of the numerous interviewing skills on which other training programs focus *independent* of empathy, warmth, and genuineness, but communication of the core conditions in a variety of ways, depending on the problem and situation. Different techniques may be used, but their significance, at least for this training, is not emphasized.

Similarly, students often display a tendency to want to learn everything there is to know about clinical practice in this one experience ("O.K., I'm warm; now what do I do?"). There are frequent questions about use of behavior modification, problem-solving processes, and other "action" approaches. Where possible, such questions are dealt with, often in the context of suggesting the importance of the core conditions as a way of geometrically increasing the potency of whatever procedures are under discussion. But, again, this is not intended as a total curriculum in therapeutic practice. It is a course in the core ingredients of therapeutic practice, with important implications for the use of other approaches. And it is a course based on research showing that the core conditions are related to effective practice—predictive of success in helping clients. Thus, the focus, and the final reference for this training, including the interviewing skills that *are* provided, are the scales measuring the core conditions not so much as ends in themselves or the "last word" but as means for facilitating whatever measures the student eventually does take in work with clients.

Principle 2: Effective Training and Learning Operate from a Didactic Base

This program emphasizes the setting of structured, operational goals toward which the student can move in a step-by-step way. Further, there is a clear basis in research for the training which the instructor (or teacher or trainer) can and should transmit to students. The core conditions are presented through readings, discussions, and listening to tapes. The instructor is called upon not only to be thoroughly grounded in this literature, but to be familiar with a range of potential preferred modes of helping. Students are helped to develop an intellectual understanding of material presented in class.

Principle 3: Effective Training and Learning Operate from an Experiential Base

Students in the course are *involved* in what they are doing through a series of structured exercises. Perhaps the most important of these is role playing, which is intended not only to implement the learning of the core conditions, but to enable the student to actually *experience* what it means to be the client as well as the practitioner. The focus of the course is on *doing*, actual practice by students of what they are learning. When blocks in learning (or teaching) are reached, these problems and corresponding feelings are discussed as openly as possible. Through this experiencing, the student becomes more and more deeply involved in the process. The student also is able to experiment with different modes of functioning, to practice their communication, and to experience being the recipient of different modes of communication.

Principle 4: Effective Training and Learning Operate from a Base in Modeling

A key ingredient of training involves the modeling of the instructor. The instructor sets the atmosphere for the training experience—one of personalness, openness, and spontaneity. The instructor strives to provide high levels of the core conditions to the students—training can be only as effective as the instructor is effective. If the instructor provides low levels of the core conditions, the students likely will end with low levels of the core conditions (Carkhuff, 1969a, 1969b). If the instructor provides high levels, the students will tend to end with higher levels. These conclusions have been clearly validated in research examining the relationships between instructor level of empathy, warmth, and genuineness and the outcome of training (Carkhuff, 1969a, 1969b).

Beyond the provision of high levels of the core conditions throughout the course, the instructor is called upon to demonstrate ways of handling a variety of problems and situations. Students, especially at first, will tend to imitate the instructor's methods. If these methods are effective, students will tend to learn effective methods. If the instructor is an effective person, students will tend to become more effective people. The basis for the significant amount of learning in life that occurs through modeling is well established in research (Bandura, 1969). Used intentionally and systematically here, it can prove a key ingredient in developing more effective practitioners. The processes of effective training and effective helping are likely the same. This course is an attempt to illustrate that.

Principle 5: Effective Training and Learning Operate Through a Series of Small Steps

The whole course or training experience is organized on the basis of moving from small, very simple steps to increasingly complex ones. Thus, each early phase of the course is intended to deal with only one aspect of the total process of the communication of empathy, warmth, and genuineness. Similarly, within phases, where possible, each is broken down into small units, which are practiced until accomplished (the proximal goal is reached), and then the next unit is attempted.

This process is akin to the behavioral procedure of shaping through use of successive approximations, as described and implemented in the training program for therapeutic practice, microcounseling (Ivey, 1971). In terms of the course on the core conditions, specific goals are established dealing with concrete, operationalized units of student behavior, each of which is a step on the continuum leading to the terminal goal. Each unit is then practiced in the context of high levels of the core conditions, modeling, and extensive use of positive reinforcement from the instructor. When one step is accomplished, the next step is begun. This focus on specific skills not only keeps students from being overwhelmed by the overall experience, but allows them to practice and demonstrate each skill, and also allows for the clear evaluation of whether each specific goal was accomplished.

Principle 6: Effective Training and Learning Operate Through Feedback

Crucial to this conception of the educational process is the use of feedback for specific performances by the student. This feedback is from three sources: (a) peers, (b) the instructor, and (c) the students themselves. This feedback provides students with a picture of their own behavior and its consequences on others. Centered around the scales, the feedback includes not only consistent ratings of the levels of the core conditions at which students are operating, but specific suggestions from others as to how to improve performance. The focus of the feedback as much as possible is positive—i.e., on what to do, and reinforcing efforts in that direction, rather than negative, dwelling on the student's faults. A range of media is used for providing this feedback and hence the student's own self-evaluation. Particularly heavy use of audio and videotape recording of role-played interviews and comments from observers are used for this purpose. Such feedback is intended to ensure that students continue to learn more effective ways of communicating the core conditions.

Principle 7: Effective Training and Learning Operate Through the Creation of Enjoyable Experiences

A primary principle of effective training is that it can be, and should be, fun. The instructor works toward establishing an enjoyable atmosphere in relationships with individual students and the group as a whole. Lighthearted jokes and a good sense of humor help make many of the more difficult exercises move quickly. Further, there is an attempt to keep any specific exercise from becoming boring. If it does, the instructor should move on to another exercise, mixing and interchanging those activities where this can be done without destroying the step-by-step sequence of the total program.

Principle 8: Effective Training and Learning Operate Through Helping Students Develop Their Own Style

The principle involving the modeling base of training suggests that students tend to imitate the instructor's methods of communicating the core conditions. This is particularly so at the beginning of training. And, of course, the job of the instructor is to help students develop a range of alternatives for responding to different problems and situations. But the goal of this course at completion is to provide a framework for the students to learn and display the core conditions using any techniques or in the context of any personal style with which they are compatible. This is the heart of the course. The goal is to shape students not to be walking, talking (and unthinking) images of the instructor, but to be able to use what the instructor offers in personally meaningful ways.

The issue of students' "real selves" often is presented in class. A student might complain, "But I'm not really that way, that isn't me talking. I don't communicate that way." Such a position implies that people actually have "real selves," some sort of concrete, living entities within themselves that have been present since birth and are immutable. But the purpose of the course is to modify the behaviors of the students. The training operates on the basis that much of what we are, much of how we communicate (even including the tone of one's voice) is learned and can be unlearned and relearned, just as the core conditions themselves are considered learned interpersonal skills. Further, it is clear that people act and behave differently in different situations and in different roles—parent, spouse, friend, teacher, caseworker, client, patient, shopper, etc.—all of which can be, and in fact are, "real" ways of relating. The course merely provides one more aspect of, or adds another dimension to, being real.

Principle 9: Effective Training and Learning Operate Through a Focus on Client Self-Exploration and Action

The communication of empathy, warmth, and genuineness, while centered on what the client says, feels, and wants, is more easily learned when the student is given some framework for his or her provision of the core conditions. This is intended to help students deal with the question of: "To what *end* does one provide the core conditions," or, "What do we *do* with all that warmth?" The framework has to be broad enough to allow the flexibility necessary to meet variations in clients, problems, and situations, yet specific enough to give the student something concrete to work with. Further, the framework should not be derived from one theoretical orientation, with all the inherent biases implied thereby. And finally, such a framework should be only a general guide, so that the student/helper does not take total responsibility for deciding what areas to work on, but rather will use the framework as a guide in working on what the *client* wants to do.

The framework, actually, has its roots in research, a range of theoretical propositions, extensive practice experience, and "common sense." The model for practice was described as having four parts: experiencing and exploration; understanding and defining; action; and goal attainment and evaluation. For the purpose of providing a concrete focus for training in the core conditions, these parts are summarized into two categories. First, the student is helped to focus on client self-exploration, a dimension that some studies have demonstrated is related to successful outcome. Thus, the general emphasis of the communication of the core conditions is presented as helping clients explore and understand themselves and their problem(s), and the interrelationships between the two. A five-point scale measuring depth of client self-exploration, which has been associated in research with positive outcome (Carkhuff, 1969b) is used for measuring this dimension.

The second focal point of communication of the core conditions is to help clients act on their understanding. Obviously, the whole purpose of any helping process is to enable people to do things differently from the ways they did them before, ways that previously were unsatisfactory. Such action is influenced by the worker's use of any number of behavior change procedures, most of which are not the subject of this course. However, the overall process that *is* included in the course, and which serves to provide sufficient focus to allow development of skills in communicating the core conditions, involves teaching students to help clients describe their problem area as fully as possible, develop goals to overcome the problems, consider alternative courses of action for achieving the goals, and discuss the development of a program for achieving the goals. In fact, "action" can consist of any number of different options, including simply the type of worker response that searches for and develops lines of inquiry that ultimately offer the client the promise of direction (Carkhuff, 1969a).

These two focal points, again, are used to facilitate learning the communication of empathy, warmth, and genuineness. Correspondingly, in actual practice, communication of empathy, warmth, and genuineness is used to facilitate self-exploration and action. (The many other potential areas for therapeutic focus, as well as the other possible explanations for the success of communicating high levels of the core conditions, were discussed previously.) For purposes of the course designed specifically to train the core conditions, this model is oversimplified. But it does provide sufficient focus for students to learn more effective ways of human relating.

Principle 10: Effective Training and Learning Operate by Providing a Range of Experiences

This principle is implemented at several levels. There are, of course, the didactic and experiential bases of training, the affective and cognitive involvement, the empirical and practical experiences, the use of a variety of media, experiences as client and worker, and the discussion of a variety of aspects of therapeutic practice in the context of the core conditions. In addition, the instructor offers a number of alternatives for dealing with clients and problems of various types. A wide range of problems and situations is utilized in the role playing, affording each student the opportunity to respond with increasing flexibility as the situation demands.

Principle 11: Effective Training and Learning Operate Through an Evaluation of Results

In addition to the ongoing evaluation of, and feedback on, student behaviors, an overall evaluation of the results of training is conducted each time the course is offered. This consists of rating student levels of communication of the core conditions both before and after training (see Fischer, 1974a and 1975c for reports of such an evaluation).

Phases of Training

There are five basic phases of the training experience, leading from introductory and largely didactic material to increasingly complex and experiential exercises. Indeed, the phases of training largely parallel the stages of the conceptual model presented earlier, in fact, operationalize the stages of the model. Later phases of training are built upon earlier phases, and, whenever possible, the relationship between one phase and another (or between steps within a phase) is pointed out. Everything is intended to be "out on the table"; each phase is explained to the students as clearly as possible, including the background, purpose, and activities that will be carried out. Each step or exercise is also explained and discussed prior to its inception, with the instructor demonstrating by role playing with students examples of what will be occurring. This type of format is carried out through the entire process with the instructor role playing any situations with which students are having trouble. Care is taken to be specific about what the course is (a training experience in communicating the core conditions) and what the course is not (a sensitivity or encounter group). Since, obviously, there is enough involved in the training process to fill at least another book in itself, what will be presented here is an outline of the phases, with brief descriptions of the steps and activities that are carried out within each phase. Each of the steps is not actually a discrete unit; i.e., there is frequent overlap between activities carried out in one step and activities in the next steps, where such overlap does not detract from the activities in the subsequent step.

Phase 1: Introduction

Step 1: Overview   The instructor presents a brief overview of the purpose of the course and some of its basic features, e.g., the step-by-step learning plan. A cursory description of the core conditions and their importance to successful practice is presented. The basic ground rules of the course are discussed, including use of first names, breaks, attendance, grading procedures (where necessary), and the informal nature of the proceedings.

Step 2: Assignments   Two books, *Beyond Counseling and Therapy* (Carkhuff & Berenson, 1977) and *Toward Effective Counseling and Psychotherapy* (Truax & Carkhuff, 1967), and one article, "Research on Certain Therapist Interpersonal Skills in Relation to Process and Outcome" (Truax & Mitchell, 1971), are suggested as introductory readings so that students can become familiar with the theory and research undergirding the course.

Copies of the scales measuring empathy, warmth, and genuineness (from Truax & Carkhuff, 1967) are distributed. Students are requested to study these intensively since they will be used repeatedly throughout the course.

Students are asked to make fifteen to thirty minute audiotape recordings—either role playing or of actual interviews with clients if the students are in practice—in which they "do their best" to help the client with whatever problem(s) are presented. (Interestingly, in several years of ratings, no consistent differences between ratings of role-played and actual interviews by the same person have emerged.) These tapes are then collected by the instructor at the following session and held until the beginning of phase III.

During the second class session each student conducts (with another student as "client") a five-minute videotaped interview during which the instructions again are to "do their best" to help their pseudo-client. These videotaped interviews are held until the end of the course when they are shown with a videotape made at that point to compare both verbal and nonverbal changes occurring over the period of the course.

Supplementary assignment is made of several prepackaged tapes by experienced counselors and therapists to give the students additional experience in rating tapes on the core conditions and to listen to and evaluate a broader range of techniques and interviewing skills.

Students are assigned a programmed manual, developed by Sydnor et al., 1973. This manual provides an excellent basic introduction to, and understanding of, the material to be covered in class. Its contents range from basic conceptions of the core conditions and ratings exercises to some 400 client statements which provide the student with an opportunity to respond and compare his or her responses with those of experienced helpers. This workbook is to be completed by the start of phase III of training.

Step 3: Warm-up   Following discussion of whatever questions students have about readings and assignments, a brief series of warm-up and introductory exercises is conducted (usually during the second or third session). In these exercises, students are arbitrarily divided into two circles, one standing inside the other. The instructor suggests several story lines which are to be acted out in (roughly) two-minute skits. First one and then the other group circles around the room, and when the instructor calls, "Stop!," individuals from one circle select a partner and proceed to act out their skits. Five or six "plots" are used in this session, with varying content (e.g., one story line consists of two old friends who have not seen each other for fifteen years meeting in a museum and filling each other in on the events of the past years as they become reacquainted). This exercise almost always produces a very relaxed and informal tone in the group.

The instructor then presents a more in-depth picture of himself or herself—interests, activities, family life, etc. This introduction originally was carried out during the first session, but students seemed far more receptive to it following the warm-up exercise. The instructor here attempts to set the atmosphere for the course by modeling a personal, informal, open attitude toward the class.

Students are then asked to introduce themselves and tell whatever they consider relevant about their participation in the class.

Step 4: The Model   An overview of the integrative model is presented. The material on client self-exploration is explained in detail as the first part of the model, followed by client understanding and definition of himself or herself and the problem, followed by the development and exploration of personally meaningful courses of action, whether this be in terms of the development of actual programs or the pointing out and exploration of new and more meaningful directions of inquiry, followed by the evaluation of outcome. Indeed, the learning experience in this course itself is used as an illustration and operationalization of the model of helping skills presented in Egan (1975a) and Carkhuff & Berenson (1977) in which attending (learning to attend in order to involve) → responding (learning to respond in order to explore) → personalizing (learning to personalize for understanding and defining) → initiating (learning to initiate for action). Hence, in the experiential model for training and learning described here, phases I and II provide the skills that compose the attending stage; phase III provides the skills for the exploration (responsive) stage: phase IV provides skills for the understanding/defining (personalizing) stage; and, with considerable overlap from the previous phases, phase V provides some basic skills and an introduction to the activities of the action (initiative) stage of the model.

Summary of Objectives, Phase I   The material presented in this phase should help the learner become familiar with and knowledgeable about:

1. The theory and research underlying the core conditions.
2. The scales of empathy, warmth, and genuineness themselves.
3. Some basic therapeutic responses to a range of client problems/statements based on the programmed manual (Sydnor et al., 1973).

4. A range of different interviewing styles learned from listening to some of the prepackaged tapes.
5. Basic concepts involved in the integrative model.

For actual participants in the course or training session, there also should be a beginning degree of comfort and familiarity with each other and with the instructor.

Phase II: Basic Interviewing Skills (Attending)

The second phase of training consists of a series of exercises intended to provide students with basic interviewing skills, which are used as a foundation for training in the core conditions. The length of this phase can vary with the skills of the students involved; this determination can be made as training progresses. It should be noted that the length of prior experience in actual practice frequently is not related to the skills demonstrated by students in this or other phases of the course. In fact, extensive practice experience often appears to be as much a dysfunctional factor in the development of facilitative practice skills (due perhaps to repeated experience with the same inappropriate skills) as it is a constructive factor in the development of effective practice methodologies. In other words, experience in itself is not the criterion for deciding whether to abbreviate any of the phases of training since experienced practitioners often are as much, or even more, in need of training in the core conditions as individuals with little or no actual practice experience. What ultimately counts is the *quality* of any individual's experience, not the length.

At the start of each session, once the actual experiential training in phase II has begun, students pair off and interview each other for roughly five minutes (plus feedback), practicing the skills learned in earlier sessions. This is an attempt to keep these skills in focus, reinforce their use, and build a cumulative effect into the training.

Step 1: Attending Behavior Paying close attention to another person indicates respect and a feeling that what he or she has to say is important. This exercise helps students concentrate on their own attending behavior.

First, students are divided into dyads, and a series of exercises, derived from Pfeiffer and Jones (1971), is utilized to illustrate the problem of nonattending behavior. First, one student (A) in each dyad is told to do nothing, i.e., whatever he does when he thinks he is doing nothing. The other student (B) observes A for thirty seconds, then tells A what A communicated. Then B is instructed to speak to, but not look at, A for thirty seconds. Then A discusses how he felt about B's behavior. Next, A speaks to B but B (the *listener*) does not look at A at all while A speaks. A's responses are elicited. Finally, B speaks to A, and A looks occasionally at B. Then B's reactions to A's (the listener's) partial attention are elicited.

Several specific aspects of attending behavior, which have been validated in research as contributing to effective interviewing (see, e.g., Dittman et al., 1965;

Ellsworth & Carlsmith, 1968; Mehrabian, 1969a, 1969b; Reece & Whitman, 1962; plus studies discussed below), are practiced in this exercise: (a) Maintaining good eye contact; (b) maintaining a relaxed, natural, comfortable posture, (c) leaning slightly toward the other person; (d) using appropriate and congruent facial expressions; (e) using relaxed, spontaneous head, arm, and body movements; and (f) using friendly greetings. (Related to this, students are also encouraged to see that the client is sitting in as comfortable a place as possible, that the discussion takes place in a quiet and private area, and that there is no desk or similar obstruction between the client and worker.) As with all exercises, the instructor models different attending behaviors and has the group comment. Also as with all exercises, the instructor uses as much positive social reinforcement (e.g., praise) as possible for appropriate student responses. The class is divided into groups of three with one person role playing the "worker," one the "client," and one serving as an observer to provide feedback. Each exercise is, of course, rotated so that all participants have an equal chance at functioning in every role. (Except where otherwise noted, this format of groups of three with rotation of worker-client-observer roles is followed. It is also possible to use dyads, but generally, the person in the client role, perhaps because of involvement in that role, provides less accurate feedback than the third-person observer.) The worker and client carry on a brief conversation on a topic of their own choosing (i.e., at this point, it need not be problem-focused), after which the worker is provided feedback on several dimensions of his or her attending behavior. A useful checklist for providing this feedback is available in Danish and Hauer (1973, pp. 19–20). This checklist contains thirty-two specific items of attending behavior and is very helpful in adding specificity to the feedback.

This step, focusing for the most part on the "worker's" nonverbal behavior, is an important component of the course and is emphasized throughout. The main reason for this emphasis is that several studies have demonstrated nonverbal behavior to be a crucial component of peoples' perceptions of such dimensions as empathy, warmth, and genuineness and of judgments as to which therapists appear to be most expert and most helpful (Strong et al., 1971; Haase & Tepper, 1972; Shapiro et al., 1968; Schmidt & Strong, 1970; Shapiro, 1968). Indeed, it is likely that a large part of empathy, warmth, and genuineness is communicated through nonverbal behavior (Shapiro et al., 1968), although judgments made from audiotapes are correlated with those based on audio *and* visual media and are thereby a reasonable abstraction of the therapeutic process for both evaluative and training purposes (Shapiro, 1968). However, it appears that a more comprehensive and more accurate picture is derived when the helping person can be both seen and heard. Particularly for training purposes, it is crucial to maintain a consistent focus on nonverbal behaviors at the same time that appropriate verbal behaviors are being taught.

Step 2: Body Language   Although most of the course deals with verbal activity, nonverbal cues, as demonstrated in body language, play an important part in understanding other people's communications. Gestures, expressions, posture, all can convey a variety of meanings. Being able to read body language can help the student in any number of ways: (a) in helping another begin to talk, (b) when a person has not spoken for some time, (c) in noting discrepancies between a person's speech and appearance, and (d) in evaluating the impact on the client of what the worker says (Sydnor et al., 1973).

The exercise used to work on skills at reading body language was adapted from Longfellow (1970). Students are divided into small groups of five or six. Several "feeling words" are selected (e.g., joy, depression, shyness, anxiety), and each student writes one of these words on four cards. Each of the four cards also contains either the term "hand," "head," or "full body." All the cards for each group are then shuffled and dealt, with at least three or four placed face down in the center. Then each member of the group selects a card and attempts to act out the emotion in body language as instructed, using only a hand, head, or the full body. The remainder of the group attempts to identify the emotion by placing a card expressing the similar emotions face down in front of them (those without similar cards, or who are unsure, can pass). After the "expresser" tells what emotion he or she was trying to express, those who identified it correctly place their similar cards at the bottom of the deck. Those who were wrong return their own cards to their hand and draw another card from the deck. The first person to run out of cards "wins" (elaborations of the game are available in the original reference). This exercise is continued until group members are competent in recognizing a variety of emotions through accurate perception of body language.

Step 3: Content Listening and Concentration   This exercise is intended to help students recognize, and then practice coping with, the difficulties most people have simply in listening to, concentrating on, and remembering what other people say. In responding to others, it is important to focus complete attention on them and listen carefully to what they are saying. The first part of the exercise—to illustrate the problems—consists of sending everyone out of the room. The instructor then calls one person back to read a brief, but somewhat complicated, prepared statement. This person attempts to remember the statement and repeats it as accurately as possible to the next person who is called back to the room, and so on through the rest of the class. By the time the last person repeats the statement for the entire group, the statement usually does not even bear a reasonable facsimile to the original statement.

The next part of the exercise consists of dividing the class into groups of three and having A tell B something which B repeats to A. C then provides a critique of, and feedback on, B's accuracy. As with subsequent exercises, each role is then switched so that all participants have a chance to be involved in the different roles.

The last part of the exercise consists of having students concentrate on and remember several prepared statements, starting with shorter and progressing to longer statements. First the instructor reads a statement to the group and calls on someone to repeat it. (Other group members can write it down.) The instructor proceeds from brief to more complex statements. Then the class is divided into groups of three, and, rotating roles within groups, each group continues this exercise using several pages of statements prepared in advance and distributed by the instructor, beginning with shorter statements and moving to longer ones. The goal of this exercise is to enhance skills at concentration by having students repeat from memory statements that are three to four lines long after hearing them only once. Of course, the point is not in the memorization but in the demonstration of how concentrating can be enhanced by focusing on content listening and memory exercises, and can therefore provide a clearer focus to the worker's understanding of the client's comments.

Step 4: Expressing and Detecting Feelings   This exercise is intended to facilitate students' awareness of the distinction between content and feelings and the ability to express their own feelings. Since the focus of empathy is on feelings, and one of the key dimensions of empathy is the intensity of the worker's response, this exercise helps students distinguish between content and feelings, then express their feelings more clearly and share them with others. The instructor provides some examples distinguishing between the expression of content and the expression of feelings (e.g., "I go to the School of Social Work,"—content, versus, "I *hate* the School of Social Work,"—feelings). Again in small groups, students are assigned several topics, e.g., school, work, television, friends, relatives. Then each student discusses each topic with another, first demonstrating an expression of content, then an expression of feeling. Students are encouraged to attend to the way they actually feel when expressing feelings (i.e., as opposed to simply pretending) and to express those feelings as fully as possible. They are also encouraged to attend to body language, to the way they look when expressing feelings, and are given feedback as to the congruence between voice and appearance. In essence, the purpose of this exercise for "expressers" is to attend to how they feel and what they say when expressing feelings. For listeners, the purpose is to be able to distinguish between content and feelings and to be able to pick up clues as to which is which.

Step 5: Open Invitation to Talk   The task of workers is to help clients speak about their problems, perhaps by providing a limited structure through the use of an open invitation to talk (Ivey, 1971). An open invitation to talk provides room for clients to express their feelings and explore themselves and their problems. A closed invitation to talk, on the other hand, which usually can be answered in one or two words, shuts off clients. (For example, "Do you get along with your children?"—closed, versus, "Maybe you could tell me a little about how you get along with your children,"—open.) Further, this open invitation to talk encourages the process of centering the interview on the concerns of the client, rather than simply on providing information for the worker. It also cuts down on the use of questions which often are focused only on collecting data and are used because the worker does not know what else to say, which do not follow from what the client has just said, or which are difficult for clients to answer, thereby eliciting defensiveness. In the exercise students divide into groups of three with two students engaging in the role playing while the observer rates the "worker" on his or her use of open invitations. The topic of the conversations can be anything (i.e., again not necessarily focused on a problem). Using examples of both open and closed invitations to talk provided by the instructor, each "worker" is rated and given feedback about his or her performance in brief conversations with the "client" on four specific uses of open invitations to talk: (a) Helping begin an interview, (b) helping the client elaborate on a point; (c) helping elicit examples of specific behavior to clarify what the client is describing, and (d) helping focus the client's attention on his or her feelings.

Step 6: Minimal Encourages to Talk   Often, once a client is speaking, it is sufficient for the worker to use only brief comments to facilitate the discussion. Such minimal encourages to talk (Ivey, 1971) consist of brief comments which let the client know the worker is there, tuned in, participating and active, but not intending to interfere or detract from what the client is trying to say. Minimal encourages are to be used, though, in conjunction with other more expressive responses by the worker. But they are focused on as a separate dimension to encourage students' awareness of how and when they are used. Examples of minimal encourages are (Ivey, 1971, p. 152): (a) "Oh?" "So?" "Then?" "And?": (b) the repetition of one of two key words; (c) "Uh huh," "Umm-hmmm." Students are divided into groups as previously and a similar format is used with two students engaging in conversation, and the third rating and giving feedback to the "identified worker" on the appropriate use of minimal encourages.

Step 7: Voice Training   The last step in phase II consists of helping students develop more expressive voices. Obviously, the voice is a most crucial medium of communication. Every time someone speaks, listeners form a picture of what sort of person the speaker is. Especially in the area of emotions, the voice can be a most marvelous and accurate indicator of feelings, or a device for hiding feelings. In terms of the core conditions, the sound of the voice can be a crucial factor in determining level of functioning and in relating to clients. The intensity of expression, e.g., manifested in the voice, is a major indicator of empathy. The modulation of the voice is an important ingredient in warmth. Speaking too fast may reveal an anxious worker, perhaps low on genuineness. A well-modulated, expressive, appropriately paced voice is particularly important in demonstrating high levels of the core conditions. It is the major means through which worker responses—content and feelings—are communicated to the client. The exercises on voice training are not an encapsulated or isolated step, but are carried over as part of several sessions to enhance their effects. (a) The first exercise consists of each person in the class reading an "intense" statement the way they would have liked to have said it in actual practice. These statements are tape recorded right in the group on a single tape and then put aside. The order of speaking is also noted. (b) The instructor then goes around the room using a variety of cue words (e.g., "Hello"), asking each student to use the word to express several different feelings. This illustrates the basic point of this exercise: It is not only what you say, but how you say it. (c) Each person in the class reads a brief passage into the tape recorder. Then on a typology based on the work of Young (1973) and Boone (1971), each voice is rated for the following dimensions: (1) Harshness (rough or smooth); (2) nasality (cheerful or complaining); (3) monotone (stimulating or boring); (4) speed (too fast, too slow, or just right; (5) faulty volume control (too loud, too soft, or just right); (6) pitch (too high, too low, or satisfactory). A "voice diagnosis" is made for each student. (d) Specific exercises are prescribed for each student according to his or her "voice diagnosis" (Boone, 1971; Young, 1973). The class is paired off and each member helps the other in working on specific problem areas. (e) When the class is together again, the instructor leads the entire group in a voice modulation exercise. A series of statements with strong feeling content is read to the group. After each statement, the instructor goes around the class, first, in order, later, calling on people randomly, and encourages them to repeat the statement in a highly exaggerated fashion. This exercise is repeated several times to illustrate the degree of control each student actually has over his or her voice and to help students speak more expressively. (Toward the end of the exercise, the exaggeration is decreased to the point that appears appropriate for the expression of whatever feelings or content the student wishes to express.) The goal is for students voluntarily to control the way they speak and express feelings and content the way they want to express them. (f) The class is divided into dyads, and students practice saying, then singing, the days of the week—going up and down the scale. This exercise is intended to increase both sensitivity to the different tones and overall expressiveness. (g) Still in dyads, students read a series of prepared statements, first in a highly exaggerated way, then gradually diminishing the exaggeration until they read the statements with the appropriate expression. (h) In the same order as at the beginning of this exercise, again using tape recorders, students read the same "intense" statement the way they would like to have it sound in actual practice. These results are compared for immediate feedback with the initial statements to determine the effects of this exercise, first playing the original statement, then the later one.

Summary of Objectives, Phase II   At the conclusion of phase II, learners should be able to:

1. Engage in appropriate attending behavior, including:
       Good eye contact
       Relaxed, comfortable posture
       Leaning slightly toward client
       Appropriate, congruent facial expressions
       Relaxed, spontaneous head, arm, and body movements
       Friendly greetings
2. Read body language, be familiar with the potential meaning of different non-verbal cues

3. Concentrate on and remember what the client is saying
4. Distinguish between content and feelings and be aware of their own behaviors when they are expressing feelings
5. Use open invitations to talk and few if any questions in speaking with clients
6. Use minimal encourages as appropriate
7. Attend to and control their voices so that they speak in unhurried, soothing, expressive, and well-modulated tones.

Phase III: Basic Training in the Core Conditions (Experiencing and Exploration)

The third phase of training builds on the previous two phases by incorporating them with introductory training in skills in communicating the core conditions of empathy, warmth, and genuineness. Most of the outside reading is finished by this point, and the completed programmed manuals also are collected and reviewed by the instructor.

Step 1 The tapes made at the start of the course are rated in class using the scales measuring empathy, warmth, and genuineness. Five-minute randomly selected excerpts are rated by students, and their ratings are compared with the instructor's. The instructor presents the reasons for his or her ratings in an effort to develop greater reliability in rating (i.e., agreement between class members). This serves the purpose of opening up considerable discussion about the scales, building on the largely cognitive understanding developed in the readings and through completion of the programmed manual. Several styles and techniques of interviewing are also illustrated. The ratings serve to teach the students to discriminate between various levels of each scale. Finally, the tapes also serve as a precourse baseline against which a tape made by the students at the end of the course can be compared.

When the course was originally designed, the tapes were made and reviewed by the class in the initial sessions, during phase I. However, because students did not have time to read and understand the conceptual and empirical background of the material, this early reviewing was premature. An even more important reason for holding off on reviewing the tapes was that phase II of training, basic interviewing (attending), skills, did not specifically utilize the scales. Hence, because of the gap between listening to the tapes and rating them on the scales and actual use of the scales for practice in class, it seemed far more appropriate to place this step immediately preceding the steps where the scales will be used in the actual training process. Of course, as in many other aspects of this training, placement of the step of listening to and evaluating the tapes can be left up to the individual instructor.

Step 2: Discrimination and Operational Indicators In conjunction with the ratings of the tapes in step 1, students are increasingly familiarized with the scales through discussion and examples of different scale levels. Four basic tasks are involved in discrimination training: (a) Articulation of the dimensions involved, (b) clarifying the functions and effects of the dimensions, (c) putting into operation the assessment of these dimensions, and (d) shaping student discriminations of the levels of these dimensions (Carkhuff, 1969a, pp. 171–172). Since the students already have completed the readings and have listened to a variety of tapes, fuller, in-depth discussion of the core conditions is accomplished. A form describing a number of additional operational indicators of each of the core conditions has been developed by the author and is supplied to the students, and they are taught how to discriminate their presence and the appropriate scale level. These indicators include such dimensions as worker voice tone, tentativeness, personalness, intensity of worker response, interchangeability of affect between worker and client statements regarding the empathy dimension (Carkhuff, 1969a), and indicators of incongruence and of possessiveness.

Step 3: Movie   The next step involves the viewing of the film *Three Approaches to Psychotherapy*. This film consists of interviews of the same client by Carl Rogers, Fritz Perls, and Albert Ellis. The film presents radically different approaches to counseling and therapy and radically different styles. Each therapist is rated on the core conditions, and the differences between the types of relationships they develop with their clients are discussed.

Step 4: Empathy and Identification of Feelings   A large part of this and the following phase revolves around training for the communication of accurate empathy. While the other two dimensions of the core conditions are, of course, not ignored, the empathy scale is the one that is most clearly operationalized, has the greatest range of procedures for instruction, and is most easily focused upon by students. Furthermore, although not necessarily the most important dimension, the communication of empathy is the "meat" of the therapeutic process and, more than the other scales, involves what the worker actually *does*. Further, increased mastery of the communication of empathy in training, by providing actual guidelines for specific interaction with clients, appears to open up students to more ready and facilitative communication of warmth and genuineness. Clearly, less concern or anxiety is generated among students about feeling free in the intervention process when they are more comfortable with what they are to do and say.

Obviously, before one can communicate about another's feelings, one must know what they are. This step begins with the instructor reading a series of client statements recorded from actual interviews. Students are asked to detect and communicate (in any way they can) the feelings which the client was trying to convey. At first, volunteers are solicited. Later, students are selected to respond on a more or less random basis to encourage concentration, attentiveness, and facility in responding. The class is then divided into groups of three, and, using the client statements passed out previously by the instructor, one student presents a statement to another while the third acts as observer, rates, and also provides feedback. Again, students are not directed to respond in any particular way but only to identify what they think the feelings are that the client was attempting to communicate. As usual, the instructor models the exercise at its inception. While the class is divided into groups (in this and all other exercises), the instructor circulates around the room, participating in all the groups, not only by providing feedback, but by helping in the identification of feelings.

Step 5: Basic Empathy Training   Once the feelings have been accurately understood, the next step is to accurately *communicate* that understanding. This is done through helping students develop the skill of reflecting feelings. Reflection is discussed not as a specific technique, but simply as any number of ways of communicating back to the client, with accuracy and the appropriate intensity, the affective message the client has presented. The client's words are not simply repeated in a robot-like, artificial manner. ("I am angry." "You are angry.") Rather, the feelings are reflected by restating in the worker's own words what the client appears to be experiencing. The goal, of course, is not only to clarify and understand what the client is feeling, but to express to the client, "I am with you."

First, the class reviews some of the operational indicators of empathy such as appropriate intensity, focus on feelings, tentativeness, following the client's lead, focus on *current* feelings, appropriate voice tone, and accuracy in communication. Then, after the instructor models the exercise, as with the previous step, the instructor reads a series of clients' statements to the whole group, with individual class members responding with an empathic statement. First, volunteers are solicited, then students are selected randomly. The goal in this phase is to aim for a "moderately" empathic response—say, 3 to 4 on the scale—one which is within most students' reach at this point. Then the students, in triads, are asked to role play brief client statements and helper responses—one to three statements, roughly thirty to forty-five seconds—for each participant. The student/worker is rated by the observer and the student/client on empathy and is given feedback on what a more empathic response might have been. The statements that are used as client statements include those the instructor has passed out, plus any statements the students themselves would like to provide (hypothetical or based on real experiences).

Step 6: Basic Warmth Training   The basic indicators of warmth are briefly reviewed—nonjudgmentalness, voice tone, a caring quality in the voice, absence of questions about concrete matters, absence of advice ("You should do such and such"), absence of negative regard, workers centering attention on clients rather than on themselves, and so on. Then the students are again divided into triads—different partners and groups are used throughout—and asked to role play brief client statements and worker responses. In this instance, however, the student/workers are to be concerned solely with the communication of warmth. They are then rated on the warmth scale and provided feedback by the student/clients and observers on ways to improve the rating, using the specific indicators outlined above. As with the previous exercise, role playing is confined to one to three statements, thirty to forty-five seconds, and the goal is to achieve a moderate rating, approximately level 3 on the warmth scale.

Step 7: Basic Genuineness Training　　As with step 6, the exercise, this time concerning genuineness, begins with a review of indicators of genuineness—voice tone, personalness, absence of "professional" sounding tones (just saying things because it seems they should be said), use of humor, absence of the appearance in the worker of saying one thing and feeling or thinking another, absence of the sound of discomfort or anxiety on the part of the worker, absence of negative effect on the client of what the worker says when the worker is congruent: nondefensiveness, nonphoniness, etc. Then, in triads, students role play one to three brief client statements and helper responses, focusing on genuineness, with ratings and appropriate feedback geared toward achieving approximately a level 3 on the scale.

Step 8: Introduction to Client Self-Exploration　　To aid in focusing their role playing efforts, students are introduced to the notion of client self-exploration. This important dimension, as described earlier, has been related in research to successful outcome (i.e., there is an association between depth of client self-exploration and successful treatment). Self-exploration is measured on a five-point scale (Carkhuff, 1969b, pp. 327–328), ranging from a low point (level 1) where the clients do not discuss any personally relevant material, to a midpoint (level 3) where the clients voluntarily introduce personally relevant material but do so mechanically, to a high point (level 5) where the clients are fully and actively, spontaneously and expressively, focusing upon themselves and inwardly probing and exploring themselves and their world. Interspersed with ratings of student/workers on the scales measuring empathy, warmth, and genuineness, then, student/clients are rated for depth of self-exploration to provide additional feedback to student/workers regarding the effects of their communication on their clients.

Step 9: Putting the Core Conditions Together　　Students are once again divided into groups of three, a "worker," a "client," and an observer (with these roles, of course, changing). Following the format described previously, students role play brief interchanges; this time, the student/worker responds and is rated and provided feedback on all three dimensions of the core conditions.

Step 10: Listening to Tapes　　The last step of this phase, with the class together again, involves the instructor playing a series of tape-recorded statements by clients in the context of actual interviews. Students are then selected to respond to these statements, first without ratings (to decrease anxiety), later with ratings on all three scales, plus feedback to shape responses toward higher scores. An interesting and enjoyable part of this exercise, once the student is through responding, is to continue the tape recording to hear the response made to the client by the real practitioner. Since the tapes include several prominent counselors and therapists, this allows students to compare their own responses with those of the "big shots." Generally, at this stage, student responses tend to be rated higher than those of many experienced professionals.

Summary of Objectives, Phase III At the conclusion of phase III, the learner should be able to:

1. Discriminate between different levels of the scales and rate interviews reliably.
2. Communicate moderate levels of empathy, centering around levels 3 to 4 on the scales.
3. Communicate moderate levels of warmth, centering around level 3 on the scale.
4. Communicate moderate levels of genuineness, centering around level 3 on the scale.
5. Be familiar with the scale on client self-exploration.

At this point, communication of the core conditions generally is rather variable, i.e., students tend to be inconsistent in maintaining moderate levels of empathy, warmth, and genuineness. Extended practice in the subsequent phase, however, is intended to correct that problem.

Phase IV: Advanced Training (Understanding and Defining)

This phase of training is intended to extend and deepen students' abilities to communicate the core conditions. Many of the exercises begun in the previous stage are extended in time to give students more in-depth, longer experiences in interviewing. The major focus remains on the scales measuring empathy, warmth, and genuineness, although some new, supplementary content is added. Particular emphasis is placed on providing skills to help students help their clients develop deeper understanding of their problems and define the problems in concrete terms as a prelude to taking action on them.

Step 1: Advanced Discrimination A series of sixteen written excerpts of expressions from clients, each of which has four possible worker responses (Carkhuff, 1969a, pp. 115–123), is presented to the students. The students rate the worker responses in terms of level of the core conditions. This exercise helps in aiding discrimination abilities and, in presenting responses to each stimulus statement which range from low on the scales to minimally facilitative to highly expressive, suggests to the students an increasingly wide range of possibilities for responding. In addition, the instructor points out the added "action" dimension of some of the statements, thus paving the way for presentation of the total model in the following phase.

Step 2: Going Around With the group sitting in a circle, one member volunteers to discuss either a role-played or personally relevant experience which is responded to by another member of the group. The responder is rated by other members of the group and provided feedback. The student/client continues and is responded to by all members of the group (including the instructor), all of whom are rated. This exercise can be tape recorded and played back, at which time feedback can be given; this eliminates the necessity for interruptions for rating and feedback after each response (Blakeman & Emener, 1971). This exercise can also be conducted without interruption by having the instructor give an overall rating of the response by holding up the number of fingers appropriate for a particular scale stage. After all students have had their turns, more specific feedback can be given. Whatever anxiety is generated by this exercise is greatly reduced by going around like this several times in a row.

Step 3: Summary of Feeling   This exercise is an extension of the basic empathy/reflection of feeling exercise from the previous phase. Summary of feeling, though, essentially covers a longer time period and involves a broad range of feelings which the client has expressed (Ivey, 1971), thereby raising the overall level of empathy by pulling together what the client has said, and adding directionality. In groups of three, one student acts as observer and rater while another, the "client," role plays a particular experience. The student/worker facilitates this statement, perhaps by using minimal encourages to talk, and after approximately five minutes, as cued by the observer, restates in his or her own words the feelings and perceptions that the client has been communicating. This exercise actually can begin with a few client statements and extend to several statements for up to ten minutes, as usual, with rating and feedback for student/worker responses. This exercise is facilitated by having students study in advance a worksheet prepared by the instructor illustrating some "summaries of feeling."

Step 4: Concreteness   Another dimension—concreteness—is added to the discussion of empathy. Actually, extensive research has revealed concreteness, or specificity of expression, to be related to successful outcome (Truax & Carkhuff, 1967; Carkhuff & Berenson, 1977), although not as substantially as the core conditions. Experimentation by the author with methods of teaching concreteness has revealed that the most efficacious, and least confusing, method appears to be to combine it with accurate empathy, in that the higher the degree of empathy, the more the worker will speak in, and facilitate the client's speaking in, concrete and specific terms (as opposed to generalities) regarding problems, feelings, etc. A five-point scale measuring concreteness (Carkhuff, 1969b, pp. 323–324) is used to facilitate understanding of this dimension.

Step 5: Levels of Empathic Response   This step is based on an article by Means (1973) which provides a conceptual focus to help guide students with regard to what they are empathic to. The model is actually based on both the empathy and concreteness scales and delineates six elements of client statements to which students can respond and communicate empathy. The elements are: (1) Client's accurately expressed feeling or obvious feeling, (2) identification of environmental stimulus, (3) identification of client's behavior pattern, (4) feelings toward self as a result of interaction with the environment, (5) expectations about self, and (6) basic beliefs about self. The exercise proceeds by taking a single client statement and then demonstrating how the worker might respond to one or any combination of these six elements in that client statement. Then in groups of three and using prepared stimulus statements, students practice responding to various of the six elements included in each client statement.

Steps 6 to 9: In-Depth Practice   The group is divided into triads, and the exercises from the previous phase are repeated, this time, however, for progressively longer periods of time. First, empathy is the focus, then warmth, then genuineness, then the three conditions together. Student/clients and student/workers expand their sequence of exchanges to practice extended periods of communication, with the focus for rating and feedback on modal levels of communication of the core conditions, i.e., the level at which the student/worker is performing most of the time. Extensive use of videotaping is made at this stage, with students recording five- to ten-minute interviews and then receiving detailed feedback by stopping the playback after each response to discuss it.

During this, or sometimes the previous, exercise, discussion often centers on just what "deeper" feelings are, i.e., what kinds of feeling one would have to be sensitive to and communicate in order to score at the higher levels of empathy. The instructor attempts to clarify this by giving examples of the range of such deeper feelings and by attempting to contrast "superficial" versus "deep" feelings. Sometimes, for instance, a deep feeling really refers to a more intense elaboration of a superficial feeling, i.e., anguish or pain or ambivalence which is hinted at in the words of the client, and of which the client is not thoroughly aware. Thus, the worker's role is to help the client explore these deeper levels. Students are encouraged not to think about "bombshell" interpretations of mystical feelings or personal configurations ("Hmm, it appears to me that the real problem is that you are suffering from a counterinverted Oedipal complex"). The idea is to take away the mystique surrounding "deep feelings" and to make students aware of the fact that most students are capable of understanding and touching these feelings without miraculous or superhuman powers.

Step 10: Focus on Immediacy of Relationship   One of the most difficult aspects of therapeutic interviewing is recognizing, and/or refocusing on, those instances where the relationship is centered around (or concerned with) the here-and-now feelings between the worker and the client. These feelings, of course, can be crucial for the success or failure of any interpersonal helping process, and detecting and dealing with them appropriately is of special importance. A separate scale for measuring immediacy of relationship is available (Carkhuff, 1969b, pp. 326–327), ranging from level 1 where the worker simply disregards all those client messages that are related to the worker, to level 5 where the worker is not at all hesitant in relating the client's expressions directly to the worker-client relationship.

A series of prepared statements is used (plus any others students wish to use in their role playing) in which a "client" expresses some feeling, positive or negative, about the worker. The class is divided into groups of three with students role playing such expressions and possible responses to them. In subsequent extended role playing, immediacy of relationship is focused on as appropriate.

If it has not come up before, the subject of transference is usually discussed here. It is acknowledged that, to some extent, all relationships are based on previous experiences with people. However, the psychoanalytic term "transference," referring to specific irrational responses of the client to the worker, as though the worker were some person in the client's previous experience, is frequently used to refer to *any* positive or negative feelings of the client for the worker. In this sense, the therapeutic relationship would be viewed as a *transference* relationship, as opposed to a *real* relationship, thus permitting the worker to insulate himself or herself from any true reactions and personally meaningful interactions with the client. Although irrational reactions to workers, as though they were actually someone else, do sometimes occur, they should be dealt with and clarified at that point in time. For the most part, however, *unless there is strong evidence to the contrary,* all reactions of the client to the worker should be explored as real, personal, and meaningful in the context of the given person-to-person relationship. Otherwise, the worker will avoid really encountering the client, and the necessary requisites for communicating empathy, warmth, and genuineness will not exist.

Step 11: Introduction to Self-Disclosure   Using the five-point scale to measure self-disclosure (Carkhuff, 1969b, pp. 321–322), students are introduced to the varying conditions of disclosing their own personal values, attitudes, and beliefs to the client. (Actually, the issue of self-disclosure is often discussed in less formal ways throughout the entire training.) The purpose of self-disclosure is clarified: in brief, it is to enhance the relationship and help the client, not to make the worker feel better (hence, this scale actually is called "facilitative self-disclosure"). In essence, self-disclosure can be used: (1) When it does not detract from centering on clients and their focus on themselves; (2) when it does not center on workers to the extent that clients wish to continue to explore more of the worker's personal life or workers become caught up in the details of what they are revealing; (3) when it does not leave clients with the feeling that because the workers have experienced whatever it is they reveal, that the workers either cannot be sufficiently objective or are too disturbed to help the clients; (4) when the self-disclosure is not a transparent and phony way of attempting to communicate empathy; (5) when the self-disclosure is not awkward, hesitant, or vague; (6) when the self-disclosure is in the ongoing context of the relationship, offered constructively, and in keeping with the client's interests.

Step 12: Introduction to Confrontation   When the issue of confrontation is formally focused upon, it is done in the context of explaining that many students have been engaging in facilitative confrontation throughout the course. Confrontation, using the five-point scale developed by Carkhuff (1969b, pp. 324–325), is described simply as the clarification of discrepancies: (1) between the clients' descriptions of what they wish to be and how they actually experience themselves; (2) between the clients' verbal expression of their awareness of themselves and their observable or reported behaviors; and (3) between the way the workers reportedly experience clients and the clients' own expressions of their experience of themselves (Carkhuff, 1969a). Thus workers communicating moderate to high levels of empathy also will be sensitive "automatically" to such discrepancies. The key aspects of confrontation that are focused on, however, are the hows and whys of confrontation—always to facilitate the clients' understanding of themselves, always constructively so that clients can deal with the confrontations in beneficial ways, and always to the clients' strengths rather than weaknesses.

Summary of Objectives, Phase IV   At the conclusion of phase IV, which essentially is the last phase of intensive role playing, the learner should be able to:

1. Consistently communicate moderate to high levels of empathy (minimum of level 3 or 4).
2. Consistently communicate moderate to high levels of warmth (minimum of level 3).
3. Consistently communicate moderate to high levels of genuineness (minimum of level 3).
4. Consistently deal with and help the client deal with feelings concretely and specifically.
5. Consistently help the client focus on and explore himself or herself with spontaneity and expressiveness (level 4 on the self-exploration scale).

Because of time limitations, the focus on the other aspects of the helping relationship—immediacy, confrontation, self-disclosure—is less intense (a problem that easily could be alleviated by extending the time limit for the training in accord with the requirements of whatever agency or institution is sponsoring the training). Thus, rather than consistent high-level communication of these dimensions, the learner by the end of this phase should be at least sensitized and familiar with and have some basic competence in:

1. Focusing on immediacy of relationship.
2. Providing facilitative self-disclosures.
3. Constructively confronting the client regarding perceived discrepancies.

Phase V: The Conclusion of Training: A Beginning (Action)

The last phase of training involves putting everything together, adding material regarding the complete model of the helping process, and some concluding exercises. This phase is the wrap-up, where students are encouraged to demonstrate what they have learned in terms of inducing meaningful action on the part of student/clients.

Step 1: Role Playing the Complete Model   After review and discussion of the stages of the overall model, students spend extended periods of time role playing with each other. The entire process of helping is focused on. Through the communication of high levels of the core conditions, student/clients are helped to, first, explore themselves, second, gain some degree of understanding, and third, develop a course of action. Observers rate, evaluate, and provide feedback and suggestions as to ways student/workers can be more effective in facilitating any of these dimensions.

Step 2: The Real Self   This exercise involves having all the students role play, as worker/therapists, a situation twice: once as they would have done it prior to the course or at least in ways they perceive as their "natural" or "real" selves, and again demonstrating as well as possible new learnings regarding the core conditions as taught in the course. The purpose of this exercise is to illustrate that at this point in training most participants in the course have difficulty in reverting to their old style, have integrated much of the learning into their personal styles in ways that can be immediately identified, or, at times cannot even distinguish in role playing between their old and new styles so that observers can rate the differences. The final exercises (steps 3 and 4) are intended to answer the question of the importance of this issue—whether the higher levels of the core conditions actually were learned.

Step 3: Videotaping   While videotaping of any stage of the process can be very helpful, providing an immediate and effective form of feedback, it is used at this stage to record and then play back student efforts at actualizing the content and experiences of the course and to compare their post-videotapes with the ones they made at the beginning of the course. As previously, students are given several minutes to role play situations in front of the cameras. Then, the entire group, including the participants in the role playing process, view each individual's pre and post-videotapes together, rating and providing feedback on the core conditions, body language, physical appearance, and so on. Apart from being particularly instructive, this exercise is one of the most enjoyable of all as clear and obvious differences between the two videotapes are generally apparent for most students, to the extent that students often cannot believe those pretapes were actually themselves.

Step 4: Tape Recording: Once More with Feeling   The final exercise involves making one more audiotape recording outside of class (either role playing or an actual interview). These tapes can be used to supplement the videotaping or replace it if videotape equipment is not available. The class and instructor listen to and rate the audiotapes to examine systematically any changes between the first and last tape (see Fischer, 1974a, 1975c for controlled evidence on the positive outcome for this course).

Step 5: Follow-Up   Although no formal follow-up is included in the course, participants are encouraged to continue to develop these skills, or at least be sure they maintain them at postcourse levels, both in their student practicum experiences and once they become practicing professionals. They are urged to tape record several of their actual therapeutic sessions with clients and to engage, at least monthly, in peer reviews of those tapes using the scales measuring the core conditions for rating, feedback, and discussion.

Summary of Objectives, Phase V   At the conclusion of phase V, the learner should be able to:

1. Demonstrate maintenance or enhancement of levels of communication achieved in phase IV, particularly as compared with pretraining levels of interpersonal skills.
2. Demonstrate knowledge of and familiarity with the conceptual model of helping and the ability to engage in the behaviors and activities required of each stage.

References

Bandura, A. (1969). *Principles of behavior modification*. New York: Holt.

Blakeman, J. E., & Emener, W. G. (1971). Training in interpersonal communication: Suggested techniques and approaches. *Journal of Research and Development in Education, 4*, 36–46.

Boone, D. (1971). *The voice and voice therapy*. Englewood Cliffs, NJ: Prentice-Hall.

Bullmer, K. (1975). *The art of empathy*. New York: Human Sciences Press.

Carkhuff, R. R. (1969a). *Helping and human relations* (vol. 1). New York: Holt.

Carkhuff, R. R. (1969b). *Helping and human relations* (vol. 2). New York: Holt.

Carkhuff, R. R. (1971). *The development of human resources*. New York: Holt.

Carkhuff, R. R., & Berenson, R. (1977). *Beyond counseling and therapy* (2nd ed.). New York: Holt.

Danish, S. J., & Hauer, A. L. (1973). *Helping skills: A basic training program*. New York: Behavioral Publications.

Dittman, A. T., Parloff, M. B., & Boomer, D. S. (1965). Facial and bodily expression: a study of emotional cues. *Psychiatry, 28*, 239–244.

Egan, G. (1975a). *The skilled helper*. Monterey, CA: Brooks/Cole.

Egan, G. (1975b). *Exercises in helping skills*. Monterey, CA: Brooks/Cole.

Ellsworth, P. C., & Carlsmith, J. M. (1968). Effects of eye contact and verbal content on affective response to a dyadic interaction. *Journal of Personality and Social Psychology, 10*, 15–20.

Fischer, J. (1974). *Effective training for effective practice.* Unpublished Paper. Honolulu: University of Hawaii School of Social Work.

Fischer, J. (1975). Training for effective therapeutic practice. *Psychotherapy: Theory, research, and practice, 12,* 118–123.

Haase, R. F., & Tepper, D. T. (1972). Nonverbal components of empathic communication. *Journal of Counseling Psychology, 19,* 417–424.

Ivey, A. E. (1971). *Microcounseling: Innovations in interviewing training.* Springfield, IL: Charles C Thomas.

Longfellow, L. A. (1970). Body talk: The game of feeling and expression. October. *Psychology Today.*

Means, B. L. (1973). Levels of empathic response. *Personnel and Guidance Journal, 52,* 23–28.

Mehrabian, A. (1969a). Significance of posture and position in the communication of status relationships. *Psychological Bulletin, 71,* 359–372.

Mehrabian, A. (1969b). Some referents and measures on nonverbal behavior. *Basic Research Method and Instruction, 1,* 203–207.

Pfeiffer, J., & Jones, J. A. (1971). *Handbook of structured experiences for human relations training.* Iowa City, IA: University Associates.

Reece, M. N., & Whitman, R. N. (1962). Expressive movements and verbal reinforcement. *Journal of Abnormal and Social Psychology, 64,* 204–236.

Schmidt, L. D., & Strong, S. R. (1970). "Expert" and "Inexpert" counselors. *Journal of Counseling Psychology, 17,* 115–118.

Shapiro, J. G. (1968). Relationships between visual and auditory cues of therapeutic effectiveness. *Journal of Clinical Psychology, 24,* 236–239.

Shapiro, J. G., Foster, C. P., & Powell, T. (1968). Facial and bodily cues of genuineness, empathy, and warmth. *Journal of Clinical Psychology, 24,* 233–236.

Strong, S. R., et al. (1971). Nonverbal behavior and perceived counselor characteristics. *Journal of Counseling Psychology, 18,* 554–561.

Sydnor, G. L., Akridge, R. L., & Parkhill, N. L. (1972). *Human Relations: A manual for trainers.* Minden, LA: Human Resources Development Training Institute.

Sydnor, G. L., Akridge, R. L., & Parkhill, N. L. (1973). *Systematic human relations training: A programmed manual.* Minden, LA: Human Resources Development Training Institute.

Truax, C. B., & Carkhuff, R. R. (1967). *Toward effective counseling and psychotherapy.* Chicago: Aldine.

Truax, C. B., & Mitchell, K. (1971). Research on certain therapist interpersonal skills in relation to process and outcome. In A. Bergin & S. Garfield (Eds.), *Handbook of Psychotherapy and Behavior Change* (pp. 299–344). New York: Wiley.

Young, W. (1973). Is your voice the real you? November 18. *Kansas City Star Magazine.* Kansas City.

Appendix B
Flowcharts of Techniques and Technique Packages

Techniques and References	Population	Problem
1. Assertion training and social skills training[7,10,23]	Full range of clients from severely disturbed psychiatric patients to unhappy couples	Wide range of skill/behavior: deficits ranging from self-care and assertion skills to communication training
2. Contingency management (including positive reinforcement, token economy, etc.)[3]	Almost all populations including children and adults; individuals, couples, families	Full range of problems from mild to severe
3. Systematic Desensitization[4,24]	Mainly adults, moderate disorders	Decreasing maladaptive anxiety, especially related to specific stimuli
4. (Behavioral) Contracting[17]	Individuals, families, couples	Weight loss, marital and family problems, academic behaviors, medication compliance
5. Problem-solving[11,15]	Adults, moderate to severe problems	Problem-solving skills in a variety of contexts; decrease in some specific problem behaviors
6. Self-instruction training[2,20]	Children and adults, moderate disorders	Impulsive children, public speaking, and test anxiety
7. Stress-inoculation training[2,20,21]	Adults, moderate disorders	Interpersonal and general anxiety, stress and anger control
8. Cognitive restructuring[12,14,2]	Adults, mild to moderate disorders	Unrealistic expectations, misconceptions, dysfunctional self-statements
9. Modeling and participant modeling[2,3,4]	Children and adults; individuals, groups, couples, and families, slight to severe impairment	Decrease in anxiety, increase in social skills
10. Covert sensitization[3,9,16]	Adults	Unwanted sexual behaviors, alcohol abuse, smoking, and overeating

Techniques and References	Population	Problem
11. Covert positive reinforcement[4,16]	Adults, mild to moderate disorders	Negative self-statements, test anxiety, weight control, animal phobias
12. Covert modeling[2,16]	Adults, mild to moderate disorders	Phobias, lack of assertiveness, mild fears
13. Exposure and response prevention[3,13,18,19]	Adults, mild to moderate disorders	Simple and social phobias, agoraphobia, compulsive rituals
14. Thought stopping[2,3,4]	Adults, mild to moderate thoughts	Obsessive thoughts
15. Habit reversal[5,6,22]	Adults and children	Tics, nailbiting, trichotillomania
16. Paradoxical[25] instruction	Adults, mild to moderate disorders	Procrastination, depression, anxiety, sleep disorders

General
[1] Bellack, A. S. & Hersen, M. (eds.). *Dictionary of Behavior Therapy Techniques.* New York: Pergamon, 1985.
[2] Cormier, W. H. & Cormier, L. S. *Interviewing Strategies for Helpers* (2nd edition). Monterey, California: Brooks/Cole, 1985.
[3] Rimm, D. C. & Masters, J. C. *Behavior Therapy: Techniques and Empirical Findings* (2nd edition). New York: Academic Press, 1979.
[4] Walker, C. E. et al. *Clinical Procedures for Behavior Therapy.* Englewood Cliffs, N.J.: Prentice-Hall, 1981.

Specific Techniques
[5] Azrin, N. H. & Nunn, R. C. *Habit Control.* New York: Simon & Shuster, 1977.
[6] Azrin, N. H. & Nunn, R. C., "Habit Reversal: A Method of Eliminating Nervous Habits and Tics," *Behavior Research and Therapy,* Vol. 11, 1982, 619–628.
[7] Bellack, A. S. & Hersen, M. (eds.). *Research and Practice in Social Skills Training.* New York: Plenum, 1979.
[8] Brehony, K. A. & Celler, E. S., "Agoraphobia: Appraisal of Research and a Proposal for an Integrative Model," in M. Hersen et al. (eds.). *Progress in Behavior Modifications,* Vol. 12. New York: Academic Press, 1981, 1–66.
[9] Cautela, J. R., "Covert Sensitization." *Psychological Reports,* Vol. 20, 1967, 459–468.
[10] Curran, J. P. & Monti, P. M. (eds.). *Social Skills Training.* New York: Guilford, 1982.
[11] D'Zurilla, T. J. & Nezu, A., "Social Problem Solving in Adults," in Kendall P. C. (ed.). *Advances in Cognitive-Behavioral Research and Therapy,* Vol. 1. New York: Academic Press, 1982, 201–274.
[12] Ellis, A. & Greiger, R. (eds.). *Handbook of Rational-Emotive Therapy.* New York: Springer, 1977.
[13] Foa, E. B. & Steketee, G. S., "Obsessive Compulsives: Conceptual Issues and Treatment Considerations," in M. Hersen et al. (eds.). *Progress in Behavior Modification,* Vol. 8. New York: Academic Press, 1979, 1–53.
[14] Goldfried, M. R., "Anxiety Reduction Through Cognitive-Behavioral Intervention," in P. C. Kendall & S. D. Hollon (eds.). *Cognitive-Behavioral Interventions.* New York: Academic Press, 1979, 117–152.
[15] Janis, I. L. & Mann, L. *Decision-Making.* New York: Free Press, 1977.
[16] Kadzin, A. E. & Smith, G. A., "Covert Conditioning: A Review." *Advances in Behavior Research and Therapy,* Vol. 2, 57–98, 1979.
[17] Kirschenbaum, D. S. & Flannery, R. C., "Behavioral Contracting: Outcomes and Elements," in M. Hersen et al. (eds.). *Progress in Behavior Modification,* Vol. 15, New York: Academic Press, 1983, 217–275.
[18] Marshall, W. L. et al., "The Current Status of Flooding Therapy," in M. Hersen et al. (eds.). *Progress in Behavior Modification,* Vol. 7. New York: Academic Press, 1974, 205–275.
[19] Matthews, A. M. et al. *Agoraphobia: Nature and Treatment.* New York: Guilford, 1981.
[20] Meichenbaum, D. *Cognitive-Behavior Modification.* New York: Plenum, 1977.
[21] Novaco, R. W., "The Cognitive Regulation of Anger and Stress," in P. C. Kendall and S. D. Hollon (eds.). *Cognitive-Behavioral Interventions.* New York: Academic, 1979, pp. 241–286.
[22] Turpin, G., "The Behavioral Management of Tic Disorders: A Critical Review." *Advances in Behavior Research and Therapy,* Vol. 5, 1983, 203–245.
[23] Twentyman, C. T. & Zimering, R. T., "Behavioral Training of Social Skills: A Critical Review." In M. Hersen et al. (eds.). *Progress in Behavior Modification,* Vol. 7, New York: Academic Press, 1979, 319–400.
[24] Wolpe, J. *The Practice of Behavior Therapy,* 3rd edition. New York: Pergamon, 1982.
[25] Dowd, E. T. and Trutt, S. D., "Paradoxical Interventions in Behavior Modification," in M. Hersen et al. (eds.). *Progress in Behavior Modification,* Vol. 23. New York: Academic Press, 1988, 96–130.

ASSERTIVE TRAINING

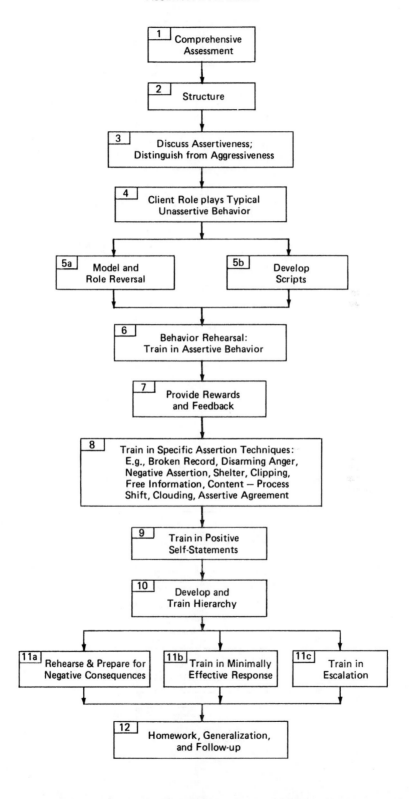

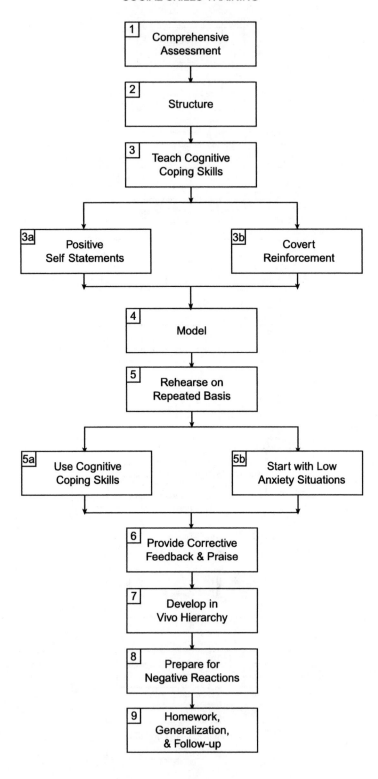

SOCIAL SKILLS TRAINING

1 Comprehensive Assessment

2 Structure

3 Teach Cognitive Coping Skills

3a Positive Self Statements

3b Covert Reinforcement

4 Model

5 Rehearse on Repeated Basis

5a Use Cognitive Coping Skills

5b Start with Low Anxiety Situations

6 Provide Corrective Feedback & Praise

7 Develop in Vivo Hierarchy

8 Prepare for Negative Reactions

9 Homework, Generalization, & Follow-up

CONTINGENCY MANAGEMENT

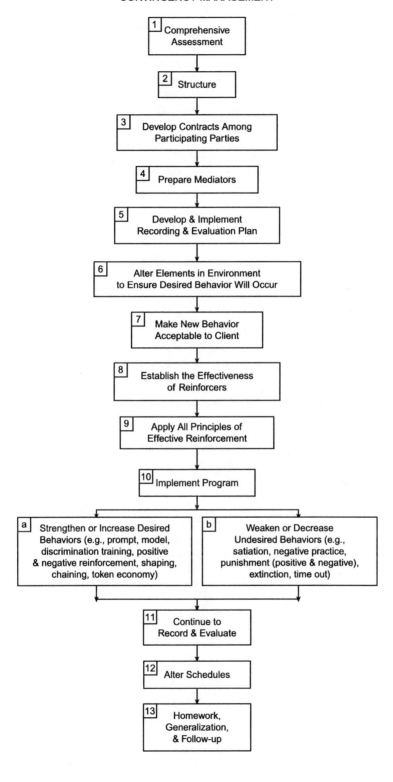

SYSTEMATIC DESENSITIZATION

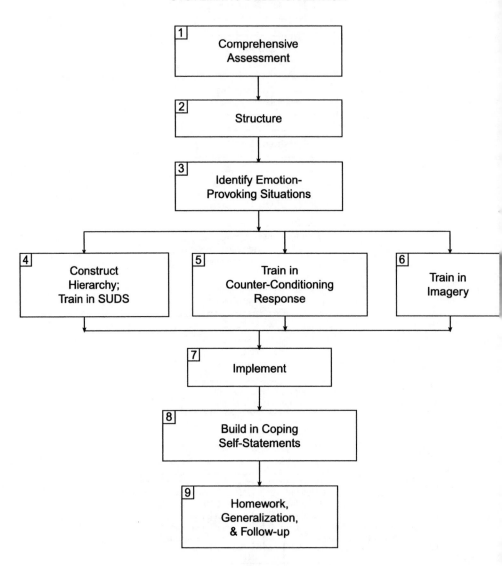

RELAXATION

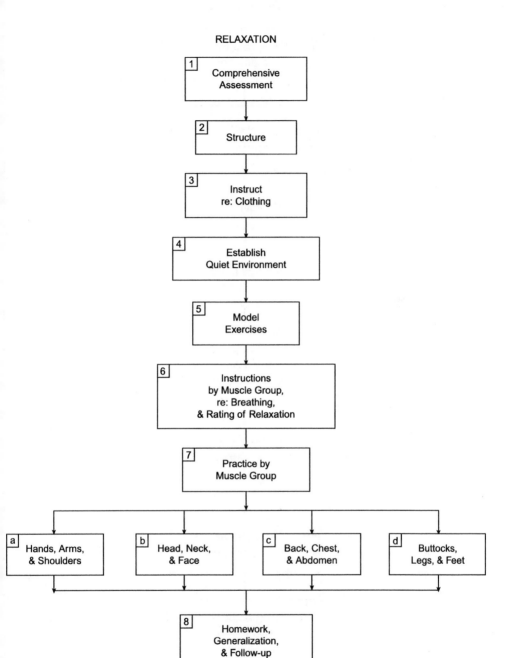

MEDITATION

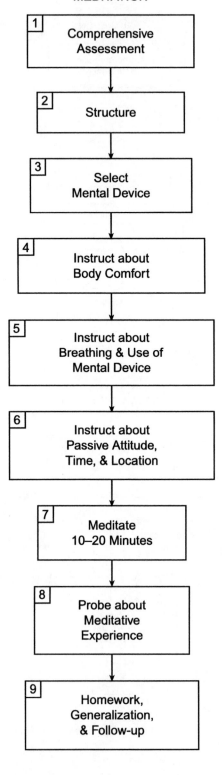

PROBLEM SOLVING AND DECISION MAKING:
THE BALANCE SHEET

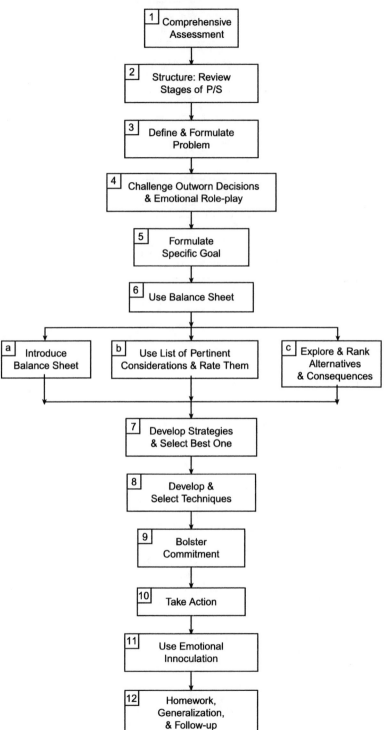

STRESS INOCULATION TRAINING

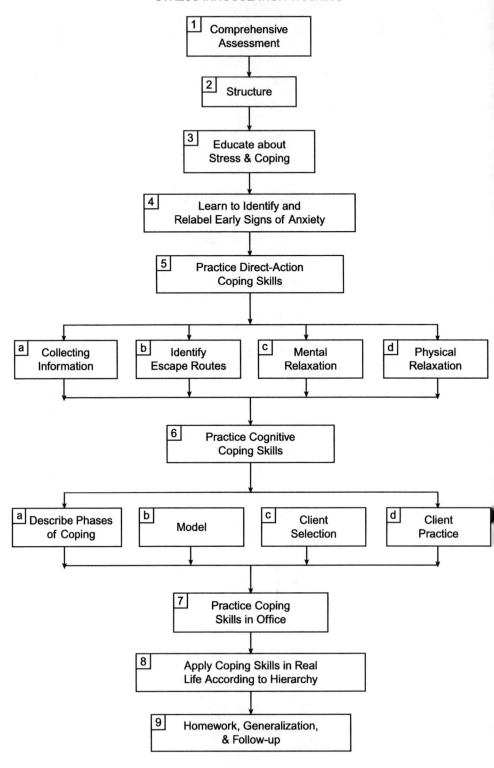

COGNITIVE MODELING AND
SELF-INSTRUCTION TRAINING

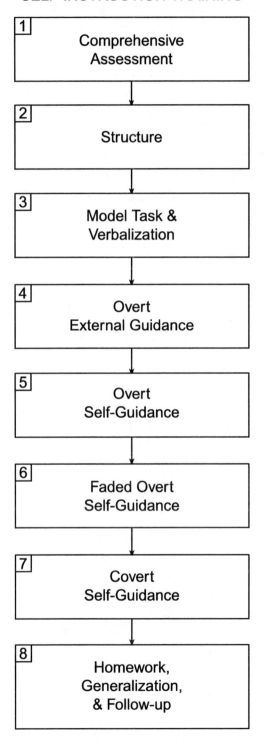

COGNITIVE RESTRUCTURING

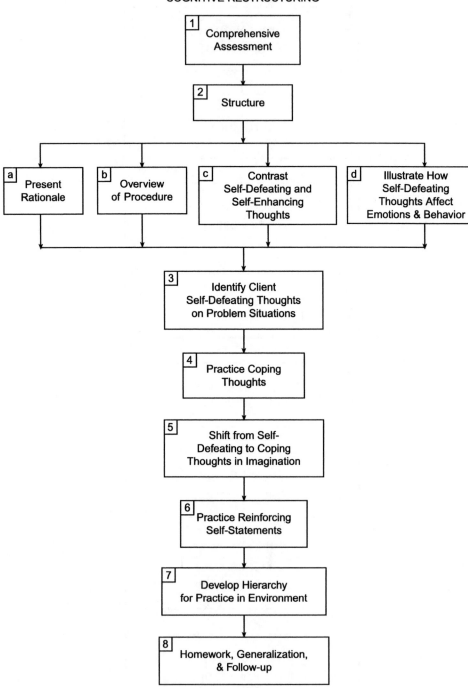

MODELING

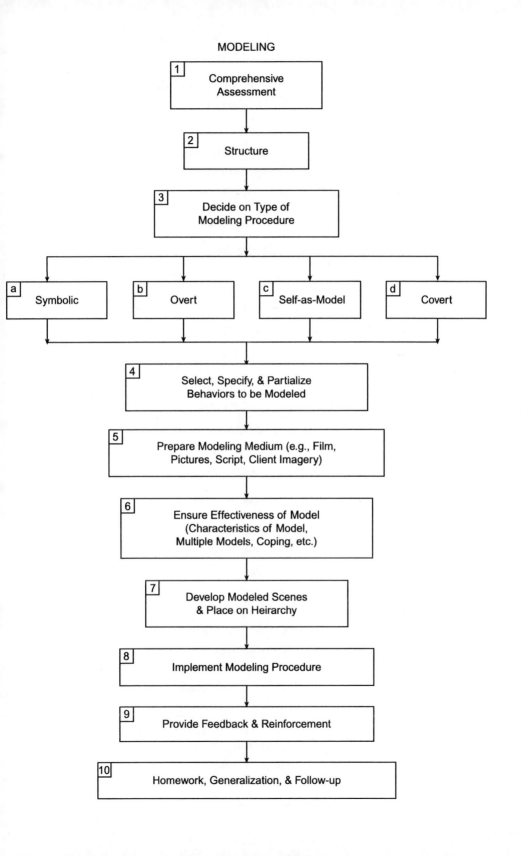

PARTICIPANT MODELING/
CONTACT DESENSITIZATION

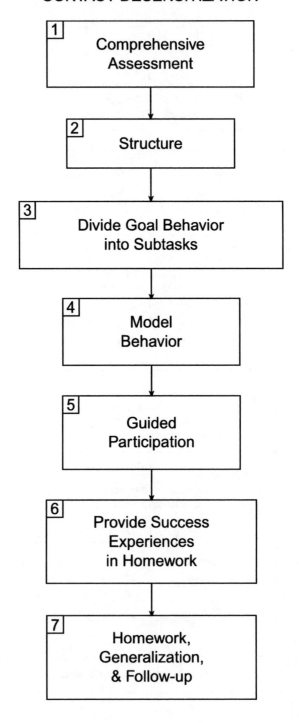

COVERT SENSITIZATION

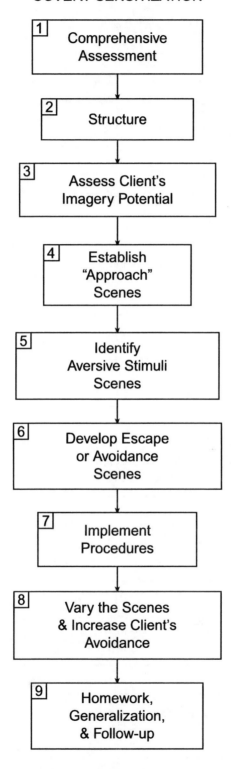

COVERT REINFORCEMENT

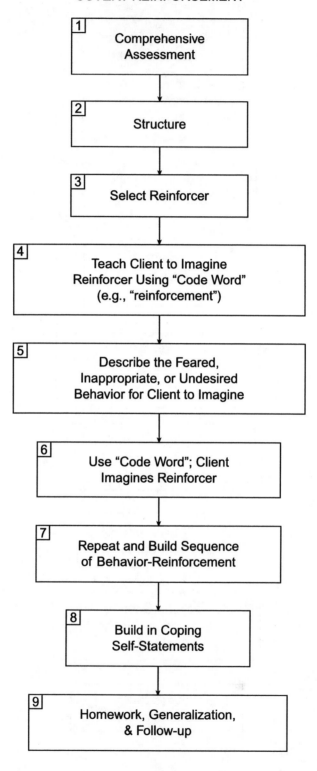

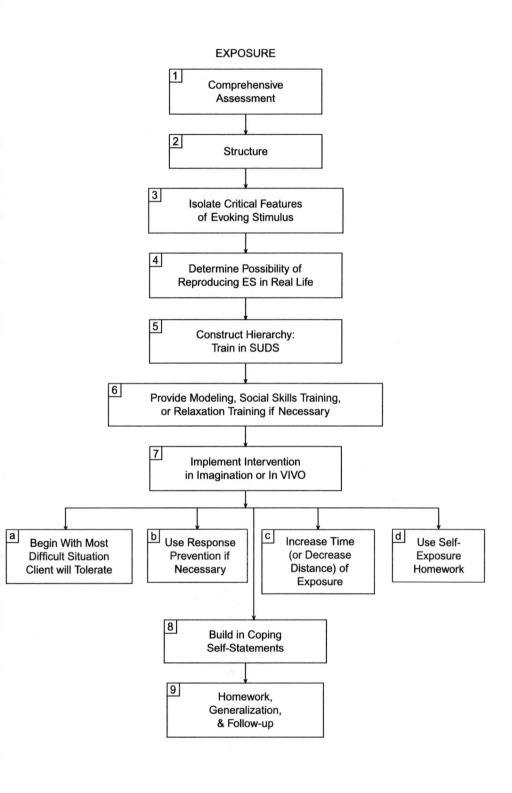

THOUGHT-STOPPING

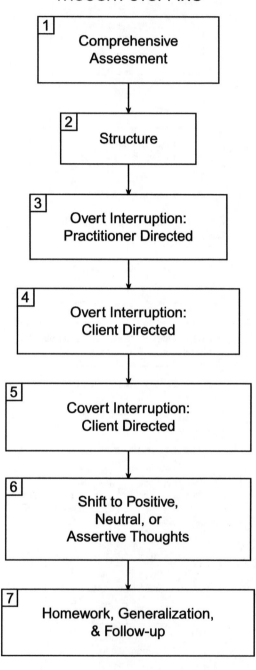

HABIT REVERSAL

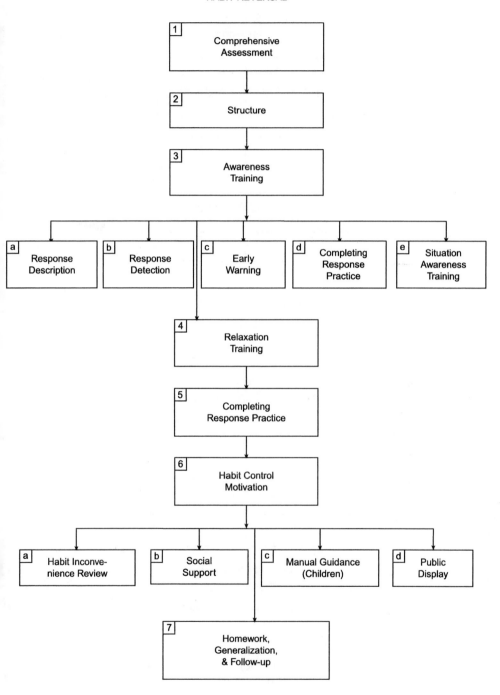

STRUCTURED LEARNING THERAPY

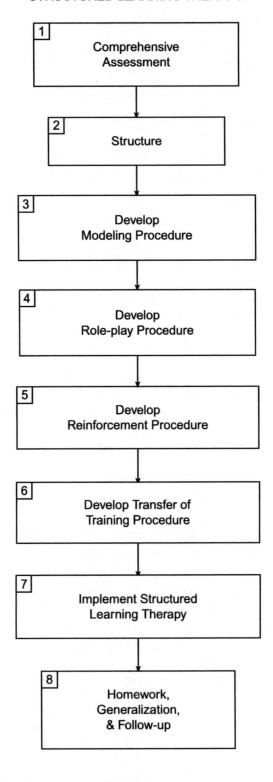

1. Comprehensive Assessment
2. Structure
3. Develop Modeling Procedure
4. Develop Role-play Procedure
5. Develop Reinforcement Procedure
6. Develop Transfer of Training Procedure
7. Implement Structured Learning Therapy
8. Homework, Generalization, & Follow-up